Agora Paperback Editions
GENERAL EDITOR: ALLAN BLOOM

Introduction to the Reading of Hegel: Lectures on the Phenomenology of
Spirit, by Alexandre Kojève
Medieval Political Philosophy, edited by Ralph Lerner and Muhsin Mahdi
The Roots of Political Philosophy: Ten Forgotten Socratic Dialogues,
by Thomas L. Pangle
Politics and the Arts, by Jean-Jacques Rousseau

CONTRIBUTORS

George N. Atiyeh, Universidad de Puerto Rico
Lawrence Berman, Dropsie College
S. B. Chrimes, University College, Cardiff
Ernest L. Fortin, Assumption College
Alan Gewirth, University of Chicago
George F. Hourani, University of Michigan
Ralph Lerner, University of Chicago
Charles I. Litzinger, St. Stephen's Priory, Dover, Mass.
Donald McCarthy, Boston College
Muhsin Mahdi, University of Chicago
Richard McKeon, University of Chicago
Michael E. Marmura, University of Toronto
Fauzi M. Najjar, Michigan State University
Francis Oakley, Williams College
Peter D. O'Neill, Assumption College
Robert Sacks, St. John's College, Annapolis
Joseph Sheerin, Assumption College
Philip H. Wicksteed

MEDIEVAL POLITICAL
PHILOSOPHY: *A Sourcebook*

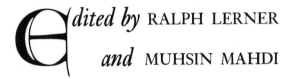

Edited by RALPH LERNER

and MUHSIN MAHDI

WITH THE COLLABORATION OF ERNEST L. FORTIN

Cornell Paperbacks

CORNELL UNIVERSITY PRESS

ITHACA, NEW YORK

Library of Congress Cataloging-in-Publication Data
(For library cataloging purposes only)

Lerner, Ralph, ed.
  Medieval political philosophy.

  (Cornell paperbacks) (Agora paperback editions)
  Bibliography: p.
  ISBN-13: 978-0-8014-9139-9 (pbk.: alk. paper)
  ISBN-10: 0-8014-9139-8 (pbk.: alk. paper)
  1. Political science—Early works to 1700—Addresses, essays, lectures.
2. Philosophy, Medieval—Addresses, essays, lectures. I. Mahdi, Muhsin, joint
ed. II. Title.
[JA82.L4 1972]   320.9'02   72-4326

Cornell University Press strives to use environmentally responsible
suppliers and materials to the fullest extent possible in the publishing
of its books. Such materials include vegetable-based, low-VOC inks
and acid-free papers that are recycled, totally chlorine-free, or partly
composed of nonwood fibers. For further information, visit our website
at www.cornellpress.cornell.edu.

Paperback printing   20   19   18   17   16   15   14   13

FOREWORD

W I T H the publication of this Sourcebook in Medieval Political Philosophy the Agora Paperback Editions presents a volume that can enable the general reader to get a serious introduction to the sources of all modern theological-political thought. On the basis of this book one can study not only the adaptation of the philosophic teaching about politics made by each of the three great revealed religions, but also the interrelations between these three doctrines. No attempt to understand the Western tradition can be undertaken without consideration of these works, which are the immediate sources of our thought. It is in the political domain in particular that the alternative teachings about the relation between reason and revelation can be most clearly grasped. Hence the editor believes this to be a capital volume for the study of political philosophy and a unique contribution to our available sources.

Many of the texts are translated for the first time into English; all are translated by competent scholars. Fidelity to the text was the first principle of the translations so that the English reader can, with some real assurance of reliability, make his own interpretations. The selections were made so as to present, in so far as possible, complete works or at least the whole of the relevant sections of the works; in this way the reader is not at the mercy of the selections, and hence interpretations, of the editors. No framework is imposed from the outside; each author is meant to be understood in his own terms and on his own grounds.

This volume should be of value to serious scholars as well as to students. It is the result of an extraordinary effort of cooperation. As such, it gives evidence to the fact that the truest and deepest source of understanding between the faiths is a return to, and respect for, the profound *teachings* which are their inspiration.

ALLAN BLOOM
General Editor, Agora Paperback Editions

PREFACE

S E V E N centuries ago Roger Bacon could lament the neglect of moral philosophy by the scholars of his age, adding ruefully: "But the books on this science by Aristotle and Avicenna, Seneca and Tullius and others, cannot be obtained except at great cost, both because the principal works are not translated into Latin and because copies of the others are not found in the usual schools or elsewhere." It is perhaps remarkable that what Bacon held to be true of his situation should also be applicable in part to our age, which has labored more than any other at the task of recovering all kinds of information about every conceivable period and civilization, and which has the further advantages of rapid translation and cheap printing. Everyone knows that the political philosophy that developed in Greece first spread throughout the classical world and, at some later date, penetrated into the three monotheistic religions, which among them commanded the allegiance of almost all men living between the Indus and the North Atlantic. Some people know that the encounter between political philosophy and revealed religion manifested itself in different ways in Islam, Judaism, and Christianity; but the study of these noteworthy confrontations has, by and large, been limited to the case of Christianity. This narrowing of the field of investigation is, in our judgment, regrettable. We believe that this judgment would be concurred in, above all, by the Christian scholastics themselves, who were diligent students of the works of many of the Muslims and Jews represented in this volume. These Christians wrote with a deep awareness of the work of those who, loosely speaking, might be regarded as their counterparts in Islam and Judaism. For one reason or another the mutual interest that figured so prominently in the medieval concourse of scholars waned. This change was followed by the rise of a radically new kind of political philosophy in the West—one that progressively narrowed its field of inquiry to the point where the questions that had preoccupied the greatest medieval thinkers no longer seemed relevant or even intelligible. Today we find ways of defining our inquiries so as to avoid such problems, though it may be doubted whether the role of science and religion in politics has ceased to be problematical for us. The student of political life can hardly do better than to turn to the writings of those political philosophers for whom this was the central political problem. Nowhere will he find a fuller and more sober account of the political implications of the encounter of science and religion.

The aim of this Sourcebook is to provide the student for whom these problems still retain a spark of life with a more direct access to medieval political philosophy than is afforded presently by footnotes in general histories of that subject. We do so out of the conviction that only a direct confrontation with the texts will enable him to discover for himself such insights as they may contain, and supply him with material for further reflection and inquiry. In delimiting our subject matter and selecting the works to be included here, we have borne in mind a number of difficulties that might be raised by intelligent readers. These are dealt with in the course of the introductory essay. It suffices to state here that we distinguish political philosophy from the political thought of theologians, legists, and so forth. We have tried to look at this vast medieval literature with eyes uninformed by any prejudgment, however scholarly, that would assure us in advance that political philosophy could not conceivably be found in the writings of this particular man or of this particular religious community.

In every case we began with the attempt to ascertain the state of the text in the language in which it originally was written. In a number of cases we found that texts existed only in manuscript form and these first had to be edited before a reliable translation could be attempted. In other cases the existing vulgate text had to be compared with additional manuscripts. In all cases the translations included here were made directly from the Arabic, Hebrew, or Latin originals. There is much in this literature that deserves close study even though it is not, strictly speaking, political philosophy. We have included some of this related literature in the bibliography at the end of this volume. (There are important works of political philosophy whose original texts have not as yet been found; such works, as for example Averroes' commentaries on the *Republic* and the *Ethics*, must await the discovery of their Arabic originals, or at least a satisfactory edition of their Hebrew translations, before they are ready to be translated.) The majority of the texts included in this volume are translated into English for the first time, and in some cases these are the first translations ever to be made from the originals.

This Sourcebook is divided into three Parts, corresponding to the order in which political philosophy made its appearance within the three religious communities. The authors in any given Part are presented chronologically; but where an author is represented by more than one work, the texts are in what we regard as a logical order and not necessarily in the order of composition. Certain editorial devices have been used that require explanation. Where present, italic numbers in brackets inserted in the body of the translation refer to the pagination of the critical edition or the vulgate text that is cited in the preceding introduction. It is hoped that these will help students who plan to read the present volume in conjunction with the original texts or to consult the latter on particular points. *All footnote references are to these pages* and not to the pages of this Sourcebook. Citations from the Old Testament, the New Testament, and the Koran are given in italics. References to the Koran, which appear in Part One in the form of Roman and Arabic numerals, indicate the chapter and verse numbering of the Egyptian edition; references to the Old Testament in Part Two follow the Masoretic text; references to the Old and New Testaments in Part Three follow the Vulgate, which may be consulted in the Douay-Rheims and Knox translations. All such references are inserted in the body of the translation. (Not infrequently, an author will use a near-quotation from the Bible or the Koran in apparent disregard for its original wording. Where these have been recognized, they have been identified also.) Usually we have adopted the names that common usage in the Latin West assigned to Muslim and Jewish writers and that remain current in medieval studies; their full Arabic or Hebrew names are given in the biographical notices that precede the first text of each author.

The responsibility for this Sourcebook as a whole, the inclusion or exclusion of any materials, and the introductory essay is shared by the two co-editors. Each Part is under the supervision of a single editor; in preparing Part Three, we sought the collaboration of the Reverend Ernest L. Fortin, A.A., of Assumption College, Worcester, Massachusetts. The editor of each Part shares with the individual translator the responsibility for the general integrity and accuracy of the translation. Where previously published translations have been used, the editor has compared these with the original text and has made the necessary changes to secure as high a degree of literalness as is compatible with intelligible English and to preserve a certain measure of uniformity in the translation of technical terms. In addition, the editor of each Part wrote the short introductions that preface each translation.

Many have contributed toward the publication of this Sourcebook. Foremost among them is Father Ernest L. Fortin. He has fully shared in, and reinforced, our enthusiasm for this project. We have taught, and learned from, one another, and we have agreed and disagreed, in a spirit that we saw exemplified in the very works we were editing. We wish to thank the individuals who contributed their talents and labors in the form of new translations made especially for this volume. They have borne our detailed criticisms with remarkable patience, and they have accepted our suggested revisions, even where these have been extensive. A number of scholars have benefited us through their constructive criticisms at various stages of this enterprise: Joseph Cropsey, William Daley, Father I. Th. Eschmann, Father Theodore Fortier, Etienne Gilson, George F. Hourani, Father George A. Laberge, Father Armand Maurer, the late Rabbi Maurice B. Pekarsky, Shlomo Pines, Joseph Sheerin, Leo Strauss, J. L. Teicher, and Richard Walzer.

The co-editors have each received generous grants from the Rockefeller

Foundation's program in Legal and Political Philosophy; these grants have contributed substantially toward completing the research for this volume. We are happy to acknowledge our thanks to the Foundation. The Publication Fund of the College of the University of Chicago has helped in meeting the costs of manuscript preparation. Finally, the following publishers have kindly permitted us to reprint or to make use of translations to which they hold the copyright: Cambridge University Press (Sir John Fortescue, *De Laudibus Legum Angliae*, trans. S. B. Chrimes, pp. 3-41); Columbia University Press (Marsilius of Padua, *The Defender of Peace*, trans. Alan Gewirth, Vol. II, pp. 3-55, 95-97, 187-92); J. M. Dent and Co. (*The Latin Works of Dante Alighieri*, trans. Philip H. Wicksteed, pp. 127-72, 275-79); the Trustees of the Gibb Memorial Fund (*Averroes on the Harmony between Religion and Philosophy*, trans. George F. Hourani, pp. 44-71); from *Selections from Medieval Philosophers*, Vol. II, edited and translated by Richard McKeon, pp. 81-99, 100-106. Copyright 1929 Charles Scribner's Sons; renewal copyright © 1957. Used by permission of Charles Scribner's Sons. Henry Regnery Co. (St. Thomas Aquinas, *Commentary on the Ethics of Aristotle*, trans. Father Charles I. Litzinger, O.P.); University of Chicago Press (Moses Maimonides, *The Guide of the Perplexed*, trans. Shlomo Pines).

We thank all of the aforementioned individuals and institutions for their aid and counsel, while absolving them of any responsibility for this Sourcebook.

R.L.
M.M.

Chicago, Illinois

CONTENTS

xi

PART THREE   *Political Philosophy in Christianity*
EDITED BY ERNEST L. FORTIN

Introduction

[handwritten note: distinguish classical political teaching from political point of their teaching of their religion]

I F O N E were to try to state the theme and problem of medieval political philosophy with the utmost conciseness and at the price of considerable oversimplification, the following statement might be made. Medieval political philosophy, as far as it is accessible to us in the form
of extant treatises, commentaries, and other written records, consists of
the inquiries and conclusions of individuals, living as Muslims or Jews
or Christians, who attempted to identify the classical political teaching
and to distinguish it from, or to harmonize it with, the political teaching
of their particular religion. Or one might say, somewhat more pointedly:
medieval political philosophy is the attempt by men, living in communities that were defined by a particular religion, to understand the differences between the political teaching of certain pagan philosophers and
the political teaching of the revelation that constituted their religious
community, and as far as possible to reconcile the two. For the moment—
but only for the moment—we may disregard, not only the profound
differences that separate Islam from Judaism and each of these from
Christianity, but also the differing practical situations in which men who
would pursue philosophy found themselves within these religious communities. What at first glance appear to be the most striking elements
are shared by all three: a divinely-revealed religion, the appearance of
Greek political philosophy within a community that is constituted—
either wholly or in its highest aims—by a divinely-revealed Law, and the
disagreement or conflict between the demands of the divine Law and
the political teaching of the philosophers. These are the elements of the
enterprise that we call medieval political philosophy.

It is almost impossible to exaggerate the size or number of the obstacles
that stand in the way of the modern reader's effort to understand that
enterprise and enter into its spirit. Brushing aside vulgar notions that see
only dark ages or ingenious exercises in logic-chopping, we still must
take account of the intellectual baggage that the modern reader typically
drags along with him, baggage that well-nigh blocks the subject matter
from his view. Even an open-minded reader might be expected to regard

[handwritten note: communities defined by a religion to understand differences]

the texts of medieval political philosophy as utterly incomprehensible by virtue of the bizarreness of the themes, as irrelevant by virtue of the religious adherence of the authors, or as superfluous because of the vast over-complication of the material. Such reactions, we believe, account in large measure for the curious treatment (or nontreatment) of medieval political philosophy today. It is no exaggeration to say that a text by Plato or Aristotle seems less exotic to the modern reader than a text by Aquinas, let alone Alfarabi or Maimonides, though the latter group, both in time and in their adherence to a monotheistic religion, stand in a closer relationship to today's reader than do the pagans of classical Greece. Why is this so?

The three kinds of reaction just mentioned are at bottom the products of three characteristically modern prejudgments. First, we tend to assume that the particular form of expression that political philosophy takes is that which is most familiar to us: there will be a book wholly or largely devoted to a systematic discussion of forms of government, law, justice, and so forth; we think of the *Leviathan* or the *Social Contract*. We are not accustomed to looking for an author's political philosophy in the interstices, so to speak, of his work—especially if his work takes the form of a commentary on yet another work, or a resumé (sometimes rather fanciful in appearance if compared with the text it claims to summarize), or if his work seems largely concerned with religious and doctrinal questions arising from revealed religion. Generally speaking, we find it hard to see why someone who had a contribution to make to political philosophy did not go about it in a straightforward manner; hence the impatient judgment that sees most medieval thinkers as doing little more than dotting the *i*'s and crossing the *t*'s of Aristotle's texts. This first reaction, then, rests on the erroneous view that political philosophy has a typical or normal form of expression and that it should be judged solely in terms of its originality or its manifest innovations. Second, we tend to draw hard and fast lines between reason and revelation and then summarily to dispose of medieval authors by placing them on the one side or the other. Averroes, Albo, and Roger Bacon all filled a certain religious office or belonged to a religious order; this fact, in itself, does not mean that these men were fitted with theological blinders that kept them from casting sidelong glances. It may safely be granted that these were not rationalists cut to the pattern of the Enlightenment, but then neither were they "know-nothings" blindly led by a blind faith in their religion. This second reaction, then, rests on the erroneous notion that every adherent of a religious Law is completely incapable of freeing himself—if only provisionally—from the fundamental views enjoined by that Law. Third, we tend to underestimate the very formidable difficulties that stood in the way of the medieval enterprise. Exaggeration in any direction may be misleading; minimizing the tension between philosophy and revela-

search for political wisdom religious problems posed by philosophy for the divine law

tion is no surer way to proper understanding than is magnifying that tension. Although pious and learned men had dismissed philosophy as having nothing to say to them, and although equally pious men detested philosophy, men of the stature of Avicenna, Maimonides, and Aquinas devoted their lives and thoughts to achieving some measure of clarity, for themselves and for others, about the problem posed by philosophy for the divine Law. As intelligent men, they were in search of wisdom; as political philosophers, they were in search of practical or political wisdom. We have argued that their search was not foreclosed or predetermined in some crude fashion by their membership in a religious community. At the same time, however, their search for political wisdom was conducted within a religious community. As men of practical wisdom, they were no more disposed than is a responsible lawyer to posit cases upon the ruin of the constitution. Unlike a lawyer or jurist, however, they were able to examine their constitution critically from the highest vantage point available to man. However easily we may say today that the medieval political philosophers tried to prove that the goals of the divine Law and of philosophy were in large measure identical, we ought never to forget what they constantly bore in mind: that clarifying the differences between the divine Law and philosophy and clarifying their relationships is a difficult and, not seldom, hazardous undertaking. This third reaction, then, follows from an inadequate appreciation of the fact that classical political philosophy initially had the status of a newly-arrived alien in an established community.

We have dwelt at length upon these preliminary obstacles to understanding solely because common prejudices of these kinds preclude even the most rudimentary recognition of the subject matter of medieval political philosophy. But if our reader succeeds in freeing himself from the sway of unexamined certainties, he has done so only to become more perplexed than he had any reason to anticipate. One of the first thoughts that will cross his mind is that the themes of medieval political philosophy, as represented here, do not correspond to the commonly-received accounts of that subject matter. He may be surprised by some things he reads in the Christian Part; he may be at a loss to understand how some passages in the Islamic and Jewish Parts can be comprehended under political philosophy; above all, he will wonder how it came about that the reception or adaptation of classical political philosophy by the three great monotheistic religions should have taken such diverse forms.

However unfamiliar and perplexing these questions may be, there is much that suggests that a determined effort to pursue them will be rewarding. A moment's reflection should make it clear that all the arguments that support the comparative study of cultures and political institutions apply with at least equal force to the comparative study of

adaption of political philosophy took diverse forms

medieval political philosophy. Social scientists recognize that it is necessary to know and understand cultures other than our own. The proper study of man is seen to require the ability to transcend the horizons of one's own time and place. From Herodotus' time down to ours, men have left the familiar surroundings they called their own in search of the different and the strange, in the expectation that breadth of view would provide a truer perspective by which to take in social life as a whole. The benefits of a broad view are at least as great in the study of political philosophy, giving the student a more comprehensive picture of the uniformity and diversity characteristic of a distinctively human activity. Needless to say, the benefits will not be reaped if other men and other ways are not first studied in their own terms. We must make the greatest effort to see things as these men saw them—that is, to take seriously what they took seriously—rather than to impose upon their thoughts whatever added wisdom hindsight may appear to have given us. The least one can say is that such a methodological device seems in order initially, or until such time as we put this methodology aside and try to determine, on the basis of the available evidence, the worth or worthlessness of these men's thoughts and ways.

We have maintained that arguments supporting a comparative approach apply to the field of medieval political philosophy. One might go further and argue that medieval political philosophy stands in special need of such an approach. As regards medieval studies generally, we have learned to broaden rather than to narrow our views. One example must suffice: the study of medieval economic history has shown the advantage of considering the Mediterranean world as a unit. What is necessary in understanding the traffic in goods is at least as necessary in understanding the traffic in ideas. It is common knowledge that the classical tradition of science and philosophy originally and in part moved through the Muslims to the Jews to the Christians of Western Europe. Important as this linear transmission is in the history of medieval political philosophy, it is by no means sufficient for our understanding of its subject matter. The reason is that political philosophy combines both theory and practice in an exceptionally intimate connection. In view of this, the way in which men conduct themselves as philosophers becomes itself a political question, linked to the particular political and social conditions that prevail in the community within which that activity is being carried on. Hence any comparative investigation of medieval political philosophy has to consider, not only what was held in common (for example, the broad features of classical political philosophy and of revealed monotheistic religion), but also the significant and specific differences between the three religious communities of Islam, Judaism, and Christianity.

We may now summarize the advantages accruing from this kind of comparative study. The medieval world is sufficiently foreign and removed from our own for us to view it with some measure of detachment. We are in a good position to learn about a number of matters that have passed out of currency; we are in a good position to be reminded of considerations that we tend, without sufficient reflection, to dismiss as irrelevant or that we tend simply to ignore. At the same time, the medieval world is, in some respects, closer to us than the present-day Antipodes or Yucatan. The medieval world has formed our own history and heritage and remains a part of it. We still can recognize in our world much that we share with it: the classical tradition, the religious tradition, and the interest in science. Furthermore, a part of this medieval world is, for many millions of men living today, more than tradition or cultural legacy. In states where any one of these religions is the official church, or in enclaves within secular societies, there are to be found men for whom this past still lives.

In speaking of the themes or subject matter of medieval political philosophy, the first thing to be noted is that for men in all three religious communities, political philosophy was both possible and important. They did not doubt the possibility of their enterprise: they believed that, in principle, it is within the grasp of the human mind to attain knowledge of the nature of political things. Moreover, they regarded political philosophy (or political science, as it was sometimes called) as the highest of the practical sciences. In their eyes its importance lay in its comprehensive treatment of the ways of life and opinions of human communities, or of man's political life in the broadest sense. Any misgivings that the modern reader may entertain with respect to this estimate of the feasibility and scope of political philosophy may have to be suspended temporarily if he is to gain any access to the thoughts or aims of these men. It also is important to note in this connection that political philosophy, as pursued by these medieval thinkers, was not an abstract exercise in speculation idly indulged in by men in the privacy of their closets. The medieval political philosopher did not write for the man in the street, but neither did he write for himself. He did not regard his activity as falling into what is today called the "policy sciences"; but then again neither did he regard his activity as unrelated to the amelioration of the political conditions and political opinions of ordinary men. However "theoretical" the speculation became, it was and remained speculation about political things and, as such, had a practical end. Finally, it ought to be noted that the medieval political philosophers were concerned with recovering the political teaching of the classics and with making that teaching meaningful or relevant for their own times. This concern frequently expressed itself in the writing of summaries, paraphrases, and commentaries. While there are some remarkable differences between the religious communities in the extent to which the classical teaching was incorporated into the medieval philosopher's teaching and in the manner in which that incorporation was effected, there is a common regard for what the classics taught.

Political philosophy is concerned with every kind of governance, especially with the best governance. We may sketch very broadly the themes of the medieval political philosophers by considering the varieties of governance that they discussed and the kinds of questions that they then were led to investigate. Most familiar to us is the discussion of the governance of men by men. Here we are faced with a great variety in the kinds of governance, corresponding both to the differences in the size or scale of governance and to the great variety in the things that men honor. A common distinction is that drawn between man's governance of himself (ethics) and the governance of the household (economics) and the governance of the city, of the nation, or of many nations or of the great nation. Similarly, a distinction is drawn between the political forms of governance in terms of the differing goals or ends to which they are directed. These governances, however they are distinguished, are based upon human—that is, man-made—laws. The status of these laws requires study; the relation of these laws to other kinds of law (natural, divine, and so forth) also requires investigation. In the Christian religious community, there is a need to clarify the relationship of a governance based on human law to a governance based on divine Law: that is, the relationship of civil law and human government—state or emperor—to canon law and divine government—church or pope. Another form of governance is that of men by God. This inquiry begins with an investigation of the divine Law (*lex divina*) or religious Law (*sharīʿa* or *torah*) and its distinctive features. In Islam and Judaism, the all-inclusive character of the religious Law leads to a special emphasis upon the intentions of the Law or upon the intentions of the prophet who promulgated that Law. In this way, revelation, the agency of the prophet-legislator in defining a particular religious community, and religion itself, all become major themes of political philosophy. Finally, and as a special branch of the individual's governance of himself, it is possible to speak of the philosopher's governance of himself. This emerges as a theme of medieval political philosophy in two ways: in so far as the philosopher is a solitary, he is guided by some kind of natural law in his occasional relations with others; and inasmuch as he lives in the midst of a religious community, he is guided by the Law of that community. It is in this way that the place of philosophy in the religious community and the philosopher's own activity become parts of the subject matter of medieval political philosophy.

Not all of these themes were the exclusive province of political philosophy as distinguished from political thought. One can hardly turn to a single text of medieval political thought that does not evince a concern for such problems as well as an effort to deal with them at some level of understanding. Most of these themes appear in medieval political literature, but not all of that literature is able to articulate or to discuss these themes with an equal degree of insight and authority. The study of the law is a case in point. There was a multitude of jurists and lawyers who were daily involved in this study, but it is evident (no less today than in medieval times) that, as jurists and lawyers, these men could at best ascertain and seek to interpret or reinterpret the fundamentals of the law with a view to applying it to particular cases; but they were not equipped to raise and consider the broad questions lying at the bottom of the law. Nor could they, as jurists and lawyers, reflect on the relation between the principles of the law and, say, the principles of the theoretical or practical sciences. We must distinguish, then, a treatment of these themes that is sufficient for most practical purposes, from a truly comprehensive treatment of these themes. In the middle ages such a comprehensive treatment—that is, the investigation of the principles of political things in the highest and most orderly form—was the subject matter of two distinct disciplines: political philosophy and political theology. Any study of medieval political thought presupposes an awareness of this distinction and an understanding of the complex relationship between these two disciplines.

Political philosophy is a branch of philosophy. Just as philosophy is the love and quest of wisdom or universal and comprehensive knowledge, so political philosophy is the love or quest of wisdom about the nature or principles of all human affairs or political things. Just as philosophy seeks to understand the whole and the parts of the whole and the place of the parts within the whole, so political philosophy seeks to understand the principles of political life, the relation of these principles to each other, and the relation of political things to all other things. Political theology is an integral part of theology. (In speaking of theology here, we do not mean what Aristotle, for example, called theology—the inquiry into divine things, as distinguished from the account of divine things given by mythographers, poets, legislators, and the ancestral tradition. The medievals themselves distinguished natural theology from sacred theology. Natural theology is the inquiry into divine things, as far as these are accessible to the human mind without the aid of any revelation. This belongs to metaphysics and constitutes its highest theme. When speaking of theology in the present context, we are referring to sacred theology—that is, the inquiry into divine things based upon a divine revelation whose highest principles are, as such, not accessible to the unassisted human mind.) As a part of sacred theology, political theology is the elucidation of the political teachings of a divine revelation or the inquiry into political things based upon a divine revelation.

Both of these comprehensive treatments were "political" with respect to their subject matter. But by virtue of the fact that each claimed to present a comprehensive account of political things, there arose the possibility of a conflict between them and, accordingly, the need to define and establish a proper relationship between the two. Every medieval political philosopher had to face this problem at some point: he had to distinguish political philosophy from political theology, and he had to relate the two kinds of activity. A number of inconclusive compromises were reached, but two particular approaches are of paramount importance. One or the other of these was followed by all of the great figures among the medieval political philosophers.

One approach was to consider political theology within the framework of political philosophy. This was the dominant mode among all of the Muslim political philosophers; it was used by Maimonides in so far as he followed their political teaching; and it was an important aspect of so-called Latin Averroism in the Christian West. This mode was justified in the following way. The principles of political theology are derived from a particular revelation and divine Law; political theology has to accept and cannot question these principles. On the other hand, the comprehensive inquiry into political things, an inquiry that goes to the roots, cannot take these principles for granted; it must broaden its horizon and ask questions about the intentions of the Lawgiver, questions that ultimately cannot be answered except through an inquiry into the end of man, his place within the whole, and the nature of political things. Nor can these questions be answered by accepting, without further investigation, the answers given to them in that divine Law. For these answers, too, were given as a part of the legislative activity of the Lawgiver. Through these beliefs, the Lawgiver intended to found a particular religious community; he regarded these beliefs as best for those men. This does not exclude the possibility that the political teaching based upon such beliefs is indeed simply the best political teaching. But this cannot be granted prior to inquiry; and if the argument is not to be circular, it must begin from principles accessible to the unassisted human mind. Whatever the results of this investigation, political philosophy must begin with the attempt to replace the beliefs held by the followers of a given divine Law with knowledge of the essential character of any divine Law; similarly, the inquiry into political things based on belief in a given divine Law must be replaced by knowledge of the nature of political things and especially of the nature of all kinds of law. Given the possibility of such knowledge—or at least the possibility of knowledge of the fundamental political questions as questions—political philosophy becomes a higher and a more comprehensive science than political theology. It inquires into the things that political theology accepts as its unquestioned point of departure. More generally stated: the principles of political theology are the fundamentals of a particular religious polity. These fundamentals were revealed for the sake of that body and they constitute its basic beliefs. Political philosophy, on the other hand, is not relative or bound to any particular religious or nonreligious polity. If political theology probes to the roots or principles of a particular religious polity, political philosophy inquires into these principles and roots, and attempts to probe to the roots of the roots, of all kinds of polity. Such an inquiry cannot presuppose any principles or roots as articles of faith or as unquestioned beliefs. This subordination of political theology to political philosophy does not lessen the need for the former or diminish its importance as a political and practical discipline. It is both necessary and useful for the particular religious community in which it is pursued, although it is not of any use to other religious communities, which do not share or accept these beliefs. The political teaching of every divine revelation needs to be identified, clarified, interpreted, and defended. This is the specific function of the political theologian. The political philosopher himself may, and normally does, engage in this activity, which is an integral part of his practical or political activity as a teacher, reformer, and so forth, within his own religious community. Nevertheless, the distinction between the two is settled and so is the subordination of political theology to political philosophy. (We have included a number of texts in which medieval political philosophers treat the political teaching of their revealed Law as political philosophers or as political theologians or as both. In order to understand these texts the reader needs to remind himself of the distinctive character of these two approaches and of the practical importance of political theology in helping to elucidate the revealed Law.)

The other approach was to consider political philosophy within the framework of political theology. This mode itself does not rest upon philosophic principles. It took many forms and was represented by various theologians and theological schools in Islam, Judaism, and Christianity. It could, for instance, be based on a purely practical consideration. As members of this religious community, the most important thing is to live the kind of life prescribed by our divine Law; everything else, including all foreign or mundane sciences, either should not be pursued at all or should be pursued only to the extent necessary to promote the life of faith and virtue. Political philosophy, especially, has become superfluous because our divine Law provides us with everything needed to conduct our lives and to promote our welfare both in this world and in the next. Only where it can be shown that the study of political philosophy can contribute in some way to this end should it be admitted; its contribution, in any case, is of limited importance and its place clearly subordinate. While from a practical point of view this position is under-standable, it does not properly meet the problems posed by political philosophy that were sketched above.

A far more adequate approach is rendered possible by making an effort to meet political philosophy on its own ground. Theology is conceived of as a comprehensive theoretical and practical science, just as philosophy is. Political theology is conceived of as a more comprehensive science than political philosophy; it sees further and more deeply than political philosophy. Political theology, in this sense, does not begin by inquiring whether, beyond the knowledge based on revelation and the divine Law, we need political philosophy. Rather it begins by asking whether, beyond the knowledge that is provided (or that can be provided) by political philosophy, we need something more, a higher knowledge than that which political philosophy offers or can offer. This question is not asked by the simple believer in a revelation or a divine Law. For him, belief or faith means that he is convinced or certain that following the precepts of the divine Law and the beliefs prescribed by it is the only way to salvation and hence that no other law and no other kind of knowledge is sufficient for this purpose. Furthermore, he is not troubled by the multiplicity of laws and even of divine Laws, for he believes that the others are either false or incomplete. Nevertheless, the simple believer holds to two essential elements of the political theology about which we are speaking: that he must follow his own divine Law and no other, and that his divine Law goes beyond all the precepts of a merely human science. It remained for certain theologians in the three religious com-munities to support these beliefs, which the simple believer accepts on faith, through a science of political theology. The development of such a science required drawing the fundamental distinction between the poli-tical teaching, based on revealed principles, that is *essentially* not acces-sible to the unaided human mind, and the revealed political teaching that is accessible to the unaided human mind but which, for one reason or an-other, needed to be stated for all members of the religious community. The political theologian treats the revealed teaching as principles from which he deduces their necessary consequences. In so doing, and because he has access to principles higher than the highest principles accessible to the political philosopher, he develops a comprehensive political doctrine. He will include in it the teaching of the political philosophers. But being the possessor of a higher knowledge, he has the right to incorporate as much of the lower (political philosophy) as he sees fit, as he judges to be in harmony with or to support or to promote the higher (sacred) political teaching. Again, in so doing, he does not think that he is in any way limiting, to say nothing of corrupting, the teaching of the political philosophers. Quite the contrary. When he selects from it or corrects it or refutes certain parts of it, he believes that he is improving it and improving on it. He is placing it in the broader context within which it properly belongs, and he is providing it with the benefit of a higher light that enables it to see and judge more clearly the truth of its principles, including its practical function and aim. It was in the Christian world that this mode of placing political philosophy within a theological framework received its most elaborate expression—not only in the patristic period (when Christians first had to come to terms with pagan philosophy), but also in the work of Thomas Aquinas. Aquinas' insistence on the distinction between the domains of philosophy and sacred doctrine represents a departure from some earlier Christian theologians who sought to incorporate or absorb philosophy into the "one wisdom." Much of the Thomistic teaching is devoted to defining the separate realms of theology and of philosophy; and when speaking as a commentator on the *Nicomachean Ethics* or the *Politics*, Aquinas is indeed speaking about political things as far as these are known to natural reason. But the Thomistic teaching about society goes beyond commentaries on Aristotle and includes his view of the church, as elaborated in his theological works and in the treatise *On Kingship*. In other words, the Thomistic teaching about society is neither complete nor fully clear unless one takes into account, not only his distinction between man's earthly end—which may be attained through civil society and earthly kings—on the one hand, and man's supernatural end—which must be ordered through the church and the priests—on the other, but also Aquinas' subordination of the former to the latter. This relationship, which in his view constitutes a Christian society, cannot be properly treated except within a theological framework.

We may now summarize these two heterogeneous approaches to the study of political things. The first is based on the position that philosophy alone is capable of giving a comprehensive account of the highest principles and that it alone can illuminate the understanding of all political things, including the political teaching of the divine Law, which occupies an honored place within political philosophy. The second approach is based on the position that the highest political teaching is contained in that revelation or divine Law in which the theologian believes. Only the science of that revelation or divine Law (that is, the theology that takes revelation or the divine Law as its premise) can illuminate fully the understanding of all political things, including the teaching of political philosophy, which occupies an honored but subordinate place within political theology.

These two approaches, as well as varying combinations of the two, were followed by men in all three religious communities in their study of political things. The predominance of one mode over another in any particular community requires explanation, though in the nature of the

case an explanation can only be tentative and suggestive. We shall attempt
to sketch the outlines of an explanation by considering the relative positions of theology and jurisprudence in Christianity, Islam, and Judaism.
Broadly stated, theology was the paramount science in Christianity. The
Christian community was constituted, not by a single divine Law that
comprehensively prescribed opinions and actions of every kind, but
rather by a sacred doctrine. The custodians of this doctrine were
apostolic successors, the hierarchy, and the theologians, not the jurists.
In Islam it is the all-embracing Law and its study that are supreme.
Theology occupies a prominent, though subordinate, position. Judaism,
like Islam, is constituted by a comprehensive revealed Law. That Law
and the jurists' activity in interpreting, elaborating, and applying it are
paramount. Theology does not appear to have a significant or even a
well-defined position. These broad differences in the relative prominence
of theology and jurisprudence within the religious communities seem
to have had important consequences for the way in which political
philosophy was regarded, the definition of its subject matter, and the
place it came to occupy.

Christianity begins by rescinding the Old Law and replacing it with
a New Law, the Law of Grace. This New Law is not a comprehensive
Law in the sense that the Pentateuch is; it does not include, as an integral
part, the regulation of men's private and public lives as citizens. There
is no penal legislation in the New Testament. The New Law prescribes
beliefs that complement, rather than supplant, the civil and public law
of Caesar; the latter develops independently and continues, as before, to
regulate men's political and social lives. To be sure, certain changes
were made in Caesar's law: for example, the old laws prescribing cults
and forms of worship and governing the pagan priests were rescinded,
and new laws consonant with Christianity were substituted; then, too,
the civil and public law was restrained from hindering the exercise of
the Christian virtues. As a result there developed a twofold system of
law—canon and civil—that has no analogue in Islam or Judaism. In general, the Christian divine Law, more than the Koran and to a vastly
greater extent than the Jewish Bible, is largely directed to a transpolitical,
other-worldly goal. There were no medieval Christian counterparts to
the Islamic *faqīhs* or the Jewish talmudists, whose task it was to ascertain
the text of the original revelation, take it as a body of premises, and
deduce from it a more elaborate set of rules—all this without paying,
or needing to pay, much attention to the foreign sciences of the pagans.
Even more important than the foregoing features is the way in which
Christian theology received effective institutional support. This theology
developed in an intimate relation with a church that claimed to be
catholic. In the councils, the church had at once the authority and the

effective instrument by which it could define an article of faith and make binding decisions as to its correct interpretation. This institution was almost a millennium old by the thirteenth century, that is, by the time the Latin West felt the impact of the newly acquired Islamic and Jewish learning and the impact of the newly recovered works of Aristotle. Concomitantly with the rise of political philosophy, there arose the need to define its relation to the existing traditional theology. (The latter consisted in the study of Christian dogmas as found in the New Testament, the decisions of councils, Peter Lombard's *Book of Sentences,* certain works by Augustine and other church fathers, and those elements from the writings of Cicero, Plotinus, Alfarabi, Avicenna, and a number of others, that had been incorporated into traditional theology.) A number of attempts were made to reform this theology in the light of the newly acquired learning. The penetration of political philosophy into the Christian community raised the question as to which one of the reformed versions of theology is correct.

In Islam and Judaism, on the other hand, the penetration of classical political philosophy led to the posing of a quite different question. There the primary issue was whether these new and alien sciences are permitted or prohibited by the religious Law. This was a juridical, rather than theological, question; the jurist, and only the jurist, could render a decision, and that decision would take the form of a judicial ruling. In Islam and Judaism it was quite possible to rule that the Law permits the pursuit of all or most of these sciences and of the various modes of integrating them with one another. It was quite possible to leave the differing advocates to argue their case against one another, provided that in doing so they did not gainsay or interfere with the beliefs and way of life prescribed by the Law, as defined by the jurists. Furthermore, neither in Islam nor in medieval Judaism was there an ecclesiastical institution that had the authority to determine the correct interpretation of the beliefs prescribed by the Law. The far-reaching consequences of these differences may be seen in this extreme example: Averroes could present the case of *Philosophy* vs. *Theology* before the tribunal of the Law, and ask for a decision to the effect that theology is the enemy of the Law and that the Law demands the truly scientific—that is, the philosophic—interpretation of certain doctrines. Within Christianity, certain Averroists appear to have envisaged a reformation of traditional theology along these lines. They wished the Christian church to remove itself from the controversy between theology and philosophy, rather than sit in judgment on the conflicting interpretations of the proper relation of the two. The church, however, declined to withdraw from the controversy. Certain bishops availed themselves of their authority to determine the curriculum of the schools, and proceeded to condemn some of the more notable attempts at reforming traditional theology. In general, some of the reformed versions of theology were approved, others condemned, and still others left free. In time one version came to be approved by the church itself; other competing versions, never having been rehabilitated, failed to enter into the mainstream of Christian thought. In Islam and Judaism, in contrast, the preference of individual jurists for a certain theological or philosophic school or interpretation could find no institutional channel through which this could be declared as the correct catholic doctrine and through which its opponents could be condemned or persecuted as being beyond the pale of the true religion. There was no instrument for establishing a universal or permanent doctrine.

We may now summarize this discussion of the relative positions of theology and jurisprudence with a view to its bearing upon the *content* of political philosophy. The separation of canon and civil law, in the Christian community, left the civil law as the domain of the legists. By the same token it could also become the domain of the political philosophers, who could raise such questions as: what is the natural law? what is human law? what is the common good? In other words, the political philosophers could reflect upon the foundations of the civil law without necessarily having to touch upon the divine Law and the sacred doctrine. A political philosophy that was restricted or that restricted itself to such questions could be incorporated into a political theology that proceeded beyond it to the study of the divine Law and the sacred doctrine. Where there is no such separate civil law, as in Islam and Judaism, political philosophy has no such limited area of human law to which it can be confined. If political philosophy was to reflect upon any law, it had to be *the* Law; political philosophy had to inquire into the roots of a single comprehensive divine Law, which itself preempts any place that might be left to a human law. Consequently, when political philosophy plunged into a study of the Law, it was inevitably drawn to inquire into revelation (or the source of that Law), prophecy (or the agency through which the Law was revealed), and the religious polity as a species of governance (or the political community organized under such a Law).

Nothing that we have said ought to be interpreted as meaning that the Thomistic synthesis was a foregone conclusion in Christianity or, similarly, that the Averroistic synthesis was a foregone conclusion in Islam and Judaism. The fundamental differences we have sketched in the character of the divine Laws of Islam, Judaism, and Christianity, and in the relative positions of theology and jurisprudence in these communities do not, of themselves, necessitate the one mode or the other. *How* one accommodated the conflicting claims of the revealed teaching and the political philosophers' teaching turned on a still more fundamental question. Is, or is not, man directed to an end that surpasses the grasp of his reason, and ordained to an end that is not proportionate to, but exceeds, his natural ability? Muslims, Jews, and Christians alike divided among themselves when they interpreted their revelation with a view to answering this question. Both interpretations—let us call them the philosophic and the theological—found ardent and powerful supporters within each community. We have already made it clear that only in medieval Christianity was it institutionally possible to convert one of these interpretations of the revelation into a catholic teaching and, with authority, to condemn an alternative interpretation as contrary to the faith. In Islam, to take the other extreme, it was possible for both interpretations to be pursued and advocated side by side. In the light of this difference, it is not perhaps fortuitous that those who favored the philosophic interpretation of the revelation in Islam and in Judaism were all staunch supporters of the Law who labored to uphold its authority. At the same time, their counterparts in Christianity developed an anticlerical tendency. Men like Marsilius argued against the plenitude of power of the Popes, against their authority to define articles of the faith, and especially against their claim to have coercive power to compel anyone in this world (that is, by temporal pain or punishment) to observe the commands of the evangelical Law, let alone a particular interpretation of it. Whatever the broader political implications of this anticlericalism may have been, it was certainly an integral part of philosophic politics; it was aimed at removing the practical impediment to the pursuit of the philosophic interpretation of revelation within the Christian community. In this respect, some of the so-called Latin Averroists and their Islamic and Jewish counterparts shared the same goal, despite the apparent differences in their approach.

Going hand in hand with these differences in the character of the divine Law and in the relative positions of theology and jurisprudence in the three religious communities, is the presence of two rather distinct classical political traditions in the middle ages. This fact has significance only if one takes seriously the fact of which all medieval political philosophers were fully aware: that political philosophy had been handed down to them from the pagan philosophers. The medieval political philosophers themselves did not claim to have developed their teaching solely on the basis of direct reflection upon medieval political life without any regard for earlier conventions and traditions. The analyses of the political life of their own communities, the very terms employed, were largely borrowed from classical political philosophy. In this respect, the medieval political philosophers were like the Romans before them and the moderns after them. If they added to, or modified, or radically changed the framework of the classical political tradition, it was nonetheless to that tradition that they first turned. This classical tradition was, as it were, a pair of spectacles that all of them wore and through which they looked at political life. Depending on our estimate of the fundamental soundness or ultimate worth of classical political philosophy, we may think that these spectacles enabled them to see the nature of political life more clearly or that these spectacles distorted their vision. But the fact remains that there is no medieval political philosopher who did not directly or indirectly make use of the classical tradition in approaching the study of political things.

Not all of the classical political writings were available to, or utilized by, all of the medieval political philosophers. While the Muslim political philosophers frequently refer to Aristotle's *Politics* by name and occasionally quote from it, none of them wrote a commentary on that work. By the late twelfth century, Averroes could state that he had not been able to obtain a copy of it. Moreover, the entire Latin tradition of political philosophy, both pagan and Christian, was not translated into Arabic and remained inaccessible to the Muslims. Instead, the main classical political writings of which they made constant use were the works of Plato and the Eastern Hellenistic Platonic tradition. Plato's *Republic* and *Laws* were known to the Muslims from the tenth century onward. Alfarabi wrote commentaries on both. Avicenna considered Plato's *Laws* to be the fundamental philosophic work on prophecy and the divine Law. And Averroes, the Commentator of Aristotle, wrote a commentary on Plato's *Republic*, but not on Aristotle's *Politics*. Plato, however, by no means appears only as the author of works expounded in commentaries; his political philosophy dominates the entire approach of the Islamic tradition of political philosophy and of that part of Jewish political philosophy which had access to the Arabic philosophic literature.

The situation in Latin Christianity and in the Jewish political philosophy that had access to the Latin philosophic literature is somewhat different. Here Plato's *Republic* and *Laws* are absent throughout the entire medieval period. They were not translated until the Renaissance. Neither were the Arabic commentaries on these works translated into Latin. (Averroes' *Republic* was translated into Latin from the Hebrew version in the sixteenth century.) Aristotle's *Politics*, on the other hand, was translated in the thirteenth century, and at least seven commentaries on it were written within a generation (including those of Albert the Great, Aquinas, Peter of Auvergne, and Siger of Brabant). Aristotle's *Politics*, not Plato's *Republic* and *Laws*, was the fundamental work of political philosophy in the Latin-Christian tradition. In addition, the Christians had access to the Roman pagan political philosophers, particularly Cicero. One may note in this connection a feature of Christian political philosophy that is absent from Islamic political philosophy (and from the writings of Jews who followed its lead): the great interest in the question of natural law, which was a hallmark of the Roman political tradition.

This difference in the classical traditions available to the medieval readers of Arabic and Latin is clear. It also seems clear that this difference is somehow related to the previously discussed differences as to the ways in which political philosophy was regarded, the formulations of its subject matter, and the relations between it and political theology. As a result, political philosophy in Islam and Christianity took distinctive forms, and Jewish political philosophy was, by and large, divided into Judaeo-Arabic and Judaeo-Latin branches. What is not clear is whether the presence or absence of Plato's *Republic* and *Laws*, and of Aristotle's *Politics*, as the case may be, was due purely to chance. Was it the availability in Arabic of Plato's political writings that gave Islamic political philosophy its decidedly Platonic character? Or was it the need to investigate the Islamic divine Law, revelation, prophecy, and so forth, that directed these Muslim philosophers to Plato, whose writings in turn proved more pertinent and helpful to them in their efforts to inquire into these Islamic political problems? Similarly, was the availability of Aristotle's *Politics* in Latin what led the Christian tradition to regard political philosophy as confined to human laws and mundane governance? Or was it the existence of a civil law, with its distinct and restricted area of operation, that directed these Christian philosophers to Aristotle's *Politics*, where political things are discussed as a relatively restricted and independent field of inquiry and where divine Law and the divine origins of laws are not discussed as political themes? While we have no intention of underestimating the role of chance in the transmission of manuscripts, we may note the following facts in passing. There is strong circumstantial evidence that Aristotle's *Politics* was translated into Arabic, and it is certain that Aristotle's political teaching was known to the Muslims at least in the form of quotations from the *Politics*, and from the *Nicomachean Ethics* and his other works. Again, the Latins, up to some time in the thirteenth century, had neither Plato's *Republic* or *Laws* nor Aristotle's *Politics* at hand. These texts had to be searched for before they could be translated; the first Latin translation of the *Politics* appears to have been made at the request of Albert the Great or of Aquinas. Finally, there is the affinity between the facts of political life in Islam and the issues discussed by Plato, on the one hand, and the facts of political life in Christianity and the way in which Aristotle proceeds in the *Politics*, on the other. However this may be understood, it would be misleading to leave it at that. The three religious communities shared a large and important part of the classical tradition. There was the other Aristotle, the Aristotle of the *Organon*, *Physics*, *Metaphysics*, and the *Nicomachean Ethics*. These works provided a common basis in all three religious communities for the distinction between the theoretical and practical sciences. The political philosophers in all three religious communities were as one in maintaining the superiority of theory to practice and in regarding man's ultimate end as the study and contemplation of divine, rather than merely human, things.

No general account of the themes and problems of medieval political philosophy, however detailed, can give an adequate notion of the richness, variety, and refinement (both in style and thought) of the writings of the medieval political philosophers. Like all great writings, these must be confronted directly. The reader must be prepared to be led by the hand by their authors into strange and wondrous lands, to follow them as they present the great themes of political philosophy as they saw them, and to listen to them as they discourse on the beliefs and the ways of life of these religious polities. These medieval political philosophers remain our best guides to the understanding of what is important and lasting in medieval political life. They had access to it as it was actually lived rather than through pages in history books. They participated in it as we can never hope to do. And they were competent and intelligent judges who, in looking at these religious polities, combined sympathy and understanding with dispassionate inquiry to a degree that is rarely equalled by their modern counterparts. The modern student of medieval politics cannot hope to form an adequate notion of his subject without encountering their writing.

This encounter will not be fruitful, however, if the reader is not conscious of the gulf that separates us from those authors, as well as of the many elements that we share with them. To begin with the latter, we must first remember that the Reformation was restricted to the Christian community, and that even here it was not universal or comprehensive: not everybody or everything was reformed. There are many individuals and communities today, in Islam, Judaism, as well as in Christianity, for whom the political teaching represented in this volume remains the true teaching in its classical form. That is, they not only retain the beliefs and ways of life prescribed by these religions, but consider the medieval formulation of their political teaching as either the valid formulation or the treasured heritage whose recovery is a precondition for further achievements in political philosophy. But even where men revolted against the medieval tradition of political philosophy and ventured into novel modes of thought, they nevertheless retained certain elements of it. One need only consider the doctrine of the law of nature, which found its way from Aquinas through Hooker to Locke and which remains of central importance for a number of modern political philosophers. Also retained were more than a few doctrines normally associated with so-called Latin Averroism; these are important directly as the background of Machiavelli's political philosophy, and indirectly for all the modern political philosophers who were influenced by Machiavelli.

There were, of course, many other elements in medieval political philosophy that were suppressed, although never completely so, or in a satisfactory or decisive manner. Perhaps the most important of these suppressed elements is the doctrine of the supremacy of theoretical knowledge over the practical. The medieval thinkers maintained that the highest end of man consists in contemplation rather than action, without in any way belittling the great importance of action and the necessity, for men in general and for the philosopher in particular, of leading a virtuous life. The dethronement of theoretical knowledge is a fundamental change that in one way or another marks modern political philosophy as a whole. One can see it exemplified most dramatically by comparing Ibn Tufayl's *Hayy the Son of Yaqzan* and Daniel Defoe's *Robinson Crusoe*. Ibn Tufayl's story was popular in late seventeenth-century England, and Defoe may have taken it as a model for his own story. Ibn Tufayl's hero, who is convinced of the necessity of reforming the multitude and is willing to do his duty toward his fellowmen, spends his remaining days back on his deserted island contemplating God. Defoe's hero, in contrast, returns to England, enjoying the comforts of the material civilization of his time. To champion the doctrine that the end of man consists in the enjoyment of material civilization, or in comfortable self-preservation, would have looked human, all too human, to the medieval political philosophers. But apart from their difficulty in seeing anything particularly pious about such a doctrine, they did not think that it was reasonable.

The dethronement of theoretical knowledge is an aspect of modern political philosophy that is not universally recognized or admitted: modern political philosophy emerged as a revolt, not only against the medieval tradition, but also—and more specifically—against the classical tradition of political philosophy, which the middle ages had found in the writings of Plato and Aristotle. We do not always recognize the fact that medieval political philosophy gives testimony to the great vitality of the classical tradition and supplies the most damaging evidence against the hypothesis that classical political philosophy was purely a Greek affair. The times seemed most unpropitious: revealed religions had arisen claiming the privilege of having received the very word of God Himself, directly or through His chosen messengers. Why should anyone attach importance to what certain pagans had thought about God, the ultimate end of man, and the best political order? Yet classical political philosophy asserted its claim that it can offer the best, if not the only, way to investigate the truth of the claims of these religions, even the truth of their revelations and prophecies and divine Laws. Everyone who cared to pursue the truth of these matters was forced to listen to it, come to terms with it, and, curiously enough, learn from it how to investigate divine and human things, how to reform the beliefs and way of life of his own community, and how to act in a manner conducive to the common interest of his community and to his own interest as an investigator.

In contrast, the break with classical political philosophy has led modern political philosophy progressively to simplify and oversimplify the complexity of the relation between philosophy or science and society: first by narrowing the horizon within which knowledge is pursued (notwithstanding the great expansion of the material of investigation within this narrowed horizon), then by lowering the aims pursued in political life, and finally by reducing the possibilities of action open to man within society by emphasizing the causal determination exercised by the lower elements of life over the higher. In its anxiety to free itself from medieval dogmatism, modern political philosophy has shown a tendency to substitute new forms of dogmatism whose scientific claims cannot entirely conceal their dogmatic foundation or their harmful practical consequences. Today we are becoming increasingly aware of the fact that the revolt against medieval political theology did not liberate modern political philosophy; it only led to the substitution of new political theologies for the old one. We moderns are willing to admit this fact about almost the entire modern tradition, and even about all the contemporary schools of thought, with the sole exception of contemporary scientific social science. But we refuse to consider the possibility that the reason for the failure of modern political philosophy and for our dissatisfaction with it may be due not so much to its revolt against medieval political theology as to its revolt against classical political philosophy. Medieval political philosophy can teach us many things, but perhaps its most telling lesson is that classical political philosophy has both the theoretical and practical possibilities to humanize a barbarous age and to free men from the darkness of their prisons.

PART ONE

Political Philosophy
in Islam

EDITED BY MUHSIN MAHDI

1.

Alfarabi

THE ENUMERATION

OF THE SCIENCES

Translated by Fauzi M. Najjar

Alfarabi (Abū Naṣr Muḥammad al-Fārābī, *ca.* 870–950) was born in Transoxania and studied in Khorasan and Baghdad. In 942 he left Baghdad for the court of the Syrian Prince Sayf al-Dawlah in Aleppo. While in Syria, he visited Egypt and lived in Damascus, which was seized by his patron prince three years after Alfarabi's departure from Baghdad. He died at the age of eighty and was buried with full honors in Damascus. Among others, Alfarabi studied under Yūhannā Ibn Haylān, a Syriac-speaking Christian who taught in Harrān (Carrhae) and Baghdad (where he died in the first third of the tenth century), and he traces the philosophic tradition represented by this Yūhannā to the school of Alexandria, where philosophy survived despite the restrictions imposed by church authorities. The decline of the cultural position of Alexandria after the

Muslim conquest seems to have forced this school to move first to Antioch (early in the eighth century) and then to Harrān (in the middle of the ninth century), where Greek learning and paganism continued to flourish in the midst of Syriac-speaking Christian neighbors and under Islamic rule. (According to certain reports, Alfarabi studied there himself.)

Alfarabi was the first Muslim philosopher to head a "school" and to become known as a "teacher." He was acknowledged by subsequent Muslim philosophers as the true founder of philosophy in Islam, and Muslim historians of philosophy called him *the* Muslim philosopher and the "second Master" (after Aristotle). His commentaries on Aristotle's works established the latter's authority in logic, physics, and metaphysics. Simultaneously, he recovered the significance of

Plato and introduced him as the supreme authority on political philosophy and the investigation of human and divine laws.

In his preface to the *Enumeration of the Sciences*, Alfarabi states that his intention is to give an enumeration of the well-known sciences, and make known the basic themes of each, its subdivisions, and the basic themes of each of the subdivisions. This will be done in five chapters: (1) the science of language, (2) logic, (3) mathematics, (4) physics and metaphysics, and (5) political science, jurisprudence, and dialectical theology. He concludes the preface by enumerating the uses of the book's content: it will enable the student who wishes to study a particular science to know where to begin, what he will gain from his study, and so forth, and to be aware of what he is undertaking rather than plunge into it blindly. It enables one to compare the various sciences and learn which of them is more excellent, more useful, more precise, and so forth. It enables one to uncover the ignorance of whoever pretends to know a particular science; by asking about its subdivisions and basic themes, one will be able to show his false claim. It enables one who knows a particular science to find out whether he knows all or only certain parts of it, and to what extent he knows it. Finally, it is useful to the educated man whose intention is to

acquaint himself with only the basic themes of every science and to the man who seeks to resemble the men of science and be considered one of them. Despite its terseness, Chapter V contains the earliest and most significant comprehensive account of the basic themes and subdivisions of political science in Islamic philosophy.

In the Arabic original, the *Enumeration of the Sciences* became an indispensable introduction to the study of the sciences and was freely copied and paraphrased by many encyclopedists and historians of the sciences. Judaeo-Arabic authors used it in the Arabic original, and substantial extracts from it were translated into Hebrew by Shemtob ben Falaquera (who lived in Spain and Provence during the thirteenth century) and Kalonymos ben Kalonymos of Arles (in 1314). Dominicus Gundisalvi (perhaps in collaboration with John of Spain [Ibn Dāwūd]) extracted about half of it in his composite work *De Scientiis* (middle of the twelfth century; printed in Paris, 1638); and Gerard of Cremona made a complete Latin translation from the Arabic in Toledo in about 1175. The following translation is based on Osman Amine's second edition of the Arabic original: *Iḥṣā' al-'ulūm* (Cairo, 1948), pp. 102-13. The notes to the translation specify whether the readings adopted here occur in the notes to this edition.

CHAPTER V

ON POLITICAL SCIENCE, JURISPRUDENCE

AND DIALECTICAL THEOLOGY

POLITICAL SCIENCE

POLITICAL SCIENCE investigates the various kinds of voluntary actions and ways of life;[1] the positive dispositions, morals, inclinations, and states of character that lead to these actions and ways of life;[1] the ends for the sake of which they are performed; how they must exist in man; how to order them in man in the manner in which they must exist in him; and the way to preserve them for him. It distinguishes among the ends for the sake of which actions are performed and ways of life[1] are practiced. It explains that some of them are true happiness, while others are presumed to be happiness although they are not. That which is true happiness cannot possibly be of this life, but of another life after this, which is the life to come; while that which is presumed to be happiness consists of such things as wealth, honor, and the pleasures, when these are made the only ends in this life. Distinguishing the actions and ways of life,[1] it explains that the ones through which true happiness is attained are the goods, the noble things, and the virtues, while the rest are the evils, the base things, and the imperfections; and that they [must] exist in man in such a way that [103] the virtuous actions and ways of life[1] are distributed in the cities and nations according to a certain order and are practiced in common. It explains that this comes about only through a rulership (ri'āsah) by which [the ruler] establishes these actions, ways of life,[2] states of character, positive dispositions, and morals in the cities and nations, and endeavors to preserve them so that they do not perish; and that this rulership comes about only by virtue of a craft and a positive disposition that lead to the actions that establish [these virtues] and to the actions that preserve what has been established among them [that is, the cities and nations]. This is the royal craft or kingship, or whatever one chooses to call it; politics (siyāsah) is the operation of this craft.

[Political science explains] that rulership is of two kinds. (a) A rulership that establishes the voluntary actions, ways of life,[2] and positive dispositions, with which to attain what is truly happiness. This is the virtuous rulership; the cities and nations that submit to this rulership are the virtuous cities and nations. (*b*) A rulership that establishes in the cities the actions and states of character with which to attain the things that are presumed to be happiness although they are not. This is the ignorant rulership. It has many divisions, each of which is designated by the purpose it seeks and strives for; there are thus as many of them as there are ends and purposes for this rulership to pursue. If it pursues wealth, it is called the vile[3] rulership; if honor, timocracy; and if something else, it is given the name of its particular end.

[Political science] further explains that the virtuous royal craft is composed of two faculties. The one is the faculty for [*104*] general rules. The other is the faculty that man acquires through long practice in political deeds, dealing with the morals and the individuals existing in actual[4] cities, and becoming practically wise through experience and long observation, as is the case in medicine. For the physician becomes a perfect practitioner by virtue of two faculties. The one is the faculty for the generalities and the rules he has acquired from medical books. The other is the faculty he acquires by the long practice of medicine on the sick and by becoming practically wise in this through long experience and observation of the bodies of individuals. By virtue of this latter faculty, the physician is able to determine the medicaments and the cure with a view to a particular body in a particular state. Similarly, it is by means of such a faculty and experience that the royal craft is able to determine what is to be done with a view to a particular accident, state, and time.[5]

Regarding the voluntary actions, ways of life,[1] positive dispositions, and so forth, that it investigates, political philosophy gives an account of the general rules. It gives an account of the patterns according to which they should be determined with due regard to particular states and times: how, with what, and by how many things, they are to be determined. Beyond this, it leaves them undetermined, because actual determination belongs to another faculty, with a different function, which should be joined to this one. Moreover, the states and the accidents with a view to which the determination is made are indefinite and uncircumscribable. This science is divided into two parts:

(*A*) One part comprises making known what happiness is; distinguishing between true and presumed happiness; enumerating the general voluntary actions, ways of life, morals, and states of character that are to be distributed in the cities and nations; and distinguishing between the ones that are virtuous and the ones that are not.

(*B*) Another part comprises the way of ordering the virtuous states of character and ways of life in the cities and nations; and making known the royal functions by which the virtuous ways of life and actions are established [*105*] and ordered among the citizens of the cities, and the activities by which to preserve what has been ordered and established among them. It then enumerates the various kinds of the nonvirtuous royal crafts—how many they are, and what each one of them is; and it enumerates the functions each one of them performs, and the ways of life[1] and the positive dispositions that each seeks to establish in the cities and nations under its rulership. (These things are to be found in the *Politics,* the book on the regime by Aristotle. They are to be found also in Plato's *Republic* and in [other] books by Plato and others.) It explains that all of these actions, ways of life, and positive dispositions are like diseases to the virtuous cities: the actions that pertain to the royal crafts and the royal ways of life [in the nonvirtuous cities] are diseases to the virtuous royal craft; and the ways of life and the positive dispositions that pertain to these cities are like diseases to the virtuous cities. It then enumerates the grounds and the directions because of which the virtuous rulerships and the ways of life[1] of the virtuous cities are in danger of being transformed into the ignorant ways of life[1] and positive dispositions. Furthermore, it enumerates the various kinds of actions by which virtuous cities and rulerships are regulated so that they do not become corrupt and transformed into nonvirtuous ones. It enumerates also the various measures, devices, and methods that should be used to restore them to their previous state once they have been transformed into ignorant [cities and rulerships]. It then explains of how many things the virtuous royal craft is composed; [*106*] that they include the theoretical and the practical sciences; and that to these should be joined the faculty acquired through the experience arising from long practice in cities and nations—this last is the ability to discover well the conditions according to which the actions, ways of life, and positive dispositions are determined with a view to a particular group, city, or nation, and with a view to a particular state and accident. It explains that the virtuous city remains virtuous and escapes transformation only if its princes continue to succeed one another in time and possess identical qualifications, so that the successor would possess the same attributes and qualifications as his predecessor and their succession would be without break or interruption. It makes known what must be done in order to avoid a break in the succession of princes. It explains which natural qualifications and attributes must be sought in the sons of the princes and in others, so that they may qualify their possessor to assume authority after the ruling prince. It explains how the one who is endowed with these natural qualifications must grow up and how he ought to be educated, so that he may possess the royal craft and become an accomplished prince. It explains, further, that those whose rulership is ignorant should not at all be called[6] princes, and that they do not need either theoretical or practical philosophy in any of their states, activities, or policies. Rather, each one of them can achieve his purpose in the city or nation under his rule by virtue of the experiential faculty that he acquires through the continual practice in the kind of actions with which he attains his goal and achieves whatever goods he aims at, [*107*] provided he happens to possess a fine natural perceptive faculty with which to discover what he needs to do in order to attain the good that is his goal—be it pleasure, honor, or something else—supplemented by the ability to follow in the footsteps of the preceding princes whose goal was the same as his.

THE SCIENCE OF JURISPRUDENCE

Jurisprudence (*fiqh*) is the art that enables man to infer the determination of whatever was not explicitly specified by the Lawgiver, on the basis of such things as were explicitly specified and determined by him; and to strive to infer correctly by taking into account the Lawgiver's purpose with the religion he had legislated for the nation to which he gave that religion. Now every religion comprises certain opinions and certain actions. Examples of the opinions are those legislated about God (praise be to Him) and His attributes, about the world, and so forth. Examples of the actions are those by which God (the Mighty and Majestic) is magnified, and the actions by means of which transactions are conducted in the cities. For this reason, the science of jurisprudence has two parts, one part dealing with the opinions and another dealing with the actions.

THE SCIENCE OF DIALECTICAL THEOLOGY

The art of dialectical theology (*kalām*) is a positive disposition that enables man to argue in the defense of the [*108*] specific opinions and actions stated explicitly by the founder of the religion, and against everything that opposes these opinions and actions. This art is also divided into two parts; one part deals with the opinions, and another deals with the actions. It is different from jurisprudence. For the jurist takes the opinions and the actions stated explicitly by the founder of the religion and, using them as axioms, he infers the things that follow from them as consequences. The dialectical theologian, on the other hand, defends the things that the jurist uses as axioms, without inferring other things from them. If it should happen that a certain man possesses the ability to do both, then he is both a jurist and a dialectical theologian. He defends the axioms in his capacity as a dialectical theologian, and he infers from them in his capacity as a jurist.

As far as the ways and opinions that must be employed in defending

religions are concerned [dialectical theologians hold a variety of views
that can be summed up as follows]:

(*A*) There is a group of dialectical theologians who are of the opinion
that they should defend religions by arguing that religious opinions and
all their postulates are not susceptible of examination by human opinions,
deliberation, or intellects, because they are superior to these in rank since
they are received through divine revelation, and because they comprise
divine mysteries that human intellects are too weak to comprehend or
approach. Again, man is such that, through revelation, religions can
offer him what [*109*] he cannot apprehend by his intellect, and before
which his intellect is impotent. Otherwise, revelation would be meaning-
less and useless, for it would only offer man that which he knows already
or what he could, upon reflection, come to apprehend by his intellect.
Were this the case, man would have been left to depend on his intellect,
and he would have had no need for prophecy or revelation. But this
is not the way he is treated. Consequently, the knowledge supplied by
religions must be what our intellects are unable to apprehend and, what
is more, also what our intellects reject; for the more intensely we reject it,
the greater the possibility that it is vastly advantageous. That is because
the things that are brought forth by religions and that the [human]
intellects reject and [human] fancies regard as abominable, are in reality
neither objectionable nor absurd, but are valid for the divine intellects.
For even though man were to reach the limit of human perfection, his
position in relation to the possessors of divine intellects is like that of the
child, the adolescent, and the callow youth in relation to the perfect man.
Most children and callow youths consider as objectionable by their intellects many things that are not in reality objectionable or impossible—
although to them they are impossible. The one who has reached the
limit of human perfection occupies a similar position in relation to the
divine intellects. Also, prior to his being trained and experienced, man
considers many things objectionable, [*110*] regards them as abominable,
and imagines that they are absurd. But once he is trained in the sciences
and acquires practical wisdom through experience, he is freed from such
beliefs: the things he had considered absurd prove to be necessary, and
he would wonder about the opposite of what formerly used to cause
him wonder. Similarly, it is possible that the man who is perfect in
humanity may consider certain things objectionable and imagine that
they are impossible, although in reality they are not. The reasons why
these [dialectical theologians] held the opinion that religions must be
considered valid are as follows. He who brought us revelation from God
(praised be His name) is veracious and it is inadmissible that he may
have lied. That he is such, may be attested in one or both of two ways:
the miracles that he performs[7] or that take place through him, or the

testimonies to his veracity and his place with God (the Mighty and Majestic) of the veracious and trustworthy ones who preceded him. Once we validate his veracity in these ways, and [acknowledge] that it is inadmissible that he may have lied, there ought not to remain any room for intellecting, reflection, deliberation, or speculation with respect to the things he says. It is with such and similar arguments that these [dialectical theologians] thought they should defend religions.

(B) Another group of them are of the opinion that they should defend religion by first presenting everything stated explicitly by the founder of the religion in the very words he used to express them. Then they look around for the various sensible, generally accepted, and intelligible things. Whenever they find that one of these, or something that follows from it as consequence, [111] supports, though remotely, anything in the religion, they use the former to defend the latter; and whenever it contradicts anything in the religion, and they are able to interpret, no matter how remote the interpretation may be, the words in which the founder of the religion has expressed it [that is, what is in the religion] in such a manner as to make it harmonious with that which contradicts it, they would proceed to interpret it in this manner. If this were not possible for them, but it were possible to argue against that contradicting thing, or to construe it in a manner that would make it accord with what is in the religion, they would do so. When, however, the testimony of the generally accepted opinions and of the objects of sense contradict each other—for instance, when the objects of sense or their consequences require one thing and the generally accepted opinions or their consequences require the contrary—they would look for the one whose testimony in support of what is in the religion is stronger and adopt it, and they would dismiss the other and argue against it. Now, when it proves impossible to construe the religious text to accord with either of these [that is, the objects of sense or the generally accepted opinions], or to construe any of these to accord with the religion, or to dismiss or argue against any of the objects of sense, the generally accepted opinions, or the intelligibles that contradict a certain thing in the religion, they then hold the opinion that this thing [in the religion] should be defended by arguing that it is true on the ground that it is reported by him who could not have lied or erred. These [dialectical theologians] argue concerning this part of the religion as the first group argued concerning all of it. This, then, is the way in which these [dialectical theologians] thought they should defend religions. [112]

A certain group of them[8] hold the opinion that they should defend things of this sort [in their religion] (namely, the ones that they imagine to be absurd)[9] by looking into all other religions and selecting the absurd things in them, so that when a follower of one of the other religions seeks to vilify something in theirs, they will confront him with the absurd things in the religions of others and thus ward off his assault upon their own.

Another group of them, realizing that the arguments they advance in the defense of things of this sort are insufficient to prove their complete validity—so that their adversary's silence would result from his accepting the validity of these things rather than from his inability to argue against them—were then forced to use certain things that would drive him to cease arguing against them,[10] either from shame and his inability to express himself adequately, or from fear of being harmed.

And still others, convinced of the validity of their own religion beyond any doubt, [*113*] hold the opinion that they should defend it before others, show it to be fair and free it of suspicion, and ward off their adversaries from it, by using any chance thing. They would not even disdain to use falsehood, sophistry, confounding, and contentiousness because they hold the opinion that only one of two men would oppose their religion. He is either an enemy, and it is admissible to use falsehood and sophistry to ward him off and to defeat him, as is the case in war (*jihād*) and combat. Or he is not an enemy, but one who, owing to weak intellect and poor judgment, is ignorant of the advantage he would derive from this religion; and it is admissible to use falsehood and sophistry to make man seek his well-being, just as is done in the case of women and children.

NOTES

1. Reading *siyar* (n.) for *sunan* (laws).
2. Reading *siyar* for *sunan;* cf. preceding note.
3. For a detailed description of this and other regimes, see Alfarabi, *Political Regime*, pp. 57 ff. (below, Selection 2).
4. Literally: "experiential" (*tajrībiyyah*).
5. See Alfarabi, *Attainment of Happiness*, pp. 17 ff. (below, Selection 3).
6. Reading *yusammaw* (n.) for *yakūnū* (be).

7. Reading *ya'maluhā* (n.) for *ya-'qiluhā* (intellects them).
8. From the manner in which Alfarabi introduces and concludes the description of (*A*) and (*B*), it appears that this and the following two subdivisions belong to group (*B*).
9. The phrase in parentheses appears to be an interpolation.
10. Adding *bi-l-qawl* (n.).

2.

Alfarabi

THE POLITICAL REGIME

Translated by Fauzi M. Najjar

In a famous letter to his translator Ibn Tibbon, Maimonides wrote: "Do not busy yourself with books on the art of logic except for what was composed by the wise man Abū Naṣr al-Fārābī [Alfarabi]. For, in general, everything that he composed—and particularly his book on the *Principles of Beings*—is all finer than fine flour. His arguments enable one to understand and comprehend, for he was very great in wisdom." The work referred to by Maimonides is known under two titles: the *Principles of Beings* (or the *Six Principles*) and the *Political Regime*. The first title seems to have been extracted from the opening passage of the work, which gives the impression that it is a treatise on the principles of the natural world and their respective ranks of order: (1) the First Cause, (2) the Second Causes, (3) the Active Intellect, (4) the soul, (5) form, and (6) matter. The entire

first part of the work consists of an account of these six principles and of how they constitute the bodies and their accidents. Only when one proceeds to the second part (the human and political part translated here) does one perceive that this account is an introduction to, and a preparation for, an account of political life and a classification of political regimes. Alfarabi wrote a parallel book, the *Principles of the Opinions of the Citizens of the Virtuous City*, which discusses the same themes in similar terms. As the titles indicate, however, the *Political Regime* is concerned more with regimes or constitutions while the *Virtuous City* is concerned more with the opinions of the citizens in these regimes.

The *Political Regime* is frequently cited by Muslim authors as one of the fundamental works of Alfarabi. It was translated into Hebrew in the middle

31

Being philosopher — highest goal
different kinds of recurring 4/in those 4
there is
hierarchy. — #1 philosophy

of the thirteenth century. The following translation is based on the critical edition of the Arabic text prepared by Fauzi M. Najjar. The page numbers inserted in the translation refer to the Hyderabad text: *al-Siyāsāt al-madaniyyah* (1346 A.H.). This edition is incomplete, and so are all the manuscripts, with the possible exception of Feyzullah 1279.

MAN BELONGS to the species that cannot accomplish their necessary affairs or achieve their best state, except through the association of many groups of them in a single dwelling-place. Some human societies are large, others are of a medium size, still others are small. The large societies consist of many nations that associate and cooperate with one another; the medium ones consist of a nation; the small are the ones embraced by the city. These three are the perfect societies. Hence the city represents the first degree of perfection. Associations in villages, quarters, streets, and households, on the other hand, are the imperfect associations. Of these the least perfect is the household association, which is a part of the association in the street, the latter being a part of the association in the quarter, and this in turn a part of the political association. Associations in quarters and villages are both for the sake of the city; they differ, however, in that the quarters are parts of the city while the villages only serve it. [*40*] The political [or civic] society is a part of the nation, and the nation is divided into cities. The absolutely perfect human societies are divided into nations. A nation is differentiated from another by two natural things—natural make-up and natural character—and by something that is composite (it is conventional but has a basis in natural things), which is language—I mean the idiom through which men express themselves. As a result some nations are large and others are small.

The primary natural cause of the differences between nations in these matters consists of a variety of things. One of them is the difference in the parts of the celestial bodies that face them, namely, the first [that is, the outermost] sphere and the sphere of the fixed stars, then the difference in the positions of the inclined spheres from the various parts of the earth and the variation in their proximity and remoteness. From this follows the difference between the parts of the earth that are the nations' dwelling-places; for from the outset, this difference results from the difference in the parts of the first sphere that face them, from the difference in the fixed stars that face them, and from the difference in the positions of the inclined spheres with respect to them. From the difference between the parts of the earth follows the difference in the vapors rising from the earth; since each vapor rises from a certain soil, it is akin to that soil. From the difference in the vapors follows the difference in the air and water, inasmuch as the water of each country is generated from its underground vapors, and the air of each country is mixed with the vapors that work their way up to it from the soil. In the same manner, the difference in the air and water [of each country] follows from the difference [in the parts] of the fixed stars and of the first sphere that face it, and from the difference in the positions of the inclined spheres. From all these differences, in turn, follows the difference in the plants and in the species of irrational animals, [*41*] as a result of which nations have different diets. From the difference in their diets follows the difference in the materials and crops that go into the composition of the individuals who succeed the ones who die. From this, in turn, follows the difference in the natural make-up and natural character. Moreover, the difference in the parts of the heaven that face them causes further differences in their make-up and character, in a different manner from the one mentioned above. The difference in the air, too, causes differences in make-up and character in a different manner from the one mentioned above. Furthermore, out of the cooperation and combination of these differences there develop different mixtures that contribute to differences in the make-up and character of the nations. It is in this manner and direction that natural things fit together, are connected with each other, and occupy their respective ranks; and this is the extent to which the celestial bodies contribute to their perfection. The remaining perfections are not given by the celestial bodies but by the Active Intellect;[1] and the Active Intellect gives the remaining perfections to no other species but man.

In giving [these perfections] to man, the Active Intellect follows a course similar to that followed by the celestial bodies. First, it gives him a faculty and a principle with which, of his own accord, he seeks, or is able to seek, the remaining perfections. That principle consists of the primary knowledge and the first intelligibles present in the rational part of the soul; but it gives him this kind of knowledge and those intelligibles only after man (*a*) first develops the sensitive part of the soul and the appetitive part, which gives rise to the desire and aversion that adhere to the sensitive part. [*42*] (The instruments of the last two faculties develop from the parts of the body.) They, in turn, give rise to the will. For, at first, the will is nothing but a desire that follows from a sensation; and desire takes place through the appetitive part of the soul, and sensation through the sensitive. (*b*) Next, there has to develop the imaginative part of the soul and the desire that adheres to it. Hence a second will develops after the first. This will is a desire that follows from [an act of the] imagination. After these two wills develop, it becomes possible for the primary knowledge that emanates from the Active Intellect to the rational part to take place. At this point a third kind of will develops in man—the desire that follows from intellecting—which is specifically called "choice." This choice pertains specifically to man, exclusive of all other animals. By virtue of it, man is able to do either what is commendable or blamable, noble or base; and because of it there are reward and punishment. (The first two wills, on the other hand, can exist in the irrational animals too.) When this will develops in man, with it he is able to seek or not to seek happiness, and to do what is good or evil, noble or base, in so far as this lies in his power.

Happiness is the good without qualification. Everything useful for the achievement of happiness or by which it is attained, is good too, not for its own sake, however, but because it is useful with respect to happiness; and everything that obstructs the way to happiness in any fashion is unqualified evil. The good that is useful for the achievement of happiness may be something that exists by nature or that comes into being by the will, and the evil that obstructs the way to happiness may be something that exists by nature or that comes into being by the will. That of it which is by nature is given by the celestial bodies, but not because they intend to assist the Active Intellect toward its purpose or [43] to hamper it. For when the celestial bodies give something that contributes to the purpose of the Active Intellect, they do not do so with the intention of assisting the Active Intellect; neither are the natural things that obstruct the way to its purpose intended by the celestial bodies to hamper the Active Intellect. Rather, it is inherent in the substance of the celestial bodies to give all that it is in the nature of matter to receive, without concerning themselves with whether it contributes to, or harms, the purpose of the Active Intellect. Therefore it is possible that the sum total of what is produced by the celestial bodies should comprise at times things that are favorable, and at other times things that are unfavorable, to the purpose of the Active Intellect.

As to voluntary good and evil, which are the noble and the base respectively, they have their origin specifically in man. Now there is only one way in which the voluntary good can come into being. That is because the faculties of the human soul are five: the theoretical-rational, the practical-rational, the appetitive, the imaginative, and the sensitive. Happiness, which only man can know and perceive, is known by the theoretical-rational faculty and by none of the remaining faculties. Man knows it when he makes use of the first principles and the primary knowledge given to him by the Active Intellect. When he knows happiness, desires it by the appetitive faculty, deliberates by the practical-rational faculty upon what he ought to do in order to attain it, uses the instruments of the appetitive faculty to do the actions he has discovered by deliberation, and his imaginative and sensitive faculties assist and obey the rational and aid it in arousing man to do the actions with which he attains happiness, then everything that originates from man will be good. It is only in this way that the voluntary good comes into being. As to voluntary evil, it originates in the manner that I shall state. Neither the imaginative nor the appetitive faculty perceives [44] happiness. Not even the rational faculty perceives happiness under all conditions. The rational faculty perceives happiness only when it strives to apprehend it. Now there are many things that man can imagine that they ought to be the aim and end of life, such as the pleasant and the useful, honor, and the like. Whenever man neglects to perfect his theoretical-rational part, fails to perceive happiness and hasten toward it, holds something other than happiness—what is useful, what is pleasant, domination, what is honorable, and the like—as an end toward which he aims in his life, desires it with the appetitive faculty, uses the practical-rational faculty to deliberate in the discovery of what enables him to attain this end, uses the instruments of the appetitive faculty to do the things he has discovered, and is assisted in this by the imaginative and the sensitive faculties, then everything that originates from him is evil. Similarly, when man apprehends and knows happiness but does not make it the aim and the end of his life, has no desire or has only a feeble desire for it, makes something other than happiness the end that he desires in his life, and uses all his faculties to attain that end, then everything that originates from him is evil.

Since what is intended by man s existence is that he attain happiness, which is the ultimate perfection that remains to be given to the possible[2] beings capable of receiving it, it is necessary to state the manner in which man can reach this happiness. Man can reach happiness only when the Active Intellect first gives the first intelligibles, which constitute the primary knowledge. However, not every man is equipped by natural disposition to receive the first intelligibles, because individual human beings are made by nature with unequal powers and different preparations. Some of them are not prepared by nature to receive any of [45] the first intelligibles; others—for instance, the insane—receive them, but not as they really are; and still others receive them as they really are. The last are the ones with sound human natural dispositions; only these, and not the others, are capable of attaining happiness.

* * *

Since what is intended by man's existence is that he attain supreme happiness, he—[48] in order to achieve it—needs to know what happiness is, make it his end, and hold it before his eyes. Then, after that, he needs to know the things he ought to do in order to attain happiness, and then do these actions. In view of what has been said about the differences in the natural dispositions of individual men, not everyone is disposed to know happiness on his own, or the things that he ought to do, but needs a teacher and a guide for this purpose. Some men need little guidance, others need a great deal of it. In addition, even when a man is guided to these two [that is, happiness and the actions leading to it], he will not, in the absence of an external stimulus and something to arouse him, necessarily do what he has been taught and guided to. This is how most men are. Therefore they need someone to make all this known to them and to arouse them to do it.

Besides, it is not in the power of every man to guide others nor in the power of every man to induce others to do these things. He who does not possess the power to arouse another to do anything whatever, nor to employ him in it, but only has the power always to do what he has been guided to, is never a ruler in anything at all; he is always ruled in everything. He who has the power to guide another to a certain thing, to induce him to do it, and to employ him in it, is in that thing a ruler over the one who cannot do it on his own. And he who cannot discover something on his own, but does it when he is guided to it and instructed in it, and has the power to arouse another to do, and to employ him in, that thing in which he himself has been instructed and to which he has been guided, is a ruler over one man and is ruled by another. Thus the ruler may be a supreme or a subordinate ruler. The subordinate ruler is one who is subject to one man [49] and in turn rules over another. These two types of rule can be in one kind [of art], such as husbandry, trade, or medicine, and can pertain to all kinds of human [arts].

The supreme ruler without qualification is he who does not need anyone to rule him in anything whatever, but has actually acquired the sciences and every kind of knowledge, and has no need of a man to guide him in anything. He is able to comprehend well each one of the particular things that he ought to do. He is able to guide well all others to everything in which he instructs them, to employ all those who do any of the acts for which they are equipped, and to determine, define, and direct these acts toward happiness. This is found only in the one who possesses great and superior natural dispositions, when his soul is in union with the Active Intellect. He can only attain this [union with the Active Intellect] by first acquiring the passive intellect, and then the intellect called the acquired; for, as it is stated in *On the Soul*,[3] union with the Active Intellect results from possessing the acquired intellect. This man is the true prince according to the ancients; he is the one of whom it ought to be said that he receives revelation. For man receives revelation only when he attains this rank, that is, when there is no longer an intermediary between him and the Active Intellect; for the passive intellect is like matter and substratum to the acquired intellect, and the latter is like matter and substratum to the Active Intellect. It is then that the power that enables man to understand how to define things and actions and how to direct them toward happiness, emanates from the Active Intellect to the passive intellect. [50] This emanation that proceeds from the Active Intellect to the passive through the mediation of the acquired intellect, is revelation. Now because the Active Intellect emanates from the being of the First Cause, it can for this reason be said that it is the First Cause that brings about revelation to this man through the mediation of the Active Intellect. The rule of this man is the supreme rule; all other human rulerships are inferior to it and are derived from it. Such is his rank.

The men who are governed by the rule of this ruler are the virtuous, good, and happy men. If they form a nation, then that is the virtuous nation; if they are associated in a single dwelling-place, then the dwelling-place that brings together all those subject to such a rule is the virtuous city; and if they are not associated together in a single dwelling-place, but live in separate dwelling-places whose inhabitants are governed by rulerships other than this one, then these are virtuous men who are strangers in those dwelling-places. They happen to live separately either because no city happens to exist as yet in which they can be associated, or because they were [associated] in a city, but as a result of certain disasters—such as an enemy attack, pestilence, failure of crops, and so forth—they were forced to separate. If at any one time a group of these princes happens to reside in a single city, in a single nation, or in many nations, then this group is as it were a single prince because they agree in their endeavors, purposes, opinions, and ways of life. If they follow one another in time, their souls will form as it were a single soul, the one who succeeds will be following the way of life of his predecessors, and the living will be following in the way of the ones who have died. Just as it is permissible for each of them to change a Law he had legislated at one time [51] for another if he deems it better to do so, similarly it is permissible for the living who succeeds the one who died to change what the latter had legislated, for the one who died also would have changed it had he been able to observe the new conditions. But if it does not happen that a man exists with these qualifications, then one will have to adopt the Laws prescribed by the earlier ones, write them down, preserve them, and govern the city by them. The ruler who governs the city according to the written Laws received from the past imams will be the prince of the law (*sunnah*).

As every citizen of the city does what is entrusted to him—either by knowing it on his own or by being guided and induced to it by the ruler—he acquires, by these actions, the good states of the soul, just as by continued practice in good writing a man acquires excellence in the art of writing, which is a state of the soul; and the more he continues practicing, the more firm his excellence in writing becomes, the greater the pleasure he takes in the resulting state, and the stronger the delight of his soul in that state. Similarly, the actions that are determined and directed toward happiness strengthen the part of the soul that is naturally equipped for happiness, and actualize and perfect it—to the extent that the power resulting from the perfection achieved by it enables it to dispense with matter; having been thus freed from matter, it is not destroyed by the destruction of matter, since it is no longer in need of matter in order to exercise its power or to exist—at which time it attains happiness. It is evident that the kinds of happiness attained by the citizens of the city differ in quantity and quality as a result of the difference in the perfections they acquire through political activities. Accordingly, [52] the pleasures they attain vary in excellence. When the soul becomes separated from matter and incorporeal, it is no longer subject to any of the accidents that are attached to bodies as such; therefore it cannot be said of it that it moves or that it rests. Rather one ought then to apply to it the statements appropriate to what is incorporeal. Every one of the things adhering to the human soul and that fits the description of the body as body, ought to be considered as one of the negative attributes of the separate soul. The comprehension and conception of the states of the separate soul are extremely difficult and at variance with common usage, just as it is difficult to conceive the substances that are not bodies or in bodies.

As one group of them passes away, and their bodies are destroyed, their souls have achieved salvation and happiness, and they are succeeded by other men who assume their positions in the city and perform their actions, the souls of the latter will also achieve salvation. As their bodies are destroyed, they join the rank of the former group that had passed away, they will be together with them in the way that incorporeal things are together, and the kindred souls within each group will be in a state of union with one another. The more the kindred separate souls increase in number and unite with one another, the greater the pleasure felt by each soul; and the more they are joined by those who come after them, the greater the pleasure felt by each of the latter through their encounter with the former as well as the pleasure felt by the former through their union with the latter. For each soul will then be intellecting, in addition to itself, many other souls that are of the same kind; and it will be intellecting more souls as the ones that had passed away are joined by the ones succeeding them. Hence the pleasure felt by the very ancient ones will continue to increase indefinitely. Such is the state of every group of them. This, then, is true and supreme happiness, which is the purpose of the Active Intellect.

When the activities of the citizens of a city are not directed toward happiness, they lead them to acquire [53] bad states of the soul—just as when the activities of [the art of] writing are badly performed, they produce bad writing, and similarly, when the activities of any art are badly performed, they produce in the soul bad states, corresponding to the [badly performed] art. As a result their souls become sick. Therefore they take pleasure in the states that they acquire through their activities. Just as because of their corrupt sense [of taste], those with bodily sickness—for example, the ones affected by fever—take pleasure in bitter things and find them sweet, and suffer pain from sweet things, which seem bitter to their palates; similarly, because of their corrupt imagination, those who are sick in their souls take pleasure in the bad states [of the soul]. And just as there are among the sick those who do not feel their malady and those who even think that they are healthy, and such sick men do not at all listen to the advice of a physician; similarly, the sick in their souls who do not feel their sickness and even think that they are virtuous and have sound souls, do not listen at all to the words of a guide, a teacher, or a reformer. The souls of such individuals remain chained to matter and do not reach that perfection by which they can separate from matter, so that when the matter ceases to exist they too will cease to exist.

The ranks of order among the citizens of the city, as regards ruling and serving, vary in excellence according to their natural dispositions and according to the habits of character they have formed. The supreme ruler is the one who orders the various groups and every individual in each group, in the place they merit—that is, gives each a subservient or a ruling rank of order. Therefore, there will be certain ranks of order that are close to his own, others slightly further away, and still others that are far away from it. Such will be the ruling ranks of order: beginning with the highest ruling rank of order, they will descend gradually until they become subservient ranks of order devoid of any element of ruling and below which there is no other rank of order. After having ordered these ranks, if the supreme ruler wishes to issue a command about a certain matter that [54] he wishes to enjoin the citizens of the city or a certain group among them to do, and to arouse them toward it, he intimates this to the ranks closest to him, these will hand it on to their subordinates, and so forth, until it reaches down to those assigned to execute that matter. The parts of the city will thus be linked and fitted together, and ordered by giving precedence to some over the others. Thus the city becomes similar to the natural beings; the ranks of order in it similar to the ranks of order of the beings, which begin with the First and terminate in prime matter and the elements; and the way they are linked and fitted together will be similar to the way the beings are linked and fitted together. The prince of the city will be like the First Cause, which is the cause for the existence of all the other beings. Then the ranks of order of the beings gradually keep descending, each one of them being both ruler and ruled, until they reach down to those possible beings—that is, prime matter and the elements—that possess no ruling element whatever, but are subservient and always exist for the sake of others.

The achievement of happiness takes place only through the disappearance of evils—not only the voluntary but also the natural ones—from the cities and nations, and when these acquire all the goods, both the natural and the voluntary. The function of the city's governor—that is, the prince—is to manage the cities in such a way that all the city's parts become linked and fitted together, and so ordered to enable the citizens to cooperate to eliminate the evils and acquire the goods. He should inquire into everything given by the celestial bodies. Those of them that are in any way helpful and suitable, or in any way useful, in the achievement of happiness, he should maintain and emphasize; [55] those of them that are harmful he should try to turn into useful things; and those of them that cannot be turned into useful things he should destroy or reduce in power. In general, he should seek to destroy all the evils and bring into existence all the goods.

Each one of the citizens of the virtuous city is required to know the highest principles of the beings and their ranks of order, happiness, the supreme rulership of the virtuous city, and the ruling ranks of order in it; then, after that, the specified actions that, when performed, lead to the attainment of happiness. These actions are not merely to be known; they should be done and the citizens of the city should be directed to do them.

The principles of the beings, their ranks of order, happiness, and the rulership of the virtuous cities, are either cognized and intellected by man, or he imagines them. To cognize them is to have their essences, as they really are, imprinted in man's soul. To imagine them is to have imprinted in man's soul their images, representations of them, or matters that are imitations of them. This is analogous to what takes place with regard to visible objects, for instance, man. We see him himself, we see a representation of him, we see his image reflected in water and other reflecting substances, and we see the image of a representation of him reflected in water and in other reflecting substances. Our seeing him himself is like the intellect's cognition of the principles of the beings, of happiness, and so forth; while our seeing the reflection of man in water and our seeing a representation of him is like imagination, for our seeing a representation of him or our seeing his reflection in a mirror is seeing that which is an imitation of him. Similarly, when we imagine those things, we are in fact having a cognition of matters that are imitations of them rather than a cognition of them themselves.

Most men, either by nature or by habit, are unable to comprehend and cognize those things; these are the men for whom one ought to represent the manner in which the principles of the beings, their ranks of order, the Active Intellect, and the supreme rulership, exist through things that are imitations of them. Now while the meanings and essences [56] of those things are one and immutable, the matters by which they are imitated are many and varied. Some imitate them more closely, while others do so only remotely—just as is the case with visible objects: for the image of man that is seen reflected in water is closer to the true man than the image of a representation of man that is seen reflected in water. Therefore, it is possible to imitate these things for each group and each nation, using matters that are different in each case. Consequently, there may be a number of virtuous nations and virtuous cities whose religions are different, even though they all pursue the very same kind of happiness. For religion is but the impressions of these things or the impressions of their images, imprinted in the soul. Because it is difficult for the multitude to comprehend these things themselves as they are, the attempt was made to teach them these things in other ways, which are the ways of imitation. Hence these things are imitated for each group or nation through the matters that are best known to them; and it may very well be that what is best known to the one may not be the best known to the other.

Most men who strive for happiness, follow after an imagined, not a cognized, form of happiness. Similarly, most men accept such principles as are accepted and followed, and are magnified and considered majestic, in the form of images, not of cognitions. Now the ones who follow after happiness as they cognize it and accept the principles as they cognize them, are the wise men. And the ones in whose souls these things are found in the form of images, and who accept them and follow after them as such, are the believers.

The imitations of those things differ in excellence: some of them are better and more perfect imaginative representations, while others are less perfect; some are closer to, others are more removed from, the truth. In some the points of contention are few or unnoticeable, or it is difficult to contend against them, while in others the points [57] of contention are many or easy to detect, or it is easy to contend against them and to refute them. It is also possible that those things be presented to the imagination of men by means of various matters, but that, despite their variety, these matters bear a certain relation to each other: that is, there are certain matters that are the imitations of those things, a second set that are the imitations of these matters, and a third set that are the imitations of the second. Finally, the various matters that are the imitations of those things —that is, of the principles of the beings and of happiness—may be on the same level as imitations. Now if they are of equal excellence as regards imitation, or with respect to having only a few or unnoticeable points of contention, then one can use all or any one of them indifferently. But if they are not of equal excellence, one should choose the ones that are the most perfect imitations and that either are completely free of points of contention or in which the points of contention are few or unnoticeable; next, those that are closer to the truth; and discard all other imitations.

The virtuous city is the opposite of (*A*) the ignorant city, (*B*) the immoral city, and (C) the erring city. (D) Then there are the Weeds in the virtuous city. (The position of the Weeds in the cities is like that of the darnel among the wheat, the thorns growing among the crop, or the other grass that is useless or even harmful to the crop or plants.) Finally, there are the men who are bestial by nature. But the bestial by nature are neither political beings nor could they ever form a political association. Instead, some of them are like gregarious beasts and others are like wild beasts, and of the latter some are like ravenous beasts. Therefore some of them live isolated in the wilderness, others live there together in depravity like wild beasts, and still others live near the cities. Some eat only raw meats, others graze on wild vegetation, and still others prey on their victims like [58] wild beasts. These are to be found in the extremities of the inhabited earth, either in the far north or in the far south. They must be treated like animals. Those of them that are gregarious and are in some way useful to the cities, should be spared, enslaved, and employed like beasts of burden. Those of them from whom no use can be derived or who are harmful, should be treated as one treats all other harmful animals. The same applies to those children of the citizens of the cities who turn out to have a bestial nature.

[A. THE IGNORANT CITIES]

As for the citizens of the ignorant cities, they are political beings. Their cities and their political associations are of many kinds, which comprise (i) indispensable associations, (ii) the association of vile men in the vile cities, (iii) the association of base men in the base cities, (iv) timocratic association in the timocratic city, (v) despotic association in the despotic cities, (vi) free association in the democratic city and the city of the free.

[i. THE INDISPENSABLE CITY]

only to obtain bare necessities

The indispensable city or the indispensable association is that which leads to cooperation to acquire the bare necessities for the subsistence and the safeguarding of the body. There are many ways to acquire these things, such as husbandry, grazing, hunting, robbery, and so forth. Both hunting and robbery are practiced either by stealth or openly. There are certain indispensable cities that possess all the arts that lead to the acquisition of the bare necessities. In others the bare necessities are obtained through one art only, such as husbandry alone or any other art. The citizens of this city regard the best man to be the one who is most excellent in skill, management, and accomplishment in obtaining the bare

no attempt to reach supreme happiness minimal necessities of life necessities through the ways of acquisition that they employ. Their ruler is he who can govern well and is skillful in [59] employing them to acquire the indispensable things, who can govern them well so as to preserve these things for them, or who generously provides them with these things from his own possessions.

[ii. THE VILE CITY]

The vile city or the association of the vile citizens is that whose members (a) cooperate to acquire wealth and prosperity, the excessive possession of indispensable things or their equivalent in coin and in money,[4] and their accumulation beyond the need for them and for no other reason than the love and covetousness of wealth; and (b) avoid spending any of it except on what is necessary for bodily subsistence. This they do either by pursuing all the modes of acquisition or else such modes as are available in that country. They regard the best men to be the wealthiest and the most skillful in the acquisition of wealth. Their ruler is the man who is able to manage them well in what leads them to acquire wealth and always to remain wealthy. Wealth is obtained through all the methods employed to obtain the bare necessities, that is, husbandry, grazing, hunting, and robbery; and also through voluntary transactions like commerce, lease, and so forth.

[iii. THE BASE CITY]

think what life is for - hedonistic enjoyment

The base city or the base association is that in which the citizens cooperate to enjoy sensual pleasures or imaginary pleasures (play and amusement) or both. They enjoy the pleasures of food, drink, and copulation, and strive after what is most pleasant of these, in the pursuit of pleasure alone, rather than what sustains, or is in any way useful to, the body; and they do the same as regards play and amusement. This city is the one regarded by the citizens of the ignorant city as the happy and admirable city; for they can attain the goal of this city only after having acquired the bare necessities and acquired wealth, and only by means of much expenditure. They regard whoever possesses more resources for play and the pleasures as the best, the happiest, and the most enviable man.

[iv. THE TIMOCRATIC CITY]

Best of worst

The timocratic city or the timocratic association is that in which the citizens cooperate with a view to be [60] honored in speech and deed:

that is, to be honored either by the citizens of other cities or by one another. Their honoring of one another consists in the exchange of either equal or unequal honors. The exchange of equal honors takes place through someone bestowing on someone else a certain kind of honor at a certain time so that the latter may at another time return the same kind of honor or another kind of honor that, in their eyes, is of equal worth. The exchange of unequal honors takes place through someone bestowing a certain kind of honor on someone else, with the latter bestowing on the former another kind of honor of greater worth than the first. In every case, moreover, this [exchange of unequal honors] among them takes place on the basis of merit (one of two men merits an honor of a certain worth, while the other merits a greater one), depending on what they consider merit to be. In the eyes of the citizens of the ignorant city, merits are not based on virtue, but (*a*) on wealth, or (*b*) on possessing the means of pleasure and play and on obtaining the most of both, or (*c*) on obtaining most of the necessities of life (when man is served and is well provided with all the necessities he needs), or (*d*) on man's being useful, that is, doing good to others with respect to these three things. (*e*) There is one more thing that is well liked by most of the citizens of the ignorant cities, that is, domination. For whoever achieves it is envied by most of them. Therefore this, too, must be regarded as one of the merits in the ignorant cities. For, in their eyes, the highest matter for which a man must be honored is his fame in achieving domination [that is, superiority] in one, two, or many things; not being dominated, because he himself is strong, because his supporters are either numerous or strong, [61] or because of both; and that he be immune to being harmed by others, while able to harm others at will. For, in their eyes, this is a state of felicity for which a man merits honor; hence the better he is in this respect, the more he is honored. Or the man [whom they honor] possesses, in their eyes, distinguished ancestors. But ancestors are distinguished because of the things mentioned above: namely, one's fathers and grandfathers were either wealthy, abundantly favored with pleasure and the means to it, had domination [that is, were superior] in a number of things, were useful to others—be they a group or the citizens of a city—with respect to these things, or were favored with the instruments of these things, such as nobility, endurance, or the contempt of death, all of which are instruments of domination. Honors of equal worth, on the other hand, are sometimes merited by virtue of an external possession, and sometimes honor itself is the reason for the merit, so that the one who begins and honors someone else merits thereby to be honored by the other, as is the case in market transactions.

Thus, in their eyes, the one who merits more honor rules over the one who merits less of it. This inequality continues on an ascending scale terminating in the one who merits more honors than anyone else in the city. This, therefore, will be the ruler and the prince of the city. By virtue of this office, he ought to be of greater merit than all the rest. Now we have already enumerated what they consider to be the bases of merit. Accordingly, if honor, according to them, is based on distinguished ancestry alone, the ruler ought to have a more distinguished ancestry than the others; and similarly if honor, according to them, is based on wealth alone. Next, men are distinguished and given ranks of order according to their wealth and ancestry; [62] and whoever lacks both wealth and a distinguished ancestry will have no claim to any rulership or honor. Such, then, is the case when merits are based on matters that are good to their possessor alone; and these are the lowest among timocratic rulers. When, on the other hand, the ruler is honored because of his usefulness to the citizens of the city in their pursuits and wishes, it is then because he benefits them with regard to wealth or pleasure; or because he brings others to honor the citizens of the city or to provide them with the other things desired by them; or because he supplies them with these things from his own or he enables them to obtain and preserve them through his good governance. Of such rulers, they consider the best to be the one who provides the citizens of the city with these things without seeking anything for himself except honor: for instance, the one who provides them with wealth or the pleasures without desiring any for himself, but rather seeks only honor (praise, respect, and exaltation in speech and deed), to become famous for it among all nations in his own lifetime and after, and to be remembered for a long time. This is the one who, in their eyes, merits honor. Often, such a man requires money and wealth to spend it on what enables the citizens of the city to fulfil their desires for wealth or pleasure or both, and on what helps them to preserve these things. The more he does in this respect, the greater his wealth must be. His wealth becomes a reserve for the citizens of the city. This is the reason why some of these rulers seek wealth and regard their expenditures as an act of generosity and liberality. They collect this money from the city in the form of taxes, or they conquer another group—other, that is, than the citizens of the city—for its money, which they bring to their treasury. They keep it as a reserve [63] out of which they disburse great expenditures in the city in order to obtain greater honor. The one who covets honor by whatever means, may also claim distinguished ancestry for himself and his offspring after him; and so that his fame survive through his offspring, he designates his immediate offspring or members of his family as his successors. Furthermore, he may appropriate a certain amount of wealth for himself to be honored for it, even though it is of no benefit to others. Also, he honors a certain group so that they may honor him in return. He thus possesses all the things for which men may honor him, reserving for himself alone the things regarded by them as manifesting splendor, embellishment, eminence, and magnificence—such as buildings, costumes, and medals, and, finally, inaccessibility to people. Further, he lays down the laws concerning honors. Once he assumes a certain office and people are accustomed to the fact that he and his family will be their princes, he then orders the people into ranks in such a way as to obtain honor and majesty. To each kind of rank, he assigns (*a*) a kind of honor and (*b*) things by virtue of which one merits honor, such as wealth, building, costume, medal, carriage, and so forth, and which contribute to his majesty; and he arranges all this in a definite order. Furthermore, he will show special preference for those men who honor him more or contribute more to the enhancement of his majesty, and he confers honor and distributes favor accordingly. The citizens of his city who covet honor keep honoring him until he acknowledges what they have done and confers honors on them, because of which they will be honored by their inferiors and superiors.

For all these reasons, this city can be likened to the virtuous city, especially when the honors, and men's ranks of order with respect to honors, are conferred because of other, more useful things: for example, wealth, pleasures, or anything else that is desired by whoever seeks after useful things. This city is the best among the ignorant cities; unlike those of the others, its citizens are [more properly] called "ignorant" [64] and so forth. However, when their love of honor becomes excessive, it becomes a city of tyrants, and it is more likely to change into a despotic city.

[V. THE DESPOTIC CITY]

The despotic city or the despotic association is that in which the members cooperate to achieve domination. This happens when they are all seized by the love of domination, provided that it is in different degrees, and that they seek different kinds of domination and different things for the sake of which to dominate other men; for instance, some like to dominate another man in order to spill his blood, others, to take his property, still others, to possess him so that they may enslave him. People occupy different ranks of order in this city depending on the extent of one's love of domination. Its citizens love to dominate others in order to spill their blood and kill them, to possess them so that they may enslave them, or in order to take their property. In all this, what they love and aim at is to dominate, subdue, and humiliate others, and that the subdued should have no control whatever over himself or any of the things because of which he has been dominated, but should do as the subduer commands and wishes. (Indeed when the lover of domination and subjugation—who is inclined to, or desires, a certain thing—obtains it without having to subdue someone else, he does not take it and pays no attention to it.) Some of them choose to dominate through wiliness, others, through open combat alone, and still others, through both wiliness and open combat. Therefore many of those who subjugate others in order to spill their blood, do not kill a man when asleep and do not seize his property until they first wake him up; they prefer to engage him in combat and to be faced with some resistance in order to subdue him and harm him. Since every one of them loves to dominate the others, each one loves to dominate everyone else, [65] whether a fellow citizen or not. They refrain from dominating one another as regards the spilling of blood or the taking of property, only because they need one another so as to survive, cooperate in dominating others, and defend themselves against outside domination.

Their ruler is he who shows greater strength in governing well with a view to employing them to dominate others; who is the wiliest of them; and who has the soundest judgment about what they ought to do in order to continue to dominate forever and never be dominated by others. Such is their ruler and prince. They are the enemies of all other men.

All their laws and usages are such that, when followed, they enable them better to dominate others. Their rivalries and contentions center on how many times they dominate others or on the extent of their domination, or else on the abundant possession of the equipment and instruments of domination. (The equipment and instruments of domination exist either in man's mind, in his body, or in what is external to his body: in his body, like endurance; external to his body, like arms; and in his mind, like sound judgment regarding that which enables him to dominate others.) At times, such men become rude, cruel, irascible, extravagant, and excessively gluttonous; they consume great quantities of food and drink, overindulge in copulation, and fight each other for all the goods, which they obtain through subjugating and humiliating those who possess them. They think that they should dominate everything and everybody.

(1) Sometimes this is true of the entire city, whose citizens will then choose to dominate those outside the city for no other reason than the citizens' need for association [and hence for a common cause that would promote it]. (2) Sometimes the vanquished and the subjugators live side by side in a single city. [66] The subjugators then either (a) love to subjugate and dominate others to the same degree and hence have the same rank of order in the city, or (b) they occupy various ranks of order, each one of them having a certain kind of domination over their vanquished neighbors, which is lesser or greater than that of the other. In this way, and depending on the power and judgment through which

they achieve domination, they occupy their respective places next to a prince who rules them and manages the subjugators' affairs as regards the instruments they use for subjugation. (3) And sometimes there is but a single subjugator, with a group of men as his instruments for subjugating all other men. The group in question does not seek to enable him to dominate and seize something for someone else's sake, but so that he dominate something that would belong to him alone. The single subjugator, in turn, is satisfied with what maintains his life and strength; he gives [the rest] to the others and dominates for the sake of the others, like dogs and falcons do. The rest of the citizens of the city, too, are slaves to that one, serving his every wish; they are submissive and humiliated, possessing nothing whatever of their own. Some of them cultivate the soil, others trade, for him. In all this, he has no other purpose beyond seeing a certain group subjugated and dominated and submissive to him alone, even though he derives no benefit or pleasure from them except that of seeing them humiliated and dominated. This (3), then, is the city whose prince alone is despotic, while the rest of its citizens are not despotic. In the one that preceded it (2), half of the city is despotic. In the first (1), all the citizens are despotic.

The despotic city may thus have such a character that it employs one of these methods in the pursuit of domination alone and the enjoyment of it. But if domination is loved only as a means for the acquisition of bare necessities, prosperity, the enjoyment of pleasures, honors, or all of these together, then this is a despotic city of a different sort; and its citizens belong to the other cities mentioned above. [67] Most people call such cities despotic; but this name applies more properly to the one among them that seeks all of these (three?)[5] things by means of subjugation. There are three sorts of such cities: that is,[6] (3) one of the citizens, (2) half of them, or (1) all of them are despotic. But they [that is, the citizens of these cities], too, do not pursue subjugation and maltreatment for their own sake; rather they pursue, and aim at, something else.

There are, further, other cities that aim at something else and at domination as well. The first of these cities, which aims at domination however and for whatever it may be, may include someone who inflicts harm on others without any benefit to himself, such as to murder for no other reason than the pleasure of subjugation alone; its citizens fight for the sake of base things, as it is told about some of the Arabs. In the second, the citizens love domination for the sake of certain things that they regard as praiseworthy and lofty, not lowly; and when they attain these things without subjugating others, they do not resort to it. The third city does not harm or murder, unless it knows that this enhances one of its noble qualities. Hence when one [of its citizens] gets to the things he wants, without having to dominate and subjugate others—for instance, when the thing exists in abundance, when someone else takes care of seizing it for him, or when someone else gives him the thing voluntarily—he will not harm others, remains indifferent to the thing in question, and does not take it from others. Such individuals are also called high-minded and manly. The citizens of the first city confine themselves to such subjugation as is indispensable for the achievement of domination. Sometimes they strive and struggle very hard to possess a certain property or human soul that is denied to them, and they persist until they get it and are able to do with it whatever they please; but at this point they turn away and do not seize it. Such men may also be praised, honored, and respected for what they do; also, [*68*] those who seek honor do most of these things so that they may be honored for them. Despotic cities are more often tyrannical than timocratic.

Sometimes the citizens of the [vile or] plutocratic city and the citizens of the [base] city that is dedicated to play and amusement imagine that they are the ones who are lucky, happy, and successful, and that they are more excellent than the citizens of all other cities. These delusions about themselves sometimes lead them to become contemptuous of the citizens of other cities and to suppose that others have no worth, and to love to be honored for whatever caused their happiness. Consequently, they develop traits of arrogance, extravagance, boastfulness, and the love of praise, and suppose that others cannot attain what they themselves have attained, and that the others are therefore too stupid to achieve these two kinds of happiness [which result from wealth, and play and amusement, respectively]. They create for themselves titles with which they embellish their ways of life, such as that they are the talented and the elegant, and that the others are the rude. Therefore they are supposed to be men of pride, magnanimity, and authority. Sometimes they are even called high-minded.

When the lovers of wealth and the lovers of pleasure and play do not happen to possess any of the arts by which wealth is obtained except the power to dominate, and they achieve wealth and play by subjugation and domination, then they become extremely arrogant and join the ranks of tyrants (in contrast, the former group are simply idiots). Similarly, it is possible to find among the lovers of honor some who love it, not for its own sake, but for the sake of wealth. For many of them seek to be honored by others in order to obtain wealth, either from those others or from someone else. They seek to rule, and to be obeyed by, the citizens of the city in order to obtain wealth alone. Many of these seek wealth for the sake of play and pleasure. Thus they seek to rule and to be obeyed in order to obtain wealth to make use of it in play; and they think that the greater and the more complete their authority and the obedience of others to them, the greater their share of these things. Hence they desire to be the sole rulers over the citizens of the city in order to possess majesty, by which to achieve great and incomparable wealth [69] in order to make use of it in obtaining a measure of play and pleasures (food, drink, sex) that no one else can obtain both as regards its quantity and quality.

[vi. THE DEMOCRATIC CITY]

The democratic city is the one in which each one of the citizens is given free rein and left alone to do whatever he likes. Its citizens are equal and their laws say that no man is in any way at all better than any other man. Its citizens are free to do whatever they like; and no one, be he one of them or an outsider, has any claim to authority unless he works to enhance their freedom. Consequently, they develop many kinds of morals, inclinations, and desires, and they take pleasure in countless things. Its citizens consist of countless similar and dissimilar groups. This city brings together the groups—both the base and the noble—that existed separately in all the other cities; and positions of authority are obtained here by means of any one of the things we have mentioned. Those from among the multitude of this city, who possess whatever the rulers possess, have the upper hand over those who are called their rulers. Those who rule them do so by the will of the ruled, and the rulers follow the wishes of the ruled. Close investigation of their situation would reveal that, in truth, there is no distinction between ruler and ruled among them. However, they praise and honor those who lead the citizens of the city to freedom and to whatever the citizens like and desire, and who safeguard the citizens' freedom and their varied and different desires against [infringement] by one another and by outside enemies; and who limit their [70] own desires to bare necessities. Such, then, is the one who is honored, regarded as the best, and is obeyed among them. As to any other ruler, he is either (*a*) their equal or (*b*) their inferior. (*a*) He is their equal when it happens that, when he provides them with the good things that they want and desire, they reciprocate with comparable honors and wealth. In this case they do not consider him to be superior to them. (*b*) They are his superiors when they accord him honors and allot him a share of their possessions, without receiving any benefit from him in return. For it is quite possible to find in this city a ruler in this situation: he happens to be magnified in the eyes of the citizens either because they take a fancy to him or because his ancestors ruled them well and they let him rule in gratitude for what his ancestors did. In this case, the multitude would have the upper hand over the rulers.

All the endeavors and purposes of the ignorant cities are present in this city in a most perfect manner; of all of them, this is the most admirable and happy city. On the surface, it looks like an embroidered garment full of colored figures and dyes. Everybody loves it and loves to reside in it, because there is no human wish or desire that this city does not satisfy. The nations emigrate to it and reside there, and it grows beyond measure. People of every race multiply in it, and this by all kinds of copulation and marriages, resulting in children of extremely varied dispositions, with extremely varied education and upbringing. Consequently, this city develops into many cities, distinct yet intertwined, with the parts of each scattered throughout the parts of the others. Strangers cannot be distinguished from the residents. All kinds of wishes and ways of life are to be found in it. Consequently, it is quite possible that, with the passage of time, virtuous men will grow up in it. Thus it may include [71] philosophers, rhetoricians, and poets, dealing with all kinds of things. It is also possible to glean from it certain [men who form] parts of the virtuous city; this is the best thing that takes place in this city. Therefore, this city possesses both good and evil to a greater degree than the rest of the ignorant cities. The bigger, the more civilized, the more populated, the more productive, and the more perfect it is, the more prevalent and the greater are the good and the evil it possesses.

There are as many aims pursued by the ignorant rulerships as there are ignorant cities. Every ignorant rulership aims at having its fill of bare necessities; wealth; delight in the pleasures; honor, reputation, and praise; domination; or freedom. Therefore, such rulerships are actually bought for a price, especially the positions of authority in the democratic city; for here no one has a better claim than anyone else to a position of authority. Therefore, when someone finally holds a position of authority, it is either because the citizens have favored him with it, or else because they have received from him money or something else in return. In their eyes the virtuous ruler is he who has the ability to judge well and to contrive well what enables them to attain their diverse and variegated desires and wishes, safeguards them against their enemies, and takes nothing of their property, but confines himself to the bare necessities of life. As for the truly virtuous man—namely the man who, if he were to rule them, would determine and direct their actions toward happiness —they do not make him a ruler. If by chance he comes to rule them, he will soon find himself either deposed or killed or in an unstable and challenged position. And so are all the other ignorant cities; each one of them only wants the ruler who facilitates the attainment of its wishes [72] and desires, and paves the way for their acquisition and preservation. Therefore, they refuse the rule of virtuous men and resent it. Nevertheless, the construction of virtuous cities and the establishment of the rule of virtuous men are more effective and much easier out of the indispensable and democratic cities than out of any other ignorant city.

Bare necessity, wealth, the enjoyment of the pleasures and of play, and honors may be attained by subjugation and domination, or they may be attained by other means. Hence the four cities [the indispensable, vile, base, and timocratic] can be subdivided accordingly. Similarly, the rule that aims at these four things, or any one of them, pursues the achievement of its aim by domination and subjugation, or else pursues it by other means. Those who acquire these things by domination and subjugation, and safeguard what they have acquired by force and compulsion, need to be strong and powerful in body, and to be fierce, rough, rude, and contemptuous of death in moral traits, and not to prefer life to these pursuits; they need skill in the use of arms, and good judgment as regards the means of subjugating others: all this applies to all of them.

But as to the pleasure seekers [that is, the citizens of the base city], they develop, in addition, gluttony and lust for food, drink, and sex. Some of them are dominated by softness and luxury, weakening their irascible faculty to the extent that none or very little of it remains. Others are dominated by anger and its psychical and bodily instruments, and by the appetite and its psychical and bodily instruments, which strengthens and intensifies these two faculties, and facilitates the performance of their functions. Their judgment will be equally devoted to the actions of these two faculties, and their souls equally subservient to them. Of these, the final objective of some are the actions of the appetite. Thus they turn their irascible faculties and actions into instruments by which to achieve the appetitive actions, thus subordinating lofty and higher faculties to the lower; that is, they subordinate their rational faculty to [73] the irascible and appetitive, and further, the irascible faculty to the appetitive. For they devote their judgment to the discovery of what fulfils the irascible and appetitive actions, and devote the actions and instruments of their irascible faculties to what enables them to attain the enjoyment of the pleasures of food, drink, and sex, and all that enables them to seize and safeguard them for themselves, such as you see in the notables of the dwellers of the steppes from among the Arabs and the Turks. For the dwellers of the steppes generally love domination, and have insatiable lust for food, drink, and sex. Consequently, women are of great importance to them, and many of them approve of licentiousness, not considering it as being a degeneration and vileness since their souls are subservient to their appetites. You also see that many of them try to please women in everything they do, in order to gain importance in the eyes of women, considering disgraceful whatever women consider to be disgraceful, fair what women consider to be fair. In everything they do, they follow the desires of their women. In many cases, their women have the upper hand over them

and control the affairs of their households. For this reason many of them
accustom their women to luxury by shielding them from hard work and
keeping them instead in luxury and comfort, while they themselves undertake to do everything that requires toil and labor and the endurance of
pain and hardship.

[B. THE IMMORAL CITIES]

Immoral cities are the ones whose citizens once believed in, and cognized, the principles [of beings]; imagined, and believed in, what happiness is; and were guided toward, knew, and believed in, the actions by
which to attain happiness. Nevertheless, they did not adhere to any of
those actions, but came to desire and will one or another of the aims
of the citizens of the ignorant cities—such as honor, domination, and so
forth—and directed all their actions and faculties toward them. There
are as many kinds [74] of these [immoral] cities as there are ignorant
cities, inasmuch as all their actions and morals are identical with those
of the ignorant cities. They differ from the citizens of the ignorant cities
only in the opinions in which they believe. Not one of the citizens of
these cities can attain happiness at all.

[C. THE ERRING CITIES]

Erring cities are those whose citizens are given imitations of other
matters than the ones we mentioned[7]—that is, the principles that are established for, and imitated to, them are other than the ones we mentioned; a kind of happiness that is not true happiness is established for,
and represented to, them; and actions and opinions are prescribed for
them by none of which true happiness can be attained.[8]

[D. THE WEEDS IN VIRTUOUS CITIES]

The Weeds within the virtuous cities are of many classes. (i) [Mem-
bers of] one class adhere to the actions conducive to the attainment of
happiness; however, they do not do such actions in the pursuit of happiness, but rather of other things that man can attain by means of virtue,
such as honor, rulership, wealth, and so forth. Such individuals are
called opportunists (*mutaqanniṣūn*). Some of them have an inclination

to one of the ends of the citizens of the ignorant cities and they are prevented by the Laws and the religion of the city from pursuing such ends. Therefore they resort to the expressions of the lawgiver and the statements that embody his precepts, and interpret them as they wish, by which interpretation they make the thing they are after appear good. Such men are called the misinterpreters (*muharrifah*). Others among them do not deliberately misinterpret but, because they do not rightly understand the lawgiver and because of their misconception of his statements, they understand the Laws of the city in a different way than the one intended by the lawgiver. Their actions will therefore not conform to the intention of the supreme ruler. Hence they err without realizing it. These men are the apostates (*māriqah*).

(ii) [Members of] another class do imagine the things we mentioned,[9] yet they are not convinced of what they have imagined of them. Hence they use arguments to falsify them for themselves and for others. [75] In so doing, they are not contending against the virtuous city; rather they are looking for the right path and seeking the truth. He who belongs to this class, should have the level of his imagination raised to things that cannot be falsified by the arguments he has put forward. If he is satisfied with the level to which he has been raised, he should be left alone. But if he is again not satisfied, and discovers here certain places susceptible to contention, then he should be raised to a higher level. This process should continue until he becomes satisfied with one of these levels. And if it happens that he is not satisfied with any one of these levels of imagination, he should be raised to the level of the truth and be made to comprehend those things as they are, at which point his mind will come to rest.

(iii) [Members of] another class falsify whatever they imagine. Whenever they are raised to a higher level, they falsify it, even when they are conducted to the level of the truth—all this in the pursuit of domination alone, or in the pursuit of ennobling another of the aims of the ignorant cities that is desired by them. They falsify them in every way they can; they do not like to listen to anything that may establish happiness and truth firmly in the soul, or any argument that may ennoble and imprint them in the soul, but meet them with such sham arguments as they think will discredit happiness. Many of them do that with the intention of appearing as having a pretext for turning to one of the aims of the ignorant cities.

(iv) [Members of] another class imagine happiness and the principles [of beings], but their minds are totally lacking in the power to cognize them, or it is beyond the power of their minds to cognize them adequately. Consequently, they falsify the things they imagine and come upon the places of contention in them, and whenever they are raised to a level of imagination that is closer to the truth, they find it to be false.

Nor is it possible to raise them to the level of the truth because their minds lack the power to comprehend it. And many of them may find most of what they imagine to be false, not because what they imagine truly contains places of contention, [76] but because they have a defective imagination, and they find these things false because of their defective minds, not because these things contain a place of contention. Many of them—when unable to imagine something sufficiently or discover the real points of contention and in the places where they are to be found, or are unable to comprehend the truth—think that the man who has apprehended the truth and who says that he has apprehended it, is a deliberate liar who is seeking honor or domination, or else think that he is a deluded man. So they try hard to falsify the truth also, and abase the man who has apprehended it. This leads many of them to think that all men are deluded in everything they claim to have apprehended. It leads (1) some of them to a state of perplexity in all things, and (2) others to think that no apprehension whatever is true, and that whenever someone thinks that he has apprehended something that he is lying about it[10] and that he is not sure or certain of what he thinks. These individuals occupy the position of ignorant simpletons in the eyes of reasonable men and in relation to the philosophers. (For this reason it is the duty of the ruler of the virtuous city to look for the Weeds, keep them occupied, and treat each class of them in the particular manner that will cure them: by expelling them from the city, punishing them, jailing them, or forcing them to perform a certain function even though they may not be fond of it.) (3) Others among them think that the truth consists of whatever appears to each individual and what each man thinks it to be at one time or another, and that the truth of everything is what someone thinks it is. (4) Others among them exert themselves to create the illusion that everything that is thought to have been apprehended up to this time is completely false, and that, although a certain truth or reality does exist, it has not as yet been apprehended. (5) Others among them imagine—as if in a dream or as if a thing is seen from a distance—that there is a truth, and it occurs to them that the ones who claim to have apprehended it may have done so, or perhaps that one of them may have apprehended it. They feel that they themselves have missed it, either because they require a long time, and have to toil and exert themselves, in order to apprehend it, when they no longer have sufficient time or the power to toil and persevere; or because they are occupied by certain pleasures and so forth to which they have been accustomed and from which they find it very difficult to free themselves; or because they feel that they cannot apprehend it even if they had access to all the means to it. Consequently, they regret and grieve over what they think others may have attained. Hence, out of jealousy for those who may have apprehended the truth, they think it wise to endeavor, using sham argument, to create the illusion that whoever claims to have apprehended the truth is either deluded or else a liar who is seeking honor, wealth, or some other desirable thing, from the claim he makes. Now many of these perceive their own ignorance and perplexity; they feel sad and suffer pain because of what they perceive to be their condition, they are overcome by anxiety, and it torments them; and they find no way to free themselves of this by means of a science leading them to the truth whose apprehension would give them pleasure. Hence they choose to find rest from all this by turning to the various ends of the ignorant cities, and to find their solace in amusements and games until death comes to relieve them of their burden. Some of these—I mean the ones who seek rest from the torment of ignorance and perplexity—may create the illusion that the [true] ends are those that they themselves choose and desire, that happiness consists of these, and that the rest of men are deluded in what they believe in. They exert themselves to adorn the ends of the ignorant cities and the happiness [that they pursue]. They create the illusion that they have come to prefer some of these ends after a thorough examination of all that the others claim to have apprehended, that they have rejected the latter only after finding out that they are inconclusive, and that their position was arrived at on the basis of personal knowledge—therefore, theirs are the ends, not the ones claimed by the others.

These, then, are the classes of the Weeds growing among the citizens of the city. With such opinions, they constitute neither a city nor a large multitude; rather they are submerged by the citizen body as a whole.[11]

NOTES

1. Cf. Aristotle *De Anima* iii. 5. Alfarabi gives an account of the Active Intellect at the beginning of the *Political Regime*, pp. 2–3, 6–7.

2. As distinguished from the "necessary" being that is not caused. The reference here is to the human species.

3. Aristotle *De Anima* iii. 5, 7. The term "acquired intellect" (*nous epiktētos*) does not occur in Aristotle's *De Anima* but in Alexander of Aphrodisias' commentary on that book. Its function is implied by Aristotle, however.

4. Alfarabi says: "dirhem and dinar."

5. This word appears to be an interpolation. It is, however, present in all the manuscripts. Feyzullah punctuates the preceding enumeration in such a manner that it is subdivided into three parts: "bare necessities, prosperity, or the enjoyment of pleasures; honors; or all of these together."

6. Cf. above, pp. 65–66.

7. Above, pp. 55 ff.

8. See n. 11, below.

9. Above, pp. 55 ff.

10. Here ends the Hyderabad edition and all of the manuscripts with the exception of Feyzullah.

11. This terminates the discussion of the "opposites" of the virtuous cities enumerated on p. 58 above. Feyzullah contains an additional paragraph, which is practically identical with the beginning of the account of the "opinions of the citizens of the ignorant and erring cities" in Alfarabi's *Virtuous City* (corresponding to pp. 73:23–74:10 in Dieterici's edition [Leiden, 1895]). This paragraph may be simply misplaced here, in which case the work would be complete at this point. If, however, it belongs to the *Political Regime*, then the text of Feyzullah, too, is clearly incomplete since it ends with an incomplete sentence and lacks the part corresponding to the *Virtuous City*, pp. 74:10–85:7. The paragraph in question reads in Feyzullah as follows:

"The erring cities develop when the religion is based upon certain ancient and corrupt opinions. For instance, a group of men say: 'We see that the beings we observe are contradictory, each seeking to destroy the others. We also see that when each one of them comes into being, it is provided—in addition to existence—with something by which it preserves its existence from destruction, with something by which it repels its contradictory away from itself and safeguards itself against its contradictory, and with something that enables it to employ all other things in what is useful for achieving its best existence and the continuity of its existence. Many of these beings are provided also with what enables them to dominate what resists them. All contradictory beings are placed in this position with regard to their contradictories and to all other beings, so that each one of them tends to achieve the best existence of itself alone, regardless of the others: therefore it is provided with what enables it to destroy. . . .'"

3.

Alfarabi

THE ATTAINMENT OF

HAPPINESS

Translated by Muhsin Mahdi

The *Attainment of Happiness* is the first part of a trilogy entitled the *Philosophy of Plato and Aristotle*, of which the second part is the *Philosophy of Plato* and the third part is the *Philosophy of Aristotle*. It has four subdivisions. The first gives an account of (1) the theoretical virtues or theoretical sciences (including "theoretical" political science) and explains the relationship among them. The second raises and answers the question of the need for something beyond theoretical science, which answer unfolds into an account of (2) prudence or deliberation, (3) the moral virtues, and (4) the practical arts; and discusses the relationship among these four things in an individual. The third gives an account of the methods through which these four are realized in a nation or a city, which unfolds into a discussion of the qualities of the ruler and the structure of the city,

and its opinions and actions. The fourth begins with the praise of theoretical science or philosophy, but proceeds to discuss the relation between the philosopher and the prince, between philosophy and religion, and between true and false philosophy. This is perhaps Alfarabi's most fundamental work; it provides the philosophic framework on the basis of which his didactic and political works ought to be understood. The sections omitted here (secs. 2–15 [sec. 1 is given in n. 6]) deal with logic, mathematics, and physics.

A Hebrew paraphrase of the *Attainment of Happiness* is included in Shemtob ben Falaquera's *Introduction to Science*, which in turn was translated into Latin. The following translation is based on the revised edition cited below. The numbers in the translation refer to the Hyderabad text: *Taḥṣīl al-saʿādah* (1345 A.H.), pp. 12-47. The variants adopted here have been given in "Notes to the Arabic Text of the *Attainment of Happiness*," in Alfarabi's *Philosophy of Plato and Aristotle*, tr. with intro- duction by Muhsin Mahdi (New York: The Free Press of Glencoe, 1962; rev. ed., Ithaca: Cornell Paper- backs, 1969), pp. 149 ff.

I

16　When one finally comes to inquire into the heavenly bodies and investigate the principles of their being, this inquiry into the principles of their being will force one to look for principles that are not natures or natural things, but beings more perfect than nature and natural things. They are also not bodies or in bodies. Therefore one needs another kind of investigation here and another science that inquires exclusively into beings that are metaphysical. At this point he is again standing between two sciences: the science of nature and [metaphysics, or] the science of what is beyond natural things [*13*] in the order of investigation and instruction and above them in the order of being.

17　When his inquiry finally reaches the stage of investigating the principles of the being of animals, he will be forced to inquire into the soul and learn about psychical [or animate] principles, and from there ascend to the inquiry into the rational animal. As he investigates the principles of the latter, he will be forced to inquire into (1) *what, by what*, and *how*, (2-3) *from what*, and (4) *for what* it is.[1] It is here that he acquaints himself with the intellect and things intelligible. He needs to investigate (1) *what* the intellect is and *by what* and *how* it is, and (2-3) *from what* and (4) *for what* it is. This investigation will force him to look for other principles that are not bodies or in bodies, and that never were or will be in bodies. This inquiry into the rational animal will thus lead him to the same conclusion as the inquiry into the heavenly bodies. He now acquaints himself with incorporeal principles that are to the beings below the heavenly bodies as those incorporeal principles (with which he became acquainted when investigating the heavenly bodies) are to the heavenly bodies. He will acquaint himself with the principles for the sake of which the soul and the intellect are made, and with the ends and the ultimate perfection for the sake of which man is made. He will know that the natural principles in man and in the world are not sufficient for man's coming to that perfection for the sake of whose achievement he is made. It will become evident that man needs some rational, intellectual principles with which to work toward that perfection.

18   At this point the inquirer will have sighted another genus of things, different from the metaphysical. It is incumbent on man to investigate what is included in this genus: that is, the things that realize for man his objective through the intellectual principles that are in him, and by which he achieves that perfection which became known in natural science. It will become evident concomitantly that these rational principles are not mere causes by which man attains the perfection for which he is made. Moreover, he will know that these [*14*] rational principles also supply many things to natural beings other than those supplied by nature. Indeed man arrives at the ultimate perfection (whereby he attains that which renders him truly substantial) only when he labors with these principles toward achieving this perfection. Moreover, he cannot labor toward this perfection except by exploiting a large number of natural beings and until he manipulates them to render them useful to him for arriving at the ultimate perfection he should achieve. Furthermore, it will become evident to him in this science that each man achieves only a portion of that perfection, and what he achieves of this portion varies in its extent, for an isolated individual cannot achieve all the perfections by himself and without the aid of many other individuals. It is the innate disposition of every man to join another human being or other men in the labor he ought to perform: this is the condition of every single man. Therefore, to achieve what he can of that perfection, every man needs to stay in the neighborhood of others and associate with them. It is also the innate nature of this animal to seek shelter and to dwell in the neighborhood of those who belong to the same species, which is why he is called the social and political animal. There emerges now another science and another inquiry that investigates these intellectual principles and the acts and states of character with which man labors toward this perfection. From this, in turn, emerge the science of man and political science.

19   He should begin to inquire into the metaphysical beings and in treating them use the methods he used in treating natural things. He should use as their principles of instruction[2] the first premises that happen to be available and are appropriate to this genus, and in addition, the demonstrations of [*15*] natural science that fit as principles of instruction in this genus. These should be arranged according to the order mentioned above,[3] until one covers every being in this genus. It will become evident to whoever investigates these beings that none of them can possess any matter at all; one ought to investigate every one of them only as to (1) *what* and *how* it is, (2–3) *from what agent* and (4) *for what* it is. He should continue this investigation until he finally reaches a being that cannot possess any of these principles at all (either *what* it is or *from what* it is or *for what* it is) but is itself the first principle of all the aforementioned beings: it is itself that *by which, from which,* and *for which*

they are, in the most perfect modes in which a thing can be a principle for the beings, modes free from all defects. Having understood this, he should investigate next what properties the other beings possess as a consequence of their having this being as their principle and the cause of their being. He should begin with the being whose rank is higher than the rest (that is, the one nearest to the first principle), until he terminates in the being whose rank is inferior to the rest (that is, the one farthest from the first principle). He will thus come to know the ultimate causes of the beings. This is the divine inquiry into them. For the first principle is the divinity, and the principles that come after it—and are not bodies or in bodies—are the divine principles.

20   Then he should set out next upon the science of man and investigate the *what* and the *how* of the purpose for which man is made, that is, the perfection that man must achieve. Then he should investigate all the things by which man achieves this perfection or that are useful to him in achieving it. These are the good, virtuous, and noble things. He should distinguish them from [*16*] the things that obstruct his achieving this perfection. These are the evils, the vices, and the base things. He should make known *what* and *how* every one of them is, and *from what* and *for what* it is, until all of them become known, intelligible, and distinguished from each other. This is political science.[4] It consists of knowing the things by which the citizens of cities attain happiness through political association in the measure that innate disposition equips each of them for it. It will become evident to him that political association and the totality that results from the association of citizens in cities correspond to the association of the bodies that constitute the totality of the world. He will come to see in what are included in the totality constituted by the city and the nation the likenesses of what are included in the total world. Just as in the world there is a first principle, then other principles subordinate to it, beings that proceed from these principles, other beings subordinate to these beings, until they terminate in the beings with the lowest rank in the order of being, the nation or the city includes a supreme commander,[5] followed by other commanders,[5] followed by other citizens, who in turn are followed by other citizens, until they terminate in the citizens with the lowest rank as citizens and as human beings. Thus the city includes the likenesses of the things included in the total world.

21   This, then, is theoretical perfection. As you see, it comprises knowledge of the four kinds of things[6] by which the citizens of cities and nations attain supreme happiness. What still remains is that these four be realized and have actual existence in nations and cities while conforming to the account of them given by the theoretical sciences.

II

22   Do you suppose that these theoretical sciences have also given an account of the means by which these four can be [*17*] actually realized in nations and cities, or not? They have indeed given an account of the latter as they are perceived by the intellect. Now if it were the case that to give an account of these things as they are perceived by the intellect is to give an account of their [actual] existence, it would follow that the theoretical sciences have given an account of them as actually existent. (For instance, if it were the case that giving an intelligible account of architecture and perceiving by the intellect what constitutes architecture and what constitutes a building make an architect of the man who has intellected what manner of thing the art of building is, or, if it were the case that giving an intelligible account of a building is to give an account of its actual existence, then the theoretical sciences do both.) But if it is not the case that the intellection of a thing implies its existence outside the intellect and that to give an intelligible account of it is to give an account of its actual existence, then, when one intends to make these four things exist, he necessarily requires something else beside theoretical science.

23   That is because things perceived by the intellect are as such free from the states and accidents that they have when they exist outside the [thinking] soul. In what remains numerically one these accidents do not vary or change at all; they do vary, however, in what remains one, not numerically, but in the species. Therefore when it is necessary to make the things perceived by the intellect and remaining one in their species exist outside the soul, one must join to them the states and accidents that must accompany them if they are to have actual existence outside the soul. This applies to the natural intelligibles, which are and remain one in their species, as well as to the voluntary intelligibles.[7]

24   However, the natural intelligibles, which exist outside the soul, exist from nature only, and it is by nature that they are accompanied with their accidents. As for the intelligibles that can be made to exist outside the soul by will, the accidents [*18*] and states that accompany them when they come into being are willed too. Now voluntary intelligibles cannot exist unless they are accompanied with these accidents and states. Since everything whose existence is willed cannot be made to exist unless it is first known, it follows that when one plans to bring any voluntary intelligible into actual existence outside the soul, he must first know the states that must accompany it when it exists. Because voluntary intelligibles do not belong to things that are one numerically, but in their species or genus, the accidents and states that must accompany them vary constantly, increase and decrease, and fall into combinations

that cannot be covered at all by invariable and unchangeable formal rules. Indeed for some of them no rule can be established. For others rules can be established, but they are variable rules and changeable definitions. Those for which no rule at all can be established are the ones that vary constantly and over short periods. The others, for which rules can be established, are those whose states vary over long periods. Those of them that come to exist are for the most part realized by the agency of whoever wills and does them. Yet because of obstacles standing in their way—some of which are natural and others voluntary, resulting from the wills of other individuals—sometimes none of them at all is realized. Furthermore, they suffer not only temporal variations, so that they may exist at a certain time with accidents and states different from those that accompany them at another time before or after; their states also differ when they exist in different places. This is evident in natural things, for example, Man. For when it [that is, the intelligible idea Man] assumes actual existence outside the soul, [*19*] the states and accidents in it at one time are different from the ones it has at another time, after or before. The same is the case with respect to different places. The accidents and states it has when existing in one country are different from the ones it has in another. Yet, throughout, the intellect perceives Man as a single intelligible idea. This holds for voluntary things as well. For instance, Moderation, Wealth, and the like are voluntary ideas perceived by the intellect. When we decide to make them actually exist, the accidents that must accompany them at a certain time will be different from the accidents that must accompany them at another time, and the accidents they must have when they exist in one nation will be different from those they must have when existing in another. In some of them, these accidents change from hour to hour, in others from day to day, in others from month to month, in others from year to year, in others from decade to decade, and in still others they change after many decades. Therefore, whoever should will to bring any of them into actual existence outside the soul ought to know the variable accidents that must accompany it in the specific period at which he seeks to bring it into existence and in the determined place in the inhabited part of the earth. Thus he ought to know the accidents that must accompany what is willed to exist from hour to hour, from month to month, from year to year, from decade to decade, or in some other period of determinate length, in a determined locality of large or small size. And he ought to know which of these accidents are common to all nations, to some nations, or to one city over a long period, common to them over a short period, or pertain to some of them specifically and over a short period.

25   The accidents and states of these intelligibles vary [*20*] whenever certain events occur in the inhabited part of the earth, events common to all of it, to a certain nation or city, or to a certain group within a

city, or pertaining to a single man. Such events are either natural or willed.

26   Things of this sort are not covered by the theoretical sciences, which cover only the intelligibles that do not vary at all. Therefore another faculty and another skill is required with which to discern the voluntary intelligibles [not as such, but] in so far as they possess these variable accidents: that is, the modes according to which they can be brought into actual existence by the will at a determined time, in a determined place, and when a determined event occurs. That is the deliberative faculty.[8] It is the skill and the faculty by which one discovers and discerns the variable accidents of the intelligibles whose particular instances are made to exist by the will, when one attempts to bring them into actual existence by the will at a determined time, in a determined place, and when a determined event takes place, whether the time is long or short, whether the locality is large or small.

27   Things are discovered by the deliberative faculty only in so far as they are found to be useful for the attainment of an end and purpose. The discoverer first sets the end before himself and then investigates the means by which that end and that purpose are realized. The deliberative faculty is most perfect when it discovers what is most useful for the attainment of these ends. The ends may be truly good, may be evil, or may be only believed to be good. If the means discovered are the most useful for a virtuous end, then they are noble and fair. [21] If the ends are evil, then the means discovered by the deliberative faculty are also evil, base, and bad. And if the ends are only believed to be good, then the means useful for attaining and achieving them are also only believed to be good. The deliberative faculty can be classified accordingly. Deliberative virtue is that by which one discovers what is most useful for some virtuous end. As for the deliberative faculty by which one discovers what is most useful for an evil end, it is not a deliberative virtue but ought to have other names. And if the deliberative faculty is used to discover what is most useful for things that are only believed to be good, then that deliberative faculty is only believed to be a deliberative virtue.

28   (1) There is a certain deliberative virtue that enables one to excel in the discovery of what is most useful for a virtuous end common to many nations, to a whole nation, or to a whole city, at a time when an event occurs that affects them in common. (There is no difference between saying most useful for a virtuous end and most useful and most noble, because what is both most useful and most noble necessarily serves a virtuous end, and what is most useful for a virtuous end is indeed the most noble with respect to that end.) This is political deliberative virtue. The events that affect them in common may persist over a long period or vary within short periods. However, political deliberative virtue is the deliberative virtue that discovers the most useful and most noble that

is common to many nations, to a whole nation, or to a whole city, irrespective of whether what is discovered persists there for a long period or varies over a short period. When it is concerned exclusively with the discovery of the things that are common to many nations, to a whole nation, [22] or to a whole city, and that do not vary except over many decades or over longer periods of determinate length, then it is more akin to a legislative ability. (2) The deliberative virtue with which one discovers only what varies over short periods. This is the faculty that manages the different classes of particular, temporary tasks in conjunction with, and at the occurrence of, the events that affect all nations, a certain nation, or a certain city. It is subordinate to the former. (3) The faculty by which one discovers what is most useful and noble, or what is most useful for a virtuous end, relative to one group among the citizens of a city or to the members of a household. It consists of a variety of deliberative virtues, each associated with the group in question: for instance, it is economic deliberative virtue or military deliberative virtue. Each of these, in turn, is subdivided inasmuch as what it discovers (*a*) does not vary except over long periods or (*b*) varies over short periods. (4) The deliberative virtue may be subdivided into still smaller fractions, such as the virtue by which one discovers what is most useful and noble with respect to the purpose of particular arts or with respect to particular purposes that happen to be pursued at particular times. Thus it will have as many subdivisions as there are arts and ways of life. (5) Furthermore, this faculty can be divided also in so far as (*a*) it enables man to excel in the discovery of what is most useful and noble with respect to his own end when an event occurs that concerns him specifically, and (*b*) it is a deliberative virtue by which he discovers what is most useful and noble with respect to a virtuous end to be attained by somebody else—the latter is consultative deliberative virtue. These two may be united in a single man or may exist separately.

29 It is obvious that the one who possesses a virtue by which he discovers what is most useful and noble, and this for the sake of a virtuous end that is good (irrespective of whether what is discovered is a true good that he wishes [23] for himself, a true good that he wishes someone else to possess, or something that is believed to be good by whomever he wishes it for), cannot possess this faculty without possessing a moral virtue. For if a man wishes the good for others, then he is either truly good or else believed to be good by those for whom he wishes the good although he is not good and virtuous. Similarly he who wishes the true good for himself has to be good and virtuous, not in his deliberation, but in his moral character and in his acts. It would seem that his virtue, moral character, and acts, have to correspond to his power of deliberation and ability to discover what is most useful and noble. Hence if he discovers by his deliberative virtue only those most useful and noble

means that are of great force (such as what is most useful for a virtuous end common to a whole nation, to many nations, or to a whole city, and does not vary except over a long period), then his moral virtues ought to be of a comparable measure. Similarly, if his deliberative virtues are confined to means that are most useful for a restricted end when a specific event occurs, then this is the measure of his [moral] virtue also. Accordingly, the more perfect the authority and the greater the power of these deliberative virtues, the stronger the authority and the greater the power of the moral virtues that accompany them.

30   (1) Since the deliberative virtue by which one discovers what is most useful and noble with respect to the ends that do not vary except over long periods and that are common to many nations, to a whole nation, or to a whole city when an event that affects them in common occurs, has more perfect authority and greater power, the [moral] virtues that accompany it should possess the most perfect authority and the greatest power. [24] (2) Next follows the deliberative virtue with which one excels in the discovery of what is most useful for a common, though temporary end, over short periods; the [moral] virtues that accompany it are of a comparable rank. (3) Then follow the deliberative virtues confined to individual parts of the city—the warriors, the rich, and so on; the moral virtues that have to do with these parts are of a comparable rank. (4) Finally, one comes to the deliberative virtues related to single arts (taking into account the purposes of these arts) and to single households and single human beings within single households (with attention to what pertains to them as events follow one another hour after hour or day after day); they are accompanied by a [moral] virtue of a comparable rank.

31   Therefore one ought to investigate which virtue is the perfect and most powerful virtue. Is it the combination of all the virtues? Or, if one virtue (or a number of virtues) turns out to have a power equal to that of all the virtues together, what ought to be the distinctive mark of the virtue that has this power and is hence the most powerful virtue? This virtue is such that when a man decides to fulfil its functions, he cannot do so without making use of the functions of all the other virtues. If he himself does not happen to possess all of these virtues—in which case he cannot make use of the functions of particular virtues present in him when he decides to fulfil the functions of that virtue—that virtue of his will be a moral virtue in the exercise of which he exploits the acts of the virtues possessed by all others, whether they are nations, cities within a nation, groups within a city, or parts within each group. This, then, is the leading virtue that is not surpassed by any other in authority. [25] Next follow the virtues that resemble this one in that they have a similar power with respect to single parts of the city. For instance, together with the deliberative faculty by which he discovers what is most useful and

noble with respect to that which is common to warriors, the general ought to possess a moral virtue. When he decides to fulfil the functions of the latter, he exploits the virtues possessed by the warriors as warriors. His courage, for instance, ought to be such as to enable him to exploit the warriors' particular acts of courage. Similarly, the one who possesses a deliberative virtue by which he discovers what is most useful and noble for the ends of those who acquire wealth in the city ought to possess the moral virtue that enables him to exploit the particular virtues of the classes of people engaged in acquiring wealth.

32   The arts, too, ought to follow this pattern. The leading art that is not surpassed by any other in authority is such that when we decide to fulfil its functions, we are unable to do so without making use of the functions of all the arts. It is the art for the fulfilment of whose purpose we require all the other arts. This, then, is the leading art and the most powerful of the arts—just as the corresponding moral virtue was the most powerful of all the moral virtues. It is then followed by the rest of the arts. An art of a certain class among them is more perfect and more powerful than the rest in its class if its end can be fulfilled only by making use of the functions of the other arts in its class. Such is the status of the particular leading arts. For instance, the art of commanding armies is such that its purpose can be achieved only by making use of the functions of the particular arts of warfare. Similarly, the [26] leading art of wealth in the city is such that its purpose with regard to wealth can be achieved only by exploiting the particular arts of acquiring wealth. This is the case also in every other major part of the city.

33   Furthermore, it is obvious that what is most useful and noble is in every case either most noble according to generally accepted opinion, most noble according to a particular religion, or truly most noble. Similarly, virtuous ends are either virtuous and good according to generally accepted opinion, virtuous and good according to a particular religion, or truly virtuous and good. No one can discover what is most noble according to the followers of a particular religion unless his moral virtues are the specific virtues of that religion. This holds for everyone else; it applies to the more powerful virtues as well as to the more particular and less powerful. Therefore the most powerful deliberative virtue and the most powerful moral virtue are inseparable from each other.

34   It is evident that the deliberative virtue with the highest authority can only be subordinate to the theoretical virtue; for it merely discerns the accidents of the intelligibles that, prior to having these accidents as their accompaniments, are acquired by the theoretical virtue. If it is determined that the one who possesses the deliberative virtue should discover the variable accidents and states of only those intelligibles of which he has personal insight and personal knowledge (so as not to make discoveries about things that perhaps ought not to take place), then the

deliberative virtue cannot be separated from the theoretical virtue. It follows that the theoretical virtue, the leading deliberative virtue, the leading moral virtue, and the leading practical art are inseparable from each other; otherwise the latter [three] will be unsound, imperfect, and without complete authority. [27]

35 But if, after the theoretical virtue has caused the intellect to perceive the moral virtues, the latter can only be made to exist if the deliberative virtue discerns them and discovers the accidents that must accompany their intelligibles so that they can be brought into existence, then the deliberative virtue is anterior to the moral virtues. If it is anterior to them, then he who possesses the deliberative virtue discovers by it only such moral virtues as exist independently of the deliberative virtues. Yet if the deliberative virtue is independent of the moral virtue, then he who has the capacity for discovering the (good) moral virtues will not himself be good, not even in a single virtue.[9] But if he himself is not good, how then does he seek out the good or wish the true good for himself or for others? And if he does not wish the good, how is he capable of discovering it without having set it before himself as an end? Therefore, if the deliberative virtue is independent of the moral virtue, it is not possible to discover the moral virtue with it. Yet if the moral virtue is inseparable from the deliberative, and they coexist, how could the deliberative virtue discover the moral and join itself to it? For if they are inseparable, it will follow that the deliberative virtue did not discover the moral virtue; while if the deliberative virtue did discover the moral virtue, it will follow that the deliberative virtue is independent of the moral virtue. Therefore either the deliberative virtue itself is the virtue of goodness or one should assume that the deliberative virtue is accompanied by some other virtue, different from the moral virtue that is discovered by the deliberative faculty. If that other moral virtue is formed by the will also, it follows that the deliberative virtue discovered it—thus the original doubt recurs. It follows, then, that there must be some other moral virtue—other, that is, than the one discovered by the deliberative virtue—that accompanies the deliberative virtue and enables the possessor of the deliberative virtue to wish the good and the virtuous end. [28] That virtue must be natural and must come into being by nature, and it must be coupled with a certain deliberative virtue [that is, cleverness] that comes into being by nature and discovers the moral virtues formed by the will. The virtue formed by the will then will be the human virtue by which man, after acquiring it in the way in which he acquires voluntary things, acquires the human deliberative virtue.

36 But one ought to inquire what manner of thing that natural virtue is. Is it or is it not identical with this voluntary virtue? Or ought one to say that it corresponds to this virtue, like the states of character that

exist in irrational animals?—just as it is said that courage resides in the lion, cunning in the fox, shiftiness in the bear, thievishness in the magpie, and so forth. For it is possible that every man is innately so disposed that his soul has a power such that he generally moves more easily in the direction of the accomplishment of a certain virtue or of a certain state of character than in the direction of doing the opposite act. Indeed man moves first in the direction in which it is easier for him to move, provided he is not compelled to do something else. For instance, if a man is innately so disposed that he is more prone to stand his ground against dangers than to recoil before them, then all he needs is to undergo the experience a sufficient number of times and this state of character becomes voluntary. Prior to this, he possessed the corresponding natural state of character. If this is so in particular moral virtues that accompany particular deliberative virtues, it must also be the case with the highest moral virtues that accompany the highest deliberative virtues. If this is so, it follows that there are some men who are innately disposed to a [natural moral] virtue that corresponds to the highest [human moral] virtue and that is joined to a naturally superior deliberative power, others just below them, and so on. [29] If this is so, then not every chance human being will possess art, moral virtue, and deliberative virtue with great power.

37   Therefore the prince occupies his place by nature and not merely by will. Similarly, a subordinate occupies his place primarily by nature and only secondarily by virtue of the will, which perfects his natural equipments. This being the case, the theoretical virtue, the highest deliberative virtue, the highest moral virtue, and the highest practical art are realized only in those equipped for them by nature: that is, in those who possess superior natures with very great potentialities.

III

38   After these four things are realized in a certain man, the realization of the particular instances of them in nations and cities still remains; his knowing how to make these particular instances exist in nations and cities remains: he who possesses such a great power ought to possess the capacity of realizing the particular instances of it in nations and cities.

39   There are two primary methods of realizing them: instruction and the formation of character. To instruct is to introduce the theoretical virtues in nations and cities. The formation of character is the method of introducing the moral virtues and practical arts in nations. Instruction proceeds by speech alone. The formation of character proceeds through habituating nations and citizens in doing the acts that issue from the practical states of character by arousing in them the resolution to do

these acts; the states of character and the acts issuing from them should
come to possess their souls and they should be, as it were, enraptured by
them. The resolution to do a thing may be aroused by speech or by
deed.

40 Instruction in the theoretical sciences should be given either to
the imams and the princes, or else to those who should preserve the
theoretical sciences. The instruction of these two groups proceeds by
means of identical approaches. These are the approaches [30] stated
above.[10] First, they should know the first premises and the primary
knowledge relative to every kind of theoretical science. Then they should
know the various states of the premises and their various arrangements
as stated before,[10] and be made to pursue the subjects that were mentioned. (Prior to this, their souls must have been set aright through the
training befitting the youths whose natures entitle them to this rank in
the order of humanity.) They should be habituated to use all the logical
methods in all the theoretical sciences. And they should be made to
pursue a course of study and form the habits of character from their
childhood until each of them reaches maturity, in accordance with the
plan described by Plato.[11] Then the princes among them will be placed
in subordinate offices and promoted gradually through the ranks until
they are fifty years old. Then they will be placed in the office with the
highest authority. This, then, is the way to instruct this group; they are
the elect who should not be confined to what is in conformity with
unexamined common opinion. Until they acquire the theoretical virtues,
they ought to be instructed in things theoretical by means of persuasive
methods. They should comprehend many theoretical things by way of
imagining them. These are the things—the ultimate principles and the
incorporeal principles—that a man cannot perceive by his intellect except
after knowing many other things. The vulgar ought to comprehend
merely the similitudes of these principles, which should be established
in their souls by persuasive arguments. One should draw a distinction
between the similitudes that ought to be presented to every nation, and
in which all nations and all the citizens of every city should share, and
the ones that ought to be presented to a particular nation and not to
another, to a particular city and not to another, or to a particular group
among the citizens of a city [31] and not to another. All these [persuasive
arguments and similitudes] must be discerned by the deliberative virtue.

41 They [the princes and the imams] should be habituated in the
acts of the practical[12] virtues and the practical arts by either of two
methods. First, by means of persuasive arguments, passionate arguments,
and other arguments that establish these acts and states of character in
the soul completely so as to arouse the resolution to do the acts willingly.
This method is made possible by the practice of the rational arts—to
which the mind is naturally inclined—and by the benefits derived from

such practice. The other method is compulsion. It is used with the re-
calcitrant and the obstinate among those citizens of cities and nations
who do not rise in favor of what is right willingly and of their own
accord or by means of arguments, and also with those who refuse to
teach others the theoretical sciences in which they are engaged.

42 Now since the virtue or the art of the prince is exercised by exploiting the acts of those who possess the particular virtues and the arts
of those who practice the particular arts, it follows necessarily that the
virtuous and the masters of the arts whom he [the prince] employs to
form the character of nations and citizens of the cities comprise two
primary groups: a group employed by him to form the character of
whoever is susceptible of having his character formed willingly, and a
group employed by him to form the character of those who are such
that their character can be formed only by compulsion. This is analogous
to what heads of households and superintendents of children and youths
do. For the prince forms the character of nations and instructs them,
just as the head of a household forms the character of its members and
instructs them, and the superintendent of children and youths forms their
character and instructs them. Just as each of the last two forms the
character of some of those who are in his custody [32] by being gentle
to them and by persuasion and forms the character of others by compulsion, so does the prince. Indeed it is by virtue of the very same skill
that the classes of men who form the character of others and superintend
them undertake both the compulsory formation of character and the
formation of character received willingly; the skill varies only with
respect to its degree and the extent of its power.[13] Thus the power required for forming the character of nations and for superintending them
is greater than the power required for forming the character of children
and youths or the power required by heads of households for forming
the character of the members of a household. Correspondingly, the
power of the princes, who are the superintendents of nations and cities
and who form their character, and the power of whomever and whatever
they employ in performing this function, are greater. The prince needs
the most powerful skill for forming the character of others with their
consent and the most powerful skill for forming their character by compulsion.

43 The latter is the craft of war: that is, the faculty that enables him
to excel in organizing and leading armies and utilizing war implements
and warlike people to conquer the nations and cities that do not submit
to doing what will procure them that happiness for whose acquisition
man is made. For every being is made to achieve the ultimate perfection
it is susceptible of achieving according to its specific place in the order
of being. Man's specific perfection is called supreme happiness; and to
each man, according to his rank in the order of humanity, belongs the

specific supreme happiness pertaining to his kind of man. The warrior
who pursues this purpose is the just warrior, and the art of war that
pursues this purpose is the just and virtuous art of war.

44   The other group, employed to form the character of nations and
the citizens of cities with their consent, is composed of those who possess
the rational virtues and arts. For it is obvious that the prince needs to
return to the theoretical, intelligible things [33] whose knowledge was
acquired by certain demonstrations, look for the persuasive methods that
can be employed for each, and seek out all the persuasive methods that
can be employed for it (he can do this because he possesses the power
to be persuasive about individual cases). Then he should repair to these
very same theoretical things and seize upon their similitudes. He ought
to make these similitudes produce images of the theoretical things for
all nations jointly, so establish the similitudes that persuasive methods can
cause them to be accepted, and exert himself throughout to make both
the similitudes and the persuasive methods such that all nations and cities
may share in them. Next he needs to enumerate the acts of the particular
practical virtues and arts that fulfil the above-mentioned requirements.[14]
He should devise methods of political oratory with which to arouse the
resolution to such acts in nations and cities. He should employ here:
(1) arguments that support [the rightness of] his own character; (2) passionate and moral arguments that cause (*a*) the souls of the citizens to
grow reverent, submissive, muted, and meek. But with respect to everything contrary to these acts he should employ (*b*) passionate and moral
arguments by which the souls of the citizens grow confident, spiteful,
insolent, and contemptuous. He should employ these same two kinds of
arguments [*a* and *b*], respectively, with the princes who agree with him
and with those who oppose him, with the men and the auxiliaries employed by him and with the ones employed by those who oppose him,
and with the virtuous and with those who oppose them. Thus with respect to his own position, he should employ arguments by which souls
grow reverent and submissive. But with respect to his opponents he
should employ arguments that cause souls to grow spiteful, insolent, and
contemptuous; arguments with which he contradicts, using persuasive
methods, those who disagree with his own opinions and acts; and arguments that show the opinions and acts of the opponent as base and make
their meanness and notoriety apparent. He should employ here [34] both
classes of arguments: I mean the class that should be employed period-
ically, daily, and temporarily, and not preserved, kept permanently, or
written down; and the other class, which should be preserved and kept
permanently, orally and in writing. [The latter should be kept in two
Books.] He should place in these two Books the opinions and the acts
that nations and cities were called upon to embrace, the arguments by
which he sought to preserve among them and to establish in them the

things they were called upon to embrace so that they will not be forgotten, and the arguments with which he contradicts the opponents of
these opinions and acts. Therefore the sciences that form the character
of nations and cities will have three orders of rank; each kind will have a
group to preserve it who should be drawn from among those who possess the faculty that enables them to excel in the discovery of what had not
been clearly stated to them with reference to the science they preserve, to
defend it, to contradict what contradicts it, and to excel in teaching all
of this to others. In all of this they should aim at accomplishing the purpose of the supreme ruler with respect to nations and cities.

45   Then he [the supreme ruler] should inquire next into the different
classes of nations by inquiring into every nation and into the human
states of character and the acts for which all nations are equipped by
that nature which is common to them, until he comes to inquire into
all or most nations. He should inquire into that in which all nations
share—that is, the human nature common to them—and then into all the
things that pertain specifically to every group within every nation. He
should discern all of these, draw up an actual, if approximate, list of the
acts and the states of character with which every nation can be set
aright and guided toward happiness, and specify the classes of persuasive
argument (regarding both the theoretical and the practical virtues) that
ought to be employed among them. He will thus set down what every
nation is capable of, having subdivided every nation and inquired whether
or not there is a group fit for preserving the theoretical sciences [35] and
others who can preserve the popular theoretical sciences or the image-
making theoretical sciences.[15]

46   Provided all of these groups exist in nations, four sciences will
emerge. First, the theoretical virtue through which the beings become
intelligible with certain demonstrations. Next, these same intelligibles
acquired by persuasive methods. Subsequently, the science that comprises
the similitudes of these intelligibles, accepted by persuasive methods.
Finally, the sciences extracted from these three for each nation. There
will be as many of these extracted sciences as there are nations, each
containing everything by which a particular nation becomes perfect
and happy.

47   Therefore he [the supreme ruler] has to secure certain groups of
men or certain individuals who are to be instructed in what causes the
happiness of particular nations, who will preserve what can form the
character of a particular nation alone, and who will learn the persuasive
methods that should be employed in forming the character of that nation.
The knowledge which that nation ought to have must be preserved by a
man or a group of men also possessing the faculty that enables them to
excel in the discovery of what was not actually given to this man or this
group of men but is, nevertheless, of the same kind for which they act

as custodians, enables them to defend it and contradict what opposes it, and to excel in the instruction of that nation. In all of this they should aim at accomplishing what the supreme ruler had in mind for the nation, for whose sake he gave this man or this group of men what was given to them. Such are the men who should be employed to form the character of nations with their consent.

48   The best course is that each member of the groups to which the formation of the character of nations is delegated should possess a warlike virtue and a deliberative virtue for use in case there is need to excel in leading troops in war; [*36*] thus every one of them will possess the skill to form the [nation's] character by both methods. If this combination does not happen to exist in one man, then he [the supreme ruler] should add to the man who forms the character of nations with their consent, another who possesses this craft of war. In turn, the one to whom the formation of the character of any nation is delegated should also follow the custom of employing a group of men to form the character of the nation with its consent or by compulsion, either by dividing them into two groups or employing a single group that possesses a skill for doing both. Subsequently, this one group, or the two groups, should be subdivided, and so on, ending in the lowest divisions or the ones with the least power in the formation of character. The ranks within these groups should be established according to the deliberative virtue of each individual: that is, depending on whether this deliberative virtue exploits subordinate ones or is exploited by one superior to it. The former will rule and the latter have a subordinate office according to the power of their respective deliberative virtues. When these two groups are formed in any nation or city, they, in turn, will order the rest.

49   These, then, are the modes and methods through which the four human things by which supreme happiness is achieved are realized in nations and cities.

I V

50   Foremost among all of these [four] sciences is that which gives an account of the beings as they are perceived by the intellect with certain demonstrations. The others merely take these same beings and employ persuasion about them or represent them with images so as to facilitate the instruction of the multitude of the nations and the citizens of cities. That is because nations and the citizens of cities are composed of some who are the elect and others who are the vulgar. The vulgar confine themselves, or should be confined, to theoretical cognitions that are in conformity with unexamined common opinion. [*37*] The elect do not

confine themselves in any of their theoretical cognitions to what is in conformity with unexamined common opinion, but reach their conviction and knowledge on the basis of premises subjected to thorough scrutiny. Therefore whoever thinks that he is not confined to what is in conformity with unexamined common opinion in his inquiries, believes that in them he is of the "elect" and that everybody else is vulgar. Hence the competent practitioner of every art comes to be called one of the "elect" because people know that he does not confine himself, with respect to the objects of his art, to what is in conformity with unexamined common opinion, but exhausts them and scrutinizes them thoroughly. Again, whoever does not hold a political office or does not possess an art that establishes his claim to a political office, but either possesses no art at all or is enabled by his art to hold only a subordinate office in the city, is said to be "vulgar"; and whoever holds a political office or else possesses an art that enables him to aspire to a political office, is of the "elect." Therefore, whoever thinks that he possesses an art that qualifies him for assuming a political office or thinks that his position has the same status as a political office (for instance, men with prominent ancestors and many who possess great wealth), calls himself one of the "elect" and a "statesman."

51 Whoever has a more perfect mastery of the art that qualifies him for assuming an office is more appropriate for inclusion among the elect. Therefore it follows that the most elect of the elect is the supreme ruler. It would appear that this is so because he is the one who does not confine himself in anything at all to what is in conformity with unexamined common opinion. He must hold the office of the supreme ruler and be the most elect of the elect because of his state of character and skill. As for the one who assumes a political office [38] with the intention of accomplishing the purpose of the supreme ruler, he adheres to thoroughly scrutinized opinions. However, the opinions that caused him to become an adherent[16] or because of which he was convinced that he should use his art to serve the supreme ruler, were based on mere conformity to unexamined opinions; he conforms to unexamined common opinion in his theoretical cognitions as well. The result is that the supreme ruler and he who possesses the science that encompasses the intelligibles with certain demonstrations belong to the elect. The rest are the vulgar and the multitude. Thus the methods of persuasion and imaginative representation are employed only in the instruction of the vulgar and the multitude of the nations and the cities, while the certain demonstrative methods, by which the beings themselves are made intelligible, are employed in the instruction of those who belong to the elect.

52 This is the superior science and the one with the most perfect [claim to rule or to] authority. The rest of the authoritative sciences are subordinate to this science. By "the rest of the authoritative sciences"

I mean the second and the third, and that which is derived from them,[17] since these sciences merely follow the example of that science and are employed to accomplish the purpose of that science, which is supreme happiness and the final perfection to be achieved by man.

53   It is said that this science existed anciently among the Chaldeans,[18] who are the people of al-'Irāq,[19] subsequently reaching the people of Egypt,[20] from there transmitted to the Greeks, where it remained until it was transmitted to the Syrians,[21] and then to the Arabs. Everything comprised by this science was expounded in the Greek language, later in Syriac, and finally in Arabic. The Greeks who possessed this science used to call it true wisdom and the highest wisdom. They called the acquisition of it, science, and the scientific state of mind, philosophy (by which they meant the quest and the love for the highest wisdom). [39] They held that potentially it subsumes all the virtues. They called it the science of sciences, the mother of sciences, the wisdom of wisdoms, and the art of arts (they meant the art that makes use of all the arts, the virtue that makes use of all the virtues, and the wisdom that makes use of all wisdoms). Now, "wisdom" may be used for consummate and extreme competence in any art whatsoever when it leads to performing feats of which most practitioners of that art are incapable. Here "wisdom" is used in a qualified sense. Thus he who is extremely competent in an art is said to be "wise" in that art. Similarly, a man with penetrating practical judgment and acumen may be called "wise" in the thing regarding which he has penetrating practical judgment. However, true wisdom is this science and state of mind alone.

54   When the theoretical sciences are isolated and their possessor does not have the faculty for exploiting them for the benefit of others, they are defective philosophy. To be a truly perfect philosopher one has to possess both the theoretical sciences and the faculty for exploiting them for the benefit of all others according to their capacity. Were one to consider the case of the true philosopher, he would find no difference between him and the supreme ruler. For he who possesses the faculty for exploiting what is comprised by the theoretical matters for the benefit of all others possesses the faculty for making such matters intelligible as well as for bringing into actual existence those of them that depend on the will. The greater his power to do the latter, the more perfect is his philosophy. Therefore he who is truly perfect possesses with sure insight, first, the theoretical virtues, and subsequently the practical. Moreover, he possesses the capacity for bringing them about in nations and cities in the manner and the measure possible with reference to each. Since it is impossible for him to possess the faculty for bringing them about except by employing certain demonstrations, persuasive methods, [40] as well as methods that represent things through images, and this

either with the consent of others or by compulsion, it follows that the true philosopher is himself the supreme ruler.

55 Every instruction is composed of two things: (*a*) making what is being studied comprehensible and causing its idea to be established in the soul and (*b*) causing others to assent to what is comprehended and established in the soul. There are two ways of making a thing comprehensible: first, by causing its essence to be perceived by the intellect, and second, by causing it to be imagined through the similitude that imitates it. Assent, too, is brought about by one of two methods, either the method of certain demonstration or the method of persuasion. Now when one acquires knowledge of the beings or receives instruction in them, if he perceives their ideas themselves with his intellect, and his assent to them is by means of certain demonstration, then the science that comprises these cognitions is philosophy. But if they are known by imagining them through similitudes that imitate them, and assent to what is imagined of them is caused by persuasive methods, then the ancients call what comprises these cognitions religion. And if those intelligibles themselves are adopted, and persuasive methods are used, then the religion comprising them is called popular, generally accepted, and external philosophy. Therefore, according to the ancients, religion is an imitation of philosophy. Both comprise the same subjects and both give an account of the ultimate principles of the beings. For both supply knowledge about the first principle and cause of the beings, and both give an account of the ultimate end for the sake of which man is made—that is, supreme happiness—and the ultimate end of every one of the other beings. In everything of which philosophy gives an account based on intellectual perception or conception, religion gives an account based on imagination. In everything demonstrated by philosophy, religion employs persuasion. Philosophy gives an account of the ultimate principles (that is, the essence of the first principle and the essences of the incorporeal second principles[22]), [*41*] as they are perceived by the intellect. Religion sets forth their images by means of similitudes of them taken from corporeal principles and imitates them by their likenesses among political offices.[23] It imitates the divine acts by means of the functions of political offices.[23] It imitates the actions of natural powers and principles by their likenesses among the faculties, states, and arts that have to do with the will, just as Plato does in the *Timaeus*.[24] It imitates the intelligibles by their likenesses among the sensibles: for instance, some imitate matter by "abyss" or "darkness" or "water," and nothingness by "darkness." It imitates the classes of supreme happiness—that is, the ends of the acts of the human virtues—by their likenesses among the goods that are believed to be the ends. It imitates the classes of true happiness by means of the ones that are believed to be happiness. It imitates the ranks of the beings by

their likenesses among spatial and temporal ranks. And it attempts to bring the similitudes of these things as close as possible to their essences.[25] Also, in everything of which philosophy gives an account that is demonstrable and certain, religion gives an account based on persuasive arguments. Finally, philosophy is prior to religion in time.

56   Again, it is evident that when one seeks to bring into actual existence the intelligibles of the things depending on the will supplied by practical philosophy, he ought to prescribe the conditions that render possible their actual existence. Once the conditions that render their actual existence possible are prescribed, the voluntary intelligibles are embodied in laws. Therefore the legislator is he who, by the excellence of his deliberation, has the capacity to find the conditions required for the actual existence of voluntary intelligibles in such a way as to lead to the achievement of supreme happiness. It is also evident that only after perceiving them by his intellect should the legislator seek to discover their conditions, and he cannot [42] find their conditions that enable him to guide others toward supreme happiness without having perceived supreme happiness with his intellect. Nor can these things become intelligible (and the legislative craft thereby hold the supreme office) without his having beforehand acquired philosophy. Therefore, if he intends to possess a craft that is authoritative rather than subservient, the legislator must be a philosopher. Similarly, if the philosopher who has acquired the theoretical virtues does not have the capacity for bringing them about in all others according to their capacities, then what he has acquired from it has no validity. Yet he cannot find the states and the conditions by which the voluntary intelligibles assume actual existence, if he does not possess the deliberative virtue; and the deliberative virtue cannot exist in him without the practical virtue. Moreover, he cannot bring them about in all others according to their capacities except by a faculty that enables him to excel in persuasion and in representing things through images.

57   It follows, then, that the idea of Imam, Philosopher, and Legislator is a single idea. However, the name "philosopher" signifies primarily theoretical virtue. But if it be determined that the theoretical virtue reach its ultimate perfection in every respect, it follows necessarily that he must possess all the other faculties as well. "Legislator" signifies excellence of knowledge concerning the conditions of practical[26] intelligibles, the faculty for finding them, and the faculty for bringing them about in nations and cities. When it is determined that they be brought into existence on the basis of knowledge, it will follow that the theoretical virtue must precede the others—the existence of the inferior presupposes the existence of the higher. The name "prince" signifies sovereignty and ability. To be completely able, one has to possess [43] the power of the greatest ability. His ability to do a thing must not result

only from external things; he himself must possess great ability as a result of his art, skill, and virtue being of exceedingly great power. This is not possible except by great power of knowledge, great power of deliberation, and great power of [moral] virtue and art. Otherwise he is not truly able nor sovereign. For if his ability stops short of this, it is still imperfect. Similarly, if his ability is restricted to goods inferior to supreme happiness, his ability is incomplete and he is not perfect. Therefore the true prince is the same as the philosopher-legislator. As to the idea of Imam in the Arabic language, it signifies merely the one whose example is followed and who is well-received: that is, either his perfection is well-received or his purpose is well-received. If he is not well-received in all the infinite activities, virtues, and arts, then he is not truly well-received. Only when all other arts, virtues, and activities seek to realize his purpose and no other, will his art be the most powerful art, his [moral] virtue the most powerful virtue, his deliberation the most powerful deliberation, and his science the most powerful science. For with all of these powers he will be exploiting the powers of others so as to accomplish his own purpose. This is not possible without the theoretical sciences, without the greatest of all deliberative virtues, and without the rest of those things that are in the philosopher.

58   So let it be clear to you that the idea of the Philosopher, Supreme Ruler, Prince, Legislator, and Imam is but a single idea. No matter which one of these words you take, if you proceed to look at what each of them signifies [44] among the majority of those who speak our language, you will find that they all finally agree by signifying one and the same idea.

59   Once the images representing the theoretical things[27] demonstrated in the theoretical sciences are produced in the souls of the multitude and they are made to assent to their images, and once the practical things (together with the conditions of the possibility of their existence), take hold of their souls and dominate them so that they are unable to resolve to do anything else, then the theoretical and practical things are realized. Now these things are philosophy when they are in the soul of the legislator. They are religion when they are in the souls of the multitude. For when the legislator knows these things, they are evident to him by sure insight, whereas what is established in the souls of the multitude is through an image and a persuasive argument. Although it is the legislator who also represents these things through images, neither the images nor the persuasive arguments are intended for himself. As far as he is concerned, they are certain. He is the one who invents the images and the persuasive arguments, but not for the sake of establishing these things in his own soul as a religion for himself. No, the images and the persuasive arguments are intended for others, whereas, so far as he is concerned, these things are certain. They are a religion for others, whereas,

so far as he is concerned, they are philosophy. Such, then, is true philosophy and the true philosopher.

60 As for mutilated philosophy: the counterfeit philosopher, the vain philosopher, or the false philosopher is the one who sets out to study the theoretical sciences without being prepared for them. For he who sets out to inquire ought to be innately equipped for the theoretical sciences—that is, fulfil the conditions prescribed by Plato in the *Republic*:[28] He should excel in comprehending and conceiving that which is essential. Moreover, he should have good memory and be able to endure the toil of study. He should love truthfulness and truthful people, and justice and just people; [45] and not be headstrong or a wrangler about what he desires. He should not be gluttonous for food and drink, and should by natural disposition disdain the appetites, the dirhem, the dinar, and the like. He should be high-minded and avoid what is disgraceful in people. He should be pious, yield easily to goodness and justice, and be stubborn in yielding to evil and injustice. And he should be strongly determined in favor of the right thing. Moreover, he should be brought up according to laws and habits that resemble his innate disposition. He should have sound convictions about the opinions of the religion in which he is reared, hold fast to the virtuous acts in his religion, and not forsake all or most of them. Furthermore, he should hold fast to the generally accepted virtues and not forsake the generally accepted noble acts. For if a youth is such, and then sets out to study philosophy and learns it, it is possible that he will not become a counterfeit or a vain or a false philosopher.

61 The false philosopher is he who acquires the theoretical sciences without achieving the utmost perfection so as to be able to introduce others to what he knows in so far as their capacity permits. The vain philosopher is he who learns the theoretical sciences, but without going any further and without being habituated to doing the acts considered virtuous by a certain religion or the generally accepted noble acts. Instead he follows his own inclination and appetites in everything, whatever they may happen to be. The counterfeit philosopher is he who studies the theoretical sciences without being naturally equipped for them. Therefore, although the counterfeit and the vain may complete the study of the theoretical sciences, in the end their possession of them diminishes little by little. By the time they reach the age at which [46] a man should become perfect in the virtues, their knowledge will have been completely extinguished, even more so than the extinction of the fire [sun] of Heraclitus mentioned by Plato.[29] For the natural dispositions of the former and the habit of the latter overpower what they might have remembered in their youth and make it burdensome for them to retain what they had patiently toiled for. They neglect it, and what they retain begins to diminish little by little until its fire becomes in-

effective and extinguished, and they gather no fruit from it. As for the false philosopher, he is the one who is not yet aware of the purpose for which philosophy is pursued. He acquires the theoretical sciences, or only some portion of them, and holds the opinion that the purpose of the measure he has acquired consists in certain kinds of happiness that are believed to be so or are considered by the multitude to be good things. Therefore he rests there to enjoy that happiness, aspiring to achieve this purpose with his knowledge. He may achieve his purpose and settle for it, or else find his purpose difficult to achieve and so hold the opinion that the knowledge he has is superfluous. Such is the false philosopher.

62   The true philosopher is the one mentioned before.[30] If after reaching this stage no use is made of him, the fact that he is of no use to others is not his fault but the fault of those who either do not listen or are not of the opinion that they should listen to him. Therefore the prince or the imam is prince or imam by virtue of his skill and art, regardless of whether or not anyone acknowledges him, whether or not he is obeyed, whether or not he is supported in his purpose by any group; just as the physician is physician by virtue of his skill and his ability to heal the sick, whether or not there are sick men for him to heal, whether or not he finds tools to use in his activity, whether he is prosperous or poor—not having any of these things does not do away with his physicianship. Similarly, neither the imamate of the imam, [47] the philosophy of the philosopher, nor the princeship of the prince is done away with by not having tools to use in his activities or men to employ in reaching his purpose.

63   The philosophy that answers to this description was handed down to us by the Greeks from Plato and Aristotle only. Both have given us an account of philosophy, but not without giving us also an account of the ways to it and of the ways to re-establish it when it becomes confused or extinct. We shall begin by expounding first the philosophy of Plato and the orders of rank in his philosophy. We shall begin with the first part of the philosophy of Plato, and then order one part of his philosophy after another until we reach its end. We shall do the same with the philosophy presented to us by Aristotle, beginning with the first part of his philosophy.

64   So let it be clear to you that, in what they presented, their purpose is the same, and that they intended to offer one and the same philosophy.

NOTES

1. These are the four ways of interpreting and asking the question *why*, which Alfarabi has indicated previously in sections 5 ff.; they ask after (1) the form, (2-3) the agent and the material, and (4) the end.

2. For the source of the distinction between the "principle of instruction" and the "principle of being," between "what is better known to us" and "what is better known by nature," or between the *causa cognoscendi* and the *causa essendi,* consider Aristotle *Physics* i. 1. 184ᵃ16–23, i. 5. 189ᵃ4 (cf. *Posterior Analytics* i. 2. 71ᵇ34–72ᵃ6), *Nicomachean Ethics* i. 4. 1095ᵃ30 ff., vi. 3. 1139ᵇ25 ff.

3. Sections 4 ff.

4. That is, the "theoretical" part of it. Cf. below, section 26; Alfarabi, *Enumeration of the Sciences,* pp. 103–4 (above, Selection 1).

5. Alfarabi says "first principle" and "principles" respectively; cf. the physical-metaphysical and political connotations of *archē (archōn)* : *principium-princeps,* "principle"-"prince."

6. Enumerated by Alfarabi in section 1: "The human things by which nations and citizens of cities attain earthly happiness in this life and supreme happiness in the life beyond are of four kinds: theoretical virtues, deliberative virtues, moral virtues, and practical arts."

7. The distinction between "natural" and "voluntary" intelligibles and the meaning of "voluntary" intelligibles are stated below, sections 24 ff.

8. The "rationative," "thinking," "calculative" or "reflective" faculty (*fikriyah*).

9. Cf. Aristotle *Nicomachean Ethics* vi. 12, 13.

10. Sections 4 ff.

11. *Republic* ii. 376E–iv. 427C, vii. 521C-41B.

12. That is, deliberative and moral.

13. Note, however, the end of the section and the following sections where the dual aspect of this skill is emphasized.

14. Sections 41-43, perhaps also sections 28 ff.

15. The latter two sciences are (derivatively) "theoretical" (or "philosophic," cf. section 55 [40:12-13]) inasmuch as (*a*) they deal with opinions (vs. acts) and (*b*) their subjects were originally seized upon in the theoretical sciences properly so-called (above, section 44, below, section 46).

16. Or "follower," "successor" (*tābi').* He functions as an "aide" or "subordinate" who is employed by the supreme ruler to apply and preserve his law (above, sections 44, 47-48). In the absence of the supreme ruler, the "adherent" is envisaged as his "successor." This is a second-best arrangement, because the ruler will then lack theoretical knowledge and hence the ability to be a true lawgiver (above, sections 45 ff.). Cf. Alfarabi, *Political Regime,* pp. 51, 54 (above, Selection 2).

17. Above, section 46.

18. For an account of the "philosophic" sciences (mathematics, astronomy, etc.) of the "Chaldeans," cf., e.g., Ṣā'id al-Andalusī, *Classes of Nations (Ṭabaqāt al-umam),* ed. Louis Cheikho (Beirut, 1912), iv. 3.

19. Southern Mesopotamia, the alluvial region bounded in the north by a line from al-Anbār to Takrīt. Cf. *ibid.* i.

20. *Ibid.* iv. 6. Ṣā'id al-Andalusī reports the popular myⁿʰ of the "prophetic" origin of the philosophic sciences. In addition to claiming that philosophy *alone* is true wisdom, Alfarabi insists (below, section 55 [41:12]) that "philosophy is prior to religion *in time.*"

21. *al-Siryān:* the Jacobite and Nestorian (Monophysite) Christians using Syriac as a literary medium in Syria, Mesopotamia, and the Persian Empire.

22. The causes or principles of the heavenly bodies.

23. Alfarabi says "principles." Cf. above, n. 5.

24. 19D, 21B-C, 29B ff.

25. See Alfarabi, *Political Regime,* pp. 56-57 (above, Selection 2).

26. "Practical" as distinguished from "incorporeal" and "natural." They are the intelligibles whose realization depends on deliberation, moral character, and art. Above, sections 22 ff., 40.

27. "Things" (*ashyā'*). The term *shay'* is used throughout in a variety of senses (roughly corresponding to "being"). It can signify particulars or universals, what exists outside the mind or the intelligible ideas (as here), the objects of knowledge or of opinion and imagination (as in the rest of the section).

28. ii. 375A ff., vi. 487B ff., *passim.*

29. *Republic* vi. 498B; cf. Aristotle *Meteorologica* ii. 2. 355ᵃ9 ff.

30. Sections 53, 57, 59.

4.

Alfarabi

PLATO'S LAWS

Translated by Muhsin Mahdi

Plato's Laws consist of an introduction and summaries of the first nine books of Plato's *Laws*, of which only the first two are given here. In the introduction, Alfarabi explains Plato's art of writing in general and the method he follows in writing the *Laws* in particular. He also states his own method of summarizing Plato's *Laws*, points to the two groups of readers for whom the work was written, and indicates the benefit that each can derive from reading it. In the preceding texts, especially in the *Attainment of Happiness*, Alfarabi treats of the place of laws and legislation in the broader context of political philosophy. Here, the question of laws becomes the object of a specialized study. In the guise of a commentary on Plato's *Laws*, Alfarabi shows the relevance of Plato's investigation of Greek divine laws to the study and understanding of all divine laws; hence Avicenna's statement (below, Selection 5) that Plato's *Laws* treat of prophecy and the Law. The term *nāmūs* (nomos) is translated throughout as "law."

The translation is based on F. Gabrieli's edition: *Alfarabius Compendium Legum Platonis* (London, 1952), pp. 3-16, and takes into account the additional evidence presented by Muhsin Mahdi, "The *Editio Princeps* of Fārābī's *Compendium Legum Platonis*," *Journal of Near Eastern Studies*, XX (1961), 1-24.

[INTRODUCTION]

1 Whereas the thing by which man excels all other animals is the faculty that enables him to discern the means and the affairs with which he deals and that he observes, in order to know which of them

is useful so as to want and obtain it, and to reject and avoid the useless; whereas that faculty emerges from potentiality into actuality only through experience ("experience" means reflection upon the particular instances of a thing and, from what one finds in these particular instances, passing judgment upon its universal characteristics)—therefore, whoever acquires more of these experiences is more excellent and perfect in his humanity. However, the man of experience may err in what he does and experiences, so that he conceives the thing to be in a different state than the one in which it really is. (There are many reasons for error, which have been enumerated by those who have discussed the art of sophistry. Of all men, the wise men are the ones who have acquired the experiences that are truly sound.) Nevertheless, all men are naturally disposed to pass a universal judgment after observing only a few particular instances of a thing ("universal" means here that which covers all the particular instances of the thing as well as their duration in time); so that once it is observed that an individual had done something in a certain way on a number of occasions, it is judged that he does that thing in that way all the time. For instance, when someone has spoken the truth on one, two, or a number of occasions, men are naturally disposed to judge that he is simply truthful, and similarly when someone lies; and when someone is observed on a number of occasions to act with courage or as a coward, or to give evidence of any other moral habit, he is judged to be so, wholly and always.

2   Whereas the wise men know this aspect of men's natural disposition, sometimes they have repeatedly shown themselves as possessing a certain character until men judged that this is how they always are. Then, afterwards, they acted in a different manner, which went unnoticed by men, who supposed that they were acting as they had done [4] formerly. It is related, for example, that a certain abstemious ascetic was known for his probity, propriety, asceticism, and worship, and became famous for this. He feared the tyrannical sovereign and decided to run away from his city. The sovereign's command went out that he is to be searched for and arrested wherever he is found. He could not leave from any one of the city's gates and was apprehensive lest he fall into the hands of the sovereign's men. So he went and found a dress that is worn by vagabonds, put it on, carried a cymbal in his hand, pretended to be drunk early at night, and came out to the gate of the city singing to the accompaniment of that cymbal of his. The gatekeeper said to him, "Who are you?" "I am so and so, the ascetic!" he said in a jocular vein. The gatekeeper thought he was poking fun at him and he did not interfere with him. So he saved himself without having lied in what he said.

3   Our purpose in making this introduction is this: the wise Plato did not feel free to reveal and uncover the sciences for all men.

Therefore he followed the practice of using symbols, riddles, obscurity, and difficulty, so that science would not fall into the hands of those who do not deserve it and be deformed, or into the hands of one who does not know its worth or who uses it improperly. In this he was right. Once he knew and became certain that he had become well-known for this practice, and that all men came to know that this was what he did, he sometimes turned to the subject he intended to discuss and stated it openly and literally; but the one who reads or hears his discussion thinks that it is symbolic and that he intended something different from what he has stated openly. This notion is one of the secrets of his books. Moreover, no one is able to understand that which he states openly and that which he states symbolically unless he is trained in that art itself, and no one is able to distinguish between the two unless he is skilled in the science that is being discussed. This is how his discussion proceeds in the *Laws*. In the present book, we have resolved upon extracting the notions to which he alludes in that book and grouping them together, following the order of the Discourses it contains, in order that the present book become an aid to whoever wants to know that book and sufficient for whoever cannot bear the hardship of study and reflection. God accommodates to what is right. [5]

FIRST DISCOURSE

1 A questioner asked about the cause of laying down the laws: "cause" means here the maker, the maker of the laws being the one who legislates them. The interlocutor answered that the one who legislated them was Zeus; among the Greeks, Zeus is the father of men who is the last cause.

2 Then he mentioned another legislation in order to explain that there are many laws and that their multiplicity does not detract from their validity. He supported this by the testimony of generally accepted and popular poems and traditions in praise of some ancient legislators.

3 Then he indicated that, because there are some who detract from the validity of the laws and tend to argue that they are foolish, it is right to examine them. He explained that the laws occupy a very high place and that they are superior to all wise sayings. He examined the particulars of the law that was generally accepted in his time.

Plato mentioned the cypress trees; he mentioned the path that was being taken by the interlocutor and the questioner, and its stations. Most people thought that beneath this there are subtle notions: that by "trees" he meant "men," and similar difficult, forced, and offensive notions, which it would take too long to state. But the case is not as they think.

Rather, he intended thereby to prolong his discourse, and to establish a link between the literal sense of the discussion and something that corresponds to it, but that refers to other matters—this being his purpose—in order to hide his intention.

4 Then he turned to some of the rules of that law which was generally accepted by them and he examined them (he sought to determine in what way that law was right and whether it agreed with the requirements of sound judgment)—that is, messing in common and carrying light armor. He explained that such rules have many advantages —for instance, they promote friendship and mutual aid—and that they were called for because their roads were rugged and most of them were infantrymen rather than cavalrymen.

5 Then he explained that because men in general, and those people in particular, are naturally disposed to perpetual war, the carrying of appropriate arms and their acquisition, and association and friendship, are necessary things. He explained also the advantages reaped from war, gave an exhaustive account of the kinds of war, and explained the specific and general forms of war.

6 Then he expanded on the discourse on wars until he stated [6] many things about the advantages of the law: it enables an individual to control himself, to obtain the power to suppress evil things (both the ones that are in the soul and the external ones), and to pursue what is just. Moreover, he explained in this connection what is the virtuous city and who is the virtuous man. He explained that they are the city and the man that conquer by virtue of truth and rightness. He explained also the true need for a judge, the obligation to obey him, and how this promotes the common interests. He described who is the agreeable judge, how he ought to conduct himself in suppressing the evil ones and protecting men against wars by gentleness and good governance, and that he should begin with what is most needed, that is, the lowest. He explained that men are badly in need of avoiding wars among themselves, and that they intensely desire to avoid wars because this promotes their well-being. But it is impossible without adhering to the law and applying its rules. When the law commands waging wars, it does so in the pursuit of peace, not in the pursuit of war—just as someone may be commanded to do something undesirable because its final consequence is desirable. He stated also that it is not sufficient for an individual to live in prosperity without security. He supported this statement by the testimony of a poem by a man well-known among them, that is, the poem of Tyrtaeus. He explained also that the courageous and praiseworthy man is not the one who is first to attack in external wars, but he who, in addition, controls himself and manages to uphold peace and security whenever he can. He supported this statement by poems commonly known among them.

7 Then he explained that the purpose of the legislator's forbearance and accomplishment is to seek the face of God, the Mighty and Majestic, look for reward and the last abode, and acquire the highest virtue, which is higher than the four moral virtues. He explained that there may be certain men who imitate the legislators. These are individuals with various purposes, who legislate hastily to achieve their bad aims. (He turned to mention these individuals only so that men guard against being beguiled by the like of them.) [7]

He divided the virtues and explained that some of them are human and others are divine; the divine are preferable to the human; and the one who has acquired the human may have missed the divine. The human virtues—like power, beauty, prosperity, science, and so forth—are the ones enumerated in the books on ethics. He stated that the true lawgiver is the one who orders these virtues in a suitable manner leading to the acquisition of the divine virtues; for when the human virtues are practiced by the one who possesses them as the law requires him to do, they become the divine virtues.

8 Then he explained that the lawgivers turn to the means that lead to the acquisition of the virtues, and they command and impress upon men that they should adhere to them so that, through the realization of these means, the virtues would be realized. Examples of these means are legal marriage, the ordering of the appetites and the pleasures, and indulging in each only to the extent permitted by the law. The same applies to fear and anger, base and noble matters, and everything else that serves as a means to the virtues.

9 Then he explained that Zeus and Apollo had used all those means in their two laws. He explained the many advantages of each one of the rules of their Law—for instance, those dealing with hunting, messing in common, war, and so forth.

He explained also that war may take place by necessity or because of the appetite and desire. He explained which war is desirable and pleasant and which is the one caused by necessity.

He stated in the oblique part of his discussion that the argument that runs between the speaker and the interlocutor may lead to debasing and degrading certain noble and desirable things; but what is intended by this is to examine them and reflect upon them so as to explain their excellence, clear them of suspicion, and ascertain their validity and desirability. This is right. He presented this as an excuse for whoever argues for reflecting upon [8] any of the rules of the law, for such a one is the lover of moderation and inquiry, not of contention or mischief.

10 Then he proceeded to condemn certain rules that were known to them in those laws. He stated that to accept such rules, regardless of one's suspicion from the outset that they may be defective, is to

act like children and ignorant men; an intelligent man must examine such rules in order to overcome his doubt and understand the truth about them.

11   Then he stated that to carry out the demands of the law is one of the most difficult things, while to censure and make unfounded claims is very easy.

12   Then he mentioned some of the generally accepted rules that had been laid down in earlier laws—for instance, the ones concerning festivals—and how they are extremely correct because they involve pleasure, to which all men are naturally inclined; and he mentioned the established law that renders the pleasure divine. He praised it, approved of it, and explained its advantages. Another example is that of wine-drinking, its advantages when practiced as the law demands, and its consequences when practiced differently.

13   Then he warned against believing that the victors are always right and that the vanquished are always wrong. Victory may be due to large numbers, and they may very well be in the wrong. Therefore a man ought not to be deluded by their victory, but reflect upon their qualities and the qualities of their laws. If they are in the right, it makes no difference whether they are victors or vanquished. Nevertheless, in most cases the one who is in the right is the victor; it is only accidentally that he is vanquished.

14   Then he stated that not anyone who wishes to legislate is a true legislator, but only the one whom God creates and equips for this purpose. This is true of every master in an art—like the navigator and others—who then deserves to be called a master both when practicing his art and when not practicing it. Just as the one who is known for his mastery of an art deserves to be called a master regardless of whether he is practicing it, the one who practices an art without being good or proficient in it does not deserve to be called a master. [9]

15   Then he explained that the legislator ought first to practice his own laws and only then command others to practice them. For if he does not practice what he commands others, and does not require of himself what he requires of others, his command and argument will not be received well and properly by the ones whom he commands— just as when the general is not a hero who is himself able to fight, his leadership will not take proper effect. He gave an example of this drawn from the drinking party. He said that when their leader and master, too, is drunk like the rest, he will not be able to conduct the party in the right way; rather, he ought to be sober, and extremely sharp-witted, knowledgeable, and vigilant so as to be able to conduct a drinking party. What he said is certainly true. For a legislator who is as ignorant as his people will not be able to legislate the law that benefits them.

16   Then he stated that the formation of character and training are useful in preserving the laws, and that the one who neglects himself or his subordinates ends up in great confusion.

17   Then he explained that when an individual becomes generally known for his ability as a good dialectician and discussant, and as a copious speaker, then whenever he turns to a thing in order to praise and describe it, it will be suspected that the thing itself is not as excellent as he describes, but that his description of it results from his ability as a discussant. This is a disease that often afflicts the men of science. Thus the one who listens to a discussion must use his intellect to reflect, soundly and exhaustively, upon the thing itself, and determine whether the stated descriptions exist in it or whether they are things that the discussant describes because of his capacity for discussion and refutation or because he loves that thing and thinks well of it. If he finds that the thing itself is noble and deserves these descriptions, let him drive from his mind the suspicion we have described. In itself, the law is noble and excellent; it is more excellent than anything said of it and in it.

18   Then he explained that there is no way of knowing the truth of the laws and their excellence, and the truth [*10*] of all things, except through reason and training in reasoning; and that men must train and exercise themselves in it. Although initially their aim may not be the understanding of the truth of the law, this can be of benefit to them later on. He gave an example of this drawn from the arts, for example, the child who sets up doors and houses for play, whereby he obtains certain states of mind and accomplishments in the art in question, which become useful to him when he plans to acquire the art seriously.

19   Then he turned to the lawgiver and stated that exercise from childhood in political matters and reflecting upon their rightness and wrongness benefit him when he becomes seriously engaged in politics. Because of his earlier exercise and training, he will be able to control himself and face what confronts him with perseverance.

20   Then he began to explain that there are in the soul of every man two contrary powers that attract it in opposite directions, and that man is also subject to sorrow and gladness, pleasure and pain, and the other contraries. One of these two powers is the power of discernment, and the other is the bestial. The law operates through the power of discernment, not through the bestial. He explained that the attraction exercised by the bestial power is strong and hard, while the attraction exercised by the power of discernment is softer and more gentle. The individual man ought to reflect on how his soul is faring in the presence of these attractions, and follow the one exercised by the power of discernment. So also the whole citizen body: if by themselves they are incapable of discernment, they must accept the truth from their law-

givers, from those who follow in the latter's footsteps, from those among themselves who speak the truth, and from those who are good and righteous.

21   Then he explained that it is just and extremely right that one should bear the toil and the discomfort commanded by the lawgiver because it leads to comfort and virtue—just as the pain experienced by the one who drinks distasteful drugs is commendable because, at the end, it leads to the comfort of health.

22   Then he explained that moral habits follow from, and resemble, one another, and that one ought to distinguish them from their contraries. For instance, modesty is commendable, but the excess of it becomes impotence and is blameworthy; having a good opinion of men is commendable and an expression of openheartedness, but if it is of one's enemies it becomes blameworthy; and [11] caution is commendable, but the excess of it becomes cowardice and inaction and thus blameworthy. He explained that it is blameworthy for an individual to use blameworthy means to reach his intended purpose—even though it may be extremely good and virtuous—and that it would be better if he could achieve his intended purpose through fair and desirable means.

23   Then he mentioned something useful, that is, that an intelligent man must draw near evil things and know them in order to be able to avoid them and be more on guard against them. He gave an example drawn from wine-drinking. He explained that the sober man ought to draw near to the drunkards and attend their parties in order to know the blemishes generated from drunkenness and in order to know how to avoid the blemishes and the blameworthy things that occur among them: that, for instance, after drinking a few cups, the one with a weak body may think that he is strong although he is nothing of the sort (because he thinks he is strong, he wants to shout and fight, but his strength fails him), and numerous other things that happen to wine-drinkers.

24   Then he explained that he who wants to acquire one of the virtues ought first to exert himself in driving away the vice that opposes it. For it is very rare that virtue is acquired without the prior departure of vice.

25   Then he explained that every natural disposition has an activity especially suitable to it. Hence the lawgiver must know this in order to match the duties he lays down with the suitable and appropriate natural dispositions so that his rules would not be dissipated. For when the thing is not placed properly, it will be dissipated and no trace of it will be left.

SECOND   DISCOURSE

1   He explained in this Discourse that there are in man certain natural things that are the causes of his moral habits and of his actions. Therefore the legislator ought to reach for these natural things and set them aright. For when these natural things are set right, so will the moral habits [12] and the actions. (I suspect that by "children" he means [in this connection] all beginners, whether in age, knowledge, or religion.) He explained that these natural things are based upon, and originate from, pleasure and pain; it is through these two that the virtues and the vices—and, at the end, practical judgment and the sciences—are acquired. The ordering of these two [that is, pleasure and pain] is called education and training. Had the lawgiver commanded men to avoid the pleasures altogether, his law would not have been rightly established and men would not have followed it, because of their natural inclination to the pleasures. Instead, he appointed for them certain festivals and times during which they could pursue the pleasures; for this reason these pleasures become divine. This is also the case with the various kinds of music that they [the lawgivers] have permitted, knowing that men are naturally inclined toward them and in order that the pleasure in them becomes divine. He gave such examples of this as were well-known among them, such as dancing and flute-playing.

He explained that everything is made up of that which is noble and that which is base. The noble kind of music is that which is suitable to noble and useful moral habits—for instance, generosity and courage—and the base kind is that which promotes the contrary moral habits. He gave examples of this drawn from the tunes and the figures that had existed in the temples of Egypt and among the inhabitants of that country, and had been instrumental in sustaining the traditions (*sunan*); he explained that they were divine.

He explained that whoever is younger in age is more prone to take delight in those pleasures, while the older he is the more calm and firm he will be. The skilled lawgiver is the one who lays down the law that charms everyone toward goodness and happiness. Again, every group, every generation, and the inhabitants of every region, have their own natural dispositions, which differ from those of the others. The skilled [lawgiver] is the one who introduces the kind of music and other rules of law (*sunan*) that control these natural dispositions and compel them to accept the law, regardless of the difference and the multiplicity in the natural dispositions, and the variety of their moral habits; and not the one who introduces certain rules that control one group and not another, for the latter [13] can be accomplished by the

majority of the members of each group, who practice these rules because they are naturally disposed to them. Moreover, the one who lays
down a law that commands the obedience of a man of science and
experience is more excellent than the one who lays down a law that
commands the obedience of a group of men who are men neither of
science nor of experience: the former is like the singer who excites
an old, experienced, rugged, and tenacious man.

The lawgiver and those who undertake to apply the law and assume
the responsibilities it entails, ought to control the many and different
human affairs in every respect and in all their details so that nothing
of these human affairs would escape them. They should not neglect
any of these affairs; for once [the citizens] become used to neglect on
their part, they slip away from their hands whenever they can. For
when a thing is neglected once, twice, or more, it is lost sight of and
its edges are blunted—just as when it is employed once or twice, it
becomes an inescapable habit: it is fixed or obliterated to the extent that
it is, respectively, used or neglected. The young in age and children
have no knowledge of this; they should be made to accept it and to
act accordingly. For if they get used to enjoying themselves, to following
their appetites, and to taking pleasure in what is contrary to the law,
it is then very hard to set them aright by the law. Rather, they must
experience pleasure to the extent determined by the law; both men
and children should be required to be in intimate association with the law
and to follow it in practice.

The lawgiver ought to address every group of men with what is
closer to their comprehensions and intellects, and to set them aright with
what they are capable of doing. For sometimes it is difficult for men
to comprehend a thing, or they are incapable of doing it; its difficulty
causes them to reject it and prompts them to neglect and discard it.
He gave as an example of this the skilled and gentle physician who offers
the sick man the drugs that are useful to him in his familiar and ap-
petizing food.

2   Then he intended to explain that the good is relative and not
absolute. He supported the soundness of his statement by the testimony
of an ancient poem that mentions the things—for instance, health, beauty,
and wealth—that a certain group considers good, while others do not.
He explained that all these things are good [*14*] for good men; for the
evil and unjust men, however, they are not good and do not lead
them to happiness. Indeed, even life is evil for evil men, just as it is
good for good men. Therefore it is correct to say that the good is
relative. This is a notion to which the lawgiver, and the poets too,
must pay great attention, and also those who write down their sayings,
so that they will not be misunderstood.

3   Then he explained that the assertion that all good things are
immediately pleasant, that everything that is noble and good is pleasant

and good, and that the contrary assertion is also true, is not demonstrable. For many pleasant things—that is, everything in which men of weak intellects take pleasure—are not good. Upon my life, the good can be pleasant to the one who knows its outcome, but not to the one who has not ascertained that outcome. The same applies to the assertion concerning the just ways of life and that they are opposed to [the enjoyment of] the good things.

4 Then he explained that not all men need follow the same rule of law, but that there are rules of law for each group that the others need not follow. He gave an example of this drawn from the dancing performed by different age groups, and how the conditions that call for dancing and the use made of it differ among different men, whether they differ in age or in some other states that adhere to them at particular times. For when a thing is not used in its proper place, it will not have the glitter, the fair look, the approval, and the praise, that pertain to it when it is used in its proper place. He gave many examples of this: it is not appropriate for an old man to play the flute or to dance, and if he does these or similar things in a public gathering, the public will not cheer or approve of it. Similarly, it is extremely disapproved and base for one to play the flute or dance on an occasion that does not call for such things. This is the case with everything that is done by one for whom it is not proper to do it, or in a place or time [*15*] in which it is unseemly for such things to be done by the like of him, or when the occasion does not call for them—all this is repulsive, improper, and disapproved; it prompts the onlookers to reject it, and to consider it base and repulsive, especially if they happen to be inexperienced.

5 Then he explained that pleasures vary with respect to different men, their conditions, natural dispositions, and moral habits. To explain this, he gave the examples of the courageous men and the practitioners of the arts. For what is pleasant to the practitioner of one art is different from what is pleasant to the practitioner of another art. The case is the same with what is right, what is noble, and what is just.

6 Then he spoke at length about this subject in order to explain that all these things are noble and base relative to other things, and not noble and base in themselves. He said that if one asks the practitioners of the arts about this notion, they would undoubtedly confirm it.

7 Then he explained that the one who does not know *what* the thing is, its essence, or *that* it is, cannot order its parts, what suits it, its concomitants, and the things that adhere to it, simply by going a-chasing after it; and if someone should claim that he can do so, he is making a false claim. Also, the one who knows *what* the thing is, may not have noticed how fair or fine, or bad and base it is. The one who possesses a perfect knowledge of a thing is he who knows *what* the thing is, and also how fair and how fine, or bad and base it is. This

is true of laws and of all the arts and the sciences. Therefore the one who judges their fineness, or deficiency and badness, ought to have learned about them the three things mentioned above and mastered them well; only then should he judge them, so that his judgment be correct and well-founded. The best judge is the one who constructs and institutes a thing; for the one who constructs and institutes it, because he has the three kinds of knowledge mentioned above, is able to institute what is appropriate for each condition. As for the one who lacks these three kinds of knowledge about a thing, and that power too, how could he be able to institute and construct it? Nor is this peculiar to the laws alone; it is true of every science and every art. He gave examples of this drawn from poems and their meters and tunes, and from music and those who compose it and play its various modes. [16]

8   Then he spoke at length, mentioning dancing and flute-playing. His entire purpose with these examples is to explain that each rule of Law and of tradition ought to be applied in its proper place, and to those who are able to perform it; and that the corruption resulting from misplacing and misusing a thing is worse and uglier than what results from abandoning it altogether. He mentioned the praise that was bestowed upon those who played certain tunes, which were well-known among them, in their proper places and to a suitable audience, and the blame bestowed upon the ones who altered these tunes, tampered with them, and played them at improper times, with the result that they stirred up many afflictions and evils. The art of singing occupied a marvelous position among the Greeks, and their legislators paid full attention to it. And it is truly very useful, especially because its working penetrates the soul; and since the law concerns itself with the soul, he spoke at length about this subject. For such training as the body needs is but for the sake of the soul; when the body is made fit, it leads to the fitness of the soul.

9   Then he explained another notion that is suitable for what he was describing, that is, that the same thing may be used in one law and abandoned in another law. This is neither infamous nor base, for the law is given with a view to the requirements of an existing condition so as to lead men to the ultimate good and to the obedience of the gods. He gave an example of this drawn from wine and the drinking of it, and how it was practiced by one group among the ancient Greeks, while it was shunned by another group even in case of necessity. The condition that necessarily demands the drinking of wine is that in which one needs to be deprived of his intellect and knowledge—for instance, in childbirth, cauterization, and the painful doctoring of the body; this is also the case when wine is used as a remedy by means of which to obtain the kind of health that nothing else could bring about.

5.

Avicenna

ON THE DIVISIONS

OF THE RATIONAL SCIENCES

Translated by Muhsin Mahdi

Avicenna (Abū 'Alī al-Ḥusayn Ibn Sīnā, 980–1037) was born in Afshana, near Bukhara, where his father was governor. Bukhara (the capital of the Samanid kingdom, one of the many principalities into which Persia, nominally still a province of the caliph in Baghdad, was divided) was at the time a respectable center of learning. Here Avicenna had his early training, distinguished himself as a capable physician, was enrolled in the service of the sultan Nūḥ Ibn Manṣūr, and was able to make use of the excellent court library. In 999 the Samanid kingdom broke up and Avicenna began to wander among the warring Persian principalities, entering the service of various princes. Between 1015 and 1022 he acted as the physician and, twice, as the vizier of the Buyid prince Shams al-Dawlah in Hamadhan. He refused to take office under his son Tāj al-Mulk and made secret overtures to join the service of the Kakuyid prince 'Alā' al-Dawlah (in Isfahan), who was preparing to overthrow the Buyids. After a short period in hiding and four months in prison, he finally succeeded in escaping—disguised in the habit of Sufis—from Hamadhan to Isfahan, where he pursued his scientific work as the intimate friend and learned courtier of the prince until his death. In Eastern Islam, Avicenna replaced Alfarabi as the leading philosopher, and Algazel's attacks on him do not seem to have diminished his authority among the students of philosophy, the sciences, and mysticism. In Western Islam, on the other hand, he was criticized (by Averroes and others) as having departed from Aristotle and as having compromised with dialectical theology on a number of important issues. There, Alfarabi continued to be regarded as the great master, with Avicenna occupying an important but secondary position. This was true also of his place among Judaeo-Arabic authors, as is evident from Maimonides' remarks. Among the Latins, the differences between Avicenna and Averroes had significant repercussions beginning with the twelfth century.

On the Divisions of the Rational Sciences (or the *Divisions of Wisdom*) is a short epistle composed by Avicenna in answer to someone who asked him to present a summary account of the rational sciences, an account that is short, complete, clear, true, easy to understand, well arranged, and well ordered. Avicenna begins with a definition of the essence of wisdom, followed by the account of the primary divisions of science (or wisdom); then he presents the divisions of theoretical science, followed by the divisions of practical science. The remaining parts deal with the principal parts and branches of natural science, mathematics, metaphysics, and logic. The "branches" of metaphysics or divine science deal again with revelation and prophecy (see below,

Selection 6). Unlike Alfarabi's classification in the *Enumeration of the Sciences* (above, Selection 1), Avicenna here follows the more traditional Aristotelian classification of the sciences into theoretical and practical, and subdivides the latter into ethics, economics, and politics. Nevertheless, it is noteworthy that he considers the study of prophecy and the divine Law as integral parts of political science.

This work, like Alfarabi's *Enumeration of the Sciences*, was popular among students of philosophy in Islam, and among historians of science and authors of scientific encyclopedias. It was translated into Hebrew and Latin. The following translation is based on a composite text resulting from the collation of a number of manuscripts of the original Arabic text, preserved in the libraries of Constantinople. The two sections correspond to *Fī aqsām al-ʿulūm al-ʿqliyyah* in *Tisʿ rasāʾil* (Cairo, 1908), pp. 105 and 107-108, respectively.

ON   THE   PRIMARY   DIVISIONS   OF   SCIENCE

SCIENCE IS DIVIDED into a theoretical, abstract part and a practical part. The theoretical part is the one whose end is to acquire certainty about the state of the beings whose existence does not depend on human action. Here the aim is only to acquire an opinion. Examples of it are the science of [God's] unity and astronomy. The practical part is the one whose aim is not merely to acquire certainty about the beings; its aim can be the acquisition of a sound opinion about a matter that exists through man's endeavor, with a view to acquiring by it what is good. Thus the aim here is not merely to acquire an opinion, but rather to acquire an opinion for the sake of action. Therefore, the end of the theoretical part is truth, and the end of the practical is the good.

*   *   *

ON   THE   DIVISIONS   OF   PRACTICAL   SCIENCE

Since human governance either pertains to a single individual or does not pertain to a single individual, since the one that does not pertain to a single individual takes place through partnership, and since partnership is formed within the context of a household association or of a political association, there are three practical sciences.

One of these sciences pertains to the first division. Through this science one knows how man ought to be in his moral habits and in his actions so as to lead a happy life here and in the hereafter. This part is contained in Aristotle's book on ethics [that is, the *Nicomachean Ethics*].

The second science pertains to the second division. Through this science one knows how man ought to conduct the governance of his household—which is common to him, his wife, his children, his servants, and his slaves—so as to lead a well-ordered life that enables him to gain happiness. It is contained in Bryson's *On the Governance of the Household*[1] and in books by many others.

The third science pertains to the third division. Through this science one knows the kinds of political regimes, rulerships, and associations, both virtuous and bad; and it makes known the way of preserving each, the reason for its disintegration [*108*] and the manner of its transformation. Of this science, the treatment of kingship is contained in the book by Plato and that by Aristotle on the regime, and the treatment of prophecy and the Law is contained in their two books on the laws.[2] By the nomoi, the philosophers do not mean what the vulgar believe, which is that the nomos is nothing but a device and deceit. Rather, according to them, the nomos is the law and the norm that is established and made permanent through the coming-down of revelation. The Arabs, too, call the angel that brings down the revelation, a nomos (*nāmūs*). Through this part of practical wisdom one knows the necessity of prophecy and the human species' need of the Law for its existence, preservation, and future life. One knows through it the wisdom in the universal penalties that are common to all Laws and in the penalties pertaining to particular Laws, having to do with particular peoples and particular times. And one knows through it the difference between divine prophecy and false pretensions to it.

NOTES

1. On Bryson's *Economist*, see Martin Plessner, *Der Oikonomikos des neupythagoreers 'Bryson' und sein Einfluss auf die islamische Wissenschaft* (Heidelberg, 1928).

2. While in the case of Plato the references are unmistakably to the *Republic* and the *Laws*, the references to Aristotle are less certain. Avicenna may be referring to the two books given in the bibliographies of Aristotle's writings, which bear the same titles as the two works by Plato.

6.

Avicenna

HEALING: METAPHYSICS X

Translated by Michael E. Marmura

The *Healing* (or "Sufficiency," as it was called by some Latin writers) is perhaps Avicenna's most important, comprehensive, and detailed work. It is composed of four parts: *Logic, Physics, Mathematics,* and *Metaphysics* or *Divine Science.* In *Physics* VI ("Psychology") Avicenna gives an account of practical intellect, of the prophetic faculties, and of certain related political questions, within the framework provided by natural science. The specific treatment of political science, however, is reserved for the end of the *Metaphysics,* with the implication that the understanding of political science has to be based on the conclusions arrived at in metaphysics. *Metaphysics* X is composed of five chapters. The first chapter gives a summary of the preceding nine books and serves as a transition to the subject of the tenth book. It is entitled: "On Beginning and Return (a Concise Statement); on Inspirations, Dream-visions, Prayers that are Answered, and Heavenly Punishments; on the States of Prophecy and the Status of Astrology."

The *Metaphysics* (*Philosophia Prima*) was translated into Latin about the middle of the twelfth century and was printed a number of times in Venice (first in 1495). The first critical edition of the Arabic original was made by G. C. Anawati and others: *al-Shifā': al-Ilāhiyyāt* (2 vols.; Cairo, 1960). The following translation is based on this edition, Vol. II, pp. 441-55.

98

CHAPTER 2

PROOF OF PROPHECY.

THE MANNER OF THE PROPHET'S

CALL TO GOD, THE EXALTED.

THE "RETURN" TO GOD.

WE NOW SAY: it is known that man differs from the other animals in that he cannot lead a proper life when isolated as a single individual, managing his affairs with no associates to help him satisfy his basic wants. One man needs to be complemented by another of his species, the other, in turn, by him and one like him. Thus, for example, one man would provide another with vegetables while the other would bake for him; one man would sew for another while the other would provide him with needles. Associated in this way, they become self-sufficient. For this reason men have found it necessary to establish cities and form associations. Whoever, in the endeavor to establish his city, does not see to the requirements necessary for setting up a city and, with his companions, remains confined to forming a mere association, would be engaged in devising means [to govern] a species most dissimilar to men and lacking the perfection of men. Nevertheless, even the ones like him cannot escape associating with the citizens of a city, and imitating them.

If this is obvious, then man's existence and survival require partnership. Partnership is only achieved through reciprocal transactions, as well as through the various trades practiced by man. Reciprocal transactions demand law (*sunnah*) and justice, and law and justice demand a lawgiver and a dispenser of justice. This lawgiver must be in a position that enables him to address men and make them adhere to the law. He must, then, be a human being. Men must not be left to their private opinions concerning the law so that they disagree, each considering as just what others owe them, unjust what they owe others.

Thus, with respect to the survival and actual existence of the human species, the need for this human being is far greater than the need for such benefits as the growing of the hair on the eyebrow, the shaping of the arches in the feet, and many others that are not necessary [*442*] for survival but at best are merely useful for it. Now the existence of the righteous man to legislate and to dispense justice is a possibility, as we have previously remarked.[1] It becomes impossible, therefore, that divine providence should ordain the existence of those former benefits and not the latter, which are their bases. Nor is it possible that the First Principle and the angels after Him should know the former and not the latter. Nor yet is it possible that that which He knows to be in itself within the realm of possibility but whose realization is necessary for introducing the good order, should not exist. And how can it not exist, when that which depends and is constructed on its existence, exists? A prophet, therefore, must exist and he must be a human. He must also possess characteristics not present in others so that men could recognize in him something they do not have and which differentiates him from them. Therefore he will perform the miracles about which we have spoken.[1]

When this man's existence comes about, he must lay down laws about men's affairs by the permission of God, the Exalted, by His command, inspiration, and the *descent of His Holy Spirit* on him [cf. xvi, 102]. The first principle governing his legislation is to let men know that they have a Maker, One and Omnipotent; that *He knows the hidden and the manifest* [cf. xvi, 19]; that obedience is due Him since *command* must belong to *Him who creates* [cf. vii, 54]; that He has prepared for those who obey Him an afterlife of bliss, but for those who disobey Him an afterlife of misery. This will induce the multitude to obey the decrees put in the prophet's mouth by the God and the angels.

But he ought not to involve them with doctrines pertaining to the knowledge of God, the Exalted, beyond the fact that He is one, the truth, and has none like Himself. To go beyond this and demand that they believe in His existence as being not referred to in place, as being not subject to verbal classifications, as being neither inside nor outside the world, or anything of this kind, is to ask too much. This will simply confuse the religion (*dīn*) they have and involve them in something from which deliverance is only possible for the one who receives guidance and is fortunate, whose existence is most rare. For it is only with great strain that they can comprehend the true states of such matters; it is only the very few among them that can understand the truth of divine "unicity" and divine "remoteness." The rest would inevitably come to deny the truth of such an existence, fall into dissensions, and indulge in disputations and analogical arguments that stand in the way of their political duties. This might even lead them [*443*] to adopt views contrary to the city's welfare, opposed to the imperatives of truth. Their complaints and doubts will multiply, making it difficult for a man to control them. For divine wisdom is not easily acquired by everyone.

Nor is it proper for any man to reveal that he possesses knowledge he is hiding from the vulgar. Indeed, he must never permit any reference to this. Rather, he should let them know of God's majesty and greatness through symbols and similitudes derived from things that for them are majestic and great, adding this much—that He has neither equal, nor companion, nor likeness. Similarly, he must instill in them the belief in the resurrection in a manner they can conceive and in which their souls find rest. He must tell them about eternal bliss and misery in parables they can comprehend and conceive. Of the true nature of the afterlife he should only indicate something in general: that it is something that "no eye has seen and no ear heard,"[2] and that there are pleasures that are great possessions, and miseries that are perpetual torture.

Know that God, exalted be He, knows that the good lies in such a state of affairs. It follows, then, that that which God knows to be the good, must exist, as you have known [from the preceding discussion]. But there is no harm if the legislator's words contain symbols and signs that might stimulate the naturally apt to pursue philosophic investigation.

CHAPTER 3

ACTS OF WORSHIP: THEIR BENEFITS IN THIS WORLD AND THE NEXT.

Moreover, this individual who is a prophet is not one whose like recurs in every period. For the matter that is receptive of a perfection like his occurs in few bodily compositions. It follows necessarily, then, that the prophet (may God's prayers and peace be upon him) must plan with great care to ensure the preservation of the legislation he enacts concerning man's welfare. [444] Without doubt, the fundamental principle here is that men must continue in their knowledge of God and the resurrection and that the cause for forgetting these things with the passage of the generation succeeding [the mission of] the prophet (may God's prayers and peace be on him) must be absolutely eliminated. Hence there must be certain acts and works incumbent on people that the legislator must prescribe to be repeated at frequent specified intervals.[3] In this way memory of the act is renewed and reappears before it can die.

These acts must be combined with what brings God and the afterlife necessarily to mind; otherwise they are useless. Remembering is achieved through words that are uttered or resolutions made in the imagination and by telling men that these acts bring them closer to God and are richly rewarded. And these acts must in reality be of such a nature. An example of these are the acts of worship imposed on people. In general, these should be reminders. Now reminders consist of either motions or the absence of motions that lead to other motions. An example of motion is prayer; of the absence of motion, fasting. For although the latter is a negative notion, it so greatly moves one's nature that he who fasts is reminded that what he is engaged in is not a jest. He will thus recall the intention of his fasting, which is to draw him close to God.

These conditions must, if possible, be mixed with others useful for strengthening and spreading the law. Adding these will also be beneficial to men's worldly interests, as in the case of war (*jihād*) and the pilgrimage (*hajj*). Certain areas of land must be designated as best suited for worship and as belonging solely to God, the Exalted. Certain acts, which people must perform, must be specified as belonging exclusively to God—as, for example, sacrificial offerings—for these help greatly in this connection. Should the place that is of such a benefit contain the legislator's home and abode, this will then also be a reminder of him. Remembrance of him in relation to the above benefits is only next in importance to the remembrance of God and the angels. Now, the one abode cannot be within proximate reach of the entire community (*ummah*). It therefore becomes fitting [445] to prescribe a migration and a journey to it.

The noblest of these acts of worship, from one point of view, should be the one in which the worshiper considers himself to be addressing God, beseeching Him, drawing close to Him, and standing in His presence. This is prayer. The legislator should therefore prescribe for the worshiper in preparation for prayer those postures men traditionally adopt when they present themselves to human kings, such as purification and cleanliness (indeed, he must prescribe fully in these two things). He should also prescribe for the worshipers the behavior traditionally adopted in the presence of kings: reverence, calm, modesty, the lowering of the eyes, the contracting of the hands and feet, the avoidance of turning around, composure. Likewise, he must prescribe for each time of prayer praiseworthy manners and customs. These acts will benefit the vulgar inasmuch as they will instill in them remembrance of God and the resurrection. In this way their adherence to the statutes and laws will continue. For without such reminders they will forget all of this with the passing of a generation or two. It will also be of great benefit for them in the afterlife inasmuch as their souls will be purified in the manner you have known [in our discourse].[4] As for the elect, the greatest benefit they derive from these things pertains to the afterlife.

We have established[4] the true nature of the afterlife and have proved that

true happiness in the hereafter is achieved through the soul's detaching itself by piety from the acquisitions of bodily dispositions opposed to the
means for happiness. This purification is realized through moral states and
habits of character acquired by acts that turn the soul away from the body
and the senses and perpetuate its memory of its true substance. For if the
soul continues to turn unto itself, it will not be affected by the bodily
states. What will remind and help the soul in this respect are certain arduous acts that lie outside natural habit—indeed they are more on the side of
exertion. These tire the body and curb the [natural] animal desire for rest,
for laziness, for the rejection of toil, for the quieting of the hot humor,
and for avoiding all exercise except that which is conducive [*446*] to
bestial pleasure. In the performance of these acts the soul must be required
to recall God, the angels, and the world of happiness, whether it desires
to do so or not. In this way the soul is instilled with the propensity to be
repelled from the body and its influences and with the positive disposition
to control it. Thus it will not be affected by the body. Hence when the
soul encounters bodily acts, these will not produce in it the propensities
and positive disposition that they would normally produce when the soul
submits to them in everything. For this reason, the one who speaks truth
has said: *Surely the good deeds drive away the bad deeds* [xi, 114]. If this
act persists in man, then he will acquire the positive disposition of turning
in the direction of truth and away from error. He thus becomes well
prepared to be delivered unto [true] happiness after bodily separation.

If these acts were performed by someone who did not believe them to
be divine obligations and who, nonetheless, had to remember God in every
act, rejecting everything else, this one would be worthy of some measure
of this virtue. How much more worthy will be the one who performs
these acts knowing that the prophet comes from God and is sent by God,
that his being sent is necessitated by divine wisdom, that all the prophet's
legislation is an obligation demanded of him by God, that all he legislates
comes from God? For the prophet was obligated by God to impose these
acts of worshiping Him. These acts benefit the worshipers in that they
perpetuate in the latter adherence to the laws and religion (*shari'ah*) that
insure their existence and in that, by virtue of the goodness they inspire,
they bring the worshipers closer to God in the hereafter.

Moreover, this is the man who is charged with administering the affairs
of men, for insuring their livelihood in this world and their well-being in
the world to come. He is a man distinguished from the rest of mankind
by his godliness. [*447*]

CHAPTER 4

ESTABLISHMENT OF THE CITY, THE

HOUSEHOLD (THAT IS, MARRIAGE),

AND THE GENERAL LAWS

PERTAINING TO THESE MATTERS.

The legislator's first objective in laying down the laws and organizing the city must be to divide it into three groups: administrators, artisans, and guardians. He must place at the head of each group a leader, under whom he will place other leaders, under these yet others, and so forth until he arrives at the common run of men. Thus none in the city will remain without a proper function and a specific place: each will have his use in the city. Idleness and unemployment must be prohibited. The legislator must leave the way open to no one for acquiring from another that share of a livelihood necessary for man while exempting himself from any effort in return. Such people he must vigorously restrain. If they fail to refrain from such a practice, he must then exile them from the land. But should the cause here be some physical malady or defect, the legislator must set aside a special place for such cases, under someone's charge.

There must exist in the city a common fund, part of it consisting of duties imposed on acquired and natural profits such as fruit and agricultural produce, part of it imposed as punishment, while another part should consist of property taken from those who resist the law, that is, of war-booty. Thus the fund will serve to meet the exigencies of the common good, to meet the needs of the guardians who do not work in any craft, and those prevented from earning their livelihood by maladies and chronic diseases. Some people have held the opinion that the diseased whose recovery is not to be expected should be killed. But this is base; for their sustenance will not hurt the city. If such people have relatives enjoying a superfluity of means, then the legislator must impose on these relatives the responsibility for their people. [*448*]

All fines must not be imposed on the criminal alone. Some of these must be imposed on the criminal's protectors and relatives who fail to reprimand and watch over him. But the fines legislated in the latter case should be mitigated by allowing delay in payment. The same should apply to crimes committed inadvertently. These must not be ignored even though they do occur by mistake.

Just as idleness must be prohibited, so should professions like gambling, whereby properties and utilities are transferred without any benefit rendered in exchange. For the gambler takes without rendering any service at all. Rather, what one takes must always be a compensation given in return for work, a compensation that is either substance, utility, good remembrance, or any other thing considered a human good. Similarly, professions that lead to the opposite of welfare and usefulness, such as the learning of theft, brigandage, leadership of criminal bands, and the like, must be prohibited. Professions that allow people to dispense with learning those crafts pertaining to the association—professions such as usury—must be prohibited. For usury is the seeking of excess profit without practicing a craft to achieve it, even though it does render a service in return. Also those acts—which, if once permitted, would be detrimental to the city's growth—like fornication and sodomy, which dispense with the greatest pillar on which the city stands, that is, marriage, must be prohibited.

The first of the legislator's acts must pertain to marriage resulting in issue. He must call and urge people to it. For by marriage is achieved the continuity of the species, the permanence of which is proof of the existence of God, the Exalted. He must arrange it in such a way that matrimony takes place as a manifest affair, so that there will be no uncertainties concerning progeny causing defects in the proper transfer of inheritances, which [449] are a source of wealth. For wealth is indispensable for a livelihood. Now wealth divides into source and derivatives. Sources consist of wealth that is inherited, found, or granted. Of these three sources, the best is inherited wealth; for it does not come by way of luck or chance but is of an order akin to the natural. Through this also—I mean the concealment of marriage—defects in other respects occur: for example, in the necessity that one party should undertake expenditure over the other, in rendering mutual assistance, and in other matters that will not escape the wise person after reflection.

The legislator must take firm measures to assure the permanence of the union so that not every quarrel should result in a separation that disrupts the bond between children and parents and renews the need of marriage for everyone. In this there are many sorts of harm. Also, because what is most conducive to the general good is love. Love is only achieved through friendship; friendship through habit; habit is produced only through long association. This assurance, with respect to the woman, consists in not placing in her hands the right to make the separation. For in reality she is not very rational and is quick to follow passion and anger. But a way for separation must be left open and not all doors closed. To prevent separation under all circumstances results in all kinds of harmful consequences. Of these is the fact that some natures cannot adapt themselves to others: the more they are brought together, the greater the resulting evil, aversion, and unpleasantness. Or again, someone might get an unequal partner, or one who is of bad character, or repellent in nature. This will induce the other partner to desire someone else—for desire is natural—and this in turn leads to many harmful consequences. It also might so happen that the married couple do not cooperate for procreation and if exchanged for other partners they would. Hence some means for separation is necessary. But the law must be strict about it. [450]

The means for separation must not be placed in the hands of the less rational of the two, the one more prone to disagreement, confusion, and change. Instead, this must be relegated to the judges who will affect the separation when they ascertain the woman's mistreatment by the other partner. In the case of the man, an indemnity must be imposed on him so that he will approach separation only after ascertainment and after he finds it to be the right thing for him in every way.

The legislator must, nevertheless, leave the way open for reconciliation, without, however, emphasizing it lest this encourage thoughtless action. On the contrary, he must make reconciliation more difficult than separation. How excellent was that which [Muhammad] the greatest of legislators commanded [cf. ii, 229-30]—that the man, after thrice pronouncing the formula for divorce, is not allowed to remarry the woman until he brings himself to drink a cup unsurpassed in bitterness, which is, to first let another man marry her by a true marriage and have real relations with her. If such a prospect awaits a man, he will not approach separation recklessly, unless he has already determined that the separation is to be permanent, or unless he is of a defective character and takes perverted pleasure in scandal. But the likes of these fall outside the pale of men who deserve the seeking of their welfare.

Since woman by right must be protected inasmuch as she can share her sexual desire with many, is much inclined to draw attention to herself, and in addition to that is easily deceived and is less inclined to obey reason; and since sexual relations on her part with many men cause great disdain and shame, which are well-known harms, whereas on the part of the man they only arouse jealousy, which should be ignored as it is nothing but obedience to the devil; it is more important to legislate that the woman should be veiled and secluded from men. Thus, unlike the man, she should not be a bread-earner. It must be legislated that her needs be satisfied by the man upon whom must be imposed her sustenance. For this the man must be compensated. He must own her, but not she him. [451] Thus she cannot be married to another at the same time. But in the case of man this avenue is not closed to him though he is forbidden from taking a number of wives whom he cannot support. Hence the compensation consists in the ownership of the woman's "genitalia." By this ownership I do not mean sexual intercourse. For both partake of its pleasure and the woman's share is even greater, as is her delight and pleasure in children. But by this I mean that no other man can make use of them.

It must be legislated with respect to the child that both parents must undertake his proper upbringing—the woman in her special area, the man by provision. Likewise it must be prescribed that the child must serve, obey, respect, and honor his parents. For they are the cause of his existence and in addition have borne his support, something we need not enlarge upon as it is evident.

CHAPTER 5

CONCERNING THE CALIPH AND THE
IMAM: THE NECESSITY OF OBEYING
THEM. REMARKS ON POLITICS,
TRANSACTIONS, AND MORALS.

Next, the legislator must impose as a duty obedience to whosoever succeeds him. He must also prescribe that designation of the successor can only be made by himself or by the consensus of the elders.[5] The latter should verify openly to the public that the man of their choice can hold sole political authority, that he is of independent judgment, that he is endowed with the noble qualities of courage, temperance, and good governance, and that he knows the law to a degree unsurpassed by anyone else. Such a verification must be openly proclaimed and must find unanimous agreement by the entire public. The legislator must lay down in the law that should they disagree and quarrel, succumbing to passion and whim, or should they agree to designate someone [452] other than the virtuous and deserving individual, then they would have committed an act of unbelief. Designation of the caliph through appointment by testament is best: it will not lead to partisanship, quarrels, and dissensions.

The legislator must then decree in his law that if someone secedes and lays claim to the caliphate by virtue of power or wealth, then it becomes the duty of every citizen to fight and kill him. If the citizens are capable of so doing but refrain from doing so, then they disobey God and commit an act of unbelief. The blood of anyone who can fight but refrains becomes free for the spilling after this fact is established in the assembly of all. The legislator must lay down in the law that, next to belief in the prophet, nothing brings one closer to God than the killing of such a usurper.

If the seceder, however, verifies that the one holding the caliphate is not fit for it, that he is afflicted with an imperfection, and that this imperfection is not found in the seceder, then it is best that the citizens accept the latter. The determining factor here is superiority of practical judgment and excellence in political management. The one whose attainment in the rest of the virtues [including knowledge] is moderate—although he must not be ignorant of them nor act contrary to them—but excels in these two is more fit than the one who excels in the other virtues but is not foremost in these two. Thus the one who has more knowledge must join and support the one who has better practical judgment. The latter, in turn, must accept the former's support and seek his advice, as was done by 'Umar[6] and 'Alī.[7]

He must then prescribe certain acts of worship that can be performed only in the caliph's presence, in order to extol his importance and make them serve his glorification. These are the congregational affairs, such as festivals. He must prescribe such public gatherings; for these entail the call for solidarity, the use of the instruments of courage, and competition. It is by competition that virtues are achieved. Through congregations, supplications are answered and blessings are received in the manner discussed in our statements.

Likewise, there must be certain transactions in which the imam participates. These are the transactions that lead to the building of the city's foundation, such as marriage and communal activities. He must also prescribe, in the transactions involving exchange, laws that prevent treachery and injustices. He must forbid unsound transactions where the objects of exchange change before being actually received or paid, as with money-changing, [453] postponement in the payment of debt, and the like.

He must also legislate that people must help and protect others, their properties, and lives, without this, however, entailing that the contributor should penalize himself as a result of his contribution.

As for enemies and those who oppose his law, the legislator must decree waging war against them and destroying them, after calling on them to accept the truth. Their property and women must be declared free for the spoil. For when such property and women are not administered according to the constitution of the virtuous city, they will not bring about the good for which property and women are sought. Rather, these would contribute to corruption and evil. Since some men have to serve others, such people must be forced to serve the people of the just city. The same applies to people not very capable of acquiring virtue. For these are slaves by nature as, for example, the Turks and the Zinjis and in general all those who do not grow up in noble [that is, moderate] climes where the conditions for the most part are such that nations of good temperament, innate intelligence, and sound minds thrive. If a city other than his has praiseworthy laws, the legislator must not interfere with it unless the times are such that they require the declaration that no law is valid save the revealed law. For when nations and cities go astray and laws are prescribed for them, adherence to the law must be assured. If the adherence to the law becomes incumbent, it might very well be the case that to ensure this adherence requires the acceptance of the law by the whole world. If the people of that [other] city, which has a good way of life, find that this [new] law, too, is good and praiseworthy and that the adoption of the new law means restoring the conditions of corrupted cities to virtue, and yet proceed to proclaim that this law ought not to be accepted and reject as false the legislator's claim that this law has come to all cities, then a great weakness will afflict the law. Those opposing it could then use as argument for their rejecting it that the people of that [other] city have rejected it. In this case these latter must also be punished and war (*jihād*) waged on them; but this war must not be pursued with the same severity as against the people utterly in error. Or else an indemnity must be imposed on them in lieu of their preference. In any case, it must be enunciated as a truth that they are negators [of the true law]. For how are they not negators, when they refuse to accept the divine Law, which God, the Exalted, has sent down? Should they perish, they would have met what they deserve. For their death, though it means the end of some, results in a permanent good, particularly when the new law is more complete and better. [454] It should also be legislated with regard to these, that if clemency on condition that they pay ransom and tax is desired, this can be done. In general, they must not be placed in the same category as the other nonbelievers.

The legislator must also impose punishments, penalties, and prohibitions to prevent disobedience to the divine Law. For not everyone is restrained from violating the law because of what he fears of the afterlife. Most of these [penalties and so forth] must pertain to acts contrary to law that are conducive to the corruption of the city's order; for example, adultery, theft, complicity with the enemies of the city, and the like. As for the acts that harm the individual himself, the law should contain helpful advice and warning, and not go beyond this to the prescription of obligatory duties. The law concerning acts of worship, marriage, and prohibitions should be moderate, neither severe nor lenient. The legislator must relegate many questions, particularly those pertaining to transactions, to the exercise of the individual judgment (*ijtihād*) of the jurists. For different times and circumstances call for decisions that cannot be predetermined. As for the further control of the city involving knowledge of the organization of guardians, income and expenditure, manufacture of armaments, legal rights, border fortifications, and the like, it must be placed in the hands of the ruler in his capacity as caliph. The legislator must not impose specific prescriptions concerning these. Such an imposition would be defective since conditions change with time. Moreover, it is impossible to make universal judgments that cover every contingency in these matters. He must leave this to the body of counsellors.

It is necessary that the legislator should also prescribe laws regarding morals and customs that advocate justice, which is the mean. The mean in morals and customs is sought for two things. The one, involving the breaking of the dominance of the passions,[8] is for the soul's purification and for enabling it to acquire the power of self-mastery so that it can liberate itself from the body untarnished. [455] The other, involving the use of these passions, is for worldly interests. As for the use of pleasures, these serve to conserve the body and procreation. As for courage, it is for the city's survival. The vices of excess are to be avoided for the harm they inflict in human interests, while the vices of deficiency are to be avoided for the harm they cause the city. By wisdom as a virtue, which is the third of a triad comprising in addition temperance and courage, is not meant theoretical wisdom—for the mean is not demanded in the latter at all—but, rather, practical wisdom pertaining to worldly actions and behavior. For it is deception to concentrate on the knowledge[9] of this wisdom, carefully guarding the ingenious ways whereby one can attain through it every benefit and avoid every harm, to the extent that this would result in bringing upon one's associates the opposite of what one seeks for oneself and result in distracting oneself from the attainment of other virtues. To cause the hand to be thus fettered to the neck, means the loss of a man's soul, his whole life, the instrument of his well-being, and his survival to that moment at which he attains perfection. Since the motivating powers are three—the appetitive, the irascible, and the practical—the virtues consist of three things: (*a*) moderation in such appetites as the pleasures of sex, food, clothing, comfort, and other pleasures of sense and imagination; (*b*) moderation in all the irascible passions such as fear, anger, depression, pride, hate, jealousy, and the like; (*c*) moderation in practical matters. At the head of these virtues stand temperance, practical wisdom, and courage; their sum is justice, which, however, is extraneous to theoretical virtue. But whoever combines theoretical wisdom with justice, is indeed the happy man. And whoever, in addition to this, wins the prophetic qualities, becomes almost a human god. Worship of him, after the worship of God, becomes almost allowed. He is indeed the world's earthly king and God's deputy in it.

NOTES

1. In *Metaphysics* X, ch. 1.

2. A "sacred" Tradition.

3. More literally: "to be repeated at such short intervals that they recommence soon after they end."

4. *Metaphysics* IX, ch. 7.

5. Strictly, "forerunners" or "predecessors," a term usually applied to those who had been close to Muhammad.

6. 'Umar Ibn al-Khaṭṭāb, the second orthodox caliph (d. 644).

7. 'Alī Ibn Abī Ṭālib, the fourth orthodox caliph (d. 661).

8. Literally: "powers."

9. Reading *ta'arrufihā* (n.) for *ta'rīfihā* (making it known).

7.

Avicenna

ON THE PROOF OF PROPHECIES

AND THE INTERPRETATION

OF THE PROPHETS' SYMBOLS

AND METAPHORS

Translated by Michael E. Marmura

Avicenna's *On the Proof of Prophecies* is noteworthy for singling out the "essence" of prophecy for a specialized treatment; and it is clear from *On the Divisions of the Rational Sciences* and from *Metaphysics* X that, not only the general question of prophecy, but the prophecy of Muhammad, has become of central importance in Avicenna's political science. The work is written in the form of an epistle to someone who had already discussed the question orally with Avicenna. The interlocutor had "misgivings about accepting prophecy" that could not be dispelled by "the claims of the advocates of prophecy."

Avicenna now sums up the substance of what he had said to him before with a view to eliminating these misgivings. The treatise is made up of two parts. The first part summarizes the proof of prophecy and shows its essence. The second part offers an interpretation of certain symbols taken from the Koran and the sayings of Muhammad.

The following translation is based on the critical edition of the Arabic text prepared by Michael E. Marmura. The numbers inserted in the translation refer to the text printed in Cairo: *Fī ithbāt al-nubuwwāt* in *Tis' rasā'il* (1908), pp. 120-32.

THE LEADING [MASTER] Abū 'Alī al-Ḥusayn Ibn Sīnā [Avicenna], may God have mercy on him, said:

You have asked—may God set you aright—that I sum up for you in a treatise the substance of what I said to you with a view to eliminating your misgivings about accepting prophecy. You were confirmed in these misgivings because the claims of the advocates of prophecy are either logically possible assertions that are treated as necessary without the benefit of demonstrative argument or even of dialectical proof, or else impossible assertions on the order of fairy tales, such that the very attempt on the part of their advocate to expound them deserves derision. I answer your request—may God extend your life for the purpose—and begin by saying:

Anything that inheres in another essentially, exists in it in actuality as long as the latter exists; and anything that inheres in another accidentally, exists in it potentially at one time and actually at another time. Whatever has this essential inherence is always actual and is itself the thing that changes whatever is potential into actuality, mediately or without mediation. Examples of this are light, which is the visible in essence [121] and the cause that changes whatever is potentially visible into actuality; and fire, which is the hot in essence and which heats other things, either mediately—as, for example, when it heats water through the mediation of the copper pot—or without mediation—as when it heats the copper pot by itself, I mean by direct contact. Many examples could be given of this. Moreover, if anything is composed of two things, if one of the two can be found without the other, the other can be found without the first. An example of this is oxymel, which is composed of vinegar and honey: if vinegar can be found without honey, honey can be found without vinegar. Another example is the formed statue composed of bronze and the human form: if bronze can be found without the human form, the human form can be found without the bronze. This can be found by induction and has many examples.

I now say: there exists in man a faculty by which he is differentiated from the rest of animals and other things. This is called the rational soul. It is found in all men without exception, but not in all its particulars since its powers vary among men. Thus there is a first power ready to become informed with the universal forms abstracted from matter, which in itself has no form. For this reason it is called the material intellect by analogy with prime matter. It is an intellect in potentiality in the same way that fire in potentiality is a cold thing, not in the sense in which fire is said to have the potentiality to burn. Then there is a second power, which has the capability and the positive disposition to conceive the universal forms because it contains the generally accepted opinions. It also is an intellect in potentiality, but in the sense in which we say that fire has the potentiality to burn. There is, besides these two, a third power that is actually informed with the forms of the universal intelligibles [*122*] of which the other two form a part when these have become actualized. This third power is called the acquired intellect. It does not exist actually in the material intellect and thus does not exist in it essentially. Hence the existence of the acquired intellect in the material intellect is due to something in which it exists essentially and that causes existence; through it, what was potential becomes actual. This is called the universal intellect, the universal soul, and the world soul.

The reception of whatever possesses essentially the power of being received occurs in two ways, directly and indirectly. The reception from the universal active intellect occurs, similarly, in two ways, either directly —like the reception of the common opinions and the self-evident truths[1]— or indirectly—like the reception of the second intelligibles through the mediation of the first, and of the intelligibles acquired through the media-tion of organs and materials such as the external sense, the common sense, the estimative faculty, and the cogitative faculty. Now the rational soul, as we have shown, receives at times directly and at others indirectly; hence the capacity to receive directly does not belong to it essentially but accidentally. This capacity, therefore, must exist essen-tially in something else whence the rational soul acquires it. This is the angelic intellect, which receives essentially without mediation and by its very reception causes the powers of the soul to receive. (The property peculiar to the first intelligibles that allows their reception without mediation is due only to two factors: briefly, it is because these intelli-gibles in themselves are easily receivable, or because the recipient can receive without mediation only that which is easily receivable.)

We have also seen that there are different degrees of strength and weakness, ease and difficulty, in that which receives and that which is received. Now, it is impossible for the capacity to receive to be infinite. For [*123*] there is finitude in the direction of weakness, which consists of the inability of the power to receive even one intelligible, directly or indirectly, and there is finitude in the direction of strength, which consists in the ability of the power to receive directly. [Hence, the affirmation that the capacity to receive is infinite would involve our saying that] it is both finite and infinite in both directions, and this is an impossible contradiction. Moreover, it has been shown that in the case of that which is composed of two things, if one of them can be found without the other, the other can be found without the one. We have also seen that some things receive at one time directly and at other times indirectly. Moreover, we have found that there are things that cannot receive emanations from the [Active] Intellect without mediation, while there are other things that receive all the intellectual emanations without mediation; also that when the capacity to receive is finite in the direction of weakness, it is also necessarily finite in the direction of strength.

Now the degrees of excellence among the causes run along the lines I say: some individual essences are self-subsisting while others are not, and the first are better. The self-subsisting are either immaterial, essential forms or forms that are in matter, and the first are better. Let us proceed and subdivide the latter group since here lies what we seek: the forms and materials that constitute bodies are either organic[2] or inorganic, and the first are better. The organic are either animals or not animals, and the first are better. The animals, in turn, are either rational or irrational, and the first are better. The rational either possess reason by positive disposition or do not, and the first are better. That which is rational by positive disposition either becomes completely actual or does not, and the first is better. That which becomes completely actual does so without mediation or through mediation, and the first is better. This is the one called prophet and in him the degrees of excellence in the realm of material forms culminate. Now, if that which is best stands above and rules the inferior, [*124*] then the prophet stands above and rules all the genera above which he excels.

Revelation is the emanation and the angel is the received emanating power that descends on the prophets as if it were an emanation continuous with the universal intellect. It is rendered particular, not essentially, but accidentally, by reason of the particularity of the recipient. Thus the angels have been given different names because [they are associated with] different notions; nevertheless, they form a single totality, which is particularized, not essentially, but accidentally, because of the particularity of the recipient. The message, therefore, is that part of the emanation termed "revelation" which has been received and couched in whatever mode of expression is deemed best for furthering man's good in both the eternal and the corruptible worlds as regards knowledge and political governance, respectively. The messenger is the one who conveys what he acquires of the emanation termed "revelation," again in whatever mode of expression is deemed best for achieving through his opinions the good of the sensory world by political governance and of the intellectual world by knowledge.

This, then, is the summary of the discourse concerning the affirmation of prophecy, the showing of its essence, and the statements made about revelation, the angel, and the thing revealed. As for the validity of the prophethood of our prophet, of Muhammad (may God's prayers and peace be on him), it becomes evident to the reasonable man once he compares him with the other prophets, peace be on them. We shall refrain from elaboration here.

We will now take up the interpretation of the symbols you asked me about. It has been said that a condition the prophet must adhere to is that his words should be symbols and his expressions hints. Or, as Plato states in the *Laws*: whoever does not understand the apostles' symbols will not attain the Divine Kingdom.[3] Moreover, the foremost Greek philosophers and prophets made use in their books of symbols and signs in which they hid their secret doctrine—men like Pythagoras, [*125*] Socrates, and Plato. As for Plato, he had blamed Aristotle for divulging wisdom and making knowledge manifest so that Aristotle had to reply: "Even though I had done this, I have still left in my books many a pitfall which only the initiate among the wise and learned can understand."[4] Moreover, how could the prophet Muhammad (may God's prayers and peace be on him) bring knowledge to the uncouth nomad, not to say to the whole human race considering that he was sent a messenger to all? Political guidance, on the other hand, comes easily to prophets; also the imposition of obligations on people.

The first thing you asked me about was what the prophet Muhammad (may God's prayers and peace be on him) conveyed from his Lord (may He be honored and glorified), saying: *God is the light of the heavens and the earth. The likeness of His light is as a niche wherein is a lamp (the lamp in a glass, the glass is as it were a brilliant star) kindled from a blessed tree, an olive neither from the east nor from the west. Its oil almost shines even if no fire touched it. Light upon light! God guides to His light whom He will. God strikes similitudes for men. God has knowledge of everything* [xxiv, 35].

I say: *light* is an equivocal term partaking of two meanings, one essential, the other metaphorical. The essential stands for the perfection of the transparent inasmuch as it is transparent, as Aristotle said.[5] The metaphorical meaning is to be understood in two ways: either as the good, or as the cause that leads to the good. Here, the sense is the metaphorical one in both meanings. I mean that God, the Exalted, is in Himself the good and the cause of everything good. The same judgment applies to the essential and to the nonessential. *The heavens and the earth* stands for the "whole." The *niche* stands for [*126*] the material intellect and the rational soul. For the walls of a niche are close to each other and it is thus excellently predisposed to be illuminated since the closer the walls of a place are to each other, the greater the reflection and the light it holds. And just as the actualized intellect is likened to light, its recipient is likened to the recipient of light, which is the transparent. The best of transparent things is air and the best [transparent] air is in the niche. Thus what is symbolized by the niche is the material intellect, which is to the acquired intellect as the niche is to the light. The *lamp* stands for the acquired actualized intellect. For light, as the philosophers defined it, is the perfection of the transparent and that which moves it from potentiality to actuality. The acquired intellect is to the material intellect as the lamp is to the niche.

The expression *in a glass* is used because between the material and the acquired intellects there exists another [intermediate] level or place that is related to these two as that which intervenes between what is transparent and the lamp is related to the latter two. Here, in visual sight, the lamp does not reach [and hence could not be seen through] the transparent [air] without a medium. This is the oil vessel with the wick, from which the glass protrudes. For glass is one of the transparent things receptive of light. Hence the subsequent utterance, *is as it were a brilliant star*, is given to convey that it is pure transparent glass, not opaque colored glass, since nothing colored is transparent. By *kindled from a blessed tree, an olive*, is meant the cogitative power, which stands as subject and material for the intellectual acts in the same way that oil stands as subject and material for the lamp.

Neither from the east nor from the west is explained as follows: "East" lexically [*127*] derives from the place whence light emanates and "west" where it is quenched; and *east* is used metaphorically for the place where there is light and *west* for the place where there is no light. (Notice how the rules of simile are adhered to: *light* was made the basis of the statement and the simile constructed thereon; *light* was conjoined with the apparatus and materials that produce it.) Thus what is symbolized by the expression, *neither from the east nor from the west*, is as follows: the cogitative power, in the absolute sense, is not one of the pure rational powers where light emanates without restriction. This is the meaning of the saying, *a . . . tree . . . neither from the east*. Nor is it one of the animal powers where light is utterly lost. This is the meaning of *nor from the west*.

The saying, *its oil almost shines even if no fire touched it*, is in praise of the cogitative power. In this expression, *even if no fire touched it*, the word *touch* stands for connection and emanation. The saying *fire* is explained as follows: when the similarity between metaphorical *light* and real light and between the instruments and the consequences of the former and those of the latter was drawn, the essential subject that causes a thing to be in another was likened to what is customarily considered a subject, that is to say, fire. For although in reality fire is colorless, custom takes it to be luminous. (Observe how the rules of simile are adhered to!) Moreover, since fire surrounds the elements (*ummahāt*), that which surrounds the world, not in the spatial sense, but in a verbal metaphorical sense, is likened to fire. This is the universal intellect. This intellect, however, is not as Alexander of Aphrodisias believed—attributing the belief to Aristotle—the true God, the First. For although in one respect this first intellect is one, it is multiple inasmuch as it consists of the forms of numerous universals. [*128*] It is thus one, not essentially, but accidentally, acquiring its oneness from Him who is essentially one, the one God (may He be magnified).

As for that which the Prophet [Muhammad] (may God's prayers and peace be upon him) conveyed from his Lord (may He be honored and glorified), saying: *and upon that day eight shall carry above them the throne of thy Lord* [lxix, 17], I say: religious Laws generally state that God is on the throne. Among other things this expression means that the throne is the last of the created corporeal existents. The anthropomorphists among the adherents of religious Laws claim that God, the Exalted, is on the throne, though not in the sense of His indwelling there. The philosophers in their language, however, regard the ninth sphere, which is the sphere of all the spheres, the last of the corporeal existents. They state that God is there and is on it, but not in the sense of indwelling, as was made clear by Aristotle at the end of the *Physics*.[6] The philosophers who adhere to religious Laws have agreed that what is meant by the throne is this very same celestial body. They maintained, in addition, that the sphere is moved by its soul by way of desire. They maintained this because movements are either essential or nonessential. They then showed that this movement is not nonessential. Essential movement, they continued, is either natural or is caused by the soul. Then they showed that this movement is not natural and hence that it must be caused by the soul. They showed that the soul of the sphere is the rational, the perfect, and the active, and also that the spheres neither perish nor change throughout eternity. Now it is a widely spread notion in the disciplines based on religious Laws that angels are living beings and that, unlike man who perishes, they never perish. Once it is said that the spheres are rational living beings and the rational living being that does not perish is called an angel, the spheres are then called angels. And once these premises are put forth, it becomes clear that the throne [*129*] is carried by eight and so does the interpretation of the exegetes who take these to be eight spheres. "Carrying" is used in two senses: (*a*) in a human sense—and this is the more appropriate use of the term carrying—as when we speak of the stone that is carried on the back of a man, and (*b*) in a natural sense as when we say that water is carried on earth and fire on air. The sense is the natural one, not the first.

The expressions *upon that day, the hour,* and *the resurrection*[7] are meant to convey what the Lawgiver [Muhammad] spoke of when he said: "Each soul after death is resurrected." Moreover, since the soul's scrutiny after its separation from the body is certain, punishment and reward and the like have been deferred to that day.

As for what the Prophet [Muhammad] (may God's prayers and peace be on him) conveyed from his Lord (may He be honored and glorified), saying: "Across the fire lies a path, the description of which is that it is sharper than the sword and finer than a hair. None can enter paradise without crossing it. Those who cross it are saved, while those who fall off it are lost." You will first be required to know what "punishment" and "reward" are, and what is meant by "paradise" and "fire." I say: Reward is to dwell eternally within divine providence devoid of all striving for things unattainable in the realm of the practical and the cognitive. This is only achieved after attaining perfection in the realm of knowledge and after shunning the vices in the realm of the practical so that they do not become a habit and a positive disposition for which the soul longs as one longs for intimate things, making impossible the patient endurance of their absence. It will only happen when one resists the animal soul in its practical activities and in its cognitions, excepting the necessary. Indeed, all who have perished have suffered thus because they have conformed with the estimative faculty, which is the animal faculty [130] that gives false judgments regarding the abstracted images when the senses are dormant. No wonder, then, that this audacious faculty, calling itself "the material intellect," by taking away reason, renders suspect whoever imitates it and an apostate whoever believes it, leading them to inevitable corruption and future destruction. When thus corrupted with his believed images, such an individual finds that the rational soul, whose activities to some degree correspond to his, is devoid of the noble intellectual forms that actualize it. The soul is then naturally impelled to seek the impeding cause in the same way that a stone, raised to its unnatural place and then released, descends seeking its natural place when separated from the impediment. But this happens to the soul when the instruments used to attain the acquired intellect, such as the external and inner senses, estimation, memory, and the faculty of cogitation, have been corrupted. The individual thus remains longing for the soul's natural activity of acquiring the things by which it realizes its essence, at a time when none of the instruments for such an acquisition exists. What greater calamity can there be, particularly that the soul continues eternally in this state?

Moreover, inasmuch as the soul had acted in agreement with such an individual's indulgence in practical vices, it is doubtful that the soul should remain thereafter unattached to its evil kindred. For it becomes accustomed to the things it had acted in agreement with, having never opposed the appetitive pleasures of the senses. But how can an individual achieve these pleasures, now that the sensitive and appetitive faculties exist no more? His state is well exemplified by the saying: "Never fall in love with someone who is a traveller. For he will inevitably travel or will die. You will then be left in the anguish of love, tortured."

Since the meaning of punishment and reward has been briefly shown, we will now discuss the essence of paradise and fire. We say: [131]

If the worlds are three, the sensory, the imaginative and estimative, and the intellectual, it is the intellectual world that is the place of dwelling. This is paradise. The imaginative and estimative world, as has been shown, is the world of corruption. The world of the senses is the world of the graves. Know then that the intellect, in acquiring most universals, needs to study the particulars inductively. This necessarily requires the external senses. You will then know that the intellect takes a narrow and difficult path or way: from the external sense, through the faculties of imagination, estimation, and cogitation—all of which belong to the infernal realm—until it arrives unto itself and perceives intellectually. It is thus seen how the intellect takes a path or a way in the infernal world. If it crosses this path, it arrives at the intellectual world. But if it stops in the infernal world, mistaking the estimative faculty for the intellective and accepting as true what this faculty points to, then it remains in the infernal world, dwells in hell, and suffers enormous loss. This then is the explanation of the saying concerning the path.

As for what the prophet Muhammad (may God's prayers and peace be with him) conveyed from his Lord, the Mighty and Majestic, saying: *Upon it there are nineteen* [lxxiv, 30], it is explained as follows. It has already been shown what the inferno is. In brief, we have shown that it is the animal soul, and we have shown that this soul rests eternally in hell. Now the animal soul is divided into two parts, the cognitive and the practical. The practical, in turn, consists of the appetitive and the irascible. The cognitive, on the other hand, consists of the apprehensions of sensible things by the imaginative faculty through the external senses. These sensible things are sixteen in number. In addition to these, there is the estimative faculty that judges these images in a logically possible way, and it is one in number. Hence we have two, plus sixteen, plus one: these make nineteen. Thus the saying, *Upon it there are nineteen*, is evidently true.

As for the saying: *Only the [132] angels have we made the masters of hell* [lxxiv, 31], it is to be explained as follows: It is customary in the religious Law to call the subtle powers that are not perceived by the senses "angels."

As for that which the prophet Muhammad (may God's prayers and peace be on him) conveyed from his Lord, the Mighty and Majestic, saying: "Hell has seven gates and paradise eight,"[8] it is explained in the following manner. It is known that the cognitive faculties of the soul are of two sorts: there are those like the external senses, which are five in number, that apprehend the particulars. These apprehend the sensible form together with its matter. Then there are the faculties that apprehend and become informed with the sensible forms without their matters. An example of these is the storing place of the sense-perceptions, known as the imagination. In addition to these, there is the faculty that judges these forms in a logically possible way; this is the estimative faculty.

Then there is further the faculty that judges these forms in a necessary way; this is the intellect. These add up to eight. Now when all the faculties are present, they lead to eternal happiness and entry into paradise. But when only seven are present, without the eighth that completes them, they lead to eternal misery. According to usage in language, whatever leads to a thing is termed its gate. Thus the seven faculties that lead to hell are called its gates, while the eight that lead to paradise are called the latter's gates.

This, in brief, is the explanation of all the questions you asked about.

NOTES

1. Literally: "the beginning [that is, the primary knowledge or the first intelligibles] of the intellects."

2. Literally: "growing."

3. Not a quotation from Plato's *Laws*.

4. Avicenna is quoting from the "correspondence" between Plato and Aristotle translated into Arabic from Hellenistic sources.

5. Aristotle *De Anima* ii. 7. 418ᵇ5–14.

6. viii. 10. 267ᵇ5–10.

7. Koran, *passim*.

8. A Tradition; cf. Koran xv, 44.

8.

Avempace

THE GOVERNANCE

OF THE SOLITARY

Translated by Lawrence Berman

Avempace (Abū Bakr Muḥammad Ibn Bājjah [or Ibn al-Ṣā'igh], d. 1138) was born in Saragossa toward the end of the eleventh century, lived in Seville, Granada, and later in North Africa (where he seems to have enjoyed a favored position at the Almoravid court), and died in Fez. He is celebrated as the first Spanish-Muslim philosopher, and is credited with extensive knowledge of medicine, mathematics, astronomy, and music. Most of his surviving works are short treatises, many of which are incomplete and do not appear to have been properly revised by the author.

The *Governance of the Solitary* is noteworthy for having the character and position of the philosopher in the imperfect cities as its central theme. This theme, in a sense, complements Alfarabi's discussion of the solitary individuals (or Weeds) in the virtuous city in his *Political Regime* (above,

Selection 2). "Abū Bakr Ibn al-Ṣā'igh sought to establish a way for the 'Governance of the Solitary' in these lands," says Averroes, "but this book is, incomplete, and besides, it is not always easy to understand its meaning. . . . He is the only one to treat this subject, and none of his predecessors surpassed him in this respect." The central theme of the work is interwoven with another theme, that of "spiritual" or incorporeal "forms." Only such parts as treat the main theme are given here.

Moses Narboni made a Hebrew paraphrase of the book in his commentary on Ibn Tufayl's *Hayy the Son of Yaqzan*, composed in 1349. This paraphrase was published by David Herzog: *Die Abhandlung des Abu Bekr Ibn al-Saig "Vom Verhalten des Einsiedlers" nach Mose Narbonis Auszug* (Berlin, 1896). The first edition of the Arabic text was published by Miguel

Asín Palacios: *Tadbīr al-mutawaḥḥid*
(Madrid-Granada, 1946). At about
the same time, D. M. Dunlop published the first two chapters of the
text: "Ibn Bājjah's Tadbīru'l-Muta-
waḥḥid (Rule of the Solitary)," *Journal of the Royal Asiatic Society of
Great Britain and Ireland* (1945),
pp. 63–73 (corresponding to Asín Palacios' ed., pp. 3–17). Both editions are
based on the same manuscript (Bod-
leian, Pococke, No. 206) and present
numerous difficulties, some of which
are no doubt due to the unfinished
character of the work as left by
Avempace. The following translation
is based on Asín Palacios' edition, pp.
3–12, 37, 54–55, 58–62, 78–79.

I

1 The word "governance" (*tadbīr*) is used in Arabic in many senses,
enumerated by the experts in that language. Most commonly, it is used
to signify, in a general way, the ordering of actions to an end that is
being pursued. Therefore they do not apply it to someone who performs
a single action with a view to accomplishing a particular end: one does
not call an activity "governance" if he believes that it consists of a
single action; whereas the one who believes that the activity consists
of many actions and considers it inasmuch as it possesses an order, he
then calls that order a governance. (For this reason, they say of God
that He is the "governor" of the world.) This [order] may be potential
or actual; but the more frequent use of the word "governance" signifies
the potential [order].

It is evident that when certain affairs are ordered potentially, they
are so ordered by means of calculation; for this [kind of order] pertains
to calculation and can exist through calculation alone. Therefore [4] it
can exist in man alone, and the use of "governor" [cited above] is merely
analogical. Hence governance is used in a primary and a derivative
sense.[1] Governance may also designate the bringing of this [potential]
order into being and in so far as order is on its way into being, which
is more frequent and apparent in human action, less so in the actions of
the irrational animal. Applied in this manner, governance has a general
and a restricted sense. Used in a general sense, it designates all human
activities of whatever kind. It is applied to the crafts as well as to the
faculties, except that it is more frequent and common to apply it [in the
restricted sense] to the faculties. Therefore it is applied to the ordering
of military affairs and hardly ever to the arts of shoemaking and weaving.
When applied in this [restricted] manner, again it has a general and a
restricted sense. Used in a general sense, it designates all that is covered
by the arts called "faculties." I have given an account of this in [my
work(s) on]' political science. Used in a restrictive sense, it designates
the governance of cities.

Governance is applied to matters some of which are prior to others in dignity and perfection. Of these, the most dignified are the governance of cities and the governance of the household. But governance is seldom applied to the household, to the extent that the expression "governance of the household" is used in a metaphorical and qualified sense. As for the governance of war and so forth, they form parts of these two kinds of governance. As for God's governance of the world, this is certainly governance of a different kind, only distantly related to even that meaning of the word [that is, the one referring to the city] which resembles[2] it most closely. The latter is governance in the unqualified sense. It is also the most dignified, for it receives the designation [5] "governance" because of the supposed similarity between it and bringing the world into existence by God, the Exalted.

It is evident that this class of ambiguous nouns [to which "governance" belongs] is the farthest removed from univocity; it is almost completely equivocal. The multitude uses it ambiguously. The philosophers use it with complete equivocity; they consider it ambiguous only in the sense in which we give *A* the name of *B* because *A* contains something that is similar to *B*—a class of which they did not give an account in [their discussions of] ambiguous nouns because of its rarity. Therefore the multitude does not use the adjective "right" in connection with God's governance [of the world] and does not say of the governance of the world that it is "right" governance. Instead it says that it is "perfect," "precise," and the like, because these expressions imply the presence of rightness and some other dignified thing in addition. For in the eyes of the multitude, right activity is like a species of perfect and precise activity. The account of this matter is presented elsewhere.

2   When governance is used in an unqualified sense, as we have used it above, to designate[3] the governance of cities, and when used in a restricted sense [to designate the governance of the household], it is divided into right and wrong governance. It is sometimes supposed that governance may be free of these two opposite [qualifications], but investigation and close study will reveal that they adhere to it necessarily. This can be ascertained easily by anyone with a minimal understanding of political philosophy. Therefore the two types of governance properly so called can be divided into right and wrong governance.

As far as the governance of cities is concerned, Plato has explained it in the *Republic*. He explained [6] what is meant by the right governance of cities and the source of the wrongness that adheres to it. To trouble oneself with the task of dealing with something that has been adequately dealt with before is superfluous, a result of ignorance, or a sign of evil intent.

As for the governance of the household, the household as household is a part of the city. He [Plato] explained there that man alone forms the natural household [of which he spoke]. He explained that the most excellent existence of that which is a part, is to exist as a part. Therefore he did not formulate the governance of the household as a [separate] part of the political art, since it is treated by him within the political art. He explained there what the household is and how it exists, that[4] it exists most excellently when the [city conducts a] common household, and he describes its communal character.

As for the household existing in cities other than the virtuous—that is, in the four [imperfect] cities enumerated [in the *Republic*[5]]—the household exists in them imperfectly, and there is something unnatural in it. Only that household is perfect to which nothing can be added without resulting in an imperfection, like the sixth finger; for the distinguishing feature of what is well constructed is that it becomes imperfect by adding to it. All other households are imperfect and diseased in comparison with the [natural] household, for the conditions that differentiate them from the virtuous household lead to the destruction of the household and its ruin. Therefore these conditions are like a disease. Certain authors have gone through the trouble of treating the governance of these imperfect—that is, the diseased—households. Those of them whose books on the governance of the household have reached us employ rhetorical arguments. In contrast, the position we stated is clear: except for the virtuous household, the households are diseased; they are all corrupt; and they do not exist by nature but only by convention. Therefore whatever virtue they may possess, [7] is by convention too, except perhaps so far as they have something in common with the virtuous household. The virtuous household can be treated following a fixed and necessary order of exposition. Understand,[2] then, that the treatment of that common element can be scientific as well, for no household is without many of the common features that are to be found in the virtuous household. For without them a household cannot endure or even be a household except equivocally. Let us, then, turn aside and leave the treatment of imperfect households to those who devote themselves to the treatment of such matters as exist at particular times.

Moreover, the perfection of the household is not something desired for its own sake, but only for the sake of rendering perfect either the city or the natural end of man, and the treatment of the latter clearly forms part of man's governance of himself [that is, ethics]. In any case, the household is either a part of the city and its treatment forms part of the treatment of the city, or a preparation for another end and its treatment forms part of the treatment of that end. This explains why the treatment of the household in the popular manner is pointless and does not constitute a science. If it has any advantage, then this is only temporary, as is the case with what the rhetoricians present in their works on "manners" (which they call psychological), such as *Kalilah and Dimnah* and the *Book of Arab Sages,* which contain maxims and sayings of counsel. For the most part, this topic is treated in certain sections of a book, such as in the chapters[2] dealing with the companionship of the sultan, the social relations with friends, and the like. In the majority of cases, these things are true[2] for a particular time and a particular [8] way of life. When that way of life changes,[2] those opinions—expressed as universal statements—change;[2] their application becomes restricted after having been universal; they become harmful or rejected after having been useful. You will understand this if you acquaint yourself with the contents of the books composed on this topic and try to apply what is said in each case to later times.

3   The virtuous city is characterized by the absence of the art of medicine and of the art of judication. For friendship binds all its citizens, and they do not quarrel among themselves at all. Therefore, it is only when a part of the city is bereft of friendship and quarrelsomeness breaks out, that recourse must be had to the laying down of justice and the need arises for someone, who is the judge, to dispense it. Moreover, since all the actions of the virtuous city are right—this being the distinguishing characteristic that adheres to it—its citizens do not eat harmful foods. Therefore they do not need to know about the cures for the suffocation caused by mushrooms and the like, nor do they need to know about the treatment for excessive wine-drinking, for nothing there is not properly ordered. When the citizens forego exercise, this too, gives rise to numerous diseases; but it is evident that the virtuous city is not subject to such diseases. It may not even need any remedies aside from those for dislocation and the like, and, in general, for such diseases whose specific causes are external and that the healthy body cannot ward off by its own effort. For it has been observed in many a healthy man that his serious wounds heal [9] by themselves, and there are other kinds of evidence for this. It is, then, characteristic of the perfect city that there is neither doctor nor judge, while it is inherent in the four [imperfect simple regimes or] unmixed[6] cities that they are in need of doctor and judge. The more removed a city is from the perfect, the more it is in need of these two and the more dignified the station of these two types of men in it.

It is evident that in the virtuous and perfect city, every man is offered the highest excellence he is fit to pursue. All of its opinions are true and there is no false opinion in it. Its actions alone are virtuous without qualification. When any other action is virtuous, it is so only in relation to some existing evil. For instance, the amputation of a limb from the body is harmful in itself, but, by accident, it may prove beneficial to someone who has been bitten by a snake and whose body achieves health by that amputation. Similarly, scammony is harmful in itself, but it is beneficial to someone with a disease. An account of these matters is given in the *Nicomachea*.[7]

It is, then, evident that every opinion arising in the perfect city that is different from the opinions of its citizens is false, and every action arising in it that is different from the actions customarily performed in it is wrong. Now the false does not have a defined nature and cannot be known at all; this is explained in the *Book of Demonstration*.[8] As to the wrong action, it may be performed in order to achieve some other end. There are books composed to enable one to study these actions, such as the *Book of Devices* by the Banū Shākir.[9] But everything contained in them is in the nature of play—things intended to excite rather than to contribute [*10*] to the essential perfection of man. To discuss such things is a sign of evil intent and results from ignorance.

In the perfect city, therefore, one does not introduce arguments dealing with those who hold an opinion other than that of its citizens or perform an action other than their action. In the four [imperfect] cities, on the other hand, this can be done. For here, there may be an unknown[10] action that a man discovers by nature or learns from someone else, and does it. Or there may be a false opinion, and some man becomes aware of its falsehood. Or there may be erroneous sciences in all or most of which the citizens do not believe because they involve accepting[2] contradictory positions; and, by nature or instruction, a man may find which of the two contradictory propositions is the true one.

Now the ones who discover a right action or learn a true science that does not exist in the city, belong to a class that has no generic name. As for the ones who stumble upon a true opinion that does not exist in the city or the opposite of which is believed in the city, they are called Weeds.[11] The more such opinions they hold and the more crucial the opinions, the more appropriate the appellation. Strictly speaking, the term applies to these men alone. But it may be applied, more generally, to anyone who holds an opinion other than the opinion of the citizens of the city, regardless of whether his opinion is true or false. The name has been transferred to these men from the weeds that spring up of themselves among plants. But let us restrict the use of this term to the ones who hold true opinions. It is evident that one of the characteristics of the perfect city is that it is free of Weeds [in both its strict and more general senses]; in the strict sense, because it is free of false opinions; and in the general sense, because their presence means that the city is already diseased and disintegrating and has ceased to be [*11*] perfect. The Weeds can, however, exist in the four [imperfect] ways of life. Their existence is the cause that leads to the rise of the perfect city, as explained elsewhere.[12]

4   All the ways of life that exist now or have existed before (accord-

ing to the great majority of the reports reaching us about them, with
the possible exception of what Abū Naṣr [Alfarabi] narrates concerning
the early Persians' way of life), are mixtures of the five ways of life
[that is, the perfect and the four imperfect ones], and for the most part
we find them to be mixtures of the four [imperfect] ways of life. We
leave it to those who devote themselves to the investigation of the ways
of life that exist in this time to supply the details. We merely remark
that the three types of men—the Weeds, the judges, and the doctors—
exist, or can exist, in these ways of life. The happy, were it possible for
them to exist in these cities, will possess only the happiness of an isolated
individual; and the only right governance [possible in these cities] is the
governance of an isolated individual, regardless of whether there is one
isolated individual or more than one, so long as a nation or a city has
not adopted their opinion. These individuals are the ones meant by the
Sufis when they speak of the "strangers"; for although they are in their
homelands and among their companions and neighbors, the Sufis say that
these are strangers in their opinions, having travelled in their minds to
other stations that are like homelands to them, and so forth.

5   We intend to discourse here about the governance of this solitary
man. It is evident that he suffers from something that is unnatural. We
will therefore state how he should manage himself so that he may achieve
the best existence proper to him, just as the doctor states how the isolated man in these cities should manage himself in order to be healthy:
that is, either how to preserve his health (for instance, [*12*] what Galen
writes in his *Preservation of Health*), or how to recover it once it is
lost, which is laid down in the art of medicine. Similarly, this discourse
is addressed to the isolated Weed: (*a*) How he is to achieve happiness
if he does not possess it, or how to remove from himself the conditions
that prevent his achieving happiness or achieving the portion he can
achieve of it, which in turn depends either on how far his insight takes
him or on [a belief] that had seized him. (*b*) As to the preservation
of his happiness, which is similar to the preservation of health, it is
impossible in the three [four?] ways of life and those mixed of them;
what Galen and others prescribe in this situation is similar to alchemy
and astrology. What we are laying[2] down here is the medicine of the
soul, as distinguished from the other medicine, which is the medicine
of the body, and from judication, which is the medicine of social relations. It is evident that the latter two arts disappear completely in the
perfect city and are, therefore, not to be reckoned among the sciences.
Similarly, the subject we are treating would disappear if the city were
perfect, and so would the utility of this subject, just as would the
science of medicine, the art of judication, and every other art devised
to meet [the predicaments characteristic of] the imperfect [kinds of]
governance. Just as the true opinions contained in medicine revert [in

the perfect city] to the natural sciences,[13] and those contained in the art of judication to the art of politics, similarly those contained in the present subject revert to natural science[13] and the art of politics.

* * *

VII

4 [37] Every one of these [particular spiritual forms, that is, the ones present in common sense, in the imagination, and in memory] is beloved of man by nature, and hardly a man can be found who does not have a liking for at least one of these spiritual forms. If man is a part of the city, then the city is the end that is served in all of his actions. But this obtains in the virtuous city alone. In the other four cities and the ones mixed of them, on the other hand, each citizen establishes for himself any of these spiritual forms as an end and has a predilection for the pleasures resulting from them. Hence things that are mere preparations in the virtuous city become the ends in the other cities.

* * *

XII

1 [54] The ends that the solitary individual establishes[14] for himself are three: his corporeal form, his particular spiritual form, or his universal spiritual form [that is, his intellectual perception of the intelligible ideas]. The account of his ends when he[15] is a part of a lasting [that is, perfect or virtuous] city has been given in political science. As regards the ends he establishes for himself in each one of the other cities—in so far as he is a part of one of them—here, the solitary individual performs, among others, certain activities appropriate to him as he pursues any of these ends. Now these ends are (a) pursued in the city,[16] and the general account of the city has been given in [55] political science. To achieve any of them, one has to use reflection, investigation, inference, and, in general, calculation; for without the use of calculation, an activity is bestial, not partaking of the human in any way beyond the fact that its object is a body that has a human form. (b) When, on the other hand, one pursues a bestial purpose— whether this purpose can be achieved through human calculation or not[17]—his kind of man is not different from the beast, and there is no difference at this point whether this being possesses a human form that conceals a beast or it is a beast living in isolation. It is also evident

that no city can be formed from beings that act in the bestial manner, and that they cannot at all form parts of a city. Only the solitary individual can act in this manner, and we have stated the ends of the solitary. Hence the end of the bestial man is among these three ends. However, it cannot be the universal spiritual form; for this pertains to the intellect, which achieves it through inquiry. It is, then, evident that they must be two, that is, the particular spiritual and the corporeal forms.

*   *   *

XIII

1 [58] Some men, as we stated previously, are merely concerned with their corporeal form; they are the base. Others occupy themselves only with their [particular] spiritual form; they are the high-minded and the noble. Just as the basest among the men concerned with their corporeal form would be the one who disregards his spiritual form for the sake of the corporeal and does not pay any attention to the former, so the one who possesses [59] nobility in the highest degree would be the one who disregards his corporeal form and does not pay any attention to it. However, the one who disregards his corporeal form completely, reduces his longevity; like the basest of men he deviates from nature; and like him he does not exist. But there are men who destroy their corporeal form in obedience to the demands of their spiritual form. Thus Ta'abbata Sharran[18] says:

> Our lot is either captivity to be followed by the favor
> [of manumission]
> Or to shed our blood; death is preferable for the free.

Thus he considers death better than having to bear the favor of manumission. Others choose to kill themselves. This they do either by seeking certain death in the battlefield, as did, for example, the Marwanite[19] in the war with 'Abd Allāh Ibn 'Alī Ibn al-'Abbās; he is the author of the following lines:

> Life with dishonor and the dislike of death,
> Both I consider evil and hard.
> If there is no escape from one or the other,
> Then I choose to march nobly to death.

[Or else they choose to take their life with their own hands.] Zenobia did this when 'Amr was about to kill her: "I would rather do it with my own hands than let 'Amr kill me."[20] So did the queen of Egypt whose story[21] with Augustus is given in the histories. So also did certain peoples [60] whom Aristotle mentions when treating of the magnanimous man:[22] they burned themselves and their city[23] when they became certain that their enemy was about to defeat them. All this borders on excess, except in certain situations in which the destruction of the corporeal form (but not the spiritual form) results from magnanimity and high-mindedness. This, for instance, applies to what Fāṭimah the mother of al-Rabīʿ (and the rest of the Banū Ziyād) did when Qays Ibn Zuhayr caught up with her. She threw herself off the camel she was riding, and died.[24] But this is one of the special cases in which it is better to die than to live, and in which the choice of death over life is the right thing for man to do. We shall give an account of this later on.

2   There is another and lower type of the noble and the magnanimous man, which forms the majority. This is the man who disregards his corporeal form for the sake of the spiritual, but does not destroy the former, either because his spiritual form does not compel him to do so, or—despite its compelling him to destroy his corporeal form—because he decides in favor of keeping it. We believe this to be what Ḥātim al-Ṭāʾī[25] did when he slaughtered his horse and sat hungry, not eating any of it himself or feeding any of it to his family, while his young children were convulsing with hunger. Another example is what thieves do [when they endure hardships and face danger]. However, in the former case, the purpose is to control the body and improve it, while these thieves expend[26] their bodies for the sake of their bodies and have a predilection for one corporeal state rather than another. In the former case—the case of Ḥātim al-Ṭāʾī and his like—no argument can be adduced for not acknowledging that the action is noble and highminded, and the nature responsible for it is honorable, sublime, [61] and free of corporeality; it occupies the most sublime position, next only to that occupied by wisdom; and it must necessarily be one of the qualities of the philosophic nature, for without it the philosophic nature would be corporeal and mixed.

In order to achieve its highest perfection, the philosophic nature must, then, act nobly and high-mindedly. Therefore, whoever prefers his corporeal existence to anything pertaining to his spiritual existence will not be able to achieve the final end. Hence no corporeal man is happy and every happy man is completely spiritual. But just as the spiritual man must perform certain corporeal acts—but not for their own sake—and perform [particular] spiritual acts for their own sake, similarly, the philosopher must perform numerous [particular] spiritual acts—but not for their own sake—and perform all the intellectual acts for their own sake: the corporeal acts enable him to exist as a human, the [particular] spiritual acts render him more noble, and the intellectual acts render him divine and virtuous. The man of wisdom is therefore necessarily a man who is virtuous and divine. Of every kind of activity, he takes up the best only. He shares with every class of men the best states that characterize them. But he stands alone as the one who performs the most excellent and the noblest of actions. When he achieves the final end—that is, when he intellects simple essential intellects, which are mentioned in the *Metaphysics, On the Soul,* and *On Sense and the Sensible*—he then becomes one of these intellects. It would be right to call him simply divine. He will be free from the mortal sensible qualities, as well as from the high [particular] spiritual qualities: [62] it will be fitting to describe him as a pure divinity.

All these qualities can be obtained by the solitary individual in the absence of the perfect city. By virtue of his two lower ranks [that is, the corporeal and the particular spiritual] he will not be a part, the end, the agent, or the preserver of this perfect city. By virtue of this third rank he may not be a part of this perfect city, but he nevertheless will be[27] the end aimed at in this city. Of course, he cannot be the preserver or the agent of the perfect city while a solitary man.

*   *   *

XVII

2   [78] . . . It is clear from the situation of the solitary that he must not associate with those whose end is corporeal nor with those whose end is the spirituality that is adulterated with corporeality. Rather, he must associate with those who pursue the sciences. Now since those who pursue the sciences are few in some ways of life and many in others, there even being ways of life in which they do not exist at all, it follows that in some of the ways of life the solitary must keep away from men completely so far as he can, and not deal with them except in indispensable matters and to the extent to which it is indispensable for him to do so; or emigrate to the ways of life in which the sciences are pursued—if such are to be found. This does not contradict what was stated in political science and what was explained in natural science. It was explained there [that is, in natural science] that man is political by nature, and it was explained in political science that all isolation is evil. But it is only evil as such; accidentally, it may be good, which happens with reference to many things pertaining to nature. For instance, bread and meat are by nature beneficial and nourishing, while opium and colocynth are mortal poisons. But the body may possess certain unnatural states in which the latter two are beneficial [79] and must be employed, and the natural nourishment is harmful and must be avoided. However, such states are necessarily diseases and deviations

from the natural order. Hence the drugs are beneficial in exceptional cases and by accident, while [natural] nourishment is beneficial in the main and essentially. These states are to the body as the ways of life are to the soul. Just as health is believed to be one in opposition to these many [diseased] states, and health alone is the natural state of the body while the many [diseased states] are deviations from nature, similarly the lasting way of life is the natural state of the soul and is one in opposition to the rest of the ways of life, which are many, and these many [ways of life] are not natural to the soul.

NOTES

1. Literally: "is said in [accordance with an order of] priority and posteriority."

2. With Dunlop.

3. Reading <wa->dall.

4. Reading wa-inn for fa'inn (indeed).

5. That is, timocracy, oligarchy, democracy, and despotism. Plato *Republic* viii–ix.

6. See above, n. 5.

7. Aristotle *Nicomachean Ethics* v. 11. 1138ᵇ1 ff., vii. 5 ff., *passim*.

8. Aristotle *Posterior Analytics* i. 16, *passim*.

9. Aḥmad, al-Ḥasan, and Muḥammad, the sons of Mūsā Ibn Shākir, collaborated in writing numerous works on mathematics, astronomy, and mechanics. The *Book of Devices* is attributed to Muḥammad (d. 873).

10. Reading yujhal for yuhill (permitted).

11. Cf. Alfarabi, *Political Regime*, pp. 57, 74 ff. (above, Selection 2).

12. Cf., e.g., *ibid.*, pp. 70–71 (above, Selection 2).

13. Avempace says "arts" and "art" respectively. He is perhaps alluding to the arts that treat dislocation and the like; see above, p. 8.

14. Reading yanṣubuhā for yataḍammanuhā with Narboni?

15. Reading wa-huw for wa-hiy.

16. Bracketing al-fāḍilah (virtuous).

17. Adding aw before lam.

18. A pre-Islamic Arab poet.

19. The event took place in the decisive battle of the Greater Zab (in 750) in which the Abbasides, led by 'Abd (not 'Ubayd) Allāh, defeated the last Umayyad caliph Marwān. The Umayyad (Marwanite) Yaḥyā Ibn Mu'āwiyah refused 'Abd Allāh's offer of safety and preferred to die.

20. According to an apocryphal story (reported by al-Mas'ūdī, *Les prairies d'or*, eds. C. Barbier de Meynard and Pavet de Courteille, Vol. III [Paris, 1864], pp. 189-96), the pre-Islamic Arab queen of Syria, Zenobia (captured by Aurelian in 272), was trapped by the Lakhmid king 'Amr Ibn 'Adī, who was about to kill her in revenge for his maternal uncle, king Jadhīmah, whom she had invited to her court and treacherously murdered. Zenobia sucked at her ring, which contained poison, while addressing 'Amr (read bi-yad for yā with al-Mas'ūdī).

21. Reading khabaruhā for ḥarruhā.

22. Cf. Aristotle *Nicomachean Ethics* iv. 3–4; *Eudemian Ethics* iii. 5; *De Virtutibus et Vitiis* chs. 3, 5. No such story is related by Aristotle in these places.

23. Reading ḥaraqū anfusahum wa-madīnatahum with Narboni.

24. The event took place during the pre-Islamic battle days of Dāḥis (second half of the sixth century).

25. Famous for his hospitality (d. *ca.* 605).

26. Reading yabdhulūn for yubdilūn (change).

27. Reading yakūn for takūn.

9.

Ibn Tufayl

HAYY THE SON OF YAQZAN

Translated by George N. Atiyeh

Ibn Tufayl (Abū Bakr Muḥammad IbnṬufayl, d. 1185) was born in the first decade of the twelfth century in Guadix near Granada. He practiced medicine in the city of Granada, became secretary to the governor of the province of Granada, and in 1154 was appointed by the founder of the Almohad dynasty 'Abd al-Mu'min as secretary to his son Abū Sa'īd, governor of Ceuta and Tangier. He became the chief physician and vizier of the second Almohad prince Abū Ya'qūb (reigned, 1163–1184) who "was most affectionate and friendly to him." "I was told," says the historian al-Marrākushī, "that he [Ibn Tufayl] used to stay with him for many days and nights without leaving the palace." In 1182 he retired as chief physician to be succeeded in this function by his protégé Averroes, whom he had introduced to the prince in 1168/9. After Abū Ya'qūb's death in 1184, his son

and successor Abū Yūsuf seems to have kept Ibn Tufayl as vizier and honored courtier until the latter's death in Marrakesh.

Hayy the Son of Yaqzan is an epistle addressed to a disciple and friend seeking information about the secrets of the Oriental or Illuminative philosophy mentioned by Avicenna. It consists of an introduction, which is a critical survey of the history of Islamic philosophy; the narrative relating the birth of *ḥayy* (alive) the son of *yaqẓān* (awake) and his development on a deserted island; the narrative of the development of *salāmān* (sound?) and *āsāl* (questioner?) in a religious community on a neighboring island; and the narrative of Asal's retirement to Hayy's island, their meeting, their decision to go back to Asal's island to educate and improve the religious community, their failure in their mission, and their return to

Hayy's island. A number of the names and the elements of the story are borrowed from popular Hellenistic stories and from Avicenna's story that bears the same title.

Ibn Tufayl's *Hayy the Son of Yaqzan* was translated into Hebrew by an unknown author; and Moses Narboni wrote a commentary on it in 1349. The Arabic original was first published together with a Latin translation by Edward Pococke, Jr.: *Philosophus Autodictatus, sive Epistola Abi Jaafar ebn Tophail de Hai ebn Yokdan, quomodo ex Inferiorum contemplatione ad Superiorum notitiam Ratio humana ascendere possit* (Oxford, 1671; 2nd ed.: Oxford, 1700). Pococke's Latin version was translated into English by the Quaker George Keith (1674) and by Ashwell (1686). A third English translation, made directly from the Arabic, was done by Simon Ockley: *The Improvement of the Human Reason, Exhibited in the Life of Hai Ebn Yokdhan* (London, 1708). The reason for the interest in this book during that period may be seen in Ockley's subtitle: "In which is demonstrated, by what Methods one may, by the meer *Light of Nature*, attain the Knowledg of things *Natural* and *Supernatural;* more particularly the Knowledg of God, and the Affairs of another Life." Ockley found it useful to add an Appendix "In which the Author's Notion concerning the Possibility of Man's attaining the True Knowledg of God, and Things necessary to Salvation, without the Use of external Means [*Instruction*], is briefly consider'd" because "the preceding History . . . contains several things co-incident with the Errors of some Enthusiasts of these present Times. . . ." The following translation and summary are based on the critical edition of the Arabic text by Léon Gauthier: *Hayy Ben Yaqdhân* (2nd ed.; Beirut, 1936).

[INTRODUCTION]

YOU HAVE ASKED ME, my noble, sincere, and affectionate brother (may God bestow upon you eternal life and infinite happiness), to convey to you what I can of [4] the secrets of the illuminative [or oriental] philosophy referred to by the Leading Master Abū 'Alī Ibn Sīnā [Avicenna]. Know, then, that he who desires to know the perfect truth should seek after this philosophy and assiduously endeavor to possess it.

Your question has awakened in me a noble intention that led me, praise be to God, to partake in the vision of a state I had not experienced before. It made me reach a point so extraordinary that words cannot describe and clear exposition cannot render an account thereof, because it is of an order and realm not belonging to them. Nonetheless, because of the joy, exuberance, and the pleasure radiating from that state, whoever attains it or reaches one of its limits is incapable of remaining reticent about it or of concealing its secret. He is overwhelmed with such rapture, liveliness, gaiety, and cheerfulness that drive him to divulge the gist, though not the details, of its secret.

Now, if the one who experiences this state lacks scientific skill, he will speak about it inconclusively. One such man went so far as to declare while in this state, "Glory to me, how great I am."[1] Another said, "I am the Truth."[2] And still another said, "He who wears this garment is none other than God."[2] As to the Master Abū Ḥāmid [Algazel],[3] when he attained this state, he described it by reciting the following verse:

> What took place, I will not say;
> So take it well, and do not ask for an account.[4] [5]

But then he was a man refined with knowledge and made skillful through the pursuit of science.

Consider, further, the discourse of Abū Bakr Ibn al-Ṣā'igh [Avempace] in connection with his doctrine on the character of conjunction (*ittiṣāl*).[5] He says, "If . . . someone comes to grasp the (intended) meaning, then it becomes evident to him that no knowledge of the ordinary sciences can be placed in the same category. His conception of that meaning takes place on a level in which he finds himself cut off from all that preceded, and holding new convictions free of corporeality, too sublime to be attributed to natural life, and free from the ephemeral composition inherent in natural life. They are rather worthy to be considered as divine states, bestowed by God upon whomsoever He pleases of His servants."[6] This level to which Abū Bakr [Avempace] has alluded is attained by way of theoretical science and by rational investigation. Doubtlessly, he must have attained such a level although he did not go beyond it.

Regarding the level to which we have alluded first, it is different although it is the same in the sense that there is nothing revealed in the first that is not revealed also in the second. The first, however, differs by its superior clarity and in the way it is beheld through something that we call "force," but only metaphorically because we fail to find terms, [6] whether current or technical, that designate the thing by virtue of which that kind of vision is experienced. The state we have just described—of which, moved by your question, we have had a taste (*dhawq*)[7]—is one of the states indicated by the Master Abū 'Alī [Avicenna] when he says, "Then, when by will and discipline one is carried to a limit where he catches delightful glimpses of the Truth, strokes of lightning as it were, which no sooner flash than they disappear. . . . Now, if he persists in his disciplinary practice, these ecstatic glimpses multiply. Then he goes deeper and deeper until he is capable of catching these glimpses without any more discipline. Every time he glances at a thing, he turns toward the August Divinity, and remembers something of that state. An ecstasy takes hold of him until he would see the Truth in almost all things. . . . Finally discipline leads him to the point where his [troubled] time turns into tranquillity. What was only evanescent becomes common and what was just a gleam [7] becomes a shining star. He acquires a firm intimacy, a constant association as it were." He then goes on to describe the orderly gradation of the levels and how they terminate in attaining the goal as the seeker's most intimate soul turns into "a polished mirror facing the Truth." At this point the sublimest pleasures flow upon him, and "the traces left by the Truth" in his soul fill him with happiness. And at this level, he hesitatingly fluctuates between "looking at the Truth and at himself," until finally "all consciousness of himself is lost and he notices nothing but the August Divinity. If he ever happens to glance aside at his soul, he does so only inasmuch as his soul is the glancing agent. . . . It is then that true union takes place."[8] Now by these states that he described, Avicenna intended that he [the initiate] acquire a taste that is not acquired by way of theoretical perception, which results from syllogistic reasoning, the assumption of premises, and the drawing of conclusions.

If you wish a comparison to illustrate the difference between the perception attained by this group of men and that attained by others, then imagine the case of a man born blind, but endowed with keen innate intelligence, penetrating insight, tenacious memory, and determined will. Since the day he is born, he grows up in a [8] certain town. By means of his other powers of perception, he continues to acquaint himself with the individual men living there, the many species of animate and inanimate beings, the streets of the city and alleys that cut through it, its houses, and its markets, to the extent that he can walk around in that city without a guide, and recognize instantly everyone he meets. Colors form an exception; he knows them by means of the explanations of their names and by certain definitions designating them. Then, when he reaches this grade, his eyes are open of a sudden, and his eyesight is restored to him. He runs all over town only to discover that in fact nothing is different from what he has believed it to be, nor does he fail to recognize anything he lays eyes upon. He finds the colors truly corresponding to the descriptions given him. In all this he experiences, nevertheless, two great things, the one a consequence of the other: a greater lucidity and clarity, and an exalted pleasure. The state of the speculators who have not attained the phase of sanctity is comparable to the first state of the blind man; the colors, which, [9] in this state, are known through the description of their names, are comparable to those things of which Abū Bakr [Avempace] said that they are too sublime to be attributed to natural life and that they are bestowed by God upon whomsoever He pleases of His servants. The state of the speculators who attain sanctity and to whom God grants that thing of which we said that it is not called "force" except metaphorically, is the second state.

In very rare cases, one may find someone with piercing intelligence, keen, and not in need of speculation. Here I do not mean—may God bestow His sanctity upon you—by "the perception of the speculators" what they perceive of the physical world and by "the perception of the men of sanctity" what they perceive of the metaphysical, for these two kinds of perception in themselves are very different from each other and it is hardly possible to confound the one with the other. What we mean by the perception of the speculators is what they apprehend of the metaphysical order, such as was apprehended by Abū Bakr [Avempace]. When this perception is true and valid, it is possible to compare it with the perception of the men of sanctity who are concerned with these very same [metaphysical] things, but who perceive them with greater clarity and pleasure. However, [*10*] Abū Bakr [Avempace] censures the men of sanctity for this pleasure and ascribes it to the imaginative faculty. He promised to describe in a clear and precise manner how the state of the happy ones ought to be. One ought to answer him in this context with the saying: "Do not call sweet what you have not tasted, nor step over the necks of the veracious." Our man did not do any of the things he said he would do; he did not fulfil his promise. It seems, as he himself mentions, he was impeded by shortage of time and the trip he took to Wahrān [Oran]. Or, it could be he realized that if he described that state, he would find himself obliged to say things that decry his own conduct, and belie what he had continually maintained concerning the efforts one should exert to accumulate and hoard riches and the use of all kinds of artifices to obtain them.

We have deviated somewhat from the course to which your question had led us, as this seemed necessary. However, it is now clear from what has been said that your goal can only be one of two things: (1) That you are seeking to understand that which is beheld by those who experience the vision, the taste, and the presence [of God] in their moment of sanctity. This is one of those things whose real nature cannot be entrusted to the pages of a book; and once you try to do that, constraining yourself either through the spoken or the written word, the very nature of the experience is altered by passing to [*11*] the other realm, that is, the speculative. Because whenever such an experience is wrapped in sounds and letters and brought nearer to the sensible world, its nature does not remain the same, no matter how we look at it. Hence it lends itself to a great many different and varied expressions. As a result many are led astray from the right path, and others are thought to have gone astray although in reality they have not. This is because [one is trying to explain] an infinite entity within a divine epiphany of enormous dimensions, an epiphany that contains but is not itself contained. (2) The second of the two goals to which your question could possibly lead is that you are seeking that this thing be made known to you in accordance with the method of the speculators. This—may God honor you with sanctity—is a thing that could be entrusted to books and it lends itself to being expressed, although [this knowledge] is rarer than red sulphur, especially in the region we live in [that is, Andalusia and Northwest Africa]. Such [knowledge] is so extremely uncommon that only now and then someone acquires small portions of it. Moreover, whoever comes to acquire any portion of it does not communicate it to others except through symbols. The Ḥanīfite [Islamic] religion and the true [Islamic] Law have prohibited delving into it and warned against pursuing it.

Do not think that the philosophy that reached us [*12*] in the works of Aristotle, Abū Naṣr [Alfarabi], and in [Avicenna's] *Healing* is sufficient to achieve your purpose. Furthermore, no Andalusian has as yet written enough on the subject. This is because all those Andalusians with brilliant talent—and who received their education before the diffusion of logic and philosophy in that country—dedicated themselves to the science of mathematics, reaching a high degree in it. But they were not able to do more than that. The generation that succeeded them went beyond and into the science of logic. They studied it, but it failed to bring them to true perfection. One of them recited:

> Afflicted I am, because all that mortals know
> Are two things and no more;
>
> A truth whose acquisition is impossible,
> And a falsehood whose acquisition is of no use.[9]

Then followed another generation with a greater perspicacity and closer to the truth. There was none among them of a finer genius, of a greater understanding, or of a truer insight than Abū Bakr Ibn al-Ṣā'igh [Avempace]. Yet, the things of this world kept him busy until death overtook him before the treasures of his science could be brought to light and the secrets of his wisdom made available. The greatest part of his extant writings are in an imperfect state and incomplete, [*13*] such as *On the Soul* and the *Governance of the Solitary*, as well as his books on logic and physics. As for his finished works, they include only concise books and hastily written treatises. He himself declared this when he mentioned that the idea he meant to demonstrate in his treatise *On Conjunction* cannot be clearly understood without hard struggle and great effort, that the order of his explanations, in some places, is not the best, and that he was inclined to change them, had time permitted him to do so. This is what has come down to us concerning this man's knowledge; we never met his person. With regard to his contemporaries who are described as being of the same rank as he, we have not found any written works by them. Regarding their successors who are our contemporaries, they are either in the stage of development, or have stopped short of perfection, or else we are not sufficiently informed about them.

As to the books of Abū Naṣr [Alfarabi] that have reached us, the majority are on logic. The ones that deal with philosophy proper are plagued with doubts. For example, he affirms in the *Virtuous Religion* that the souls of the wicked are doomed after death to infinite suffering for an infinite time. Then he declares in the *Political Regime* that they dissolve into nothingness and that only [14] the virtuous and perfect souls survive. Then in his commentary on the *Ethics*, he describes an aspect of human happiness and affirms that this is achieved only in this life and in this very world. He then adds a remark whose meaning can be summed up as follows: all that is said contrary to this is senseless jabber and tales told by old women. A doctrine like this leads all men to despair of God's mercy, and places the wicked and the good in the same category since, according to this doctrine, all men are destined for nothingness. This is a slip that cannot be rectified, and a false step that cannot be remedied. This, aside from his declared disbelief in prophecy, namely, his assertion that it is the exclusive property of the imaginative faculty; and not to mention his preference for philosophy over prophecy, and many other things into which we need not now go.

As for the works of Aristotle, the Master Abū 'Alī [Avicenna] under-took to explain their contents. He followed Aristotle's doctrine and philosophic method in his *Healing*. At the beginning of that book, he declares that the truth in his opinion is otherwise, that the above work expounds the peripatetic teaching, and that he who seeks pure truth should look for it in his [15] *Illuminative* [or *Oriental*] *Philosophy*. He who takes the trouble of reading the *Healing* and the books of Aristotle cannot but recognize their agreement on most points, though there are things in the *Healing* that have not come down to us as Aristotelian. Now, were one to accept the literal meaning of everything presented in the books of Aristotle as well as in the *Healing* without penetrating into the secret and esoteric sense, this would not enable him to attain perfection—as the Master Abū 'Alī [Avicenna] warned us in the *Healing*.

As for the books of the Master Abū Ḥāmid [Algazel], what he says in them depends on his public; he says one thing in one place and a different thing in another. He charges others with unbelief because they hold certain doctrines, then turns about and accepts them as lawful. Among other things, he charges the philosophers with unbelief, in his *Incoherence* [*of the Philosophers*], for their denial of the resurrection of the body and their affirmation that only the souls receive rewards and punishments. But at the outset of his *Criterion* [*of Action*], he says that this very same tenet is definitely held by the Sufi masters. Then, in his *Deliverer from Error and the Explainer of the States*, he says that he himself holds the same belief as the Sufis and that he had arrived

[*16*] at this conviction after a long and detailed study. His books are packed with things of this kind, and anyone who takes the pain to consider and examine them can see that for himself. In fact he apologizes for such conduct at the end of his *Criterion of Action*, where he maintains that opinion is of three classes: (1) An opinion in which one agrees with the multitude. (2) An opinion that is in conformity with the way one addresses all questioners and seekers of counsel. (3) An opinion that one holds intimately within himself, and does not disclose except to those who share his convictions. Then he says: "Even if there were no value in these words except to make you doubt your inherited beliefs, that in itself would be useful enough. He who does not doubt does not look, he who does not look does not see, he who does not see remains blind and perplexed." Then he recites the following verse:

> Accept what you see and let go what you hear;
> When the sun comes out you will need no saturn.[10]

So this is how he presents his teaching. It is mainly symbols and allusions of little use except for the one who is capable of grasping them first by his own perspicacity and then by listening to his [Algazel's] explanations, or the one who is naturally disposed to understand and is endowed with great intelligence and for whom the slightest allusion is enough. He mentions [*17*] in his *Jewels* [*of the Koran*] that he composed some esoteric books in which he incorporated the unveiled truth. But as far as we know none of these books has reached Andalusia. The books that have in fact reached us and are alleged to be his esoteric works, are in reality not so. These books are: the *Intellectual Cognitions* and the *Blowing and Levelling*, and a work in which certain other problems are brought together. Although these books contain certain allusions here and there, they nevertheless contain little else that could reveal more than what is already to be found in his more familiar books. In fact one may find in his *Supreme Purpose* things that are more ambiguous than what is found in these [allegedly esoteric books]. Since he himself declares that the *Supreme Purpose* is not esoteric, it must follow if this is so, that these books that have reached Andalusia are not the esoteric books. A recent author imagines that what is said at the end of the *Niche* [*of Light*] presents a grave difficulty that supposedly caused al-Ghazālī [Algazel] to fall in a pit from which there is no salvation. The reference is to what [Algazel] says after enumerating the different classes of those who are veiled by [divine] lights, and his passing to mention the ones who attained [union with God]—he says that the latter have learned that this Being is characterized by an attribute [*18*] incompatible with pure unity. [Our author] tries to infer from this that [Algazel] must believe in some kind of multiplicity in the very essence of the First Truth (may God be exalted far and above what the unjust say of

Him). We, on the other hand, do not doubt that the Master Abū Ḥāmid [Algazel] was one of those who were blessed with supreme happiness and who have consummated that most honorable of unions [the union with God]. Yet his esoteric books, which contain the science of unveiling [the truth], have not come down to us.

Now the truth at which we have arrived, which was the end of our quest, would have been impossible to obtain had we not scrutinized his [Algazel's] teaching and the teaching of Abū 'Alī [Avicenna], compared the one with the other, and then related both to the opinions that appeared in our times and are being professed by some who pretend to philosophize, until the truth dawned upon us—at first by means of investigation and speculation, and now we enjoy also this slight degree of the taste [that we experienced] through vision. It was at this stage that we felt ourselves worthy of saying something of our own. And we deem it an obligation that you be made the first to be presented with what we have and to be acquainted with what we possess, in recognition of your sincere loyalty and candor. However, to hand you the conclusions at which we arrived before making sure that you possess the principles upon which they rest, will be of as little value to you as giving you a conventional [19] summary. In return, we trust that you will approve what we say because of our intimate friendship rather than because we are worthy of saying things that ought to be accepted. However, we do not accept this level for you, and we will not be content until you achieve a higher one, since this level does not insure salvation, much less the winning of the highest dignities. It is our desire to take you along the same path through which we have passed, and to make you swim in the very sea we had to cross first, until you are carried to where we have been carried. You will then see what we have seen; you will ascertain for yourself all the things we ascertained for ourself. In this way you will not need to make your knowledge dependent upon ours.

This requires an appreciable length of time, freedom from all concerns, and complete dedication to this art. Now, if you are sincerely decided and resolutely set on seeking this end, gratefully will you rise after a *nocturnal journey* [cf. xvii, 1] and blessed will be your endeavor. Both your Lord and yourself will be *satisfied* [cf. lviii, 22]. I will be at your side as you expect,[11] to guide you along [20] the shortest road and the one safest from mishaps and accidents, although now I am only pointing to a little glimpse just to stimulate and exhort you to get going. I shall narrate to you the story of Ḥayy the son of Yaqẓān and of Asāl and Salāmān, who are mentioned by the Master Abū 'Alī [Avicenna].[12] In *their story is surely a lesson for men of understanding* [xii, 111], and *surely in that there is a reminder to him who has a heart, or will give ear with a present mind* [l, 37].

[Summary of the Tale]

After this introduction, Ibn Tufayl proceeds to narrate the experiences of Hayy the son of Yaqzan. Starting with his birth, he offers the reader a choice between two alternative accounts. According to the first, Hayy would have been born on a desert island south of the equator, not from a father and a mother, but from clay in fermentation. The author expounds the importance of the island's perfect geographic position and temperate climate in order to indicate the possibility of spontaneous human generation without the need for mother and father. According to the second story, Hayy would be the illegitimate son of a princess and daughter of the tyrant of a large inhabited island next to the desert island. In order to save him from certain death if she were discovered, she puts him in a box and entrusts him to the waves. Overnight the tides toss it on the desert island. The author then gives a detailed description of the successive phases in the spontaneous generation of the human embryo, following the account of those who hold the first version. First the clay ferments, then sticky and aerated bubbles appear, a heart is formed from the bubbles, and finally a soul descends from heaven and enters the heart. There follows a comparison between the soul and the continually emanating light of the sun. The soul sheds its light on the human body, whereas the sun sheds its light on the different classes of substance that constitute this world. The two stories coincide from here on.

Then the author begins his description of Hayy's self-education. A gazelle who had lost her doe hastens to the sound of a crying baby. She adopts, feeds, and raises him until he is over seven years old. As the boy, endowed with keen intelligence, grows up, he begins to observe nature and the animal world around him. To provide for his needs, he learns how to dress himself, how to shelter himself, and also how to domesticate animals. One day, however, the gazelle dies. Frightened, but wanting to save her, he reasons that the gazelle's inertness must be due to an invisible impediment. He decides to open her up and look for the seat of the impediment. He finds it in the left ventricle of the heart. He discovers that the obstacle is nothing but the permanent departure of a vital principle located in the ventricle. And that leads him to think of the body as a mere instrument of a life-sustaining principle, without which the body is nothing. After burying his "mother," he wonders what that principle is, what unites it to the body, and where it goes. For a time he roams around the island until one day he sees a fire break out in a bush. Taking a firebrand to the cave in which he now lives, he keeps it alive night and day. He studies the properties of the flame and observes that it tends to go upward and to radiate warmth. This convinces him that it belongs by nature to the celestial bodies and that it may somehow be related to the life-sustaining principle. In order to find out whether that principle possesses things like fire, light, and heat, he opens the heart of a living animal. In the left ventricle, which he had found empty in the heart of the gazelle, he senses with his finger a whitish vapor of such warmth that his finger is almost burned. The immediate death of the animal convinces him that the hot vapor is the principle of motion in all living beings, and that its absence spells death. Devoured with curiosity, he now wants to know how this vapor holds together and how it imparts life to all the bodily organs. Hayy dissects live and dead animals until his scientific knowledge equals that of the greatest naturalists. He recognizes that what gives unity to the body, in spite of the multiplicity of its parts and the variety of its sensations and movements, is the animal spirit radiating from a central abode and using the bodily organs as instruments to perform specific functions.

When Hayy reaches his twenty-first birthday, he has already learned how to stew meat, dress, use a knife made from the spines of fish, build himself a refuge, and domesticate animals. But then his mind begins to move from the consideration of the physical order of things to the metaphysical. He starts with the world of generation and corruption. After examining all kinds of objects such as animals, plants, and minerals, he notices that they possess a great variety of attributes and perform a number of varied functions; moreover, their movements are either concordant or discordant. Looking at them carefully, he notices that they coincide in certain attributes but differ in others. They form a unity if one looks at them from the angle of their congruencies, and form a multiplicity if one looks at them from the angle of their discrepancies. He observes in every animal a certain unity in spite of the multiplicity of its parts. Also, all classes of animals coincide in sensation, in the need for food, and in voluntary motion, all of which are functions of the animal spirit. This must be, he thinks, one in essence in spite of the small differences that exist between the species. He then mentally reduces the animal and vegetable kingdoms to their smallest units; and in the inanimate kingdom he observes a tighter unity in all corporeal bodies. From the attributes common to corporeal bodies, he infers the general notion of a body as a three-dimensional extension. He begins then to look for

that quality which makes a body, that is, the essence of a body. He had observed that bodies are either light or heavy. Nonetheless, these two attributes, lightness and heaviness, do not belong to the body as body; they are added to corporeality, which is common to all bodies. This is how Hayy arrives at the notion of form and thus comes nearer to the spiritual world. He comes to realize that a body, aside from being an extension, is also a form, and that a substance is made up of matter, extension, and form. He discovers along with this duality in substance the notion of a first matter that is apt to receive all forms through change. Now, if bodies change, that is, if the same matter receives different forms, this implies a giver of forms. He looks for a giver of forms among the bodies that surround him, but he realizes that they are all *produced*, which implies the existence of a *producer*.

When Hayy reaches his twenty-eighth year, he looks into the sky and among the stars, but comes to the conclusion that the sky and what is in it are all corporeal since they all have length, width, and depth. He proves to himself that an infinite body is impossible. He later demonstrates to himself that the celestial body is finite, and tries to find out what form the sky could have. He arrives at the conclusion that it is spherical in shape, but composed of a series of concentric spheres, the outermost of which causes the movement of the rest. He also infers that the world is a huge animal. Asking himself whether the world is eternal or produced in time, he finds that there are two plausible answers to this question, which he leaves unanswered. But in each case he is led to the conclusion that there exists a necessary being who is the creator of all other beings and who is exempt from all corporeal qualities and inaccessible to the senses or the imagination. He maintains the world and is superior to it in the order of His being as well as by His eternity. Hayy then determines the degree of His power on all created things, also His eternity and omnipotency. He finds Him, furthermore, endowed with complete perfection and exempt from all imperfection.

When Hayy reaches his thirty-fifth year, he is completely absorbed in thinking about this producer. Sure of the existence of a Perfect Being, Hayy wants to find out how he came to know Him. He realizes that he could not have known Him through the senses. These, being divisible, are not capable of knowing what is indivisible, spiritual, and not subject to corruption. He must have come to know Him through something to which corporeality cannot be attributed, and that must be the very essence of his own being, that is, his soul. This, consequently, is indivisible, spiritual, and not subject to corruption. After he reaches the knowledge that his soul is not subject to corruption, he wants to know what happens to it after it departs from the body. Examining all the faculties of perception, he finds out that they perceive sometimes in actuality and at other times in potentiality. Whenever the perception is in a state of potentiality, it desires to pass into actuality, this being a state more perfect than potentiality. In fact, the more perfect a being is, the greater is the craving for actuality and the sadness at being deprived of it. He thus comes to know that the Necessary Being is perfect and exempt from all privation, and that He is known by something whose nature is unlike the corporeal bodies. This leads him to see that the perfection of the soul consists in the constant use of reason in this life. If, on the other hand, one does not use reason, his soul becomes a nothingness after death. Also, if he has known the Necessary Being, but turned away from Him in order to follow his passions, he will be deprived of the intuitive vision and will suffer infinitely; whereas if one turns wholly toward God and dies while enjoying the intuitive vision, he will enjoy eternal bliss. These considerations lead Hayy to seek divine ecstasy by concentrating his thoughts on the Necessary Being. However, the senses, sensible images, plus the physical needs of the body, would obstruct him. He is afraid death would overtake him while he is still being distracted from the Necessary Being. Hoping to find a remedy for his plight, he examines the actions and goals of all animals to find out whether they seek after God so that he could learn from them how to save himself. To his dismay, he discovers that they do not seek after God. He next examines the celestial bodies and finds out that they possess an intelligent substance, like his, and that they eternally behold the Necessary Being. Among all the animals, he thinks of himself as the only one who could know the Necessary Being. The reason lies in his possession of a perfectly balanced substance that abides in the heart and presents unmistakable similarities to the celestial bodies. Moreover, he realizes that he resembles, on the one hand, the Necessary Being through that noble part of himself—the immaterial intelligent substance, his soul—and, on the other, the animals through that vile part of himself that is his body. From this he concludes that his action should be carried out on three levels: (1) the actions emulating those of the animals, (2) those emulating the celestial bodies, and (3) those emulating the Necessary Being [20-107].

[HAYY'S THREE EMULATIONS]

He was obliged to undertake the first emulation by virtue of having a murky body with separable members, different faculties, and a variety of passions. He was obliged to undertake the second emulation by virtue of his animal spirit, which has its seat in the heart and which is a principle for the whole body and the faculties existing in it. He was obliged to undertake the third emulation by virtue of his being what he is, that is, by virtue of being the essence through which he came to know the Necessary Being. He had come to know before that his happiness and his triumph over misery consisted in a continuous intuitive vision of this Necessary Being and not parting from it for so much as the twinkling of an eye. Then he considered the means by which this continuity might be secured, and his considerations led him to conclude the necessity of continuous practice in the three levels of emulation. The first emulation, he realized, could not contribute to his acquiring any portion of [*108*] this vision, but on the contrary it was a deterrent and a hindrance to it because it concerned sensible things, and all sensible things are curtains that interfere with that vision. The reason for practicing such an emulation, therefore, was to preserve the animal spirit that makes possible the second emulation, namely, emulating the celestial bodies. Sheer necessity demands that one take this road, although it is not exempt from the harm indicated. Through the second emulation, he realized, he might obtain a great portion of this continuous vision. However, it is an adulterated vision since whosoever beholds after this manner of vision, remains, while experiencing the vision, conscious of his own essence and turns toward it, as will be shown afterwards. Finally, through the third emulation one might obtain pure vision and absolute absorption, without being diverted from it in any direction except in the direction of the Necessary Being. The very essence of the one who experiences this vision disappears from his consciousness, it melts and fades away, and so do all the other essences, irrespective of their number, except the essence of the One, the True, the Necessary [*109*] Being (may His name be exalted).

Now it became clear to him that his ultimate end consists in the third emulation, that this is not obtained without long exercise and practice in the second, and that the continuation of the second depends on his first emulation. And he also realized that the first emulation, although necessary, is as such a hindrance and a help only accidentally. Consequently, he forced himself to reduce the first emulation to bare necessity, that is, the strictly required amount below which the animal spirit would not subsist. He found two things necessary for the subsistence

of the animal spirit. One, what maintains it internally by restoring what
is wasted of it, namely food. The other, what preserves it externally
and guards it against all kinds of possible damage coming from cold,
heat, rain, sunburn, harmful animals, and the like. And he perceived
that if he were to take his necessities from these elements haphazardly,
he would fall into excess and take more than the strictly required amount.
He might thus [*110*] injure himself unawares. Whereupon he thought
it prudent to set for himself certain limits that he would not pass and
measures that he would not exceed; and it became clear to him that
this prescription should apply to the kind, content, and quantity of his
nourishment as well as its frequency.

Examining first the types of his food, he discovered that they are
three in number: (1) Either plants that have not yet finished, or reached
the limit of, their growth—that is, the different kinds of green vegetables
proper for nourishment. (2) Fruit of the plants that have reached their
full growth and developed seeds for the reproduction of the same
species—that is, the different kinds of fruit, fresh or dry. (3) Or some
kind of edible animal, either terrestrial or marine. Hayy had ascertained
that all these types of food are made by the Necessary Being; and it
had become evident to him that his happiness consists in the nearness
to, and the desire to imitate Him. Doubtless, he thought, to eat these
different foods [*111*] must prevent them from reaching their perfection
and obstruct the realization of the end for which they are destined. This
would be like an objection against the work of the Maker, an objection
that is contrary to what he was seeking—the nearness to, and emulation
of, Him. He perceived that the correct thing for him to do, if possible,
would be to abstain from eating altogether. But this was impossible. He
found that by completely abstaining from eating, his body tended to
dissolve, a thing that constituted a much greater objection against his
Maker than the former; since he is nobler [by nature] than the other
things whose very destruction is the cause of his preservation. He chose
the lesser of the two evils and indulged in the milder of the two objections. Now, it seemed proper to him that, whenever some of these
classes of food are not available, he should partake of whatever can
be obtained, and in quantities that he will decide about later. But if all
the classes of food are available, then he should make sure to choose
those foods whose consumption will not constitute a major objection
against the work of the Maker, such as the flesh of fully ripe fruit
whose seeds have so matured as to produce [*112*] others of the same
class. But always with the condition that he preserve the seeds by not
eating them or spoiling them or throwing them in places not fit for
plants to grow in, such as rocks, briny soil, and the like. And whenever
such fruit with nourishing flesh—such as apples, plums, and the like—
are not accessible, he should then eat of those fruits that had nothing

edible in them but their seeds—such as walnuts and chestnuts or the vegetables that had not yet reached the limit of their perfect growth— but on condition in both cases that he should prefer the vegetables that are more abundant and endowed with greater force of reproduction. He was never to extract any of their roots or destroy their seeds. And if none of these [edible plants] was to be had, then he could take some animals or their eggs, on condition—inasmuch as the animals were con- cerned—that he take the more numerous and not exterminate any one species. This was what he considered prudent in regard to the kind of his nourishment. Regarding the quantity, he perceived that it should be in accordance with what satisfies a man's hunger and no more. As to the lapse of time between meals, he ruled that once he had satisfied [*113*] his needs, he was to remain content with that and not touch any- thing until he suffered a weakness that would hinder him from the performance of some of the actions to which he was committed in the second emulation and that will be mentioned afterwards. Regarding the necessities required for the subsistence of the animal spirit, protecting it from external harm, he had very little to worry about, for he clothed himself with skins and he had a dwelling that protected him against external harm. This satisfied him, and hence he did not see any further need to worry about it. And as far as his diet was concerned, he observed the rules he had set for himself, which we have already explained.

Then he applied himself to the second exercise—that is, to emulate the celestial bodies, imitate them, acquire their attributes, and look for their qualities, which he found to be of three kinds. First, the qualities the celestial bodies possess by virtue of the relations they maintain with what is below them in the world of generation and corruption: impart- ing heat, by essence, and cold, by accident, illumination, rarefaction, condensation, and the other actions [*114*] by means of which they dispose the things of this world to receive the overflow of the spiritual forms from the Agent, the Necessary Being. The second kind of qualities are qualities that belong to their very essence—such as that they are translucent, luminous, pure, free from turbidness and any kind of vile- ness, and that they move circularly, some of them moving around their own center and some around the center of another. The third kind of qualities are the ones they possess by virtue of their relation to the Necessary Being, such as that they possess continuous vision of Him without any deviation, and that they yearn for Him and act according to His command, constrain themselves in order to do His will, and do not move save in accordance with His wish and within His control. So he proceeded to emulate them [the celestial bodies] in every one of these three kinds of qualities to the utmost of his power.

In the first case, his emulation of the celestial bodies consisted in obliging himself, whenever he could, to remove [the cause of the plight] of every animal or plant he sees to be in need, diseased, injured, or facing an impediment. Thus whenever he saw a plant that was deprived of sunlight by the interference of another object, or that was entwined with another harmful plant, or that was suffering from extreme dryness, he would remove the object [115] if it was something that could be removed, and he would separate the harmful plant from the other without injuring the harmful one, and he would take care to water it whenever that was possible. Whenever he happened to see any animal endangered by a wild beast, or trapped in a snare, or pricked with thorns, or that had something harmful fallen into its eyes or ears, or was hungry or thirsty, he would take infinite care to relieve it and give it food and drink. Or whenever he happened to see any watercourse, flowing to irrigate a plant or to quench the thirst of an animal, stopped by a stone that has fallen in it or by a fallen cliff, he took care to remove all that. He persisted in this kind of emulation until he attained its highest end.

In the second case, his emulation consisted in obliging himself to remain pure, to remove all dirt and filth from his body, washing himself often and keeping his nails, teeth, and the hidden parts of his body clean, and perfuming himself [116] with every kind of fragrant herb and all sorts of aromatic pomades that he could find. He took care to maintain his clothes clean and fragrant until he was resplendent with beauty, cleanliness, and fragrance. In addition, he took upon himself to perform all sorts of circular movements. One time he would walk around the island compassing its shores and journeying to its remotest areas. Sometimes he would walk or run around his house or a rock for a number of times. At other times he would spin himself until he lost consciousness.

In the third case, his emulation of the celestial bodies consisted in concentrating his thoughts on the Necessary Being and suppressing all connection with the sensible world. He would close his eyes, stop his ears, and restrain himself from following his imagination. He would wish, to the utmost of his power, to think of nothing else but Him, and to associate nobody with Him. To accomplish this, he would have recourse to spinning himself more rapidly. As his spinning increased, sensible objects would vanish out of his sight, his imagination would grow weaker and so would all the faculties that make use of [117] bodily organs. Meanwhile, the work of his essence, which is independent of the body, grew stronger; so that at times his thoughts freed themselves from all confusion, and he beheld the Necessary Being. But the corporeal faculties would return upon him and spoil this state for him, bringing him back to the lowest of levels; thus he would go back to his former condition. Whenever he felt any weakness that interrupted him from pursuing his purpose, he partook of some food, but always according to the established conditions. Henceforth he moved to the performance of his emulation of the celestial bodies in the three mentioned respects. He applied himself assiduously to this for some time, struggling against his corporeal faculties—just as they were resisting him. Whenever he got the better of them and his thoughts were free from confusion, he briefly experienced something of the state of those who have attained the third emulation.

Then he started to seek after the third emulation and tried hard to attain it by pondering over the attributes of the Necessary Being. He had come to know, during the period of his [*118*] scientific speculation on the subject before he had entered upon any action, that these attributes were of two kinds: positive, such as knowledge, power, and wisdom; and negative, such as His complete freedom from corporeality and from the bodily attributes, and from whatever adheres to these attributes or is related to them even remotely. The negative attributes are a condition that renders the positive attributes absolutely exempt from the attributes of the bodies, one of which is multiplicity, so that His essence would not be multiplied by these positive attributes, and so that all of them would be reduced to a single notion which is that of His real essence. He started thereupon to seek a way by which to emulate Him in both these kinds [of attributes]. As for the positive attributes, when he came to know that they are all to be reduced to His real essence and that they are free from multiplicity in every respect —since multiplicity is one of the attributes of bodies—and that His knowledge of His essence is not a notion superimposed on His essence, but that His essence is His knowledge of His essence and His knowledge of His essence is His essence, it became evident to him that if he could know his own essence, the knowledge with which he would come to know it could not be something superimposed on his essence, but identical with it. Therefore he perceived that to emulate Him in His positive attributes would be to know Him alone without association with [*119*] any of the corporeal attributes. He took it upon himself to do exactly that. As for the negative attributes, they are all reduced to exemption from the corporeal.

He began therefore to strip himself of all corporeal attributes. He had cast off a great deal of them during his former exercises in which he sought to emulate the celestial bodies. However, a great many relics had been left, such as spinning around—and movement is one of the most characteristic attributes of bodies—and his care for animals and plants, the feeling of pity toward them, and the preoccupation he had to remove whatever inconvenienced them. The latter, too, are corporeal attributes. For, to begin with, they can be seen only with the help of

a corporeal faculty. Furthermore, the hard labor they require is performed with a corporeal faculty too. Therefore he began to rid himself
of all this, for it is in no way befitting the state to which he now aspired.
Henceforth he confined his activities to repose in the bottom of his
cave with his head tilted down, his eyes closed, disregarding all sensible
things and all corporeal faculties, concentrating all his effort and thoughts
on the Necessary Being alone, without associating Him with anything
whatsoever. Whenever a thought that was not of God crossed his
imagination, he tried to drive it away [120] and put it off with all his
force. He exercised himself in this, persisting for a long time, so much
so that several days would pass without his having anything to eat and
without ever stirring. At those moments when he would reach a high
pitch in his exercise, all things might vanish from his memory and
thought except his own essence, which would continue to be present
when he was deeply immersed in the vision of the True Being, the
Necessary Being.

This used to cause him great concern, for he knew that it was a
mixture perturbing the sure vision and an intrusion in the observation
[of Him]. Nevertheless, he kept seeking the disappearance of his soul
and the utmost sincerity in his vision of the Truth, until finally he
achieved what he was after. Thereupon, *the sky, the earth, and everything that is between* [xv, 85; lxxviii, 37], vanished from his memory
and thought. And so did all the spiritual forms[13] and corporeal faculties
and all the powers separate from the elements, namely the essences that
know the True Being. Also, his own essence disappeared like the other
essences. The universe vanished and dwindled away, *a scattered dust*
[lvi, 6]. There remained only the One, the True Being, the Permanent
Being, and he recited His speech (which is not a notion superimposed
on His essence): "*Whose is the Kingdom today?*" "*God's, the One, the
Omnipotent*" [xl, 16]. He understood [121] His words and heard His call,
and not even his ignorance of words and his inability to speak could
hinder the understanding of Him. He immersed himself in this state, and
beheld "that which no eye has ever seen nor an ear ever listened to,
neither has it ever presented itself to the heart of a man."[14]

Do not let your heart be chained to the description of something
that has never presented itself to the heart of a man. Many are the things
that present themselves to the heart of a man but are hard to describe.
How much harder, therefore, would be the description of something
that has no chance of ever presenting itself to the heart, and that is
not of the same world nor of the same category. And I do not mean
by "heart" the body out of which the heart is constituted or the spirit
contained in its ventricle, but rather the form of the spirit whose
powers extend throughout the body. Now, each one of these three

things might be called "heart," but it is impossible for this thing [ecstasy] to occur to any of these three. And yet there is no way of expressing anything beyond what occurs to these three. Therefore, he who seeks to express this state is seeking the impossible. He is like someone who wants to taste the dyed colors inasmuch as they are colors, and at the same time requests that black should taste, for example, sweet or [*122*] sour. However, in spite of all this, we will not let you go without some allusions by which we shall hint at the wonderful things Hayy saw when he was in that station. We will do this in the form of an allegory without knocking upon the door of the truth; for there is no other way to ascertain what is in that station without actually reaching it. So listen now with the ear of your heart to what I shall indicate to you and gaze at it with your mind's eye; perhaps you will find in it some form of guidance that may bring you to the highway. I demand that you not ask me at present for any oral explanation in addition to what I have entrusted to these pages. For my hands are tied, and it is dangerous to express arbitrarily something that cannot be expressed.

[Summary of the Tale—continued]

Hayy, in spite of his superior intelligence and philosophic preparation, falls into the error of identifying himself with God. But with the help of divine mercy, he corrects his error. Furthermore, he comes to understand that the separate essences cannot be said to be one or multiple, since they are beyond the reach of any human logical classification and since the divine world can only be known through vision. Reason only observes the particulars and abstracts universal notions from them. Then the author describes in an allegorical form the descending hierarchy of the separate essences that Hayy perceives during his ecstasy, namely, the intelligences of the spheres, the fixed stars, and those of all the other spheres until one reaches the sublunary world. They are compared to a series of mirrors of diminishing perfection that reflect from the first to the last the image of the divine essence in a descending order of clarity. The mirror of the sublunary world is the last and least perfect of them all. The image of the divine essence seems to be reflected in it as in troubled waters and divided into a multitude of indefinite individual essences each of which is united to a body (this refers to human souls), some virtuous and happy, the others perverse and miserable. However, one should not think that these souls disappear when the body to which they are united disappears, as happens to the image reflected in a mirror once the mirror is destroyed. The comparison should not be taken literally since it is not the body that sustains the soul, but the soul the body. Likewise, since the sensible world is sustained by the divine, it necessarily follows the divine world just as the shadow necessarily follows the body [122-34].

[CONCLUSION]

This is as much as I could indicate to you now concerning what Hayy the son of Yaqzan intuitively beheld in that noble station. Do not expect any more than this through mere words. For this is almost impossible. As for the rest of his story, that I will tell you.

After he had come back to the sensible world from the excursions he had undertaken, he became weary of the concerns of this life and he strongly yearned for the ultimate life. He sought to return to that station through the same means by which he had sought it at first, till he was able to attain it with less effort than before and also to stay there longer than he had stayed before. Then he returned to the sensible world, and [*135*] attempted later to attain his station once more and attained it with less effort than in both the first and the second preceding attempts, and his stay there was longer too. And so it grew easier and easier for him to attain that noble station and to continue in it longer and longer until he could attain it whenever he pleased and stay in it for as long as he pleased. He used to keep himself in that station and not turn away from it except when the necessities of his body, which he had cut down to the bare minimum, demanded it. In all this, he used to wish that it would please God, the Mighty and Majestic, to deliver him altogether from his body, which caused his separation from that station, so as to give himself up perpetually to his [supreme] pleasure and so as to be relieved from the pain he suffered every time he had to retire from his station to attend to the necessities of the body. He continued in this state of affairs until he was past the seventh septenary of his birth, that is, he was fifty years old. Then he happened to come together with Asal; the story of what took place between them will be narrated—God willing—in what follows.

It is told that on an island close to [*136*] the one on which Hayy the son of Yaqzan was born—according to one of the two different accounts of the circumstances of his birth—there arrived one of the true religions received from one of the old prophets—upon whom be the blessings of God. It was a religion that imitated all the true beings through parables that present images of those things and establish their descriptions in the souls, as is customary in addressing the multitude. This religion continued to spread on the island and kept growing and gaining in power until the king adopted it himself and made the people embrace it.

Now there had grown in that island two young men of virtue and good will, called respectively Asal and Salaman, who embraced that religion and accepted it eagerly. They took it upon themselves to observe all its Laws and to follow regularly its practices; this formed the basis of their friendship. Sometimes they used to study the wording of that religious Law concerning the attributes of God, the Mighty and Majestic, and His angels, and also the character of resurrection, rewards, and punishments. Of the two, Asal delved deeper into the esoteric meaning; he was more apt to find [137] spiritual notions, and was a more ambitious interpreter. As for Salaman, he was more apt to keep to the apparent meaning, to avoid interpretation, and to abstain from examination and reflection. However, both assiduously performed the external practices [of the religious Law], disciplined themselves, and controlled their passions.

Now there were in this religious Law certain arguments that favored seclusion and solitude, indicating that these led to salvation and [ultimate] success; and there were other arguments that favored sociability and adherence to the whole body of the community (*jamā'ah*). Asal devoted himself to the search for seclusion and favored the argument for it, because he was naturally inclined to continued meditation, to heeding the warnings [of the religious Law], and to penetrating deeply into the meanings [of the things mentioned in it]; and it was through solitude that he most frequently accomplished these objectives. Salaman, on the other hand, devoted himself to adhering to the whole body of the community and favored the argument for this position, because he was naturally timid as regards thought and examination. Following the majority, he thought, would lead to the suppression of evil thoughts and the removal of the promptings of the devil. Their differences on this issue caused [138] them to separate.

Asal had heard about the island on which it was said that Hayy the son of Yaqzan was formed. He knew also of its fertility, conveniences, and temperate climate, and that the one who seeks solitude can achieve it there. Resolved to move there and to retire from the company of men for the rest of his life, he gathered together what money he possessed; with a part of it he hired a ship to carry him to that island, and the rest he distributed among the poor. He bade farewell to his friend [Salaman] and went aboard. The mariners transported him to the island, set him ashore, and withdrew. Asal remained there worshiping God, the Mighty and Majestic, magnifying Him, sanctifying Him, and meditating upon His most beautiful names and exalted attributes without any interruption in the presence of his mind or disturbance in his thoughts. Whenever he felt the need for food, he took from the fruits or game of the island enough to satisfy his hunger. He remained in this state a while, enjoying the most complete felicity and the greatest delight through an intimate intercourse with his Lord, experiencing every day His kindness, the excellence of His gifts, and the ease with which He enabled him to satisfy his necessary needs and nourishment— all of which confirmed his belief in Him and consoled Asal's heart. [139]

In the meantime, Hayy the son of Yaqzan was wholly immersed in his sublime stations. He never left his cave but once a week to take whatever nourishment was at hand. This is the reason why Asal did not discover his presence at first; he used to walk around the island and go over all its parts without seeing a human being or observing the traces of any footsteps. This swelled his joy and gladdened his heart as he was firmly resolved to lead the most retired and solitary life that was possible, until Hayy the son of Yaqzan happened to go out one day to seek his provisions at a place where Asal happened to be. They both spied one another. Asal did not entertain any doubt but that Hayy was a retired worshiper who must have come to that island in search of solitude as he himself had done, and feared that should he come up and make his acquaintance, this might disturb Hayy's state and disrupt the pursuit he was engaged in. Hayy the son of Yaqzan, on the other hand, did not know what Asal was; for of all the animals [*140*] he had seen, he had never seen anything with such a form. Now Asal had on a black coat made out of hair and wool, which Hayy the son of Yaqzan thought was a natural part of him and at which he stood wondering for quite a while. Asal turned and fled from fear that he might distract Hayy. But Hayy the son of Yaqzan ran after him out of his natural curiosity to look for the truth of things. When he saw that Asal began to run faster, he slowed down and hid himself from him, so that Asal thought he had left him and gone off far from the place where he was. Asal then proceeded with his prayer, recitation, invocation, supplication, and lamentation, until this made him forget everything else. Then Hayy the son of Yaqzan started to draw closer and closer, with Asal unaware of his presence, until he came so close as to hear his recitation and praise [of God], observing in him a sense of humility and that he was weeping. Hayy heard a pleasant voice and harmonious sounds such as he had never heard before in any kind of animal. Then he considered Asal's shape and lineaments and saw that he was of the same form as himself. He also found that the coat he had on was not a natural skin but an artificial attire like [*141*] his own. Upon watching the sincere humility of Asal, his supplication and weeping, he did not doubt but that he was one of those essences who know the True One. He felt himself seized by an affection toward him and a desire to know what was the matter with him, and what caused his weeping. He drew closer to him till Asal felt his presence and took to flight. Hayy the son of Yaqzan chased him energetically until he caught up with him—as the result of the vigor and the capacity, intellectual as well as physical, that God had bestowed upon him—seized him, held him fast, and would not let go of him. When Asal looked at him and saw that he was clothed with animal furs, his hair grown so long as to cover a great part of his body, and perceived his alertness and great strength, he trembled from fear and began to implore and entreat him with words that Hayy the son of Yaqzan could not understand and did not know what they were meant to convey. He could, however, see the signs of alarm on Asal's face; whereupon he endeavored to allay his fear with such voices as he had learned from some of the animals. He stroked his head and both sides of his neck, and caressed him, showing him a great joy and gladness, until Asal's agitation calmed and he understood that he meant him no harm.

Asal had formerly [*142*] studied most languages as a result of his love for the science of interpretation and had become an expert in them. So he began to speak to Hayy the son of Yaqzan in every language he knew, asking him about himself and trying to make himself understood, but without success. Hayy the son of Yaqzan wondered all the while at what he heard, not knowing what it was. Nevertheless, he showed gladness and good disposition; and they mutually wondered at each other. Asal had conserved some of the provisions he had brought along from the inhabited island. He offered it to Hayy the son of Yaqzan, who, having never seen such food before, did not know what it was. Asal ate a little of it and signaled Hayy to eat too. Hayy the son of Yaqzan remembered the dietary obligation he had resolved to abide by. Not knowing the constitution of the food he had been offered, nor whether or not he should permit himself to partake of it, he declined to eat. Asal, nonetheless, kept asking him and urging him beseechingly. As Hayy the son of Yaqzan had become fond of Asal and was afraid lest he might be vexed if he should continue to refuse, he went ahead and ate some of the food. As soon as [*143*] he had tasted it and liked it, Hayy realized that he had done wrong by violating the covenant he made with himself as regards diet. He repented what he did and wanted to separate from Asal and go back to his former condition, seeking to return to his sublime station. But he could not attain the vision quickly. Thereupon he decided to stay with Asal in the sensible world until he discovered what he really was and until he felt no more desire to be with him, after which he might apply himself to his station without any interruption. Thus he remained in the company of Asal. Now as Asal perceived Hayy's inability to speak, he felt secure since no harm could threaten his faith from his company. He hoped to instruct him in speaking, in science, and in the faith, so that he [Asal] might obtain a great reward and be favored by God. Asal began to teach him how to speak, first, by pointing at particular beings and pronouncing their names, repeating them several times, and then making Hayy pronounce them. Hayy pronounced them at the same time as he in turn pointed to each being, until Asal taught him all the names. He helped him to improve gradually, until, in a very short time, Hayy could speak.

Then Asal began to ask him about his condition, and whence he came [*144*] to that island. Hayy the son of Yaqzan told him he knew nothing of his origin, nor of a father or a mother beyond the gazelle that reared him. Then Hayy described his experiences from beginning to end, and how he ascended in knowledge until he attained a degree of union [with God]. Asal heard him describe those truths and the essences separate from the sensible world, which know the essence of the Truth, the Mighty and Majestic. Then Hayy described the essence of the Truth, the Exalted and Majestic, with His beautiful qualities. And finally Hayy described, as far as he could, what he beheld when he attained union [with God], the joys of those who unite [with God], and the pains of those who are veiled from Him. After hearing all this, Asal had no doubt that all the things given in his own religious Law concerning God, the Mighty and Majestic, His angels, His books, His messengers, the last day, and His paradise and hell, are the similitudes of these things that Hayy the son of Yaqzan had beheld. The eye of his heart was thereby opened, the fire of his mind kindled. He found that reason and tradition agree, and he found a better access to the ways of interpretation. There remained not one difficulty in the religious Law that he did not now see clearly, nor anything locked up that was not opened, nor anything obscure that did not become plain. Thereupon he passed into the ranks of the *men of understanding* [xii, 111]. From that moment, Asal looked upon Hayy the son of [*145*] Yaqzan with veneration and respect, and he was convinced that Hayy was one of the saints of God who *need have no fear, neither shall they suffer* [ii, 38, 262, 274]. He took it upon himself to wait upon him, to follow in his steps, and to accept his directions in regard to the fulfilment of the religious-legal practices that his religion had taught him, but had seemed to be contradictory.

Hayy the son of Yaqzan, in his turn, began to inquire from him about himself and his present condition. Whereupon Asal proceeded to describe the island from which he came, the people who inhabit it, and their way of life before and after religion reached them. He described to him all the content of the religious Law concerning the divine world, paradise, hell, the quickening of the dead, the resurrection, the assembly for a final judgment, the balance, and the bridge.[15] Hayy the son of Yaqzan understood all this, not finding in it anything that disagreed with what he had intuitively seen in his sublime station. He recognized that the one who described these things and brought them forth was truthful in his description, veridical in his words, and a messenger from his Lord. He believed in him, accepted his truthfulness, and bore witness to his mission.

Then he began to find out from Asal what were the acts of worship that he [the messenger] ordained as duties. Asal described prayer, almsgiving, fasting, pilgrimage, and similar [*146*] external practices. Hayy accepted them, and he took it upon himself to carry them out in compliance with the command of whose author's veracity he had become convinced. There only remained two points that kept him wondering and whose wisdom he could not understand. One point was why this messenger, in the greatest part of his description of the divine world, used parables? Why he avoided the clear disclosure [of the truth] and thus led men to fall into the great error of attributing corporeality to Him and believe certain things about the essence of the Truth from which He is completely exempt? And why he did the same concerning rewards and punishments? The other point was why he confined himself to those duties and acts of worship and permitted acquisition of wealth and excessive consumption of food so that people gave themselves up to vain occupations and turned away from the Truth. Hayy's own opinion was that nobody ought to eat anything more than necessary to keep body and soul together. As for riches, they meant nothing to him. He saw no point to the [*147*] rules of the religious Law in regard to wealth, such as alms-giving in its various forms, trading, and usury, and in regard to penalties and punishments. All this he found strange and considered it superfluous. He said that if people understood the truth of the matter they would avoid these vanities, turn toward the Truth, and dispense with all this. Nobody will then own private property for which alms would have to be paid, hands cut off for stealing it, or people die for robbing it. What misled Hayy was his belief that all men were endowed with excellent natures, clear-sighted sagacity, and resolute souls. He was not aware how stupid, deficient, ill-opinioned, and weak in resolution they were, *as the cattle; nay, they are further astray from the way* [xxv, 44].

As his pity toward men increased and he entertained the ambition of becoming the instrument of their salvation, he made up his mind to reach them, and to lay bare the truth before them and make it clear for them. He discussed [*148*] his intention with Asal and asked him if a way could possibly be contrived to reach them. Asal informed him of their deficient nature and how they turn away from God. But Hayy could not comprehend that and still hoped to be able to pursue his intention. Asal, too, entertained the ambition that God might, through Hayy, lead into the right path some of his acquaintances, who were initiates and closer to salvation than the others: so he helped him to carry out his design. They resolved to keep close to the seashore without leaving it night or day, till God should please to offer them the opportunity to cross the sea. So they stayed by the shore supplicating and praying to God, the Mighty and Majestic, *that He may guide them to the right path in their design* [cf. xviii, 10].

It happened, by God's command, that a ship that had lost its course was driven [*149*] by the winds and the tumultuous waves upon the shore

of that island. As the ship drew closer to the land, the people on board
saw the two men on shore and made toward them. Asal spoke to them
and asked that the two of them be taken along. The [mariners] re-
sponded favorably and took them aboard. God sent a fair wind, which
in a short time brought the ship to the island they were seeking. There
they landed and went into the city. Asal's friends met with him, and
he told them the story of Hayy the son of Yaqzan. They flocked around
Hayy, showed him great admiration, met with him, and esteemed and
venerated him. Asal let Hayy know that this group was superior to all
other men in understanding and sagacity; should he prove unable to
instruct them, his chances of instructing the multitude were slim. Now
the ruler [*150*] and chief of that island was Salaman, Asal's friend who
believed in adhering to the whole body of the community and argued for
prohibiting seclusion. Hayy the son of Yaqzan began to teach and to
disclose the secrets of wisdom. But no sooner had he gone a little beyond
the apparent, and started to describe what they had previously learned to
be otherwise, than they began to feel ill at ease in his presence, to feel
in their souls an abhorrence for what he told them; and they resented
it in their hearts, although in his face they showed that they were
pleased, out of respect for his being a stranger as well as for the sake of
their friend Asal. Hayy the son of Yaqzan kept entreating them night
and day, and kept explaining to them the truth both in private and in
public. But this did not produce any effect except to increase their
disdain and aversion, despite their love of goodness and their desire for
the truth. Nonetheless, because of their deficient natures, they did not
pursue the truth in the proper way, nor did they receive it in the proper
manner nor [*151*] call for it at its own doors. On the contrary, they
wanted to learn the truth on the authority of other men. So Hayy
despaired of reforming them and lost hope in their ability to receive
the truth.

Examining afterwards the different categories of men, he found that
each party was rejoicing in what it had [xxiii, 53; xxx, 32], *taking their
caprice to be their god* [cf. xxv, 43] and worshiping their desires. They
were fighting desperately to collect the crumbs of this world, and *they
were absorbed in amassing* [*wealth*] *until the day they reached their
graves* [cf. cii, 1-2]. All good advice is lost upon them, and kind words
have no effect. Discussion only makes them more obstinate; and as for
wisdom, there is no way they could acquire it, neither have they any
portion of it. They were submerged in ignorance, and *what they were
earning has rusted upon their hearts* [lxxxiii, 14]. *God has set a seal
on their hearts and their hearing and on their eyes is a covering, and
there awaits them a mighty chastisement* [ii, 7]. When he saw the
pavilion of punishment surrounding them and the darkness of the veils
covering them—all of them, except a few, do not take seriously anything

but the worldly aspects of their religion; they disregard the observance of its practices [*152*] regardless of their easiness, and *they sold it for a small price* [cf. iii, 187]; *commerce did divert them from the remembrance of God, the Exalted,* and *they had no fear of a day when hearts and eyes shall be turned about* [cf. xxiv, 37]—it became clear to him, indeed he was absolutely sure, that it was impossible to address them by way of unveiling [the pure truth], and that to enjoin upon them any works beyond the measure [laid down by their messenger] was not expedient; and further, that the greatest benefit the multitude could get from the religious Law concerned their mundane life alone, so that they might live forthrightly and no man trespass the private property of the others. Only the exceptional and the rare among them would attain the happiness of the hereafter, namely *the one who desires the tillage of the hereafter, and strives after it as he should—being a believer* [cf. xvii, 19]. As *for him who is impious, and prefers the life of this world, then surely hell is his abode* [lxxix, 37-39]. What weariness can be greater, or what misery more overwhelming than that of the one who, if you examined his activities from the moment he wakes up till the time he goes to sleep, you would find does nothing but seek [*153*] after one or another of the vile sensible things: riches to collect, pleasures to partake of, lusts to satisfy, a rage for which he seeks relief, glory to obtain, or practice commended by the religious Law with which to make a vainglorious show or defend his own neck. All these things are *darkness upon darkness in a deep sea* [cf. xxiv, 40], and *there is not one of you, but he shall go down to it, that for thy Lord is a thing decreed, determined* [xix, 71].

Upon comprehending that this is the condition of men and that the majority are like irrational animals, he knew that all wisdom, guidance to the right path, and good fortune reside in the utterances of the apostles of God and what is set forth by religious Law: nothing else is possible and nothing more could be added to it. Certain kinds of men are fit for certain kinds of work and each man is more fit to do that for which he is made. *Such has been God's way with the ones who had passed away, and you shall find no change in God's way* [cf. xlviii, 23]. Hence Hayy went back to Salaman and his friends, apologized for what he had said to them, and asked that he be forgiven for it. He informed them that he now shared their opinion and has been guided to the right path that they were following. He also exhorted them to keep firm in their observance of the prescriptions of the religious Law and the performance of the external [religious] practices and not to delve into what does not concern them. They should believe, furthermore, in the ambiguous [statements of the Law] and assent readily to them. They should avoid [*154*] innovations and private opinions and follow in the footsteps of their pious ancestors, forsaking all unprecedented novelties.

He commanded them to avoid the indifference of the vulgar toward the religious Law, and their love of this world, and cautioned them with insistence against it. He and his friend Asal knew now that this is the only way in which this group, which has the desire but not the capacity for salvation, can achieve it. Should one try to raise them to the height of personal vision, this would upset their present order without enabling them to attain the grade of the happy ones. They will waver and suffer a relapse, ending in evil. On the other hand, if this same group should continue in this same condition till death overtook them, they would gain security and belong to the *Companions of the Right* [lvi, 90, 91]. As for *the Outstrippers, they are the ones brought nigh* [*to God's Throne*] [lvi, 10–11].

Asal and Hayy took their leave and separated from the group. They sought an opportunity to go back to their island, till it pleased God, the Mighty and Majestic, to help them and facilitate their passage back. Hayy sought his previous sublime station the same way he had sought it before, till he recovered it. Asal followed in Hayy's footsteps till he came close to him or almost did so. They both *worshiped God* [*155*] in that island *until death overtook them* [cf. xv, 99].

This—may God assist you *through his inspiration* [cf. lviii, 22]—is the story of what happened to Hayy the son of Yaqzan, Asal, and Salaman. It contains certain statements that are not to be found in any book, nor heard in a common discourse. It is a part of that well-protected science which only those who know God accept and only those *deluded concerning God* ignore [cf. xxxi, 33; lvii, 14; lxxxii, 6]. We have taken a road contrary to that of the pious ancestors who grudged its dissemination and parsimoniously guarded it. The reason that the disclosure of this secret and the tearing of its veil were made easy for us was the appearance, in our present time, of corrupt opinions aired and broached by some contemporaneous pretenders to philosophy, till they spread all over the countries, and the mischief caused by it has now become common. Fearing lest the weak ones who have rejected the authority of the prophets and who would want to imitate the fools, should think that these opinions are the secrets guarded [*156*] against the ones unworthy of them,[16] and so increase their inclination to, and love of, them, we decided to give them a glimpse of the secret of secrets in order to attract them to the side of self-fulfilment and avert them from this road. Nevertheless, we have not left whatever secrets we confided to these pages without a thin veil and a delicate curtain, which is easy to break by those worthy of doing so, but which turns thick for the ones unworthy of going beyond it so that they would be unable to go any further.

I ask my brothers who read this book to accept my apologies for my indulgence in explaining whatever I explained and for my liberality in writing it down. I did not do so except because I climbed heights that the eyes fail to see, and wished to simplify my discourse about them in order to attract others and make them desire to take to the way. I ask for God's indulgence and forgiveness, and that He may lead us unto the pure knowledge of Him. He is gracious and generous. Peace be with you, my brother whom it is my duty to help, and the mercy and blessing of God.

NOTES

1. Attributed to the Sufi al-Bisṭāmī (d. 875 or 877).

2. Attributed to the Sufi al-Ḥallāj (d. 922).

3. The well-known Muslim dialectical theologian, jurist, and Sufi (1059-1111).

4. The verse is by the poet Ibn al-Mu-'tazz (d. 908). It is quoted by Algazel in his *Deliverer from Error* (tr. by W. Montgomery Watt in *The Faith and Practice of al-Ghazālī* [London, 1953], p. 61).

5. A Sufi term meaning union with God. Avempace uses it to mean conjunction with the Active Intellect.

6. Avempace, *On Conjunction (Fī ittiṣāl al-'aql bi-l-insān)*: M. Asín Palacios, "Tratado de Avempace sobre la unión del intelecto con el hombre," *Al-Andalus*, VII (1942), pp. 22-23 (text), 46–47 (Spanish tr.).

7. A Sufi term meaning the first immediate experience of the intuition of God; it is characterized by its instability and furtiveness.

8. Avicenna, *Directives and Remarks (al-Ishārāt wa-l-tanbīhāt)*, ed. J. Forget (Leiden, 1892), pp. 202-4 (French tr. A.–M. Goichon, *Livre des directives et remarques* [Paris, 1951], pp. 493-97).

9. The verse is by the Toledan poet al-Waqqāshī (d. 1095).

10. The verse is by the poet al-Taghrā'ī (d. 1120).

11. Or "He [that is, God] will enable you to reach where you want."

12. Avicenna, *Recital of Ḥayy Ibn Yaqẓān* (in Henri Corbin, *Avicenna and the Visionary Recital*, tr. W. R. Trask [New York, 1960], pp. 137-50).

13. See Avempace, *Governance of the Solitary*, pp. 37, 54 ff. (above, Selection 8).

14. Cf. I Cor. 2:9.

15. Or the "way," "path" (*sirāt*), which separates hell from paradise. See Avicenna, *On the Proof of Prophecies*, pp. 129 ff. (above, Selection 7).

16. Above, pp. 17–18.

10.

Averroes

THE DECISIVE TREATISE,

DETERMINING WHAT THE

CONNECTION IS BETWEEN

RELIGION AND PHILOSOPHY

Translated by George F. Hourani

Averroes (Abū al-Walīd Muḥammad Ibn Aḥmad Ibn Rushd, 1126–1198) was born in Cordova to a distinguished family of jurists; both his grandfather and father occupied posts as judges in that city. Little is known of his life and activities prior to 1168/9. He is reported to have studied Islamic jurisprudence and dialectical theology; in 1153 he went to Marrakesh where he was received by the founder of the Almohad dynasty 'Abd al-Mu'min (reigned, 1132/3–1163), apparently in connection with the prince's plans to establish a school; and he composed a work on medicine. In 1168/9 he went to Marrakesh again, where he was introduced to 'Abd al-Mu'min's son and successor, Abū Ya'qūb (reigned, 1163–1184) by his aged vizier and chief physician Ibn Tufayl. Shortly afterwards, Ibn Tufayl reported to Averroes that the sovereign had complained to him about the lack of coherence in Aristotle's style, or rather in the style of his translators, and about the obscurity of Aristotle's aims, and that he had expressed the hope that someone would paraphrase them and make their aims more accessible. Ibn Tufayl himself was prevented from doing it because of his age and his occupation with government service (concentrating on "what I hold more important"), and he charged Averroes with this task. Subsequently, Averroes was named judge in Seville in 1169, where he started composing his commentaries, a work that he continued after returning to Cordova in 1171, probably as a judge too. Later, he became chief justice of Cordova and must have travelled in Andalusia and Morocco. In 1182, upon the retirement of Ibn Tufayl as chief physician to Abū Ya'qūb, Averroes replaced him in this function. He kept his favored position under Abū Ya-'qūb's son and successor Abū Yūsuf from 1184 to 1195, when he fell in disgrace, his works (except those that dealt with the practical sciences) were ordered burned, and he was exiled to the little town of Lucena near Cordova. But soon afterwards the prince revoked his decision and Averroes was called to Marrakesh where he led a retired life until his death.

Although the *Decisive Treatise* was written probably shortly before 1180, its theme is closely related to this episode and to the status of philosophy and the position of the philosopher in the Islamic world in general and under the Almohad dynasty in North Africa and Andalusia in particular. The Almohad·princes were interested in philosophy and patronized its study. But they owed their rule to the revival of a popular religion based on "the Koran and the sword." Thus they encouraged simultaneously the private study of the philosophic sciences and the public attachment to the letter of the divine Law. There were, however, many jurists and dialectical theologians who took the position that philosophic teachings were contrary to the revealed teaching and that philosophers were unbelievers; they were able to arouse the multitude of believers to adopt this view; and they were thus able at times to exert pressure on the rulers to patronize them, rather than the philosophers, as the learned men of the community. Faced with such popular indignation against philosophy at a time when he was in need of public support for his campaign in Spain, Abū Yūsuf quelled it with a temporary public censure of Averroes, which he revoked as soon as he

ended the campaign and returned to Marrakesh. The relatively constant alliance between philosophy and the Almohad rulers stands in curious contrast to the equally constant opposition between the Almohad rulers and such jurists and dialectical theologians as attempted to gain political support for their interpretation of the religious Law. The *Decisive Treatise* attempts to support the position taken by the Almohad rulers on the basis of the religious Law and of philosophy. It addresses itself to the relation between philosophy and the religious Law, argues that the objections against philosophy are devoid of legal foundation, and censures the dialectical theologians for confusing the public. But it also goes beyond this and offers a solution in the form of peaceful coexistence between philosophy and the religious Law, based on mutual understanding and benefits, and a common enemy: dialectical theology.

The *Decisive Treatise* was translated into Hebrew late in the thirteenth or early in the fourteenth century. The Arabic original was first edited by M. J. Müller: *Philosophie und Theologie von Averroes* (Munich, 1859). The text was re-edited in an extensively revised and improved version by George F. Hourani: *Ibn Rushd (Averroes): Kitāb faṣl al-maqāl* (Leiden, 1959). The following translation is based on this text, but the page numbers, like those in Hourani's text and translation, refer to Müller's edition. Hourani's translation was published with a valuable introduction, summaries, and extensive notes in *Averroes on the Harmony of Religion and Philosophy* ("E. J. W. Gibb Memorial Series," N.S., XXI [London: Luzac, 1961]).

THUS SPOKE THE LAWYER, imam, judge, and unique scholar, Abū al-Walīd Muḥammad Ibn Aḥmad Ibn Rushd [Averroes]:

Praise be to God with all due praise, and a prayer for Muhammad His chosen servant and apostle. The purpose of this treatise is to examine, from the standpoint of the study of the Law, whether the study of philosophy and logic is allowed by the Law, or prohibited, or commanded—either by way of recommendation or as obligatory.[1]

We say: if the activity of philosophy is nothing more than study of existing beings and reflection on them as indications of the Artisan, that is, inasmuch as they are products of art (for beings only indicate the Artisan through knowledge of the art in them, and the more perfect this knowledge is, the more perfect the knowledge of the Artisan becomes), and if the Law has recommended and urged reflection on beings, then it is clear that what this name signifies is either obligatory or recommended by the Law.

That the Law summons to reflection on beings, and the pursuit of knowledge about them, by the intellect is clear from several [2] verses of the Book of God, Blessed and Exalted, such as the saying of the Exalted, *Reflect, you have vision* [lix, 2]: this is textual authority for the obligation to use intellectual reasoning, or a combination of intellectual and legal reasoning. Another example is His saying, *Have they not studied the kingdom of the heavens and the earth, and whatever things God has created?* [vii, 185]: this is a text urging the study of the totality of beings. Again, God, the Exalted, has taught that one of those whom He singularly honored by this knowledge was Abraham, peace on him, for the Exalted said, *So we made Abraham see the kingdom of the heavens and the earth, that he might be* [and so on to the end of] the verse [vi, 75]. The Exalted also said, *Do they not observe the camels, how they have been created, and the sky, how it has been raised up?* [lxxxviii, 17-18]; and He said, *and they give thought to the creation of the heavens and the earth* [iii, 191], and so on in countless other verses.

Since it has now been established that the Law has rendered obligatory the study of beings by the intellect, and reflection on them, and since reflection is nothing more than inference and drawing out of the unknown from the known, and since this is reasoning or at any rate done by reasoning, therefore we are under an obligation to carry on our study of beings by intellectual reasoning. It is further evident that this manner of study, to which the Law summons and urges, is the most perfect kind of study using the most perfect kind of reasoning, and this is the kind called demonstration.

The Law, then, has urged us to have demonstrative knowledge of God, the Exalted, and all the beings of His creation. But it is preferable and even necessary for anyone, who wants to understand God, the Exalted, and the other beings demonstratively, to have first understood the kinds of demonstration and their conditions [of validity], and in what respects demonstrative reasoning differs from dialectical, rhetorical, and sophistical reasoning. But this is not possible unless he has previously learned what reasoning as such is, and how many kinds it has, and which of them are valid and which invalid. This in turn is not possible unless he has previously learned the parts of reasoning, of which it is composed, that is, the premises and their kinds. Therefore he who believes in the Law, and obeys its command to study beings, ought prior to his study to gain a knowledge of these things, which have the same place [3] in theoretical studies as instruments have in practical activities.

For just as the jurist infers from the divine command to him to acquire knowledge of the juridical categories that he is under obligation to know the various kinds of juridical syllogisms, and which are valid and which invalid, in the same way he who would know [God] ought to infer from the command to study beings that he is under obligation to acquire a knowledge of intellectual reasoning and its kinds. Indeed it is more fitting for him to do so, for if the jurist infers from the saying of the Exalted, *Reflect, you have vision*, the obligation to acquire a knowledge of juridical reasoning, how much more fitting and proper that he who would know God should infer from it the obligation to acquire a knowledge of intellectual reasoning!

It cannot be objected: "This kind of study of intellectual reasoning is a heretical innovation since it did not exist among the first believers."[2] For the study of juridical reasoning and its kinds is also something that has been discovered since the first believers, yet it is not considered to be a heretical innovation. So the objector should believe the same about the study of intellectual reasoning. (For this there is a reason, which it is not the place to mention here.) But most followers of this religion support intellectual reasoning, except a small group of gross literalists, who can be refuted by [sacred] texts.

Since it has now been established that there is an obligation by the Law to study intellectual reasoning and its kinds, just as there is an obligation to study juridical reasoning, it is clear that, if none of our predecessors had formerly examined intellectual reasoning and its kinds, we should be obliged to undertake such an examination from the beginning, and that each succeeding scholar would have to seek help in that task from his predecessor in order that knowledge of the subject might be completed. For it is difficult or impossible for one man to find out by himself and from the beginning all that he needs on that subject, as it is difficult for one man to discover all the knowledge that he needs of the kinds of juridical reasoning; indeed this is even truer of knowledge of intellectual reasoning.

But if someone other than ourselves has already examined that subject, it is clear that we ought to seek help toward our goal from what has been said by such a predecessor on the subject, regardless of whether this other one shares our religion or not. For when a valid sacrifice is performed with a certain instrument, [4] no account is taken, in judging the validity of the sacrifice, of whether the instrument belongs to one who shares our religion or to one who does not, so long as it fulfils the conditions for validity. By "those who do not share our religion" I refer to those ancients who studied these matters before Islam. So if such is the case, and everything that is required in the study of the subject of intellectual syllogisms has already been examined in the most perfect manner by the ancients, presumably we ought to lay hands on their books in order to study what they said about that subject; and if it is all correct we should accept it from them, while if there is anything incorrect in it, we should draw attention to that.

When we have finished with this sort of study and acquired the instruments by whose aid we are able to reflect on beings and the indications of art in them (for he who does not understand the art does not understand the product of art, and he who does not understand the product of art does not understand the Artisan), then we ought to begin the examination of beings in the order and manner we have learned from the art of demonstrative syllogisms.

And again it is clear that in the study of beings this aim can be fulfilled by us perfectly only through successive examinations of them by one man after another, the later ones seeking the help of the earlier in that task, on the model of what has happened in the mathematical sciences. For if we suppose that the art of geometry did not exist in this age of ours, and likewise the art of astronomy, and a single person wanted to ascertain by himself the sizes of the heavenly bodies, their shapes, and their distances from each other, that would not be possible for him—for example to know the proportion of the sun to the earth or other facts about the sizes of the stars—even though he were the most intelligent of men by nature, unless by a revelation or something resembling revelation. Indeed if he were told that the sun is about 150 or 160 times[3] as great as the earth, he would think this statement madness on the part of the speaker, although this is a fact that has been demonstrated in astronomy so surely that no one who has mastered that science doubts it.

But it is hardly even necessary to use the example of the art of mathematics; for here is the art [5] of the principles of jurisprudence and jurisprudence itself, both of which were perfected only over a long period of time.[4] And if someone today wanted to find out by himself all the arguments that have been discovered by the theorists of the legal schools on controversial questions, about which debate has taken place between them in most countries of Islam (even if one excluded the West),[5] he would deserve to be ridiculed, because such a task is impossible for him, apart from the fact that the work has been done already. Moreover, this is a situation that is self-evident not in the scientific arts alone but also in the practical arts; for there is not one of them that a single man can construct by himself. Then how can he do it with the art of arts, philos-

ophy? If this is so, then whenever we find in the works of our predecessors of former nations a theory about beings and a reflection on them
conforming to what the conditions of demonstration require, we ought
to study what they said about the matter and what they set down in their
books. And we should accept from them gladly and gratefully whatever
in these books accords with the truth, and draw attention to and warn
against what does not accord with the truth, at the same time excusing
them.

From this it is evident that the study of the books of the ancients is
obligatory by Law, since their aim and purpose in their books is just
the purpose to which the Law has urged us, and that whoever forbids
the study of them to anyone who is fit to study them—that is, anyone
who unites two qualities, (1) natural intelligence and (2) legal integrity
and moral virtue—is blocking people from the door by which the Law
summons them to knowledge of God, the door of theoretical study that
leads to the truest knowledge of Him; and such an act is the extreme
of ignorance and estrangement from God, the Exalted.

And if someone errs or stumbles in the study of these books owing to
a deficiency in his natural capacity, or bad organization of his study of
them, or being dominated by his passions, or not finding a teacher to
guide him to an understanding of their contents, or a combination of all
or more than one of these causes, it does not follow that one should
forbid them to anyone [6] who is qualified to study them. For this
manner of harm that arises owing to them is something that is attached
to them by accident, not by essence; and when a thing is beneficial by
its nature and essence, it ought not to be shunned because of something
harmful contained in it by accident. This was the thought of [the
Prophet], peace on him, on the occasion when he ordered a man to
give his brother honey to drink for his diarrhea, and the diarrhea increased after he had given him the honey: when the man complained to
him about it, he said, "God spoke the truth; it was your brother's stomach
that lied." We can even say that a man who prevents a qualified person
from studying books of philosophy, because some of the most vicious
people may be thought to have gone astray through their study of them,
is like a man who prevents a thirsty person from drinking cool, fresh
water until he dies of thirst, because some people have choked to death
on it. For death from water by choking is an accidental matter, but death
from thirst is essential and necessary.

Moreover, this accidental effect of this art is a thing that may also
occur accidentally from the other arts. To how many jurists has jurisprudence been a cause of lack of piety and immersion in this world!
Indeed we find most jurists in this state, although their art by its essence
calls for nothing but practical virtue. Thus it is not strange if the same

thing that occurs accidentally in the art that calls for practical virtue should occur accidentally in the art that calls for intellectual virtue.

Since all this is now established, and since we, the Muslim community, hold that this divine Law of ours is true, and that it is this Law that incites and summons us to the happiness that consists in the knowledge of God, Mighty and Majestic, and of His creation, that [end] is appointed for every Muslim by the method of assent that his temperament and nature require. For the natures of men are on different levels with respect to [their paths to] assent. One of them comes to assent through demonstration; another comes to assent through dialectical arguments, just as firmly as the demonstrative man through demonstration, since his nature does not contain any greater capacity; while another comes to assent through rhetorical arguments, again just as firmly as the demonstrative man through demonstrative arguments.

Thus since this divine Law of ours has [7] summoned people by these three methods, assent to it has extended to everyone, except to him who stubbornly denies it with his tongue or for whom no method of summons to God, the Exalted, has been appointed in the Law owing to his own neglect of such matters. It was for this purpose that [the Prophet], peace on him, was sent with a special mission to "the red [white] man and the black man"[6] alike; I mean because his Law embraces all the methods of summons to God, the Exalted. This is clearly expressed in the saying of God, the Exalted, *Summon to the way of your Lord by wisdom and by good preaching, and debate with them in the most effective manner* [xvi, 125].

Now since this Law is true and summons to the study that leads to knowledge of the truth, we the Muslim community know definitely that demonstrative study does not lead to [conclusions] conflicting with what is given in the Law; for truth does not oppose truth but accords with it and bears witness to it.

This being so, whenever demonstrative study leads to any manner of knowledge about any being, that being is inevitably either unmentioned or mentioned in the Law. If it is unmentioned there is no contradiction, and it is in the same case as an act whose category is unmentioned so that the jurist has to infer it by reasoning from the Law. If the Law speaks about it, the apparent meaning of the words inevitably either accords or conflicts with the conclusions of demonstration about it. If this [apparent meaning] accords there is no argument. If it conflicts there is a call for interpretation[7] of it. The meaning of "interpretation" is: extension of the significance of an expression from real to metaphorical significance, without forsaking therein the standard metaphorical practices of Arabic, such as calling a thing by the name of something resembling it or a cause or consequence or accompaniment of it, or other things such as are enumerated in accounts of the kinds of metaphorical speech.

Now if the jurist does this in many legal decisions, with how much more right is it done by the possessor of demonstrative knowledge! For the jurist has at his disposal only reasoning based on opinion, while he who would know [God] has at his disposal reasoning based on certainty. So we affirm definitely that whenever the conclusion of a demonstration is in conflict with the apparent meaning of the Law, [*8*] that apparent meaning admits of interpretation according to the rules for such interpretation in Arabic. This proposition is questioned by no Muslim and doubted by no believer. But its certainty is immensely increased for those who have had close dealings with this idea and put it to the test, and made it their aim to reconcile the assertions of intellect and tradition. Indeed we may say that whenever a statement in the Law conflicts in its apparent meaning with a conclusion of demonstration, if the Law is considered carefully, and the rest of its contents searched page by page, there will invariably be found among the expressions of the Law something that in its apparent meaning bears witness to that interpretation or comes close to bearing witness.

In the light of this idea the Muslims are unanimous[8] in holding that it is not obligatory either to take all the expressions of the Law in their apparent meaning or to extend them all from their apparent meaning by interpretation. They disagree [only] over which of them should and which should not be so interpreted: the Ash'arites[9] for instance give an interpretation to the verse about God's directing Himself [ii, 29] and the Tradition about His descent,[10] while the Hanbalites[11] take them in their apparent meaning.

The reason why the Law came down containing both an apparent and an inner meaning lies in the diversity of people's natural capacities and the difference of their innate dispositions with regard to assent. The reason why the Law came down containing apparent meanings that contradict each other is in order to draw the attention of those who are *well grounded in science* to the interpretation that reconciles them. This is the idea referred to in the words of the Exalted, *He it is who has sent down to you the Book, containing certain verses clear and definite* [and so on] down to the words, *those who are well grounded in science* [iii, 7].

If it is objected: "There are some things in the Law that the Muslims have unanimously agreed to take in their apparent meaning, others [that they have agreed] to interpret, and others about which they have disagreed; is it permissible, then, that demonstration should lead to interpreting what they have agreed to take in its apparent meaning, or to taking in its apparent meaning what they have agreed to interpret?" We reply: if [the existence of] the unanimous agreement could be established with certainty, it is not permissible; but if [the existence of] the unanimous agreement on those things is a matter of opinion, then it may be permissible. This is why Abū Ḥāmid [Algazel], Abū al-Maʿālī,[12] and other leaders of thought said that no one should be definitely called an unbeliever for violating unanimity on a point of interpretation in matters like these.

That unanimity on theoretical matters is never determined with certainty, as it can be on practical matters, may be shown to you by the fact that it is not possible [9] for unanimity to be determined on any question at any period unless that period is strictly limited by us, and all the scholars existing in that period are known to us (that is, known as individuals and in their total number), and the doctrine of each of them on the question has been handed down to us on unassailable authority, and, in addition to all this, unless we are sure that the scholars existing at the time were in agreement that there is not both an apparent and an inner meaning in the Law, that knowledge of any question ought not to be kept secret from anyone, and that there is only one way for people to understand the Law. But it is recorded [in Tradition] that many of the first believers used to hold that the Law has both an apparent and an inner meaning, and that the inner meaning ought not to be learned by anyone who is not a man of learning in this field and who is incapable of understanding it. Thus, for example, al-Bukhārī[13] reports a saying of ʿAlī Ibn Abī Ṭālib[14] (may God be pleased with him): "Speak to people about what they know. Do you want God and His Prophet to be accused of lying?" Other examples of the same kind are reported about a group of early believers. So how can it possibly be conceived that a unanimous agreement can have been handed down to us about a single theoretical question, when we know definitely that not a single period has been without scholars who held that there are things in the Law whose true meaning should not be learned by all people?

The situation is different in practical matters: everyone holds that the truth about these should be disclosed to all people alike, and to establish the occurrence of unanimity about them we consider it sufficient that the question [at issue] should have been widely discussed and that no report of controversy about it should have been handed down to us. This is enough to establish the occurrence of unanimity on matters of practice, but on matters of doctrine the case is different.

You may object: "If we ought not to call a man an unbeliever for violating unanimity in cases of interpretation, because no unanimity is conceivable in such cases, what do you say about the Muslim philosophers like Abū Naṣr [Alfarabi] and Ibn Sīnā [Avicenna]? For Abū Ḥāmid [Algazel] called them both definitely unbelievers in the book of his known as the *Incoherence [of the Philosophers]*, on three counts: their assertions of the pre-eternity of the world and that God, the Exalted, does not know particulars" (may He be Exalted far above that [ignorance]!), "and their [*10*] interpretation of the passages concerning the resurrection of bodies and states of existence in the next life."

We answer: it is apparent from what he said on the subject that his calling them both unbelievers on these counts was not definite, since he made it clear in the [*Decisive*] *Distinction* that calling people unbelievers for violating unanimity can only be tentative.

Moreover, it is evident from what we have said that a unanimous agreement cannot be established in questions of this kind, because of the reports that many of the early believers of the first generation, as well as others, have said that there are interpretations that ought not to be expounded except to those who are qualified to receive them. These are *those who are well grounded in science;* for we prefer to place the stop after the words of God, the Exalted, *and those who are well grounded in science* [iii, 7], because if the scholars did not understand the interpretation, there would be no superiority in their assent that would oblige them to a belief in Him not found among the unlearned. God has described them as those who believe in Him, and this can only be taken to refer to the belief that is based on demonstration; and this [belief] only occurs together with knowledge of the interpretation. For the unlearned believers are those whose belief in Him is not based on demonstration; and if this belief that God has attributed to the scholars is peculiar to them, it must come through demonstration, and if it comes through demonstration it only occurs together with knowledge of the interpretation. For God, the Exalted, has informed us that those [verses] have an interpretation that is the truth, and demonstration can only be of the truth. That being the case, it is not possible for general unanimity to be established about interpretations, which God has made peculiar to scholars. This is self-evident to any fair-minded person.

In addition to all this we hold that Abū Ḥāmid [Algazel] was mistaken about the Peripatetic philosophers, in ascribing to them the assertion that God, Holy and Exalted, does not know particulars at all. In reality they hold that God, the Exalted, knows them in a way that is not of the same kind as our way of knowing them. For our knowledge of them is an effect of the object known, originated when it comes into existence and changing when it changes; whereas Glorious God's knowledge of existence is the opposite of this: it is the cause of the object known, which is existent being. Thus to suppose [*11*] the two kinds of knowledge similar to each other is to identify the essences and properties of opposite things, and that is the extreme of ignorance. And if the name of "knowledge" is predicated of both originated and eternal knowledge, it is predicated by sheer homonymy, as many names are predicated of opposite things: for example, *jalal* of great and small, *ṣarīm* of light and darkness. Thus there exists no definition embracing both kinds of knowledge at once, as the dialectical theologians of our time imagine.

We have devoted a separate essay to this question,[15] impelled by one of our friends.

But how can anyone imagine that the Peripatetics say that God, the Glorious, does not know particulars with His eternal knowledge, when they hold that true dream-visions include premonitions of particular events due to occur in future time, and that this warning foreknowledge comes to people in their sleep from the eternal knowledge that governs and rules the universe? Moreover, it is not only particulars that they say God does not know in the manner in which we know them, but universals as well; for the universals known to us are also effects of the nature of existent being, while with His knowledge the reverse is true. Thus the conclusion to which demonstration leads is that His knowledge transcends qualification as "universal" or "particular." Consequently there is no point in disputing this question, that is, whether to call them unbelievers or not.

Concerning the question whether the world is pre-eternal or came into existence, the disagreement between the Ash'arite dialectical theologians and the ancient philosophers is in my view almost resolvable into a disagreement about naming, especially in the case of certain of the ancients. For they agree that there are three classes of beings: two extremes and one intermediate between the extremes. They agree also about naming the extremes; but they disagree about the intermediate class.

(1) One extreme is a being that is brought into existence from something other than itself and by something, that is, by an efficient cause and from some matter; and it, that is, its existence, is preceded by time. This is the status of bodies whose generation is apprehended [12] by sense, for example, the generation of water, air, earth, animals, plants, and so on. All alike, ancients and Ash'arites, agree in naming this class of beings "originated." (2) The opposite extreme to this is a being that is not made from or by anything and not preceded by time; and here too all members of both parties agree in naming it "pre-eternal." This being is apprehended by demonstration; it is God, Blessed and Exalted, who is the Maker, Giver of being, and Sustainer of the universe; may He be praised and His Power exalted!

(3) The class of being that is between these two extremes is that which is not made from anything and not preceded by time, but which is brought into existence by something, that is, by an agent. This is the world as a whole. Now they all agree on the presence of these three characters in the world. For the dialectical theologians admit that time does not precede it, or rather this is a necessary consequence for them since time according to them is something that accompanies motion and bodies. They also agree with the ancients in the view that future time is infinite and likewise future being. They only disagree about past time and past being; the dialectical theologians hold that it is finite (this is the

doctrine of Plato and his followers), while Aristotle and his school hold that it is infinite, as is the case with future time.

Thus it is clear that (3) this last being bears a resemblance both to (1) the being that is really generated and to (2) the pre-eternal Being. So those who are more impressed with its resemblance to the pre-eternal than its resemblance to the originated name it "pre-eternal," while those who are more impressed with its resemblance to the originated name it "originated." But in truth it is neither really originated nor really pre-eternal, since the really originated is necessarily perishable and the really pre-eternal has no cause. Some—Plato and his followers—name it "originated and coeval with time," because time according to them is finite in the past.

Thus the doctrines about the world are not so very far apart from each other that some of them should be judged as constituting unbelief and others not. For [*13*] this to happen, opinions must be divergent in the extreme, that is, contraries such as the dialectical theologians suppose to exist on this question; that is, [they hold] that the names "pre-eternity" and "coming into existence" as applied to the world as a whole are contraries. But it is now clear from what we have said that this is not the case.

Over and above all this, these opinions about the world do not conform to the apparent meaning of the Law. For if the apparent meaning of the Law is searched, it will be evident from the [Koranic] verses that give us information about the bringing into existence of the world that its form really is originated, but that being itself and time extend continuously at both extremes, that is, without interruption. Thus the words of God, the Exalted, *He it is who created the heavens and the earth in six days, and His throne was on the water* [xi, 7], taken in their apparent meaning imply that there was a being before this present being, namely the throne and the water, and a time before this time, that is, the one that is joined to the form of this being, namely the number of the movement of the celestial sphere. And the words of the Exalted, *On the day when the earth shall be changed into other than earth, and the heavens as well* [xiv, 48], also in their apparent meaning imply that there will be a second being after this being. And the words of the Exalted, *Then He directed Himself toward the sky, and it was smoke* [xli, 11], in their apparent meaning imply that the heavens were created from something.

Thus the dialectical theologians too in their statements about the world do not conform to the apparent meaning of the Law but interpret it. For it is not stated in the Law that God was existing with absolutely nothing else: a text to this effect is nowhere to be found. Then how is it conceivable that the dialectical theologians' interpretation of these verses could meet with unanimous agreement, when the apparent meaning of the Law, which we have mentioned about the existence of the world, has been accepted by a group of philosophers!

It seems that those who disagree on the interpretation of these difficult questions earn merit if they are in the right and will be excused [by God] if they are in error. For assent to a thing as a result of an indication [of it] arising in the soul is something compulsory, not voluntary: that is, it is not for us [to choose] not to assent or to assent, as it is to stand up or not to stand up. And since free choice is a condition of obligation, a man who assents to an error as a result of a consideration that has occurred to him is excused, if he is a scholar. [*14*] This is why [the Prophet], peace on him, said, "If the judge after exerting his mind makes a right decision, he will have a double reward; and if he makes a wrong decision, he will [still] have a single reward." And what judge is more important than he who makes judgments about being, that it is thus or not thus? These judges are the scholars, specially chosen by God for [the task of] interpretation, and this error that is forgivable according to the Law is only such error as proceeds from scholars when they study the difficult matters that the Law obliges them to study.

But error proceeding from any other class of people is sheer sin equally whether it relates to theoretical or to practical matters. For just as the judge who is ignorant of the law (*sunnah*) is not excused if he makes an error in judgment, so he who makes judgments about beings without having the proper qualifications for [such] judgments is not excused but is either a sinner or an unbeliever. And if he who would judge what is allowed and forbidden is required to combine in himself the qualifications for exercise of personal judgment, namely knowledge of the principles [of the Law] and knowledge of how to draw inferences from those principles by reasoning, how much more properly is he who would make judgments about beings required to be qualified, that is, to know the primary intellectual principles and the way to draw inferences from them!

In general, error about the Law is of two types: either error that is excused to one who is a qualified student of that matter in which the error occurs (as the skillful doctor is excused if he commits an error in the art of medicine and the skillful judge if he gives an erroneous judgment), but not excused to one who is not qualified in that subject; or error that is not excused to any person whatever, and which is unbelief if it concerns the principles of the Law, or heresy if it concerns something subordinate to the principles.

This [latter] error is that which occurs about (1) matters, knowledge of which is provided by all the different methods of indication, so that knowledge of the matter in question is in this way possible for everyone. Examples are acknowledgment of God, Blessed and Exalted, of the prophetic missions, and of happiness and misery in the next life; for these three principles are attainable by the three classes of indication, [*15*] by which everyone without exception can come to assent to what he is obliged to know: I mean the rhetorical, dialectical, and demonstrative indications. So whoever denies such a thing, when it is one of the principles of the Law, is an unbeliever, who persists in defiance with his tongue though not with his heart, or neglects to expose himself to learning the indication of its truth. For if he belongs to the demonstrative class of men, a way has been provided for him to assent to it, by demonstration; if he belongs to the dialectical class, the way is by dialectic; and if he belongs to the class [that is convinced] by preaching, the way for him is by preaching. With this in view [the Prophet], peace on him, said, "I have been ordered to fight people until they say, 'There is no god but God' and have faith in me"; he means, by any of the three methods of attaining belief that suits them.

(2) With regard to things that by reason of their recondite character are only knowable by demonstration, God has been gracious to those of His servants who have no access to demonstration, on account of their natures, habits, or lack of facilities for education: He has coined for them images and likenesses of these things, and summoned them to assent to those images, since it is possible for assent to those images to come about through the indications common to all men, that is, the dialectical and rhetorical indications. This is the reason why the Law is divided into apparent and inner meanings: the apparent meaning consists of those images which are coined to stand for those ideas, while the inner meaning is those ideas [themselves], which are clear only to the demonstrative class. These are the four or five classes of beings mentioned by Abū Ḥāmid [Algazel] in the [*Decisive*] *Distinction*.

But when it happens, as we said, (1) that we know the thing itself by the three methods, we do not need to coin images of it, and it remains true in its apparent meaning, not admitting of interpretation. If an apparent text of this kind refers to principles, anyone who interprets it is an unbeliever, for example, anyone who thinks that there is no happiness or misery in the next life, and that the only purpose of this teaching is that men should be safeguarded from each other in their bodily and sensible lives, that it is but a practical device, and that man has no other goal than his sensible existence.

If this is established, [*16*] it will have become clear to you from what we have said that there are (1) apparent texts of the Law that it is not permitted to interpret; to do so on fundamentals is unbelief, on subordinate matters, heresy. There are also (2) apparent texts that have to be interpreted by men of the demonstrative class; for such men to take them in their apparent meaning is unbelief, while for those who are not of the demonstrative class to interpret them and take them out of their apparent meaning is unbelief and heresy on their part.

Of this [latter] class are the verse about God's directing Himself and the Tradition about His descent.[16] That is why [the Prophet], peace on him, said in the case of the black woman, when she told him that God was in the sky, "Free her, for she is a believer." This was because she was not of the demonstrative class; and the reason for his decision was that the class of people to whom assent comes only through the imagination, that is, who do not assent to a thing except in so far as they can imagine it, find it difficult to assent to the existence of a being that bears no relation to any imaginable thing. This applies as well to those who understand from this relation merely [that God has] a place; these are people who have advanced a little in their thought beyond the position of the first class by rejecting belief in corporeality. Thus the [proper] answer to them with regard to such passages is that they belong to the ambiguous texts, and that the stop is to be placed after the words of God, the Exalted, *And no one knows the interpretation thereof except God* [iii, 7]. The demonstrative class, while agreeing unanimously that this class of text must be interpreted, may disagree about the interpretation, according to the level of each one's knowledge of demonstration.

There is also (3) a third class of texts in the Law falling uncertainly between the other two classes, on which there is doubt. One group of those who devote themselves to theoretical study attach them to the apparent texts that it is not permitted to interpret, others attach them to the texts with inner meanings that scholars are not permitted to take in their apparent meanings. This [divergence of opinions] is due to the difficulty and ambiguity of this class of text. Anyone who commits an error about this class is excused, I mean any scholar.

If it is asked, "Since it is clear that the texts in the Law in this respect fall into three grades, to which of these three grades, according to you, do the descriptions of the future life and its states belong?" we reply: the position clearly is that this matter belongs to the class (3) about which there is disagreement. For we find [*17*] a group of those who claim to be men of demonstration saying that it is obligatory to take these passages in their apparent meaning, because there is no demonstration leading to the impossibility of the apparent meaning in them—this is the view of the Ash'arites; while another group, who devote themselves to demonstration, interpret these passages, and these people give the most diverse interpretations of them. In this class must be counted Abū Ḥāmid [Algazel] and many of the Sufis; some of them combine the two interpretations of the passages, as Abū Ḥāmid [Algazel] does in some of his books.

So it is likely that a scholar who commits an error in this matter is excused, while one who is correct receives thanks or a reward; that is, if he acknowledges the existence [of a future life] and merely gives a certain sort of interpretation, that is, of the mode of the future life not of its existence, provided that the interpretation given does not lead to denial of its existence. In this matter only the negation of existence is unbelief, because it concerns one of the principles of the Law and one of those points to which assent is attainable through the three methods common to "the red [white] man and the black man."[17]

But anyone who is not a man of learning is obliged to take these passages in their apparent meaning, and interpretation of them is for him unbelief because it leads to unbelief. That is why we hold that, for anyone whose duty it is to believe in the apparent meaning, interpretation is unbelief, because it leads to unbelief. Anyone of the interpretative class who discloses such [an interpretation] to him is summoning him to unbelief, and he who summons to unbelief is an unbeliever.

Therefore interpretations ought to be set down only in demonstrative books, because if they are in demonstrative books they are encountered by no one but men of the demonstrative class. But if they are set down in other than demonstrative books and one deals with them by poetical, rhetorical, or dialectical methods, as Abū Ḥāmid [Algazel] does, then he commits an offense against the Law and against philosophy, even though the fellow intended nothing but good. For by this procedure he wanted to increase the number of learned men. But this increased the number of the mischievous, although not without some increase in the number of the learned.[18] As a result, one group came to slander philosophy, another to slander the Law, and another to reconcile the two. It seems that this [last] was one of his objects [*18*] in his books; an indication that he wanted by this [procedure] to arouse minds is that he adhered to no one doctrine in his books but was an Ashʿarite with the Ashʿarites, a Sufi with the Sufis, and a philosopher with the philosophers, so that he was like the man in the verse:

> One day a Yamanite if I meet a man of Yaman,
> And if I meet a Maʿaddite, I am an ʿAdnānite.[19]

The imams of the Muslims ought to forbid those of his books which contain learned matter to all save the learned, just as they ought to forbid demonstrative books to those who are not capable of understanding them. But the damage done to people by demonstrative books is lighter, because for the most part only persons of superior natural intelligence become acquainted with demonstrative books, and this class of persons is only misled through lack of practical virtue, unorganized reading, and tackling them without a teacher. On the other hand their total prohibition obstructs the purpose to which the Law summons, because it is a wrong to the best class of people and the best class of beings. For to do justice to the best class of beings demands that they should be known profoundly, by persons equipped to know them profoundly, and these are the best class of people; and the greater the value of the being, the greater is the injury toward it, which consists of ignorance of it. Thus the Exalted has said, *Associating [other gods] with God is indeed a great wrong* [xxxi, 13].

This is as much as we see fit to affirm in this field of study, that is, the correspondence between the Law and philosophy and the rules for interpretation in the Law. If it were not for the publicity given to the matter and to these questions that we have discussed, we should not have permitted ourselves to write a word on the subject; and we should not have had to make excuses for doing so to the interpretative scholars, because the proper place to discuss these questions is in demonstrative books. God is the Guide and helps us to follow the right course!

You ought to know that the purpose of the Law is simply to teach true science and right practice. True science is knowledge of God, Blessed and Exalted, and the other beings as they are, and especially of noble beings, and knowledge of happiness [*19*] and misery in the next life. Right practice consists in performing the acts that bring happiness and avoiding the acts that bring misery; and it is knowledge of these acts that is called "practical science." They fall into two divisions: the first are outward bodily acts; the science of these is called "jurisprudence"; and the second are acts of the soul such as gratitude, patience, and other moral habits that the Law enjoins or forbids; the science of these is called "asceticism" or "the sciences of [that is, concerned with] the future life." To these Abū Ḥāmid [Algazel] turned his attention in his book: as people had given up this sort [of act] and become immersed in the other sort, and as this sort involves the greater fear of God, which is the cause of happiness, he called his book the *Revival of the Sciences of Religion*. But we have digressed from our subject, so let us return to it.

We say: the purpose of the Law is to teach true science and right practice; and teaching is of two classes, [of] concepts and [of] judgments, as the logicians have shown. Now the methods available to men of [arriving at] judgments are three: demonstrative, dialectical, and rhetorical; and the methods of forming concepts are two: either [conceiving] the object itself or [conceiving] a similitude of it. But not everyone has the natural ability to take in demonstrations, or [even] dialectical arguments, let alone demonstrative arguments, which are so hard to learn and need so much time [even] for those who are qualified to learn them. Therefore, since it is the purpose of the Law simply to teach everyone, the Law has to contain every method of [bringing about] judgments of assent and every method of forming concepts.

Now some of the methods of assent comprehend the majority of people, that is, the occurrence of assent as a result of them [is comprehensive]: these are the rhetorical and the dialectical [methods]—and the rhetorical is more comprehensive than the dialectical. Another method is peculiar to a smaller number of people: this is the demonstrative. Therefore, since the primary purpose of the Law is to take care of the majority (without neglecting to arouse the elect), the prevailing methods of exposition in the Law are the common methods by which [20] the majority comes to form concepts and judgments.

These [common] methods in the Law are of four classes:

One of them occurs where the method is common, yet specialized in two respects: that is, where it is certain in its concepts and judgments, in spite of being rhetorical or dialectical. These syllogisms are those whose premises, in spite of being generally accepted notions, or opinions, are accidentally certain, and whose conclusions are accidentally to be taken in their direct meaning rather than as similitudes. This class of statements in the Law has no interpretation, and anyone who denies it or interprets it is an unbeliever.

The second class occurs where the premises, in spite of being generally accepted notions, or opinions, are certain, and where the conclusions are similitudes for the things that it was intended to conclude. [Statements of] this [class], that is, their conclusions, admit of interpretation.

The third is the reverse of this: it occurs where the conclusions are the very things that it was intended to conclude, while the premises are generally accepted notions, or opinions, without being accidently certain. [Statements of] this [class] also, that is, their conclusions, do not admit of interpretation, but their premises may do so.

The fourth [class] occurs where the premises are generally accepted notions, or opinions, without being accidentally certain, and where the conclusions are similitudes for what it was intended to conclude. In these cases the duty of the elect is to interpret them, while the duty of the multitude is to take them in their apparent meaning.

In general, everything in these [statements] that admits of interpretation can only be understood by demonstration. The duty of the elect here is to apply such interpretation; while the duty of the multitude is to take them in their apparent meaning in both respects, that is, in concept and judgment, since their natural capacity does not allow more than that.

But there may occur to students of the Law interpretations due to the superiority of one of the common methods over another in [bringing about] assent, that is, when the indication contained in the interpretation is more persuasive than the indication contained in the apparent meaning. Such interpretations are popular; and [the making of them] is possibly a duty for those whose powers of theoretical understanding have attained the dialectical level. To this sort belong [21] some of the interpretations of the Ash'arites and Mu'tazilites[20]—though the Mu'tazilites are generally sounder in their statements. The multitude on the other hand, who are incapable of more than rhetorical arguments, have the duty of taking these [statements] in their apparent meaning, and they are not permitted to know such interpretations at all.

Thus people in relation to the Law fall into three classes:

One class is those who are not people of interpretation at all: these are the rhetorical class. They are the overwhelming multitude, for no man of sound intellect is exempted from this kind of assent.

Another class is the people of dialectical interpretation: these are the dialecticians, either by nature alone or by nature and habit.

Another class is the people of certain interpretation: these are the demonstrative class, by nature and training, that is, in the art of philosophy. This interpretation ought not to be expressed to the dialectical class, let alone to the multitude.

When something of these interpretations is expressed to anyone unfit to receive them—especially demonstrative interpretations because of their remoteness from common knowledge—both he who expresses it and he to whom it is expressed are led into unbelief. The reason for that [in the case of the latter] is that interpretation comprises two things, rejection of the apparent meaning and affirmation of the interpretation; so that if the apparent meaning is rejected in the mind of someone who can only grasp apparent meanings, without the interpretation being affirmed in his mind, the result is unbelief, if it [the statement in question] concerns the principles of the Law.

Interpretations, then, ought not to be expressed to the multitude nor set down in rhetorical or dialectical books, that is, books containing arguments of these two sorts, as was done by Abū Hāmid [Algazel]. They should not be expressed to this class; and with regard to an apparent statement, when there is a self-evident doubt whether it is apparent to everyone and whether knowledge of its interpretation is impossible for them, they should be told that it is ambiguous and [its meaning] known by no one except God; and that the stop should be put here in the sentence of the Exalted, *And no one knows the interpretation thereof except God* [iii, 7]. The same kind of answer should also be given to a question about abstruse matters, which there is no way for the multitude to understand; just as the Exalted has answered in His saying, *And they will ask you about the Spirit. Say, 'The Spirit is by the command of my Lord; you have been given only a little knowledge'* [xvii, 85].

As for [22] the man who expresses these interpretations to unqualified persons, he is an unbeliever on account of his summoning people to unbelief. This is contrary to the summons of the Legislator, especially when they are false interpretations concerning the principles of the Law, as has happened in the case of a group of people of our time. For we have seen some of them thinking that they were being philosophic and that they perceived, with their remarkable wisdom, things that conflict with the Law in every respect, that is, that they are not susceptible of interpretation; and that it was obligatory to express these things to the multitude. But by expressing those false beliefs to the multitude they have been a cause of perdition to the multitude and themselves, in this world and the next.

The relation between the aim of these people and the aim of the Legislator [can be illustrated by] a parable, of a man who goes to a skillful doctor. [This doctor's] aim is to preserve the health and cure the diseases of all the people, by prescribing for them rules that can be commonly accepted, about the necessity of using the things that will preserve their health and cure their diseases, and avoiding the opposite things. He is unable to make them all doctors, because a doctor is one who knows by demonstrative methods the things that preserve health and cure disease. Now this [man whom we have mentioned] goes out to the people and tells them, "These methods prescribed by this doctor for you are not right"; and he sets out to discredit them, so that they are rejected by the people. Or he says, "They have interpretations"; but the people neither understand these nor assent to them in practice. Well, do you think that people in this condition will do any of the things that are useful for preserving health and curing disease, or that this man who has persuaded them to reject what they formerly believed in will now be able to use those [things] with them, I mean for preserving health? No, he will be unable to use those [things] with them, nor will they use them, and so they will all perish.

This [is what will happen] if he expresses to them true interpretations about those matters, because of their inability to understand them; let alone if he expresses to them false interpretations, because this will lead them to think that there are no such things as health which ought to be preserved and disease which ought to be cured—let alone [23] that there are things that preserve health and cure disease. It is the same when someone expresses interpretations to the multitude, and to those who are not qualified to understand them, in the sphere of the Law; thus he makes it appear false and turns people away from it; and he who turns people away from the Law is an unbeliever.

Indeed this comparison is certain, not poetic as one might suppose. It presents a true analogy, in that the relation of the doctor to the health of bodies is [the same as] the relation of the Legislator to the health of souls: that is, the doctor is he who seeks to preserve the health of bodies when it exists and to restore it when it is lost, while the Legislator is he who pursues this [end] for the health of souls. This health is what is called "fear of God." The precious Book has told us to seek it by acts conformable to the Law, in several verses. Thus the Exalted has said,

Fasting has been prescribed for you, as it was prescribed for those who were before you; perhaps you will fear God [ii, 183]. Again the Exalted has said, *Their flesh and their blood shall not touch God, but your fear shall touch Him* [xxii, 37]; *Prayer prevents immorality and transgression* [xxix, 45]; and other verses to the same effect contained in the precious Book. Through knowledge of the Law and practice according to the Law, the Legislator aims solely at this health; and it is from this health that happiness in the future life follows, just as misery in the future life follows from its opposite.

From this it will be clear to you that true interpretations ought not to be set down in popular books, let alone false ones. The true interpretation is the deposit that man was charged to hold and which he held, and from which all beings shied away, that is, that which is mentioned in the words of the Exalted, *We offered the deposit to the heavens, the earth, and the mountains,* [and so on to the end of] the verse [xxxiii, 72].

It was due to interpretations—especially the false ones—and the supposition that such interpretations of the Law ought to be expressed to everyone, that the sects of Islam arose, with the result that each one accused the others of unbelief or heresy. Thus the Mu'tazilites interpreted many [Koranic] verses and Traditions, and expressed their interpretations to the multitude, and the Ash'arites did the same, although they used [24] such interpretations less frequently. In consequence they threw people into hatred, mutual detestation, and wars, tore the Law to shreds, and completely divided people.

In addition to all this, in the methods that they followed to establish their interpretations they neither went along with the multitude nor with the elect: not with the multitude, because their methods were more obscure than the methods common to the majority, and not with the elect, because if these methods are inspected they are found deficient in the conditions [required] for demonstration, as will be understood after the slightest inspection by anyone acquainted with the conditions of demonstration. Further, many of the principles on which the Ash'arites based their knowledge are sophistical, for they deny many necessary truths such as the permanence of accidents, the action of things on other things, the existence of necessary causes for effects, of substantial forms, and of secondary causes.

And their theorists wronged the Muslims in this sense, that a sect of Ash'arites called an unbeliever anyone who did not attain knowledge of the existence of the Glorious Creator by the methods laid down by them in their books for attaining this knowledge. But in truth it is they who are the unbelievers and in error! From this point they proceeded to disagree, one group saying, "The primary obligation is theoretical study," another group saying, "It is belief"; that is, [this happened] because they did not know which are the methods common to everyone, through whose doors the Law has summoned all people [to enter]; they supposed that there was only one method. Thus they mistook the aim of the Legislator, and both were themselves in error and led others into error.

It may be asked: "If these methods followed by the Ash'arites and other theorists are not the common methods by which the Legislator has aimed to teach the multitude and by which alone it is possible to teach them, then what are those [common] methods in this Law of ours?" We reply: they are exclusively the methods set down in the precious Book. For if the precious Book is inspected, there will be found in it the three methods that are available for all the people, namely the common methods for the instruction of the majority of the people and the special method. And if their merits are inspected, it becomes apparent that no better common methods for the instruction of the multitude can be found than the methods mentioned in it.

Thus whoever tampers with them, by making an interpretation not apparent in itself, or [at any rate] more apparent to everyone than they are (and that [greater apparency] is something nonexistent), is rejecting [25] their wisdom and rejecting their intended effects in procuring human happiness. This is very apparent from [a comparison of] the condition of the first believers with the condition of those who came after them. For the first believers arrived at perfect virtue and fear of God only by using these sayings [of the Book] without interpreting them; and any one of them who did find out an interpretation did not think fit to express it [to others]. But when those who came after them used interpretation, their fear of God grew less, their dissensions increased, their love for one another was removed, and they became divided into sects.

So whoever wishes to remove this heresy from the Law should direct his attention to the precious Book, and glean from it the indications present [in it] concerning everything in turn that it obliges us to believe, and exercise his judgment in looking at its apparent meaning as well as he is able, without interpreting any of it, except where the interpretation is apparent in itself, that is, commonly apparent to everyone. For if the sayings set down in the Law for the instruction of the people are inspected, it seems that in mastering[21] their meaning one arrives at a point, beyond which none but a man of the demonstrative class can extract from their apparent wording a meaning that is not apparent in them. This property is not found in any other sayings.

For those statements of the Law in the precious Book that are expressed to everyone have three properties that indicate their miraculous character. First, there exist none more completely persuasive and convincing to everyone than they. Secondly, their meaning admits naturally of mastery, up to a point beyond which their interpretation (when they are of a kind to have such an interpretation) can only be found out by the demonstrative class. Thirdly, they contain means of drawing the attention of the people of truth to the true interpretation. This [character] is not found in the doctrines of the Ash'arites nor in those of the Mu'tazilites, that is, their interpretations do not admit of mastery nor contain [means of] drawing attention to the truth, nor are they true; and this is why heresies have multiplied.

It is our desire to devote our time to this object and achieve it effectively, and if God grants us a respite of life we shall work steadily toward it in so far as this is made possible for us; and it may be that that work will serve as a starting point for our successors. For our soul is in the utmost sorrow and pain by reason of [26] the evil fancies and perverted beliefs that have infiltrated this Law, and particularly such [afflictions] as have happened to it at the hands of people who claim an affinity with philosophy. For injuries from a friend are more severe than injuries from an enemy. I refer to the fact that philosophy is the friend and milk-sister of the Law; thus injuries from people related to philosophy are the severest injuries [to the Law]—apart from the enmity, hatred, and quarrels that such [injuries] stir up between the two, which are companions by nature and lovers by essence and instinct. It has also been injured by a host of ignorant friends who claim an affinity with it: these are the sects that exist within it. But God directs all men aright and helps everyone to love Him; He unites their hearts in the fear of Him, and removes from them hatred and loathing by His grace and His mercy!

Indeed God has already removed many of these ills, ignorant ideas, and misleading practices, by means of this triumphant rule.[22] By it He has opened a way to many benefits, especially to the class of persons who have trodden the path of study and sought to know the truth. This [He has done] by summoning the multitude to a middle way of knowing God, the Glorious, [a way] that is raised above the low level of the followers of authority but is below the turbulence of the dialectical theologians; and by drawing the attention of the elect to their obligation and to make a thorough study of the principles of the Law. God is the Giver of success and the Guide by His Goodness.

NOTES

1. The question concerning philosophy is expressed formally: in which of the legal categories is it to be placed? Averroes mentions four out of the five categories: (1) obligatory, (2) recommended —these two together are classed as "commanded"; (3) allowed; and (5) prohibited. He does not mention (4) disapproved.

2. That is, the companions of Muhammad and the first generation(s) of Muslims.

3. Actually about 109 times (diameters).

4. This rendering is based on reading *wa-mā* for *wa-ammā* (Hourani's ed., n. 57) and then following BN and E (nn. 58, 60). The edited text reads: "But what calls even more strongly for comparison with the art of mathematics in this respect is the art of the principles of jurisprudence; and jurisprudence itself was completed only over a long period of time."

5. Or "except the West," that is, Andalusia and western North Africa.

6. Averroes is quoting a Tradition.

7. "Interpretation" renders the Arabic term *ta'wil*. Averroes defines the term in the immediate sequel. "Interpretation" is used by the commentators of the Koran to mean, among other things, turning a Koranic verse from its apparent or obvious meaning to a meaning that it bears, but not according to the letter or overt sense; it is an explanation of the covert, virtual, or intended meaning of the verse. In contrast to the apparent meaning, it admits of many levels. See below, pp. 10, 15, 20.

8. Unanimous agreement, or consensus (*ijmā'*), is one of the principles of Islamic jurisprudence: a source of Law (next to the Koran and Tradition).

9. The followers of Abū al-Ḥasan 'Alī al-Ash'arī (873–935), a pupil of the Mu'-tazilites (see below, n. 20) who turned to defend orthodoxy against them.

10. Which states: "God descends to the heaven of the lower world."

11. The followers of Aḥmad Ibn Ḥanbal (780–855), who stubbornly fought the Mu'tazilites and remained attached to the letter of the Law.

12. Imām al-Ḥaramayn al-Juwaynī (1028–85), Ash'arite theologian and teacher of Algazel.

13. Muḥammad Ibn Ismā'īl (810–70), author of one of the six canonical collections of Tradition. The reference is to his *al-Jāmi' al-ṣaḥīḥ* (Bulaq, 1296 A.H.), III, 49.

14. Above, Selection 6, n. 7.

15. The reference is to the "Appendix" (*Ḍamīmah*) to the *Decisive Treatise* (included in Hourani's ed., pp. 41-45, and trans., pp. 72-75).

16. Above, p. 8.

17. Above, p. 7.

18. Note the bracketing of *laysa* in the text of Hourani's ed. (n. 250), in which case the sentence reads: "But in fact he increased the number of the mischievous not of the learned."

19. The verse is by the poet 'Imrān Ibn Ḥiṭṭān al-Sadūsī (fl., seventh century). The Ma'addites, together with other North Arabian tribes, styled themselves 'Adnānites; the Yamanites were the South Arabian tribes.

20. The Mu'tazilites formed the first school of dialectical theology in Islam. Their doctrines were championed by the Abbasid caliphs between 827 and 878, but combated by the orthodox schools of jurisprudence and then by Ash'arite dialectical theologians.

21. "Mastering" and "mastery" (below), or "defending" and "defense."

22. The reference is to the Almohad ruler Abū Ya'qūb Yūsuf (reigned 1163–84), the patron of Averroes.

PART TWO

Political Philosophy in Judaism

EDITED BY RALPH LERNER

11.

Maimonides

LOGIC

Translated by Muhsin Mahdi

Moses Maimonides (Moshe ben Maimon, 1135–1204) was born in Cordova. He received his early training in Jewish studies from his father, who was a scholar of some note. In addition, he was instructed in philosophy and the natural sciences by local Muslim scholars. With the fall of Cordova to the Almohads in 1148, his father fled with his family and wandered about Spain for over a decade. In 1160 the family settled in Fez, where Maimonides continued studying with Muslim scholars. But, again, the pressure of religious persecution forced the family to leave in 1165. After passing through Acre and Jerusalem, Maimonides settled in al-Fusṭāṭ (Old Cairo). Here he entered into a medical career as a means of livelihood, finally serving as court physician to Saladin. Maimonides was a communal leader, and much of his time was occupied in answering legal and doctrinal questions addressed to him by Jews in all lands. He died in Cairo and was buried at Tiberias. Maimonides' work comes close to being encyclopedic. He was the author of works on logic, astronomy, and medicine. His *Commentary on the Mishnah* (1168) and the *Mishneh Torah* (*Code*) (1180) are comprehensive attempts to represent the immense complexities of talmudic legislation in a clear and systematic fashion. In the *Guide of the Perplexed* (1185–90?) Maimonides addressed himself to the challenge posed by Greek philosophy to the believer in a divinely-revealed Law.

The *Treatise on the Art of Logic* (*Maqālah fī ṣināʿat al-manṭiq; Millot ha-higgayon*) was written by Maimonides when he was about sixteen years old. It is addressed to a man who is described as being an authority on the sciences based on the Law and an authority on Arabic eloquence. This man has asked one who has studied the art of logic (that is, Maimonides) to explain to him the various technical terms used in logic, briefly, without going into details, and without necessarily being exhaustive. The following statement on political science occurs in the fourteenth (final) chapter of the treatise. It is preceded in this chapter by a classification of the sciences. Philosophy or science is divided into (1) theoretical philosophy, and (2) what is variously called practical philosophy, human philosophy, political philosophy, or political science. (1) Theoretical philosophy is divided into (a) mathematics, (b) physics, and (c) theology. (a) Mathematics, in turn, is divided into (i) arithmetic, (ii) geometry, (iii) astronomy, and (iv) music. (c) Theology is divided into (i) speech about God and the angels, and (ii) divine science or metaphysics. (2) Practical philosophy is divided into (a) ethics, (b) economics, (c) governance of the city or politics in

the strict sense, and (d) governance of the large nation.

Maimonides' statement on political science is here, for the first time, translated into a Western language from a text in the original Arabic. Two complete Arabic manuscripts have only recently been discovered. They have been edited, with a Turkish translation, by Mubahat Türker in: *Ankara Üniversitesi Dil ve Tarih-Coğrafya Fakültesi Dergisi*, XVIII (1960), 40–64. (The passage printed below corresponds to p. 63 of the Arabic text in the Türker edition.) An earlier critical edition, containing the Arabic text of the first half of the *Logic* (all that had hitherto been available), medieval Hebrew translations of the whole work by Moses Ibn Tibbon, Ahitub, and Vivas, and an English translation, was edited by Israel Efros under the title: *Maimonides' Treatise on Logic* (New York: American Academy for Jewish Research, 1938).

CHAPTER XIV

[POLITICAL SCIENCE]

POLITICAL SCIENCE FALLS INTO four parts: first, the individual man's governance of himself; second, the governance of the household; third, the governance of the city; and fourth, the governance of the large nation or of the nations.

Man's governance of his self consists in his making it acquire the virtuous moral habits and removing from it the vile moral habits if these are already present. Moral habits are the settled states that form in the soul until they become habitual dispositions from which the actions originate. The philosophers characterize moral habit as being a virtue or a vice; they call the noble moral habits, moral virtues, and they call the base moral habits, moral vices. The actions stemming from the virtuous moral habits, they call good; and the actions stemming from the base moral habits, they call evil. Similarly, they characterize intellecting, too—that is, conceiving the intelligibles—as being a virtue or a vice. Thus they speak of intellectual virtues and of intellectual vices. The philosophers have many books on morals. They call every governance by which a man governs another, a regime.

The governance of the household consists in knowing[1] how they [that is, the members of the household] help each other, and what is sufficient for them, so that their conditions may be well ordered, as far as this is possible in view of the requisites of that particular time and place.

The governance of the city is a science that imparts to its citizens knowledge of true happiness and imparts to them the [way of] striving to achieve it; and knowledge of true misery, imparting to them the [way of] striving to guard against it, and training their moral habits to abandon what are only presumed to be happiness so that they not take pleasure in them and doggedly pursue them. It explains to them what are only presumed to be miseries so that they not suffer pain over them and dread them. Moreover, it prescribes for them rules of justice that order their associations properly. The learned men of past religious communities (*milal*) used to formulate,[2] each of them according to his perfection, regimens and rules through which their princes governed the subjects; they called them nomoi; and the nations used to be governed by those nomoi. On all these things, the philosophers have many books that have been translated into Arabic, and the ones that have not been translated are perhaps even more numerous. In these times, all this—I mean the regimes and the nomoi—has been dispensed with, and men are being governed by divine commands.

NOTES

1. Reading *ya'lam* for *ta'allam* with Ibn Tibbon (*yēda'*).
2. Reading *taṣna'* with the printed text and Vivas, or perhaps *taḍa'* (lay down) with Ibn Tibbon and Ahitub.

12.

Maimonides

GUIDE OF

THE PERPLEXED

Translated by Ralph Lerner and Muhsin Mahdi

The *Guide of the Perplexed* (*Dalā-lat al-ḥā'irin; Moreh Nebukhim*) is addressed to a certain young man and to those like him who are troubled by the disparity that exists between the teaching of the Law, literally understood, and the teaching of the philosophers. To help such men—believers who have some acquaintance with the writings of the philosophers—in their perplexity, Maimonides has composed this work. The *Guide* is not addressed to the ordinary run of mankind or to those who have not engaged in any study beyond the jurisprudence based on the Law. Maimonides is speaking to individuals who have attained a certain measure of theoretical understanding and who have developed certain habits of reading. In his instructions for studying this work, he pointedly remarks that the diction used by him in the *Guide* has been chosen "with great exactness

and exceeding precision." The following chapters have been chosen from each of the three parts into which the work is divided. Chapter 71 of Part I serves as an introduction to Maimonides' discussion of the demonstrations of God's existence, unity, and incorporeality. It might be regarded as a history of philosophy, down to his time, reduced to the compass of a single chapter. The chapters translated here from Part II are all taken from that section of the *Guide* whose theme is prophecy; special attention is given to the prophet's legislative function. The last group of chapters (from Part III) is selected from the section in which Maimonides examines the actions commanded by God in the Law. Here his theme is the rationality of the Law's commandments (in terms of the Law's intention) and the limits to that rationality.

The *Guide* was written in Arabic.

It was twice translated into Hebrew and was available to readers of Latin within fifty years of Maimonides' death. The critical edition of the Arabic text, together with a French translation, was published by S. Munk in three volumes under the title *Le Guide des Égarés* (Paris, 1856–66). This text was revised and re-issued by Issachar Joel (Jerusalem, 1931). The present translation is based on a new English translation by Shlomo Pines (Chicago: University of Chicago Press, 1963). The italic numbers in brackets in the body of the text refer to the pagination of Munk's edition.

PART   I

CHAPTER   7 I

KNOW THAT THE MANY SCIENCES that have existed in our religious community, devoted to establishing the truth of these matters, have perished because of the length of the time that has passed, because of our being dominated by the ignorant nations, and because, as we have made clear, those matters were not permitted to all men. The only thing that was permitted to all men were the texts of the books. You already know that even the [traditionally] transmitted jurisprudence was not put down in writing in the olden times because of the command, which is widely known in the nation: "Words that I have communicated to you orally you are not allowed to put down in writing."[1] This was extremely wise with regard to the Law, for it avoided what ultimately befell it. I mean the multiplicity of opinions, the proliferation of schools, the uncertainties occurring in the expression of what is put down in writing, the negligence that accompanies what is written down, the rise of dissension among men who are separated into sects, and the introduction of perplexity in actions. All these matters instead were entrusted to the Great Court of Law, as we have explained in our juridical compositions[2] and as the text of the Torah indicates.[3]

Now if there was insistence that jurisprudence should not be perpetuated in a written compilation accessible to all men in view of the harm that would be caused by such a procedure, still less could any of the mysteries of the Torah be set down in writing and be made accessible to men. On the contrary, they were transmitted by a few of the elect to a few of the same kind, as I explained to you from their saying: "The mysteries of the Torah may only be transmitted to a counsellor, wise in crafts," and so on.[4] This was the cause that necessitated the disappearance [*94a*] of these great roots [of knowledge] from the nation. You will not find anything of them except slight indications and pointers occurring in the Talmud and the Midrashoth. These are a few kernels of grain, which are overlaid by many layers of husks, so that people were occupied with these layers of husks and thought that beneath them there was no kernel whatever.

As for that scanty bit of argument[5] regarding the notion of the unity of God and regarding what depends on this notion, which you will find in the writings of some Geonim and in those of the Qaraites, these are matters that they have taken over from the dialectical theologians of Islam and they are scanty indeed as compared to what the Muslims have composed on this subject.

Also it has so happened that the first Muslims to take this way were a certain sect, namely the Mu'tazilites,[6] from whom our coreligionists borrowed and whose way they followed. After a certain time another sect arose in Islam, namely the Ash'arites,[7] among whom other opinions arose, none of which you will find among our coreligionists. This was not because they preferred the first opinion to the second, but because it so happened that they had taken over and adopted the first opinion and assumed it to be a matter proved by demonstration.

As for the Andalusians[8] among the people of our nation, all of them cling to the affirmations of the philosophers and incline to their opinions, as long as these do not contradict a foundation of the Law. You will not find them in any way taking the paths of the dialectical theologians. Therefore in such few matters as are found [in the writings] belonging to the later ones among them, in many things they go in the same direction as our doctrine in this Treatise.

Know also that all the statements that the Muslims—both the Mu'tazilites and the Ash'arites—have made concerning these notions are all of them opinions [94b] founded upon premises that are taken over from the books of the Greeks and the Syrians who wished to disagree with the opinions of the philosophers and to disprove their statements. The reason for this was that when the Christian community came to include those communities (the Christian preaching being what it is known to be) and since the opinions of the philosophers were widespread in those communities—philosophy had first risen there, and kings rose who protected religion—the learned of those periods from among the Greeks and the Syrians saw that those preachings are greatly and clearly opposed to the philosophic opinions. Thus there arose among them this science of dialectical theology. They started to establish premises that would be useful to them with regard to their belief and to counter those opinions that undermine the foundations of their Law. When thereupon the community of Islam arrived and the books of the philosophers were translated for them, those counterarguments composed against the books of the philosophers were also translated for them. Thus they found the dialectical theology of John Philoponus,[9] Ibn 'Adī,[10] and of others with regard to these notions, held on to it, and they thought that they had achieved something great. They also selected from among the opinions of the earlier philosophers everything that the one who selected considered as useful for him, even if the later philosophers had already demonstrated the falseness of these opinions—as for instance the existence of atoms and the vacuum. And they considered that these were conceptions common to all and premises that every follower of a Law is obliged to admit. Afterward dialectical theology became wider in scope, and these people went down to other strange roads that had never been taken by the dialectical theologians from among the Greeks and others, for these were near to the philosophers. Then there arose among the Muslims assertions of the Law that were particular to them and that they [95a] necessarily had need to defend. Furthermore, differences occurred between them with regard to these questions, so that every sect among them established premises useful to it in the defense of its opinion. There is no doubt that there are things that are common to all three of us, I mean the Jews, the Christians, and the Muslims: namely, the assertion of the temporal creation of the world, the validity of which entails the validity of miracles and other things. As for the other things into which these two communities undertook to plunge—for instance, the notion of trinity into which the Christians plunged and the dialectical theology into which certain sects of the Muslims plunged—so that they found it requisite to establish premises and to establish, by means of these premises that they had chosen, the notions into which they had plunged and the notions that are peculiar to each of the two communities, having been postulated in it: these are things that we do not require in any respect.

To sum up, all the first dialectical theologians from among the Greeks who had adopted Christianity and from among the Muslims did not conform to the appearance of what exists in their premises; but rather they considered how existence ought to be in order that it should furnish a proof for the correctness of a particular opinion, or at least should not refute it. And when such a fantasy held good, they assumed that what exists corresponds to that form and started to argue in order to establish the truth of those claims from which are taken the premises that show the correctness of the doctrine or that at least do not refute it.

This is the way of the intellectuals who first used this method, put it down in books, and claimed that speculation alone impelled them to do so, without regard for a prior doctrine or opinion. As for the later ones who study these books, they know nothing about all this and consequently find in [95b] these ancient books powerful arguments and a mighty endeavor to affirm a certain thing or to disprove a certain thing, and think thereupon that there is no need in any way to prove or to disprove this matter for such foundations of the Law as require it. [They also believe] that their predecessors did what they did only in order to confuse the opinions of the philosophers and to make them doubt that which they regarded as a demonstration. Those who say this are not aware, and do not know, that the case is not as they assume, but that their predecessors toiled to affirm what they desired to affirm and to disprove what they desired to disprove because of the harm that would come if this were not done—even if it were after a hundred propositions—to the opinion that they sought to affirm. These ancient dialectical theologians did away with the disease starting with its root.

To sum up, I shall say to you that the matter is as Themistius puts it: that which exists does not conform to the various opinions, but rather the correct opinions conform to that which exists.

When I studied the books of these dialectical theologians, as far as I had the opportunity—as I studied the books of the philosophers, as far as my capacity went—I found that the method of all the dialectical theologians was one and the same in kind, though the subdivisions differed from one another. For the foundation of everything is that one need have no regard for the way in which being is, for it is merely a custom; and from the point of view of the intellect, it could well be different. Furthermore, in many places they follow the imagination and call it intellect. Thus when they propound the premises that we will let you hear, they reach the judgment, through their demonstrations, that the world is created in time. And when it is thus established that the world is created in time, it is likewise undoubtedly established that it has a maker [96a] who has created it in time. Then they infer that this maker is one; whereupon, basing themselves upon His being one, they affirm that He is not a body. This is the way of every dialectical theologian from among the Muslims in anything concerning this subject. Thus also do those belonging to our community who imitate them and follow their ways. As for the ways in which they make their inferences and propound the premises with regard to the affirmation of the temporal creation of the world or to the refutation of its pre-eternity, they differ from one another. The universal thesis of all of them, however, consists in the first place in the affirmation of the temporal creation of the world. And by means of its temporal creation it is established as correct that the deity exists.

Now when I considered this method, my soul felt a very strong aversion to it, and had every right to do so. For every argument deemed to be a demonstration of the temporal creation of the world is accompanied by doubts and is not a decisive demonstration except among those who do not know the difference between demonstration, dialectic, and sophistry. As for those who know these arts, it is clear and evident to them that there are doubts with regard to all these proofs and that premises that have not been demonstrated have been used in them. According to me, the utmost power of one who seeks to ascertain the truth (among those who follow a Law) consists in his refuting the proofs of the philosophers bearing on the eternity of the world. How sublime a thing it is when it is possible for him to do it! And everyone who engages in speculation, who is perceptive, and who seeks to ascertain the truth and does not deceive himself, knows that with regard to this question—namely, the eternity of the world or its temporal creation—no decisive demonstration can be reached and that it is a point at which the intellect rests. Later we shall speak about this at length. At present it will be enough for you to know with regard to this question that the philosophers of the various epochs disagree with respect to it for three thousand years down to our time, as we can find in their works and in the reports concerning them.

Now if this is the state of this question, how [*96b*] can we take the doctrine of the temporal creation of the world as a premise upon which we found the existence of the deity? For in that case the existence of the deity would be doubtful: if the world were created in time, there would be a deity; and if it were eternal, there would be no deity. Things either would be like that or we would claim that we have a demonstration of the creation of the world in time and we would use the sword to prove it so that we should claim to know God by means of a demonstration. All this is remote from the truth. Rather, the correct way, according to me, which is the method of demonstration about which there can be no doubt, is to establish the existence and the oneness of the deity and the negation of corporeality through the methods of the philosophers, which methods are founded upon the doctrine of the eternity of the world—not because I believe in the eternity of the world or because I concede this point to the philosophers, but because it is through this method that the demonstration becomes valid and perfect certainty is obtained with regard to those three things: I mean the existence of the deity, His oneness, and His not being a body; all this without regard to reaching a judgment as to the world's being eternal or created in time. When these three great and sublime problems have been validated for us through a correct demonstration, we shall thereafter return to the question of the creation of the world in time and we shall enounce with regard to it all the argumentation that is possible.

If you are one of those who are persuaded by what the dialectical theologians say, and if you believe that the demonstration with regard to the creation of the world in time is correct, that's just fine. If it is not demonstrated in your opinion, and if you take over from the prophets, through obeying their authority, the doctrine that it was created in time, there is no harm in that. And you should not ask how prophecy can be true if the world is eternal, before you have heard our discourse concerning prophecy in this Treatise; however at present we are not dealing with this notion.

You ought to know that the premises that are laid down by those concerned with the roots, [97a] I mean among the dialectical theologians, with a view to affirming the creation of the world in time, imply—in a measure that you will hear defined—an upsetting of the world and a change in the order established at the time of creation. For I have to state to you their premises and their way of drawing inferences.

As to this my method, it is as I shall describe to you in a general way now. Namely I shall say: the world cannot but be either eternal or created in time. If it is created in time, it undoubtedly has a creator who created it in time. For it is a first intelligible that what has appeared at a certain moment in time has not created itself in time and that its creator is other than itself. Accordingly the one who created the world in time is the deity. If, however, the world is eternal, it follows necessarily because of this and that proof that there is some being other than all the bodies to be found in the world; a being who is not a body and not a power in a body and who is one, permanent, and everlasting; who has no cause and who cannot change: this, then, is the deity. Thus it has become manifest to you that the proofs for the existence and the oneness of the deity and of His not being a body ought to presuppose the eternity of the world, for in this way the demonstration will be perfect, both if the world is eternal and if it is created in time. For this reason you will always find me—in what I have written in the books of jurisprudence, whenever I happen to mention the foundations and start upon establishing the existence of the deity—establishing it by arguments that tend toward the eternity of the world, not because I believe in the eternity of the world, but because I wish to establish in our belief the existence of God, the Exalted, through a demonstrative method as to which there is no dispute in any respect. (We do not place this true opinion, which is of immense importance, upon a foundation that everyone can shake and wish to destroy, and that other men think has never been constructed.) This is especially [in order] since these philosophic proofs of the three problems in question are taken [97b] from the visible nature of existence that is not denied except with a view to safeguarding certain opinions.

The proofs of the dialectical theologians, on the other hand, are taken from premises that run counter to the visible nature of existence so that they resort to maintaining that nothing has a nature in any respect. In this Treatise, when speaking of the creation of the world in time, I shall devote for your benefit a chapter in which I shall explain to you a proof for the creation of the world in time. I will reach the goal that every dialectical theologian desires, without abolishing the nature of existence and without disagreeing with Aristotle on any point he has demonstrated. For whereas the proof, with the aid of which some dialectical theologians prove by inference the creation of the world in time and which is their most powerful proof, is not consolidated for them until they abolish the nature of all existence and disagree with everything that the philosophers have explained, I reach a similar proof without running counter to the nature of existence and without contending against sense-perception. I saw fit to mention to you the general premises of the dialectical theologians by means of which they establish the creation of the world in time, the existence of the deity, His oneness, and the rejection of His corporeality; and I shall show you their way in this and shall make clear to you what follows necessarily from each of those premises. After that I shall mention to you the proximate premises of the philosophers regarding this and I shall show you their way.

Do not, however, demand from me in this Treatise that I should establish the correctness of those philosophic premises that I shall condense for your benefit. For doing this constitutes the greater part of natural and divine science. Likewise you should not desire that I should let you hear in this Treatise the arguments of the dialectical theologians that are intended to establish the correctness of their premises. For [*98a*] their lives passed away in this, and the lives of those who will come after them will likewise pass away in this, and their books have grown numerous. For every one of their premises, with few exceptions, is contradicted by what is visible of the nature of being, so that doubts arise regarding them. Accordingly, they resort to compilations and disputations in order to affirm the premise and to dispel the doubts coming with regard to it, and, if necessary, even to gainsay the visible [nature of existence], which contradicts it. As for the philosophic premises that I shall condense for your benefit to demonstrate these three problems—I mean the existence and oneness of the deity and the negation of corporeality—most of them are premises regarding which you achieve certainty as soon as you first hear them and understand their meaning. However some of them refer you to the passages in which their demonstration occurs in the books concerning natural science or metaphysics; you will turn to these passages and establish the correctness of what may be required to have its correctness established.

I have already let you know that there exists nothing except God, the Exalted, and this existing [world] and that there is no possible inference proving His existence, the Exalted, except those deriving from this existent taken as a whole and from its details. It follows necessarily that this existent be considered as it is and that premises be taken from what can be observed of its nature. For this reason it follows that you should know its observable form and nature, and then it will be possible to make an inference from it with regard to what is other than it. For this reason

I judged that first I ought to set down a chapter in which I would explain to you that which exists as a whole by informing you of what is demonstrated and is indubitably correct. After that I shall set down for your benefit other chapters in which I shall mention the premises of the dialectical theologians and shall make clear their methods by means of which they explained the four problems in question. After that I shall set down for your benefit other chapters in which I shall explain to you [98b] the premises of the philosophers and their methods of inference with regard to these problems. After that I shall summarize for your benefit the method that I shall adopt, as I have already informed you, with regard to these four problems.

PART II

CHAPTER 3 2

The opinions of people concerning prophecy are like their opinions concerning the eternity of the world or its creation in time. I mean by this that just as the people to whose mind the existence of the deity is firmly established, have, as we have explained, three opinions concerning the eternity of the world or its creation in time, so are there also three opinions concerning prophecy. I shall not pay attention to the opinion of Epicurus, for he does not believe in the existence of a deity, let alone believe in a prophecy. I only aim to state the opinions of those who believe in the deity.

The first opinion—that of the multitude of the ignorant communities who accept prophecy and also believed by some of the vulgar among the followers of our Law—is that God, the Exalted, chooses whom He wishes from among men, turns him into a prophet, and sends him with a mission. According to them it makes no difference whether this individual is a man of knowledge or [73a] ignorant, aged or young. However, they also posit as a condition his having a certain goodness and sound morality. For up to now people have not gone so far as to say that God sometimes turns a wicked man into a prophet unless He has first, according to this opinion, turned him into a good man.

The second opinion—that of the philosophers—is that prophecy is a certain perfection in the nature of man. This perfection is not achieved in any individual from among men except after a training that makes that which exists in the potentiality of the species pass into actuality, provided an obstacle due to temperament or to some external cause does not hinder this, as is the case with regard to every perfection whose existence is possible in a certain species. For the existence of that perfection in its extreme and ultimate form in every individual of that species is not possible. It must, however, exist necessarily in at least one particular individual; if, in order to be achieved, this perfection requires something that actualizes it, that something necessarily exists. According to this opinion it is not possible that an ignoramus should turn into a prophet; nor can a man who is not a prophet become a prophet overnight, as though one has made a find. Things are rather as follows: a virtuous individual who is perfect with respect to his rational and moral qualities, when his imaginative faculty is in its most perfect state and when he has been prepared in the way that you will hear, he will necessarily become a prophet, inasmuch as this is a perfection that belongs to us by nature. According to this opinion an individual cannot be fit for prophecy and prepared for it and not become a prophet, any more than an individual having a healthy temperament can be nourished with excellent food without sound blood and similar things being generated from that food.

The third opinion—the opinion of our Law and the foundation of our doctrine—is identical with the [73b] philosophic opinion except in one thing. For we believe that it may happen that one who is fit for prophecy and prepared for it should not become a prophet, namely, on account of the divine will. To my mind this is like all the miracles and takes the same course as they. For the natural thing is that everyone who is fit by his natural disposition and who trains himself in his education and study will become a prophet. He who is prevented from it is like him who has been prevented (like Jeroboam) from moving his hand or (like the King of Aram's army going out to seek Elisha) from seeing.[11] As for preparation and perfection in the moral and rational qualities being basic for us, this is their saying: "Prophecy only rests upon a wise, strong, and rich man."[12] We have explained this in the *Commentary on the Mishnah* and in the great compilation [namely, the *Code* or *Mishneh Torah*], and we have narrated that the disciples of the prophets were always engaged in preparation. As for the fact that one who prepares is sometimes prevented from becoming a prophet, you may know it from the history of Baruch, son of Neriah. For he followed Jeremiah, who trained, taught, and prepared him. And he aspired to become a prophet, but was prevented. As he says: *I am weary with my groanings and I find no rest* [Jer. 45:3]. Thereupon he was told through Jeremiah: *Thus shalt thou say unto him: Thus saith the Lord*, and so on. *And seekest thou great things for thyself? Seek them not* [Jer. 45:4–5]. It is possible to say that this is a clear statement that prophecy is too great a thing for Baruch. Similarly it may be said, as we shall explain, that in the passage:

Yea, her prophets find no vision from the Lord [Lam. 2:9], this was the case because they were in Exile. However we find many texts, some of them scriptural and some of them dicta of the sages, all of which follow this fundamental: that God turns whom He wills, whenever He wills it, into a prophet—but only someone perfect and virtuous to the utmost degree. But as regards one of the ignorant among the vulgar, [*74a*] this is not possible according to us—I mean that He should turn one of them into a prophet—except as it is possible that He should turn an ass or a frog into a prophet. It is our fundamental that there must be training and perfection, whereupon the possibility arises to which the power of the deity becomes attached. You should not be led astray by His saying: *Before I formed thee in the belly I knew thee, and before thou camest forth from the womb I sanctified thee* [Jer. 1:5]. For this is the state of every prophet: he must have a natural preparedness in his original natural disposition, as shall be explained. As for his saying: *For I am young* [Jer. 1:6], you know that in the Hebrew language Joseph the righteous was called *young* [cf. Gen. 41:12] though he was thirty years old, and that Joshua was called *young* though he was near his sixtieth year. For it says with reference to the time of the doings concerning the calf: *But his servant Joshua, son of Nun, a young man, departed not,* and so on [Exod. 33:11]. Now Moses our Master was at that time eighty-one years old, and his whole life lasted one hundred and twenty years. Joshua lived after him fourteen years, and the life of Joshua lasted one hundred and ten years. Accordingly it is clear that Joshua was at that time at least fifty-seven years old, and was nevertheless called young. Again you should not be led astray by His dictum figuring in the promises: *I will pour out My spirit upon all flesh, and your sons and your daughters shall prophesy* [Joel 3:1]; for He interprets this and lets us know what kind of prophecy is meant, for He says: *Your old men shall dream dreams, your young men shall see visions* [Joel 3:1]. For everyone who tells of the unseen, whether this be by way of soothsaying and divination or by way of a true dream, is likewise called a prophet. For this reason prophets of Baal and prophets of Asherah are called prophets. Do you not see that He, the Exalted, says: *If there arise among you a prophet or a dreamer of dreams* [Deut. 13:2]? As for the Presence at Mount Sinai, though through a miracle all the people saw the great fire and heard the frightening and terrifying voices, [*74b*] only those who were fit for it achieved the rank of prophecy, and even those in varying degrees. Do you not see that He says: *Come up unto the Lord, thou and Aaron, Nadab and Abihu, and seventy of the elders of Israel* [Exod. 24:1]? He (peace be upon him) had the highest rank, as He said: *And Moses alone shall come near unto the Lord; but they shall not come near* [Exod. 24:2]. Aaron was below him; Nadab and Abihu below Aaron; the seventy elders below Nadab and Abihu; and the other people below the latter according to their degrees of perfection. A text of the sages (may their memory be a blessing) reads: "Moses is an enclosure apart, and Aaron an enclosure apart."[13]

As we have come to speak of the Presence at Mount Sinai, in a separate chapter we shall give indications as to what becomes clear regarding that Presence as it was—from the scriptural texts, if they are well examined, and from the dicta of the sages.

CHAPTER 36

Know that the truth and essence of prophecy consist in its being an emanation from God, the Mighty and Majestic, through the mediation of the Active Intellect to the rational faculty in the first place and thereafter to the imaginative faculty. This is the highest degree of man and the ultimate perfection that [*78a*] can exist for his species; and this state is the ultimate perfection of the imaginative faculty. This is something that can in no way exist in every man. And it is not something that may be attained through perfection in the theoretical sciences and through improvement of moral habits (to the end that all of them become as fine and beautiful as can be) without there being in addition the highest possible degree of perfection of the imaginative faculty in respect of its original natural disposition. Now you already know that the perfection of these bodily faculties to which the imaginative faculty belongs follows from the best possible temperament, the best possible size, and the purest possible matter, of the part of the body that is the substratum for the faculty in question. It is not a thing whose lack could be made good or whose deficiency could be remedied in any way by means of a regimen. For with regard to a part of the body whose temperament was bad in the original natural disposition, the utmost that the corrective regimen can achieve is to keep it in some sort of health; it cannot restore it to its best possible condition. If, however, its defect derives from its size, position, or substance (I mean the substance of the matter from which it is generated), there is no device that can help. You know all this; it is therefore useless to explain it at length.

You already know also the actions of this imaginative faculty that are in its nature, such as retaining sense-perceptions, combining them, and imitation, and that its greatest and noblest action takes place only when the senses rest and are not performing their actions. It is then that a certain emanation flows to this faculty according to its preparation, and it is the cause of the true dreams. This same emanation is the cause of prophecy. There is only a difference in degree, not in kind. You already know that [the sages] have said time and again: "A dream is the sixtieth part of prophecy."[14] [78b] No proportion, however, can be established between two things differing in kind. One is not justified in saying, for instance, that the perfection of a man is a certain number of times greater than the perfection of a horse. They reiterated this point in Bereshith Rabbah, saying: "Dream is the unripe fruit of prophecy."[15] This is an extraordinary comparison. For unripe fruit is the individual fruit itself, but one that has fallen before it was perfect and before it had matured. Similarly the action of the imaginative faculty in the state of sleep is also its action in the state of prophecy; there is, however, a deficiency in it and it does not reach its ultimate term. Why should we teach you by means of the dicta of [the sages] (may their memory be a blessing) and leave aside the texts of the Torah? *If there be a prophet among you, I the Lord do make Myself known unto him in a vision, I do speak with him in a dream* [Num. 12:6]. Thus He, the Exalted, has informed us of the truth and essence of prophecy and has let us know that it is a perfection that comes in a dream or in a vision (*mar'eh*). The word *mar'eh* (vision) derives from the verb *ra'oh* (to see). This signifies that the imaginative faculty achieves so great a perfection of action that it sees the thing as if it were outside, and that the thing whose origin is due to it appears to have come to it by way of external sensation. In those two groups, I mean vision and dream, all the degrees of prophecy are included, as shall be explained. It is already known that a matter that occupies a man greatly—he being bent upon it and desirous of it—while he is awake and while his senses function, is the one with regard to which the imaginative faculty acts while he is asleep when the Intellect emanates to it in accordance with its [that is, the imagination's] preparation. It would be superfluous to cite examples of this and to expatiate on it as this is a manifest matter that everyone already knows. It is similar to the apprehension of the senses with regard to which no one with sound natural disposition would disagree.

After these premises, you should know that if[16] a [79a] human individual the substance of whose brain at the origin of his natural disposition is extremely well-proportioned as regards the purity of its matter and the particular temperament of each of its [that is, the brain's] parts and as regards its size and position, and is not affected by hindrances due to temperament that derive from another part of the body. Then that individual obtains knowledge and wisdom until he passes from potentiality to actuality and acquires a perfect and complete human intellect and pure and well-tempered human moral habits. All his desires are directed to acquiring the science of the secrets of this existence and knowledge of its causes, and his thought always goes toward noble matters, and he is interested only in the knowledge of the deity and in reflection on His works and on what ought to be believed with regard to that. His thought is detached from, and his desire abolished for, bestial things. (I mean the preference for the pleasures of eating, drinking, copulation, and, in general, of the sense of touch, which Aristotle explained in the *Ethics*, saying that this sense is a disgrace for us.[17] How fine is what he said, and how true it is that it is a disgrace! For we have it only in so far as we are animals like the other beasts, and nothing that belongs to the notion of humanity pertains to it. As for the other sensual pleasures—those, for instance, that derive from the sense of smell, from hearing, and from seeing—there may be found in them sometimes, though they are bodily, pleasure for man as man, as Aristotle has explained. We have been led to speak of things that are not to the purpose, but there was need for it. For most of the thoughts of those who are outstanding among men of science are preoccupied with the pleasures of this sense and are desirous of them. And then they wonder how it is that they do not become prophets, if prophecy is something natural.) It is [79b] likewise necessary that the thought of that individual be detached from the spurious kinds of rulership and that his desire for them should be abolished—I mean the wish to dominate or to be held great by the vulgar and to obtain from them honor and obedience for its own sake—but rather regard all people according to their various states with respect to which they are undoubtedly either like domestic animals or like beasts of prey. (Concerning these, the perfect man who lives in solitude, if he thinks of them at all, does so only with a view to saving himself from the harm coming from those among them who are harmful if he happens to associate with them, or to obtaining an advantage that may be obtained from them if he is forced to it by some of his needs.) There is no doubt that whenever—in an individual of this description—his imaginative faculty, which is as perfect as possible, acts and receives from the Intellect an emanation corresponding to his theoretical perfection, this individual will only apprehend divine and most extraordinary matters, will see only God and His angels, and will only be aware, and achieve knowledge of, matters that constitute true opinions and general directives for the well-being of men in their relations with one another. It is known that with regard to these three aims that we have given—namely, the perfection of the rational faculty through study, the perfection of the imaginative faculty through natural disposition, and the perfection of moral habit through turning the thought away from all bodily pleasures and putting an end to the desire for the various kinds of ignorant and evil glorification—there are among those who are perfect very many differences in rank; and on the differences in rank with regard to these three aims depend the differences in rank that subsist among the degrees of all the prophets.

You know that every bodily faculty sometimes grows tired, is weakened, and is corrupted, [80a] and at other times is in a sound state. Now this imaginative faculty is undoubtedly a bodily faculty. Accordingly you will find that the prophecy of the prophets ceased when they were sad or angry or the like. You know their saying that "prophecy does not descend during sadness or languor"[18]; that revelation did not come to Jacob our Father as long as he was mourning because of the fact that his imaginative faculty was preoccupied with the loss of Joseph;[19] and that, after the disastrous incident of the spies and until the whole generation of the desert had perished, revelation did not come to Moses (peace be on him) in the way that it had come before,[20] because—seeing the enormity of their crime—he suffered greatly because of this matter. This was so even though the imaginative faculty did not enter into his prophecy (peace be on him); rather the Intellect emanated to him without its mediation. For, as we have mentioned several times, he did not prophesy like the other prophets by means of parables. This will be made clear later on, for it is not the purpose of this chapter. Similarly you will find that several prophets prophesied during a certain time and that afterwards prophecy departed from them and did not continue because of an accident that had supervened. This is undoubtedly the essential proximate cause of the departure of prophecy during the time of the Exile. For what languor or sadness can befall a man in any state that would be stronger than that due to his being a thrall slave in bondage to the ignorant immoral communities who combine the privation of true reason with the perfection of the lusts of the beasts? *And there shall be no might in thine hand* [Deut. 28:32]. This was what we have been threatened with. And this was what he meant by saying: *They shall run to and fro to seek the word of the Lord, and shall not find it* [Amos 8:12]. And it also says: *Her king and her princes are among the nations, the Law is no more; yea, her prophets find no vision from the Lord* [Lam. 2:9]. This is true and the cause thereof is clear. For the instrument has ceased to function. This also will be the cause for the return of prophecy [*80b*] to us in its customary form, as has been promised in the days of the Messiah, may he be revealed soon.

CHAPTER 37

You ought to turn your attention to the nature of that which is in this divine emanation coming to us, through which we perceive intellectually and because of which our intellects vary in excellence. For sometimes something comes from it to a certain individual, the measure of that something being such that it renders him perfect and nothing more. Sometimes, on the other hand, the measure of what comes to the individual, beyond rendering him perfect, emanates to render others perfect. This is what happens to all beings: some of them achieve perfection to an extent that enables them to govern others, whereas others achieve perfection only in a measure that enables them to be governed by others, as we have explained.

After this, you should know that when this intellectual emanation flows only to the rational faculty and none of it overflows to the imaginative faculty—either because of the scantiness of what flows or because of some deficiency existing in the imaginative faculty in its natural disposition that makes it impossible for it to receive the emanation of the Intellect—then this is the class of men of science, theoretical men. If, on the other hand, this emanation is to both faculties—I mean both the rational and the imaginative (as we and others among the philosophers have explained)—and if the imaginative faculty is in its ultimate perfection as regards the natural disposition, then this is the class of prophets. If, again, the emanation is only to the imaginative faculty, the defect of the rational faculty deriving either from its original natural disposition or from insufficiency of training, then this class are those who govern cities [*81a*] and are the legislators, the soothsayers, the augurs, and those who have true dreams. Likewise, all those who do extraordinary things by means of strange devices and secret arts, although they are not men of science, belong to this third class. One of the things that you must ascertain is that some of those belonging to this third class have extraordinary imaginings, dreams, and amazed states while they are awake, similar to the vision of prophecy, so that they think of themselves as prophets. And they greatly marvel at what they apprehend of those imaginings and think that they acquired sciences without instruction; and they bring great confusion into theoretical matters of great import; true notions and imaginary ones are strangely confused for them. All this is due to the power of the imaginative faculty and the weakness of the rational faculty, and to [the latter's] not having obtained anything—I mean thereby that it has not passed into actuality.

It is known that in each of these three classes there are very many differences of degree and that each of the first two classes is divided into two parts, as we have explained. For the measure of the emanation reaching each of these two is either such as only to render the individual who receives it perfect and nothing more, or such that from that individual's perfection there is something left over that renders others perfect. As regards the first class—that of the men of science—that which emanates to the rational faculty of an individual [among them] is sometimes such that it makes him into a man who inquires and is endowed with understanding, who knows and discerns, but is not moved to teach others or to compose works, neither finding in himself a desire for this nor having the ability to do it. And sometimes that which emanates to him is such that it moves him of necessity to compose works and to teach. The same holds good for the second class. Sometimes the revelation that comes to him only renders that prophet perfect and nothing more. And sometimes what comes to him [*81b*] of it compels him to address a call to the people, teach them, and let his own perfection flow to them.

It has already become clear to you that, were it not for this additional perfection, sciences would not be set forth in books and prophets would not call upon people to know the truth. For a man of science does not compose anything for himself in order to teach himself what he already knows. Rather the nature of this Intellect is such that it always flows and extends from the one who receives that emanation to another one who receives it after him, until it reaches an individual beyond whom that emanation cannot go, but only renders him perfect, as we have stated in a parable in one of the chapters of this Treatise. The nature of this matter makes it necessary for someone to whom this additional measure of emanation has come, to address a call to people, regardless of whether that call is listened to or not, and even if it leads to his being harmed in his body. We even find that prophets addressed a call to people until they were killed; this divine emanation moves them and does not leave them to rest and be quiet in any way, even if they meet with great misfortunes. For this reason you will find that Jeremiah (peace be on him) explicitly stated that because of the contempt he received from those disobedient ones and unbelievers who lived in his time, he wished to conceal his prophecy and not to call them to the truth that they rejected; but he was not able to do it. He says: *Because the word of the Lord is made a reproach unto me, and a derision, all the day. And if I say: I will not make mention of Him, nor speak any more in His name; then there is in my heart as it were a burning fire shut up in my bones, and I weary myself to hold it in, but cannot* [Jer. 20:8–9]. This is the meaning of the words of the other prophet: *The Lord God hath spoken, who shall not prophesy?* [Amos 3:8] Know this. [*82a*]

CHAPTER 38

Know that in every man there is necessarily the faculty of courage. Were this not so, he would not be moved in his thought to ward off what harms him. Among the faculties of the soul, this faculty is, according to me, similar to the faculty of repulsion among the natural faculties. This faculty of courage varies as to strength and weakness, as do other faculties, so that you find among people some who will advance upon a lion, while others flee from a mouse. You find someone who advances against an army and fights it, and find another who trembles and fears if a woman shouts at him. There also must be a kind of temperamental preparation in the original natural disposition, which in turn increases and applies itself to bringing out what is potential [into actuality] and in accordance with a certain opinion. It may also diminish through a deficiency of application and in accordance with a certain opinion. The abundance or the weakness of this faculty in the young is made clear to you from their infancy.

Similarly this faculty of divination exists in all men, but varies in degree. It exists especially with regard to things with which a man is greatly concerned and about which his thought turns, so that you find in your soul that so and so spoke or acted in such and such a manner in such and such an episode, and the thing is really so. You find among men one whose conjecturing and divination are very strong and habitually hit the mark, so that he hardly imagines that a thing comes to pass without its happening wholly or in part as he imagined it. The causes of this are many—they are various anterior, posterior, and present circumstances. [*82b*] But in virtue of the strength of this divination, the mind goes over all these premises and draws from them conclusions in the shortest time, so that it is thought to happen in no time. In virtue of this faculty, certain people give warnings concerning great future events.

These two faculties must necessarily be very strong in prophets, I mean the faculty of courage and that of divination. And when the Intellect emanates to them, these two faculties become very greatly strengthened so that this may finally reach the point you know: namely, the lone individual, having only his staff, went boldly to the great king in order to save a religious community from the burden of slavery, and had no fear or dread because it was said to him: *I will be with thee* [Exod. 3:12]. This too is a state that varies in them [that is, the prophets] but it is indispensable. Thus it was said to Jeremiah: *Be not afraid of them*, and so on. *Be not dismayed at them*, and so on. *For, behold, I have made thee this day a fortified city*, and so on [Jer. 1:8, 17, 18]. And it was said to Ezekiel: *Be not afraid of them or of their words* [Ezek. 2:6]. Similarly you will find all of them (peace be on them) to be endowed with great courage. Also, because of the abundance of the faculty of divination in them, they give information as regards future events in the shortest time. This faculty likewise varies in them as you already know.

Know that the true prophets obtain theoretical apprehensions without doubt; by theory alone, man is unable to grasp the causes from which that known thing necessarily follows. This has a counterpart in their giving information as regards matters about which man, using only common conjecture and divination, is unable to give information. For the very emanation that flowed to the imaginative faculty (so as to render it perfect so that its act brings about its giving information as to what will happen and its apprehending such matters as though they had been perceived by the senses and had reached this imaginative faculty from the senses) [*83a*] also perfects the act of the rational faculty, so that its act brings about its knowing things that are true; and it achieves this apprehension as if it had apprehended it by starting from theoretical premises. This is the truth that is believed by whoever chooses to be equitable toward himself. For all things bear witness to one another and indicate one another. It is even more fitting that this should pertain to the rational faculty. For the Active Intellect truly emanates only to it [that is, to the rational faculty], and that is what brings it into actuality. It is from the rational faculty that the emanation comes to the imaginative faculty. How then could the perfection of the imaginative faculty reach this measure [that is] the apprehension of what has not reached it from the senses, without the rational faculty being affected in a similar way [that is] apprehending without having apprehended by way of premises, inference, and reflection?

This is the true meaning of prophecy, and those are the opinions that are peculiar to the prophetic teaching. I have stipulated in my saying, "the true prophets," in order not to involve myself with the people belonging to the third class, who are utterly devoid of rational [notions] and knowledge, but have mere imaginings and thoughts. Perhaps they —I mean what these people apprehend—are merely opinions that they once had had and of which traces have remained impressed upon their imaginings together with everything else that is in their imaginative faculty. But after they voided and annulled many of their imaginings, the traces of these opinions remained alone and reappeared to them; and they thought them to be something that had unexpectedly occurred to them and something that had come from outside. According to me, they are comparable to a man who had with him in his house thousands of individual animals. Then all of them except one individual, which was one of those that were there, went out of that house. When the man remained alone with that individual, [*83b*] he thought that it had just now come to his house, whereas that was not the case; rather he was one of those who did not leave. This is one of the positions that are sophistical and destructive. How many among those who have aspired to obtain discernment have perished through this! Because of this you will find that certain groups of people establish the truth of their opinions by means of dreams that they have seen, thinking that what they have seen in sleep is something else than the opinion that they believed in or heard while awake. Therefore one ought not to pay attention to one whose rational faculty has not become perfect and who has not attained utmost theoretical perfection. For only one who achieves theoretical perfection is able to apprehend other objects of knowledge when the divine intellect emanates to him. It is he who is truly a prophet. This is explicitly stated: *And the prophet [possesseth] a heart of wisdom* [Ps. 90:12]. It says here that one who is truly a prophet has *a heart of wisdom.* This too ought to be known.

CHAPTER 39

Having spoken of the essence of prophecy and made known its truth and explained that the prophecy of Moses our Master is different from the prophecy of the others, we shall say that the call to the Law followed necessarily from that apprehension alone. That is because this call addressed to us by Moses our Master was not preceded by a similar call by any one of those we know who lived from the time of Adam to him; nor was a call similar to that one made by one of our prophets after him. Such is the fundamental of our Law: that there will never be another Law. Hence, according to our opinion, there never has been any Law and there never will be any other than the one Law, which is the [*84a*] Law of Moses our Master. The explanation of this as stated in the texts of the prophetic books and as is found in the traditions, is as follows. Not one of the prophets—such as the Patriarchs, Shem, Eber, Noah, Methuselah, and Enoch—who came before Moses our Master has ever said to a class of people: "God has sent me to you and has commanded me to say to you such and such things; He has forbidden you to do such and such things and has commanded you to do such and such things." This is a thing that is not attested to by any text of the Torah and does not figure in any true tradition. These men only received revelation from God, as we have explained. He who received an emanation of great magnitude, as for instance Abraham, assembled the people and called upon them by way of teaching and instruction to a truth that he had apprehended. In this manner Abraham taught the people and explained to them by means of theoretical proofs that the world has but one deity, that He has created all other things, and that these forms[21] ought not to be worshiped nor any of the created things. This is what he enjoined the people to do, attracting them by means of beautiful speeches and by means of the benefits he conferred upon them. But he never said: "God has sent me to you and has given me commandments and prohibitions." Even when the commandment of circumcision was laid upon him, his sons, and his servants, he circumcised them and did not call upon men to do so in the form of prophetic call. Do you not see the text of the Torah referring to him that reads: *For I have known him*, and so on [Gen. 18:19]?[22] Thus it is made clear that he acted only through injunction. Isaac, Jacob, Levi, Kohat, and Amram also addressed their call to the people in this form. You will find likewise that the sages say with reference to the prophets who came before him: "the court of justice of Eber, the court of justice of Methuselah, the school of Methuselah."[23] All of them (peace be on them) were prophets who merely taught the people as instructors, teachers, [*84b*] and guides, rather than saying: "The

Lord said to me: 'Speak to the sons of so and so.'" Things were like that before Moses our Master. As for Moses, you know what was said to him, what he said, and what all the people said to him: *This day we have seen that God doth speak*, and so on [Deut. 5:21]. As for all the prophets from among us who came after Moses our Master, you know the text of all their stories and the fact that they had the same position as preachers calling men to the Law of Moses, threatening those who turn away from it, and holding out promises to those who are forthright in following it. We likewise believe that things will always be this way. As it says: *It is not in heaven*, and so on [Deut. 30:12]; *for us and for our children for ever* [Deut. 29:28]. And that is as it ought to be. For when a thing is as perfect as it is possible to be within the species, it is impossible that within that species there should be found another thing that does not fall short of that perfection either because of excess or deficiency. Thus in comparison with the balanced temperament that has the highest degree of balance in a particular species, every other temperament that deviates from that degree of balance will have either deficiency or excess. Things are similar with regard to this Law, as is clear from its balance. For it says: *Just statutes and judgments* [Deut. 4:8]; now you know that the meaning of *just* is balanced. For these are manners of worship in which there is no burden and excess—such as monastic life and pilgrimage and similar things—nor a deficiency necessarily leading to greed and being engrossed in indulgence, so that the perfection of man is diminished with respect to his moral habits and to his speculation—this being the case with regard to all the other nomoi of past religious communities. When we speak in this Treatise about the reasons of the Laws, their balance and wisdom will be made clear to you in so far as this is necessary. For this reason it is said with reference to them: *The Law of the Lord is perfect* [Ps. 19:8]. As for those who deem that its burdens are hard, heavy, and difficult to bear—all of this is due to an error in considering them. I shall explain later on [*85a*] how easy they truly are in the eyes of the perfect ones. For this reason it says: *What doth the Lord thy God require of thee*, and so on [Deut. 10:12]. And it says: *Have I been a wilderness unto Israel*, and so on [Jer. 2:31]. However all this refers to the virtuous; whereas in the eyes of those who are unjust, violent, and tyrannical, the existence of a judge who renders tyranny impossible is a most harmful and hard thing. Similarly for the greedy and the vile, the hardest thing in their eyes is that which hinders their abandoning themselves to debauchery and which punishes those who indulge in it. Similarly everyone who is deficient in any respect considers that a hindrance in the way of the evil that he prefers because of his moral viciousness is a great burden. Accordingly the ease or difficulty of the Law should not be measured on the basis of the passion of every wicked, vile, and morally corrupt man, but should be considered with reference to the man who is perfect among the people, for it is the aim of this Law that everyone should be such a man. Only this Law is called by us divine Law; whereas the other political governances—such as the nomoi of the Greeks and the ravings of the Sabians and of others—are all due to the activity of certain rulers, rather than prophets, as I have explained several times.

CHAPTER 40

It has been explained with utmost clarity that man is political by nature and that it is his nature to associate with others. He is not like the other animals for whom association is not a necessity. Because of the manifold composition of this species—for, as you know, it is the last one to have been composed—there are many differences between the individuals belonging to it, so that you can hardly find two individuals who are alike in [*85b*] any one of the species of moral habits, any more than their visible forms are alike. The cause of this is the difference of the temperaments; the material [constituents] differ, and so do the accidents that adhere to the form. For every natural form has certain accidents adhering specifically to it, other than those that adhere to the material. Nothing like this great individual difference is found among any other animal species. Rather the differences between the individuals of every species are slight, except for man. For you find among us two individuals who seem to belong to two different species with regard to each moral habit; so that you find in an individual cruelty that reaches a point at which he kills the youngest of his sons in his great anger, whereas another individual is full of pity at the killing of a bug or any other insect, his soul being too tender for this. The same holds good for most accidents.

Now as the nature of the human species requires that there be those differences among the individuals belonging to it and as, in addition, association is a necessity for this nature, it is by no means possible that his association should be accomplished except—and this is necessarily so—through a ruler who gauges the actions of the individuals, perfecting that which is deficient and reducing that which is excessive, and who lays down actions and moral habits for all of them to practice always in the same way, until the natural diversity is hidden through the multiple points of conventional accord, and so the society becomes well-ordered. Therefore I say that the Law, although it is not natural, has a basis in what is natural. It was a part of the wisdom of the deity with regard to the continuance of this species, that He put it into its nature (when He willed its existence), that individuals belonging to it should have the faculty of ruling. Among them there is one to whom that governance has been revealed by prophecy directly; he is the prophet or the one who lays down the nomos. Among them there are also those who have the faculty to compel people to accomplish, observe, [*86a*] and actualize that which has been laid down by those two. They are the sovereign who adopts that nomos and the one who claims to be a prophet and who adopts the Law of the prophet—either the whole of it or a portion. His adopting a portion and abandoning another portion may be due either to this being easier for him or, out of jealousy, to make people think that those matters came to him through revelation and that with regard to them he does not follow somebody else. For among the people there are men who admire a certain perfection, take pleasure in it, have a passion for it, and wish that people should imagine that they have this perfection, though they know that they possess no perfection. Thus you see that there are many who lay claim to, and give out as their own, the poetry of someone else. This has also been done with regard to certain works of men of science and to particular points of many sciences. An envious and lazy individual comes upon a thing invented by somebody else and claims that it was he who invented it. This has also happened with regard to this prophetic perfection. For we find people who laid a claim to prophecy and said things with regard to which there had never been at any time a revelation coming from God—such as Zedekiah, son of Chenaanah.[24] And we find other people who laid a claim to prophecy and said things that God has undoubtedly said—I mean things that had come through a revelation, but a revelation addressed to other people; thus, for instance, Hananiah, son of Azzur.[25] Accordingly they adopted them as their own and adorned themselves with them. The knowledge and discernment of all this are very clear. I shall explain this to you in order that the matter should not be obscure to you and that you should have a distinction by which you can separate the governances of nomoi that have been laid down, the governances of the divine Law, and the governances of those who took over something from the dicta of the prophets, raised a claim to it, and gave it out as their own.

As regards the nomoi with respect to which those who have laid them down have stated explicitly that these are nomoi that they have laid down by following their own thoughts, there is no need to adduce proofs for this; for, with its being recognized by the adversary, no further evidence is needed. I only want to make known to you the governances [*86b*] that are claimed to be prophetic; some of them are truly prophetic—I mean divine—others are [established on the basis of a human] nomos, and still others are plagiarisms.

Accordingly, if you find a Law the whole end of which and the whole purpose of the chief thereof, who determined the actions required by it, are exclusively the ordering of the city and of its circumstances and the removal of injustice and oppression from it; and if in that Law attention is not at all directed toward theoretical matters, no heed is given to perfecting the rational faculty, and no regard is accorded to opinions being correct or faulty—the whole purpose of that Law being, on the contrary, the arrangement, in whatever way this may be brought about, of the circumstances of people in their relations with one another and their obtaining, in accordance with the opinion of that chief, some presumed happiness—you will then know that that Law [has the character of] a nomos and that its promulgator belongs, as we have mentioned, to the third class, I mean to those who are perfect only in their imaginative faculty.

And if you find a Law all of whose governances attend to the aforementioned soundness of the bodily states and also to the soundness of belief—a Law that takes pains to give correct opinions regarding God, the Exalted, in the first place, and with regard to the angels, and that desires to make man wise, to give him understanding, and to awaken his attention, so that he knows the whole of existence as it truly is—you must know that this governance comes from Him, the Exalted, and that this Law is divine.

It remains for you to know whether he who lays claim to such a governance is a perfect man to whom a revelation of that governance has been made, or whether he is an individual who lays claim to these dicta, having plagiarized them. The way of putting this to a test is to consider the perfection of that individual, carefully to examine his actions, and to study his way of life. The strongest of the indications you should attend to is his renunciation of, and contempt for, the bodily pleasures, for this is the first of the degrees of the people of science and, all the more, of the prophets. In particular this holds good with regard to the sense [*87a*] that is a disgrace for us—as Aristotle has stated —and especially in what belongs to it with regard to the foulness of copulation. For this reason God has stigmatized with it everyone who lays claim to prophecy, so that the truth should be made clear to those who seek it and they should not go astray and fall into error. Do you not see how Zedekiah, son of Maaseiah, and Ahab, son of Kolaiah, claimed prophecy, were followed by the people, and gave forth dicta deriving from a revelation that had come to others; and how they plunged themselves into the vileness of the pleasure of copulation so that they fornicated with the wives of their companions and followers so that God made them notorious, just as He disgraced others, and the King of Babylon burned them? As Jeremiah has explained, saying: *And of them shall be taken up a curse by all the exiles of Judah that are in Babylon, saying: The Lord make thee like Zedekiah and like Ahab, whom the King of Babylon roasted in the fire; because they have wrought vile*

deeds in Israel, and have committed adultery with their neighbors' wives,
and have spoken words in My name falsely, which I commanded them
not; but I am He that knoweth and am witness, saith the Lord [Jer.
29:22–23]. Understand this intention.

CHAPTER 45

After the preceding explanation of the truth of prophecy according
to the requirements of theory together with the explanation supplied
by our Law, I ought to mention to you the degrees of prophecy according to these two roots. Now not everybody who is found in one of the
degrees, which I call degrees of prophecy, is a prophet. For the first and
second degree are steppingstones toward prophecy, and he who has
attained one of them is not to be considered among the prophets discussed previously. And even though he may sometimes be called a
prophet, this term is applied to him in a general sort of way, because
he is very close to the prophets. You should not be misled with regard
to these degrees by the fact that sometimes you find in the books [*93a*]
of prophecy that a revelation came to a prophet in the form characteristic
of one of their degrees and then it is explained with regard to the very
same prophet that a revelation came to him in the form characteristic
of another degree. For as regards the degrees I shall mention, it sometimes happens that some of the revelation of one particular prophet comes
to him in a form characteristic of a certain degree, whereas another
revelation, which comes to him at another time, corresponds to a degree
inferior to that of the first revelation. For just as a prophet may not
prophesy continuously the whole of his life, but prophesies at a certain
moment and is abandoned by prophecy at other moments, so may he
also prophesy at a certain moment in a form characteristic of a high
degree and at another moment in a form characteristic of an inferior
degree. Sometimes perhaps he may not attain this high degree more
than once in his lifetime and then is deprived of it and perhaps remains
fixed in a degree inferior to this until the cessation of his prophesying.
For there is no doubt that the prophesying of all the prophets comes to
an end before their death, either shortly or a long time before, as was
explained with regard to Jeremiah by the saying: *At the termination of*
the word of the Lord by the mouth of Jeremiah [Ezra 1:1], and as was
explained with regard to David by the saying: *Now these are the last*
words of David [II Sam. 23:1]. From this, one must draw an inference
to all the prophets. After having made this introduction and explained
it, I shall begin to set forth the degrees that have been alluded to, and
shall say:

The First Degree: The first of the degrees of prophecy is that an individual is accompanied by divine help, which moves and activates him to a righteous, great, and important action—such as the deliverance of a community of virtuous people from a community of wicked people, or the deliverance of a virtuous and great man, or the conferring of benefits on numerous people. The individual in question finds in himself something [*93b*] that moves and incites him to the action, and this is called "the spirit of the Lord." And it is said of the individual who is accompanied by this state that *the spirit of the Lord came upon him,*[26] or that *the spirit of the Lord clothed him,*[27] or that *the spirit of the Lord rested upon him,*[28] or that *the Lord was with him;*[29] or other similar expressions are applied to him. This is the grade of all the judges of Israel of whom it is said in general that: *And when the Lord raised them up judges, then the Lord was the judge, and delivered them* [Judg. 2:18]. This is also the grade of all the virtuous messiahs[30] of Israel. This is explained especially as regards some judges and kings: *Then the spirit of the Lord came upon Jephthah* [Judg. 11:29]. And it is said of Samson: *And the spirit of the Lord came upon him* [Judg. 14:19]. And it is said: *And the spirit of God came upon Saul when he heard [those] tidings* [I Sam. 11:6]. Similarly it is said of Amasai when the Holy Spirit moved him to help David: *Then the spirit clothed Amasai who was chief of the captains: Thine are we, David, and on thy side, thou son of Jesse; peace,* and so on [I Chron. 12:19]. Know that such a power did not abandon Moses our Master from the moment he reached manhood. It was because of this that he was moved to slay the Egyptian and to reprove the one who was in the wrong among the two men that struggled.[31] The strength of this power in him shows in the fact that when—after having been filled with fear and having fled—he came to Midian as a stranger full of fear and saw some wrong that was done, he could not refrain from putting an end to it and was incapable of patience with regard to it, as it says: *But Moses stood up and helped them* [Exod. 2:17]. David likewise was accompanied by such a power from the time that he was anointed with the oil of anointment, as is found in the text: *And the spirit of the Lord came upon David from that day forward* [I Sam. 16:13]. And it was for this reason that he attacked the lion, the bear, and the Philistine. Such a spirit of the Lord by no means caused one of these to speak of anything; rather the end of this power was to move the one strengthened by it to a certain action: not to any [*94a*] chance action, but only to the defense of the wronged—whether one great man or a community—or to what leads to that result. And just as not everyone who has seen a true dream is a prophet, not everyone who is accompanied by [divine] help in some matter—whatever it may be, such as the acquisition of property or the achievement of an end that concerns him alone—is said to have been accompanied by the spirit of the Lord, or to have the Lord with him, or to have done what he has done through the Holy Spirit. We only say this about one who has performed a very great good or what leads to that result—as, for instance, the success of Joseph in the house of the Egyptian,[32] which was, as is clear, the first cause for great things that occurred afterwards.

The Second Degree: It consists in an individual's finding that a certain thing has descended upon him and that another power has come upon him and has made him speak; so that he talks wise sayings or in words of praise or in useful admonitory dicta, or concerning governmental or divine matters—and all this while he is awake and his senses function as usual. This is the one of whom it is said that he "speaks through the Holy Spirit." It is through this kind of Holy Spirit that David composed "Psalms," and Solomon "Proverbs," "Ecclesiastes," and "Song of Songs." "Daniel" and "Job" and "Chronicles" and all the other Writings[33] have likewise been composed through this kind of Holy Spirit. For this reason people call them Writings, meaning thereby that they are written through the Holy Spirit. The sages have stated explicitly that "the Scroll of Esther was spoken through the Holy Spirit."[34] It is of this kind of Holy Spirit that David has said: *The spirit of the Lord spoke by me and His word was upon my tongue* [II Sam. 23:2]; he meant that it caused him to speak the words in question. [*94b*] It was to this group that the seventy elders belonged, of whom it is said: *And it came to pass, that, when the spirit rested upon them, they prophesied, but they did so no more* [Num. 11:25]. Eldad and Medad and every High Priest who was questioned through the Urim and Thummim also belong to this class, I mean that as the sages have mentioned: "The divine Presence rests upon him, and he speaks through the Holy Spirit."[35] Yahaziel, son of Zechariah, likewise belongs to this class, as it is he of whom it is said in Chronicles: *The spirit of the Lord came upon him in the midst of the congregation; and he said: Hearken ye, all Judah, and ye inhabitants of Jerusalem, and thou king Jehoshaphat. Thus saith the Lord unto you,* and so on [II Chron. 20:14–15]. So does Zechariah, the son of Jehoiada the priest, belong to this group, for it is said of him: *And the spirit of God clothed Zechariah, the son of Jehoiada the priest; and he stood above the people, and said unto them: Thus saith God* [II Chron. 24:20]. Similarly Azariah, son of Oded, of whom it is said: *And the spirit of God came upon Azariah, son of Oded; and he went out to meet Asa,* and so on [II Chron. 15:1–2]. The same applies to all those of whom something similar is said. Know too that Balaam, when he was righteous, also belonged to this kind. This is the meaning that it intends to convey in the dictum: *And the Lord put a word in Balaam's mouth* [Num. 23:5]. It is as if it said that he spoke through the Holy Spirit. It is for this reason that [Balaam] says of himself, *who heareth the words of God* [Num. 24:4]. One of the things to which we must draw attention is that David and

Solomon and Daniel belong to this class and not to that of Isaiah and Jeremiah and Nathan the prophet and Ahijah the Shilonite and men similar to them. For they—I mean David and Solomon and Daniel—spoke and said what they said through the Holy Spirit. As for David's saying: *The God of Israel said, the Rock of Israel spoke to me* [II Sam. 23:3], it means that [God] gave him a promise through a prophet, either through Nathan or somebody else; as: *And the Lord said unto her* [Gen. 25:23]; and as: *Wherefore the Lord said [95a] unto Solomon: Forasmuch as this is done of thee, and thou hast not kept My covenant* [I Kings 11:11]— a saying that undoubtedly is a threat to him made through the prophet Ahijah the Shilonite or somebody else. Similarly the saying concerning Solomon: *In Gibeon the Lord appeared to Solomon in a dream by night; and God said,* and so on [I Kings 3:5], is not pure prophecy like: *The word of the Lord came unto Abram in a vision, saying* [Gen. 15:1], nor is it like: *And God spoke unto Israel in the visions of the night* [Gen. 46:2], nor is it like the prophecy of Isaiah and Jeremiah. For even if revelation came to each of these in a dream, that revelation informs him that it is a prophecy and that revelation has come to him; whereas in this story about Solomon it says at the end: *And Solomon awoke, and, behold, it was a dream* [I Kings 3:15]; and similarly in the second story it says: *The Lord appeared to Solomon the second time, as He had appeared unto him at Gibeon* [I Kings 9:2], which has been explained to be a dream. This grade is below the one of which it is said: *I will speak unto him in a dream* [Num. 12:6]. For those who prophesy in a dream, by no means call this state a dream after prophecy has come to them in a dream, but state decidedly that it was a revelation. Just as Jacob our Father said; for when he awoke from that prophetic dream, he did not say that this is a dream, but stated decidedly and said: *Surely the Lord is in this place,* and so on [Gen. 28:16]. And he said: *God Almighty appeared unto me at Luz in the land of Canaan* [Gen. 48:3]; he thus decided that that was a revelation. Whereas with regard to Solomon, it says: *And Solomon awoke, and, behold, it was a dream.* Similarly you will find that Daniel applies the expression "dreams" to them, even though he saw an angel in those dreams and heard words spoken in them. He calls them dreams even after having learned what he did through them. Thus it says: *Then was the secret revealed unto Daniel in a vision of the night* [Dan. 2:19]. It also says: *Then he wrote the dream,* and so on [Dan. 7:1]; *I saw in my vision by night,* and so on [Dan. 7:2]; *And the visions [95b] of my head affrighted me* [Dan. 7:15]. And he says: *And I was appalled at the vision, but understood it not* [Dan. 8:27]. There is no doubt that this degree is below the degree of those of whom it is said: *I will speak unto him in a dream* [Num. 12:6]. For this reason the religious community has reached a consensus to classify the Book of Daniel among the Writings, and not among the Prophets. For this reason I called your attention to the fact that in this kind of prophecy that came to Daniel and Solomon—even though an angel was seen in a dream—as long as they did not find in themselves that that was a pure prophecy, but rather that it was a dream prophesying the truth of certain matters, it is like those who speak through the Holy Spirit. This is the second degree. Similarly when arranging the Holy Scriptures, they[36] made no difference between "Proverbs" and "Ecclesiastes" and "Daniel" and "Psalms," on the one hand, and the "Scroll of Ruth" or the "Scroll of Esther" on the other; all of them have been written through the Holy Spirit. Also all these are called, in a general way, prophets.

The Third Degree: This is the first of the degrees of those who say: "The word of the Lord came to me," or expressions having a similar sense. That is, a prophet sees a parable in a dream according to all the conditions set forth before with regard to the truth of prophecy. And it is in this very dream of prophecy that the meaning of that parable— what was intended thereby—is made manifest to him, as in most of the parables of Zechariah.

The Fourth Degree consists in his hearing articulate and clear speech in the dream of prophecy, but without seeing the speaker—as has happened to Samuel in the first revelation that came to him, as we have explained with regard to him. [96a]

The Fifth Degree: This consists in his being addressed by a man in a dream—as it says in one of Ezekiel's prophecies: *And the man said unto me: Son of man,* and so on [Ezek. 40:4].

The Sixth Degree consists in his being addressed by an angel in a dream. This is the state of the majority of the prophets. Thus it says: *And the angel of God said unto me in the dream,* and so on [Gen. 31:11].

The Seventh Degree consists in his seeing in the dream of prophecy, as it were, that He, the Exalted, addresses him. Thus Isaiah says: *I saw[37] the Lord,* and so on [Isa. 6:1]. *And He said:*[38] *Whom shall I send,* and so on [Isa. 6:8]. Thus Micaiah, son of Imla, says: *I saw the Lord,* and so on [I Kings 22:19; II Chron. 18:18].

The Eighth Degree consists in revelation coming to him in a vision of prophecy and his seeing parables—as Abraham in the vision between the pieces,[39] since these parables came in a vision during the day, as has been explained.

The Ninth Degree consists in his hearing speech in a vision—as is said with regard to Abraham: *And, behold, the word of the Lord came unto him, saying: This shall not be thine heir* [Gen. 15:4]. [96b]

The Tenth Degree consists in his seeing a man who addresses him in a vision of prophecy—as Abraham again by the terebinths of Mamre and as Joshua in Jericho.

The Eleventh Degree consists in his seeing an angel who addresses him in a vision—as Abraham at the time of the binding. According to

me, this is the highest of the degrees of the prophets whose states are
attested by the books, assuming what has been determined concerning
the perfection of the rational faculties of the individual according to the
requirements of theory, and assuming that one exempts Moses our Master.
As regards the question whether it is possible that a prophet would also
see in a vision of prophecy that God, as it were, addressed him—this,
according to me, is improbable; the power of the act of the imagination
does not reach this point, and we have not found this state in the other
prophets. For this reason it is clearly said in the Torah: *I will make
Myself known unto him (elav ethvada) in a vision, and will speak unto
him in a dream* [Num. 12:6]. Thus it assigns speech to dreams only,
assigning to visions the union and emanation of the Intellect, this being
signified by its saying: *elav ethvada.* For [*ethvada*] is a reflexive form of
the verb *yado'a* (to know). Thus it is not explicitly stated that speech
coming from God can be heard in a vision.

Inasmuch as I found scriptural texts attesting that prophets heard
speech—it having been made clear that this was in a vision—I said by way
of conjecture that it is possible that, in this speech that is heard in a dream
and the like of which may not occur in a vision, it is God who is making
him imagine that He is addressing him; all this is based on the external
meaning. One could also say that every vision in which you find the
hearing of an address, was in its beginning a [*97a*] vision, but ended in a
state of submersion [in sleep] and became a dream, as we have explained
with regard to the saying: *And a deep sleep fell upon Abram* [Gen.
15:12]. [The sages] have said: "This is the deep sleep of prophecy."[40]
Therefore all speech that is heard, whatever the way may be in which
it is heard, was heard only in a dream; as the text has it: *I will speak unto
him in a dream* [Num. 12:6]. On the other hand, in a vision of prophecy
only parables or intellectual unions[41] are apprehended, which lead to the
attainment of scientific matters similar to those attained through speculation, as we have explained. This is the meaning of its saying: *I will make
Myself known unto him in a vision* [Num. 12:6]. Consequently, according
to this last interpretation, there are eight degrees of prophecy; the highest
and most perfect among them being the one in which [the prophet]
prophesies in a vision—taking this in a general way—even though, as has
been mentioned, he is merely addressed by a man. Perhaps you will raise
the objection against me, saying: "You have counted among the degrees
of prophecy the prophet's hearing an address from God who addresses
him, as in the cases of Isaiah and Micaiah. How can this be when our
fundamental is that all prophets hear an address only through the intermediary of an angel, with the exception of Moses our Master, of whom
it is said: *With him do I speak mouth to mouth* [Num. 12:8]?" Know
then that this is in fact so, and that the intermediary here is the imaginative faculty. For he only hears in a dream of prophecy that God has

spoken to him. Moses our Master, on the other hand, heard Him *from above the ark-cover, from between the two cherubim* [Exod. 25:22], without action on the part of the imaginative faculty. We have already explained in *Mishneh Torah* the differentia of that prophecy and have commented on the meaning of: *Mouth to mouth* [Num. 12:8], and: *As a man speaketh unto his friend* [Exod. 33:11], and others. Understand it from there, for there is no need to repeat what has already been said.

PART   III

CHAPTER   2 7

The Law as a whole aims at two things: the well-being of the soul and the well-being of the body. As for the well-being of the soul, it consists in the multitude acquiring correct opinions corresponding to their respective capacity. Therefore some of them [namely, the opinions] are set forth explicitly and some of them are set forth in parables. For it is not within the nature of the common multitude[42] that its capacity should suffice for apprehending that subject matter as it is. As for the well-being of the body, it comes about by the improvement of their ways of living one with another. This matter is achieved through two things. One of them is the removal of reciprocal wrongdoing from among them. This consists in not allowing any human individual to act according to his will and up to the limits of his power, but compelling him to do that which is useful to all. The second consists in the acquisition by every human individual of moral qualities that are useful for social intercourse so that the affair of the city may be well ordered. Know that as between these two aims, one is undoubtedly greater in nobility, namely the well-being of the soul, I mean the giving of correct opinions; while the second aim, I mean the well-being of the body, is prior in nature and time. The latter aim consists in the governance of the city and the well-being of the states of all its people according to their capacity. This second is the more urgent one, and it is the one regarding which every effort has been made to expound it and to expound all its particulars. For the first aim can only be achieved after achieving this second one. For it has already been demonstrated that man has two perfections: a first perfection, which is the perfection of the body, and an ultimate perfection, which is the perfection of the soul. His first perfection [*60a*] consists in his being healthy and in the very best bodily state, and this is only possible through his finding the things necessary for him whenever he seeks them. These are his food and the rest of the things needed for the governance of his body, such as shelter, bathing, and so forth. This cannot be achieved in any way by one isolated individual. An individual can only attain all this through a political association, it being already known that man is political by nature. His ultimate perfection is to become rational in actuality, I mean to have an intellect in actuality; and that is to know everything concerning all the beings that it is within the capacity of man to know in accordance with his ultimate perfection. It is clear that this ultimate perfection does not comprise either actions or moral habits and that it consists only of opinions arrived at through speculation and made necessary by investigation. It is also clear that this noble ultimate perfection can only be achieved after the first perfection has been achieved. For a man cannot cognize an intelligible even when made to comprehend it, and still less become aware of it of his own accord, while in pain or very hungry or thirsty or hot or very cold. But once the first perfection has been achieved it is possible to achieve the ultimate perfection, which is undoubtedly more noble and is the only cause of lasting life.

As for the truth-telling Law, of which, as we have already explained, there is only one and no other, namely the Law of Moses our Master, it has come to give us both perfections—I mean the well-being of the states of people in their relations with one another through the removal of reciprocal wrongdoing and through the adoption of noble and excellent moral character, to make possible the preservation of the population of the country and the perpetuation of their being under a single order, so that [6ob] every one of them achieves his first perfection; and the soundness of the beliefs and the giving of correct opinions through which ultimate perfection is achieved. The text of the Torah has spoken of both perfections and has informed us that the end of this Law in its entirety is the achievement of these two perfections. He, the Exalted, said: *And the Lord commanded us to do all these statutes (ḥuqqim), to fear the Lord our God, for our good always, that He might preserve us alive, as it is at this day* [Deut. 6:24]. Here He puts the ultimate perfection first on account of its nobility, just as we have explained that it is the ultimate end. Hence His saying here: *For our good always.* You know already what [the sages] (may their memory be a blessing) have said in commenting on the saying of the Exalted: *That it may be well with thee, and that thou mayest prolong thy days* [Deut. 22:7]. They said: "That it may be well with thee in a world in which everything is well and that thou mayest prolong thy days in a world the whole of which is long."[43] Similarly the intention of His saying here, *For our good always,* is this same notion: I mean the attainment of "a world in which everything is well and [the whole of which is] long." And this is lasting life. On the other hand, His saying, *That He might preserve us alive, as it is at this day*, refers to this first and bodily life, which lasts for a certain duration and which can only be well ordered through political association, as we have explained.

CHAPTER 28

Among the things to which your attention must be directed is that you should know that as regards the correct opinions through which the ultimate perfection is obtained, the Law has given only their end and has called to believe in them in a summary way—namely, in the existence of the deity, the Exalted, His unity, His knowledge, His power, His will, and His eternity. All these are ultimate ends that do not become evident [61a] in detail and with precision except after knowing many opinions. In the same way the Law has called to adopt certain beliefs, the belief in which is necessary for the sake of the well-being of political conditions—like our belief that the Exalted becomes violently angry with those who disobey Him and that it is therefore necessary to fear Him and to dread Him and to take care not to disobey. As regards all the other correct opinions concerning the whole of this existence— opinions that constitute all the theoretical sciences in their many kinds through which those opinions forming the ultimate end are validated— the Law, although it does not call to them explicitly as it does with regard to the former, does do this in summary fashion by saying: *To love the Lord* [Deut. 11:13,22; 19:9; 30:6,16,20]. You already know what is found regarding the expression "love": *With all thy heart, and with all thy soul, and with all thy might* [Deut. 6:5]. We have already explained in *Mishneh Torah* that this love becomes valid only through the apprehension of the whole of existence as it is and through the consideration of His wisdom in it. We have also mentioned there that the sages (may their memory be a blessing) call attention to this notion.

What results from all that we have now stated as a premise regarding this subject is that whenever a commandment, be it a prescription or a prohibition, requires removing reciprocal wrongdoing, or urging to a noble moral habit leading to a good social relationship, or giving a correct opinion that ought to be believed either on account of itself or because it is necessary for the removal of reciprocal wrongdoing or for the acquisition of a noble moral habit, such a commandment has a clear cause and is of manifest utility. No question as to the end need be posed with regard to such commandments. For at no time at all was anyone perplexed or asked why we were commanded by the Law that God is one, or why we were forbidden to [61b] kill and to steal, or why we were forbidden to exercise vengeance and retaliation, or why we were ordered to love one another. Rather the things about which people were perplexed and opinions differed—so that some said that they are completely useless except as mere commands, whereas others said that they are useful, but their utility is hidden from us—are the commandments from whose external meaning it does not appear that they are useful according to one of the three notions we have mentioned; I mean that they neither give one of the opinions nor instill a noble moral habit nor remove a reciprocal wrongdoing. Apparently these commandments are not related to the well-being of the soul, as they do not give a belief, or to the well-being of the body, as they do not give rules useful for the governance of the city or for the governance of the household—the prohibition of the mingled stuff, of the mingling [of diverse species], and of meat in milk,[44] and the commandment concerning the covering of blood, the heifer whose neck was broken, and the firstling of an ass,[45] and others of the same kind. You will hear my explanation for all of them and the exposition of their correct and demonstrated causes, with the sole exception—as I have mentioned to you—of certain details and a few commandments. I shall explain that all these and others of the same kind have to be related to one of the three notions—either to the soundness of a belief or to the well-being of the circumstances of the city, which is achieved through two things: removal of reciprocal wrongdoing and acquisition of excellent moral habit.

Sum up what we have said concerning beliefs as follows. In some cases a commandment gives a correct belief, which is the one and only thing aimed at—like the belief in the unity and eternity of the deity and in His not being a body. In other cases the belief is necessary for the removal of reciprocal wrongdoing or for the acquisition of a noble moral habit—like the belief that He, the Exalted, has a violent anger against those who do injustice, according to what is said: *And My wrath shall wax hot, and I will kill,* and so on [Exod. 22:23], and as the belief that He, the Exalted, [62a] responds instantaneously to the prayer of someone wronged or deceived: *And it shall come to pass, when he crieth unto Me, that I will hear; for I am gracious* [Exod. 22:26].

CHAPTER 34

Among the things that you likewise ought to know is that the Law does not pay attention to the exceptional, and legislation is not made with a view to things that are rare. Rather, in everything that it wishes to bring about, be it an opinion or a moral habit or a useful work, it is directed only toward the things that occur in the majority of cases and pays no attention to what happens rarely or to the harm occurring to a single human being resulting from this determination and governance of the Law. For the Law is a divine thing. It is your business to reflect on the natural things in which those general utilities, which are in them, comprise and necessarily lead to harms that befall certain individuals, as became clear from our discourse and the discourse of others. In view of this consideration also, do not wonder that the purpose of the Law is not perfectly achieved in each individual and that, on the contrary, it necessarily follows that there should be individuals whom this governance of the Law does not make perfect. For not everything that derives necessarily from the natural specific forms is actualized in each and every individual. Indeed, all things proceed from one deity and one agent and *have been given from one shepherd* [Eccles. 12:11]. The contrary of this is impossible, and we have already explained that the impossible has a permanent nature that never changes. In view of this consideration it also will not be possible that the Laws be dependent on changes in the circumstances of the individuals and of the times, as is the case with regard to medical treatment, which is particularized for every individual in conformity with his present temperament. On the contrary, the governance of the Law ought to be unqualified and common for the generality, [75a] even if that is required only for certain individuals and not required for others; for if it were made to fit individuals, corruption would befall the generality, and "you would make out of it something that varies."[46] For this reason, matters that are primarily intended in the Law, ought to be dependent on neither time nor place; rather, the decrees ought to be unqualified and common, in accord with what He, the Exalted, says: *As for the congregation, there shall be one statute (ḥuqqàh) for you* [Num. 15:15]. However, only the common interests, those of the majority, are considered in them, as we have explained.

After I have set forth these premises, I shall begin to explain what I have intended to explain.

NOTES

1. *Babylonian Talmud, Gittin,* 60b.
2. Cf. *Mishneh Torah,* Introduction.
3. Cf. Deut. 17:8–12.
4. *Babylonian Talmud, Ḥagigah,* 14a.
5. Or: "of dialectical theology" (*kalām*).
6. See Part One, Selection 10, n. 19.
7. See Part One, Selection 10, n. 8.
8. Or: "the Spaniards."
9. A late Neoplatonist.
10. Yaḥyā Ibn ʿAdī was a Christian theologian and Aristotelian philosopher who

died in 974, more than two centuries after the beginning of the Mu'tazilite *kalām*.

11. Cf. I Kings 13:4; II Kings 6:18.

12. *Babylonian Talmud, Shabbath,* 92a.

13. *Mekhilta,* Commentary on Exod. 19:24.

14. *Babylonian Talmud, Berakhoth,* 57b.

15. *Genesis Rabbah,* XVII and XLIV.

16. The apodosis of this conditional sentence begins with the words, "there is no doubt," on p. 79b.

17. Cf. *Nicomachean Ethics* iii. 10. 1118^{b}2 ff. "Hence the sense to which profligacy is related is the most universal of the senses; and there appears to be good ground for the disrepute in which it is held, because it belongs to us not as human beings but as animals" (Rackham).

18. *Babylonian Talmud, Shabbath,* 30b.

19. Cf. *Chapters of Rabbi Eliezer,* XXXVIII.

20. Cf. *Babylonian Talmud, Ta'anith,* 30b.

21. I.e., the forms of the stars, etc.

22. The verse continues: *to the end that he may command his sons and his house after him, that they may keep the way of the Lord, to do righteousness and judgment.*

23. *Genesis Rabbah,* XLIII.

24. Cf. I Kings 22:11,24.

25. Cf. Jer. 28:1 ff.

26. Cf. Judg. 14:6,19; I Sam. 10:6, 16:13.

27. Cf. Judg. 6:34; I Chron. 12:19; II Chron. 24:20.

28. Cf. Num. 11:25–26; Isa. 11:2.

29. Cf. Judg. 2:18; I Sam. 3:19, 18:12.

30. Or: "anointed ones."

31. Cf. Exod. 2:11–13.

32. Cf. Gen. 39:2.

33. The Hebrew Bible is divided in three parts: the Torah (Pentateuch), the Prophets, and the Writings (Hagiographa).

34. *Babylonian Talmud, Megillah,* 7a.

35. *Babylonian Talmud, Yoma,* 73b.

36. The ones who did this.

37. The verb has a different tense in the Bible.

38. The verb has a different form in the Bible.

39. Cf. Gen. 15:9–10.

40. *Genesis Rabbah,* XVII and XLIV.

41. I.e., the union of the Active Intellect with the intellect of the prophet.

42. Or: "within the common nature of the multitude."

43. *Babylonian Talmud, Qiddushin,* 39b.

44. Cf. Deut. 22:11; Lev. 19:19; Exod. 23:19.

45. Cf. Lev. 17:13; Deut. 21:1–9; Exod. 13:13.

46. A talmudic expression; cf., e.g., *Babylonian Talmud, Shabbath,* 35b.

13.

Maimonides

LETTER ON ASTROLOGY

Translated by Ralph Lerner

This letter (also known as the letter to Marseilles) by and large explains the circumstances attending its composition. A long and detailed series of questions relating to astrology has been sent to Maimonides by a group of Provençal rabbis. Maimonides is, as it were, compelled to answer even though he has already discussed the problems posed by astrology in the *Mishneh Torah* (*Code*) and in the *Guide of the Perplexed*. The rabbis have to be informed of the difference between the pseudo-science of astrology and the genuine science of the stars. This leads to an account of the controversy between the philosophers and the Jews concerning the origin of the universe and, further, to the controversy between philosophers, astrologers, and Jews with respect to the workings of providence. Maimon-ides' discussion of the fall of the Jewish commonwealth (at the end of the second paragraph) attributes the political disaster of defeat and conse-quent world-wide dispersion of the people to the ancient Jews' preoccu-pation with astrology. It is note-worthy that astrology is here re-garded less as a transgression of the Second Commandment than as a wit-less diversion from the activities that help to preserve political communities.

The Hebrew text of this letter, together with variant readings, has been edited by Alexander Marx in *Hebrew Union College Annual*, III (1926), 349–58. Italic numbers in brackets refer to this edition. The letter on astrology has not previously been translated into English. Marx's paragraphing has not been followed.

Who is she that looketh forth as the dawn, fair as the moon, clear as the sun, terrible as an army with banners? [Song of Songs 6:10] The inquiry of *our companions and familiar friends* [cf. Ps. 55:14], the skillful sages *who know law and decree* [cf. Esth. 1:13], who dwell at Montpellier, has arrived. May the Name shield them and increase their wisdom and enlarge their learning and *command the blessing upon them in their storehouses and in all that they put their hands unto* [cf. Deut. 28:8]. Such is the wish of their brother and friend, who prays on their behalf and rejoices in their tranquillity, Moses, son of Rabbi Maimon (may the memory of the righteous be a blessing), the Spaniard. This inquiry testifies to the purity of their soul and the excellence of their understanding and shows that they pursue science and search into the chambers of understanding and hasten to ascend the steps of knowledge in order *to find out desired words and that which was written uprightly* [cf. Eccles. 12:10], and to understand the *word* and the *interpretation* [cf. Eccles. 8:1]. May the hand of the Lord be their help and lay open for them everything that is hidden and *make level every rugged place* [cf. Isa. 40:4]. Amen. I perceive in this inquiry that although its boughs are many, they are all branches of a single tree, which is their common root: namely, all the statements of *the astrologers, the stargazers* [cf. Isa. 47:13]. It is evident that the compilation we have made of the statutes of the Torah, which we entitled *Mishneh Torah*, has not reached you. If it had, you would have known directly my opinion regarding all those things of which you have inquired; for we have made this entire matter clear in [the section of that work called] "Laws Concerning Idolatry and the Ordinances of the Nations." It seems to me that it will come to you before this reply, since it is already widespread on the island of Sicily, as well as in the West and in the East and in the South. In any case, I myself need to make this clear to you. [*350*]

Know, my masters, that it is not proper for a man to accept as trustworthy anything other than one of these three things. The first is a thing for which there is a clear proof deriving from man's reasoning—such as arithmetic, geometry, and astronomy. The second is a thing that a man perceives through one of the five senses—such as when he knows with certainty that this is red and this is black and the like through the sight of his eye; or as when he tastes that this is bitter and this is sweet; or as when he feels that this is hot and this is cold; or as when he hears that this sound is clear[1] and this sound is indistinct; or as when he smells that this is a pleasing smell and this is a displeasing smell and the like. The third is a thing that a man receives from the prophets or from the righteous. Every reasonable man ought to distinguish in his mind and thought all the things that he accepts as trustworthy, and say: "This I accept as trustworthy because of tradition, and this because of sense-perception, and this on grounds of reason." Anyone who accepts as trustworthy anything that is not of these three species, of him it is said: *The simple believeth everything* [Prov. 14:15]. Thus you ought to know that fools have composed thousands of books of nothingness and emptiness. Any number of men, great in years but not in wisdom, wasted all their days in studying these books and imagined that these follies are science. They came to think of themselves as wise men because they knew that science. The thing about which most of the world errs, or all of it—save for a few individuals, *the remnant whom the Lord shall call* [cf. Joel 3:5]— is that thing of which I am apprising you. The great sickness and the *grievous evil* [cf. Eccles. 5:12, 15] consist in this: that all the things that man finds written in books, he presumes to think of as true—and all the more so if the books are old. And since many individuals have busied themselves with those books and have engaged in discussions concerning them, the rash fellow's mind at once leaps to the conclusion that these are words of wisdom, and he says to himself: *Has the pen of the scribes wrought in vain* [cf. Jer. 8:8], and have they vainly engaged in these things? This is why our kingdom was lost and our Temple was destroyed and we were brought to this: for our fathers sinned and are no more because they found many books dealing with these themes of the star-gazers, these things being the root of idolatry, as we have made clear in "Laws Concerning Idolatry." They erred and were drawn after them, imagining them to be glorious science and to be of great utility. They did not busy themselves with the art of war or with the conquest of lands, but imagined that those studies would help them. Therefore the prophets called them *fools* and *dolts* [cf. Jer. 4:22]. And truly fools they were, *for they walked after confused things that do not profit* [cf. I Sam. 12:21, and Jer. 2:8]. [*351*]

Know, my masters, that I myself have investigated much into these matters; the first thing I studied is that science which is called judicial astrology—that is, [the science] by which man may know what will come to pass in the world or in this or that city or kingdom and what will happen to a particular individual all the days of his life. I also have read in all matters concerning all of idolatry, so that it seems to me there does not remain in the world a composition on this subject, having been trans-lated into Arabic from other languages, but that I have read it and have understood its subject matter and have plumbed the depth of its thought. From those books it became clear to me what the reason is for all those commandments that everyone comes to think of as having no reason at all other than the decree of Scripture. I already have a great composition on this subject in the Arabic language [namely, the *Guide of the Per-plexed*] with lucid proofs for every single commandment, but this is not required of us now. I now return to the subject of your inquiry.

Know, my masters, that every one of those things concerning judicial astrology that [its adherents] maintain—namely, that something will hap-pen one way and not another, and that the constellation under which one is born will draw him on so that he will be of such and such a kind and so that something will happen to him one way and not another—all those assertions are far from being scientific; they are stupidity. There are lucid, faultless proofs refuting all the roots of those assertions. Never did one of those genuinely wise men of the nations busy himself with this matter or write on it; no [nation] wrote such compositions or committed the error of calling it a science, other than the Chasdeans, Chaldeans, Canaanites, and Egyptians, for that was their religion in those days. But the wise men of Greece—and they are the philosophers who wrote on science and busied themselves with all the species of science (*madda'*)—mock and scorn and ridicule these four nations that I have mentioned to you, and they rally proofs to refute their entire position—*root and branch* [cf. Mal. 3:19]. The wise men of Persia also recognized and understood that all that science which the Chasdeans, Chaldeans, Egyptians, and Canaanites produced is a falsehood and a lie. Do not imagine that those refutations are mere assertions and that we therefore should not put our trust in them; rather there are lucid and correct, faultless proofs to refute that entire position, and the only one who would cling to it would be *a simple one who believes everything* [cf. Prov. 14:15] or one who wishes to deceive others.

And know, my masters, that the science of the stars that is genuine science is knowledge of the form of the spheres, their number, their measure, the course they follow, each one's period of revolution, their declination to the North [*352*] or to the South, their revolving to the East or to the West, and the orbit of every star and what its course is. On all this and the like, the wise men of Greece, Persia, and India wrote compositions. This is an exceedingly glorious science. By means of it the onset of the eclipses of luminaries may be known and when they will be eclipsed at any given place; by means of it there may be known the cause (*'ilah*) for the moon's (*yareah*) appearing just like a bow, then waxing great until it is full, and then gradually waning; by means of it there may be known when the moon (*lebanah*) will or will not be seen; and the reason why one day will be long and another day short; and the reason why two stars will rise as one, but not set together; and the reason why a given day at a given place is thirteen hours long and in another place fifteen or sixteen or twenty hours long, yet being a single day. (In one place the day and the night will be of equal duration; in another place the day will be like a month or two months or three—so that a place may be found where the entire year is a single day, six months daytime and six months nighttime.) How many amazing conditions are made intelligible by this science, all of which is undoubtedly true. It is this calculation of astronomical cycles of which the [talmudic] sages said that it is wisdom and understanding in the sight of the [Gentile] peoples.[2] But as for these assertions of the stupid astrologers, they are nothing. I am now making clear to you the main points of those matters that are the mystery of the world.[3]

Know, that all the wise men of the Gentile nations—and they are the great philosophers, men of intellect and science (*madda'*)—were all in accord that the world has a Governor; He makes the sphere revolve, the sphere not revolving of itself. They have many books advancing a lucid proof for this; on this point there is no controversy among men of science (*madda'*). There is, however, a great controversy among them regarding this entire world, namely, the sphere and what is beneath it. (1) Most of them say that it is not subject to generation and corruption, but that as it is now, it was and it will be for ever and ever. Just as the Holy One (blessed be He), who was always the same as He is now, is making it revolve, so was He always making it revolve, and it was always being revolved; the two of them were always together, never was one without the other. (2) Among them there are those who maintain[4] that this sphere has come into being and that the deity has created it, but that there is a single thing that exists together with the Creator, *like the clay in the potter's hand* [cf. Jer. 18:6]. From that thing which exists together with Him, He makes whatever He pleases. Sometimes He will use some of that clay, as it were, to make heaven and some of it to make earth; and sometimes, if He pleases, He takes some of that out of which He has made heaven and makes something else out of it. But to bring forth something out of nothing is impossible. [353] (3) Among the philosophers there are those who maintain[5]—just as the prophets maintained—that the Holy One (blessed be He) created all created things out of nothing and that there is no other thing with the Creator aside from the creation that He has brought forth. Now the great controversy is over this point, and this is the very point that Abraham our Father discerned. A thousand books have already been written on this, with proofs that each and every one of them rallies to support its position. It is the root of the Torah that the deity alone is primordial and that He has created the whole out of nothing; whoever does not acknowledge this is guilty of radical unbelief and is guilty of heresy. I myself have already written a great composition in Arabic [namely, the *Guide of the Perplexed*] on these matters. I have explained the lucid proofs of the existence of the Creator and that He is one and that He is not a body or corporeal in any respect. I have shattered all those proofs that the philosophers advance as proving that the world was not created. In addition I have resolved all the great difficulties that they have raised against us on account of our maintaining that the deity has created everything that exists out of nothing. ——All these, then, are the three sects into which the wise men of the world fall, from the earliest antiquity down to now. (1) Those who maintain that the sphere is not a created thing, but that it eternally has been and will be just as it is. (2) Those who maintain that the deity has created it out of that matter which always exists by Him. (3) Those who maintain —just as all the prophets did—that there is no other thing that is with the deity, just He Himself; and that when He wished, He brought forth this world out of nothing, in conformity with His will. All of these three sects are in accord on the following point. Everything that comes into being in this lower world—namely, every *living soul* [cf. Gen. 1:30] and every tree and every species of grass and every one of the species of minerals—the whole has the deity as its maker, through a power coming from the spheres and the stars. And they are in accord that the power of the Creator flows first upon the spheres and the stars; from the spheres and the stars it flows and spreads through this [lower] world—everything that is, thereby coming into being. Just as we maintain that the Holy One (blessed be He) performs signs and wonders through the angels, so do these philosophers maintain that all these occurrences in the nature of the world come through the spheres and the stars. They maintain that the spheres and the stars possess souls and knowledge. All these things are true. I myself have already made it clear, with proofs, that all these things involve no damage to religion. And not only this, but what is more I have understood from the sayings of the sages in all of the Midrashoth that they maintain as the philosophers maintained. There is no controversy whatever between the sages of Israel and the philosophers on these matters, as I have made clear in those chapters [in the *Guide of the Perplexed*]. [354] All three of these sects of the philosophers, which maintain that everything is made by means of the spheres and the stars, also maintain that whatever happens to each and every human being is due to chance; it is not due to any cause (*'ilah*) coming from above, and neither the constellation under which one is born nor nature will avail against it. There is no difference for them between this individual who was torn to pieces by a lion that happened upon him, or this mouse that was torn to pieces by a cat, or this fly that was torn to pieces by a spider. Neither is there a difference between a roof's falling upon and killing someone, or a rock's breaking loose from a mountain and falling upon a tree or upon another rock and breaking it. All this, they maintain, is simply fortuitous. It is said as well of those human beings who are warring with one another over a great kingdom, that they are like a pack of dogs warring over a carcass. This is not due to any cause (*sibbah*) coming from the stars. Further, this one's being poor and that one rich, this one's having children and that one's being childless—all the philosophers maintain that this is due to chance. The summary of the matter is that they maintain that what happens to each and every thing—be it man or beast or trees and minerals—is all due to chance. But the being of all the species[6] and the things comprehended in the entire world—in which there is not the activity of a living[7] soul—all of this stems from the power of the spheres whose root, in turn, comes from the Holy One (blessed be He). The controversy lies in this, that the true religionists, and that is the religion of Moses our Master, maintain that what happens to individuals is not due to chance, but rather to judgment—as the Torah says: *For all His ways are judgment* [Deut. 32:4]. The prophet explained: *Whose eyes are open upon all the ways of the sons of men, to give every one according to his ways, and according to the fruit of his doings* [Jer. 32:19]. It is regarding this that the Torah warned and bore witness and told Israel: *But if ye will not hearken unto Me* [Lev. 26:14], I shall bring hardship upon you. If you maintain that that hardship is not an affliction brought on by your sins, but rather due to chance and one of those things that happen by chance, why then I Myself shall heap more of that chance upon you—as it is written: *And if ye walk with Me [in the way of] chance, . . . then I will walk with you in the fury of chance* [Lev. 26:21, 28]. This is a root of the religion of Moses our Master, that everything happening to human beings is a [just] decree and judgment. Hence [the talmudic] sages maintained: "There is no death without sin and no affliction without transgression."[8]

And know, my masters, that it is one of the roots of the religion of Moses our Master—and one that all the philosophers also acknowledge—that every action of human beings is left to them and that there is nothing to constrain or draw them. Rather, if he so pleases, a man will worship God and become wise and sit in the house of study. And if he so pleases, he will follow the counsel of the wicked and run with thieves and hide with adulterers. There is no influence or constellation under which one is born that will draw him in any manner toward any one of those ways. Hence it was commanded and told to him: "Do this and do not do that." We have made clear many of the things involved in these matters in most of our [355] Arabic compositions, in the *Commentary on the Mishnah* and in the rest of the compositions. Thus we ought to know that what happens to human beings is not—as the philosophers maintain—like what happens to the beast. Three disagreements are to be found in these matters. Imagine this situation. Here is Reuben, a tanner, poor, and his children have died in his own lifetime. And here is Simon, a perfumer, rich, and his children stand before him. (1) The philosopher will maintain that this is due to chance. It is possible that Reuben could become a perfumer, grow rich, and have children; and it is possible that Simon could become impoverished, turn into a tanner, and witness his children's death. All this is simply fortuitous. There is no nature in the world and no power emanating from a star that caused this individual to be or not to be thus. This is the position of the philosophers. (2) The second position is that of those who believe in judicial astrology and whose sayings you have heard and whose follies are widespread among you. They maintain that it is impossible that a given thing should ever change. Never will Reuben be anything other than a tanner and poor and childless, for it was thus fixed by the power of the sphere at the time of his birth. Similarly, it is impossible for Simon to be anything other than a perfumer and rich and with surviving children, just as it was fixed by the power of the sphere at the time of his birth.——These two ways or these two positions are regarded as falsehoods by us. The position of the astrologers is given the lie by reason, for correct reasoning has already refuted, by means of lucid proofs, all those follies that they have maintained. It also is regarded as a falsehood by us because of the religious tradition, for if the matter stood thus, of what utility would the Torah and the commandment and the Talmud be to a particular individual? For in that event, every single individual would lack the power to do anything he set his mind to, since something else draws him on—against his will—to be this and not to be that; of what use then is the command or the Talmud? The roots of the religion of Moses our Master, we find, refute the position of these stupid ones—in addition to reason's doing so with all those proofs that the philosophers maintain to refute the position of the Chasdeans and the Chaldeans and their associates. The position of the philosophers who maintain that these things are due to chance is also regarded as a falsehood by us because of the religious tradition. (3) The true way upon which we rely and in which we walk is this: we say regarding this Reuben and Simon, that there is nothing that draws on the one to become a perfumer and rich, and the other to become a tanner and poor. It is possible that the situation will change and be reversed, as the philosopher maintains. But the philosopher [356] maintains that this is due to chance. We maintain that it is not due to chance, but rather that this situation depends on the will of *Him who spoke, and the world came into being* [cf. Ps. 33:9]; all of this is a [just] decree and judgment. We do not know the end of the Holy One's wisdom (blessed be He) so as to know by what [just] decree and judgment He required that this should be this way and that that should be the other way; *for His ways are not like our ways, neither are His thoughts like our thoughts* [cf. Isa. 55:8]. We rather are obliged to fix in our minds that if Simon sins, he will be punished with stripes and impoverished and his children will die and the like. And if Reuben repents and mends his ways and searches his deeds and walks in a straight path, he will grow rich and will succeed in all his undertakings and *see [his] seed and prolong [his] days* [cf. Isa. 53:10]. This is a root of the religion. If a man says, "But look, many have acted in this way and yet have not succeeded," why this is no proof. Either some iniquity of theirs caused this, or they are now afflicted in order to inherit something even better than this. The summary of the matter is that our mind cannot grasp how the decrees of the Holy One (blessed be He) work upon human beings in this world and in the world to come. What we have said about this from the beginning is that the entire position of the stargazers is regarded as a falsehood by all men of science (*madda'*). I know that you may search and find sayings of some individual sages in the Talmud and Midrashoth whose words appear to maintain that at the moment of a man's birth, the stars will cause such and such to happen to him. Do not regard this as a difficulty, for it is not fitting for a man to abandon the prevailing law and raise once again the counterarguments and replies [that preceded its enactment]. Similarly it is not proper to abandon matters of reason that have already been verified by proofs, shake loose of them, and depend on the words of a single one of the sages from whom possibly the matter was hidden. Or there may be an allusion in those words; or they may have been said with a view to the times and the business before him. (You surely know how many of the verses of the holy Law are not to be taken literally. Since it is known through proofs of reason that it is impossible for the thing to be literally so, the Translator[9] rendered it in a form that reason will abide.) A man should never cast his reason behind him, for the eyes are set in front, not in back. Now *I have told you all my heart* [cf. Judg. 16:18] on this subject.

What has reached you in my name concerning the Messiah does not correspond to the facts; it was not in the East, in Isfahan. It was rather in Yaman that an individual arose (it is now some twenty-two years ago), and proclaimed that he was a messenger come to prepare the way for the King Messiah and told them that the Messiah was in the land of Yaman. Many people—Jews and Arabs—gathered about him, and they would move around in the hills. Our brethren in Yaman wrote me a long letter informing me of his way and judgment, of the innovations he had made for them in the prayers, [357] and of what he was saying. They said that they had already seen certain marvels of his. They questioned me about this. I gathered from all the circumstances that this poor individual is ignorant and god-fearing, indeed he possesses no wisdom at all, and that everything that they say he did or that came to sight through him is a falsehood and a lie. I trembled for the Jews who were there, and composed some three or four tablets for them on the subject of the Messiah and his signs and the signs of the time during which he shall appear; and I warned them to beware of this individual lest he be ruined and ruin the [Jewish] communities. The summary of the matter is that after a year he was seized, and all who had joined with him fled. The king of the Arabs who had seized him asked him: "What is this that you have done?" He replied: "What I have done, I have indeed done,[10] and according to God's word." Then he said: "What is your authenticating wonder?" He replied: "Chop off my head and I shall revive at once." He said to him: "You [can] have no greater sign than this. Certainly I—and the whole world—shall trust and know that my forefathers have bequeathed a falsehood." At once they killed the poor fellow. May his death be an atonement for him and for all Israel. The Jews in most places were punished by fines, and even now there are some ignoramuses there who maintain that presently he will come to life and rise. Such were the circumstances. If you heard that my letter has come to Fez, it is only because those remarks of mine that I sent to Yaman were copied and arrived in Fez.

I have already told you that all the details of your inquiries on this subject are all branches of a single tree. I myself command you, out of my knowledge: *Hew down the tree and cut off its branches,* and so on [Dan. 4:11]. Plant in its stead *the tree of the knowledge of good and evil* [cf. Gen. 2:9], and *eat of its goodness and its fruit* [cf. Jer. 2:7], and put forth your hands and take also from the tree of life. The Holy One (blessed be He) will absolve us and will absolve you for plucking off its fruit and for eating our fill of its goodness until we live forever. Amen. Written in great haste on 11 Tishri 1507 (of the Seleucid era) [= A.D. 1194] in the land of Egypt. May salvation be nigh.——Do not censure me, my masters, for the brevity of these remarks, for the writing makes it clear that I wrote it to fill a present need. For I was very busy with many Gentile affairs. The deity knows that if Rabbi Pinhas had not sent a messenger who *urged me till I was ashamed* [cf. II Kings 2:17] and did not leave my presence until I had written it, I would not be replying now since [358] I have no leisure. On this account, judge in my favor. Farewell, my brothers, friends, and masters; may you increase and be exalted forever. Amen.

NOTES

1. Reading *ṣalul*, as two MSS have it. If one reads *ṣarud* with Marx, the phrase would be: "that this sound is harsh and this sound is indistinct."

2. Cf. *Babylonian Talmud, Shabbath,* 75a.

3. Cf. *Babylonian Talmud, Ḥagigah,* 13a.

4. Or: "there is one who maintains."

5. Or: "there is one who maintains."

6. Reading *ha-minim,* as four MSS have it, rather than *hamonim* (multitudes).

7. Correcting a misprint in the text (354:12) to read *ḥayah*.

8. *Babylonian Talmud, Shabbath,* 55a.

9. The reference is to the Targum Onqelos, an Aramaic translation of the Bible.

10. Or: "I have dealt truly . . ."

14.

Albo

BOOK OF ROOTS

Translated by Ralph Lerner

Joseph Albo (*ca.* 1380–1444) spent his entire life in Christian Spain, but little is known about him apart from that. He is mentioned as having participated in the religious disputations of 1413–14 convened by the Avignon pope, Benedict XIII, in Tortosa and San Mateo, in Aragon. His long treatise on law, the *Book of Roots* (1425?), indicates that Albo was acquainted with works on the natural sciences and the writings of the Muslim philosophers as well as those of the Jews.

The announced intention of the *Book of Roots* is to give the reader a clear and systematic account of the foundations of laws in general and of divine laws in particular. Albo says that he was moved to compose this work because of the inadequacy and superficiality of earlier treatments of this subject. In view of the fact that all men of whom we have any knowl-

edge are under some law, it is necessary that every one of them attain some measure of understanding of the roots of his law. That understanding may reach a genuine verification of the roots of the law or may not progress beyond the preliminary imaginative and formal stage. Albo's book will constitute an "adequate investigation" of a subject of which no one ought to remain ignorant. The passages translated here consist of the opening statement, which precedes the table of contents, and chapters five through ten of the First Treatise. In the first four chapters, Albo has discussed the grave dangers involved in an inquiry of this kind, argued that such an investigation is permitted to the wise, defined the word "root" and distinguished it from "true belief," and, finally, stated what he takes to be the roots of divine law in general. In the remainder of the First Treatise

237

(chapters 11–26), Albo goes on to an elaborate discussion of the roots of divine law and of its derivative roots. The Law of Moses is chosen for analysis "since all agree that it is divine." The subsequent three treatises were added, according to the author, at the request of his friends—"believers and men of speculation"—who wanted him to explain these primary and derivative roots in a manner that more closely approximates religious or theological speculation.

The Hebrew text of this work has been edited by Isaac Husik. His critical edition, containing Albo's text, variant readings, and an English translation, appears under the title: *Sefer ha-'ikkarim, Book of Principles* (5 vols., "Schiff Library of Jewish Classics" [Philadelphia: Jewish Publication Society of America, 1946]). The Hebrew text corresponding to the present translation may be found in the first volume of Husik's edition, to whose pagination the italic numbers in brackets refer. Albo's summary description has been transposed from the table of contents (3:16–4:17) to the beginning of the respective chapters. Husik's paragraphing has been followed.

[handwritten margin notes: goal to make clear how many roots for divine law; divine law; revelation God]

SINCE HUMAN HAPPINESS depends upon speculation and action, as the Philosopher has made clear in the book *On the Soul*, and since true knowledge and praiseworthy actions cannot be properly grasped by human reason—because man's reason is not capable of grasping things as they truly are (as will appear further on)—there must, then, necessarily be something that is above human reason and by which the praiseworthy actions are defined and true knowledge cognized in such a way that there will be no doubt whatever concerning them. This can only be through divine guidance. Hence [2] it is fitting and necessary that every man discern that divine law[1] (from among the other laws) which leads to this. But this [discernment] presupposes knowledge of the roots[2] without which the divine law cannot exist. That [knowledge] is the intention of this composition: to make clear how many roots there are that are necessary for divine law. That is why it is called the *Book of Roots*. It is divided into an Introduction and four treatises.

The Introduction makes known in a general way the necessity that led to the composition of this book and the investigations that properly should take place in it. In [the Introduction] the high importance of the investigation taking place in this book is made clear; and in it the verse, *And let the graciousness [of the Lord our God be upon us]* [Ps. 90:17] is explained. [3]

The First Treatise will investigate the roots of the laws, how many there are and what they are, the differences between the divine laws and the conventional laws,[3] and what the roots of the divine law are, and what the roots of the conventional law are. It will make it clear that laws have roots that are general [to more than one law] and roots that are peculiar [to a particular law], and that the general roots of divine law are three—namely, the existence of God, divine revelation,[4] and reward and punishment. It will make it clear that under these, there are other roots that derive and branch off from them. And it will make it clear how the divine law may be discerned from the sham law that pretends to be divine.

The Second Treatise is an explanation of the first root—which is the existence of the Lord—and of the roots that derive and branch off from it.

The Third Treatise is an explanation of the second root—which is divine revelation—and of the roots that derive and branch off from it.

The Fourth Treatise is an explanation of the third root—which is reward and punishment—and of the roots that branch off from it and of the matters that derive from it.

* * *

CHAPTER V. In it will be made clear the necessity of the existence of natural law for the continuance of the human species; and it will make it clear that this by itself does not suffice for the continuance of the political association unless there is another law; and it will make clear the necessity of the existence in a city of a judge or king.

All the animals live and exist in one of three ways. There are some for whom it is impossible to live and exist together, such as beasts of prey. Association and fellowship are bad and harmful for them, for if many of them would associate together in a single place, they would kill one another as prey. There are some who are the opposite of these; they are animals for whom it is impossible to live [71] and exist without company and association and for whom fellowship is necessary for their continued being, like the human species. Because of his delicacy and temperamental balance, he will be affected by cold and by heat and by every one of the extremes; hence he will be in need of clothes to protect him against heat and cold, and properly prepared foods suitable for his temperament. None of this can possibly be accomplished except through the association and fellowship of many people who help one another: one will weave and one will sew and one will make needles, and so on with each and every art, so that finally every one of the people will be able to find whatever he needs in the way of food and clothes for his life and existence. There are other species of animals who are, as it were, in the middle between these two extremes. Association and company do not harm them in their being, as they would the beasts of prey and the raptorial birds; but then neither are they necessary for them, as is the case with the human species. Rather, association and fellowship will occur among them in the interest of improvement, as, for example, many of the grazing animals and the birds that are not raptorial. These join and go together in flocks[5] in the interest of company and convenience and not otherwise, since this is not necessary for them in their being and continuance as[6] it is for the human species. [72]

Since association and fellowship are needed by the human species for its life and existence, the wise men have maintained that man is political by nature. They mean by this that it is almost necessary for man, on account of his nature, that he dwell in a city with a large association of people, so that he might find whatever he needs for his life and existence. On account of this, it is clear that there ought to be—for the whole association that is in a city or for the general association that is in a particular district or region, or for the generality of people in the entire world—some order by which they conduct themselves so as to preserve justice in general and to eliminate wrongdoing, so that people should not quarrel in their keeping company together during the business and commerce that they transact. This order would comprise protection against murder, theft, robbery, and the like, and, in general, whatever would preserve the political association and arrange it so that people might live in a proper manner. This order the wise men called by the name of natural law—that is to say, that it is something that man needs in respect of his nature—whether it is ordered by a wise man or by a prophet.

Yet this law does not suffice to arrange the needs of people and their lives and existence with one another, unless there is added to it [73] some order or convention comprising the affairs that people have with one another in all their business and in the commerce that they transact— such as the laws of the Roman emperors and the rules of governance of cities and the statutes that the people of a particular district or kingdom enact among themselves in order to preserve conventional justice. This order is called nomos or conventional law. It is impossible for this order or nomos to exist unless there is one man ruling or judging or reigning over that association or city, who compels the people regarding the elimination of wrongdoing and the maintenance of the nomos, so that the improvement of that association may be accomplished. Hence the matter of the establishment of the king or the governor or the judge is, as it were, necessary for the continuance of the human species, seeing that man is political by nature, as we have made clear.

CHAPTER VI will decide that it is proper that there be a divine Law[7] to guide the people toward human happiness.

When we speculate upon the formation of the animals and the perfection of all their organs, we find that the Creator has exercised wonderful providence in their formation with a view to arranging their affairs and all their particular needs in a wonderful manner. [He has supplied] not only what is necessary for them for the continuance of the species or of the individual, but also what is not necessary for them—neither [74] for the continuance of the species nor for the continuance of the individual—but that exists for them in the interest of improvement, such as the duplication of the sense organs, which is found in animals so that their affairs may be ordered in a more proper and more perfect manner, even though it is not necessary for them for the maintenance of their lives.

If there is this providence in the case of the inferior animals, how much more fitting is it that He exercises providence for the noblest species by arranging its condition, in accord with its specific perfection, in such a way that all its affairs may be ordered in a manner that suffices for the attainment of its perfection. Whoever speculates diligently on this will find that the existence of a divine emanation, through which are arranged those things needed for the maintenance of the human species with a view to the attainment of its perfection and its end,[8] is more necessary than any number of things found in the formation of the [inferior] animals, which are found in them only in the interest of improvement and without which it is possible for them to exist. This divine emanation, though it may be found only in a particular individual, nonetheless leads to the perfection of the human species [as a whole].

This is so [for the following reason]. No species coming under the genera is in a position to lead the others to perfection. (That is to say, [75] though among the species there may be found one particular species that is more perfect than all of the rest of them, that species by itself is not the perfection and end of that genus and does not guide that genus to its final perfection, for each and every species in itself has within it an end and perfection particular to that distinct species.) Nevertheless, within each and every species, though there are to be found within it differing sects of which one is nobler than the other (as if you were to say that the sect of chiefs is more perfect in human perfection than the sect of husbandmen, and the sect of wise men is more perfect than the sect of chiefs), and similarly in this way within each and every sect there will be an individual or individuals more perfect than others of that sect; yet neither that individual nor those individuals nor that sect in particular is the end for the sake of which that species exists. Nonetheless that individual[9] or those individuals or that sect are the cause of the attainment of that species' end in that they lead the entire species to perfection. I mean that they are like an instrument enabling the species to attain its end and its perfection, which is set for that entire species, even though there are within it degrees differing one from another. [76]

It is like this: just as each and every individual has within him many differing organs, all of them needed for the continuance of the animal, nonetheless one is more perfect than the other, and yet another more perfect than that one, so that there may be found in it one organ that is the root of the animal's continuance, thereby leading the animal to perfection. I mean that it is an instrument enabling perfect life to reach the animal as a whole. (It is as though you were to say that the heart is the root of the animal's continuance, and it is an instrument enabling life to reach all the organs in general and the brain in particular; so that by means of the life coming from the heart to the brain, sensation and motion will come from the brain to all the organs. Thus the continuance of the living being will be perfected by what comes to the organs from the heart, be it through an intermediary or without an intermediary.) So it is with humans: though all are equal in humanity, human perfection will come to some of them through the intermediacy of others. For just as all of the organs are needed for the continuance of the individual, and yet some of them will have a degree of primacy over others and life will come to some of them through the intermediacy of others; similarly in this way the sect of wise men has a degree of primacy over the rest, and there will come from the wise man to people at large an order arranging their affairs so that [they] attain human perfection. This order is called a nomos. [77]

Now since, as we have already said, it is fitting that the divine providence be exercised for the benefit of the human species (just as we find that it is exercised for trivial things found in the [inferior] animal), so is it necessary that a divine emanation flow upon whatever individual of the human species is most fitted for it, so that he may be an instrument enabling people to reach the perfection of their end—either directly through him while he is alive or through an intermediary after his death. (That would be through the wise men, who follow him, guiding people at every time and in every place according to what they have received from him or according to what they have understood from his statements that are found in his books. For it is not fitting that the divine power should fall short of gauging this benefit, which is necessary for the human species, and of perfecting it at every moment and in every place, just as it does not fall short in perfecting the benefit needed for the inferior animals in every place and at every time.) The guidance that comes to people through this individual is that which is called divine Law. Its rank in relation to the other Laws and nomoi is the same as the rank of the ruling art in relation to the other arts that are subservient to it. [78]

> CHAPTER VII will make it clear that some law is natural, some is conventional, and some is divine; and it will characterize the intention of each one of them and what its end is and how each one of them may be discerned from the others.

The term "law" (*dat*) applies to every guidance or governance that comprises a large association of people, regardless of whether it comprises many commands (as in: *All that knew law and decree* [Esth. 1:13]), or a single command (as in: *And a law was given out in Shushan* [Esth. 9:14]); and regardless of whether it is divine (as in: *At His right hand was a fiery law unto them* [Deut. 33:2]), or conventional, like the laws of Media and Persia.

There are three kinds of law: natural or conventional or divine. The natural law is the same for every man and for every time and for every place. The conventional law is what is ordered by a wise man or wise men in accord with the place and the time and the nature of those governed by it, like the laws and the statutes that were ordered in some of the cities among the ancient idolaters, or among those who worship God according to the rational order as this is required by human reason without divine direction. The divine law is what is ordered by God through a prophet like Adam or Noah, and like the governance and the law by which Abraham was teaching and training people to worship God and was circumcising them by the commandment of God, or what is ordered by God [79] through a messenger sent by Him so that a law may be given through him, like the Law of Moses.

The intention of the natural law is to remove wrongdoing and to promote justice, so that the people may keep away from theft, robbery, and murder, that association among people may endure and exist, and that everyone may be delivered *out of the grasp of the unrighteous and ruthless man* [Ps. 71:4]. The intention of the conventional law is to remove the base and to promote the noble, so that the people may keep aloof from what is generally regarded as base. In this it exceeds the natural law, for the conventional law also arranges the governance of people and orders their affairs in a proper manner so as to improve the political association, just as the natural law does. The intention of the divine law is to guide people to the attainment of true happiness (that being the happiness of the soul and everlasting immortality), show them the ways they should follow so as to reach it, make known to them the true good in order that they might try to attain it, also make known to them [80] the true evil in order that they might guard against it, and train them to abandon the illusory kinds of happiness so that they no longer desire them and grieve at their loss. It also lays down ways of justice in order that the political association may be improved in a proper and perfect manner, so that the evil order of their association will not hinder them from attaining true happiness nor crush them in the attempt to attain the happiness and final end of the human species—this being the object of the divine law. In this it exceeds the conventional law.

CHAPTER VIII. In it will be made clear some of the defects of the conventional law by which it falls short of the divine law; and it will make clear that some of them are alluded to in the verse, *The Law of the Lord is perfect* [Ps. 19:8], and the verses that follow it.

The conventional law falls short of the divine law in many respects. The first is what we have stated before: the conventional law arranges the actions of the people in such a way that the political association will be improved, but it does not suffice for giving perfection in opinions (as we shall make clear in what follows), so that the soul might endure after death. Therefore the soul will not be able to return to dwell in the Land of Life from which it had been taken, since the conventional law encompasses nothing other than the noble and the base. But the divine law does suffice for this since it comprises the two parts on which human perfection depends, namely, the moral habits and the opinions. For it encompasses the noble and the base, and distinguishes between [*81*] the true and the false—these being the opinions. Therefore David characterized it as being perfect, and said: *The Law of the Lord is perfect, restoring the soul* [Ps. 19:8]. That is to say, the conventional law is not perfect since it does not encompass the true opinions, but the divine law is perfect since it comprises perfection in moral habits and perfection in opinions, these being the two parts on which the perfection of the soul depends. Hence it *restores the soul* to the God who gave it, to the place where its home was initially.

Another respect in which the conventional law falls short of the divine is that the former is not able to discriminate the noble from the base in all things. For a thing may be noble or base for us without being noble or base in itself. For just as it is impossible that man in his initial condition should be born perfect in all the practical arts (even though in his nature he may be fitted for some of them), so is it impossible that man should be born perfect in all of the virtues and perfections and free from all of the vices and imperfections. Though he may be more fitted for a certain virtue or perfection than for another, it is impossible that he should be fitted for all of the virtues. [*82*]

It becomes clear from this that it is impossible for anyone promulgating a human nomos not to incline in his nature toward some vice and as a result judge the noble to be base and the base to be noble. Because of this, his testimony concerning the noble and the base will not be true. Do you not see that Plato erred greatly in this, declaring the base to be noble, for he maintained that the women in a city ought to be shared by the men of a given order. (It is as though you were to say that the women of the rulers be shared by all the rulers, and the women of the merchants be shared by all the merchants, and similarly the women of those practicing a particular craft be shared by all those of that craft.) This is a thing that the Law has rejected, and even the Noahidic Law[10]—for consider

divide law - guides you, gives you more than general direction

what was said to Abimelech: *Behold, thou shalt die, because of the woman thou hast taken; for she has a husband* [Gen. 20:3]; and he vindicated himself in that he did not know that she was a man's wife. Indeed, Aristotle has censured Plato's opinion in this matter.[11]

This is proof that no man's reason suffices to discriminate the truly noble from the base, and hence his testimony concerning [*83*] the noble and the base is not sure. All the more in the case of opinions, for it is impossible that his testimony be sure in the profound problems (such as whether the world is created or pre-eternal, for human reason does not suffice to know this truly). But *the testimony of God is sure, making wise the simple* [cf. Ps. 19:8], for it bears true witness as to whether the world is created or pre-eternal, and about other weighty problems, and about the noble and the base.

Another respect in which the conventional law falls short of the divine: it is not able to rejoice the heart of those who govern themselves according to its mandate, since whenever anyone is in doubt whether the thing he is doing suffices for reaching the intended end, he does not rejoice in his activity. Now he who governs himself according to the conventional law's mandate does not rejoice in his activity, since he is in doubt whether what is defined as justice in that law is truly justice or nothing but the appearance of justice. But he who governs himself according to the divine law's mandate—since he knows that the justice defined in it is truly justice—rejoices in his activity. Hence are *the precepts of God just, rejoicing the heart* [cf. Ps. 19:9].

Another respect in which the conventional law falls short of the divine: it is not able to define the particular actions that ought to be done [*84*] in the case of each and every virtue, since it is only generalities that it makes known. Just as definitions are only of general things—since the particular has no definition—so is it impossible for the conventional law to define the particular actions. Thus Aristotle, in the *Ethics*, always mentions in the case of all of the virtues that they ought to be practiced in a proper way and in the proper moment and in the proper place, but does not make clear what is the proper moment and what the proper place. To gauge this is undoubtedly not given to every man. We find him saying in many places in the *Ethics* that the particular actions ought to be gauged, but he does not make clear what the gauging of them is. It appears that his opinion was to say that the gauging of this belongs to someone other than himself.[12]

Undoubtedly if it were given to man as man to know this gauging, Aristotle would have spoken of it without any doubt; but on account of its not being in the nature of man to grasp this by himself, he [Aristotle] left it to someone other than himself—namely, divine gauging. Hence we find him speaking of the virtues in a general way. Thus, for example,

Aquina— sums up all types of law

[*85*] he says of moderation that it is a quality that is a mean between taking pleasure in food and drink and copulation and the other pleasures, on the one hand, and excessive abstinence, on the other.[13]

The authors of human nomoi say that one should have sexual intercourse in the proper manner and with the proper individual and at the proper moment, but they are not able to explain this in detail. But the divine law specifies that "sexual intercourse in the proper manner" means that which aims at raising up seed for the continuance of the species; "with the proper individual" means with one's own wife (and it forbids certain women whom it is not proper to join to oneself); and that "at the proper moment" means when the woman is clean and not during or near her menstruation.

Similarly the divine law forbids some foods and permits others, and forbids the drinking of wine when one is about to perform divine service or to pray. It makes it clear that excessive abstinence is not proper, as our rabbis (may their memory be a blessing) have explained as regards the verse: *And make atonement for him,*[14] *for that he sinned by reason of the soul* [Num. 6:11]. "By reason of what soul has he sinned? In this, that he afflicted himself by abstaining from wine."[15] [*86*]

Similarly the authors of human nomoi praise courage and maintain that a man ought not to expose himself to dangers except at a moment when death is more preferable to him than life, but they are not able to define that moment. The divine Law makes it clear that that moment is when the name of Heaven would be sanctified through him—like Hananiah, Mishael, and Azariah[16]—or in order to do battle against the idolaters so as to destroy them and blot out their names from under the heaven.

Similarly as regards mercy and cruelty: the human nomos is not able to gauge when each is proper and when each is improper. The divine law makes it clear that cruelty is to be directed toward those guilty of radical unbelief and heretics and those who transgress the law; that it is proper to punish them with stripes or with death, each one according to what the Law has meted out for his rebellion; and that it is proper that mercy be directed, in differing respects, toward believers and toward the poor and the unfortunate—for there is one to whom it is proper to give an outright gift, and another to whom it is proper to give something by way of loan. To draw attention to the impropriety of keeping to only a single course, the Psalmist has said: *Well is it with the man that dealeth graciously and lendeth, that ordereth his affairs rightfully* [Ps. 112:5]. He has said, *that dealeth graciously*, with regard to the alms given to a poor man who takes an [*87*] outright gift; *and lendeth*, is said with regard to one who does not wish to take except by way of loan. He said that one who does these two things is he who *ordereth his affairs rightfully*; and he said of him: *For he shall never be moved; the righteous shall be held in everlasting remembrance* [Ps. 112:6], because he benefits all people—be it by

way of favor and gift or by way of loan. It is not within the power of
the human nomos to gauge some such particular action. Hence he who
governs himself according to its mandate will be walking in the dark and
will not know which of these particular actions ought to be done, nor
will he know which way to follow. But *the commandment of God is
clean like the sun, and enlightens the eyes* [cf. Ps. 19:9], illuminating for
those who govern themselves by it, the way they should follow and the
deed they should do.

Another [aspect of the inferiority of] the conventional law. Since it is
ordered by a human, it is impossible for him to gauge the noble and the
base for all times, for it is possible that what is generally accepted at a
given moment will change, so that the noble will come to be regarded
as base, and the base, noble. (Just as we find in the case of Cain and Abel
and the times of the ancients, that the marriage of a sister was not base
for them; and even in the days of Abraham, as he said to Abimelech
when he was [*88*] vindicating himself before him: *And moreover she
is indeed my sister, the daughter of my father, but not the daughter
of my mother* [Gen. 20:12]; and afterward it came to be regarded as
base.) Hence it is impossible that the acquired fear of the base that
comes through the conventional law should be everlasting, for it will
change with the change of the times. But the divine law, since it is
gauged by divine wisdom, will make clear the noble and the base for
all times. Hence the acquired fear of the base that comes through it
will not be open to change and destruction, for it is free from all
dross and filth and in this respect may possibly exist forever, like silver
that is free from all dross—as the Psalmist says: *The words of the Lord
are pure words, as silver tried in a crucible on the earth, refined seven
times* [Ps. 12:7].

Its explanation is this. Some sham silver made by the art of alchemy
may be melted once without disclosing its badness, but if melted a second
time its badness will be disclosed; some may withstand two meltings, and
some may withstand three or four or five, but in the end its badness will
be disclosed. The badness of some will not be disclosed when it is melted
in a furnace, but if it is melted *in dense earth*[17] its badness will be disclosed. That silver which has been tried in dense earth and refined many
times is free [*89*] from every sham and dross and filth; it is impossible
for it to change afterward, even if melted many times. Hence he characterized *the words of the Lord,* inasmuch as they are *pure,* as pure
silver that has been *tried in a crucible on the earth* (that being in an open
place in dense earth), *refined seven times,* in which there is no suspicion
of any sham. Thus the acquired *fear* of the base that comes through the
Law is *pure, enduring for ever* [cf. Ps. 19:10], since it is not subject to
the change and the destruction to which the conventional law is subject.

Another [aspect of the inferiority of] the conventional law. It is not able to treat each individual equitably according to his conduct and to gauge punishments by measuring them in a balance—so that one receives stripes and another is stoned and another is strangled,[18] and one pays double damages and another pays four- and five-fold damages—in order that the punishments meted out to the sinner should be true, according with the measure of the sin. But the divine law recompenses each and every one according to his wickedness, not less and not more. And even if it is found, from the appearance of things, that a righteous man is undone in his righteousness and a wicked man is long-lived in his wickedness, why this is the case if the punishments are examined with regard to [*90*] the goods of this world alone. But when the goods of this world that befall a wicked man are combined with the evils and the punishments that befall him in the world to come, and similarly the evils befalling a righteous man in this world with the goods befalling him in the world to come, we shall find the two recompenses are righteous when considered together, even though each one of them is not righteous when considered separately by itself. Hence the Psalmist has said: *The judgments of the Lord are true, they are righteous altogether* [Ps. 19:10]. He said *true* as regards the gauging of the punishments, and he said *righteous altogether* as regards the punishments of this world considered with the goods of the world to come, or vice versa.

I have seen one who interprets [this verse in the following fashion]. Since we find in the Law that the same thing is prohibited and permitted —for example, the wife of one's brother is prohibited, yet the childless widow of his brother is permitted;[19] the fat of cattle is prohibited, yet the fat of a wild beast is permitted; meat in milk is prohibited, yet the udder is permitted; and more of the like, which would lead a man to think that it is impossible that both parts of the contradiction can be right— he said that *the judgments of the Lord are true* and they are *righteous* together, the permission and the prohibition. But the expression *true* does not accord with this interpretation, since the expression *true* does not apply to [*91*] the laying-down of judgments, but rather the expression "proper" or "correct" or "upright judgments." But the expression *true* does apply to recompenses; thus Scripture says: *Judge true judgment* [Zech. 7:9]. For the root of recompense is always figuratively called *judgment: The Lord hath made Himself known, He hath executed judgment, the wicked is snared in the work of his own hands* [Ps. 9:17]; *Only to execute judgment* [Mic. 6.8]. Similarly the expression *altogether* is not well explained by this interpretation.

These, then, are the defects of the conventional law, and the like might be added to them. Among them is that it is impossible for the human nomos to lay down punishments except for what is done openly, not for what is done secretly, *for man looketh on the outward appearance* [I Sam. 16:7]; but the divine Law lays down punishments for what is done secretly as well, because God *looketh on the heart* [I Sam. 16:7]. It is possible to interpret, *The judgments of the Lord are true, they are righteous altogether* [Ps. 19:10], in this way as referring to what is done openly and secretly. It is not for me to enlarge upon this. I only saw fit to enumerate these six, which the Psalmist enumerated in the Psalm beginning with the words, *The heavens declare the glory of God* [Ps. 19:1], by his saying: *The Law of the Lord is perfect* [Ps. 19:8]; *The testimony of the Lord is sure* [Ps. 19:8]; *The precepts of the Lord are just,* [92] *rejoicing the heart* [Ps. 19:9]; *The commandment of the Lord is clean, enlightening the eyes* [Ps. 19:9]; *The fear of the Lord is pure, enduring for ever* [Ps. 19:10]; *The judgments of the Lord are true, they are righteous altogether* [Ps. 19:10].

Having made clear these six points of superiority that the divine law has over the conventional law, the Psalmist turned again to making it clear that not only does the divine law give perfection to opinions—they being the true and the false—and as regards the noble and the base—that being perfection of the moral habits in the way that we have described—but that it also gives perfection to everything that can be imagined to be perfect. Now since what can be imagined to be perfect—apart from the perfection of the moral habits and the opinions—is the useful and the pleasurable, he said by way of poetic figure that the useful and the pleasurable may be found in the words of the Law. Hence his saying, *More to be desired are they than gold, yea, than much fine gold* [Ps. 19:11], alludes to the useful; *Sweeter also than honey and the honeycomb* [Ps. 19:11], alludes to the pleasurable. This means that the requital attained by means of the commandments is a *great reward* that is more useful *than gold, yea, than much fine gold,* and more pleasurable than *honeycomb.* This is so, provided the man is *careful* in fulfilling them. Hence he concluded: *Moreover of them is Thy servant careful; in keeping of them there is great reward* [Ps. 19:12]. [93]

CHAPTER IX will make it clear that the principles[20] of the conventional law in general are free choice and an end; and it will make it clear why free choice is written into the Law of Moses, seeing that it is not a principle of it as divine.

The principles of the conventional law and its roots[21] are free choice and an end. This is evident and clear. For why would he who lays down a nomos establish punishments for those who transgress the commands of the nomos if the transgressor had it not within his power to do as he pleases? Similarly, how could the king or the governor of a city compel the people to do good acts if the people had it not within their power to do evil or to do good? Even those who deny the reward and punishment of the soul acknowledge that unqualifiedly free choice is with the individual man and that he has nothing that constrains it; by it he can choose whatever he pleases and direct his actions to whatever end. Hence they say that it partakes of necessity that a nomos be ordered by a wise man or wise men to define the noble and the base and the wrong and the just among the people of a city. And there is placed over them a *chief, overseer, or ruler* [Prov. 6:7] to compel the people (*'am*) with a view to the maintenance of justice among the people and the elimination of wrongdoing, in order that through him the political association may be perfected in a proper manner.

Hence it is clear that he who places free choice and an end among the principles of the divine law has not wrought well. For though [*94*] free choice necessarily precedes divine law, it is not a principle of it as divine. But it is a principle of divine law in respect of its being a principle of all the human actions and conventions and conventional rules of governance by which the political settlement is arranged, and that is impossible without it.[22] Just as we do not say that the first intelligibles are a principle of divine law—even though they precede it necessarily inasmuch as they precede all learning and teaching and all knowledge—similarly in the case of free choice: even though it necessarily is a root (*shoresh*) of the divine law, it is not a principle of it as divine. Hence Maimonides (may his memory be a blessing) did not enumerate it among the roots[23]—even though he maintains that it is a root that is necessary for the divine Law[24] (as we have written in Chapter III)—since only those are enumerated as roots that are roots of divine law as divine.

Similarly, an end in general is not a principle of divine law as divine, but it is a principle of all human actions that are done voluntarily. In this respect it is a principle of conventional law, for just as everyone who does something consciously and voluntarily does it with respect to his intending some end—be that end [*95*] good in itself or only something that seems to him to be good—so does he who lays down a nomos intend, by the commands and warnings he establishes, that the people should attain some end in their actions: namely, the guidance of the people and the well-being of their lives, by which the political association may be perfected. Hence it is clear that an end is also a principle of conventional law, not of divine law as divine. However, inasmuch as the end that comes about with respect to the Law—namely, life in the world to come—differs from the end that comes about from the conventional law and from all the other ends, Maimonides (may his memory be a blessing) enumerated it among the roots even though he did not regard free choice in the same way.

Now you may say: "Since free choice and an end are not principles of divine law as divine, why does it say in the Law, *See, I have set before thee this day life*, and so on, *therefore choose life* [Deut. 30:15, 19], thus alluding to free choice and to the end, which is eternal life?" We have already said that though free choice and an end are not principles of divine law [*96*] as divine, they do precede it necessarily, just as the first intelligibles precede divine law, even though they are not principles of it as divine. Now since there is not one who will deny that the first intelligibles are to be found in man, though there are some[25] who will deny that free choice is to be found in man (as is the opinion of some astrologers), and there also are some[26] who will deny that there is an end in all actions (such as Epicurus and his sect who think that the world just happened by chance and that there is no end in any one of the actions, but that everything happens entirely by chance), and there are some[27] who will accept the notion of an end in all human actions but will not accept so exalted an end as this, namely, the immortality of the soul in everlasting life; therefore it was necessary for the divine law to write this[28] in order to nullify those opinions as being pernicious in themselves, since they nullify all human actions and the human end, in addition to nullifying the laws in their entirety.

> CHAPTER X. It will be made clear in it that the principles of the divine law in general are three—namely, the existence of God, reward and punishment, and divine revelation—and hence these are enumerated as general roots of divine law. And it will maintain that these three are the ones that our rabbis (may their memory be a blessing) enumerated in the Mishnah of Chapter Ḥeleq.[29]

The principles of the divine law in general are three: the first is the existence of God, the second is divine revelation, and the third is reward and punishment. [*97*] There is no doubt that these three are necessary principles of divine law as divine, for if we posit the removal of one of these, the law in its entirety would fall. This is clear from their subject matter. For if we do not believe in the existence of God who commands the law, there is no divine law; and even if we believe in the existence of God, if there is no divine revelation, there is no divine law; and if there is no reward and punishment of the body in this world and of the soul in the world to come, why then has divine law been ordered? If it is to arrange the order and governance of the people and their affairs so that the settled condition of the political association may be perfected, why the conventional law suffices for that. Rather it appears without doubt that the existence of the divine law is so as to bring the people to a perfection to which the human nomos is inadequate to bring them: namely, the human perfection that depends on the perfection of the soul (as will appear later). Hence it is clear that the reward and punishment of the soul is undoubtedly a root[30] of the divine Law; and the reward of the body in this world that comes from God (blessed be He) to the righteous one for fulfilling the commandment, is a proof of this. Hence reward and punishment in general is a necessary principle of the divine law. [*98*]

Since these three are general roots of divine law, our rabbis (may their memory be a blessing) have enumerated them in Chapter Ḥeleq in the Mishnah and have said that he who disbelieves any one of them is not among the adherents of the law and hence has no share in the world to come. They have said: "All Israel have a share in the world to come, as it is said: *Thy people also shall be all righteous, they shall inherit the land for ever* [Isa. 60:21]. And these are they who have no share in the world to come: he who says that resurrection of the dead has no basis in the Torah."[31] That is to say, he who denies the divine reward and punishment implied in resurrection of the dead, which is a divine act—in relation to souls or bodies—comprising all manner of rewards. Hence we find that the words of our rabbis (may their memory be a blessing) indicate that "resurrection of the dead" points to a general and specific meaning, referring specifically to resurrection of the dead or generally to the world of souls and the world to come and the day of judgment. They have also made it clear there that the subject matter of the Messiah, which is [likened to] a physical reward, alludes to all manner of rewards.

Afterward they enumerated the one who says that there is no divine revelation, which is the other root, and then they enumerated the Epicurean. According to what [*99*] we find among the ancients about the name "Epicurus," he was an individual who thought that the world just happened by chance and who denied the existence of God as the Maker; those who followed his opinion were called Epicureans. Here, then, is why they have enumerated these three roots and have said that whoever disbelieves in them has no share in the world to come because he leaves the community of adherents of the law.

Indeed it is said there in Chapter Ḥeleq that an Epicurean is one who contemns the learned, but [the reason] they have said this is that not every man is able on his own to come to know the existence of God. Rather we know this either by way of tradition or by way of demonstration from the mouths of the wise men. He who contemns the learned, who make the existence of God generally known to all the people, has left himself no way by which he may know it; and hence he denies, as it were, the existence of God; therefore he is called an Epicurean. Now since, in the Mishnah of [Chapter] Ḥeleq, these are the only disbelievers that are enumerated as having no share in the world to come, it would appear that these three are the general roots of divine Law that everyone who holds to divine law is obliged to believe. Indeed, in the Gemara there,[32] they enumerated others who have no share in the world to come, but they enumerated them [*100*] as branching off from these three roots, and not that they are roots in themselves.

R & Punishments - is a root
Observed stuff - consequences
Understanding law because of 3 roots

NOTES

1. The Hebrew word is *dat*. It occurs in the Bible in the sense of "law" or "decree." In post-biblical rabbinic literature it may carry the additional meaning of "religion."

2. The Hebrew word being translated as "root" (unless otherwise noted) is *'iqqar*.

3. The word "conventional," in the phrase "conventional laws," is derived from the Hebraized form of the Greek *nomos*.

4. Literally: "Torah from heaven."

5. Correcting a misprint in the text (71:18) to read *agudoth*.

6. Correcting a misprint in the text (71:20) to read *ka'asher*.

7. Literally: "a divine Torah." The Hebrew word *torah* (translated as "Law" to distinguish it from *dat*, "law"), means "law," "teaching," and, above all, "the five books of Moses." It is derived from a verb meaning "to show the way."

8. Albo uses the word *takhlith* in the sense of "final cause" or the Greek *telos*. It is uniformly translated here as "end."

9. Correcting Husik's *min* (species) (75:13) to read *ish*.

10. These are the seven commandments binding upon the descendants of Noah (i.e., the gentiles): the prohibitions of idolatry, blasphemy, murder, adultery, and robbery, the command to establish courts of justice, and the prohibition of eating the limb of a living animal. According to the rabbinic tradition, the first six of these commandments had already been given to Adam.

11. Cf. Plato *Republic* v. 457B–466D; Aristotle *Politics* ii. 1. 1261^{a}1–4. 1262^{b}36.

12. Aristotle *Nicomachean Ethics* ii. 6. 1106^{b}16–28; ii. 9. 1109^{a}25–30, 1109^{b}14–23.

13. *Ibid.* iii. 10. 1117^{b}23 ff.

14. Namely, the Nazirite. Cf. Num. 6:2–21.

15. *Babylonian Talmud, Nazir*, 19a.

16. I.e., Shadrach, Meshach, and Abednego. Cf. Dan. 3:13 ff.

17. Cf. I Kings 7:46, where the phrase may signify "clay ground" or "a foundry."

18. The Bible does not explicitly prescribe strangulation as a mode of execution.

19. Cf. Deut. 25:5–6.

20. The Hebrew word being translated as "principle" is *hathhalah*. This word, which occurs in the Talmud in the sense of "beginning" or "opening," is used by later writers as a translation of the Greek *archē* (principle), and thus points to the philosophic tradition. On the other hand, *'iqqar* (root) points to dialectical theology (*kalām*).

21. Here Albo uses the plural form of the word *shoresh*, which, unlike *'iqqar*, is biblical Hebrew. Albo appears at times to use *shoresh* to designate the particular derivative propositions that follow from a more general *'iqqar*.

22. Namely, the principle of free choice.

23. Maimonides' enumeration occurs in his *Commentary on the Mishnah*, Sanhedrin, X, Introduction.

24. Maimonides, *Mishneh Torah*, "Laws Concerning Repentance," ch. 5.

25. Or: "there is one."

26. Or: "there also is one."

27. Or: "there even is one."

28. I.e., the text of Deut. 30:15,19, cited earlier in this paragraph.

29. The tenth chapter of the tractate *Sanhedrin* in the *Mishnah*. In the *Babylonian Talmud* it is the eleventh chapter.

30. Literally: "a root (*'iqqar*) and a root (*shoresh*)."

31. *Mishnah, Sanhedrin*, X 1.

32. I.e., in the Gemara to this Mishnah. Cf. *Babylonian Talmud, Sanhedrin*, XI.

15.

Abravanel

COMMENTARY ON

THE BIBLE

Translated by Robert Sacks

Isaac Abravanel (1437-1508) was born in Lisbon of a family that for generations had enjoyed political and social prominence in Spain and Portugal. Abravanel received both a traditional Jewish and a humanistic education; he also studied and drew upon the work of Christian exegetes. Early in life, he entered into the service of King Alfonso V of Portugal as treasurer. Alfonso's trust and admiration for him lasted until that monarch's death in 1481. The new king, John II, was not so well disposed toward him. Finding himself accused of collaboration with the Duke of Braganca, Abravanel escaped to Castile under threat of execution. The banished Abravanel, all his possessions confiscated, then began his great commentaries on the Bible. Soon, however, he managed to find himself back in the sphere of practical politics—first in Spain, then in Italy. When the

Jews were forced to leave Spain in 1492, he moved to Naples, but it was not long before that city was taken by the French. He was again forced south; after holding several other positions, he was employed by the Venetian republic to conclude a commercial treaty with his native land of Portugal. He died in Venice and was buried at Padua. In addition to his extensive exegetic writings (covering all of the Bible except for the Hagiographa), Abravanel produced a number of messianological and apologetic works, as well as a commentary on Maimonides' *Guide of the Perplexed.*

The following brief selections are intended to give the reader some notion of Abravanel's political teaching and of the foundations on which it rests. At bottom, there is a general concept of nature (explicit in the discussion of the origin of the arts, but implicit in other passages as well)

that serves as a measure of Abravanel's dissatisfaction with the classical view of politics. A persistent theme running through these selections is: what kind of political life did his Creator intend man to lead? In attempting to answer this question by way of determining how the ancient Jews were governed, Abravanel reaches a position markedly closer to Aquinas than to Maimonides' teaching. Abravanel is practically unique among medieval Jewish commentators in denying that the Bible positively commanded the Jews to establish a monarchy. His denial of that institution's necessity appears to be, however, less an expression of humanistic republicanism than a part of his broader disparagement of political life as such. He preserves the monarchical principle to the extent that he sees human organization culminating in a single head. But that head is a prophet-king like Moses—a man so preoccupied with divine matters that he must be instructed by a Gentile in matters pertaining to the administration of justice. Such "low things" are no concern of the prophet. Accordingly, the transpolitical prophet is not to be understood within the confines of political philosophy.

Abravanel's commentaries on the Bible were held in particularly high regard by Christian scholars of the seventeenth and eighteenth centuries. While more than thirty Latin editions have been published, the following selections are believed to be translated here for the first time in a modern language. There is no critical edition of the Hebrew text of Abravanel's commentaries. The following passages may be found in his *Commentary on the Pentateuch* (Hanau, 1710), and in his *Commentary on the Prior Prophets* (Frankfurt, 1736). The italic numbers in brackets in the body of the translation refer to page and column in these editions.

COMMENTARY ON

THE PENTATEUCH

And the whole earth was of one language and of one speech. And it came to pass, as they journeyed east, that they found a plain in the land of Shinar; and they dwelt there. And they said one to another: "Come, let us make brick and burn them thoroughly." And they had brick for stone, and slime had they for mortar. And they said: "Come, let us build us a town, and a tower, with its top in heaven, and let us make us a name; lest we be scattered abroad upon the face of the whole earth." And the Lord came down to see the town and the tower, which the children of men builded. And the Lord said: "Behold, they are one people, and they have all one language; and this is what they begin to do; and now nothing will be withholden from them, which they purpose to do. Come, let us go down, and there confound their language, that they may not understand

*one another's speech." So the Lord scattered them abroad from thence
upon the face of all the earth; and they left off to build the town. Therefore was the name of it called Babel; because the Lord did there confound
the language of all the earth; and from thence did the Lord scatter them
abroad upon the face of all the earth* [Gen. 11:1–9].

[*41a1*] I say that according to me it is more proper and fitting to say
regarding the sin of the generation of the Tower of Babel and their transgression, that they stumbled and sinned in the same way that our First
Father and his son Cain sinned, and his seed as well. Now man[1] was created
by the Holy One (blessed be He) in His image, possessing an intellecting
soul, so that he might perfect his soul by cognizing his Creator and knowing His actions. Before him were placed all the things that were necessary
for the maintenance of his life—food and drink, like the fruits of the trees
of the Garden [of Eden] and the waters of its rivers. All this existed by
nature, without any need at all for human art, so that he did not have to
busy himself with seeking them—except for divine knowledge, since it
was for this that he was created. Man sinned in that he was not satisfied
with the natural things that He had placed before him, but was attracted
to the things of the appetite and the generally accepted actions. Because
of his sin, he was driven out of the Garden of Eden, place of rest, toward
the East, filled with disgrace; and the ground was cursed on his account.
The natural things did not satisfy him, and since he chose what was superfluous, he found it necessary to do hard work, as the Master wrote. Cain
also chose to engage in artful things and therefore became a tiller of the
ground. All day he ploughed the thicket in order to plant, broke and har-
rowed his ground. But his intellect [*41a2*] gave way to his bestial part
and served it. Therefore he was a tiller of the ground. Abel, on the other
hand, who became a shepherd, was attracted to the natural things and
satisfied himself with them; for there is neither work nor art in shepherd-
ing a flock, apart from governing them according to the way of nature.
Hence all the Holy Fathers—Abraham, Isaac, and Jacob—and the tribes
and Moses and David our Fathers were shepherds; they were not tillers
of the ground. And Noah too, though he sinned in his being attracted
to wine, is not called "a tiller of the ground" by Scripture, but rather
a man of the ground [Gen. 9:20]—that is to say, a lord and ruler over
it. But Cain, because his intellect had given way to his bestial part [by
engaging] in the arts, was called *a tiller of the ground* [Gen. 4:2]. Thus
he built a town and called its name Enoch,[2] because he educated and instructed his sons in practicing the arts that are related to the building[3]
of a town and the founding of a city. Similarly all the sons of Cain took
up the work of their fathers and were attracted to the superfluous arts.
So Jubal was *the father of all such as handle the harp and pipe.* And
Tubal-cain was the father of all such as forge *brass and iron.* And Jabal,
too, in making an effort to purchase sheep, mixed art with the work of

God, something that had not previously been done. Thus it is said of him that he was *the father of all such as dwell in tents and have cattle* [cf. Gen. 4:20-22]. All the sons of Cain pursued the superfluous things; violence and destruction increased among their people until they were punished on account of it in the days of the Flood and were wiped off the earth.

Similarly, the sins of the generation of the Tower of Babel were like the sin of Adam and Cain and his sons since, having a multiplicity of the natural things necessary for their existence, by God from heaven, freed of [any need for] art and all labor, and prepared to busy themselves with the perfection of their souls, [nevertheless] their thoughts were not set at rest by the great natural gift that their Creator had prepared for them. Rather they sought and put all their thoughts to finding the arts by which a town might be built, one comprehending all the arts and having a tower in its midst, in order to come together there and to make themselves political instead of being rustics. For they thought that the end particular to them was the political association, so that joining and company might arise among them; and that this was the highest of the human ends, together with the things that would follow from it: namely, fame, office, rulership, imaginary honors, the delight of gathering possessions, and the violence and robbery and bloodshed that follow —none of which was to be found while they were in the fields, each one by himself. As Solomon said: *God made man upright; but they have sought out many inventions* [Eccles. 7:29]. All of this unnatural superfluity hinders and frustrates man in attaining his true perfection of the soul. Thus these sinning people were punished in their souls in that He confounded their language and scattered them over the face of the entire earth—just as He had driven the first man out of the Garden of Eden, and had driven Cain out of the land in which he dwelt, and had driven his sons out of the world by means of the waters of the Flood—for their sin was the same in so far as they placed the Tree of Knowledge as their final end and abandoned the Tree of Life, which is the true end. Thus it was fitting that their punishment too be alike.

*   *   *

[*41b1*] You ought not to say: "If these superfluous arts and the association into a city or town were evil in the eyes of the Lord, why was it that He did not forbid them to Israel afterwards?" For the answer to this is clear. When He (blessed be He) saw that Adam and all his progeny had already sunk into an appetite for the superfluous arts and were drowned in them, He did not forbid them to His people; for He watched and saw that they could not be removed from him *inasmuch as he is also flesh* [Gen. 6:3]. However, He admonished[4] the Children of Israel to conduct themselves in those artful things justly and in a becom-

ing manner, not disgracefully. This is like the matter of having a king, which was loathsome in His eyes; but when He saw that they were going to choose one in any case, He commanded that the choice be made by His prophets, and that it be made from among their brethren, and several other commandments that stem from the matter of having a king, as will become clear in its place. Indeed, you see that in all the days during which the Children of Israel were traveling in the desert, under divine governance, He (blessed be He) never satisfied their need with anything other than natural divine things—from the manna, the quails, and the well, even to clothing and shoes and clouds of glory[5]—but never with anything of art. As it is written: *Thy raiment waxed not old upon thee, neither did thy foot swell* [Deut. 8:4]. But when they had come into an inhabited land, He left them to their nature in all the uses of their generally accepted arts.

*   *   *

The human arts are arranged in accordance with nature in three ways. (1) Some of them help nature to do its work—like tilling the ground and the art of medicine and the like. Of these it is said that they used to say, "Let us arise and dwell in heaven";[6] that is to say, they would take part in the heavenly causes, which are the natural agents, and help them and be like them by means of their arts. Of these it is said: *And from thence did the Lord scatter them abroad* [Gen. 11:9]; for, by His will, the things of nature are sufficient unto themselves and have no need of the help of art, as was the case at the beginning of the Creation. (2) There are arts that differ from, and are alien to, nature, for they make things in which nature plays no role—like most of the productive arts, such as the making of clothing, house-building, shipmaking, and others. Concerning this sect of those possessing sciences alien to nature, the sage says that they used to say, "Let us go up into heaven and perform worship of idols."[6] For just as the heavens perform natural acts upon this matter, so they would perform acts alien [to the acts of heaven] without following them [that is, without using the same means as heaven]. Of these it is said: *Because the Lord did there confound the language of all the earth* [Gen. 11:9]; for it was because of these alien arts that they had need of alien words and alien terms, and that was the confounding of their language, as I have explained. (3) The third way of the arts is opposed to and against nature—like throwing a stone upward or causing fire to go downward. Also like this, among men, is the attempt of some to domineer over others and to subjugate some to others, though nature has made men free and equal at their birth. Concerning this sect [it is said that] they used to say, "Let us arise and make war upon heaven";[6] that is to say, their arts were opposed to, and made war upon, the natural custom.

*   *   *

[42a2] Now in the early days, until the Generation of the Flood, the whole of mankind were influenced and overseen by Him (blessed be He) in all their affairs, without any intermediary either for good or for evil. Therefore there could always be found among them wise men who had understanding of the true divine science, like Adam and Seth and Eber and Methuselah, Lemach, Noah, and their like. Among them there was to be found pure natural custom without any quest for the superfluities and the imaginary arts. And withal, they had a single language, that which the Holy One (blessed be He) had taught to the first man. However, in departing from the Ancient of Days and leaving natural custom to pursue the arts, which hinder perfection, in the building of the town and the tower, *the Lord came down to see* [Gen. 11:5] their doings, for up until then He had truly been their overseer. He said: "Since these [men] were not satisfied with being one people having one language, and have begun to do the works of the imaginary arts, *I will hide My face from them* [Deut. 32:20] and from their governance, and I shall commit them to the princes on high [that is, the angels]." Thus His saying to these princes, *Come, let us go down* [Gen. 11:7]; that is to say, "Come with Me to oversee the nations of the human species, for each one of us shall oversee a single nation. And just as My divine providence has been removed from them, so shall the divine holy language be wrested from them in such a manner that they will be divided into fragmented and conventional languages, each of them related and particular to the governance of the princes on high," just as the holy language is particular to His governance (blessed be He).

*   *   *

And it came to pass on the morrow, that Moses sat to judge the people; and the people stood about Moses from the morning unto the evening. And when Moses' father-in-law [Jethro] saw all that he did to the people, he said: "What is this thing that thou doest to the people? Why sittest thou thyself alone, and all the people stand about thee from morning unto even?" And Moses said unto his father-in-law: "Because the people come unto me to inquire of God; when they have a matter it cometh unto me; and I judge between a man and his neighbor, and I make them know the statutes of God, and His Laws." And Moses' father-in-law said unto him: "The thing that thou doest is not good. Thou wilt surely wear away, both thou, and this people that is with thee; for the thing is too heavy for thee; thou art not able to perform it thyself alone. Hearken now unto my voice, I will give thee counsel, and God be with thee: be thou for the people before God, and bring thou the causes unto God. And thou shalt teach them the statutes and the Laws, and shalt show them the way wherein they must walk, and the work that they must do. Moreover thou shalt provide out of all the people able men, such as fear God, men of truth, hating unjust gain; and place such over them to be captains of thousands, captains of hundreds, captains of fifties, and captains of tens. And let them judge the people at all seasons; and it shall be, that every great matter they shall bring unto thee, but every small matter they shall judge themselves; so shall they make it easier for thee and bear the burden with thee. If thou shalt do this thing, and God command thee so, then thou shalt be able to endure, and all this people also shall go to their place in peace." So Moses hearkened to the voice of his father-in-law, and did all that he had said. And Moses chose able men out of all Israel, and made them heads over the people, captains of thousands, captains of hundreds, captains of fifties, and captains of tens. And they judged the people at all seasons: the hard causes they brought unto Moses, but every small matter they judged themselves. And Moses let his father-in-law depart; and he went his way into his own land [Exod. 18:13–27].

[*134a2*] Concerning the multitude of judges that Jethro advised and that Moses appointed—captains of thousands and captains of hundreds, captains of fifties and captains of tens—their number being over 71,600, as the sages (may their memory be a blessing) have mentioned. Rabbi Abraham ben Ezra [applied the verse:] *For the transgression of a land many are the captains thereof* [Prov. 28:2]. There is no doubt that this is a hard and shocking thing. For his understanding was that the captains of thousands were captains who had a thousand men in their houses serving them. And similarly, the captains of hundreds were those each one of whom had a hundred men in his house serving him, and similarly for the rest. But to me that is a worthless opinion because the Israelites in Egypt were not dukes or kings that any of them might have a thousand servants, or even a hundred. Even in the case of Moses, the Scripture only mentions that he had one servant: *And his servant Joshua, the son of Nun, a young man* [Exod. 33:11]. How could it be that any one of a people who only yesterday were humbled before mortar and bricks should have a thousand servants, or a hundred or fifty or even ten? If all of the congregation were holy, and He was in their midst, why should some of them be slaves and hirelings to others, and why should these be in subjugation to the others? If it was to find food for his life, each one could partake of the manna, *each man according to his eating* [Exod. 16:16]. And even the verse, *For the transgression of a land many are the captains thereof* [Prov. 28:2], indicates rather that they are all on one level, not that some of them are captains humbling others.

As for the captains, with each increase in their number, the governance of the people is better arranged; provided only that they are ordered one under another, all culminating in a single head, as Abū Naṣr [Alfarabi] has made clear in the *Principles of Beings.*[7] This analogy may be found in the organs of a man and in the relation that the beings have to one another within the order of the world until one reaches the First Cause (blessed be He). What stands in the way of the same occurring in this matter, that is, the captains of tens under the captains of fifties, and the latter under the captains of hundreds, and the latter under the captains of thousands? It is possible to interpret it as meaning that, because Israel's camp was great and numerous, Jethro's advice was that Moses should appoint leaders and judges. And, in order that everyone should be subject to them, he gave to each captain of those leaders, men under his control to serve him, that they might follow him as the need arises, to go out in the army, or to move camp, or to castigate and punish those who were judged.[8] Among those leaders was one whose rank was so high that he had a thousand men who would preserve his headship and give heed to his bidding. And for such as was not so elevated there were a hundred men, and for another fifty, and thus for each of the others according to his rank and perfection. But those leaders [*134b1*] were few, and they would judge the people at all times. What is correct in my eyes is that with regard to the matter of judgment and the matter of wars—which are the most comprehensive things affecting the people—Jethro, in his wisdom, and Moses our lord too, saw that each time an appointment became more encompassing, it became less ordered. Therefore they did not assign captains over tens of thousands or over hundreds of thousands or the like, since surrounding oneself with great numbers of men would confuse governance. It is sufficient that the most general appointment should be over one thousand men. For with regard to the matter of judgment, it is sufficient that one man judge a thousand individuals. (In the case of wars it is even clearer that only rarely can a single man of might be found who is able to lead and order a thousand men so that they would go and come in a proper fashion.) However the captains who are under them— that is, captains of hundreds and captains of fifties and captains of tens —are needed in addition to the captains of thousands with regard to the matter of judgment. They differ in their governance and appointment in three ways. The first way is that they [the judges] will differ in regard to kind and [type of] governance. For some of them will judge cases of criminal law, and some cases of civil law. And of these, in each tribe some will judge matters of real estate, and others matters of goods, and such various things, in such a way that it is necessary that there be many judges.

*   *   *

When thou art come unto the land that the Lord thy God giveth thee, and shalt possess it, and shalt dwell therein; and shalt say: "I will set a king over me, like as all the nations that are round about me"; thou shalt in any wise set him king over thee, whom the Lord thy God shall choose; one from among thy brethren shalt thou set king over thee; thou mayest not put a foreigner over thee, who is not thy brother. Only he shall not multiply horses to himself, nor cause the people to return to Egypt, to the end that he should multiply horses; forasmuch as the Lord hath said unto you: "Ye shall henceforth return no more that way." Neither shall he multiply wives to himself, that his heart turn not away; neither shall he greatly multiply to himself silver and gold. And it shall be, when he sitteth upon the throne of his kingdom, that he shall write him a copy of this Law in a book, out of that which is before the priests the Levites. And it shall be with him, and he shall read therein all the days of his life; that he may learn to fear the Lord his God, to keep all the words of this Law and these statutes, to do them; that his heart be not lifted up above his brethren, and that he turn not aside from the commandment, to the right hand, or to the left; to the end that he may prolong his days in his kingdom, he and his children, in the midst of Israel [Deut. 17:14–20].

[*295b2*] Even though it be admitted that the existence of a king is useful and necessary for a people to improve the political association and maintain it—a proposition that is contrary to the truth—it is not so for the people of Israel, because for them it is neither needful nor necessary. The explanation of this is that the need that a people has for kings can be grouped under three headings. The first concerns the subject of wars, [namely,] saving the people from their enemies and fighting for their land. The second is to order the nomoi and set down the Laws that are necessary for maintaining them. The third is to administer extralegal stripes and punishments occasionally, according to the need of the hour, as is proper to the absolute divine power that he has.

But the nation of Israel has no need for any of these three things. This is not [necessary] as regards wars and saving them from their enemies, because Israel is saved by the Lord, and it is He who fights for them. As it is written: *Happy art thou, O Israel, who is like unto thee? A people saved by the Lord, the shield of thy help, and who is the sword of thy excellency! And thine enemies shall dwindle away before thee; and thou shalt tread upon their high places* [Deut. 33:29]. Also, this Judge would go out and come before them in wars, as we found in the cases of Joshua and Gideon and Samuel and the rest of the judges. Nor did they have need for a king to establish Laws and nomoi, for *Moses commanded us a Law,* and so on [Deut. 33:4]. And He (blessed be He) commanded: *Ye shall not add unto the word,* and so on [Deut. 4:2]. *Behold, I have taught you statutes and judgments, even as the Lord my God has commanded me* [Deut. 4:5]. *And what great nation is there that hath God so nigh,* and so on [cf. Deut. 4:7]. *And what great nation is there that hath statutes and judgments so righteous,* and so on [Deut. 4:8]. And the king of Israel did not have it in his power to innovate anything in the Law, or to subtract from it—as it is written of him: *And that he turn not aside from the commandment, to the right hand, or to the left* [Deut. 17:20]. Nor was a king necessary in Israel to administer stripes and punishments occasionally, according to the need of the hour, for the Holy One (blessed be He) delegated that to the Great Court of Law—that is, the Sanhedrin—as I have explained in commenting [on Deut. 17:8]. And aside from that, He (blessed be He) announced to us that if a judge, relying upon a righteously-ordered judgment, should declare a wicked man to be innocent, He (blessed be He) would punish the evil-doer by His great law, as it is written: *Keep thee far from a false matter; and the innocent and righteous slay thou not; for I will not justify the wicked* [Exod. 23:7]. That is, whatever you are not able to punish by the law, I Myself will punish it.

Thus it has been made clear that these three matters—saving [the people in times of] war, setting down the Law and the commandments, and [the administration of] occasional extralegal punishments and stripes—are all done by Him (blessed be He) for His people. Thus He (blessed be He) was their king, and there was nothing whatever for which they needed a king of flesh and blood. This matter had already been written in the Law, and was repeated in the Prophets, and was repeated yet again in the Hagiographa.[9] For Moses our Master (peace be upon him) said: *The Lord shall reign for ever and ever. For the horses of Pharaoh went [in with his chariots and with his horsemen into the sea,]* and so on [Exod. 15:18–19]. That is, the Holy One (blessed be He) waged war upon [*296a1*] the sea for Israel against Egypt and caused their enemies to be drowned. Thus, He *shall reign for ever and ever*, and they have no need for any other king. In the Prophets, Isaiah said: *For the Lord is our Judge, the Lord is our Legislator, the Lord is our King and He will save us* [cf. Isa. 33:22]. In this passage he alludes to the three reasons for which a king is made. With regard to the judgment made according to the need of the hour, he says: *The Lord is our Judge.* And with regard to the ordering of statutes and nomoi, all of which are called "statute," he says: *The Lord is our Legislator;* that is, He orders statutes for us. Concerning wars, he says: *The Lord is our King and He will save us.* In the Hagiographa it is said: *Lift up your heads, O ye gates; and be ye lifted up, ye everlasting doors; that the King of glory shall come in. Who is the King of glory? The Lord strong and mighty, the Lord mighty in battle* [Ps. 24:7–8]. That is, it is not proper to call a corporeal man "King of glory," but only Him (blessed be He) for it is He who is strong and mighty in battle, waging war for His people.

Thus it is clear from all this that although it be admitted that a king is necessary for the [other] nations, that does not justify it for the Israelite nation, especially since experience has already shown of the kings of Israel and the kings of Judah that *they are of them that rebel against the light* [Job 24:13]. They turned the hearts of the Children of Israel backward— as you know in the case of Jeroboam, the son of Nebat, and all the rest of the kings of Israel and most of the kings of Judah—so that on account of them, *Judah is gone into exile because of affliction, and because of great idolatry*.[10] We do not see this among the judges of Israel or their prophets. All of them were god-fearing men of valor, and men of truth. Not one of the prophets turned his heart from the Lord to worship other gods, in contradistinction to the kings, which of whom was saved from idolatry? All of this testifies to the fact that the governance of the judges was good, but that the governance of the kings was bad, harmful, and very dangerous.

*   *   *

Now hear the interpretation of the portion [of the Scripture] concerning the king, and the commandment as it is in truth! It says: *When thou art come unto the land that the Lord thy God giveth thee, and shalt possess it, and shalt dwell therein; and shalt say: I will set a king over me, like as all the nations that are round about me* [Deut. 17:14]. This is by no means a commandment, for He (blessed be He) did not command them to say that and to ask for a king. It is only a statement regarding the future, telling what will be said after you will already have been in the chosen land, after the conquests and all the wars are over, and after the partition [of the conquered territory among the people has been completed]. That is what it means when it says: *Thou shalt possess it and shalt dwell therein*. I Myself know that you shall be ungrateful when, of yourselves, you shall say, *I will set a king over me*, not from the necessity of having to wage war against the nations [inhabiting Canaan] or of conquering the land—for it has already been conquered before you —but only to make yourselves like the other nations that set kings over themselves. This is somewhat foolish, because you should have asked for a king upon first entering the land, in order to wage your wars, since that was the time when he was most properly needed, not after the conquest and the partition and when you have been dwelling securely alone in the land. This is why it says: *And thou shalt say: I will set a king over me, like as all the nations that are round about me;* that is, not by necessity, nor from any need, but only that you might act according to the deeds of the [other] nations. It mentions that when this shall happen, they shall not cause that king to reign whom they wish, but rather that one whom the Lord shall choose from among their brethren. This is the essence of the commandment and its true import: *Then thou shalt set him king over thee . . . from among thy brethren* [Deut. 17:15].[11] Not that they are commanded to ask for one, but only that when they should ask for one out of their own wish, they should not choose him by themselves, but rather that one whom the Lord shall choose from among their brethren. Accordingly, the matter of having a king was a positive commandment stemming from a permission—as if to say, when you wish to do it, even though it is not proper, thou shalt do it in no other way than this.

COMMENTARY   ON

THE   PRIOR   PROPHETS

Then all the elders of Israel gathered themselves together, and came to Samuel unto Ramah. And they said unto him: "Behold, thou art old, and thy sons walk not in thy ways; now make us a king to judge us like all the nations." But the thing displeased Samuel, when they said: "Give us a king to judge us." And Samuel prayed unto the Lord. And the Lord said unto Samuel: "Hearken unto the voice of the people in all that they say unto thee; for they have not rejected thee, but they have rejected Me, that I should not be king over them" [I Sam. 8:4–7].

[*92a2*] I myself *in my straits have prepared* [I Chron. 22:14] three speeches that consolidate the truth of this homiletic discourse. The first speech is to investigate whether a king is necessary for the political association. The second speech—[accepting for the moment] the argument that it is necessary—is whether a king is necessary for the people of Israel as it is for the rest of the nations. The third speech is an interpretation of the portion [of the Scripture] concerning the king, and an understanding of the commandment and its truth. Now I think that all this confusion, which I have noted, befell the above-mentioned sages[12] *because, even because* [Ezek. 13:10] they did not plumb the truth of the commandment and its root (*shoresh*). All of them accepted the notion that there was a positive commandment laid upon Israel to ask for a king. But I am not of this opinion. After presenting these three speeches by way of preface, I shall resolve the above-mentioned question in accord with what I think.

The first speech maintains that we ought to know first whether the existence of a king among a people is a necessary thing, required in itself, and without which nothing is possible. Those who have investigated it (Aristotle and his companions),[13] think that this is so, and that the relation of the king to the political association is like the relation of the heart to the body of an animal possessing a heart, and like the relation of what is to the First Cause (blessed be He). They believe that kingship entails three things: the first is unity and the absence of partnership; the second is continuity and the absence of change; the third is absolute power. But in truth, their thought concerning the obligation to have a king and his necessity is false, since it is not destructive that a people have many leaders who come together and unite and agree on a single plan, and that governance and judgment be according to their decision. Why should their governance not be temporary, changing from year to year, more or less? When the term comes for other judges and officers, they would take their place and look to see whether the preceding ones had transgressed in exercising their art. Whatever their wrongdoing, God would set aright any wrongdoing they had committed. And why could their power not be limited and ordered in accord with the Laws and judgments? The law is that [if there is a dispute between] an individual and a majority, the rule goes according to the majority. It is more likely that an individual man would transgress and sin in the office of king (either through his stupidity or his lust or his anger—as it is said: *The wrath of a king is as messengers of death*[14] [Prov. 16:14]), [*92b1*] than that a large number of men would sin *while they took counsel together against him* [cf. Ps. 31:14]. For if any one of them should sin, his companions would restrain him from doing so. And since judgment is due to be given shortly, the terror of flesh and blood will be upon them, and *they shall come trembling unto the Lord and to His goodness* [Hos. 3:5], and to the punishment of the judges succeeding them who will punish them, *and their wickedness shall be revealed before the congregation* [cf. Prov. 26:26]. The divine one (Aristotle),[15] says in the beginning of the *Metaphysics* that the truth is easy when considered in relation to the knowledge that many men have and the attainment thereof by all of them together, but very hard for the individual by himself.[16] This shows that ignorance is more apt to be found in an individual, while understanding together with the comprehension of the truth are more apt to be found among the many. With the power of those who understand being limited, they will not expose themselves by doing what is not proper.

What reasonable arguments do we have to bring to bear upon this point? The wise one (Aristotle),[15] has already taught us that experience prevails over the syllogism. *Behold, and see* [Lam. 1:12] the lands whose governance has been in the hands of kings. You will see their abominations and their idols; each of them *does what is right in his own eyes* [cf. Judg. 17:6], and *the land is filled with violence because of them* [cf. Gen. 6:13], *and who may say unto him* [the king], *What doest thou?* [Eccles. 8:4].

Today we see many lands whose governance is in the hands of judges and temporary rulers chosen from among them every three months, and *a king against whom there is no rising up* [cf. Prov. 30:31]. *Let us choose for them a judgment* [cf. Job 34:4] of a defined order, and they shall have dominion over the people as they practice the art of war; *not a man shall stand against them* [cf. Josh. 21:42], *whether it be for correction, or for their land, or for mercy* [cf. Job 37:13]. But if any one of them should sin in some matter, he would receive his fitting punishment from those who are soon to replace them, and in such a way that no one would presume to do so again. *Hast thou not known? hast thou not heard* [Isa. 40:28] that *the fourth dreadful beast* [Dan. 7:7], wicked Rome, ruled the entire world *and devoured the whole earth and trod it down and broke it in pieces* [cf. Dan. 7:23]? While her governance was in the hands of consuls, *they were in full strength, and likewise many* [Nah. 1:12], but after Caesar attained sole power, *she became tributary* [Lam. 1:1]. And even today the government of Venice is a mistress *that is great among the nations, and princess among the provinces* [Lam. 1:1]; and the government of Florence *is the beauty of all lands* [Ezek. 20:6]; and the government of Genoa *is dreadful and strong* [cf. Dan. 7:7]. But Lucca, Siena, and Bologna and the other lands that are without a king, but are governed by leaders who are chosen for a limited time, are, as I have mentioned, just governments *in which there is nothing perverse or crooked* [Prov. 8:8], where *no man lifts up his hand or his foot* [Gen. 41:44] *for every matter of trespass* [Exod. 22:8]. They conquer lands that are not their own by wisdom, understanding, and knowledge. All of this shows that the existence of a king is neither necessary nor obligatory for a people. Rather, it is very harmful and involves tremendous danger—both to his people and to his servants—for him to have in his hand the power to annihilate, kill, and destroy according to his whim.

* * *

[*93a1*] The third speech is an interpretation of the portion [of Scripture] concerning the king that occurs in the Law, and the understanding of the truth of the commandment.

I say that the Scripture relates, according to my opinion, that in the latter days—after Israel will have been in the land, have inherited it, and, by God's compassion for them, have dwelt therein—without any need, ungratefully they shall request permission to set a king over themselves, not out of necessity, but only in order to make themselves like the other nations that set kings over themselves. Thus it is written: *When thou art come unto the land that the Lord thy God giveth thee, and shalt possess it, and shalt dwell therein* [Deut. 17:14]. That is to say, out of foolishness you will not ask for a king at a time when wars are being waged to conquer the land—which would be the most suitable time to need him—but only after you will have inherited the land and have divided it up [*93a2*] and have dwelt therein securely. (And all of this was under the providence of Him, blessed be He, and without a king, who thus was not necessary and for whom there was no need whatever.) Then shalt thou say: *I will set a king over me;* and that is being *like as all the nations that are round about me*—that is to say, not by necessity nor for some other end. But when this should happen, He (blessed be He) commanded that they should not cause that king to reign whom they wish, but rather that one whom the Lord their God should choose from among their brethren. This is the commandment in essence and in truth: *Then thou shalt set him king over thee, whom the Lord thy God shall choose; one from among thy brethren* [Deut. 17:15].[17] That is to say, the king for whom they shall ask should be chosen by Him (blessed be He) and from among their brethren—not that they were thereby commanded to ask for one.

According to this, the commandment depends on something that was a matter of permission. It is as if it is said: if you wish to do this (even though it is not proper), you must not do it in any other way than this. It is like the verse: *When thou goest forth to war against thine enemies and the Lord thy God hath delivered them,* and so on, *and thou seest among the captives a woman of goodly form, and thou hast a desire unto her* [*and wouldest take her to thee to wife; then thou shalt bring her into thy house, and she shall shave her head*], and so on [Deut. 21:10 ff.]. For it is not commanded that he desire her or take her or have intercourse with her in her impurity, but it is only a matter of permission, though an act of the evil desire. It is only commanded that after that first intercourse, *then thou shalt bring her into thy house,* and so on, as the sages (may their memory be a blessing) have said.[18] It is also like the verse: *When thou shalt beget children and children's children, and ye shall have been long in the land, and shall deal corruptly, and make a graven image, even the likeness of any thing,* [*and shall do that which is evil in the sight of the Lord thy God to provoke Him to anger*] [Deut. 4:25]. This is not a commandment, but only a matter of permission, though an act of sin. But the end of the passage, *And thou wilt return unto the Lord thy God* [Deut. 4:30], is a positive commandment to return in penitence [for having done that] which was dependent upon a matter of permission. Thus the matter of kingship, similarly, is to be understood in the same way. The request for one was not commanded, but only permitted, though an act of the evil desire; while the stipulation was added that they should only set up that king whom God (blessed be He) had chosen from among their brethren, and in no other way.

*   *   *

And the speech pleased the Lord, that Solomon had asked this thing. And God said unto him: "Because thou hast asked this thing, and hast not asked for thyself long life; neither hast asked riches for thyself, nor hast asked the life of thine enemies; but hast asked for thyself understanding to discern justice; behold, I have done according to thy word: lo, I have given thee a wise and an understanding heart; so that there hath been none like thee before thee, neither after thee shall any arise like unto thee" [I Kings 3:10–12].

[211a1] Even though it be admitted that the wisdom of the prophets varies according to the rank of their prophecy, it would not be proper to understand thereby those [kinds of] knowledge in which Solomon perfected himself—that is to say, the knowledge of governing a household or a city—for all that is far from the concern of prophecy. You see that

Jethro guided Moses in the matter of the administration of justice, until he had taught him the way to appoint captains and how to govern the people. That was because Moses and the rest of the prophets neither busied themselves nor troubled their souls with these low things. Nor did they bother about the knowledge of the things that come-into-being and pass-away, nor about grasping their forms and their essences. For these are not the things that a prophet needs as prophet: neither the knowledge of the natures of the spheres and the stars, nor their number, nor their movements, nor their powers over the things below and how they act upon them, nor the making of talismans—all of which were embraced by Solomon's wisdom. For the knowledge of these things does not lie within the realm of prophecy, nor is it connected with it. Nor [need the prophet] have knowledge of the separate [substances[19]] in the same way in which Solomon grasped them; for he, as I have mentioned, apprehended the changes in their actions, and their officiating over the nations and over other things, and the ways in which each of them rules, and the way in which he should serve and labor in order to cause the [divine] emanation[20] to descend from it upon his nation. Now none of these things are matters the knowledge of which is needed by the prophet. For his knowledge is only of those things that are peculiar to Him (blessed be He), and the way in which He governs His creatures and, in particular, the Israelite nation, and the way in which the emanation is made to descend from Him (blessed be He) upon the nation by means of the holy sephiroth.[21] The knowledge of the separate [substances] that is fitting [for a prophet to know extends] only in so far as they are emissaries of [211a2] providence and are connected with the affairs of the Israelite nation and are the means by which prophecy and miracles occur. In all of this, the wisdom of the prophets was according to the rank of their prophecies.

*   *   *

Therefore, with regard to the wisdom of divine things and the wisdom of the Law, it is proper that we say that the pre-eminence of the prophets was greater than the rank of Solomon, in proportion as their rank in prophecy was greater than his rank. However, in the remaining kinds of science and understanding, Solomon's wisdom was greater than theirs. It was this knowledge that the sages (may their memory be a blessing) had in mind when they said in the Midrash: "He was wiser than any other man, than the first man, than Abraham, than Moses, than Joseph, than the Generation of the Desert, which was a generation of knowledge. Since of this knowledge it was said to him [Solomon]: *Lo, I have given thee a wise and an understanding heart; so that there hath been none like thee before thee, neither after thee shall any arise like unto thee*" [I Kings 3: 12].[22]

NOTES

1. Or: "Adam."

2. The word means "education" or "initiation"; cf. Gen. 4:17.

3. Reading *be-binyan* rather than *be-'inyan*.

4. Reading *hizhir* rather than *zaru*.

5. Cf. Exod. 16:15 ff.; 16:13; Num. 21: 16 ff.; Exod. 13:21 and *passim*.

6. Cf. *Genesis Rabbah* 38:6.

7. This was the title of the Hebrew translation of Alfarabi's *Political Regime*. See Part One, Selection 2 (pp. 48 ff.).

8. Reading *ha-nishpatim* rather than *ha-shofetim*.

9. See above, Selection 12, n. 33.

10. Literally: "worship of stars and constellations." Cf. Lam. 1:3 where the last phrase quoted by Abravanel reads: *and because of great servitude.*

11. This translation of the verse follows Abravanel's interpretation.

12. Maimonides, David Kimhi, Nahmanides, Gersonides, Rav Nissim, and Paulus Burgensis.

13. This appears to be a gloss.

14. Abravanel suppresses part of this verse.

15. This appears to be a gloss.

16. Aristotle *Metaphysics* ii. 1. 993ᵃ30 ff.

17. This translation of the verse follows Abravanel's interpretation.

18. Cf. *Babylonian Talmud, Qiddushin*, 21b.

19. According to the medieval Aristotelians, the heavens were moved by a series of intellects that were separated from body and that subsisted in themselves.

20. Correcting a misprint in the text to read *ha-shefa'*.

21. According to the teaching of the Cabbalah, sephiroth were the ranks or steps through which the Infinite and Inscrutable made Himself manifest in the world.

22. *Tanḥuma*, ch. Ḥuqqath.

PART THREE

Political Philosophy
in Christianity

EDITED BY ERNEST L. FORTIN

16.

Thomas Aquinas

COMMENTARY ON

THE ETHICS

Translated by Charles I. Litzinger

Thomas Aquinas (1225–1274), born at Rocca Secca, was the youngest son of Count Landulf of Aquino, who was related to the Emperor and the King of France. He received his first education at the neighboring Benedictine monastery of Monte Cassino. In 1239 he proceeded to Naples where he completed his training in the arts and first came into contact with the writings of Aristotle. His brothers vehemently opposed his decision to enter the newly founded (1216) Dominican Order and held him prisoner for fifteen months in a vain effort to dissuade him. He later pursued his studies under Albert the Great, whose pupil he became perhaps at Paris before 1248 and certainly at Cologne from 1248 to 1252. He returned to Paris in 1252 and embarked upon a teaching and writing career that was to occupy the remaining twenty-two years of his life. From 1252 to 1259 he

received his degree in theology, lectured at the Dominican convent of St. Jacques, and composed his early works. In 1259 he was sent to Italy and taught successively at Anagni (1259–1261), Orvieto (1261–1264), Rome (1265–1267), and Viterbo (1268). It was in Italy that he met his confrere William of Moerbeke and undertook with him a series of commentaries on Aristotle. He resumed his teaching in Paris at the beginning of 1269 during the most theologically and philosophically turbulent period of the thirteenth century. At that time he became engaged in the controversy with the so-called Latin Averroists, defended the mendicants against the attacks of the seculars, and upheld his own doctrinal positions against the more traditional views of Etienne Tempier, the Franciscan John Peckham, and other contemporary theologians. In 1272 he was recalled to Naples to found a new *studium generale* at the university and directed the teaching of theology there until the following year. He died on March 7, 1274 at the Cistercian Abbey of Fossanova, between Naples and Rome, on his way to the Ecumenical Council of Lyons. At the time of his canonization by John XXII in 1323, the bishop of Paris, Etienne de Bourret, praised his teaching and withdrew the condemnation of his predecessor, Etienne Tempier, to the extent to which it was aimed at his doctrines. Aquinas was declared "Doctor of the Church" by Pius V in 1567. After a period of eclipse, he again came into his own in the nineteenth century. Leo XIII's bull, *Aeterni Patris* (1879), enjoined his study on all students of theology.

Aquinas' enormous literary output falls roughly into the following categories: (1) philosophic commentaries on Aristotle (*Peri Hermeneias, Posterior Analytics, Physics, De Caelo, De Generatione et Corruptione, Metereologica, De Anima, De Sensu et Sensato, De Memoria et Reminiscentia, Metaphysics, Nicomachean Ethics, Politics*) and on the *Liber de Causis;* (2) scriptural commentaries on Job, the Psalms, the Canticle of Canticles, Isaiah, Jeremiah, the Lamentations, Matthew, John, and the Epistles of St. Paul; (3) theological commentaries on Peter Lombard (*Liber Sententiarum*), Boethius (*De Trinitate, De Hebdomadibus*), and the pseudo-Dionysius (*De Divinis Nominibus*); (4) theological syntheses (*Summa contra Gentiles, Summa Theologiae*); (5) scholastic disputations (*Quaestiones Disputatae, Quaestiones Quodlibetales*); and, finally, various lesser theological and philosophic works.

Aquinas' teachings on political philosophy are to be found especially in his commentaries on the *Ethics* and the *Politics*, in his short treatise *On Kingship, to the King of Cyprus*, and in various articles of his *Summa Theologiae*. Of particular importance are the questions on law in the latter

work (Ia IIae, Questions 90-108). Aquinas' fullest discussion of Averroism occurs in his *Summa contra Gentiles* (especially Book I, chapters 63-71; Book II, chapters 31-38, 59-61, 68-81; Book III, chapters 41-45, 69-75, 84-87, 92-100); on the subject of the relation between faith and reason, consult Book I, chapters 1-9.

Aquinas' commentary on the *Ethics* was written *ca.* 1270–1272 and is one of the many commentaries on that work in the thirteenth century. Unlike the natural treatises and *Metaphysics* of Aristotle, the *Ethics* was never debarred from the schools by ecclesiastical authority. The first part of Aristotle's work—the so-called *Ethica Vetus* (Books II–III) and *Ethica Nova* (Book I)—had been known and used in the West since the beginning of the century. In 1240, Herman the German translated the entire *Nicomachean Ethics* from the Arabic, as well as Averroes' middle commentary on that work. Shortly afterwards, Robert Grosseteste provided the first complete translation from the Greek, *ca.* 1240–1243. The procedure observed by Aquinas in the present work is typical of all his commentaries on Aristotle. It is characterized, among other things, by its literalness (as opposed to the more or less free paraphrases of other commentators, such as Albert the Great), and by the extreme care with which it scrutinizes the text. The divisions with which each new section begins, and which form an integral part of the commentary, are calculated to bring out the over-all design of the *Ethics*, as well as the particular structure of each part in its minutest detail. Each section is thus related to the whole and explained briefly or, if necessary, at greater length. The first and most apparent aim of the commentary is to clarify the meaning of Aristotle's text, not to add to it or develop from it an original philosophic teaching. Whether or not Aquinas' interpretation remains faithful in each case to Aristotle's intention is a matter of controversy. Whatever the answer to this question, he was, and is still, regarded as one of Aristotle's greatest commentators.

The following passages are taken, with slight modifications, from the first complete English translation by Father Charles I. Litzinger, O.P.: St. Thomas Aquinas, *Commentary on the Ethics of Aristotle* ("Library of Living Catholic Thought" [Chicago: Henry Regnery Co., 1963]). This translation is based on the most recent edition of the commentary on the *Ethics* by R. Spiazzi, O.P.: S. Thomae Aquinatis, *In Decem Libros Ethicorum Aristotelis Expositio* (Turin, 1949), pp. 3-11, 556-66. Italic numbers in brackets in the body of the translation refer to the pagination of the Spiazzi edition. For reasons of space, the text of Aristotle, which precedes each

lesson in the commentary, has been left out, as also the words of Aristotle that Aquinas repeats in the text of the commentary itself in order to identify the precise passage to which he is referring. The references to Aristotle at the beginning of each lesson should suffice to enable the reader, if he so desires, to locate the passages in question without any difficulty by simply consulting a translation of the *Ethics*. Aquinas' commentary is divided into Books and Lessons. The paragraph numbers were introduced by recent editors and do not occur in the manuscripts themselves. The first three lessons of Book One deal with the subject and proper mode of moral philosophy. The last three lessons (XIV-XVI) of Book Ten treat of the necessity of legislation and hence of a legislator, and constitute a transition to the treatise on politics.

BOOK   ONE

LESSON   I

[i. 1. 1094ᵃ1–18]

[The Subject Matter and End of Moral Philosophy. The Diversity of Ends]

1   As the Philosopher says in the beginning of the *Metaphysics*, it is the business of the wise man to order.[1] The reason for this is that wisdom is the highest perfection of reason, whose characteristic is to know order. Even if the sensitive powers know some things absolutely, nevertheless it belongs to the intellect or reason alone to know the order of one thing to another. Now a twofold order is found in things. One, of parts of a whole or of a multitude among themselves, as the parts of a house are mutually ordered to one another. The second order is that of things to an end. This order is of greater importance than the first. For, as the Phi-

losopher says in Book XI of the *Metaphysics,* the order of the parts of an army among themselves exists because of the order of the whole army to the commander.[2] Now order is related to reason in a fourfold way. There is one order that reason does not establish but only considers; such is the order of things in nature. There is a second order that reason, in considering, establishes in its own act; for example, when it arranges its concepts among themselves and the signs of concepts, since they are sounds that signify something. There is a third order that reason, in considering, establishes in the operations of the will. There is a fourth order that reason, in considering, establishes in the external things that it produces, like a chest and a house.

2 Because the operation of reason is perfected by habit (*habitus*), according to these different orders that reason properly considers, there are different sciences. It pertains to natural philosophy to consider the order of things that human reason considers but does not establish— taken in such a way that with natural philosophy we also include metaphysics. The order that reason makes in its own act, by considering, pertains to rational philosophy [that is, logic], which properly considers the order of the parts of speech to one another and the order of principles to one another and to conclusions. The order of voluntary actions pertains to the consideration of moral philosophy. The order that reason, in considering, establishes in the external things produced by human reason pertains to the mechanical arts. Accordingly it is proper to moral philosophy, to which our attention is at present directed, to consider human operations in so far as they are ordered to one another and to an end.

3 I call human operations those that spring from man's will following the order of reason. For if some operations are found in man that are not subject to the will and reason, they are not properly called human but natural, as clearly appears in the operations of the vegetative soul. These in no way fall under the consideration of moral philosophy. As the subject of natural philosophy is motion, or mobile being, so the subject of moral philosophy is human action ordered to an end, or even man, as he is an agent voluntarily acting for an end.

4 It must be known that, because man is by nature a social animal, needing many things to live that he cannot get for himself if alone, it follows that man naturally is a part of a multitude, which furnishes him help to live well. He needs this help for two reasons. First, to have what is necessary for life, without which he cannot live the present life; and for this, man is helped by the domestic multitude of which he is a part. For every man is the recipient of generation and nourishment and instruction from his parents. Likewise individuals, who are members of the family, help one another to procure the necessities of life. In another way, man receives help from the multitude of which [4] he is a part to have a

perfect sufficiency for life; namely, that man may not only live but live well, having everything that suffices him for living; and in this way man is helped by the civil multitude of which he is a member, not only in regard to bodily needs—as certainly in the city there are many crafts that a single household cannot provide—but also in regard to right conduct, inasmuch as public authority restrains with fear of punishment insolent young men whom paternal admonition is not able to correct.

5 It must be known, moreover, that the whole that the political multitude or the family constitutes has only a unity of order, by reason of which it is not something absolutely one. Therefore, a part of this whole can have an operation that is not the operation of the whole, as a soldier in an army has an activity that does not belong to the whole army. However, this whole does have an operation that is not proper to its parts but to the whole, for example, a battle of the entire army. Likewise the movement of a boat is an operation of the crew rowing the boat. There is also a whole that has a unity, not of order alone, but of composition or of conjunction or even of continuity, according to which unity a thing is one absolutely; and therefore there is no operation of the part that does not belong to the whole. For in continuous things the motion of the whole and of the part is the same. Similarly in composites and in conjoined things, the operation of a part is principally that of the whole. For this reason it is necessary that such consideration of both the whole and its parts should belong to the same science. It does not, however, pertain to the same science to consider the whole that has unity only of order and the parts of this whole.

6 Thus it is that moral philosophy is divided into three parts. The first of these, which is called monastic, considers an individual's operations as ordered to an end. The second, called economics, considers the operations of the domestic group. The third, called politics, considers the operations of the civil group.

7 Aristotle, therefore, beginning the treatment of moral philosophy in the first part of this book called *Ethics* or *Morals*, first gives an introduction in which he does three things. First, he shows what he intends to do. Secondly, he determines the manner of treatment. Thirdly, he explains what manner of person the student of this science ought to be. In regard to the initial point he does two things. First, he presents in advance certain things necessary to show his intention. Secondly, he makes known his intention. In regard to the first he does two things. First, he lays down the necessity of the end. Then he compares habits and acts with the end. Concerning the first point he does three things. He states in the beginning that all things human are ordered to an end. Next, he mentions the different ends. Lastly, he establishes a comparison among ends. In regard to the first point he does two things. He states what he intends, and then he explains his purpose.

8   In regard to the first we should consider that there are two principles of human acts, namely, the intellect or reason and the appetite, which are active principles, as is said in Book III of *On the Soul*.[3] In the intellect or reason, the speculative and the practical are considered. In the rational appetite, choice and execution are considered. Now all these are ordered to some good as to an end; for truth is the end of speculation. Therefore, as regards the speculative intellect, he lists teaching, by which science is conveyed from teacher to student. In regard to the practical intellect, he lists art, which is right reason applied to things to be made, as is stated in Book VI of this work.[4] In respect to the act of the appetitive intellect, he lists choice. He does not mention prudence, which is in the practical reason as art is, because choice is properly directed by prudence. He says, therefore, that each of these obviously seeks a certain good as an end.

9   Then he manifests his intention by the effect of the good. In regard to this we should take into account that good is reckoned among primary things, to such a degree that, according to the Platonists, the good is prior to being. But, in reality, the good is convertible with being. Now primary things cannot be understood by anything prior, but by something posterior, as causes are understood through proper effects. And since the good is properly the moving principle of the appetite, the good is described by the movement of the appetitive faculty, just as a motive power is usually manifested through motion. For this reason he says that the philosophers have rightly declared that the good is what all things desire.

10   Nor is there a difficulty about those who desire evil. For they do not desire evil except under the aspect of good, that is, in so far as they think it is a good. In this way their intention primarily aims at the good and only incidentally touches on evil.

11   The expression "what all things desire" is to be understood not only of beings having knowledge, which apprehend the good, but also of beings lacking knowledge. These things by a natural desire tend toward the good, not as knowing the good, but because they are moved to the good by some knowing being, that is, by the direction of the divine intellect, in the same way that an arrow speeds toward a target by the aim of the archer. The very tending toward the good is the desiring of the good. Hence, he says all things [5] desire the good in so far as they tend toward the good. But there is not one good to which all tend, as will be said later. Therefore a particular good is not meant here, but rather the good in general. However, because nothing is good except in so far as it is a likeness and participation of the highest good, the highest good itself is in some way desired in every good. Thus it can be said that the true good is what all things desire.

12   Then he shows the diversity of ends. In this we must keep in mind

that the final good, to which the inclination of each thing tends, is its ultimate perfection. Now the first perfection is had after the manner of a form, but the second perfection in the manner of an operation. Therefore there must be this diversity of ends, namely, that some ends are the operations and other ends are the works themselves, that is, certain products, which are outside the operations.

13 For evidence of this we must consider that operation is of two kinds, as is said in Book IX of the *Metaphysics*.[5] One, which remains in the agent himself, as seeing, wishing, and understanding, is an operation of the type properly called action. The other is an operation going out into external matter and is properly called making. Sometimes a person accepts external matter only for use, as a horse for riding and a zither for playing, and at other times he takes external matter to change it into some other form, as when a carpenter constructs a house or a bed. Accordingly, the first and second of these operations do not have any product that is their end, but each of them is an end. The first, however, is more excellent than the second, inasmuch as it remains in the agent himself. But the third operation is a kind of generation whose end is a thing generated. So in operations of the third type, the works themselves are the ends.

14 Then he presents the third point, saying that whenever the products, which are outside the operations, are ends, the products necessarily are better than the operations, just as the thing generated is better than the generative action. The end is more important than the means—in fact the means have goodness from their relation to the end.

15 Then he compares habits and acts with the end. Concerning this he does four things. First, he shows that different things are ordered to different ends. He says first that, since there are many operations and arts and sciences, they must have different ends, for ends and means are proportional. This he shows by saying that the end of medical art is health; of shipbuilding, navigation; of strategy, victory; and of domestic economy or the management of a household, riches. The last is said according to a common opinion. He himself proves in the first book of the *Politics* that riches are not the end of domestic economy but the instruments.[6]

16 Secondly, he sets down the order of habits among themselves. It happens that one operative habit, which he calls virtue, is subordinated to another—as the art of bridle-making is subordinated to the art of riding because the rider tells the bridle-maker how he should make the bridle. In this way the rider is the designer, that is, the chief producer of the thing itself. The same argument holds for the other arts that make additional equipment needed for riding, such as saddles or the like. The equestrian art is again subordinated to the military, for in ancient times the army included not only mounted soldiers but everyone who fought for victory. Hence under military art there is not only the equestrian

but every art or skill ordered to war, namely, archery, gunnery, and everything else of this kind. In this same way other arts are subordinated to still others.

17   Thirdly, he lays down the order of ends according to the order of habits. He says that in all arts or skills it is commonly true that the architectonic ends are absolutely more desirable to everyone than the ends of the arts or skills that are subordinated to the chief ends. He proves this from the fact that men follow or seek the ends of the inferior arts or skills for the sake of the ends of the superior. The text, however, is suspensive, and should be read as follows: "In all such skills a subordination of one to another is found . . . , in all these the architectonic ends," and so forth.

18   Fourthly, he shows that it makes no difference in the order of ends whether the end is a product or an operation. He says that it makes no difference as regards the order that these ends be operations or some product other than the operations, as appears from the doctrine given above. The end of bridle-making is a finished bridle; but the end of horsemanship, which is of greater importance, is an operation, that is, riding. The contrary is true in medicine and gymnastics, for the end of medicine is something produced, namely, health; whereas the end of gymnastics, which is comprised under medicine, is an operation, namely, exercise.

LESSON   II

[i. 2. 1094ª19–ᵇ11]

[In Human Affairs There Is a Supreme End, Which Must Be Known, and Which Pertains to the Highest Science, Namely, Politics]

19   Having finished the things that are necessary for manifesting his intention, the Philosopher begins now to make known that intention, that is, to show what the principal purpose of this science is. Concerning this he does three things. First, he shows from what was said before that there is some supreme end of human affairs. Secondly, he shows that it is necessary to know this end. Thirdly, he shows to which science this knowledge belongs. He proves the first by three reasons. The principal one is this. Whatever end is such that we wish other things because of

it, and we wish it for itself and not because of something else, then that end is not only a good, but the supreme good. This is apparent from the fact that an end for the sake of which other ends are sought is of greater importance, as is evident from what was said before. But it is necessary that there be some such end of human affairs. Therefore, in human affairs there is an end that is good and best.

20 He proves the minor by an argument that leads to an impossible conclusion. It is evident from what we have said that one end is desired on account of another. Therefore, either we arrive at some end that is not desired on account of another, or we do not. If we do, the proposition is proved. If, however, we do not find some such end, it follows that every end will be desired on account of another end. In this case we must proceed to infinity. But it is impossible in ends to proceed to infinity. Therefore there must be some end that is not desired on account of another.

21 That it is impossible in ends to proceed to infinity is proved also by an argument that leads to an impossibility. If we should proceed to infinity in desiring ends, so that one end should always be desired on account of another to infinity, we will never arrive at the point where a man may attain the end desired. But a man desires in vain what he cannot get; therefore, the end he desires would be useless and vain. But this desire is natural, for it was said [7] above that the good is what all things naturally desire. Hence it follows that a natural desire would be useless and vain. But this is impossible. The reason is that a natural desire is nothing else but an inclination belonging to things by the disposition of the first mover, which cannot be frustrated. Therefore, it is impossible that in ends we should proceed to infinity.

22 Therefore, there must be some ultimate end on account of which all other things are desired, while this end itself is not desired on account of anything else. So there must be some supreme end of human affairs.

23 Then he shows that the knowledge of this end is necessary for man. In regard to this he does two things. First, he shows that it is necessary for man to know such an end. Secondly, he shows what man should know about it. He concludes then from what has been said that it is necessary for man to know that there is a supreme end of human affairs because this has great importance for life, that is, it is of great help in all phases of human living. This is apparent for the following reason. Nothing that is directed to another can be directly attained by man unless he knows that other to which it is to be directed. This is obvious from the example of the archer who shoots straight by keeping his eye on the target at which he is aiming. Now man's whole life ought to be ordered to the supreme and ultimate end of human life. It is necessary, therefore, to have a knowledge of the ultimate and supreme end of human life. The explanation is that the reason for the means

must always be found in the end itself, as also is proved in Book II of the *Physics*.[7]

24   Then he shows what ought to be known about that end. He says that, since it is true that the knowledge of the supreme end is necessary for human life, we must determine what is the supreme end, and to which speculative or practical science its consideration belongs. By "disciplines" he understands the speculative sciences, and by "skills" (*virtutes*) the practical sciences, since they are principles of some operations. And he says that we must "try" to determine in order to suggest the difficulty there is in grasping the ultimate end of human life, as in considering all ultimate causes. On the other hand, he says that we should understand this according to its lineaments, that is, with probability, because such a manner of understanding is suitable for human things, as will be said later on. Now the first of these two belongs to the treatise on this science because such a consideration is about the matter of this science, while the second belongs to the introduction, where the purpose of this science is explained.

25   Therefore, immediately after, he shows to which science the consideration of this end belongs. In regard to this he does two things. First, he gives a reason to prove what he proposes. Secondly, he proves something that he has taken for granted. First then he states the reason for what he proposes, which is this: the supreme end belongs to the most important and most truly architectonic science. This is clear from what was said above, for it was pointed out that the sciences or arts that treat of the means to the end are contained under the science or art treating of the end. So it is necessary that the ultimate end should belong to the most important science as concerned with the primary and most important end, and to the truly architectonic science as telling the others what they should do. But political science appears to be such, namely, the most important and the most truly architectonic. Therefore, it belongs to it to consider the supreme end.

26   Then he proves what he has taken for granted: that political science is such a science. First, he proves that it is the most truly architectonic, and secondly, that it is the most important. In regard to the first he does two things. First, he ascribes to political science or politics the things that belong to an architectonic science. Secondly, from this he infers what he intended. There are two characteristics of an architectonic science. One is that it dictates what is to be done by the art or science subject to it, as the equestrian art dictates to bridle-making. The other is that it uses it for its own ends. Now the first of these is applicable to politics or political science both in regard to the speculative and in regard to the practical sciences, in different ways, however. Political science dictates to a practical science both concerning its use—whether or not it should operate—and concerning the specification of its operation.

It dictates to the smith not only that he use his skill but also that he use it in such a fashion as to make knives of a particular kind. Both are ordered to the end of human living.

27   But political science dictates to a speculative science only concerning its use and not concerning the specification of its operation. Political science orders that some teach or learn geometry; and actions of this kind, in so far as they are voluntary, belong to the matter of ethics and can be ordered to the goal [8] of human living. But the political ruler does not dictate to geometry what conclusions it should draw about a triangle, for this is not subject to the human will nor can it be ordered to human living, but it depends on the very nature of things. Therefore he says that political science ordains which sciences, both practical and speculative, should be studied in a city, who should study them, and for how long.

28   The other characteristic of an architectonic science, the use of subordinate sciences, belongs to political science only in reference to the practical sciences. Hence, he adds, we see that the most highly esteemed, that is, the noblest, skills or operative arts fall under political science, namely, strategy, domestic economy, and rhetoric, which political science uses for its own end, that is, for the common good of the city.

29   Then he draws a conclusion from these two premises. He says that since political science uses the other practical sciences, as was said above, and since it legislates what is to be done and what is not to be done, as previously stated, it follows that the end of this science as architectonic embraces or contains under itself the ends of the other practical sciences. Hence he concludes that the end of political science is the good of man, that is, the supreme end of human things.

30   Then he shows that political science is the most important science, from the very nature of its proper end. It is evident that in so far as a cause is prior and more powerful, it extends to more effects. Hence in so far as the good, which has the nature of a final cause, is more powerful, it extends to more effects. So even though the good be the same for one man and for a whole city, it seems much better and more perfect to attain, that is, to procure and preserve the good of a whole city than the good of one man. Certainly it is a part of that love which should exist among men that a man preserve the good even of a single human being. But it is much better and more divine that this be done for a whole nation and for cities. Or it is sometimes desirable that this be done for one city only, but it is much more divine that it be done for a whole nation, which includes many cities. This is said to be more divine because it shows greater likeness to God, who is the ultimate cause of all good. But this good that is common to one or to several cities, is the object of our inquiry, that is, of the particular art called political science. Hence to it,

as the most important science, belongs in a most special way the consideration of the ultimate end of human life.

31 But we should note that he says political science is the most important, not simply, but in the genus of the practical sciences, which are concerned with human things, the ultimate end of which political science considers. The ultimate end of the whole universe is considered in divine science, which is the most important without qualification. He says that it belongs to political science to treat of the ultimate end of human life. This, however, he discusses here since the teaching of this book covers the first elements of political science.

LESSON III

[i. 3. 1094^{b}12–1095^{a}13]

[The Method of Moral Science. How It Should Be Taught and Learned]

32 After the Philosopher has shown what is the good principally intended in this science, he now determines the method proper to this science. He does this first on the part of the teacher and next on the part of the student. In regard to the first he lays down this argument. The method of manifesting the truth in any science ought to be suitable to the subject matter of that science. He shows this from the fact that certitude cannot be found, nor should it be sought, in the same degree in all discussions where we reason about anything. Likewise, the same method is not used in all products that are made by art; but each craftsman works with the material in a way suited to that material, in one way with dirt, in another with clay, in still another with metal. Now the matter of moral study is of such a nature that perfect certitude is not suitable to it. He shows this from two classes of things that seem to belong to the material with which moral study is concerned.

33 In the matter of morals the first and foremost place is held by virtuous works, which he calls here just works and which are the chief concern of political science. Regarding them there is no sure opinion among men; rather a great difference is found in what men judge about them. In this matter a variety of errors occurs, for certain actions, con-

sidered just and good by some, are looked upon as unjust and bad by others according to different times and places and persons. For a deed is considered vicious at one time and in one country, but at a different time and in a different country it is not considered to be so. Because of this difference, it happens that some people are of the opinion that nothing is just or good by nature, but only [*10*] by disposition of law. We shall treat more fully of this opinion in Book II of this work.

34   Secondly, the external goods that are used by men for a purpose have a moral consideration. In regard to them also it happens that we find the error just mentioned, because these material goods are not always used in the same way by everyone. Some men are helped by them, while others are harmed by them. Many have been ruined by having riches; for instance, those who were murdered by robbers. Others, by reason of their physical strength on which they rely, have carelessly exposed themselves to dangers. Thus it is evident that moral matters are variable and divergent and do not possess absolute certitude.

35   Because, in the art of demonstrative science, principles must conform to conclusions, it is desirable and preferable, when treating subjects so variable, and when proceeding from premises of a like nature, to bring out the truth first in a rough way by applying universal principles to singulars, and by proceeding from the simple to the complex, in which actions consist. But it is necessary in every practical science to proceed in a composite manner; whereas in a speculative science, it is necessary to proceed in an analytical manner by breaking down the complex into elementary principles. Secondly, we should present the truth in outline, that is, in an approximate way. This is to proceed from the proper principles of this science. Moral science treats of voluntary acts, and what moves the will is not only the good but the apparent good. Thirdly, we are going to speak of events as they happen in the majority of cases, that is, of voluntary acts, which proceed from the will, inclined perhaps to one alternative rather than another but not operating under compulsion. In these, too, we must proceed in such a way that principles are conformable to conclusions.

36   Then he shows that the student must accept this limitation in moral matters. He says that it is proper that each one should take whatever is said to him by another "in the same spirit," that is, as the matter warrants. The reason is that a well-educated or well-instructed man should look for as much certitude in any matter as the nature of the subject admits. There cannot be as much certainty in variable and contingent matter as in necessary matter, which is always the same. Therefore, the well-educated man ought not to look for greater nor be satisfied with less certitude than is appropriate to the subject under discussion. It seems an equal fault to allow a mathematician to use rhetorical arguments and to demand from the rhetorician conclusive demonstrations such as a mathe-

matician should give. Both of these things happen because the method appropriate to the matter is not considered. Mathematics is concerned with matter in which perfect certitude is found, whereas rhetoric deals with political matter, where variation occurs.

37 Then he shows what sort of person the student of this science ought to be. First, he shows who is an unsuitable student, and secondly, who is an unprofitable student. Thirdly, he shows who is a proper student. In respect to the first he does two things. First, he introduces certain things necessary to explain his proposition. He states that each man can judge well only the things he knows. Thus a man educated in one particular subject can judge well what belongs to that subject. But the man who is well educated in all subjects can judge well about all without restriction to a particular subject.

38 Secondly, he draws his conclusion, namely, that a young man is not a proper student of political science nor of any part of moral science, which is comprised under political science, because, as was said, a man can judge well only the things he knows. Now every student should make good judgments about what he studies, so that he may accept what is well said but not what is badly said. Therefore, no one can be a proper hearer unless he has some knowledge of what he ought to study. But a young man does not have a knowledge of things belonging to moral science, for these are known mostly through experience, and a young man is inexperienced in the ways of life because of the very brevity of his life. And yet the arguments of moral science proceed from, and are also about, things that pertain to the actions of human life. For instance, if it be said that the generous man keeps the cheaper things for himself and makes a present of the more expensive to others, a young man will perhaps judge this not to be true because of his inexperience. It is the same with other civil matters. Hence it is evident that a young man is not a proper student of political science.

39 Then he shows who is an unprofitable student of this science. Here we must consider that moral science teaches men to follow reason and to refrain from the things to which the passions incline, such as concupiscence, anger, and the like. Toward these, men are inclined in two ways. In one way by choice, for instance, when a man of set purpose intends to satisfy his concupiscence. Such a one he calls a slave of passions. The other way is when a man resolves to abstain from harmful [11] pleasures but is sometimes overcome by the urge of passions, so that contrary to his resolution he follows the promptings of passion. A man of this type is said to be incontinent.

40 He affirms, then, that the slave of the passions will study this science in vain, that is, without any result and uselessly, that is, without attaining its proper end. The end of this science is not knowledge alone, which the slaves of passion can perhaps gain; rather the end of this science,

as of all practical sciences, is human action. Now those who follow the passions do not attain virtuous acts. So in regard to this it makes no difference whether the student of this science is immature in age or immature in character, that is, a slave of the passions. The reason is that, as the immature in age fails to achieve the end of this science which is knowledge, so the immature in character fails to achieve the end which is action. His deficiency is not due to time but to the fact that he lives according to his passions, seeking everything to which the passions incline. Now, for such men the knowledge of this science is useless; the same may be said of the incontinent who do not act in accord with their knowledge of moral matters.

41   Then he shows who is a proper student of this science. He says that it is very useful to have a knowledge of moral matters for those who satisfy all their desires and act in externals according to the dictates of reason.

42   Lastly, in the conclusion he sums up what has been discussed in this introduction, stating that this much has been said in a preliminary manner about the student—this was treated last; stating also what is the method of demonstrating—this was treated in the middle of the introduction; and lastly what our purpose is, namely, what the principal aim of this science is—this was treated first.

B O O K   T E N

L E S S O N   X I V

[x. 9. 1179ª33–1180ª24]

[The Necessity of Legislation]

2137   After the Philosopher has determined the end of virtue, which in the virtuous man is pleasure or happiness, now he determines the other end, which is understood in comparison with the common good. He shows that, besides this moral science, it is necessary to have another science, the legislative, whose object is the common good. Concerning this point he does three things. First, he shows that it is necessary to have legislation. Next, he shows that it is necessary that someone become a legislator. [557] Lastly, he shows how a man can become a legislator. Concerning the first point he does two things. First, he raises the question whether we have sufficiently discussed in outline—inasmuch as it had to be discussed generally and schematically—what we should think about matters pertaining to happiness, about the virtues, friendship, and pleasure, so that the choice we made in treating of the good of man is really complete and exhaustive, or whether there is still something to be added.

2138 Next, he determines the truth, showing that something more is required. First, he shows that it is necessary that a man become good. Then he shows that the habit of good living is required for a man to become good. Lastly, he shows that to have this habit legislation is required. He says first that the end of the science concerned with operable matters is not to know and investigate each individual thing, as in the speculative sciences, but rather to do them. And since we become good and doers of good works in accordance with virtue, it is not sufficient for the science that aims at man's good that someone have a knowledge of virtue; rather we must try to make him possess it according to habit and use it according to act; or if it is thought that a man can become good in another way than by virtue, then we must try to obtain this.

2139 Then he shows that habit is required in order that a man become good. First, he shows that speech alone is not sufficient; secondly, that habit is needed. He says first that if persuasive words sufficed to make men virtuous, many great rewards would be due to a man for his art, that is, because of the art of persuading to the good; and it would be absolutely necessary to give great rewards to persuaders. But this is not generally true.

2140 We see that persuasive speech can challenge and move to good liberal youths who are not slaves of vice and passion and who have noble habits inasmuch as they are disposed to virtuous operations. And those who truly love the good can become *katokōchimon*, that is, full of virtue and honor, for such as are well-disposed to virtue are incited by good advice to the perfection of virtue.

2141 But many men cannot be induced to virtue by speech because they do not heed to the sense of shame, which fears baseness, but rather are coerced by fear of punishment. They do not abstain from evil deeds on account of their baseness but on account of the punishments feared. For they live not according to reason but according to the passions, by means of which their own desires increase, and they avoid the pains opposed to the desired pleasures—pains that are inflicted on them through punishment. They have no understanding of what is truly good and pleasant, nor can they taste its delight. People of this sort cannot be changed by any discourse.

2142   To change a man by speech one must propose to him something that he accepts. However, one who has no taste for the noble good but is inclined toward the passions does not accept anything that is proposed in a speech inducing to virtue. Hence it is impossible, or at least difficult, for anyone to be able to change a man by speech from what he holds by inveterate habit. So also in speculative matters, it would not be possible to lead back to the truth a man who firmly cleaves to the opposites of the principles, which correspond to the ends in practical matters, as has been indicated previously.

2143   Next, he shows that habit is required for a man to become virtuous. He says that to acquire virtue we ought not to be satisfied with mere speeches. But we ought to consider it a thing of great value if, even after possessing everything by which men seem to become virtuous, we attain virtue. There are three opinions on these matters. Some people maintain that men become good by nature, namely, by natural temperament together with the influence of the heavenly bodies. Others hold that men become good by practice. Still others say that men become good by instruction. All three opinions are true in some measure.

2144   Certainly the natural disposition is a help to virtue; this agrees with what was stated in Book VI that some people seem to be brave or temperate right from birth by a certain natural inclination. But natural virtue of this kind is imperfect, as we pointed out in the place just mentioned; and its completion requires that the perfection of the intellect or reason supervene. For this reason there is need of instruction, which would be enough if virtue were located in the intellect or reason only, in accordance with the opinion of Socrates, [558] who maintained that virtue is science. However, because rectitude of the appetite is required for virtue, habit is necessary to incline the appetite toward the good.

2145   But what pertains to nature manifestly is not in our power but comes to men from some divine cause: from the influence of the heavenly bodies in regard to man's physical condition, and from God Himself, who alone governs the intellect in regard to the movement of man's mind toward the good. In this men are really very fortunate to be inclined toward the good by a divine cause, as is evident in the chapter *On Good Fortune*.[8]

2146   It was explained previously that speech and instruction are not effective with everyone. But, in order that they may be effective with someone, the soul of the hearer must be prepared by many good habits to rejoice in the good and hate evil, just as the soil must be well tilled to nourish the seed abundantly. For a speech heard in the soul is like seed in the ground. Indeed the man who lives according to his passions will not willingly listen to the words of an admonisher nor will he understand it in such a way as to judge the advice to be good. Hence he cannot be persuaded by anyone.

2147 Generally speaking, a passion that is firmly rooted by habit in a man and dominates him does not yield to speech alone but must be attacked by violence to compel man to good. So, evidently, for exhortation to have an effect on anyone there must necessarily pre-exist a habit by which man may acquire the proper disposition to virtue, so that he can love the noble good and hate what is dishonorable.

2148 Then he shows that legislation is required for good habits. First, he shows that all men are made good by law. Next, he shows that this cannot be done properly without law. Concerning the first point he does two things. First, he discloses his intention. Secondly, he presents a sign for it. Concerning the first point he does two things. First, he explains his intention in relation to young men; then in relation to others. He says first that it is difficult for anyone to be guided from his early years to virtue according to good customs unless he is reared under good laws, by which a kind of necessity impels a man to good.

2149 To live temperately by abstaining from pleasures and perseveringly so that one does not forsake the good on account of labors and pains is distasteful to many, and especially to young men, who are prone to pleasures, as was said in Book VII. For this reason the rearing of children and their activities must be regulated by good laws; thus they will be forced as it were to become accustomed to good things, which will not be distasteful but pleasant after the habit has been formed.

2150 Then he shows that others, too, need legislation. He says that it is not enough for men to be reared under good laws and to receive the proper care while they are young; it is even more important that someone find honorable ways to act and become accustomed to them once he has reached manhood. For this reason we need laws, not only in the beginning when someone starts to grow into manhood, but generally throughout man's whole life. Many indeed there are who yield to necessity, that is, force, rather than argument; they pay more attention to loss, that is, to the damage they incur by way of punishment, than to what is honorable.

2151 Next, he illustrates his point by means of a sign. He says that, since the restraint induced by laws is required for the good life of man, some legislators think that men must be summoned to virtue in this way; the virtuous, who of their own free will comply with what is honorable, should be aroused to good by means of pre-existing customs, for example, by being shown the goodness of what is proposed. But the insubordinate and the degenerate are allotted corporeal punishments like scourges and various penalties, and are censured and made to suffer damage to their possessions. As for those who are absolutely incurable, they are exterminated; the robber, for instance, is hanged.

2152 This is so because the virtuous man who adjusts his life to the good needs only speech, by which the good is proposed to him. But the corrupt man, because he seeks pleasure, ought to be punished by pain or sorrow like a beast of burden, just as an ass is driven by lashes. Hence, they say, those pains should be inflicted that are directly contrary to cherished pleasures; for example, if a man was intoxicated, he should be given water to drink.

2153   Then he shows that law is necessary for men to become good, for two reasons. The first is that the man [559] who is going to become virtuous must be well reared and acquire good habits; and afterwards he must live according to his discoveries of righteous ways, so that he abstains from evil either by his own will or even through compulsion against his will. This is possible only when a man's life is directed by some intellect that has both the right order conducive to the good and firmness, that is, the coercive power to compel the unwilling. Now this coercive power is not contained in the precept of a father, nor does it belong to any other counselor who is not a ruler or a person in authority. But the law includes coercive power inasmuch as it is promulgated by the ruler or prince; likewise it is an instruction issuing from prudence and reason that gives guidance toward the good. Therefore law is obviously necessary to make men good.

2154   He gives the second reason, saying that people who wish to oppose the habits of anyone are hated by the person whom they oppose even when the opposition is just; for they are thought to act from a malicious zeal. But the law that commands honest deeds is not irksome, that is, burdensome or odious, because it is proposed in a general way. Therefore it remains that law is necessary to make men good.

LESSON   XV

[x. 9. 1180ᵃ25–ᵇ28]
[The Necessity of a Legislator]

2155   After the Philosopher has shown that legislation is necessary to make men good, now he shows that it is necessary that there be a legislator. First he states his intention. Then he proves his thesis. He says first that, as was just pointed out, legislation is needed for the rearing and the activities of men; nevertheless, only in Sparta and a few other states does the legislator seem to have given attention to regulating by law the rearing of children and the ways of acting. But matters of this kind are neglected in most cities, where each man lives as he pleases, dealing with his children and wife as he wishes, like the Cyclopes, certain barbarous tribes who do not live under laws. Therefore it is best that there be a proper supervision by public authority over the rearing of children and the virtuous activities of the citizens, and that man be so instructed that he can do this properly.

2156 But men commonly neglect this because it is plain that they show no public concern for it. Hence it seems fitting that each private person do something to help his children and friends to become virtuous; or if he cannot, at least he should choose the means to make this possible. Apparently it can best be done, according to the preceding statements, if a man becomes a legislator, that is, if he acquires the competence to be able to make good laws. So to be a legislator pertains principally to a public person; secondarily, however, also to a private person.

2157 Next he proves his thesis by two arguments. He says first that general supervision, namely, that exercised by public officials whose function it is to frame laws, obviously is done through law. Thus supervision is exercised over some people inasmuch as laws are imposed on them; and good supervision is that which is done through good laws.

2158 It makes no difference for our thesis whether this is done by means of written or unwritten laws, [562] or by laws that instruct one or many, as is clearly the case also in music, gymnastics, and other skills; it does not matter in the present work whether instruction is imparted in writing or not, for writing is used to keep information for the future. Likewise it does not matter whether instruction in such matters is offered to one or many. Therefore it seems to amount to the same thing that a father of a family should instruct his son or a few members of the household by verbal or written admonition, and that a prince should make a law in writing to govern all the people of the city. For public laws and customs introduced by rulers hold the same place in cities as paternal precepts and customs set down by fathers in their families.

2159 The only difference is this: a father's words do not have full coercive power like those of a king, as was previously noted. Now he goes on to show that to some extent this [supervision] is more suitable to a private than to a public person by reason of the relationship and benefits on account of which children love their parents and are readily obedient out of the natural friendship that sons have for their father. So then, although a king's words are more powerful by way of fear, a father's words can accomplish more by way of love—a way that is more efficacious with those who are not completely inclined to evil.

2160 Next, he gives the second reason. He says that instruction which is useful in general is subject to variation in particular cases. This is clearly the case, for example, in the art of medicine: in general, fast and rest are beneficial to people running a fever, so that nature will not be burdened with an abundance of food and heat will not be generated by activity. But perhaps this is not advisable for a particular fever-stricken patient because fast might weaken him too much; and perhaps the patient might need activity to dissolve the gross humors. The same thing is true in athletic contests, because an athlete does not fight the same way against every opponent. Accordingly, the operation of each practical art will appear more certain if the proper attention is given to each individual case; thus everyone will better acquire what is suitable to him.

2161   However, a thing will be done with the best care if a doctor or a trainer or any other skilled worker knows in a universal way what is common to all men or what will benefit all men of a particular class, for example, irascible persons. This is so because science is said to be and is actually concerned with universals. Therefore he who proceeds from universal knowledge will best be able to care for an individual case. Nevertheless this is not the only way a doctor can produce a cure; nothing prevents him from curing a particular patient without universal knowledge, provided that from experience he can properly diagnose the symptoms of each patient. Thus some people seem to be skillful in doctoring themselves because they know their own symptoms from experience, but they are not qualified to help others.

2162   Although a man can operate well in a particular situation without universal knowledge, nevertheless if he wishes to become an artist he must strive for universal knowledge, that he may know the universal in some measure. Likewise this is necessary for one who wishes to be a speculative scientist, like the geometrician or the physicist. For we said earlier that the sciences deal with this, that is, with universals. The case is the same with those who exercise supervision to make people good.

2163   It is possible that someone, without art and science by which the universal is known, can make this or that man good because of his own personal experience. However, if someone wants to make people— either a few or many—better by his supervision, he should try to acquire a universal knowledge of the things that make a man good; in other words, he should try to become a legislator, so as to know the art by which good laws are framed, since we become good by means of laws, as was pointed out earlier. The reason is that the ability properly to prepare any good habit in man by introducing it and by removing its opposite, for example, health and sickness, virtue and vice, is not possessed by everyone but only by him who has a knowledge of universals. This is evident in the medical art and in all other fields where care and human prudence are displayed. In all these a man must not only know particulars but have a knowledge of universals, because some things may occur that are contained under universal knowledge but not under the knowledge of individual incidents.

LESSON XVI

[x. 9. 1180ᵇ29–1181ᵇ24]

[How One May Become a Legislator]

2164   After the Philosopher has shown that it is necessary for man to become a legislator, he inquires how someone can become a legislator. First, he states his intention. He infers from the premises that, since it was shown to be expedient for man to become a legislator, he must inquire after these discussions how someone may become a legislator, whether from habit or from instruction, and how in this or that way.

2165   Secondly, he carries out his intention. First, he shows that the things used by earlier philosophers were not sufficient to make anyone a legislator. Next, he concludes that this has to be discussed by himself. Concerning the first point he does two things. First, he shows how someone must become a legislator. Then he shows that this is not observed. He says first that it seems [565] appropriate that the origin and manner in which one becomes a legislator is the same as in the other practical sciences, which are for the sake of political science. Nor is it out of place for me to speak of political science while inquiring about legislation. For as was stated in Book VI, legislation is a part of political prudence, since legislation is a kind of architectonic political science.

2166   Then he shows that this is not observed, and appropriately so, it seems, because of the difference among those who busy themselves about legislation. First, he states their difference. Next, he shows their deficiencies. He says first that, although there would reasonably appear to be a resemblance between this and other sciences, nevertheless the same thing does not seem to be observed in political science and the other practical arts, which are called sciences in regard to the element of knowledge that they possess, and skills (*potentiae*) in so far as they are principles of operation. Indeed in the other practical arts, the people who impart these arts by teaching them seem to be identical with those who practice them: doctors, for example, both teach medicine and practice it. The same reason holds for painters and any others who operate according to art.

2167   However, it seems to be otherwise in political science. Some people, the Sophists, profess to teach legislation, but none of them puts it into operation, whereas others, namely, the politicians, seem to practice it.

2168   Next, he shows the deficiences of both groups: first of the politicians, and then of the Sophists. Concerning the first point he does three things. First, he states what he has in mind about the deficiency of the politicians. Their public activities seem to be performed more from an aptitude or a kind of habit acquired by custom and from experience than from intellectual discernment, that is, reason or science.

2169   Secondly, he verifies his statement by means of two signs. The first is that those who work scientifically can give the reasons, orally or in writing, for the things they do. But the politicians do not seem to produce anything about political science either in speeches or writing, although writing would be much better than discourses on judicial procedure, by which people are taught how they ought to judge according to certain laws, and on eloquence, by which they are taught to speak publicly according to the rules of rhetoric.

2170   The second sign is that men who work scientifically can form other scientific workers through teaching. But men of the kind who practice politics do not make their sons or any of their friends statesmen. And yet it is reasonable that they should do so if they could. Surely they could confer on their countries no greater benefit, which would remain after them, than by making others good statesmen. Likewise there would be nothing more desirable as far as they themselves are concerned than the ability to make other men statesmen, nor could they do anything more useful even for their best friends.

2171   Thirdly, he refutes an error. Someone might think from what has been said that experience in practicing politics would not be useful. But he himself says that, although it is not enough, nevertheless it contributes not a little to making a man a statesman. Otherwise, some people would not become better statesmen by the practice of political life. And experience in political life seems necessary for those who desire to know something about politics.

2172   Then he shows the deficiency from which the Sophists suffer. Concerning this point he does three things. First, he states his intention, saying that the Sophists who promise to teach political science seem to be a long way from teaching it. Indeed they appear to be completely ignorant both of the nature of political science and of the sort of things with which it deals.

2173   Next, he verifies his thesis by means of signs, first in regard to his statement that they do not know its nature. If they understood this, they would not identify it with rhetoric; for rhetoric can give persuasive arguments in praise or censure of a person both in assemblies and in the courts, and this in three kinds of causes: demonstrative, deliberative, and judicial. But according to them, political science exercises persuasion only in judicial matters. They think men are good statesmen who know how to introduce laws in view of a particular judgment.

2174 He gives the second sign for his statement that they do not know of what things political science treats. If they knew this, they would not think it easy to frame laws in accordance with legislation, which is the principal part of political science, saying that in order to make laws it suffices to collect a variety of approved laws, choose the best, and institute them.

2175 They err in two ways on this point. They err in one way by maintaining that to become a legislator it is enough to collect laws and choose the best among them. The reason is that by legislation a man [566] must not only form a judgment about the laws in use but also devise new laws, in imitation of the other practical arts; for a doctor not only judges about the known remedies for effecting a cure but can discover new ones. They also err in another way, which he touches upon after disposing of the first error. It is not easy for a man to choose the best laws, as choice does not depend on the intellect alone, and right judgment is an important matter, as is evident in music.

2176 People who have experience with particulars make a correct judgment about the things to be done and understand by what means and in what manner works of this kind can be produced, and what kinds are suited to what persons or things. But the inexperienced understandably do not know whether a work can be done well or badly according to what they read in books, for they do not know how to apply what is presented in writing to the work. Now laws to be instituted are, as it were, political works, for they are instituted as rules for political works. Hence people who do not know what kind of works are suitable cannot know what kind of laws are suitable.

2177 Therefore one cannot become a legislator by collecting laws or by judging what kind of laws are best unless he has experience; just as it does not seem possible for men to become good doctors only from the remedies found in books, even though the authors of these books try to determine not only the cures but also the means of curing, or how remedies must be prescribed according to the individual conditions of men. Nevertheless all these things seem useful only to people with experience and not to those who are ignorant of particulars because of inexperience.

2178 Lastly, he infers from the premises the rejection of an error, according to which someone might think that a collection of written laws would be absolutely useless. He says that what we have said concerning written medical remedies applies to our problem, namely, to collect laws and constitutions, that is, ordinances of different cities, is useful for those who can consider and judge from practice which works or laws are good or bad, and what kinds are suitable in given circumstances. But those who have not the habit acquired by practice and want to review written documents of this kind cannot judge them properly except by chance. However, they do become better prepared to understand such things by the fact that they read through written laws and constitutions.

2179 Then he states that he is going to discuss how a man may become a legislator. First, he shows that this is incumbent upon him. He says that, since earlier writers, namely, the philosophers who preceded him, have not treated fully what pertains to legislation, it is better that we ourselves should attempt to treat of legislation and, in general, of the whole question of government, of which lawmaking is a part, for in this way we can extend philosophic teaching to political science, that is, the practical knowledge dealing with human affairs—a subject that he seems to have taught last according to this.

2180 Then he shows in what order he is going to carry this out. He says that he will first attempt in passing to touch upon whatever was in part well treated in political science by his predecessors, that is, by earlier philosophers. This he will do in Book II of the *Politics*. After that he will consider which of the various regimes preserve the cities (the just regimes: kingship, aristocracy, and polity), and which ones ruin them (the corrupt regimes: tyranny or the rule of one man, oligarchy, and democracy). Moreover, we must consider what things preserve or corrupt each regime, and the reasons why some cities are governed well and others badly. This he will determine in the *Politics* from Book III to Book VII. Then, after the previous discussions, he begins to inquire what is the best regime, and how it ought to be organized, and what laws and customs it should follow. But before all these things, he sets down in Book I certain principles from which he says he is going to begin. This serves as a transition to the work on the *Politics* and as a conclusion of the whole of the *Ethics*.

NOTES

1. Aristotle *Metaphysics* i. 2. 982ª18.
2. *Ibid.* xii. 10. 1075ª14.
3. Aristotle *De Anima* iii. 10. 433ª9 ff.
4. Aristotle *Nicomachean Ethics* vi. 4. 1140ª9.

5. Aristotle *Metaphysics* ix. 8. 1050ª23.
6. Aristotle *Politics* i. 9. 1257ᵇ34 ff.
7. Aristotle *Physics* ii. 9. 200ª7 ff.
8. *De Bona Fortuna.* A lost work of Aristotle.

17.

Thomas Aquinas

COMMENTARY ON

THE POLITICS

*Translated by Ernest L. Fortin
and Peter D. O'Neill*

Aquinas' commentary on the *Politics*, like his commentary on the *Ethics*, appears to have been composed between 1270 and 1272. It does not extend beyond Book III, chapter 8, and was completed by Peter of Auvergne, whose commentary follows that of Aquinas in the modern editions of the latter's works. The procedure of the commentary on the *Politics* is identical to that of the commentary on the *Ethics*. It is commonly believed that William of Moerbeke revised an earlier translation of the first three books of the *Politics* and provided the first Latin translation of the remainder of that work, *ca.* 1260. Although the division of moral philosophy into ethics, economics, and politics was already known, no use was made of any part of the *Politics* prior to that time. There is no mention of the *Politics* in the new statutes of the Arts Faculty at Paris

in 1255. The canon and civil laws and such works as Cicero's *De Officiis* constituted the standard texts in the schools. As soon as it became available, the *Politics* exerted a wide influence. Lectures on the *Politics* were introduced at the Arts Faculty in Paris and then elsewhere. The same practice was soon followed by the religious orders. Besides the one by Aquinas, no fewer than six commentaries on that work, including those of Albert the Great, Peter of Auvergne (distinct from the complement to Aquinas' commentary mentioned above), Siger of Brabant, and perhaps Giles of Rome, are known to have been written before the end of the thirteenth century. (For a critical list of these commentaries, one may consult Martin Grabmann, *Die mittelalterlichen Kommentare zur Politik des Aristoteles* [Munich, 1941].) Albert's commentary was composed at approximately the same time as that of Aquinas. It is impossible to know which one came first. The influence of the *Politics* is also perceptible in numerous other works of that period, particularly those dealing with matters of ecclesiastical or imperial polity.

The following passages are all new translations. The six lessons of Book III are here translated into English for the first time. The translation is based on the recent edition of the commentary on the *Politics* by R. Spiazzi, O.P.: S. Thomae Aquinatis, *In Libros Politicorum Aristotelis Expositio* (Turin, 1951), pp. 1-12 and 121-40. Italic numbers in brackets in

the body of the translation refer to the pagination of the Spiazzi edition. For reasons of space, the text of Aristotle, which precedes each lesson in the commentary, has been left out, as also the words of Aristotle that Aquinas repeats in the text of the commentary itself in order to identify the precise passage to which he is referring. Aquinas' Proemium discusses the nature and necessity of political philosophy. The first lesson of Book I establishes the subject of that science. The first six lessons of Book III deal with the central question of the nature of citizenship.

PROEMIUM

1   As the Philosopher teaches in Book II of the *Physics*, art imitates nature.[1] The reason for this is that operations and effects stand proportionately in the same relation to one another as their principles among themselves. Now the principle of those things that come about through art is the human intellect, and the human intellect derives according to a certain resemblance from the divine intellect, which is the principle of natural things. Hence the operations of art must imitate the operations of nature and the things that exist through art must imitate the things that are in nature. For if an instructor of some art were to produce a work of art, the disciple who receives his art from him would have to observe that work so that he himself might act in like manner. And so in the things that it makes, the human intellect, which derives the light of intelligence from the divine intellect, must be informed by the examination of the things that come about through nature so that it may operate in the same way.

2   And that is why the Philosopher says that if art were to make the works of nature, it would operate in the same way as nature; and, conversely, if nature were to make the works of art, it would make them the same way art does.[2] But nature, of course, does not achieve works of art; it only prepares certain principles and in some way supplies artists with a model according to which they may operate. Art, on the other

hand, can examine the works of nature and use them to perfect its own work. From this it is clear that human reason can only know the things that exist according to nature, whereas it both knows and makes the things that exist according to art. The human sciences that deal with natural things are necessarily speculative, therefore, while those that deal with things made by man are practical or operative according to the imitation of nature.

3 Now nature in its operation proceeds from the simple to the complex, so that in the things that come about through the operation of nature, that which is most complex is perfect and whole and constitutes the end of the other things, as is apparent in the case of every whole with respect to its parts. Hence human reason also, operating from the simple to the complex, proceeds as it were from the imperfect to the perfect.

4 Now since human reason has to order not only the things that are used by man but also men themselves, who are ruled by reason, it proceeds in either case from the simple to the complex: in the case of the things used by man when, for example, it builds a ship out of wood and a house out of wood and stones; in the case of men themselves when, for example, it orders many men so as to form a certain society. And since among these societies there are various degrees and orders, the highest is that of the city, which is ordered to the satisfaction of all the needs of human life. Hence of all the human societies this one is the most perfect. And because the things used by man are ordered to man as to their end, which is superior to the means, that whole which is the city is therefore necessarily superior to all the other wholes that may be known and constituted by human reason.

5 From what we have said then concerning political doctrine, with which Aristotle deals in this book, four things may be gathered.

First, the necessity of this science. For in order to arrive at the perfection of human wisdom, which is called philosophy, it is necessary to teach something about all that can be known by reason. Since then that whole which is the city is subject to a certain judgment of reason, it is necessary, so that philosophy may be complete, to institute a discipline that deals with the city; and this discipline is called politics or civil science.

6 Secondly, we can infer the genus of this science. For since the practical sciences are distinguished from the speculative sciences in that the speculative sciences are ordered exclusively to the knowledge of the truth, whereas the practical sciences are ordered to some work, this science must be comprised under practical philosophy, inasmuch as the city is a certain whole that human reason not only knows but also produces.

Furthermore, since reason produces certain things [2] by way of making, in which case the operation goes out into external matter—this pertains properly to the arts that are called mechanical, such as that of the smith and the shipwright and the like—and other things by way of action, in which case the operation remains within the agent, as when one deliberates, chooses, wills, and performs other similar acts pertaining to moral science, it is obvious that political science, which is concerned with the ordering of men, is not comprised under the sciences that pertain to making or mechanical arts, but under the sciences that pertain to action, which are the moral sciences.

7   Thirdly, we can infer the dignity and the order of political science with reference to all the other practical sciences. The city is indeed the most important of the things that can be constituted by human reason, for all the other human societies are ordered to it.

Furthermore, all the wholes constituted by the mechanical arts out of the things that are used by men are ordered to man as to their end. If the most important science, then, is the one that deals with what is most noble and perfect, of all the practical sciences political science must necessarily be the most important and must play the role of architectonic science with reference to all the others, inasmuch as it is concerned with the highest and perfect good in human affairs. And that is why the Philosopher says at the end of Book X of the *Ethics* that the philosophy that deals with human affairs finds its perfection in politics.[3]

8   Fourthly, from what has already been said we can deduce the mode and the order of this science. For just as the speculative sciences, which treat of some whole, arrive at a knowledge of the whole by manifesting its properties and its principles from an examination of its parts and its principles, so too this science examines the parts and the principles of the city and gives us a knowledge of it by manifesting its parts and its properties and its operations. And because it is a practical science, it manifests in addition how each thing may be realized, as is necessary in every practical science.

BOOK   ONE

LESSON   I

[i. 1. 1252ª1–2. 1253ª38]

9   After these preliminary remarks, then, it should be noted that in this book Aristotle begins with a preamble of some kind in which he manifests the aim of this science; then he proceeds to manifest what he has proposed. Concerning the first point, he does two things. First, he

shows the dignity of the city, with which politics is concerned, from its end; secondly, he shows the relation of the city to the other societies.

10   Concerning the first point, he intends to prove two things: first, that the city is ordered to some good as to its end; secondly, that the good to which the city is ordered is the highest human good.

Concerning the first point, he sets down the following argument. Every society is established for the sake of some good. But every city is a society of some kind. Therefore, every city is established for the sake of some good. Since then the minor premise is evident, he proves the major as follows. All men perform everything they do for the sake of that which is seen as a good, whether it is truly good or not. But every society is established through the work of someone. Therefore, all societies seek some good, that is to say, they aim at some good as an end.

11   Then he shows that that good to which the city is ordered is the highest among human goods by means of the following argument. If every society is ordered to a good, that society which is the highest necessarily seeks in the highest degree the good that is the highest among all human goods. For the importance of the means to an end is determined according to the importance of the ends.

Now he makes clear which society is the highest by what he adds. A society is indeed a certain whole. But in all wholes is found an order such that that whole which includes another whole within itself is the higher; a wall, for example, is a whole, and because it is included in that whole which is the house, it is clear that the house is the higher of the two wholes; and likewise, the society that includes other societies is the higher. Now it is clear that the city includes all the other societies, for households and villages are both comprised under the city; and so political society itself is the highest society. Therefore, it seeks the highest among all human goods, for it aims at the common good, which is better and more divine than the good of one individual, as is stated in the beginning of the *Ethics*.[4]

12   Then he compares the city to the other societies, and in this connection he does three things. First, he states the false opinion of certain persons. Secondly, he shows how the falsity of the stated opinion can be made known. Thirdly, in accordance with the method indicated, he sets down the true relationship of the city to the other societies. Concerning the first point, he does two things. First, he states the false opinion. Secondly, he produces their reason.

13   Concerning the first point, it should be noted that there is a twofold society that is obvious to all, namely, the city and the household. The city is governed by a twofold rule, namely, the political and the kingly. There is kingly rule when he who is set over the city has full power, whereas there is political rule when he who is set over the city exercises a power restricted by certain laws of the city. Similarly, the

household has a twofold rule, namely, the domestic and the despotic. Everyone who possesses slaves is called a despot, whereas the procurator or superintendent of a family is called the domestic head.[5] Hence despotic rule is that by which a master commands slaves, [7] while domestic rule is that by which one dispenses the things that pertain to the entire family, in which are contained not only slaves but many free people as well. Some persons have maintained then, but not rightly, that these two rules do not differ but are entirely the same.

14   Then he sets forth their reason, which is as follows. Things that differ solely by reason of larger and smaller numbers do not differ specifically, because a difference according to more and less does not diversify a species. But the rules just mentioned differ solely by reason of larger or smaller numbers; this they manifested as follows. If the society that is ruled is made up of a small number of people, as in the case of some small household, he who is set over them is called the father of the family and he possesses despotic rule. If the society is made up of a larger number of people, in such a way as to contain not only slaves but a number of free men as well, he who is set over them is called the domestic head.[6] And if the society is made up of a still larger number of people, for example, not only of those who belong to one household but of those who belong to one city, then the rule is said to be political or kingly.

15   The falsity of what certain persons used to say to the effect that the household and the city differ only by reason of their magnitude and smallness, in such a way that a large household is a small city and vice versa, will become apparent from what follows. Likewise they used to assert also that political rule and kingly rule differed solely by reason of larger and smaller numbers. For, when a man himself rules absolutely and in all ways, the rule is said to be kingly. When, however, he commands in part, in accordance with the principles of a given science, that is, in accordance with the laws set down by political teaching, the rule is said to be political, as though he were in part a ruler, namely, as regards the things that come under his power, and in part a subject, namely, as regards the things in which he is subjected to the law. From all this they inferred that all the previously mentioned rules, some of which pertain to the city and others to the household, do not differ specifically.

16   Then he shows how the falsity of this opinion can be manifested. He states that what has been said is not true, and that this will become evident to those who examine the matter according to the mode indicated,[7] that is, according to the art of studying such things as will be set down below. Now the mode of this art is the following. Just as, in other things, in order to arrive at a knowledge of the whole, it is necessary to divide the compound into its elements, that is, into the indivisibles, which are the smallest parts of the whole (for instance, to understand a sentence

it is necessary to divide it into its letters, and to understand a natural mixed body it is necessary to divide it into its elements), in the same manner if we examine those things out of which the city is compounded, we shall be able to see better what each one of the previously mentioned rules is in itself, and how they differ from one another, and whether in each case something can be studied in an artful way. For in all things we see that if someone examines things as they arise from their principles, he will best be able to contemplate the truth in them. And just as this is true of other things, so also is it true of those things to which we are directing our attention. Now in these words of the Philosopher it should be noted that, in order to arrive at a knowledge of compounds, it is necessary to use the resolutive way, namely, so that we may divide the compound into its elements. Afterwards, however, the compositive way is necessary, so that from the indivisible principles already known we may judge of the things that proceed from these principles.

17   Then, in accordance with the mode just indicated, he sets down the true relationship of the other societies to the city; and in connection with this, he does two things. First, he treats of the other societies that are ordered to the city. Secondly, he treats of civil society. Concerning the first point, he does three things. First, he sets forth the society of one person to another person. Secondly, he sets down the domestic society, which comprises different associations of persons. Thirdly, he sets down the village society, which is made up of several groups. Concerning the first point, he does two things. First, he sets down two personal associations. Secondly, he compares them to each other.

Now the first of these two personal associations that he sets down is that of male and female; and he says that, since we have to divide the city into its smallest parts, it is necessary to say that the first union is that of persons who cannot be without each other, namely, the male and the female. For this union is for the sake of generation through which are produced both males and females. From this it is clear that they cannot be without each other.

18   He shows how this union is the first by what he adds. Here it should be noted that in man there is something that is proper to him, namely, reason, according to which it belongs to him to act from counsel and choice. There is also found in man something that is common to him and to others; such is the ability to generate. This then does not belong to him as a result of choice, that is, in so far as he has a reason that chooses; rather it belongs to him in so far as he has a reason that is common to him and to animals and even to plants. For there is in all these a natural [8] appetite to leave after them another being like themselves, so that in this manner, through generation, what cannot be preserved numerically the same is preserved according to its species.

There is, accordingly, a natural appetite of this kind in all other natural corruptible beings. But because living beings, namely, plants and animals, have a special way of generating in that they generate from themselves, he makes special mention of plants and animals. For even in plants a masculine and a feminine power is found, but they are joined in the same individual, even though there is a greater abundance of one or the other in this or that individual, in such a way that we can imagine a plant to be at all times such as are male and female at the time of intercourse.

19   Then he sets down the second association of persons, namely, that of ruler and subject. This association too stems from nature for the sake of preservation, for nature aims not only at generation but also at the preservation of the things generated. That among men this indeed comes about through the association of ruler and subject he shows by the fact that he who by his intellect can foresee the things that are conducive to preservation, for instance, by providing what is advantageous and repelling what is harmful, naturally commands and rules, whereas he who by reason of bodily strength is able to carry out in deed what the wise man has foreseen mentally is naturally a subject and a slave. From this it clearly appears that the same thing is profitable to both in view of their preservation, namely, that the former should rule and the latter be ruled. For he who by reason of his wisdom can foresee mentally would not be able to survive at times because of a deficiency of bodily strength if he did not have a slave to carry out his ideas, nor would he who abounds in bodily strength be able to survive if he were not ruled by the prudence of another.

20   Then he compares the associations just mentioned to each other; first, according to the truth; secondly, he rules out an error.

He infers then, first of all, from what has been said that there is a natural distinction between woman and slave. For a woman has a natural disposition to beget from another, but she is not robust in body, which is what is required in a slave. And so the two associations just mentioned differ from each other.

21   Now he establishes the cause for this distinction from the fact that nature does not make things in the same way as those who manufacture Delphic knives out of brass, that is to say, out of metal, for some poor people. For among the Delphians certain knives were made that were designed to serve several purposes, as for example, if a single knife were to be used to cut, to file, and to perform other similar duties. This was done for the benefit of the poor who could not afford several instruments. Nature, however, does not act in such a way as to order one thing to different functions; rather it assigns one thing to one function. For this reason woman is not assigned by nature to serve but to beget. Thus all things will best come about when an instrument is not used for many functions but for one only. This is to be understood,

however, of cases in which an obstacle would be encountered in one or both of the two functions to which the same instrument were to be assigned, for instance, if it were often necessary to exercise both functions simultaneously. But if the different functions are exercised one after the other, the adaptation of a single instrument to several functions does not give rise to any obstacle. Hence the tongue is suited for two functions of nature, namely, taste and speech, as is said in Book II of the [treatise] *On the Parts of Animals*.[8] For these two functions do not coincide with each other in time.

22   Then he rules out the contrary error. First, he states the error. Secondly, he shows the cause of the error.

He says then, first of all, that among the barbarians, woman and slave are considered as belonging to the same order; for they use women as slaves. There can be a doubt here, however, as to who are called barbarians. Some people say that everyone is a barbarian to the man who does not understand his tongue. Hence the Apostle says, *If I know not the power of the voice, I shall be to him, to whom I speak, a barbarian, and he that speaketh, a barbarian to me* [I Cor. 14:11]. To others it seems that those men are called barbarians who have no written language in their own vernacular. Hence Bede is said to have translated the liberal arts into the English language, lest the English be reputed barbarians. And to others it seems that the barbarians are those who are not ruled by any civil laws.

23   And in fact all these things come close to the truth in some way; for by the name "barbarian" something foreign is understood. Now a man can be said to be foreign either absolutely or in relation to someone. He who is lacking in reason, according to which one is said to be a man, seems to be foreign to the human race absolutely speaking; and so the men who are called barbarians absolutely are the ones who are lacking in reason, either because they happen to live in an exceedingly intemperate region of the sky, so that by the very disposition of the region they are found to be dull for the most part, or else because of some evil custom prevailing in certain lands from which it comes about that men are rendered irrational and almost brutal. Now it is evident that it is from the power of reason that men are ruled by reasonable laws and that they are practiced in writing. [9] Hence barbarism is appropriately manifested by this sign, that men either do not live under laws or live under irrational ones, and likewise that among certain peoples there is no training in writing. But a man is said to be foreign in relation to someone if he cannot communicate with him. Now men are made to communicate with one another above all by means of speech; and according to this, people who cannot understand one another's speech can be called barbarians with reference to one another. The Philosopher, however, is speaking here of those who are barbarians absolutely.

24 Then he establishes the cause of the error just mentioned. Its cause, he says, is that among barbarians there is no rule according to nature. For it was stated above that the man who commands according to nature is the one who is able to foresee mentally, whereas the slave is the one who is able to carry things out in deed. Now barbarians for the most part are found to be robust in body and deficient in mind. Hence the natural order of rule and subjection cannot exist among them. But there arises among them a certain association of female and male slave, that is to say, they commonly make use of a female slave, namely, a woman, and of a male slave. And because there is no natural rule among barbarians but only among those who abound in reason, the poets say that it is fitting that the Greeks, who were endowed with wisdom, should rule over the barbarians, as if to say that it is the same thing by nature to be a barbarian and to be a slave. But when the converse takes place, there ensues a perversion and a lack of order in the world, according to the words of Solomon, *I have seen servants upon horses and princes walking on the ground as servants* [Eccles. 10:7].

25 Then he treats of the domestic society, which is made up of several personal associations. In this connection he does three things. First, he shows what this society consists of. Secondly, he shows its purpose. Thirdly, he shows how those who live in this society are designated.⁹

He says then, first of all, that out of the two previously mentioned personal associations, one of which is ordered to generation and the other to preservation, the first household is constituted. For in a household there have to be a man and a woman, and a master and a slave. Now it is called the first household because there is also another personal association that is found in the household, namely, that of father and son, which arises out of the first. Hence the first two associations are primordial. To show this he adduces a saying of the poet Hesiod, who stated that a household has these three things: a master who rules, a woman, and an ox for plowing. For in a poor household the ox takes the place of a servant; man uses an ox, just as he uses a servant, to carry out some work.

26 Then he shows to what the domestic society is ordered. Here it should be noted that every human association is an association according to certain acts. Now among human acts some are performed every day, such as eating, warming oneself at the fire, and others like these, whereas other things are not performed every day, such as buying, fighting, and others like these. Now it is natural for men to communicate among themselves by helping one another in each of these two kinds of work. Thus he says that a household is nothing other than a certain society set up according to nature for everyday life, that is, for the acts that have to be performed daily. And he goes on to show this by means of

names. For a certain Charondas by name calls those who communicate in a household *homositios*, or men of one fare, because they communicate in food; and a certain other named Epimenides, a Cretan by nationality, calls them *homokapnos*, or men of one smoke, because they sit at the same fire.

27   Then he sets down the third society, namely, the village. First, he shows of what this society is made up and what its purpose is. Secondly, he shows that it is natural.

He says then, first of all, that the first association made up of several households is called a village; and it is called the first as distinguished from the second, which is the city. Now this society is not established for everyday life, as he says of the household; rather it is instituted for the sake of nondaily uses. For those who are fellow-villagers do not communicate with one another in the daily acts in which those who are members of one household communicate, such as eating, sitting at the fire, and things of this sort; rather they communicate with one another in certain external acts that are not performed daily.

28   Then he shows that the village society is natural. First, he establishes his thesis by means of a reason. Secondly, by means of certain signs.

He says then, first of all, that the proximity of households, which constitutes the village, seems to be according to nature in the highest degree. For nothing is more natural than the propagation of many from one in animals; and this brings about a proximity of households. Indeed, some people call those who have neighboring households foster brothers and children, that is, sons and children of children, that is, grandsons, so that we may understand that such a proximity of households originally springs from the fact that sons and grandsons, having multiplied, founded different households and lived close to one another. Hence, since the multiplication of offspring is natural, it follows that the village society is natural. [*10*]

29   Then he manifests the same thing by means of signs. First, according to what we see among men. Secondly, according to what used to be said about the gods.

He says then, first of all, that, since the neighborhood was established as a result of the multiplication of offspring, from this it came about that at first any city was ruled by a king; and this because cities and nations are made up of people who are subject to a king. And he shows how this sign corresponds to what has already been said by what he adds, namely, that every household is ruled by some very old member, just as sons are ruled by the father of the family. Hence it comes about that the entire neighborhood too, which was formed of blood relations, was ruled on account of this kinship by someone who was first in the order of kinship, just as a city is ruled by a king. That is why Homer has said that each one lays down laws for his wife and children, like the king in a city. Now this rule passed from households and villages to cities, because different villages are like a city spread out into different parts; and thus in former times men used to dwell dispersed through villages and not gathered in one city. So it is clear then that the rule of the king over a city or a nation derived from the rule of an older member in a household or a village.

30   Then he sets down another sign from what used to be said about the gods. He states that because of what has just been indicated, all the pagans used to say that their gods were ruled by some king and claimed that Jupiter was the king of the gods, and this because some men are still ruled by kings; but in former times almost all men were ruled by kings. This was the first rule, as will be said later. Now just as men liken the outward appearance of the gods, that is to say, their forms, to themselves, thinking the gods to be in the image of certain men, so also they liken the lives of the gods, that is to say, their behavior, to their own, thinking them to behave the way they see men behave. Aristotle is here referring, after the manner of the Platonists, to the substances separated from matter and created by only one supreme god, to whom the pagans erroneously attributed both human forms and human habits, as the Philosopher says here.

31   After having treated of the societies ordered to the city, the Philosopher treats here of civil society itself. This treatise is divided into three parts. First, he shows what kind of society the city is. Secondly, he shows that it is natural. Thirdly, he treats of the foundation of the city.

Concerning the first point, he shows the condition of the city with reference to three things. First, he shows of what things the city is made up. For, just as a village is made up of several households, so a city is made up of several villages. Secondly, he says that the city is a perfect society; and this he proves from the fact that, since every association among all men is ordered to something necessary for life, that society will be perfect which is ordered to this: that man have sufficiently whatever is necessary for life. Such a society is the city. For it is of the nature of the city that in it should be found all the things that are sufficient for human life; and so it is. And for this reason it is made up of several villages, in one of which the art of the smith is practiced, in another the art of the weaver, and so of the others. Hence it is evident that the city is a perfect society. Thirdly, he shows to what the city is ordered. It is originally made for the sake of living, namely, that men might find sufficiently that from which they might be able to live; but from its existence it comes about that men not only live but that they live well, in so far as by the laws of the city the life of men is ordered to the virtues.

32 Then he shows that civil society is natural. In this connection he does three things. First, he shows that the city is natural. Secondly, that man is by nature a political animal. Thirdly, he shows what is prior according to nature, whether it is one man, the household, or the city.

Concerning the first point, he sets down two arguments, the first of which is as follows. The end of natural things is their nature. But the city is the end of the previously mentioned societies, which were shown to be natural. Therefore, the city is natural. Now, that nature is the end of natural things he proves by the following argument. We call the nature of each thing that which belongs to it when its generation is perfect; for example, the nature of man is that which he possesses once his generation is perfect, and the same holds for a horse and for a house, in such a way, however, that by the nature of a house is understood its form. But the disposition that a thing has by reason of its perfect generation is the end of all the things that precede its generation. Therefore, that which is the end of the natural principles from which something is generated is the nature of a thing. And thus, since the city is generated from the previously mentioned societies, which are natural, it will itself be natural.

33 Then he sets down the second argument, which is as follows. That which is best in each thing is the end and that for the sake of which something comes about. But to have what is sufficient is best. Therefore, it has the nature of an end. And thus, since the city is a society that has of itself what is sufficient for life, it is itself the end of the previously mentioned societies. Hence it is clear [11] that this second argument is presented as a proof of the minor of the preceding one.

34 Then he shows that man is by nature a political animal. First, he infers this from the naturalness of the city. Secondly, he proves this from man's proper operation. Concerning the first point, he does two things. First, he establishes his thesis. Secondly, he rules out a doubt.

He infers then, first of all, from what has already been said that a city is made up of things that are according to nature. And since a city is nothing other than a congregation of men, it follows that man is a naturally political animal.

35 However, there could be a doubt in someone's mind concerning this, due to the fact that the things that are according to nature are found in all men. But not all men are found to be city dwellers. And so, in order to eliminate this doubt, he goes on to say that some men are not political on account of fortune, for instance, because they have been expelled from the city, or because poverty compels them to till fields or tend animals. And it is clear that this is not contrary to what has been said to the effect that man is naturally political, because other natural things too are sometimes lacking on account of fortune, for example,

when someone loses a hand through amputation or when he is deprived
of an eye. But if a man is such that he is not political on account of
nature, either he is bad, as when this happens as a result of the corruption
of human nature, or he is better than man, namely, in so far as he has a
nature more perfect than that generally found in other men, in such a
way that by himself he can be self-sufficient without the company of
men, as was the case with John the Baptist and Blessed Anthony the
hermit.

In support of this he adduces a saying of Homer cursing someone
who was not political because of depravity. For he says of him that he
was without tribe because he could not be contained by the bond of
friendship, and without right because he could not be contained under
the yoke of the law, and vicious because he could not be contained
under the rule of reason. Now he who is such by nature, being quarrel-
some and living without yoke, is at the same time necessarily inclined
to be avid for war, just as we see that wild fowls are rapacious.

36   Then he proves from his proper operation that man is a political
animal, more so even than the bee and any gregarious animal, by the
following argument. We say that nature does nothing in vain because
it always works for a determinate end. Hence, if nature gives to a being
something that of itself is ordered to some end, it follows that this end
is given to this being by nature. For we see that, whereas certain other
animals have a voice, man alone above the other animals has speech.
Indeed, although certain animals produce human speech, they do not
properly speak, because they do not understand what they are saying
but produce such words out of a certain habit.

Now there is a difference between language and mere voice.[10] Voice
is a sign of pain and pleasure and consequently of the other passions,
such as anger and fear, which are all ordered to pleasure and pain, as is
said in Book II of the *Ethics*.[11] Thus voice is given to the other animals,
whose nature attains the level where they sense their pleasures and pains,
and they signify this to one another by means of certain natural sounds
of the voice, as a lion by his roar and a dog by his bark, in the place
of which we use interjections.

37   Human speech, on the other hand, signifies what is useful and what
is harmful. It follows from this that it signifies the just and the unjust.
For justice and injustice consist in this, that some people are treated
equally or unequally as regards useful and harmful things. Thus speech
is proper to men, because it is proper to them, as compared to the other
animals, to have a knowledge of the good and the bad, the just[12] and the
unjust, and other such things that can be signified by speech.

Since language is given to man by nature, therefore, and since language
is ordered to this, that men communicate with one another as regards
the useful and the harmful, the just and the unjust, and other such things,

it follows, from the fact that nature does nothing in vain, that men naturally communicate with one another in reference to these things. But communication in reference to these things is what makes a household and a city. Therefore, man is naturally a domestic and political animal.

38   Then he shows from what has been said that the city is by nature prior to the household and to one individual man by the following argument. The whole is necessarily prior to the part, namely, in the order of nature and perfection. This is to be understood, however, of the part of matter, not of the part of the species, as is shown in Book VII of the *Metaphysics*.[13] And he proves this as follows: if the whole man is destroyed, neither the foot nor the hand remains, except equivocally, in the manner in which a hand made out of stone can be called a hand. This because such a part is corrupted when the whole is corrupted. Now that which is corrupted does not retain its species, from which it receives its definition. Hence it is clear that the name does not retain the same meaning, and so it is predicated in an equivocal sense. That the part is corrupted when the whole is corrupted he shows by the fact that every part is defined by its operation and by the power by which it operates. For example, the definition of a foot is that it is an organic member having the power to walk. And thus, from the fact that it no longer has this power and this operation, it is not the same according to its species but is equivocally called a foot. The same reasoning holds for other similar parts, which are called parts of matter, in whose definition the whole is included, just as circle is included in the definition of a semicircle, for [*12*] a semicircle is a half circle. Not so, however, with the parts of the species, which are included in the definition of the whole, as, for example, lines are included in the definition of a triangle.

39   So it is clear then that the whole is naturally prior to the parts of matter, even though the parts are prior in the order of generation. But individual men are related to the whole city as are the parts of man to man. For, just as a hand or a foot cannot exist without a man, so too one man cannot live self-sufficiently by himself when separated from the city.

Now if it should happen that someone is unable to participate in civil society because of his depravity, he is worse than a man and is, as it were, a beast. If, on the other hand, he does not need anyone and is, as it were, self-sufficient, he is better than a man, for he is, as it were, a god. It remains true, therefore, from what has been said, that the city is by nature prior to one man.

40   Then he treats of the foundation of the city and infers from what has been said that there is in all men a certain natural impulse toward the city, as also toward the virtues. But nevertheless, just as the virtues are acquired through human exercise, as is stated in Book II of the *Ethics*,[14] in the same way cities are founded by human industry. Now

the man who first founded a city was the cause of the greatest goods for men.

41   For man is the best of the animals if virtue, to which he has a natural inclination, is perfected in him. But if he is without law and justice, man is the worst of all the animals. This he proves as follows. Injustice is all the more cruel in proportion as it has a greater number of arms, that is, instruments for doing evil. Now prudence and virtue, which of themselves are ordered to the good, belong to man according to his nature. But when a man is evil, he makes use of these as certain arms to do evil; for example, by his shrewdness he thinks up different frauds, and through abstinence he becomes capable of bearing hunger and thirst, so that he might be more persevering in his malice, and so of the other virtues. Hence it is that a man without virtue is most vicious and savage as regards the corruption of his irascible appetite, being as he is cruel and without affection; and as regards the corruption of his concupiscible appetite, he is most evil in relation to sexual matters and greediness for food. But man is reduced to justice by means of the political order. This is clear from the fact that among the Greeks the order of political society and the judgment of justice are called by the same name, to wit, *dikē*. Hence it is evident that the man who founded the city kept men from being most evil and brought them to a state of excellence in accordance with justice and the virtues.

BOOK   THREE

LESSON   I

[iii. 1. 1274^{b}32–2. 1275^{b}33]

348   After having examined the forms of government according to the teaching of others in Book II, the Philosopher begins to treat of them according to his own opinion. This section is divided into two parts. In the first, he manifests the diversity of regimes. In the second, he teaches how to set up the best regime, in the beginning of Book VII. The first part is divided into two parts. In the first, he distinguishes the regimes. In the second, he treats of each one in particular, in Book IV. The first part is divided into two parts. In the first, he determines what pertains to the regime in general. In the second, he divides the regimes. The first part is divided into two parts. In the first, he states his intention. In the

second, he carries out his proposal. Concerning the first point, he does two things. First, he shows that, in order to treat of regimes, one must first deal with the city. Secondly, he shows that, in order to treat of the city, one must consider what a citizen is.

349 He says then, first of all, that he who wishes to study the regime and determine what each regime is according to its proper nature, and what kind of regime it is, namely, whether it is good or bad, just or unjust, must first consider what a city is. He proves this by two reasons, the first of which is that there may be some doubt concerning this point. For some people are in doubt whether certain transactions were effected by the city when, for example, they were accomplished by a tyrant or by the rich men of the city; in which case some say that the city acted, while others say that it was not the city but the rich rulers or even the tyrant. Thus there seems to be a question whether the rich rulers alone constitute the city; and because there is a question, it must be elucidated. The second reason is that the whole aim of those who treat of regimes and legislation revolves around the city, for the regime is nothing other than the order of the inhabitants of the city.

350 Then he shows that we must treat of the citizen for two reasons, the first of which is as follows. In everything that is composed of a multiplicity of parts, one must first consider the parts. The city is a certain whole made up of citizens who are, as it were, its parts, since the city is nothing other than a certain [*122*] multiplicity of citizens. Hence in order to arrive at a knowledge of the city, one must consider what a citizen is. The second reason is that concerning this point, too, there happens to be a difficulty; for not everyone is in agreement as to what a citizen is. Sometimes a common man, who is a citizen in a popular regime, where the people govern, is not reckoned a citizen under a rule of the few, where the rich govern, because it is often such that the people have no role to play in it. Hence it is evident that there is a controversy concerning the citizen, who is a citizen, and who should be called a citizen.

351 Then he carries out his aim. This section is divided into two parts. In the first, he shows what a citizen is. In the second, he shows what virtue makes a good citizen. Concerning the first point, he does two things. First, he determines what a citizen is. Secondly, he raises certain difficulties in this connection. Concerning the first point, he does two things. First, he shows what a citizen is according to virtue. Secondly, he rules out a certain false notion. Concerning the first point, he does two things. First, he sets down certain ways according to which some people are citizens in a qualified sense but not absolutely. Secondly, he shows what a citizen is absolutely speaking.

352 He says then, first of all, that for the present we must exclude those who are called citizens in a certain way, that is to say, metaphorically or by comparison, for these are not really citizens.

The first way is by residence. People are not said to be truly citizens by the fact that they reside in a city, for foreigners and slaves reside in a city and yet they are not citizens absolutely speaking.

The second way is that some people may be called citizens because they are subject to the jurisdiction of the city. Thus they share in the justice of the city in that at times they obtain a favorable verdict and at other times they are judged, that is to say, condemned. But this is also true of people who are bound by contracts and who are not citizens of the same city. In certain cities, however, foreigners do not share perfectly in this justice, like the citizens, but must present a sponsor, that is to say, someone who vouches for their obedience to the law, if they wish to litigate. Hence it is clear that outsiders share imperfectly in the interchange of justice and so, in this respect, they are not citizens absolutely speaking but can be called citizens in a qualified sense.

Likewise also, in a third sense, we call children citizens, even though they have not yet been enlisted among the ranks of the citizens, and we call old men citizens, even though they have already been dropped from the rolls since they can no longer discharge the functions of citizens. We do not refer to either group as citizens absolutely speaking but only with some qualification: to the children as imperfect citizens, and to old men as people who have gone beyond the limit required by the condition of citizens. Or if some other such qualification is added, it makes no difference, for what we are trying to say is obvious: we are now asking what a citizen is absolutely and without any qualification that would be needed in order to set forth correctly the meaning of the word "citizen."

There is a fourth way, in which we encounter the same difficulty and the same solution, and that concerns fugitives and disreputable persons, who are citizens in a qualified sense but not absolutely.

353   Then he shows what a citizen is absolutely speaking; and in this connection he does three things. First, he sets down a certain definition of the citizen. Secondly, he shows that this definition is not common to any regime. Thirdly, he shows how it may be amended so that it will become common.

He says then, first of all, that there is no better way of defining the citizen absolutely speaking than by the fact that he shares in the administration of justice in the city, so that he has the power to judge in certain matters and possesses some authority in the affairs of the city.

We must bear in mind, however, that there are two kinds of rules. Some rules are limited to a definite period of time. Thus in certain cities the same man is not allowed to hold the same office twice, or else he may hold it for a limited time, exercising a certain office for one year, for example, after which he may not be appointed to the same office for another three or four years. The other rule is that which is not limited to a certain period of time but can be exercised by one man for any length of time, as, for example, that of the praetor, who has the authority to judge certain cases, and that of the speaker, who has the authority to express his opinion in the public assembly. It may happen, however, that some such judges or speakers are not called rulers and, for this reason, it may be argued that they do not have any authority by which they may judge or address the assembly. But this is irrelevant, for the difficulty is one of words only. We do not find any name common to the judge and to the member of the assembly. Let us then give their office a name and call it "indeterminate office." Thus we assert that the men who share in this rule are citizens. This seems to be a better definition of the citizen absolutely speaking.

354   Then he shows that this definition of the citizen is not common to all regimes. He says that it must be made clear that in all matters where individual subjects differ [*123*] according to species and where one of them is first by nature, another second, and so on, either nothing is common to them absolutely, in so far as they are such, as in the case of equivocal names, or else there is something common, but only faintly and obscurely, that is to say, in some small measure. Now regimes, as we shall see later, differ according to species. Some of them are prior and others posterior; for those that are ordered according to right reason take precedence over the others, while those that are corrupt and violate the right order of the regime are by nature posterior to noncorrupt regimes, just as in any genus the perfect is by nature prior to the corrupt. Just how some regimes are perversions of the right order will become clear later on.

Hence the notion of citizen must necessarily vary with different regimes. For that reason, the definition of the citizen given above applies above all to the popular state, in which anyone among the people has the authority to judge in certain matters and to address the assembly. In other regimes, however, it sometimes happens that any citizen has this authority, but this is not necessarily so, for in some of them the people do not have any authority, nor is the assembly of the people taken into account but only others who have been especially summoned and these alone, divided into groups, judge certain cases. In Sparta, for example, the ephors judge the cases that arise among fellow-citizens and others pass sentence on other matters, and different groups judge different cases. The elders rule on homicide and other magistrates used to rule on other matters. This is also the case among the Carthaginians, for all matters are judged by certain magistrates and so the common citizens have no part in the judgment. Hence in such regimes the notion of citizen proposed above does not apply.

355 Then he amends the aforesaid definition of the citizen. He says that this definition can be rectified so as to become common, for in regimes other than the popular state the member of the assembly and the praetor do not hold office for an indeterminate period;[15] rather, these two functions pertain only to those who hold office for a determinate period; for it belongs to some of them or even to all of them to judge and to deliberate either in some matters or in all matters.

From this one can see clearly what a citizen is. He is not the one who participates in the administration of justice or in the assembly but the one upon whom the deliberative or judicial function can be conferred. For those who cannot be appointed to such offices seem to have no share in the government and hence do not appear to be citizens.

Finally, he infers from this that a city is nothing other than a large number of persons such as these, who are called citizens, [associated] in such a way that they can live self-sufficiently in an absolute sense. For a city is a self-sufficient society, as was said in Book I.[16]

356 Then he rejects a certain definition of the citizen that has some currency. He says that some people, in accordance with their custom, define the citizen as he who is born of parents both of whom are citizens, and not one only, whether it be the father or the mother. Others further require that, in order to be a citizen, one trace his ancestry back to the second or third generation and even beyond. If a citizen is so defined politically, that is to say, in accordance with the custom of certain cities, and summarily, and prior to any proper investigation, there arises a problem as to how this third or fourth ancestor was a citizen. For, according to this definition, one will not be able to call him a citizen unless his ancestry, too, is traced back to a citizen of the third or fourth generation, and so we would have an infinite regress. But this is impossible because a regime does not regress to infinity. Hence it is obvious that we must arrive at such citizens who were not born of citizens.

In this connection, he reports a saying of Gorgias, a Sicilian of Leontini, who said something regarding the aforesaid definition, either because he was not sure of the truth or because he was speaking ironically, namely, that just as mortars are things that are made by craftsmen who are mortar-makers, so Larissaeans are persons who are made, that is to say, begotten, by other Larissaeans, who are makers of Larissaeans. But this statement is naive and senseless, for if some people share in the regime according to the definition that we have given, we have to say that they are citizens even if they were not born of citizens. Otherwise, this definition that they give could not be applied to the first men who built or settled the city and who were clearly not born of citizens of that city. Hence it would follow that neither they nor, consequently, their descendants were citizens, which is absurd.

LESSON II

[iii. 2. 1275ᵇ34–3. 1276ᵇ16]

357   After having determined what a citizen is absolutely speaking, the Philosopher here points out certain difficulties concerning what has been said and treats of them. He lists four difficulties that follow upon one another.

The first difficulty has to do with those who, after a change of regime, are received as members of the political community. This, for example, is what a certain wise man by the name of Cleisthenes did in Athens after the expulsion of the tyrants. He added to the associations of the city many foreigners and even a certain number of alien slaves, so that, as a result of the increase in population, the rich would not be able to oppress the people tyrannically. By way of solving this difficulty, he says that there is no question whether these men are citizens or not, since, from the very fact that they were made citizens, they are citizens. But there is a question whether this was done justly or unjustly; and what the Philosopher seems to be driving at is that those who are instated by the person who overthrows the regime are citizens.

358   Then he raises a second difficulty: one could question whether he who is not in justice a citizen is a citizen, as if in this matter "unjust" meant the same thing as "false." For it is obvious that a false citizen is not a citizen. To this he answers that, since some people are held to be rulers notwithstanding the fact that they rule unjustly, for the same reason those who are citizens unjustly are to be called citizens, because one is called a citizen as a result of his having some share in the government, as was said earlier.

359   Then he states the third difficulty. He says that the question whether one is or is not in justice a citizen is bound up with a previous difficulty raised at the beginning of this third book. When complete changes of regimes occur in a city, one usually asks: When is that which is done an act of the city and when is it not? For example, it sometimes happens that the regime of a city changes from a tyranny or from a rule of the rich to a popular rule, and then the people, assuming control of the government, do not wish to honor the agreements that were made either by the tyrant or by the rich who once ruled. They claim that if some things were given to the tyrant or to the rich men of the city, the city did not receive them; and so it is in many such cases, for in certain

regimes, the men in power obtain certain things from others, not for the common benefit of the city, but for their private advantage. And he solves this difficulty [by saying] that, if the city remains the same once a complete change in regime has occurred, just as that which is done by the popular state is an act of the city, so, too, is that which is done when a few or a tyrant are in power. For just as the power in the city was then held by the tyrant or by the rich, so also in a popular state it is held by the people.

360   Then he states the fourth difficulty. First, he states this difficulty in general, and he says that, in order to solve the third difficulty, the proper way to speak is to ask how one should say that a city is or is not the same. Secondly, he divides the aforesaid difficulty into two parts. He says that this question on the surface appears to refer to two things, namely, the territory of the city and the men who reside in the city. For it sometimes happens that men are separated from the territory in different ways, as, for example, when all the citizens are expelled from the city and some are led away to one place and others to another. Hence, if other residents are brought in to replace them, a question may arise whether the city is or is not the same. But this difficulty is really less serious, that is to say, easier to answer. For the term "city" has many meanings. In one sense, it refers to the territory of the city, and in this sense the city is the same. In another sense, it refers to the people of the city, and in this sense it is not the same.

361   But then there remains another difficulty, [*126*] for if the same men always reside in the same place, there can be a doubt as to when the city is, or is not, one.

First, he eliminates one notion of unity. He asserts that it cannot be said that the men residing in a city preserve the identity of the city because they live within the same walls. For one whole region, for example, the Peloponnesus, could happen to be encircled by one wall and yet not constitute the same city. Such was the case with Babylon or with any other very large city that comprises one nation rather than one city. Indeed, it is said of Babylon that when one part of the city was captured, the other part did not hear about it until three days later because of the length of the walls.

362   And he remarks parenthetically that this question, namely, whether it is advantageous to have a city of that size, will have to be considered elsewhere, that is, in Book VII. For it pertains to the statesman to know how large a city should be and whether it should include men of one nation or of several. The size of the city should indeed be such that the region may be sufficiently productive and that it may be possible to repel external[17] enemies. It should also preferably be made up of a single nation in view of the fact that the men of the same nation pos-

sess the same way of life and the same customs, which foster friendship among the citizens because of their resemblance. Accordingly, the cities that were constituted out of different nations were ruined on account of the dissensions that arose in them due to the diversity of manners, for one part used to ally itself with [external] enemies out of hatred for the other part.

363   Then he investigates another notion of unity, namely, whether, when men remain in the same place, the city must be said to be the same because its inhabitants belong to the same race; for even though they are not the same numerically, one generation is succeeded by another. Just as we say that springs or rivers are the same because of the steady flow of waters, even though one part runs off and another part runs in, so we say that a city is the same, even though some men die and others are born, so long as the same race of men endures.

364   Then, by solving this difficulty, he reveals the true nature of the unity of the city. He says that, because of the aforesaid succession of men belonging to the same race, a multitude of men can be called the same in a sense; a city, however, cannot be called the same if the political order [or regime] is changed. For, since the association of citizens, which we call a regime, pertains to the nature of the city, it is evident that, if the regime is changed, the city does not remain the same. We see, for example, among those who sing in choruses, that the chorus is not the same if at one time it is a comic chorus, that is to say, if it sings comic songs about the deeds of lowly persons, and if at another time it is a tragic chorus, that is to say, if it sings tragic songs about the exploits of princes. So, too, we see in all other things that consist in a certain composition or association that, whenever there is a different species of composition, the identity is destroyed, just as, for example, a harmony is not the same if at one time it is Dorian, that is to say, if it is a harmony of the seventh or eighth tone, and at another time Phrygian, that is to say, if it is a harmony of the third or fourth tone.

Since, then, this is the case with all such things, it is evident that a city must be said to be the same with respect to the order of the regime, in such a way that, if the order of the regime is changed, though the territory and the men remain unchanged, the city is not the same, even if materially it is the same. A city changed in this manner may be called by the same name or by another name, whether the men be the same or different; but if it retains the same name, the name will be used equivocally. Now whether, due to the fact that the city does not remain the same once a complete change of regime has taken place, it is just or not that the agreements contracted by the previous regime be honored, is another matter, which will be discussed later.

LESSON III

[iii. 4. 1276ᵇ17–1277ᵇ33]

365   After having shown what a citizen is and solved certain difficulties, the Philosopher here inquires into the virtue that characterizes
the citizen. This section is divided into two parts. In the first, he shows
that the virtue of the citizen is not the same absolutely as that of the
good man. In the second, he raises certain difficulties in this connection.
Concerning the first point, he does two things. First, he shows that the
virtue of the dedicated citizen is not the same absolutely as that of the
good man. Secondly, he shows that the virtue of a certain citizen is the
same as that of the good man. Concerning the first point, he does two
things. First, he states his intention; for, after what has been said, we must
now consider whether or not we should assert that the virtue [of the
good citizen] is the same as that of the good man. This is to ask whether
the same thing prompts us to call someone a good man and a good
citizen; for virtue is that which makes the person who possesses it good.
Now, in order to investigate this question properly, we must first show
what the virtue of the citizen is in some sort of outline and likeness.

366   Secondly, he shows that the virtue of the good citizen is not
the same as that of the good man for three reasons.

In the first of these, he begins by proposing a comparison to illustrate
what the virtue of the good citizen is. He says that, just as the word
"sailor" signifies something common to many persons, so, too, does the
word "citizen." And he explains how the word "sailor" is common to
many men. Many men who differ in power, that is to say, by their art
and by their function, are called sailors: one of them is a rower, who
propels the ship by means of oars; another is a pilot, who steers the ship
by means of the rudder; another a look-out or guardian of the prow,
which is the forepart of the ship; and others have other names and
functions. Now it is obvious that each one of these men has something
that belongs to him [129] by reason of his proper competence and something that belongs to him by reason of a common competence. It pertains to the competence of each one individually to understand and look
after his own function diligently, steering, for example, in the case of
the pilot, and the same for the others. The common competence, on
the other hand, is one that belongs to all, for the work of all of them
is directed toward one end, namely, safe navigation; for it is to this

end that the aim and desire of any sailor is directed and that the common competence of sailors, which is the competence of the sailor as sailor, is ordered. In the same way also, since there are different citizens having dissimilar functions and dissimilar positions by means of which they exercise their proper operations in the city, the common work of all is the safety of the community; and this community consists in the order of the regime. Hence it is clear that the virtue of the citizen as citizen is considered in relation to the regime, so that the good citizen is the man who works well to preserve the regime.

Now there are several species of regimes, as we shall see later and as is evident to some extent from what we have already said; and men are well ordered to different regimes by means of different virtues. For a popular state is preserved in one way and a rule of the few or a tyranny in another. Hence it is evident that there does not exist a perfect virtue according to which a citizen [that is, as citizen] could be called good absolutely; but a man is called virtuous by reason of a single perfect virtue, namely, prudence, upon which all the moral virtues depend. It happens, therefore, that someone is a good citizen although he does not possess the virtue by which one is a good man; and this is the case in regimes other than the best regime.

367 Then he states the second reason. He says that by inquiring and raising objections, we can in another way reach the same conclusion even concerning the best regime, namely, that the virtue of the good citizen and that of the good man are not the same. For it is impossible, however good the regime may be, that all the citizens be virtuous; nevertheless, each one must perform his work pertaining to the city well, and this is accomplished by means of the virtue of the citizen as citizen. I say, therefore, that all the citizens cannot be alike in the sense that they would all perform the same work. From this it follows that the virtue of the good man and that of the good citizen are not identical. This consequence he manifests as follows. In the best regime, every citizen must possess the virtue of the good citizen, for in this manner the city will be most perfect. But it is impossible that all possess the virtue of the good man, because all the men in a city are not virtuous, as we have said.

368 Then he states the third reason. He says that every city is made up of heterogeneous elements, like an animal. An animal is indeed composed forthwith of heterogeneous elements, namely, soul and body; and likewise, the human soul is made up of heterogeneous parts, namely, a rational power and an appetitive power. The domestic society, in turn, is composed of heterogeneous parts, namely, man and woman, and [the art of] acquisition also requires a master and a slave. Now the city is made up of all these different parts and of many others. But we said in Book I that the virtue of the ruler is not the same as that of the subject,

either in the soul or in other things.[18] Hence it remains that the virtue of all the citizens is not one and the same, just as we see that in a chorus the virtue of the leader, that is, the one who directs the chorus, is not the same as that of the man who is next to him or his assistant. But it is obvious that the virtue of the good man is one and the same. It remains, therefore, that the virtue of the good citizen is not the same as that of the good man.

369   Then he shows that the virtue of one particular citizen is the same as that of the good man; and in this connection he does three things. First, he shows what he proposes. Secondly, he draws the conclusion arrived at in what has already been said. Thirdly, he raises a certain difficulty concerning what has already been said and resolves it.

He says then, first of all, that one will perhaps be able to say that the same virtue as that of the good man is required of a certain citizen in order that he may be good. For a man is not said to be a good ruler unless he is good as a result of his possessing the moral virtues and unless he is prudent. For it is said in Book VI of the *Ethics* that government is a certain part of prudence.[19] Hence the statesman, that is to say, the head of the regime, must be prudent and, consequently, he must be a good man.

370   Then from this he infers that the virtue of the good citizen is not the same absolutely as that of the good man. In order to prove this, he first adduces the statement made by some people to the effect that the training by which the ruler is to be educated to virtue is other than that of the citizen, as is clear from the fact that the sons of rulers are instructed in the science of horsemanship and warfare. Hence Euripides also, speaking in the person of a ruler, said, "It is not for me to know beautiful and profound things," namely, those things that are the concern of the philosopher, "but what is necessary to rule a city." This he said to indicate that there is a certain training proper to the ruler.

From this he infers that, if the training and virtue of the good ruler are the same as that of the good man, and if not every citizen is a ruler— for there are also citizens who are subjects—it follows that the virtue of the citizen is not the same absolutely as that of the good man, unless perhaps it be that of a certain citizen, namely, the one who can be a ruler. This is so because the virtue of the ruler is not the same as that of the citizen. That is why Jason said that he used to grieve when he was not a tyrant, as if he did not know how to live as a private person. [*130*]

371   Then he raises a difficulty concerning what has been said. In this connection he does two things. First, he raises an objection against what has been said. Secondly, he resolves it.

He says then, first of all, that sometimes a citizen is praised because of the fact that he is able to rule and obey well. If, therefore, the virtue of the good man is the same as that of the good ruler, and if the virtue of the good citizen is ordered to both of these things, namely, to rule and to obey, it follows that both things, namely, to be a good citizen and a good man, are not praiseworthy in the same way, but that it is much better to be a good citizen.

372   Then he resolves the aforesaid difficulty. First, he shows how the training of the ruler is the same as that of the subject and how it is not. Secondly, he shows how both ruler and subject possess the same virtue.

Concerning the first point, he does three things. First, he states his intention. He says that, because, as we have already said, both of these statements seem at times to hold, namely, that the ruler must not receive the same training as the subject and, again, that the good citizen should know both how to rule and how to obey, we must consider how each one is true from what follows.

373   Secondly, he sets down one type of rule in which one of the statements made, namely, that the training of the ruler is other than that of the subject, is verified. He says that there is a certain rule that is despotic, in which case the ruler is the master of the subjects. Such a ruler does not have to know how to do the things that pertain to the services necessary for life; rather, he should know how to make use of them. The other element, namely, to be able to serve in the things that pertain to the ministerial actions, appears to be of a servile rather than princely or despotic nature.

Now there are different kinds of slaves according to the different operations of servants. Among them, one role is played by those who work with their hands, as do craftsmen, cooks, and the like. These men live from the works of their hands, as their name indicates; and among such men must be reckoned the menial craftsmen, that is to say, those who by the work of their art dirty their bodies, as was said in Book I.[20] Because the operations of these craftsmen are not those of a ruler but are rather of a servile nature, formerly, among certain peoples, craftsmen did not have any share in the government of the city. This, I say, was the case before the advent of an extreme form of popular rule, that is to say, before the lowliest among the people were invested with power in the cities.

So it is clear, then, that neither the good statesman, or ruler of the city, nor even the good citizen should learn to perform works of subjects such as these, except occasionally because of some advantage to himself, and not because in these matters he should serve others; for then, if the masters were to exercise these servile functions, the distinction between master and slave would be obliterated.

374   Thirdly, he sets down another type of rule, in which the second statement, namely, that ruler and subject should learn the same things,

is verified. He says that there is a certain rule according to which one rules, not as a master over slaves, but over free men and equals. This is political rule, according to which now some people and now others are called upon to rule in the cities. A ruler such as this one must learn how to rule while he is still a subject, just as one learns how to command cavalrymen by having been a subject among cavalrymen, and how to be a general by having served under a general, and having been in charge of a particular unit, for example, a company or a cohort, and having laid ambushes at the general's orders. For a man learns to exercise a high office both by obedience and by training in lower offices. In this respect the proverb is right in stating that he who has not served under a ruler cannot rule well.

375   Then he shows how the virtue of the ruler is the same as that of other men and how it differs from it. He says that even in this type of rule the virtue of the ruler is other than that of the subject; the fact remains, however, that the man who is a good citizen absolutely should know both how to rule and how to be subject to a rule, not indeed to a despotic rule, which is that of slaves, but to a political rule, which is that of free men. This is the virtue of the citizen, namely, that he be well disposed toward one and the other. Good men, absolutely speaking, know both how to rule well and how to obey well. Thus the virtue of the good citizen, in so far as he is able to rule, is the same as that of the good man; but in so far as he is a subject, the virtue of the ruler and of the good man is other than that of the good citizen. For example, the temperance and justice of the ruler and the temperance and justice of the subjects are of a different species. For the subject who is free and good does not possess only one virtue, for example, justice; rather, his justice belongs to two species, according to one of which he can rule well and according to the other of which he can obey well. Such is also the case with the other virtues.

376   And he illustrates this by means of an example. The temperance and fortitude of a man and of a woman are different. A man is reputed timid if he is not more courageous than a courageous woman; and a woman, for whom silence is becoming, is reputed loquacious if she is as voluble as a good man. This is so because even in the management of the household, some things pertain to the man and other things to the woman; for it is the proper concern of the man to acquire riches and the proper concern of the woman to preserve them.

The same obtains in the city with regard to ruler and subject. For the virtue of the ruler is properly prudence, which directs and governs. The other moral virtues, whose nature it is to be governed and to obey, are [*131*] common to both subjects and rulers. Nevertheless, subjects share in prudence to the extent to which they have true opinion concerning things to be done, by which they can govern themselves in their own acts in accordance with the government of the ruler. And he cites the example of the flute-maker, who is related to the flute-player, who uses the flutes, in the same way as the subject to the ruler; for he works well in making flutes if his opinion is regulated in accordance with the orders of the flute-player. The case is the same in the city with reference to subject and ruler. Now he is speaking here of the virtue of the subject, not in so far as he is a good man, who as such must have prudence; rather, he is speaking of him in so far as he is a good subject, for this requires only that he have true opinion regarding the things that are demanded of him.

377 Finally, in an epilogue, he concludes from what has been said that it is obvious whether or not the virtue of the good man is the same as that of the good citizen, and, further, how it is the same and how it differs: it is the same in so far as he is able to rule well, and different in so far as he is able to obey well.

LESSON IV

[iii. 5. 1276^{b}34–1278^{b}6]

378 After having shown what the virtue of the dedicated citizen is and whether it is the same as that of the good man, the Philosopher raises a certain difficulty concerning the things that have already been treated. In this connection, he does three things. First, he raises the difficulty. Secondly, he resolves it. Thirdly, he clarifies the solution.

He says then, first of all, that there still remains a certain difficulty concerning the citizen, namely, whether only he who can share in the government of the city is a citizen or whether menial craftsmen, who have no share in the government, should also be ranked among the citizens. And he objects to both parts. For if laborers, who have nothing to do with the city, are called citizens, it will follow that the virtue that we said is that of the good citizen, namely, that he be able to rule and to obey well, does not apply to every citizen, because this man is ranked among the citizens despite the fact that he is not able to rule. If we say that no one of this sort is a citizen, there still remains a question, namely, in what category should laborers be placed. We cannot call them aliens, as if they came from elsewhere to reside in the city; nor can we call them strangers, like travelers who come to the city on business and not to stay; for these craftsmen make their home in the city, and were born there, and do not come from elsewhere.

379 He resolves this difficulty and says that for this last reason there is a question as to the category in which craftsmen should be placed, but the fact that they are not citizens does not pose a problem. They are men who are not citizens and yet are neither aliens nor strangers, as is clearly the case with slaves and freedmen, who have been restored from servitude to freedom. For it is true that not all who are necessary for the perfection of the city and without whom the city cannot exist are citizens, since we see that not only slaves but even sons are not perfect citizens, as are men. Men are citizens absolutely, capable as they are of discharging the functions of citizens; but sons are citizens by supposition, that is to say, with some diminishing qualification, for they are imperfect citizens. And just as slaves and children are really citizens in some way but not perfectly, so also are craftsmen. Hence in ancient times menial craftsmen and even strangers were slaves in certain cities, just as many are such even now.

380 Then he clarifies this solution, for even in the best disposed city workers could not be citizens. And if we say that a worker is a citizen in some way, then we have to say that the virtue of the citizen, which we have defined as consisting in the ability to rule and to obey well, is not that of the citizen, notwithstanding the fact that the word "citizen" is used in any way whatever. Rather, in order that this virtue may apply to them, it is necessary not only that they be free but also that they be discharged, that is to say, released from the tasks necessary for life. For if those who are assigned to such necessary tasks serve one man only, they are doing what is properly the work of slaves; for slaves used to perform such services for their masters. If, on the other hand, they perform these services for anyone indiscriminately, they are doing the work of laborers and mean persons who serve anyone for money.

381 Then he clarifies the proposed solution. And concerning this, he does three things. First, he shows how one is a citizen differently under different regimes. Secondly, he shows that he who can share in the government is most of all a citizen under any regime. Thirdly, he gathers together in an epilogue all that has been said about the virtue of the citizen.

He says then, first of all, that the truth concerning the things that have been said will become evident from a brief consideration of what follows. For if one understands perfectly what will be said, what has already been said will become obvious to him. Since there are many regimes differing in species, and since one speaks of a citizen in relation to a regime, as we have said, there must also necessarily be several species of citizens. This difference is best seen with reference to the subjects among the citizens, who are diversely related to the rulers under different regimes. Now those who are set over the others are the rulers under any regime. Hence, because of the diversity of regimes and consequently of citizens, it is necessary that under a certain regime, namely, the popular state, in which only freedom is sought, laborers be citizens; for, since they are free, they will have the possibility of being promoted to the government. Under other regimes, however, this is impossible, as is especially the case in the rule of the best, where honors are granted to those who are worthy of them by reason of their virtue. Those who live the life of laborers cannot, as rulers, provide the city with the things that pertain to virtue since they are not practiced in such things. But not even in the rule of the few are laborers capable of being citizens because in regimes of this sort some men are called upon to rule by reason of previous long-standing honors and riches. Hence it cannot easily happen that laborers are elevated to positions of honor, since throughout their whole lives they can scarcely gather enough [*134*] to become rich. But craftsmen under such regimes can be citizens and rulers because many craftsmen become rich quickly and so, by reason of their riches, can be called upon to govern in a rule of the few, when, abstaining from the practice of their art for a certain period of time after they have become rich, they have led honorable lives. Hence among the Thebans there was a statute enabling a man who had abstained from the affairs of the market place for ten years to participate in virtue, namely, ruling virtue.

381a   But even though strangers, aliens, and lowly persons cannot be citizens in the sense that they are able to rule in cities that are well established, nevertheless, in many regimes, namely, in many popular regimes, the law stipulating that strangers and aliens are not citizens is relaxed; for in certain cities he who is born of a citizen mother is considered a citizen, even if his father is an alien or a stranger. There is likewise also in many places a law to the effect that illegitimate children are citizens; but they do this on account of the scarcity of good citizens and the smallness of the population. Suffering from a deficiency of numbers, in which the power of the popular state consists, they make use of such laws so as first to choose as citizens those who were born of a male or female slave, provided one of the parents is a freeman. Then, as the population increases, they exclude all the sons of slaves but regard as citizens those whose mothers are citizens but whose fathers are aliens. Finally, they come to a point where they consider as citizens those who were born of parents both of whom are freemen and citizens. So it is evident then that there are different species of citizens according to the difference of regimes.

382   Then he shows who is most of all a citizen. He says that in any regime he who shares in the honors of the city is most of all said to be a citizen. Hence Homer says poetically of someone that he arose,

that is, to speak, after the others as one unhonored,[21] that is, as an alien who was not a citizen. But this notion of citizen is hidden; men are indeed misled due to the fact that they live together and therefore think that all those who reside together in the city are citizens. This is not proper, however, because he who does not share in the honors of the city is like an alien in the city.

383   Then in an epilogue he gathers together what has been said. He says that, concerning the question whether the virtue of the good man is the same as that of the dedicated citizen, we have shown that in a certain city, namely, that of the best, in which the ruling offices are granted according to the virtue which is that of the good man, the good man and the good citizen are identical, while in other cities, namely, in corrupt regimes, in which ruling offices are not distributed according to virtue, the good citizen is not the same as the good man. Furthermore, the one who is identical to the good man is not any citizen whatever but the ruler of the city and the master of those things that pertain to the care of the community, or the man who is capable of becoming such, either alone or with others. For we have said above that the virtue of the ruler is the same as that of the good man. Hence, if by citizen we mean he who is or is capable of being a ruler, his virtue is the same as that of the good man. But if by citizen we mean an imperfect citizen, who cannot become a ruler, then the virtue of the good citizen will not be the same as that of the good man, as is clear from what we have said.

LESSON   V

[iii. 6. $1278^{b}7-1279^{a}22$]

384   After having treated of the citizen, from the knowledge of whom we can discover what the city is, the Philosopher seeks next to divide the regime into its species. This section is divided into three parts. In the first, he distinguishes the regimes. In the second, he shows what is just in each regime. In the third, he shows which regime is preferable. Concerning the first point, he does three things. First, he states his intention. Secondly, he shows what a regime is. Thirdly, he divides the regimes.

He says then, first of all, that, now that these things have been determined, it remains to consider whether there is only one regime or whether there are several and, if several, how many there are, and what they are, and how they differ from one another.

385   Then he shows what a commonwealth is. He says that a commonwealth is nothing other than the disposition of a city with respect to all the rules that are found in it but principally with respect to the highest rule, which governs all the others. This is so because the imposition of order in a city resides entirely with the person who rules over the city; and such an imposition of order is the commonwealth itself. Hence the commonwealth consists principally in the order of the highest rule, according to the diversity of which commonwealths are diversified. Thus in a popular state the people rule and in a state of the few a few rich men. From this stems the diversity of these regimes. We must speak in the same way about the other regimes.

386   Then he distinguishes the regimes. First, he states how just regimes are distinguished from unjust regimes, and secondly, how true regimes are distinguished among themselves. Concerning the first point, he does three things. First, he shows to what the city is ordered. Secondly, he shows how the rules are distinguished from one another. Thirdly, he infers the difference between just and unjust regimes. Concerning the first point, he does two things. First, he states his intention. Secondly, he begins to carry out his proposal.

He says then, first of all, that, since we must distinguish the regimes from one another, we should begin by premising two things, the first being the reason for which the city was founded, and the second, the fact that there are differences of rules dealing with all the things that pertain to the community of life. For from these two things we shall be able to see the difference between just and unjust regimes.

387   Then he shows what the end of the city or of the regime is. He says that it was stated in Book I, in [*137*] which the question of domestic and despotic rule was treated, that man is by nature a political animal and, therefore, that men desire to live with one another and not be alone.[22] Even if one man did not have need of another for anything in order to lead a political life, there is nevertheless a great common benefit in the sharing of social life, and this with reference to two things. First, it is indeed so with reference to living well, to which each man contributes his share. For example, in any society we see that one person serves the society by performing one function, another by performing another function, and in this manner all live well together. This, then, namely, to live well, is above all else the end of the city or of the regime, both collectively with reference to all and severally with reference to each individual. Secondly, the common life is beneficial even for mere existence, since among those who share a common life one comes to the aid of another to sustain his life and preserve him against the dangers that threaten it. For this reason men come together and maintain

a political association, for even mere living considered in itself without the things that are conducive to living well is a good and desirable thing, unless perhaps a man suffers some exceedingly grave and cruel evils in his life. This is clear from the fact that, even if they bear many evils, men nevertheless persevere in their will to live and are attracted to the desire of life by a certain natural sweetness, as if life possessed in itself a certain solace and natural sweetness.

388   Then he distinguishes the species of rule, first in domestic matters, and secondly in political matters. He says that it is easy to distinguish the modes of rule that are said to exist, because he himself has made mention of them in other treatises that were not primarily concerned with them, as in Book VIII of the *Ethics*[23] and above in Book II.

In domestic affairs there is a twofold rule. One is the same as that of master over slave and is called domination. Although, according to the truth of the matter, the same thing benefits the man who is by nature a slave and the man who is by nature a master, namely, that the former be ruled by the latter, the fact remains that the master rules the slave for the benefit of the master and not for the benefit of the slave, except perhaps incidentally, in so far as when the slave dies the dominion ceases to exist. The other rule is that over free men, like that over sons, wife, and the entire family, and it is called domestic rule. What is sought in this rule is the benefit of the subjects or even the benefit common to both, but essentially and primarily the benefit of the subjects, as we see in the other arts, such as the art of medicine, which seeks principally the benefit of those who are healed, and the art of gymnastics, which seeks principally the benefit of those who exercise. Incidentally, however, it happens that the benefit redounds to those who possess the art. For he who exercises boys is also at the same time exercising himself; he, too, is sometimes among the number of those who exercise, just as the pilot is one of the crew who sail a ship. Accordingly, the exerciser of boys and the pilot of a ship consider per se the benefit of the subjects. But because they themselves are among the number of those who exercise or sail, they both share incidentally in the common benefit that they procure. In like manner, the father shares in the benefit of the household that he procures.

389   Then, in accordance with what was said, he distinguishes the political rules. He says that, since the rule over free men is primarily for the benefit of the subjects, it is therefore considered fitting that citizens particularly be governed according to political rules when they have been established in conformity with the equality and similarity of the citizens. For then it seems fitting that some persons should rule for one period of time and others for another period. It would be otherwise, however, if some of the citizens greatly surpassed others in goodness.

For then it would be fitting for them to rule all of the time, as will be said below.

Concerning this question of fittingness, however, the judgment of men differs according to different times. For in the beginning, those who ruled by serving others thought it fitting, as indeed it was, that they themselves should serve others for a time by seeking their benefit and that in turn someone else should rule for a time and seek their benefit, just as they themselves had previously sought the good of others. Afterwards, however, because of the benefits accruing from the common goods that rulers usurp for themselves and also from the very right of sovereignty, men wish to rule always, as if to rule were to be healthy and not to rule to be sick. Thus men seem to desire rulership as the sick desire health.

390   Then from what has been said he infers the distinction between just and unjust regimes. For, since it is true that the rule of free men should be for the benefit of the subjects, it is evident that any regime in which the ruler seeks the common benefit is a just regime according to absolute justice, while any regime in which the sole benefit of the ruler is sought is an unjust regime and a corruption of some sort of the just regime. For in such cases that which is simply just does not exist but only that which is just in a relative sense, as will be said later. For they rule by dominating the city and make use of the citizens as slaves, that is to say, for their own benefit. This is contrary to justice, because a city is an association of free men and a slave is not a citizen, as was said earlier.

LESSON   VI

[iii. 7. 1279ᵃ23–8. 1280ᵃ7]

391   After having distinguished just regimes from unjust ones, the Philosopher here seeks to distinguish both groups among themselves. In this connection he does two things. First, he states his aim. Secondly, he carries out his proposal. He says then, first of all, that, now that these things have been determined, we must next treat of the number and nature of the regimes in the following order: first, we shall consider the just regimes and, secondly, the unjust regimes.

392   Then he distinguishes the regimes, and in this connection he

does three things. First, he shows on what basis the distinction of the regimes is to be made. Secondly, he distinguishes the regimes. Thirdly, he raises an objection against what has been said.

He says then, first of all, that a regime is nothing other than the order of the rulers in the city; and indeed regimes must be distinguished according to the difference of rulers. In a city, either one, or a few, or the many rule; and any one of these three cases can come about in two ways: one, when they rule for the common benefit, and in this case we shall have just regimes; the other, when they rule for the private benefit of those who are in power, whether that be one man, or a few, or many, and in this case we have perversions of regimes; for we have to say either that the subjects are not citizens or that in some things they share in the benefit of the city.

393   Then he distinguishes both groups of regimes by their proper names. First, he distinguishes the just regimes and, secondly, the corrupt regimes.

He says then, first of all, that if there is a rule of one man, it is usually called kingly rule if it seeks the common benefit. The regime in which only a few, but more than one, rule for the sake of the common good is called the state of the best, either because the best, that is to say, the virtuous, rule or because such a regime is ordered to the greatest good of the city and all the citizens. And when the multitude rules and seeks the common benefit, the regime is called a commonwealth (*respublica*), which is a name common to all the regimes. And it is not without reason that this regime should chance to be called by this name; for it easily happens that in a city one or a few men are found who greatly surpass the others in virtue, but it is extremely difficult to find many who arrive at the perfection of virtue. This rather happens above all with reference to military virtue, namely, that many should excel in it. Hence in this regime, military men and men who possess arms are the ones who rule.

394   Then he distinguishes the corruptions of these regimes by name. He says that the perversions of the aforesaid regimes are the following: tyranny is a perversion of kingship, the rule of the few a perversion of the rule of the best, and the popular state a perversion of the commonwealth. From this he concludes that tyranny is the rule of one man seeking his own benefit; the rule of the few, that which seeks the benefit of the rich; and a popular state, that which seeks the benefit of the poor. None of these seeks the common benefit.

395   Then he raises an objection to what has been said; and in this connection he does three things. First, he states his aim and repeats what has been said. Secondly, he raises a difficulty. Thirdly, he proposes the solution.

He says then, first of all, that we must stand at a slightly greater distance and discuss what each one of the previously mentioned regimes is, since it presents certain difficulties. He who philosophizes in any art and considers the truth, as it were, not only looks to what is useful for action; he should not look down on or pass over anything but rather set out the truth in each instance. Now we said that a tyranny is a certain monarchy that exercises its domination over the political community because it makes use of citizens as slaves. A rule of the few exists when the regime is dominated by those who abound in riches. And a popular state exists when the regime is dominated, not by those who have an abundance of riches, but rather by the poor.

396 Then he raises the difficulty. First, he states the difficulty. Secondly, he eliminates a certain answer.

He says then, first of all, that the first difficulty concerns the definition of popular rule and of the rule of the few. Let us suppose, then, that in a certain city the rich outnumber the poor and that the rich are the masters of the city. It seems, according to this, that there exists here a rule of the many. Likewise, if it should happen, on the other hand, that the poor are fewer but better and stronger and dominate the city, it will follow, according to this, that there exists here a rule of the few. It does not seem, therefore, that we defined the regimes properly when [*140*] we said that the state of the many consists in the domination of the poor and the state of the few in the domination of the rich.

397 Then he eliminates an answer. Someone could indeed say that, in the definition of the rule of the few, fewness should be added to riches, and, in the definition of the rule of the many, multitude should be added to poverty, in such a way that the rule of the few is that in which a few rich men govern, and the rule of the many that in which many poor men govern. But this, in turn, poses another problem. For, if the regimes have been adequately divided, so that there is no other regime besides the ones mentioned, it will be impossible to say under which regime the two aforesaid regimes, the ones in which either many rich men or a few poor men rule, are comprised.

398 Then from what has been premised he infers the solution of the difficulty. He says that the nature of the difficulty just mentioned seems to indicate that the fact that there are many rulers is related only incidentally to the rule of the few, since everywhere one finds that the poor outnumber the rich; and, accordingly, these things are named as they are found to exist for the most part. But that which is incidental does not constitute a specific difference and, hence, the rules of the few are not distinguished, essentially speaking, from the rule of the many on the basis of large and small numbers. Rather, that by which they differ essentially is poverty and riches. For the nature of the rule that is ordered to opulence is other than that of the rule that is ordered to freedom, which constitutes the end of the rule of the many. And hence, wherever

some rule for the sake of riches, whether they be more numerous or less numerous, there we necessarily have a state of the few; and wherever the poor rule, there we necessarily have a rule of the many. It is incidental, however, that the latter be numerous and the former few. For those who abound in riches are few, but all share in freedom; and for this reason these two elements fight with each other. The few wish to be set over the others on account of their excess of riches, and the many wish to prevail over the few, being as it were their equals on account of freedom.

[Here ends Aquinas' commentary on the *Politics* of Aristotle.]

NOTES

1. Aristotle *Physics* ii. 2. 194ª21.
2. *Ibid.* ii. 8. 199ª13.
3. Aristotle *Nicomachean Ethics* x. 9. 1181ᵇ14.
4. *Ibid.* i. 1. 1094ᵇ9.
5. The expression "domestic head" is used here to render the Latin *oeconomus* (*oikonomos*, steward or administrator of the household), for which there seems to be no exact equivalent in the English language.
6. See the preceding note.
7. The printed text reads: *secundum hanc doctrinam* (according to this doctrine), for which we have substituted: *secundum subjectam methodum* or *secundum modum assignatum* (according to the mode [or method] indicated). The correction appears necessitated by the Latin text of Aristotle and the Thomistic context, as well as by the general meaning of the passage.
8. Aristotle *De Partibus Animalium* ii. 17. 660ª15 ff.; cf. iv. 6. 683ª20 ff., and *De Anima* ii. 8. 420ᵇ17.
9. The reading *dominantur* (rule), which occurs in the printed text, has been changed to *nominantur* (are called), in accordance with the obvious meaning of the sentence.

10. The distinction between sound, voice, and speech is discussed at greater length by Aristotle in *De Anima* ii. 8. 419ᵇ3 ff.
11. Aristotle *Nicomachean Ethics* ii. 5. 1105ᵇ23.
12. Reading *iusti* instead of *ita*, as the context demands.
13. Aristotle *Metaphysics* vii. 10. 1035ᵇ3 ff.
14. Aristotle *Nicomachean Ethics* ii. 1. 1103ª14 ff.
15. Reading *indeterminatus* instead of *determinatus*, as is clearly required by the Latin version of Aristotle and the context.
16. Aristotle *Politics* i. 2. 1252ᵇ27 ff.
17. The printed text reads *insanos*, which hardly seems appropriate in this context.
18. Aristotle *Politics* i. 13. 1259ᵇ33 ff.
19. Cf. Aristotle *Nicomachean Ethics* vi. 8. 1141ᵇ23.
20. Cf. Aristotle *Politics* i. 5. 1254ᵇ25.
21. Cf. Homer *Iliad* ix. 648; xvi. 59.
22. Cf. Aristotle *Politics* i. 2. 1252ª26 ff., i. 3. 1253ᵇ1 ff., and *passim*.
23. Cf. Aristotle *Nicomachean Ethics* viii. 10. 1160ª31 ff.

18.

CONDEMNATION OF

2 1 9   PROPOSITIONS

Translated by Ernest L. Fortin
and Peter D. O'Neill

The condemnation of the 219 Propositions by Etienne Tempier in 1277 was the most dramatic event in the history of the University of Paris during the second half of the thirteenth century. As bishop of Paris, Tempier had been requested by the Roman authorities to investigate and report on the teachings of certain masters of the faculty of arts. With the help of sixteen theologians, among them Henry of Ghent, he proceeded to draw up a list of propositions culled from various contemporary works, condemned them, threatened the promoters of these doctrines with excommunication unless they presented themselves to the bishop or his chancellor within a specified period of time, and reserved the right to impose further sanctions on them.

Tempier's sentence was only one in a series of actions designed to cope with the situation created by the rise of Aristotelianism, both in its Greek and in its Arabic forms, at the University of Paris during the course of the thirteenth century and with the latent threat that this movement presented for the Christian faith. Earlier ecclesiastical decrees in 1210 and 1215, provoked by the teachings of Almaric of Bene and David of Dinant, had cautioned against the new dangers and forbidden, under pain of excommunication, the public or private "reading" (that is, teaching) of the natural treatises and *Metaphysics* of Aristotle at Paris (but not in England or elsewhere). Also included in the ban were certain commentaries on these works, presumably those of Avicenna and perhaps those of Alfarabi. The same general policy was maintained by Gregory IX in 1231, at least until the works in question had been examined and "purged of every suspicion of error." However, the absence of any reaction to these measures in the years that follow seems to indicate that they were never enforced strictly. Further evidence suggests that, after the death of Gregory in 1241, they were in fact disregarded and in time became a dead letter. In 1255, a new statute was promulgated, reorganizing the curriculum of the faculty of arts and legalizing the study of all the known works of Aristotle, along with three Aristotelian pseudepigrapha, the *Liber de Causis*, the *De Plantis*, and the *De Differentia Spiritus et Animae*. The stage was thus set for the crisis that erupted a few years later, *ca.* 1265.

In 1270, Tempier condemned a series of thirteen errors dealing with the eternity of the world, divine providence, free will, and the unity of the intellectual soul, and likewise threatened to excommunicate all those who taught these errors knowingly. The move failed to restore order in the university, and for the next seven years the controversy raged between the faculty of theology and the faculty of arts, as well as among the representatives of the various trends within the Aristotelian camp itself. Such was the situation when Tempier again intervened, this time in a more decisive manner.

The condemnation of 1277 appears first of all as an attempt on the part of the Church to liquidate the menace engendered by the rebirth in its midst of a wholly independent (Aristotelian) philosophy; but it also bears traces of the bias entertained by Tempier and the more traditional theologians of his time against the new Christian Aristotelianism of Albert, Aquinas, and their followers. Already in 1270, fifteen propositions had originally been submitted, two of which corresponded to the teaching of Aquinas. Of the 219 propositions incriminated in 1277, some fifteen or twenty are generally regarded as reflecting his doctrine (see particularly, in the order in which they are listed

here, Props. 27, 42, 43, 50, 53, 54, 55, 110, 115, 116, 146, 147, 162, 163, 169).

The work of compiling the syllabus was completed within three weeks after the arrival of the papal bull ordering the investigation and appears to have been carried out in somewhat helter-skelter fashion by several masters working individually. One cannot say whether the propositions were extracted textually from the writings of the Aristotelians. No ostensible effort was made to introduce a logical order among them. Moreover, their precise meaning remains in some instances obscure, due to the lack of any immediate context. Although visibly influenced by Averroism, many of the propositions represent at best a crude version of the genuine Averroistic teaching.

It seems evident that by censuring these propositions in his own name, Tempier exceeded the mandate received from Rome. His resounding condemnation was nonetheless the most severe that the thirteenth century had known. Despite its purely local character, it had broad repercussions throughout the West. It provided a brutal, if momentary, solution to the problem posed by "Latin Averroism" (as it is commonly but ambiguously called since Renan), and put an end to the career of its foremost representative, Siger de Brabant, who had been teaching in Paris since *ca.* 1265. Siger appealed to Rome and, although absolved of the crime of heresy, he was forced to remain in Italy, where he was stabbed to death by a mad cleric a few years later. The condemnation also checked the spread of Thomism and gave a new impetus to the eclectic Aristotelianism favored by such men as Tempier, the Franciscan John Peckham, and the secular masters. Finally, it created an atmosphere of uneasiness that persisted for many years in university circles.

The 219 Propositions are translated here for the first time into English from the edition by P. Mandonnet, O.P., *Siger de Brabant et l'averroïsme latin au XIIIme siècle*, 2me partie, *Textes inédits* (2d ed.; Louvain, 1908), pp. 175–191. The italic numbers in brackets in the text refer to the pages of this edition. The titles of the various sections and the order in which the propositions appear are those of Mandonnet. The numbers in parentheses at the end of each proposition are those of the original list.

S T E P H E N , by divine permission unworthy servant of the church of Paris, sends greetings in the Son of the glorious Virgin to all those who will read this letter.

We have received frequent reports, inspired by zeal for the faith, on the part of important and serious persons to the effect that some students of the arts in Paris are exceeding the boundaries of their own faculty and are presuming to treat and discuss, as if they were debatable in the schools, certain obvious and loathsome errors, or rather *vanities and lying follies* [Ps. 39:5], which are contained in the roll joined to this letter. These students are not hearkening to the admonition of Gregory, "Let him who would speak wisely exercise great care, lest by his speech he disrupt the unity of his listeners," particularly when in support of the aforesaid errors they adduce pagan writings that—shame on their ignorance—they assert to be so convincing that they do not know how to answer them. So as not to appear to be asserting what they thus insinuate, however, they conceal their answers in such a way that, while wishing to avoid Scylla, they fall into Charybdis. For they say that these things are true according to philosophy but not according to the Catholic faith, as if there were two contrary truths and as if the truth of Sacred Scripture were contradicted by the truth in the sayings of the accursed pagans, of whom it is written, *I will destroy the wisdom of the wise* [I Cor. 1:19; cf. Isa. 29:14], inasmuch as true wisdom [*176*] destroys false wisdom. Would that such students listen to the advice of the wise man when he says: *If you have understanding, answer your neighbor; but if not, let your hand be upon your mouth, lest you be surprised in an unskillful word and be confounded* [Ecclus. 5:14].

Lest, therefore, this unguarded speech lead simple people into error, we, having taken counsel with the doctors of Sacred Scripture and other prudent men, strictly forbid these and like things and totally condemn them. We excommunicate all those who shall have taught the said errors or any one of them, or shall have dared in any way to defend or uphold them, or even to listen to them, unless they choose to reveal themselves to us or to the chancery of Paris within seven days; in addition to which we shall proceed against them by inflicting such other penalties as the law requires according to the nature of the offense.

By this same sentence of ours we also condemn the book *De Amore*, or

De Deo Amoris, which begins with the words, *Cogit me multum,* and so on, and ends with the words, *Cave, igitur, Galtere, amoris exercere mandata,* and so on, as well as the book of geomancy that begins with the words, *Existimaverunt Indi,* and so on, and ends with the words, *Ratiocinare ergo super eum invenies,* and so on. We likewise condemn the books, scrolls, and leaflets dealing with necromancy, or containing experiments in fortunetelling, invocations of devils or incantations endangering lives, or in which these and similar things evidently contrary to the orthodox faith and good morals are treated. We pronounce the sentence of excommunication against those who shall have taught the said scrolls, books, and leaflets, or listened to them, unless they reveal themselves to us or to the chancery of Paris within seven days in the manner described earlier in this letter; in addition to which we shall proceed to inflict such other penalties as the gravity of the offense demands.

Given in the year of the Lord 1276, on the Sunday on which *Laetare Jerusalem* is sung at the court of Paris.

I

ERRORS IN PHILOSOPHY

ON THE NATURE OF PHILOSOPHY

1. That there is no more excellent state than to study philosophy. (40)
2. That the only wise men in the world are the philosophers. (154)
3. That in order to have some certitude about any conclusion, man must base himself on self-evident principles.—The statement is erroneous because it refers in a general way both to the certitude of apprehension and to that of adherence. (151) [177]
4. That one should not hold anything unless it is self-evident or can be manifested from self-evident principles. (37)
5. That man should not be content with authority to have certitude about any question. (150)
6. That there is no rationally disputable question that the philosopher ought not to dispute and determine, because reasons are derived from things. It belongs to philosophy under one or another of its parts to consider all things. (145)

7. That, besides the philosophic disciplines, all the sciences are necessary but that they are necessary only on account of human custom.[1] (24)

ON THE KNOWABILITY OF GOD

8. That our intellect by its own natural power can attain to a knowledge of the first cause.—This does not sound well and is erroneous if what is meant is immediate knowledge. (211)

9. That we can know God by His essence in this mortal life. (36)

10. That nothing can be known about God except that He is, or His existence. (215)

ON THE NATURE OF GOD

11. That the proposition, "God is being per se positively," is not intelligible; rather God is being per se privatively. (216)

12. That the intellect by which God understands Himself is by definition different from that by which He understands other things.—This is erroneous because, although the proper reason of His understanding is different in each case, the intellect is not other by definition. (149)

ON DIVINE SCIENCE

13. That God does not know things other than himself. (3)

14. That God cannot know contingent beings immediately except through their particular and proximate causes. (56)

15. That the first cause does not have science of future contingents. The first reason is that future contingents are not beings. The second is that future contingents are singulars, but God knows by means of an intellectual power, which cannot know singulars. Hence, if there were no senses, the intellect would perhaps not distinguish between Socrates and Plato, although it would distinguish between a man and an ass. The third reason is the relation of cause to effect; for the divine foreknowledge [178] is a necessary cause of the things foreknown. The fourth reason is the relation of science to the known; for even though science is not the cause of the known, it is determined to one of two contradictories by that which is known; and this is true of divine science much more than of ours. (42)

ON DIVINE WILL AND POWER

16. That the first cause is the most remote cause of all things.—This is erroneous if so understood as to mean that it is not the most proximate. (190)

17. That what is impossible absolutely speaking cannot be brought about by God or by another agent.—This is erroneous if we mean what is impossible according to nature. (147)

18. That what is self-determined, like God, either always acts or never acts; and that many things are eternal. (52)

19. That an active potency that can exist without acting is mixed with passive potency.—This is erroneous if any operation whatsoever is understood here. (68)

20. That God of necessity makes whatever comes immediately from Him.—This is erroneous whether we are speaking of the necessity of coercion, which destroys liberty, or of the necessity of immutability, which implies the inability to do otherwise. (53)

21. That from a previous act of the will nothing new can proceed unless it is preceded by a change. (39)

22. That God cannot be the cause of a newly-made thing and cannot produce anything new. (48)

23. That God cannot move anything irregularly, that is, in a manner other than that in which He does, because there is no diversity of will in Him. (50)

24. That God is eternal in acting and moving, just as He is eternal in existing; otherwise He would be determined by some other thing that would be prior to Him. (51)

25. That God has infinite power, not because He makes something out of nothing, but because He maintains infinite motion. (62)

26. That God has infinite power in duration, not in action, since there is no such infinity except in an infinite body, if there were such a thing. (29)

ON THE CAUSATION OF THE WORLD

27. That the first cause cannot make more than one world. (34)

28. That from one first agent there cannot proceed a multiplicity of effects. (44)

29. That the first cause would be able to produce an effect equal to itself if it did not limit its power. (26)

30. That the first cause cannot produce something other than itself, because every difference between maker and made is through matter. (55)

[*179*]

31. That in heavenly things there are three principles: the subject of eternal motion, the soul of the heavenly body, and the first mover as desired.—The error is in regard to the first two. (95)

32. That there are two eternal principles, namely, the body of the heaven and its soul. (94)

ON THE NATURE OF THE INTELLIGENCES

33. That the immediate effect of the first being has to be one only and most like unto the first being. (64)

34. That God is the necessary cause of the first intelligence, which cause being posited, the effect is also posited; and both are equal in duration. (58)

35. That God never created an intelligence more than He now creates it. (28)

36. That the absolutely first unmoved being does not move save through the mediation of something moved, and that such an unmoved mover is a part of that which is moved of itself. (67)

37. That the first principle is not the proper cause of eternal beings except metaphorically, in so far as it conserves them, for unless it was, they would not be. (45)

38. That the intelligences, or separated substances, which they say are eternal, do not have an efficient cause properly speaking, but only metaphorically, in so far as they have a cause conserving them in existence; but they were not newly-made, because then they would be mutable. (70)

39. That all the separated substances are coeternal with the first principle. (5)

40. That everything that does not have matter is eternal, because that which was not made through a change in matter did not exist previously; therefore it is eternal. (80)

41. That the separated substances, having no matter through which they would be in potency before being in act and being from a cause that always exists in the same manner, are therefore eternal. (72)

42. That God cannot multiply individuals of the same species without matter. (96)

43. That God could not make several intelligences of the same species because intelligences do not have matter. (81)

44. That no change is possible in the separated substances; nor are they

in potency to anything because they are eternal and free from matter. (71)

45. That the intelligence is made by God in eternity because it is totally immutable; the soul of the heaven, however, is not. (83)

46. That the separated substances are the same as their essences because in them that by which they are and that which they are, is the same. (79) [*180*]

47. That the science of the intelligence does not differ from its substance, for where there is no distinction between known and knower, there is no distinction of thing known either. (85)

48. That an angel does not understand anything new. (76)

49. That the separated substances are infinite in act; for infinity is not impossible except in material things. (86)

50. That if there were any separated substance that did not move some body in this sensible world, it would not be included in the universe. (77)

51. That the eternal substances separated from matter have all the good possible to them when they are produced and do not desire anything that they do not have. (78)

52. That the separated substances, in so far as they have a single appetite, do not change in their operation. (69)

53. That an intelligence or an angel or a separated soul is nowhere. (218)

54. That the separated substances are nowhere according to their substance.—This is erroneous if so understood as to mean that substance is not in a place. If, however, it is so understood as to mean that substance is the reason for being in a place, it is true that they are nowhere according to their substance. (219)

55. That the separated substances are somewhere by their operation, and that they cannot move from one extreme to another or to the middle except in so far as they can will to operate either in the middle or in the extremes.—This is erroneous if so understood as to mean that without operation a substance is not in a place and that it does not pass from one place to another. (204)

ON THE FUNCTION OF THE INTELLIGENCES

56. That the separated substances by means of their intellect create things. (73)

57. That an intelligence receives its existence from God through mediating intelligences. (84)

58. That the higher intelligences create rational souls without the

motion of the heaven, whereas the lower intelligences create vegetative and sensitive souls through the medium of heavenly motion. (30)

59. That an angel is not in potency to opposite acts immediately but only through the mediating agency of something else, such as a sphere. (75)

60. That the higher intelligences are not the cause of anything new in the lower intelligences, and that the higher intelligences are the cause of eternal knowledge for the lower intelligences. (82)

61. That since an intelligence is full of forms, it impresses these forms on matter by using the heavenly bodies as instruments. (189)

62. That external matter obeys the spiritual substance.—This is erroneous if understood absolutely and according to every mode of change. (210)

63. That the higher intelligences impress things on the lower, just as one soul impresses things on another and even on a sensitive soul; and that through such an impression a spellbinder is able to cast a camel into a pitfall just by looking at it. (112) [*181*]

ON THE HEAVEN AND ON
THE GENERATION OF LOWER BEINGS

64. That God is the necessary cause of the motion of the higher bodies and of the union and separation occurring in the stars. (59)

65. That if at one time all the causes were at rest, it is necessary to assert that God is mobile. (57)

66. That God could not move the heaven in a straight line, the reason being that He would then leave a vacuum. (49)

67. That the first principle cannot produce generable things immediately because they are new effects and a new effect requires an immediate cause that is capable of being otherwise. (54)

68. That the first principle cannot be the cause of diverse products here below without the mediation of other causes, inasmuch as nothing that transforms, transforms in diverse ways without being itself transformed. (43)

69. That God cannot produce the effect of a secondary cause without the secondary cause itself. (63)

70. That God is able to produce contraries, that is, through the medium of a heavenly body which occupies diverse places. (61)

71. That the nature that is the principle of motion in the heavenly bodies is a moving intelligence.—This is erroneous if what is meant is the intrinsic nature, which is act or form. (213)

72. That the heavenly bodies have of themselves eternity of substance but not eternity of motion. (93)

73. That the heavenly bodies are moved by an intrinsic principle, which is the soul, and that they are moved by a soul and an appetitive power, like an animal. For just as an animal is moved by desiring, so also is the heaven. (92)

74. That an intelligence by its will alone moves the heaven. (212)

75. That the soul of the heaven is an intelligence, and that the heavenly spheres are not instruments but organs of the intelligences, just as the ear and the eye are organs of the sensitive power. (102)

76. That the intelligence moving the heaven influences the rational soul, just as the body of the heaven influences the human body. (74)

77. That the heaven is never at rest because the generation of lower beings, which is the end of the motion of the heaven, must not cease. Another reason is that the heaven has its existence and its power from its mover and the heaven preserves these through its motion. Hence if it ceased to move, it would cease to be. (186) [*182*]

78. That there would be nothing new if the heaven were not varied with respect to the matter of generable things. (88)

79. That if the heaven stood still, fire would not burn flax because God would not exist. (156)

80. That the reasoning of the Philosopher proving that the motion of the heaven is eternal is not sophistic, and that it is surprising that profound men do not perceive this. (91)

81. That a sphere is the immediate efficient cause of all forms. (106)

82. That if in some humor by the power of the stars such a proportion could be achieved as is found in the seed of the parents, a man could be generated from that humor; and thus a man could be adequately generated from putrefaction. (188)

ON THE ETERNITY OF THE WORLD

83. That the world, although it was made from nothing, was not newly-made, and, although it passed from nonbeing to being, the non-being did not precede being in duration but only in nature. (99)

84. That the world is eternal because that which has a nature by which it is able to exist for the whole future has a nature by which it was able to exist in the whole past. (98)

85. That the world is eternal as regards all the species contained in it, and that time, motion, matter, agent, and receiver are eternal, because the world comes from the infinite power of God and it is impossible that

there be something new in the effect without there being something new in the cause. (87)

86. That eternity and time have no existence in reality but only in the mind. (200)

87. That nothing is eternal from the standpoint of its end that is not eternal from the standpoint of its beginning. (4)

88. That time is infinite as regards both extremes, for although it is impossible for an infinity to be passed through when one of its parts had to be passed through, it is not impossible for an infinity to be passed through when none of its parts had to be passed through. (205)

89. That it is impossible to refute the arguments of the Philosopher concerning the eternity of the world unless we say that the will of the first being embraces incompatibles. (89)

90. That the universe cannot cease to exist because the first agent is able to cause transmutations one after another eternally, now into this form, now into that, and similarly it is of the nature of matter to undergo change. (203)

91. That there has already been an infinite number of revolutions of the heaven, which it is impossible for the created intellect but not for the first cause to comprehend. (101) [*183*]

92. That with all the heavenly bodies coming back to the same point after a period of thirty-six thousand years, the same effects as now exist will reappear. (6)

ON THE NECESSITY AND CONTINGENCY OF THINGS

93. That some things can take place by chance with respect to the first cause, and that it is false that all things are preordained by the first cause, because then they would come about by necessity. (197)

94. That fate, which is the disposition of the universe, proceeds from divine providence, not immediately, but mediately through the motion of the higher bodies, and that this fate does not impose necessity upon the lower beings, since they have contrariety, but upon the higher. (195)

95. That for all effects to be necessary with respect to the first cause, it does not suffice that the first cause itself be not impedible, but it is also necessary that the intermediary causes be not impedible.—This is erroneous because then God could not produce a necessary effect without posterior causes. (60)

96. That beings depart from the order of the first cause considered in itself, although not in relation to the other causes operating in the

universe.—This is erroneous because the order of beings to the first cause is more essential and more inseparable than their order to the lower causes. (47)

97. That it pertains to the dignity of the higher causes to be able to commit errors and produce monsters unintentionally, since nature is able to do this. (196)

98. That, among the efficient causes, the secondary cause has an action that it did not receive from the first cause. (198)

99. That there is more than one prime mover. (66)

100. That, among the efficient causes, if the first cause were to cease to act, the secondary cause would not, as long as the secondary cause operates according to its own nature. (199)

101. That no agent is in potency to one or the other of two things; on the contrary, it is determined. (160)

102. That nothing happens by chance, but everything comes about by necessity, and that all the things that will exist in the future will exist by necessity, and those that will not exist are impossible, and that nothing occurs contingently if all causes are considered.—This is erroneous because the concurrence of causes is included in the definition of chance, as Boethius says in his book *On Consolation*.[2] (21)

103. That the necessity of events comes from the diversity of places. (142)

104. That the differences of condition among men, both as regards spiritual gifts and temporal assets, are traced back to the diverse signs of the heaven. (143) [*184*]

105. That at the time of the generation of a man in body, and hence in soul, which follows upon the body, there is in him a disposition produced by the order of the higher and lower causes by which he is inclined to certain actions or events.—This is erroneous unless it is understood of natural events and by way of disposition. (207)

106. That one attributes health, sickness, life, and death to the position of the stars and the glance of fortune by saying that if fortune looks down on him he will live, if it does not, he will die. (206)

107. That God was not able to make prime matter save through the mediation of a heavenly body. (38)

ON THE PRINCIPLES OF

MATERIAL THINGS

108. That, just as nothing can come from matter without an agent, so also nothing can come from an agent without matter, and that God

is not an efficient cause except with respect to that which has its existence in the potency of matter. (46)

109. That a form that has to exist and come to be in matter cannot be produced by an agent that does not produce it from matter. (103)

110. That forms are not divided except through matter.—This is erroneous unless one is speaking of forms educed from the potency of matter. (191)

111. That the elements were produced from chaos by an antecedent generation, but they are eternal. (202)

112. That the elements are eternal. They were nevertheless newly produced in the disposition that they now possess. (107)

ON MAN AND THE AGENT INTELLECT

113. That a man is a man independently of the rational soul. (11)

114. That by nutrition a man can become other numerically and individually. (148)

115. That God could not make several numerically different souls. (27)

116. That individuals of the same species differ solely by the position of matter, like Socrates and Plato, and that since the human form existing in each is numerically the same, it is not surprising that the same being numerically is in different places. (97)

117. That the intellect is numerically one for all, for although it may be separated from this or that body, it is not separated from every body. (32)

118. That the agent intellect is a certain separated substance superior to the possible intellect, and that it is separated from the body according to its substance, power, and operation and is not the form of the human body. (123) [*185*]

119. That the motions of the heaven are for the sake of the intellectual soul, and the intellectual soul or intellect cannot be educed except through the mediation of a body. (110)

120. That the form of man does not come from an extrinsic source but is educed from the potency of matter, for otherwise the generation would not be univocal. (105)

121. That no form coming from an extrinsic source can form one being with matter; for that which is separable does not form one being with that which is corruptible. (111)

122. That from the sensitive and intellectual parts of man there does not result a unity in essence, unless it be a unity such as that of an intelligence and a sphere, that is, a unity in operation. (13)

123. That the intellect is not the form of the body, except in the manner in which a helmsman is the form of a ship, and that it is not an essential perfection of man. (7)

124. That humanity is not the form of a thing but of the mind. (104)

125. That the operation of the nonunited intellect is joined to the body in such a way that the operation is that of a thing that does not have a form by which it operates.—The statement is erroneous because it asserts that the intellect is not the form of man. (119)

126. That the intellect, which is man's ultimate perfection, is completely separated. (121)

127. That the human soul is in no way mobile according to place, either essentially or accidentally, and if it is placed somewhere by means of its substance, it will never move from one place to another. (108)

128. That the soul would never move unless the body moved, just as a heavy or a light thing would never move unless the air moved. (214)

129. That the substance of the soul is eternal, and that the agent intellect and the possible intellect are eternal. (109)

130. That the human intellect is eternal because it comes from a cause that is always the same and because it does not have matter by means of which it is in potency prior to being in act. (31)

131. That the speculative intellect is simply eternal and incorruptible; with respect to this or that man, however, it is corrupted when the phantasms in him are corrupted. (125)

132. That the intellect casts off the body when it so desires and puts it on when it so desires. (8)

133. That the soul is inseparable from the body, and that the soul is corrupted when the harmony of the body is corrupted. (116)

134. That the rational soul, when it departs from an animal, still remains a living animal. (114)

135. That the separated soul is not alterable, according to philosophy, although according to the faith it is altered. (113) [*186*]

136. That the intellect can pass from body to body, in such a way that it is successively the mover of different bodies. (193)

137. That the generation of man is circular, inasmuch as the form of man returns many times to the same portion of matter. (10)

138. That there was no first man, nor will there be a last; indeed, the generation of man from man always was and always will be. (9)

139. That although the generation of men could cease, by the power of the first agent it will not cease, for the first sphere promotes the generation not only of the elements but also of men. (137)

ON THE OPERATION OF
THE HUMAN INTELLECT

140. That the agent intellect is not united to our possible intellect, and that the possible intellect is not united to us substantially. And if it were united to us as a form, it would be inseparable. (118)

141. That the possible intellect is nothing in act before it understands, because in the case of an intelligible nature, to be something in act is to be actually understanding. (126)

142. That the possible intellect is simply inseparable from the body as regards that act which is the reception of species and as regards judgment, which comes about through the simple acquisition of species or the composition of intelligibles.—This is erroneous if understood of every kind of reception. (122)

143. That a man is said to understand to the same extent that the heaven is said to understand, or to live, or to move of itself, that is, because the agent performing these actions is united to him as mover to moved and not substantially. (14)

144. That from knower and known there results one substance, inasmuch as the intellect is intelligence itself formally. (127)

145. That the intellectual soul by knowing itself knows all other things; for the species of all things are co-created with it. But this knowledge does not belong to our intellect in so far as it is ours but in so far as it is the agent intellect. (115)

146. That the fact that we understand less perfectly or more perfectly comes from the passive intellect, which he says is a sensitive power.—This statement is erroneous because it asserts that there is a single intellect in all men or that all souls are equal. (187)

147. That it is improper to maintain that some intellects are more noble than others because this diversity has to come from the intelligences, since it cannot come from the bodies; and thus noble and ignoble souls would necessarily belong to different species, like the intelligences.—This is erroneous, for thus the soul of Christ would not be more noble than that of Judas. (124) [*187*]

148. That the science of master and disciple is numerically one. The reason for which the intellect is thus one is that a form is multiplied only because of the fact that it is educed from the potency of matter. (117)

149. That the intellect of the dead Socrates does not have the science of those things of which it once had science. (41)

ON THE HUMAN WILL

150. That that which by its nature is not determined to being or non-being is not determined except by something that is necessary with respect to itself. (128)

151. That the soul wills nothing unless it is moved by another. Hence the following proposition is false: the soul wills by itself.—This is erroneous if what is meant is that the soul is moved by another, namely, by something desirable or an object in such a way that the desirable thing or object is the whole reason for the movement of the will itself. (194)

152. That all voluntary movements are reduced to the first mover.—This is erroneous unless one is speaking of the simply first, uncreated mover and of movement according to its substance, not according to its deformity. (209)

153. That the will and the intellect are not moved in act by themselves but by an eternal cause, namely, the heavenly bodies. (133)

154. That our will is subject to the power of the heavenly bodies. (162)

155. That a sphere is the cause of a doctor's willing to cure. (132)

156. That the effects of the stars upon free choice are hidden. (161)

157. That when two goods are proposed, the stronger moves more strongly.—This is erroneous unless one is speaking from the standpoint of the good that moves. (208)

158. That in all his actions man follows his appetite and always the greater appetite.—This is erroneous if what is meant is the greater in moving power. (164)

159. That the appetite is necessarily moved by a desirable object if all obstacles are removed.—This is erroneous in the case of the intellectual appetite. (134)

160. That it is impossible for the will not to will when it is in the disposition in which it is natural for it to be moved and when that which by nature moves remains so disposed. (131)

161. That in itself the will is undetermined to opposites, like matter, but it is determined by a desirable object as matter is determined by an agent. (135)

162. That the science of contraries alone is the cause for which the rational soul is in potency to opposites, and that a power that is simply one is not in potency to opposites except accidentally and by reason of something else. (173)

163. That the will necessarily pursues what is firmly held by reason, and that it cannot abstain from that which reason dictates. This necessitation, however, is not compulsion but the nature of the will. (163) [*188*]

164. That man's will is necessitated by his knowledge, like the appetite of a brute. (159)

165. That after a conclusion has been reached about something to be done, the will does not remain free, and that punishments are provided by law only for the correction of ignorance and in order that the correction may be a source of knowledge for others. (158)

166. That if reason is rectified, the will is also rectified.—This is erroneous because contrary to Augustine's gloss on this verse from the Psalms: *My soul hath coveted to long*, and so on [Ps. 118:20], and because according to this, grace would not be necessary for the rectitude of the will but only science, which is the error of Pelagius.³ (130)

167. That there can be no sin in the higher powers of the soul. And thus sin comes from passion and not from the will. (165)

168. That a man acting from passion acts by compulsion. (136)

169. That as long as passion and particular science are present in act, the will cannot go against them. (129)

ON ETHICS OR MORAL MATTERS

170. That all the good that is possible to man consists in the intellectual virtues. (144)

171. That a man who is ordered as to his intellect and his affections, in the manner in which this can be sufficiently accomplished by means of the intellectual and moral virtues of which the Philosopher speaks in the *Ethics*, is sufficiently disposed for eternal happiness. (157)

172. That happiness is had in this life and not in another. (176)

173. That happiness cannot be infused by God immediately. (22)

174. That after death man loses every good. (15)

175. That since Socrates was made incapable of eternity, if he is to be eternal it is necessary that he be changed in nature and species. (12)

176. That God or the intelligence does not infuse science into the human soul during sleep except through the mediation of a heavenly body. (65)

177. That raptures and visions are caused only by nature. (33)

178. That by certain signs one knows men's intentions and changes of intention, and whether these intentions are to be carried out, and that by means of these prefigurations one knows the arrival of strangers, the enslavement of men, the release of captives, and whether those who are coming are acquaintances or thieves. (167)

179. That natural law forbids the killing of irrational animals, although not only these. (20) [*189*]

II

ERRORS IN THEOLOGY

ON THE CHRISTIAN LAW

180. That the Christian law impedes learning. (175)

181. That there are fables and falsehoods in the Christian law just as in others. (174)

182. That one does not know anything more by the fact that he knows theology. (153)

183. That the teachings of the theologian are based on fables. (152)

184. That what is possible or impossible absolutely speaking, that is, in every respect, is what is possible or impossible according to philosophy. (146)

ON THE DOGMAS OF THE CHURCH

185. That God is not triune because trinity is incompatible with the highest simplicity; for where there is a real plurality there is necessarily addition and composition. Take the example of a pile of stones. (1)

186. That God cannot beget his own likeness, for what is begotten has its beginning from something on which it depends; and that in God to beget would not be a sign of perfection. (2)

187. That creation should not be called a change to being.—This is erroneous if understood of every kind of change. (217)

188. That it is not true that something comes from nothing or was made in a first creation. (185)

189. That creation is not possible, even though the contrary must be held according to the faith. (184)

190. That he who generates the world in its totality posits a vacuum, because place necessarily precedes that which is generated in it; and so before the generation of the world there would have been a place with nothing in it, which is a vacuum. (201)

191. That the natural philosopher has to deny absolutely the newness of the world because he bases himself on natural causes and natural reasons, whereas the faithful can deny the eternity of the world because he bases himself on supernatural causes. (90)

192. That the theologians who say that the heaven rests at one time or another argue from a false supposition, and that to say that the heaven exists and does not move is to utter contradictories. (100) [*190*]

193. That it is possible for a universal deluge of fire to come about naturally. (182)

194. That a material form cannot be created. (192)

195. That without a proper agent, such as a father and a man, God could not make a man. (35)

196. That to make an accident exist without a subject has the nature of an impossibility implying contradiction.[4] (140)

197. That God cannot make an accident exist without a subject or make more than one dimension exist simultaneously.[5] (141)

198. That an accident existing without a subject is not an accident except in an equivocal sense, and that it is impossible for quantity or dimension to exist by itself, for this would make it a substance. (139)

199. That since God is not related to beings as a material or formal cause, he does not make an accident exist without a subject, inasmuch as it is of the nature of an accident to exist actually in a subject. (138)

ON THE CHRISTIAN VIRTUES

200. That no other virtues are possible except the acquired or the innate. (177)

201. That one should not be concerned about the faith if something is said to be heretical because it is against the faith. (16)

202. That one should not pray. (180)

203. That one should not confess except for the sake of appearance. (179)

204. That one should not care about burial. (155)

205. That simple fornication, namely, that of an unmarried man with an unmarried woman, is not a sin. (183)

206. That a sin against nature, such as abuse in intercourse, is not against the nature of the individual, although it is against the nature of the species. (166)

207. That the pleasure in sexual acts does not impede the act or the use of the intellect. (172)

208. That continence is not essentially a virtue. (168)

209. That chastity is not a greater good than perfect abstinence. (181)

210. That perfect abstinence from the act of the flesh corrupts virtue and the species. (169)

211. That humility, in the degree to which one does not show what

he has but depreciates and lowers himself, is not a virtue.—This is erroneous if what is meant is: neither a virtue nor a virtuous act. (171)

212. That one who is poor as regards the goods of fortune cannot act well in moral matters. (170) [*191*]

ON THE LAST ENDS

213. That death is the end of all terrors.—The statement is erroneous if it excludes the terror of hell, which is the last. (178)

214. That God cannot grant perpetuity to a changeable and corruptible thing. (25)

215. That it does not happen that a corrupted body recurs numerically the same, and it will not rise numerically the same. (17)

216. That a philosopher must not concede the resurrection to come, because it cannot be investigated by reason.—This is erroneous because even a philosopher must *bring his mind into captivity to the obedience of Christ* [cf. II Cor. 10:5]. (18)

217. That to say that God gives happiness to one and not to another is devoid of reason and fictitious. (23)

218. That nothing can be known about the intellect after its separation. (120)

219. That the separated soul in no way suffers from fire. (19)

NOTES

1. The Latin text reads: *Quod omnes scientiae sunt necessariae, praeter philosophicas disciplinas, et quod non sunt necessariae nisi propter consuetudinem hominum.*

2. Boethius *De Consolatione Philosophiae* v. Prose 2.

3. Pelagius, a British or perhaps Irish lay monk who came to Rome and then to North Africa at the beginning of the fifth century, opposed Augustine's doctrine of grace and free will on the ground that, by extolling divine grace, it minimized man's responsibility and jeopardized the entire moral order. He was condemned by the Councils at Carthage in 416 and 418. Pelagianism, the heresy to which he gave his name,

was again censured at the Council of Ephesus in 431.

4. Propositions 196–199 are directed implicitly against the theological doctrine of the Eucharist, which states that the accidents of bread and wine are left without any subject of inherence once the substance of the bread and wine has been converted into the body and blood of Christ. See Thomas Aquinas *Summa Theologiae* Part III, Questions 75–77.

5. The allusion is to the teaching according to which the quantity of Christ is present in the Eucharist despite the fact that the quantity or dimensions of the bread remain unchanged. See Thomas Aquinas, *ibid.*, Question 76, article 4.

19.

Roger Bacon

OPUS MAIUS:

MORAL PHILOSOPHY

Translated by Richard McKeon, Donald McCarthy, and Ernest L. Fortin

The details of Roger Bacon's life (*ca.* 1214/9–1292) have been the subject of much discussion in recent years. The place and the exact date of his birth are in doubt. He received his early education at Oxford and came to Paris *ca.* 1240, where he was one of the first to lecture on the natural treatises and the *Metaphysics* of Aristotle. On his return to Oxford *ca.* 1247, he attended the lectures of Adam Marsh and came into contact with Robert Grosseteste, for whom he always professed the greatest admiration. A considerable change appears to have taken place in his intellectual life at this time. For the next ten years he devoted himself wholeheartedly to the study of the various disciplines, including mathematics, languages, and experimental science. In 1257 or thereabouts, he entered the Franciscan Order but was never ordained to the priesthood. His new duties as a Friar seem to have necessitated some curtailment of his scientific work. A new milestone in his career was reached when, through his own overtures, his work was brought to the attention of Cardinal Guy de Foulques, later Pope Clement IV (1265). The latter asked to be supplied with a copy of his philosophic writings. Bacon, who had as yet composed no major treatise on philosophy, conceived the ambitious project of an encyclopedic work (the *Scriptum Principale*) embracing the whole of knowledge, but was forced to abandon the idea in favor of a work of more modest dimensions since known as the *Opus Maius*. This was followed by the *Opus Minus* and the *Opus Tertium*, which summarize and complement the teachings of his major work. All three books were written within a period of eighteen months and dispatched to Clement IV. Clement's death in 1268 deprived the author once and for all of the papal approval and financial support on which he relied for his projected reform of learning in the Church. Bacon was later condemned and imprisoned by his own superiors because of certain suspected novelties related to his astrological and alchemical pursuits, but not, it seems, because of any definite heresy. Contrary to what has been said, he was not involved in the condemnation of 1277. Neither his convictions nor his combativeness were affected by these disciplinary measures. Traces of his bitterness at the vexatious treatment meted out by his superiors and of the sharp invectives against the vices and ignorance of the clergy, with which his *Compendium Philosophiae* and other earlier writings abound, are still apparent in his last (unfinished) work, the *Compendium Studii Theologiae* (1292).

The *Opus Maius,* on which Bacon's fame chiefly rests, is a long plea (*persuasio*) designed to win Clement IV over to his views concerning the necessity of a vast educational reform. It attempts to co-ordinate the various branches of learning and vindicates for the sciences their legitimate place in the university curriculum. By the author's own repeated admission, it is written for, and uses methods and arguments suited to, "wise men," as opposed to the vulgar or the herd, for whom a simple and crude presentation of the truth is all that is needed or possible. The whole work is divided into seven parts dealing respectively with the causes of error, the relation of the profane sciences to theology, the study of languages, mathematics, optical science, experimental science, and moral philosophy. The part on moral philosophy is itself made up of six parts, the contents of which are grouped under two general heads described by the author as the "speculative part" and the "practical part" of moral philosophy. Accordingly, the first half deals with the broad principles of morality

within the traditional framework of man's relation to God (Part One), to his neighbor (Part Two), and to himself (Part Three). The second half treats of the belief in, or acceptance of, the true religion (Part Four), the love and practice of that religion (Part Five), and, in a cursory manner, the question of forensic oratory (Part Six).

By his knowledge and extensive use of Arabic materials, Bacon provides a link between Islam and Christendom in the thirteenth century. Despite his professed admiration for the Arabic philosophers, however, his moral philosophy, like that of the Franciscan masters of his time, appears to be basically Augustinian in its approach and sets out to incorporate into the old scheme new elements borrowed from the sources recently made available to the Latin writers. As such, it stands in sharp contrast with the far-reaching innovations of his contemporary, Thomas Aquinas, and the new school of Christian Aristotelians.

Parts Five and Six of the *Moral Philosophy* were unknown until a comparatively recent date and are translated here (by Donald McCarthy) for the first time from the recent edition of that work by F. Delorme and E. Massa, *Rogeri Baconis Moralis Philosophia* (Turici: Thesaurus Mundi, 1953). The translation of the remaining selections (with the exception of Part Four, Second Distinction, III 16-V 3 and VI 1-6, translated by the editor) is that of Richard McKeon, *Selections from Medieval Philosophers* (New York: Charles Scribner's Sons, 1930). II, 81-106, revised in the light of the new edition of Bacon's text. It should be noted that the Delorme-Massa edition, to which the italic numbers in brackets in the text refer, is based largely on Bacon's own manuscript (*Vat. Lat.* 4295), discovered by A. Pelzer in 1919, and represents a substantial improvement over earlier editions of the *Moral Philosophy.*

MORAL PHILOSOPHY

PART ONE

[PROEMIUM]

1. I have shown in the preceding parts that the knowledge of languages, and mathematics, and perspective as well as experimental science are extremely useful and particularly necessary in the pursuit of wisdom. Without them no one can advance as he should in wisdom, taken not only absolutely but relatively to the Church of God and to the other three sciences described above. 2. Now I wish likewise to go over the roots of the fifth science, which is better and more noble than all those previously mentioned; and it is the practical one among them all, that is, the operative one, and it deals with our actions in this life and in the other life. In fact, all other sciences are called speculative. For although certain of them are active and operative, nevertheless, they are concerned with artificial and natural actions, and they consider the truths of things and of scientific activities that have reference to the speculative intellect, and they are not related to things pertaining to the practical intellect, which is called practical because it directs *praxis*, that is, the operation of good and evil. 3. Whence the term "practical" is taken here in a restricted sense as applying to the activities of morality in accordance with which we become good or evil; although if "practical" is taken in a broad sense for all operative science, many other sciences are practical; but this one is called practical by antonomasia because of the chief operations of man, which are related to virtues and vices and to the happiness and misery of the other life. [4]

4. This practical science, then, is called moral and civil science, which places man in his proper order to God and to his neighbor and to himself, and proves these orders and invites and moves us to them efficaciously. For this science is concerned with the salvation of man, which must be accomplished through virtue and happiness; and this science aspires to that salvation so far as philosophy can. From these things, it appears in general that this science is more noble than all the other parts of philosophy. For since it is the inward end of human wisdom and since the end is what is most noble in anything, this science must of necessity be the most noble. 5. Besides, this science alone or in the

highest degree treats of the same questions as theology, because theology considers nothing other than the five subjects mentioned above, although in another manner, namely, in the faith of Christ. However, this science, too, contains many outstanding testimonies for the same faith; and it scents from afar the principal articles for the great aid of the Christian faith, as what follows will declare. But theology is the most noble of the sciences; therefore, this one, which agrees in the highest degree with it, is more noble than the others. In order that the very great utility of this science may be apparent, its parts must be investigated to the end that what we wish may be drawn from the parts and from the whole.

6. Moreover, since moral philosophy is the end of all the parts of philosophy, the conclusions of the other sciences must be the principles in it in accordance with the relation of preceding sciences to those that follow, because the conclusions of the preceding are naturally assumed in those that follow. And therefore, it is fitting that they be carefully proved and certified in the preceding sciences, that they may be worthy of acceptance in the sciences that follow, as is evident from metaphysics. 7. Therefore, the principles of moral philosophy are certified in the preceding sciences; and for that reason these principles should [5] be drawn from the other sciences, not because they belong to those sciences, but because these sciences have prepared them for their mistress. Whence, wheresoever they may be found they must be ascribed to moral philosophy, since in substance they are moral. And, although they may be repeated in the other sciences, it is by the grace of moral philosophy. Wherefore, all things of this sort must be reckoned as moral philosophy and ascribed to it. Therefore, if we wish to use them according to their right, they must be brought together in moral science from all the other sciences.

8. Nor is it strange if philosophers have spread moral philosophy through all speculative philosophy: because they knew that it is of the salvation of man; and therefore, they have mixed beautiful doctrines in all the sciences, that men might always be moved to the good of salvation, and that all might know that the other sciences are to be sought after only for this one science, which is the mistress of human wisdom. 9. Therefore, if I adduce authorities from other places than those that are contained in the books on morals, it must be considered that they should properly be placed in this science; nor can we say that they have not been written in the books of this science, since we do not have except in part in Latin the philosophy of Aristotle, Avicenna, and Averroes, who are the principal authors in this science. 10. For just as theology understands that salvation-bringing truths belong to it, wheresoever they be found, as was stated in the beginning and touched

on later, so too moral philosophy vindicates as its own whatever it finds written elsewhere on things of this sort.

11. Moreover, this moral science is called by Aristotle and [6] by others civil science, because it shows the rights of citizens and of cities. And since it was common for cities to dominate regions as Rome ruled the world, for that reason this science is called civil from the city (*civitas*), although it is formed to construct the laws of the kingdom and the empire.

12. This science, moreover, teaches in the first place to draw up the laws and the rights of living; secondly, it teaches that these rights are to be believed and approved and that men are to be stimulated to act and live according to these laws. The first part is divided into three sections; for first comes naturally the relation of man to God and in respect to the angelic substances; secondly, his relation to his neighbor; thirdly, to himself, as the Scripture states. 13. For in the first place in the books of Moses are the commands and laws concerning God and divine worship; in the second place, concerning the relation of man to his neighbor in the same books and those that follow; in the third place, there are instructions concerning customs, as in the books of Solomon. In the same way in the New Testament, these three alone are contained. For man cannot assume other relations.

14. Not only because of the first but because of all those that follow, it is necessary that the principles of this science, by which the others are verified, be set forth in the beginning. Of these principles, however, there are some that are purely principles and are capable of being stated only metaphysically. 15. Others, although they are principles with respect to the sciences that follow, are nevertheless either first conclusions of this science [that is, morals], or else, although they enjoy some of the privilege of a principle, still because of their extreme difficulty, and because they are highly controversial, and because of their excellent utility in respect to the sciences that follow, they should be sufficiently established; just as Aristotle in the beginning of his *Natural Philosophy* proves the first [7] principle of that science, namely, that there is motion, against those who suppose only the one immovable being.[1] 16. It should be noted, however, that metaphysics and moral philosophy agree with each other to the highest degree; for both have to do with God and angels and eternal life and with many subjects of this sort, although in different ways. For metaphysics investigates metaphysically the things that are proper to it by means of what is common to all the sciences, and it inquires into spiritual things by way of the corporeal, and through created things it finds the Creator, and through the present life it treats of the future life, and it sets forth many preambles to moral philosophy. 17. Hence, lest I should confuse different sciences with each other by

trying to prove here what is proper to metaphysics, I shall repeat here only the things that metaphysics investigates for the sake of civil science, so that, as is proper, I may join this science with metaphysics, in so far as what is assumed here is explained in metaphysics.

I

1. I state, therefore, that God must be, just as He must be shown to be in metaphysics. Second, that all men know naturally that God is. Third, that God is of infinite power and of infinite goodness, and together with that, that He is of infinite essence and substance, so that it follows thus that He is best, wisest, and most powerful. Fourth, that God is one in essence and not many. Fifth, that not only is He one in essence but three in another manner, which has to be explained in general by metaphysicians, but here it must be explained in its proper discipline. 2. Sixth, that He has created all things and governs them in the being of nature. Seventh, that besides corporeal things He has formed [*8*] spiritual substances, which we call intelligences and angels; for intelligence is the name of a nature, and angel is the name of a function; and how many they are and what their operations are, as it pertains to metaphysics, as far as it is possible for them to be known by human reason. Eighth, that besides angels He made other spiritual substances, which are the rational souls in men. Ninth, that He has made them immortal. 3. Tenth, that there exists the happiness of another life, that is, the highest good. Eleventh, that man is capable of this happiness. Twelfth, that God governs the human race in the way of morals just as He governs other things in the being of nature. Thirteenth, that God promises future felicity to those who live rightly in accordance with the governance of God, as Avicenna teaches in Book X of the *Metaphysics*,[2] and that a horrible future infelicity is due those who live evilly. 4. Fourteenth, that worship is due God with all reverence and devotion. Fifteenth, that as man is ordered naturally to God through the reverence due Him, so he is ordered to his neighbor by justice and peace, and to himself by honorableness of life. Sixteenth, that man cannot know by his own effort how to please God with the worship due Him, nor how he should stand in relation to his neighbor nor to himself, but he needs the revelation of truth in these things. 5. Seventeenth, that the revelation must be made to one only; that he must be the mediator of God and men and the vicar of God on earth, to whom is subjected the whole human race, and in whom one must believe without contradiction when it has been proved with certitude that he is such as I have just described him; and he is the lawgiver and the high priest who in spiritual and in temporal things has the plenitude of power, as a

"human God," as [9] Avicenna says in Book X of the *Metaphysics,* "whom it is permissible to adore after God."[3]

6. By these principles metaphysics is continuous with moral philosophy and comes down to it as its end; thus Avicenna joins them beautifully at the end of his *Metaphysics.* The other principles, however, are peculiar to this science and are not to be explained in metaphysics, although Avicenna adds a number of them. But in the beginning of his volume he gives the reason for this: that he had not constructed a moral philosophy and he did not know whether he would complete one; and therefore he mixed with these metaphysical principles many that are nevertheless proper to moral philosophy, as is evident to the inquirer. 7. And once these have been considered, the legislator should then at the beginning take up the properties of God in particular, and of angels, and the happiness and the misery of the other life, and the immortality of bodies, and things of this sort to which the metaphysician could not aspire. For the metaphysician treats in all these principally of the question of whether the thing is; because it is proper for him to take up that question in regard to all things, in that he considers that which is and being in their common properties. 8. But the other sciences take up other questions involved in things, namely, what each one is, and of what kind, and how much, and other questions of this sort, in accordance with the ten categories. The moral philosopher, however, has to explain, not all the secrets of God and of the angels and of others, but those that are necessary to the multitude, on which all men should agree, lest they fall into doubts and heresies, as Avicenna teaches in the "Roots of Moral Philosophy."[4]

II

1. I say, therefore, that moral philosophy explains first the Trinity in relation to God, which truth the legislator has by revelation [10] rather than by reason. The reason, indeed, why philosophers have said a great deal concerning divine things in particular, which exceed human reason and fall under revelation, was touched on before. For it was shown how they could have many noble truths concerning God that were had through a revelation made to them, as the Apostle says, *for God revealed* [these things] *to them* [Rom. 1:19], but more completely to the patriarchs and the prophets who, it is known, had revelation and from whom the philosophers learned all things, as was proved clearly above. 2. For the patriarchs and the prophets not only treated divine things theologically and prophetically but also philosophically, because they devised and taught all philosophy, as was proved in the second part of this work. The metaphysician, however, was able to teach sufficiently

that God is, and that He is known naturally, and that He is of infinite power, and that He is one, and that He is three. But how the Trinity is, he could not there explain to the full; and, therefore, that must be shown here.

3. There is, then, the blessed Trinity, the Father and the Son and the Holy Spirit. For Claudianus, one of the expositors of the sacred Scripture, in the book in which he combats the following heresy, that "God feels nothing with a sense of passion but with the affect of one who has compassion," brings forward this argument: Plato "with praiseworthy daring, admirable genius, unchangeable purpose, sought, found, and proclaimed three persons in the divinity: God the Father, also the paternal mind, art, or counsel, and the love of the two for each other. He taught thus not only that we must believe in one supreme equitrinal undivided divinity, but he demonstrated that He must be thus."[5] These things are clear from his book on divine things. [*11*] 4. Porphyry, too, as Augustine says in Book X of the *City of God*, spoke of "the Father and his Son," whom he called the "paternal intellect and mind," and "the medium of them, by whom," as Augustine says, "we think he meant the Holy Spirit";[6] and following our manner he called each one God, where, although he "uses words loosely," he sees nevertheless what should be maintained. And Augustine, in the same book, recounts that a certain philosopher, whose name he does not give, repeated the beginning of the Gospel according to John as far as the incarnation of Christ, in which the distinction of the divine persons is stated clearly.[7] Augustine, also in Book X of the *City of God*, insists that Porphyry says that sins cannot be purged except by the Son of God.[8] 5. And Aristotle says in the beginning of the treatise *On the Heaven and the World* that in divine worship we exercise ourselves to magnify the one God by the number three,[9] which is prominent in the properties of the things that were created. And therefore, since every creature, as is evident from the part on metaphysics, is a trace and imprint of the Trinity, there must be a Trinity in the Creator. And in the beginning of his treatise *On the Heaven and the World* he argues that there is a trinity inherent in all things because it exists in the Creator. And since Aristotle completed the philosophy of his predecessors to the limit of the possibility of his times, he had to feel far more certainly concerning the blessed Trinity of persons that he might confess the Father and the Son and the Holy Spirit. 6. For this reason there were three sacrifices in the law of Aristotle and three prayers, as [*12*] Averroes says in his commentary on the beginning of the treatise *On the Heaven and the World*;[10] and this is manifest from the *Politics* of Aristotle, which is a book of laws. Avicenna, moreover, the most outstanding expositor of Aristotle, assumes the Holy Spirit in the "Roots of Moral Philosophy."[11]

7. But he [that is, Aristotle] could perceive the truth concerning the

Father and the Son far better, because it is more difficult to understand the procession of the Holy Spirit from two distinct persons than the generation of one of them from the other. For this reason philosophers failed more in the comprehension of the Holy Spirit than in the knowledge of the Father and the Son. And therefore those who were able to have a knowledge of the Holy Spirit had far more knowledge of the other persons. 8. The philosopher Ethicus in his book on divine and human and natural things, which he wrote in the Hebrew, the Greek, and the Latin language, because of the greatness of the secrets, places in God the Father, the Word of the Father, and the Holy Spirit, and maintains that there are three persons, namely, the Father and the Son and the Holy Spirit.[12] This must also be held by reason. This reasoning, nevertheless, could not have been given before the things that have to be expressed of God in particular nor before the authorities of the moral philosophers, which are introduced to this same end in this science as in the place appropriate to them.

9. I say, therefore, that God is of infinite power; and infinite power is capable of infinite operation; therefore, something infinite can come from God, but not something different by its essence, because then there could be several gods, the contrary of which has been shown in the part on metaphysics. Therefore, that which is begotten of God must be God since it has the essence of its progenitor; but it is different in person. 10. And this which is begotten has infinite power, [*13*] since it is infinite good. Hence it can bring forth something infinite; hence it is able to bring forth another person. Either, then, the Father brings forth the same person and then the Holy Spirit will proceed from both of them; or He will be brought forth from the Son only, and in that case He will not be equal to the Father nor will there be a perfect kinship and proportion among the divine persons, which is contrary to reason. 11. Further, there cannot be parity of love according to this view, because the Father would love the Son more than the Holy Spirit, because He begets the Son and does not bring forth the Holy Spirit. But since the Holy Spirit is God, because He has the divine essence, an infinite love must be due Him; and therefore, the Father will love Him with an infinite love as He does the Son. And likewise because the love of the Father cannot be other than infinite, because His love is in accordance with His power, it remains, therefore, that the love of the Father for the Holy Spirit will be as great as the love of the Son for the Holy Spirit. Wherefore, the Holy Spirit as well as the Son must be brought forth from the Father.

12. That, however, there are not and cannot be more persons cannot and should not be explained here, but must be assumed until it is proved in the fourth part of this science [of morals], to which the full measure of the demonstration is assigned. But it was necessary that the Trinity

of persons, namely, of the Father and the Son and the Holy Spirit, be proved and expounded here because it is the radical foundation in this science for establishing divine worship and for many other things. 13. Nor should it be alleged in opposition that no science has to prove its principles. For how that is to be understood has been shown above. But other things that can be inquired concerning God and in [*14*] which there should be probable doubt, are conclusions of the fourth part and, therefore, will be determined there.

*   *   *

PART   TWO

I

1. The second part treats of the laws and statutes governing the relations of men among themselves. In the first place, the welfare of the human species is considered in the line of propagation, to bind people by laws in their increase. Therefore laws of marriage are given, and they determine how marriages must be made and how impediments are to be removed, and most of all, that fornicators and sodomites should be excluded from cities, for "they are inimical to the construction of the city," since "they draw men away from that which is better in cities, namely, marriage," as Avicenna and others maintain.[13]

2. Next, laws are given in accordance with which subjects are ordered to prelates and princes, and contrariwise, and servants to masters, according to every type of dominion and servitude; and laws are given in accordance with which the father of the family must live in guiding his offspring and family, and the master is ordered in respect to his disciples. Next, the doctors and the skilled in each of the sciences and arts are appointed; and those best suited to engage in studies and duties of this sort are chosen, according to the advice of wise men, from the youths who are to be instructed; and the rest are deputed to the military service to execute justice and to check malefactors. 3. And "it is necessary," as Avicenna says, "that this be the first intention in instituting the law, namely, to order the city in three parts, that is, into disposers, ministers, and those learned in the law, and that in each of them someone in charge be appointed. After him, other officials inferior to him should be appointed, and after these still others, until few remain; to the end that [*40*] no one should be useless in the city and not have some praiseworthy function, and that some utility to the city may be derived from each one."[14] 4. Whence, in Plato, that city is said to be most justly ordered in which each disregards his own proper desires. Therefore, as Avicenna

says, the prince of the city should prohibit "idleness and disoccupation." "As for those who cannot be curbed, they should be expelled from the city, unless the cause is infirmity or old age; and then a place should be set apart in which people of that sort should remain and have a procurator allotted to them."

5. "It is necessary, moreover, that there be in the city a certain place for the moneys of the commonwealth, which should be derived partly from the law governing contracts, partly from fines that are inflicted for punishment, partly from the estates and spoil of rebels, partly from other sources; and to the end that this public fund be available partly for those who cannot earn money for themselves because of infirmity and old age, and partly for teachers of the law and partly for public uses."[15]

6. And then, the legislator instructs men to make patrimonies and inheritances and testaments, because Avicenna says that the substance "necessary for life is partly the branch and is partly the root. But the root is the patrimony and anything bequeathed and given by testament, of which three roots the most secure is patrimony."[16] The branch of substance, however, comes from gains derived from kinds of business.

7. Then laws should be published concerning contracts in every kind of business, in buying, selling, leasing, hiring, borrowing, lending, paying, saving, and the like, "that whatever can do harm in contracts may be removed," as Avicenna says.[17]

Then, laws must be framed in accordance with which it may be shown in all lawsuits [41] and in all cases what is right or wrong, and by means of which legal processes may be terminated, that peace and justice may be fostered among the citizens.

8. Then, as Avicenna says, activities "by which inheritances and fortunes are lost" and by which the peace and concord of citizens are disturbed, must be prohibited; and the practitioners of these activities are "the people who wish to win for the sake of some gain, such as the wrestler, the gambler," and others of this sort. "In the same way, activities should be prohibited that lead to things contrary to the utilities," as, for instance, "teaching how to steal and plunder,"[18] and other things of this sort.

9. And further ordinances should be made, as Avicenna says, "that men aid and defend each other, and that they be unanimous in fighting against the enemies of the law." "If, however, there be another city or kingdom of good constitutions and laws, this is not opposed to it, unless the time should come when there must be no other law than this one, the establishment of which, since it is the best, must then be extended throughout the whole world." And in this statement the Christian law is hinted at, as will be explained below. "If, however, there should be some among them who are at variance with the law, they should first be

corrected that they may return to their senses; but if they do not wish to do that, let them be put to death."[19]

II

1. The last point that is required here is that the legislator "set up a successor to himself." This is done, according to Avicenna, in the following manner. He should do it "with the consensus of the nobles and of the people; and he should choose such a one as can rule well and be prudent and be of good morals, brave, kind, skilled [*42*] in governing and learned in the law, than whom none is more learned, and this should be manifest to all.

2. "But if thereafter they should so disagree that they wish to choose another, they have in that denied God; and therefore the legislator should interpose in his law enactments to the effect that the entire city should fall unanimously upon anyone who should wish to intrude himself by power or money and should kill him. But if they shall be able to do this and shall not have done it, they have in that contradicted God, and he is not guilty of blood who kills one of this sort, provided, however, it is previously known to the people."[20] If, on the other hand, he who is to be made successor is not worthy and has been so proved, another should be appointed.

3. And so in a summary way the design of the roots [or fundamentals] of this second part [of moral philosophy] and of those matters that proceed from such fundamentals are brought to a close. In this part is comprehended the civil law, which is now in use among the Latins, as is manifest from the roots of this part. Moreover, it is certain that the Latins have derived their rights and laws from the Greeks, that is, from the books of Aristotle and Theophrastus, his successor, as well as the laws of the twelve tables, which were taken first from the laws of Solon the Athenian.

PART   THREE

[PROEMIUM]

1. The third part of moral and civil science is concerned with the conduct of each person relative to himself, that everyone may have honorableness of life and may abandon the foulness of vices because of future

happiness and the horror of eternal punishment. That this should be the third part appears clearly, since it is plain that that part which contains the worship of God is first, as has been declared. The common good, moreover, is set before the private good, as Aristotle says in Book VII of the *Metaphysics*. But the preceding part has to do with the common good, whereas this part advances the private good. For charity is the greatest virtue, and it is ordered to the common good, and concord and peace and justice attend it, which virtues go beyond the morals of individual persons. For man is a social animal and it is one of his properties, as Avicenna says in Book V of his treatise *On the Soul* and in the "Roots of Moral Philosophy," that he should not live alone like the brute animal which in its life suffices to itself alone.[21] Therefore, the laws that order men to their neighbor are the more important.

2. According to the same Aristotle and to Averroes, [46] in Book X of the *Metaphysics*, the hermit, who is not part of the city but is concerned with himself alone, is neither good nor evil.[22] And Cicero, in his book *On Duties*, quoting the words of Plato, says that Plato wrote very truly: "We are not born for ourselves alone; our native land claims part of our origin, our friends part, and, as the Stoics are pleased to believe, all things are created for the use of men, and men are generated for the sake of men, that they may be able to aid one another."[23] As Cicero himself, in Book V of the *Academics*, says, "Nothing is so noble as the communication of benefits."[24] It is, in fact, innate in man "that he have something of the civil and the popular, which something the Greeks call *politikon*."[25] Hence, in the book *On the Happy Life*, Seneca says, "This word is required of man that he aid men; if he is able to, many; if he is less able, a few; if still less, his neighbors; if less, himself."[26]

3. Wherefore, the second principal part of moral philosophy must be concerned with common laws, as has been stated; and the third will be on the life and the honesty that each one should pursue. This, moreover, is true according to the order of the dignity of nature and absolutely speaking, although Aristotle does not adopt this manner in his books, for he proceeds according to the way of investigation and hence from the things that are better known to us and not from those better known to nature. But since we have already made certain through him and others what the power of this science requires, we can arrange its parts according to the order that the dignity of nature demands.

4. And here the philosophers have said wondrous things concerning virtues and vices; so that every Christian may be confounded when we conceive that unbelievers had such sublimities of virtues, [47] whereas we seem to fall ignominiously from the glory of virtues. For the rest, we should be greatly encouraged to aspire to the apex of virtue, and, stirred by noble examples, we should give forth more noble fruits of

virtues, since we have greater aid in life than those philosophers, and since we are assured we shall receive greater aids beyond comparison by the grace of God. I shall first repeat certain things relating to virtues and vices in general; secondly, I shall pass on to particulars.

*   *   *

PART FOUR

FIRST DISTINCTION

[PROEMIUM]

1. I have dwelt at length on this third part of moral philosophy because of the beauty and utility of moral teachings and because the books from which I have gathered these roots, flowers, and fruits of morals are rarely found. Now, however, I wish to go on to the fourth part of this science, which, although it is not so copious and so pregnant as the third, is nevertheless more wonderful and more worthy, not only than that part, but than all the preceding parts, since it consists in establishing that the true religion, which the human race should accept, is worthy of belief and approval.

2. Nor is there any branch of philosophy more necessary for man or of so great utility or dignity as the fifth part of this science, which teaches to love and acknowledge by works the religion to which we have already assented. For it is especially on account of these parts that all sciences are subordinated to moral philosophy. In fact, all wisdom is ordered with a view to knowing the salvation of the human race; and this salvation consists in the perception of the things that lead man to the happiness of the other life. Avicenna says of this happiness that it is such "as eye has not seen nor [*188*] ear heard,"[27] as has been touched on above. 3. And since Parts Four and Five of moral philosophy purpose to investigate this salvation and to attract men to it, all the sciences, arts, and functions, and whatever falls under the consideration of man, are bound to this part of the noble consideration of civil science. 4. For this reason it is most useful to consider the intention of these parts, and it belongs to every Christian to do so for the confirmation of his profession and that he may have wherewith to correct those who have wandered astray. Assuredly, God can never deny to the human race a knowledge of the way of salvation, since according to the Apostle He wishes all men to be saved.[28] And His goodness is infinite; wherefore He has always left men means by which they may be enlightened to know the way of truth.

*   *   *

SECOND DISTINCTION

[PROEMIUM]

1. Having set forth these principal religions in respect to the use of peoples as well as in respect to the ways of astronomy and in respect to the diversities of their ends, the consideration proceeds to the means of persuading men of the truth of religion.

I

1. It was said earlier in the part on mathematics, in relation to the conversion of unbelievers, that the persuasion of the true religion, which is the Christian religion alone, is brought about in a twofold manner: either by miracles, which are beyond us and beyond unbelievers, and concerning this way no man can presume; or else by a way common to unbelievers and to us, which is in our power and which they cannot deny, because it proceeds by the ways of human reasoning and by the ways of philosophy. Philosophy is indeed proper to unbelievers, since we have derived the whole of philosophy from them, and not without the greatest reason, that we may have confirmation of our faith for ourselves and that we may pray efficaciously for the salvation of unbelievers. [*196*] 2. Nor should the statement of Gregory be urged in objection, that "faith has no merit where human reason lends proof."[29] For this statement must be understood of the Christian man who would lean only or principally on human reason. But this should not be done; on the contrary, he must believe in the Church and the Scripture and the saints and the Catholic doctors, and that he should do principally. 3. But for the solace of human frailty, that it may avoid temptations and errors, it is useful for the Christian to have effective reasons for the things that he believes, and he should have a reason for his faith ready for everyone who requires it of him, as the blessed Peter teaches in his first Epistle, saying, *But sanctify in your hearts Christ as Lord; being ready always to give answer to every man that asketh you a reason concerning the faith and hope that is in you* [I Pet. 3:15]. 4. But we cannot argue here by quoting our law nor the authorities of the saints, because unbelievers deny the Lord Christ and His law and saints. Wherefore it is necessary to seek reasons in another way, and this way is common to us and to unbelievers, namely, philosophy. But the power of philosophy in this part accords with the wisdom of God; indeed, it is the trace of the divine wisdom given by

God to man, that by this trace man may be moved to divine truths. 5. Nor are these things proper to philosophy, but are common to philosophy and theology and to believers and unbelievers, given by God and revealed to philosophers, to the end that the human race might be prepared for special divine truths. And hence the reasons of which I speak are not unrelated to faith nor outside the principles of faith, but are dug from its roots, as will be manifest from what we have to say.

6. I could, of course, set forth the simple and crude methods suited to the common run of unbelievers, but that is not worthwhile. For the vulgar is too [*197*] imperfect, and therefore the argument of faith that the vulgar must have is crude and confused and unworthy of wise men. I wish, therefore, to go higher and give an argument of which wise men must judge. For in every nation there are some men who are assiduous and apt to wisdom, who are open to rational arguments, so that once they have been informed, persuasion through them of the vulgar is made easier.

7. I assume in the beginning, of course, that there are three kinds of knowledge: one is in the effort of personal discovery through experience; another is through teaching; the third precedes these, and is the way to them, and is called natural knowledge because it is common to all. 8. That, in fact, is natural which is common to all individuals of the same species, as burning is natural to fire, according to the example of Aristotle himself in Book V of the *Ethics*;[30] and Cicero says this same thing in Book I of the *Tusculan Questions*,[31] and we see it in an infinite number of examples. For we say the cries of brutes signify naturally because they are common to the individuals of their species; and things are known naturally by us of the sort in which we all agree, as that "every whole is greater than its part," and others of this sort, both simple and complex. 9. We know likewise that the rational soul is formed to know the truth and to love it, and the proof of this love is the exhibition of action, according to Gregory[32] and all the saints and philosophers. There are some, however, who think that there are two parts in the soul, or two powers, so that there is one by which the soul knows the truth, another by which it wills to love the truth known. 10. Others, on the other hand, believe that the substance [*198*] of the soul is one and that it performs both functions, because these acts are ordered to each other, in that the knowledge of truth exists on account of the love for it; for one and the same power, according to them, first apprehends the truth and then loves it and is completed in action. 11. Hence Aristotle holds, in Book III of the treatise *On the Soul*, that the speculative intellect becomes practical by the extension of knowledge of truth to the love of it.[33] Nor does he ever make a specific difference between the speculative intellect and the practical as he does between the intellect and the senses and the vegetative soul. 12. For he argues, in Book II of the treatise *On the Soul*, that these

three are diverse in species, because their operations are diverse in species, that is, understanding, perceiving, and vegetating; nor are they ordered in relation to one another.[34] But the knowledge of truth is ordered toward the love of it, and it is formed because of it; and therefore the power, or nature, or substance of the rational soul that knows the truth and loves it is one. 13. Hence in Book III of the treatise *On the Soul*, Aristotle begins thus: "However, concerning the part of the soul with which it knows and judges, I must now speak,"[35] meaning that it is the same part that has both functions, just as in the sensitive part, because it is the same power that knows and desires, as is evident in every sense; for the sense of touch knows the hot and desires it, and the sense of taste knows flavors and desires them, and so with the others. But it is not of great moment how we speak of these [that is, the senses]; for we know that the rational soul is formed to know and to love the truth.

14. But the truth of religion is perceived only so far as the knowledge of God abounds in one, for every religion is referred to God; and therefore he who wishes to arrive at certain knowledge of religion must begin with God. But the knowledge of God, so far as concerns the question of whether He is, is known to all naturally, as [*199*] Cicero teaches in his book on the immortality of the soul; and he proves this by saying, "No nation is so savage and monstrous that its mind has not been imbued with an opinion of God, nor is there a people that does not show some form of divine worship."[36] 15. But if Avicenna says in Book I of the *Metaphysics* that "this science seeks to establish the being of God by demonstration,"[37] it must be said that this is true as regards full certitude. For the natural knowledge that anyone has of God is weak, and it is weakened by sins, which are numerous in anyone, for sin obscures the soul especially as regards divine things. Therefore, it is necessary that this knowledge be aided by argument and faith.

16. But the knowledge of the unity of God, and of what God is, and how, and of what sort, is not possessed naturally. For in these matters men are always in disaccord, some maintaining several gods, others considering that the stars are gods, others, things here below, as do even now the pure pagans and the idolaters. And so they must err in religion. All others who say that there is one God do not understand other points that are true of God. 17. And therefore one who advances a religion must know at the outset how to present the attributes that are required of God in general. However, it is not necessary that he go into all the particular truths in the beginning; rather he should proceed little by little and he should begin with the easier questions in this way. For as the geometer sets down his definitions, that the things he deals with may be known in respect to what they are and what they are called, so one must proceed here, because unless one knows what it is that is meant by a name, there will be no demonstration.

18. Let us then call God the first cause, antecedent to which there is no other, which did not emerge into being, and will not be capable of ceasing to exist, of infinite power, wisdom, and goodness, creator of everything and director of everything, according to the natural capacity of each individual thing. And in this definition Tartars, Saracens, [*200*] Jews, and Christians agree. The wise men also among the idolaters and the pagans, when they have been given the reason for this, cannot contradict it; nor consequently can the multitude, over whom the wise men stand as directors and leaders. 19. For two ways of arguing to this end will be presented for them: one by the consensus of all other nations and religions. But the lesser should conform itself to the greater part, and the part that does not accord with its whole is disgraceful. It is clear that there are wiser men in the other religions; and the pagans and the idolaters are not ignorant of this. 20. For when a meeting is arranged with them, they are convinced easily, and they perceive their own ignorance clearly, as appeared in the case of the emperor of the Tartars who summoned before him Christians, Saracens, and idolaters to confer on the truth of religion, and forthwith the idolaters were confounded and convinced. This fact is evident from the book *On the Practices of the Tartars* addressed to our Lord the present King of France. 21. And when Christians confer with pagans, like the Pruceni and the other nations, they yield easily; and once they have been convinced, they believe and see that they are held by errors. The proof of this is that they are most willing to become Christians if the Church were willing to permit them to retain their freedom and to enjoy their goods in peace. 22. But the Christian princes who labor for their conversion, and most of all the brothers of the Teutonic house, wish to reduce them to servitude, as is known to the Preachers and the Friars Minor [that is, the Dominicans and the Franciscans] and other good men throughout Germany and Poland; and, therefore, they offer opposition. Hence they stand against oppression, not against the arguments of a better religion.

*   *   *

III

16. Besides, the power to know in man does not suffice for the bodies of this world and sensible objects, as is evident to anyone. For no one knows truly and adequately the nature of a single thing, however small, as, for example, one small plant or fly or some other object, and we observe an infinite discord among wise men in regard to the natures of corporeal beings. Much more, then, will man err in regard to insensible things, such as the spiritual substances and the state of the other life,

and especially in relation to the things that pertain to God and to God's will. 17. For this reason it is necessary that he have revelation. Aristotle says to this effect in Book II of the *Metaphysics* that in relation to things such as these, which are most manifest in themselves, our intellect is like the eye of a bat or an owl in relation to the sun.[38] 18. And Avicenna says in Book V of the *Metaphysics* that in relation to the things that belong to the Lord of the ages in His kingdom, man is like a person deaf from birth in relation to pleasurable harmonies and like a paralytic in relation to tasty food.[39] Hence man will not be able to arrive at certitude concerning these things, any more than the bat, the owl, and the paralytic concerning the things mentioned. 19. Furthermore, Alfarabi says in the "Morals" on this subject that "in relation to the divine truths a wise man is like an untaught child in relation to a man most wise by human wisdom; and so he will not be able to advance except through teaching and revelation." And he adds that "if man could attain by himself the truths of divine religion, then the world would not need [*210*] revelation and prophecy; but these," as he says, "have been granted to the world and are necessary."[40] Hence man cannot know these truths by himself. 20. This is also clearly taught by Avicenna in the "Roots of Moral Philosophy" when he states that "the revelation of religion must necessarily be made by God" and that "mortal man cannot rise to these immortal things,"[41] in accordance with what Seneca says in his book *On the Tranquillity of the Soul,* namely, that man is too mortal for immortal things.[42]

21. Then just as man cannot attain to these things by himself, so he must not presume to prove these things by himself without revelation and instruction; rather he should believe for three reasons. One reason consists in this, that the things that belong to the other world, and especially God's will and what pertains to God, are of infinite dignity; hence they are not commensurate with human misery. 22. Nor is man worthy of striving to explore them by his own power so as to understand them; that is why it suffices for him to believe the one who instructs him. Indeed, he is not even worthy to believe these things because of his sins and his wretchedness; let him rejoice then that he is taught by another, but not unless it is by God or by angels on God's authority. It is evident, therefore, that man should not attempt to inquire into these divine truths before he is taught and believes. 23. Moreover, God Himself knows infinitely better and with greater certitude the things that belong to Him than a creature could ever know them; and the authority and wisdom of God are infinite, and no human authority or wisdom can compare with them, especially with respect to the things that belong to God. It remains, therefore, that the authority of God alone should be sought, since His goodness is infinite and by it He wills to reveal to the human race what is necessary for salvation.

24. And beyond doubt we see this realized in the religions, namely, that all men believe that they possess their religions through revelation. [*211*] This is indeed plainly the case with Christians and Jews. The Saracens, too, believe that Muhammad received a revelation, and he himself claimed as much, for otherwise he would not have been believed; and if he did not receive this revelation from God, he received it from the demons. 25. The Tartars likewise maintain that God revealed their religion, as is written in the book already mentioned and as is certain. In like manner, the idolaters and the pagans believe that God should reveal what pertains to those religions, for otherwise man would not believe man in this matter; for every man who propounds a religion ascribes his authority to God so that he may more easily be believed.

IV

1. Since then such is the case, we must further argue that revelation should be made to only one perfect lawgiver and that a single perfect law should be given by God. And this is apparent because of divisions and heresies. For if there were several heads, the human race could not be united, since everyone strives to uphold his own view. 2. Moreover, since there is one God and one human race, which must be regulated by the wisdom of God, this wisdom must receive its unity from the two-fold unity just mentioned, or otherwise it would not be conformed either to one God or to one human race. If, indeed, there were several gods and several worlds, and, so to speak, several human races, then there could be several divine wisdoms; but it is impossible that there be many gods and many worlds; and hence it is impossible that the wisdom of God should be multiple. 3. Moreover, since the perfect religion should make known to man whatever he has to know about God and whatever is useful to man, it follows that another religion either will be superfluous if it teaches the same things, or will be erroneous if it promulgates contrary teachings. For this reason there can be only one perfect and trustworthy religion and, likewise, [*212*] only one lawgiver who receives it from God; for, if religion is one, the lawgiver is also one and vice versa. This is what Avicenna teaches in his "Roots of Moral Philosophy" as well as Alfarabi in his "Morals."[43] 4. For, as Avicenna says, there must be a single mediator of God and man, the vicar of God on earth, who receives the law from God and promulgates it, and of whom Alfarabi says that he cannot be a liar, once it is established that he comes by an inspiration from God. Once we have ascertained this truth, his word must remain unquestioned; nor should his statements be subjected to any further examination or consideration; rather he should be fully believed.

V

1. Now that this has been established, we must ask who should be proclaimed as the lawgiver and which religion should be propagated throughout the world. The principal rites, as we have said, are six. The first is that of the pagans, who live by custom alone and have no priests, but each man is his own teacher. 2. The second rite is that of the idolaters, who have priests and agree on certain regulations and assemble in one place at proper hours to perform their solemn rites; for they have large bells, like the Christians, as we have already learned. The idolaters also differ from the pagans in that they worship man-made objects, whereas the pagans worship natural things such as groves, rivers, and the like in endless number. 3. The third rite is that of the Tartars, who cultivate philosophy and the magic arts; the fourth is that of the Saracens; the fifth, that of the Jews; the sixth, that of the Christians. There are no other major religions in this world, nor will there be any others until the religion of the antichrist.

*　　*　　*

V I

1. Now one can establish that the Christian law should be preferred in the following ways. First, by means of the teachings of the philosophers indicated above in the application of mathematics to the Church and in the first part of the *Moral Philosophy*. For there noble testimonies are given concerning the articles of the Christian faith, namely, the Trinity, Christ, the Blessed Virgin, the creation of the world, angels, souls and the judgment to come, eternal life, the resurrection of bodies, the pains of purgatory, the pains of hell, and the like, which are found in the Christian religion. 2. Philosophy, however, does not agree in this manner with the religion of the Jews and of the Saracens, nor do the philosophers provide testimonies in their favor. Hence it is evident that, since philosophy is a preamble to religion and disposes men to it, the religion of the Christians is the only one that should be held. [*215*]

3. Moreover, the philosophers not only pave the way for the Christian religion, but destroy the two other religions; for Seneca, in the book that he composed against the religion of the Jews, shows in many ways that it is most irrational and erroneous in that it is bound by the letter alone, in accordance with the belief of the carnal Jews who thought that it suffices for salvation. 4. The Saracen philosophers also find fault

with their own law and calculate that it will quickly come to an end. Avicenna, in Book IX of the *Metaphysics*, takes issue with Muhammad because he spoke only of corporal pleasures and not of spiritual pleasures.[44]

5. Albumazar, too, in Book I of the *Conjunctions*, teaches that that religion will not last longer than 693 years;[45] and 665 years have already elapsed; and he asserts that it can come to an end in less time, as we mentioned earlier in the part on mathematics. It is also clear that the Tartars have nearly obliterated the entire dominion of the Saracens from the north, the east, and the west as far as Egypt and Africa, in such a way that the Caliph, who occupies the position of the Pope among them, was destroyed thirteen years ago, and Baghdad, the city of this Caliph, was captured along with an infinite multitude of Saracens.

6. But we can see this same thing in another way through the Sibyls. For, as we have made clear earlier, these Sibyls were proclaiming that Christ is God, and they set forth all the main articles of the Christian religion; but they offer no testimony in favor of the others; on the contrary, they stated that this religion alone is conducive to salvation.

*   *   *

PART FIVE

[P R O E M I U M]

1. The articles of the fourth part of moral philosophy or civil science have now been treated, which part consists in persuading men to believe and receive the true religion.[46] Now follows the fifth part, which tries to persuade believers to love that religion, and to acknowledge it by appropriate works in the observance of laws and the goodness of morals, accompanied by the desire of future happiness; also, to shrink from, hate, and vigorously detest whatever is contrary to laws, virtues, and beatitude, and to turn away from them in action.

I

1. Now our feeble intellect has great difficulty with regard to these operables; for operables are more difficult to know than are the objects of speculative knowledge. Also our corrupt will finds them exceedingly hard to bear, and does not take pleasure in them. Further, our irascible power, to which the execution of these operations is due, fails to perform better than moderately well. 2. Nor is this surprising, since these are

the highest truths concerning God and divine worship, eternal life, the laws of justice and the glory of peace, and the sublimeness of virtues. Thus our intellect is related to them as a person deaf from birth is related to the pleasure of harmony, as Avicenna pointed out in Book IX of his *Metaphysics*,[47] or as the eye of a bat is related to the light of the sun, according to Aristotle in Book I of his *Metaphysics*.[48] 3. Further, our will, according to Avicenna, in the same place,[49] is related to them in the same way as a paralyzed person is related to tasty food, which, although presented to him, he still is not able to sense. Such is our condition with respect to the things now being treated; for we have been corrupted by sins and impeded by the grossness of our body and blinded by the sensible and temporal world, whereas these matters are eternal and beyond sensation. [*248*]

4. And this is true not only of this part of moral philosophy, but also of the fourth and sixth parts. For there are three speculative parts of moral philosophy, which teach one to speculate on the nature and number of the things one should know concerning God and divine worship, eternal life, civil laws, and morals; those are the first three parts of the present work, which are concerned with the composition of the religion of the faithful. 5. There are, moreover, three practical parts as well, which teach one how and in what way a man ought to be swayed to believe the things that are required in that religion [Part Four], how he ought to be swayed to the love and fulfilment of the law once he has believed and received it [Part Five], and, thirdly, how to sway either a judge or an adversary to consent to justice in the causes that arise between fellow citizens because of the complexity of legal cases [Part Six]. 6. Hence this practical half is related to the first half as the curing of the sick and the conserving of health, which are treated in the practical part of medicine, are related to that part of medicine which teaches what health is, and what are the various illnesses, and how many there are, and what are their symptoms, causes, medicines and other remedies, and their number. For even though a man knows all these things from books, that does not mean that he also knows how to practice. 7. For there are many physicians who know these matters quite well enough to lecture on them, and to discuss and explain them, but who still do not know the precautions and ways of practice; they therefore have a speculative knowledge of medicine, but not a practical one. This distinction is also true in the cure of the soul from sin and in the preservation of spiritual health, which consists in the devout worship of God, an ardent desire of future happiness, and in a love of and zeal for laws, justice, peace, and the goodness of virtues.

8. Now it should not be a matter of surprise that within this civil science two parts are distinguished, namely the speculative and the practical, even though the science as a whole is called practical in relation

to all the other sciences; for in every science there are somehow these two parts, as Avicenna teaches in [*249*] the beginning of his *Art of Medicine*;[50] likewise the man who translated Aristotle's *Ethics* from Greek into Arabic explicitly teaches that moral science has the parts we have explained. 9. For when the phrase "practical science" is predicated absolutely and most properly, it refers exclusively to the science of our moral operations, as moral; for the Greek word *praxis* is the same as the Latin word "operation." And in this case every other science is called speculative, since every other science speculates about the truth that has been stripped of the good. For truth is the end of the speculative, while good is the end of the practical, as Aristotle says in Book II of his *Metaphysics*.[51] 10. Therefore every science that does not teach us to be good is absolutely and properly speculative, and this applies to every other science except moral science. And only that science which teaches us to become good is absolutely and most properly practical; this applies, within the various parts of philosophy, to moral science, although the complete science about these matters is to be found in Sacred Scripture.

11. Still, the words "practical" and "speculative" are also used in another way, namely relatively and less properly. And so within moral science itself, that part is called "speculative" which considers the nature and number of the truths of that science; and since these truths are concerned with our operations, that part does not lose the name "practical" taken in its absolute sense; rather, it is called "speculative" because it does not itself extend to inducing men to act morally, nor does it designate the ways or precautions of action; rather, the practical part does this. 12. Now here I speak of three kinds of moral works: the first is to sway the mind to believe and receive the truths of religion; the principles of this work have already been laid down. The second is to sway the mind to the love and fulfilment of what is good, and to the hatred and avoidance of what is evil; the fifth part will treat of these matters. The third is to sway the mind of a judge or adversary to consent to justice when cases are pleaded; this work remains to be treated in the sixth part. [*250*]

II

1. Since, however, in our mortal corruption practical matters are far better, more difficult, less pleasant, and less operable [than are speculative matters], they require stronger remedies and inducements than do the speculative. Now the first remedy that can be humanly produced is some discourse that is able to incline the mind; and this discourse is an argument taken from a group of veracious arguments, and lacks fraud

or sophistry. 2. Now because of well-known works of Aristotle on these matters, we are familiar with two kinds of arguments, namely dialectical and demonstrative. A dialectical argument moves the speculative intellect to a feeble knowledge of truth, namely, to opinion, not to science; "for a demonstration is a syllogism that produces science," as Aristotle says,[52] and therefore perfects the speculative intellect in the knowledge of truth. 3. But moral philosophy "is not for the sake of speculation, but for the sake of becoming good," as he says in the beginning of Book II of his *Ethics*;[53] and in the same place he says that "science contributes little or nothing to virtue." Hence these scientific arguments do not suffice in moral philosophy; and this is true precisely of the practical part of this science. 4. Hence Aristotle, in Book I of his *Ethics*,[54] resolves that moral science does not have to use demonstration, but rhetorical argument. For it is equally erroneous, he says there, for moral science to use demonstration as it is for a mathematical science to attempt a rhetorical argument. For a demonstration does not sway the practical intellect to its operations; rather, it is essentially related to the speculative intellect, since it does not proceed beyond a knowledge of truth. And therefore dialectical arguments are likewise invalid in matters of morals and persuasion, since if there is no room in these matters for demonstration, then neither is there room for dialectical argument. For the end of it is demonstration, in that a dialectical argument prepares the way to demonstration; for we are aroused by an opinion of the truth in order that we may more easily [*251*] arrive at the science of it. Therefore these two kinds of argument are unable to sway the mind to good, but only to a knowledge of what is true.

5. Yet it is necessary that we be swayed to what is good; in fact, it is far more necessary that we be so swayed than that we be moved to the speculation of bare truth, since virtue and happiness are better and more necessary than mere science. Therefore it is necessary that we have stronger inducements [in practical matters]. Further, the practical intellect is more noble than the speculative. 6. Further, the practical intellect is related to what is good in a more difficult and less delightful way than the speculative intellect is related to truth; and therefore it is necessary that we have better and stronger inducements to sway us to assent to the truths concerned with the good of the soul, to perform them, and so that we might be inclined to justice in cases that are pleaded. But a rhetorical argument is effective in these matters; hence it is the sort of argument that we must choose. 7. This argument, however, is not known to the ordinary run of arts students among the Latins, because the books of Aristotle and of his commentators have only recently been translated and are not yet used by students. Now Ciceronian rhetoric does not teach this argument, except in terms of cases to be pleaded, in order that an orator might persuade a judge to agree with the orator's case and be

unfavorable to that of the adversary. But as I have pointed out, there are three kinds of swaying, and therefore this argument as taught by Cicero is inadequate; rather, we need the complete doctrine, found in Aristotle and his commentators.

8. Now this rhetorical persuasion to three moral works, namely to believe, to do, and to judge rightly, follows the general principles of eloquence, which are to render the hearer docile, well disposed, and eager. Therefore it is necessary to hold the hearer by pleasure so that he will become diligent and eager; for he who takes delight in moral matters, greatly benefits his fellow citizens. [252] 9. Likewise it is necessary to explain truth clearly, distinctly, briefly, and plausibly, and to untie the knotty questions and difficulties that occur, so that the hearer may be rendered docile and grasp with ease a truth that is proposed to him. And it is necessary, if he is to become well-disposed to believing, to doing, and to judging correctly, to propose useful things. For that discourse which takes away tediousness, leaves out difficulty, and promises usefulness, is the one that lays hold of the mind and sways it to the works we have been speaking of. 10. Hence, in the book *On the Condition of the World*, Cicero gives us the beautiful aphorism: "The ideal orator is the one who, when speaking, instructs the mind, gives it pleasure, and moves it deeply. To teach is obligatory, to please is voluntary, to move is indispensable,"[55] since, as Augustine explains, teaching and pleasure do not sway.

11. Hence Augustine, in Book IV of his treatise *On Christian Doctrine*,[56] gives an excellent explanation of this aphorism of Cicero when he says: the duty of an orator is "to teach, to delight, and to sway; 'to teach is a necessity, to delight is a sweetness, to sway is a victory.[57]'" 12. Now to teach is a matter of necessity because "perhaps once the things to be taught are learned, the hearers will be so moved by them that greater powers of eloquence will be unnecessary for them to be swayed; but persuasion should be brought in when the hearers know what is to be believed,"[58] done, and thought, and yet do not so believe, do, or judge as they should. "And therefore to sway is not necessary, since it does not always have to be performed."[59] But to sway is the victory, "since it is possible that hearers be taught and delighted,"[60] and still not believe, do, or be swayed to justice. 13. But just as the hearer understands if you speak clearly and distinctly and untie his doubts, "and is delighted if you speak sweetly, so also he is swayed if he believes what you exhort, loves what you promise, fears what you threaten, hates what you censure, embraces what you command, sorrows at what you hold to be sorrowful, rejoices when you preach something joyful, [253] commiserates with those you present as in misery, flees the things that, by inspiring fear, you propose as to be avoided,"[61] sympathizes and agrees with your case, if he is a judge, and looks down on your opponent's, "and whatever

else ought to be done through the grand style of eloquence in order to move the minds of the hearers."[62]

14. For there are three styles: the humble or simple style, the moderate style, and the grand style. The humble style is content with simple eloquence; the moderate style enjoys every rhetorical ornament; but the grand style leans heavily upon words that move one affectively. For teaching, the humble or plain style is required; to please requires the moderate style, and to sway, the grand. 15. Hence Cicero says: "An eloquent man is one who can speak simply about matters of little importance, temperately about matters of moderate importance, and grandly about great things."[63] "The word 'moderate' (*modicis*) is taken from the word 'measure' (*modus*); for we are speaking improperly when we use the word 'moderate' for what is small";[64] hence moderate things are in the middle. Therefore, of these three, teaching is the least, to delight is in the middle, and to sway is the greatest. 16. And therefore not only does the simple style consist in speaking of small things, the moderate style in pleading about moderate matters, and the grand style in persuading with regard to great things, but also teaching should be done in the humble style, delighting should be provided by a moderate style, and swaying stands in need of a magnificent eloquence; for teaching holds the lowest level, delighting the intermediate, and persuading the highest of all. 17. And therefore whatever is proposed for understanding, is presented in the humble style, which consists in a simple eloquence and which stands mainly upon obvious teachings, all complicated questions having been eliminated. But whatever is presented to be loved or hated needs a moderate style: a pleasurable one for objects to be loved, a dreadful one for what is to be hated. And whatever is proposed for action, needs words that move one affectively, whereby an affection is in a wonderful way turned into a fulfilment; and these affective words pertain rather to the grand style.

III

1. Now these conditions of rhetorical argument are common to all three parts of the practical half of moral philosophy, since each uses these [254] common principles. In moral matters this argument so surpasses all demonstration that in this half of moral philosophy one rhetorical argument has more strength than a thousand demonstrations; for a demonstration either does not move the practical intellect, or moves it only in a very incidental way, whereas a rhetorical argument moves it directly and absolutely, and is able to sway the mind—something that a demonstration cannot do. 2. This fifth part, however, uses rhetorical

argument more effectively than do the other two parts, since it teaches how to sway a mind to things more difficult and less pleasurable to human corruption than do the other parts. For believing is easy compared with doing, and doing the things that pertain to divine worship, civil laws, and virtues is more difficult than to be inclined to justice in cases that are pleaded. 3. For far more and greater things are found in the works of the fifth part than in the fourth or sixth parts, since the perfection of life consists in the works of this fifth part; for the fourth part teaches us to believe and to consent, the sixth to have compassion and to commiserate, whereas this part teaches us to acknowledge in actions the things that we perceive are to be believed, and that we judge are to be commiserated, so that we might fulfil all the works of mercy. 4. Many believe that assistance should be given to the needy, fewer feel compassion, and very few actually put their hand to the task. This is because it is good to believe that assistance should be given, but it is better to have compassion, and to give actual assistance is the best of all; but with regard to what is best we are very unmanageable and lacking in ability. 5. But no wonder, in view of the fact that the better things and even the good ones, being placed as they are on a positive level, are in many ways irksome and a cause of dread for human frailty. And therefore this fifth part teaches one to make arguments in behalf of beauty, in order to carry the mind to consent suddenly and before it has had time to foresee the opposite position, as Alfarabi teaches in his book *On the Sciences*.[65]

6. And because that is the case, the rhetorical argument is divided into [255] three species. The first species is concerned with the things that pertain to the faith and the proof of the true religion. Now among believers there are six principles in which that proof is rooted: the Church, Sacred Scripture, the witness of the saints, the abundance of miracles, the power of reasons, and the consensus of all Catholic teachers. As for persuading nonbelievers, attention is paid to many of these principles as well as to others, as was pointed out previously. The second species of rhetorical argument is concerned with the things that sway one to compassion for justice; these are dealt with in Cicero's rhetorical works. The third species is concerned with the things that sway us to action as regards divine worship, laws, and virtues. 7. The first two species are simply called "rhetorical," and they do not change this name. But the third species, which is persuasive in those matters considered by the present fifth part, while it is "rhetorical," is also called by its proper name "poetic" by Aristotle[66] and the other philosophers, since veracious poets use it in swaying men to the honesty of virtues; for,

> Poets wish to be useful or to give pleasure.[67]
> He who mixes the useful with the pleasant, wins all the votes.[68]

8. Hence good poets, such as Horace and those like him, desire to be

beneficial and to delight in order to sway men, but vain and gossipy poets, such as Ovid and his like, wish to delight without caring to be beneficial, and hence do injury to the honesty of morals.

9. But the unlearned are ignorant of the way of putting this argument together, since we do not have a Latin translation of Aristotle's book on the subject. Still, diligent ones can gather much of the sense of this argument through Averroes' commentary, and through the book of Aristotle that has been translated into Latin, although it is not in common use; in the beginning of this commentary, Hermannus, the translator, says that Aristotle's text was too difficult for him to translate. 10. Likewise, Horace's *Art of Poetry* is much [256] concerned with this argument, as also are Alfarabi in his work *On Science,*[69] Avicenna in the beginning of his *Logic,*[70] which the Latins possess, and Algazel in his *Treatise on Logic.*[71]

11. Now this argument always uses the grand style, since it always speaks of great and magnificent things, and therefore requires high-sounding language, especially when the mind is swayed to action. For the grand style is not required everywhere in persuasive speech; rather, the other styles should at different times be intermixed. For, "Nothing is pleasant if not freshened up by variety,"[72] because when one style is used constantly, it engages the hearer less, and he cannot stand the grand style at all points in persuasive speech; 12. for although the hearer should be moved by grandiloquence, still his attention cannot be held by it for long; nor is the speaker up to a continuous use of this style, since it exceeds the plainness of human frailty. Therefore other styles of speech are intermingled with grandiloquence, so that it may be tempered like the waves of the sea. But the grand style always dominates, since it is the most important in this sort of persuasion, and because great matters are at stake.

13. Now the other styles of speaking should be mixed in with the grand style, not only because "Sameness is the mother of boredom,"[73] but also because the things that are to be done have to be taught and teaching requires the simple style. Likewise, they must delight the hearer and hold his attention; hence the moderate style must be inserted in praise of the things that [257] should be praised and in censure of the things that should be rendered odious. 14. But the main thing is that affective words be increased, so that the will can be deeply moved. For discourse in the grand style uses the ornaments of the moderate style, but without being either overly interested or remiss in these matters. Nor is it here that we discover its intention; rather, it aspires mainly to sway the mind by vital and affective doctrines rather than by the cultivation of speech, just as an active soldier who is decorated with weapons of gold uses them to fight, not because they are gold, but because they are able to overcome the enemy. 15. Now an especially good example of this kind of eloquence

is to be found in Cicero's letter in which he wishes the Senate well after his year of exile;[74] in this letter we are shown a concrete example of the grand style at its peak, since, according to the teachings of the philosophers on eloquence, no man ever spoke in this way.

16. This kind of argument is made up of analogies drawn from the properties of things. Thus virtue is compared to light, cleanliness, and all good and beautiful things, while sin is compared to all that is ugly; for example, a sinner is called *a sow which, even after washing, wallows in the mire* [II Pet. 2:22], and when, after penance, he reverts to sin, he is compared to *a dog which returns to his vomit* [Prov. 26:11]. 17. Likewise, favorable things are compared to whatever causes delight, while unfavorable things are pictured as dreadful. Horace employs this comparison in his *Epodes* when he says:

> A well-prepared heart hopes for a change in bad times,
>   Fears a change in good times.
> It is the same Jove who brings back the horrid winter.[75]

For a wise heart does not place confidence in prosperity, nor does a magnanimous one despair in adversity, because it is the same God who reduces prosperity into adversity and adversity into prosperity, just as summer follows winter, and winter replaces summer. 18. The happiness of the other life [258] is compared to all things beautiful and favorable, while unhappiness, its contrary, is compared to every adversity and misery. Also inserted are words having an affective meaning, and which can sway one to the desire and fulfilment of what is good, and to the hatred of and flight from what is evil. 19. And according to what Avicenna teaches in his *Logic*, this kind of argument does not care about the truth or falsity of propositions, since it moves the practical intellect, not the speculative, as is clear when a sinner is called *a sow which, even after washing, wallows in the mire* [II Pet. 2:22]. That proposition is true, not according to the property of things, but by way of analogy.

20. But if the poetic argument is to be complete, then there is required, over and above the efficacious language that moves the ears and the magnificent teaching that sways the mind, a movement of the mind and an appropriate gesture of the body in keeping with the words of the teaching, so that the hearer will be moved more by the movements of the mind expressed by the body than by the teaching or language. 21. And therefore Valerius Maximus says in Book VIII: "The ornaments of eloquence consist in an apt pronunciation and a fitting movement of the body; and when the orator has learned these, he can use them to assault his hearers in three ways: by penetrating their ears, caressing their eyes, and entering their minds."[76]

IV

1. But since the usefulness of philosophy is clear only when it is drawn to what is divine, this part of philosophy can very beautifully be of service in divine matters, according to what is beautifully and magnificently taught by the saints, and especially Saint Augustine in Book IV of his treatise *On Christian Doctrine*. For the whole of Book IV is concerned with the present subject matter, and almost everything that I have said here is found in that book, in a philosophical mode. 2. And no wonder, since Augustine was an author and teacher of rhetoric before [259] he became a Christian, and he taught this science publicly, as is written in his life.[77] Whence neither Cicero nor Seneca nor any philosopher was able to attain to the dignity of eloquence that, according to Augustine, is found in sacred doctrine. 3. He says, therefore, that the humble and moderate styles have a place in temporal matters, but not in divine things, since they are the highest, except to the extent that the grand style of speaking requires the intermixture of the other two, for the reasons previously stated. "When," as he says, "the ecclesiastical orator urges something to be done, it is necessary that he not only teach in order to instruct and delight in order to hold one's attention, but also that he persuade in order to achieve the victory."[78] "Now this orator of ours, when he speaks of what is just, good, and holy, so acts that he will be heard with understanding, freely, and obediently."[79]

4. Hence, he says: "Since both what is false and what is true can be urged by the art of rhetoric, who dares to say that the defenders of truth ought to be unarmed against falsity, in such a way that those who urge falsity shall know how to render their hearers well disposed, eager, and docile, while this is not known"[80] by those who propose the truth? 5. "Should those who teach what is false teach briefly, aptly, and plausibly, while the teachers of truth speak so as to be boring to hear, hard to understand, and unpleasant to believe? Should those who lead the minds of their hearers into error frighten, sadden, exhilarate, and exhort with ardor, while the defenders of truth are sleepy, phlegmatic, and cold,"[81] using discourse that is diffuse like a child's, disconnected like a woman's, made ugly by an asinine crudeness, and which gives birth to hearers that are languid and lazy—a birth that is accompanied with dread? 6. And he says further: "What is better than a nourishing sweetness or a sweet nourishment?"[82] And, "Wherever I understand the authors of the Canonical Scriptures, not only does it seem impossible to be wiser than they, but also to be more eloquent.

. . . Nor should they speak in any other fashion. For just as there is one eloquence that is more in keeping with a youthful speaker, [*260*] and another one with age (for that should not be called eloquence which does not fit the speaker), 7. so also there is an eloquence that is in keeping with men who are most worthy of the highest authority, and plainly divine. It is with this eloquence that the authors of the Canon spoke, an eloquence that alone is fitted to them, and they to it. For the more humble it seems, the loftier it is, and it reaches its heights, not by its windiness but by its solidity. But wherever I do not understand them, their eloquence is not so obvious to me; still I have no doubts but that even there it is the same as where I do understand them."[83] 8. And, "What surprises and amazes me more is that they have so used this eloquence of ours that it is neither absent from them nor conspicuous in them. For it is necessary for them neither to reject it nor to make a display of it; and the first would be the case if they avoided that eloquence completely, the second, if it were easily discernible."[84] "For these works were not composed by human industry; rather, they were poured forth by the divine mind."[85]

9. Now the simple style of speech is used by Paul in the Epistle to the Galatians, where he says, *Tell me, you who wish to live under the Law, have you never read the Law? For it is written that Abraham had two sons, one by a slave woman, the other by a free woman*, and so on [Gal. 4:21–22]. For here he is content to use a simple eloquence, and so to teach he opens with a clause and resolves difficult questions. But he uses the moderate style when he says, in his First Epistle to Timothy, *Do not rebuke an elderly man, rather exhort him as you would a father; exhort young men as brothers, elderly women as mothers, young girls in all chastity* [I Tim. 5:1–2]. 10. He uses it again in his Epistle to the Romans: *I exhort you therefore, brothers, by the mercy of God, that you offer your bodies as a sacrifice which is living, holy, pleasing to God, and your reasonable service* [Rom. 12:1]; *having gifts according to the grace that has been given to us, whether prophecy, according to the proportion of faith, or ministry, in ministering, or he who teaches, in teaching, he who exhorts, in exhorting*, and so on [Rom. 12:6–8]. *Rejoice with those who rejoice*, and so on [Rom. 12:15]; *Render tribute to whom tribute is due*, [*261*] and so on [Rom. 13:7]; *The night is advanced, the day approaches*, and so on [Rom. 13:12]; *not in revelry*, and so on [Rom. 13:13]. For here we see the various distinctions of clausulae; also they are rendered beautiful and proper by what is appropriate, and they contain the praise and blame they speak of. 11. And we can discern his use of the grand style with similar ornamentation, in his Second Epistle to the Corinthians: *Our mouth is open to you, O Corinthians, our heart reaches out to you* [II Cor. 6:11]. Again, in his Epistle to the Romans: *Those whom He has*

predestined, them also He has called; and whom He has called, them also He has justified . . . and glorified [Rom. 8:30]. *Who will make accusations against the elect of God? It is God who justifies; who is it that will condemn?* [Rom. 8:33–34] For here we find a cultivation of speech that by means of the separation of clausulae renders each thing in a special way; also an affective speech is proposed, and a magnificent doctrine is strengthened. 12. And in the Epistle to the Galatians we find the grand style, but without this distinction of clausulae. The noble thought and the affective speech reveal this when he says: *My little children, with whom I am in labor again until Christ be formed in you! But I wish to be with you now and change my voice, for I am confused about you* [Gal. 4:19–20].

13. And so the whole of Scripture is dotted in various places with rhetorical ornaments, and we discern in it a common eloquence, in one place more, in another place less. For in the prophets, where the sense of God is contained in wondrous enigmas, this eloquence is tempered, just as a solar ray is by the darkening of a cloud, so that our eye may be able to gaze at it. For in this way the most profound truths about God, which lack proportion to our minds, become conformed to us through prophetic discourses of this sort. 14. For the mysteries of God can be manifested to us only if beforehand we are led through such sacred veils of the Law and the Prophets, as is taught by blessed Dionysius in his books,[86] and as is confirmed by the other saints, and as is also clear from Cicero's book *On the Condition of the World*,[87] where he describes the duty of an orator even more elegantly than he does elsewhere. [*262*]

15. This kind of eloquence, however, in the proclamation of sacred truths, ought to be expressed more by appropriate dispositions and gestures than by speech—even to the extent of tears, and especially by means of example, as Augustine teaches;[88] and the ecclesiastical doctor is capable of these things "more by the piety of orisons than by his faculty of oratory."[89] 16. Therefore he ought "to pray for himself and his audience, so that as a result he is a petitioner before he is a teacher."[90] And let him, right up till the hour of his talk, think about what is said in the Gospel, *Do not think about how or what you will say! For it is not you who speaks, but the Spirit of your Father who speaks in you* [Matt. 10:19–20].

17. And if eloquence is to be perfected, the orator, whether he be ecclesiastical or secular, should consider not only the things that pertain to himself and his subject matter, concerning which we have already spoken, but also the things that pertain to the hearer. 18. For this reason the illustrious philosopher Palladius, in his book *On Agriculture*, says: "The first part of prudence is to take into consideration the person of the one to whom you wish to speak";[91] for "what is

good for a heel does not cure an eye." Rather, it is necessary that the orator take a teaching and color it, first one way, then another, according to the diversity of his hearers in terms of dignity, office, fortune, age, constitution, morals, knowledge, and all the other things pertaining to personal differences.

19. Therefore, if those things that are pertinent to the speaker, to his subject matter, and to his hearer are considered, there are elicited both the form of the whole of persuasion in life and morals, and the manner of preaching and of divine reading. 20. This is what I wanted to indicate now, prior to my *Principal Work*.[92] Now these things, and the ones that the *Principal Work* requires, are known in two ways: in one way, through authors who teach this eloquence; in another way, through [*263*] those men who have put it into practice. 21. However, the book of Aristotle on poetic argument has not been translated; but we do have explanations of it in Latin by Averroes and certain others, as is clear from Alfarabi's work *On the Sciences*, and from the *Logic* of Avicenna and of Algazel. Also Augustine, in Book IV of his treatise *On Christian Doctrine*, gives us a rather full treatment of this kind of argumentation. 22. But the letters of wise men, on the other hand, instruct us by exhibiting this eloquence in the concrete; for example, Cicero's epistles, which he pleaded before emperors, the Senate, and other princes of the world, especially the one in which he wishes the Senate well after his year of exile, where we find an infinite example of eloquence.[93] 23. Likewise, we are instructed here by the letters of Seneca and of many other philosophers, and especially by the letters of Jerome, Augustine, and of other saints, who absorbed whatever belonged to the philosophers and were also instructed according to the teaching of the High God. [*267*]

PART SIX

1. The sixth part of moral philosophy, which is also the third and final part of that half which is called "practical," consists in the pleading of cases before a judge in order to sway the judge so well that as a result he is compassionate and favorable to the just party, and displeased with its adversary. But I hold myself to be excused both because of the great length of the present work and because of the greatness of your wisdom, which, even if it should abound in others, is here superior by reason of experience.

2. But this part is treated in its principles in Aristotle's book *On the Rhetorical Argument* and in Alfarabi's commentary on that book, both of which are to be found among the Latins, although almost no

one takes them into consideration. Also the rhetorical treatises of Cicero and Seneca teach in a particular way and in the proper discipline how to compose this sort of argument. 3. Also many have the habit of this argument, for example, jurists. But the first and original art has not up to the present been found among the Latins, except what was recently and poorly translated in the book of Aristotle and the commentary on it; for the fontal art concerning this argument is given only in logic, to which belongs the task of assigning the differences and conditions of arguments.

4. We do not, however, have the full mind of Aristotle in Latin; for Aristotle's book and the commentary on it were first translated from Greek into Arabic, and then from Arabic into Latin; and, besides, the translator told me that he did not know logic, and hence he waited a long time before translating the book, and finally omitted to translate into Latin the book *On the Poetic Argument*, the reason being that he did not understand that book, as he himself confesses in the prologue to his translation of Averroes' commentary. Still, a studious person can catch a faint scent of his views, even though he cannot taste them; for a wine that is decanted from a third vase retains little of its vigor.

NOTES

1. Cf. Aristotle *Physics* i. 2. 185ᵃ12 ff.

2. Avicenna *Metaphysics* x. 2 (442). (Numbers in parentheses after Avicenna's [*Healing:*] *Metaphysics* X refer to the pages of the Arabic text translated in Part One, Selection 6. Bacon quotes the Latin translation.)

3. *Ibid.* x. 5 (455).

4. *Ibid.* x. 2 (442-43).

5. Claudianus Mamertus *De Statu Animae* ii. 7.

6. Augustine *De Civitate Dei* x. 29; cf. *ibid.* x. 23.

7. *Ibid.* x. 29.

8. *Ibid.* x. 28.

9. Aristotle *De Caelo* i. 1. 268ᵃ14-15.

10. Averroes *In De Caelo* i. 2.

11. Avicenna *Metaphysics* x. 2 (442).

12. Ethicus *Cosmographia* i. 12.

13. Avicenna *Metaphysics* x. 4 (448).

14. *Ibid.* x. 4 (447).

15. *Ibid.* x. 4 (447).

16. *Ibid.* x. 4 (449).

17. *Ibid.* x. 5 (452).

18. *Ibid.* x. 4 (448).

19. *Ibid.* x. 5 (453).

20. *Ibid.* x. 5 (451-52).

21. Avicenna *De Anima* v. 1; *Metaphysics* x. 2 (441).

22. Aristotle *Metaphysics* ix. 4. 1055ᵇ21 ff.; Averroes *Metaphysics* x. 16.

23. Cicero *De Officiis* i. 7. 22.

24. Cf. rather Cicero *De Finibus* v. 23. 65.

25. Cicero *De Finibus* v. 23. 66.

26. Seneca *De Vita Beata* 30. 5.

27. Avicenna *Metaphysics* x. 2 (443).

28. Cf. I Tim. 2:4.

29. Gregory the Great *Homiliae xl in Evangelia* ii. 26. 1, in Migne, *Patrologia*

Latina, 76, col. 1197.

30. Aristotle *Nicomachean Ethics* v. 7. 1134^{b}25–27.

31. Cicero *Tusculan Disputations* i. 13. 29–30.

32. Gregory the Great *Homiliae xl in Evangelia* ii. 30. 1, in Migne, *Patrologia Latina*, 76, col. 1220.

33. Aristotle *De Anima* iii. 10. 433^{a}9–27.

34. *Ibid*. ii. 2. 413^{b}24–33.

35. *Ibid*. iii. 4. 429^{a}10–13. This text occurs at the beginning of Book III in Averroes and in the older Latin versions.

36. Cicero *Tusculan Disputations* i. 13. 30.

37. Avicenna *Metaphysics* i. 1.

38. Aristotle *Metaphysics* ii. 1. 993^{b}9–10.

39. Cf. Avicenna *Metaphysics* ix. 7.

40. Alfarabi, *Enumeration of the Sciences*, ch. 5, p. 109. (Page numbers refer to the Arabic text translated above in Part One, Selection 1. Bacon quotes the Latin translation.)

41. Avicenna *Metaphysics* x. 2 (442).

42. Cf. rather Seneca *De Otio* 5. 7.

43. Avicenna *Metaphysics* x. 5 (452–53); Alfarabi, *Enumeration of the Sciences*, ch. 5, p. 110.

44. Avicenna *Metaphysics* ix. 7.

45. Albumazar (Abū Ma'shar al-Balkhī, d. 886) *De Magnis Conjunctionibus et Annorum Revolutionibus ac Eorum Perfectionibus* (Augsburg, 1489) ii. 7.

46. *Secta* (literally: "sect"), which has been translated as "religion" throughout this Selection.

47. Avicenna *Metaphysics* ix. 7.

48. Aristotle *Metaphysics* ii. 1. 993^{b}9.

49. Avicenna *Metaphysics* ix. 7.

50. Avicenna *Codex Totius Medicinae* i. 1. 1.

51. Aristotle *Metaphysics* ii. 1. 993^{b}20–21.

52. Aristotle *Posterior Analytics* i. 4. 73^{a}24.

53. Aristotle *Nicomachean Ethics* ii. 2. 1103^{b}26-28.

54. *Ibid*. i. 1. 1094^{b}19-27.

55. Cicero *De Optimo Genere Oratorum* i. 3.

56. Augustine *De Doctrina Christiana* iv. 12. 27.

57. Cicero *Orator* 21. 69.

58. Augustine *De Doctrina Christiana* iv. 12. 28.

59. *Ibid*. iv. 12. 28.

60. *Ibid*. iv. 12. 28.

61. *Ibid*. iv. 12. 27.

62. *Ibid*. iv. 12. 27.

63. Cicero *Orator* 29. 101.

64. Augustine *De Doctrina Christiana* iv. 18. 35.

65. Alfarabi, *Enumeration of the Sciences*, ch. 2 (see the version of Gerard of Cremona in *Catálogo de las Ciencias*, ed. G. Palencia [Madrid, 1932], p. 140, ll. 15–26).

66. Cf. Aristotle *Poetics* ch. 2. 1148^{b}24–27.

67. Horace *Ars Poetica* 333.

68. *Ibid*. 343.

69. Alfarabi, *Enumeration of the Sciences*, ch. 2 (*Catálogo de las Ciencias*, pp. 139–40).

70. Avicenna *Logic* (Venice, 1508) fol. 2.

71. Algazel *Liber Logicae* (ed. P. Liechtenstein, 1506) fol. b4.

72. Cf. Publius Syrius *Sententiae* (ed. E. Woelfflin; Lipsiae, 1869) 82, n. 239.

73. Cf. Cicero *De Inventione Rhetorica* i. 41. 76. Also cf. Alan of Lille *De Planctu Naturae*, in Migne, *Patrologia Latina*, 210, col. 459A.

74. It is not clear whether Bacon is referring to Cicero's *Oratio Post Reditum in Senatu*, or to his letter to Atticus in which he describes his speech to the Senate, i.e., *Epistulae ad Atticum* iv. 1.

75. Horace *Epodes* ii. 10, 13-16.

76. Valerius Maximus *Dictorum et Factorum Memorabilium* viii. 10, preface.

77. Cf. Possidius *Vita Sancti Augustini* 1.

78. Augustine *De Doctrina Christiana* iv. 13. 29.

79. *Ibid*. iv. 15. 32.

80. *Ibid*. iv. 2. 3.

81. *Ibid*. iv. 2. 3.

82. *Ibid*. iv. 5. 8.

83. *Ibid*. iv. 6. 9.

84. *Ibid*. iv. 6. 10.

85. *Ibid*. iv. 7. 21.

86. Cf. Dionysius *De Divinis Nominibus* 1.

87. Cicero *De Optimo Genere Oratorum* (?).

88. Cf. Augustine *De Doctrina Christiana* iv. 5. 7; 27. 60.

89. Augustine *De Doctrina Christiana* iv. 15. 32.

90. *Ibid*. iv. 15. 32.

91. Palladius *De Re Rustica* i. 1.

92. Bacon always intended to compose a *Scriptum Principale*.

93. See note 74.

20.

Giles of Rome

ON ECCLESIASTICAL

POWER

Translated by Joseph Sheerin

Giles of Rome (Aegidius Romanus, 1246/7–1316), who may have been a member of the illustrious Colonna family, entered the Augustinian Order at an early age and made his way to France, where he studied under Aquinas during the latter's second stay in Paris (1269–71). There is reason to suspect that he was implicated as an accomplice of Aquinas in the condemnation of 1277. After a few years in Italy, he returned to France and was called upon to pronounce the eulogy of Philip the Fair when the young king arrived in Paris after his consecration at Reims (1285). Because of Tempier's opposition, Giles did not receive the degree of doctor of theology until 1285, despite the fact that he had become eligible for it some five years earlier. He eventually became Superior General of the Augustinian Order and, later, archbishop of Bourges (1295). He died at Avi-

gnon. His numerous works include commentaries on the *Sentences* of Peter Lombard and on Aristotle, as well as various exegetical and theological treatises. A well-known contemporary, Godfrey of Fontaines, acclaimed him as the greatest teacher in the University of Paris. His book *On the Government of Princes (De Regimine Principum)*, composed at the request of Philip the Bold for his son, Philip the Fair, was one of the most widely read political works of the middle ages. It was often re-edited and was translated into several languages (French, Italian, Hebrew, Spanish, and perhaps Portuguese and English). Dante alludes to it in his *Convivio* (iv. 24).

Giles' treatise *On Ecclesiastical Power (De Ecclesiastica Potestate)*, composed in 1301/2, is perhaps the most thorough defense of unlimited papal supremacy written by a theologian in the middle ages. Its avowed aim is to claim for the Pope the greatest extension of power and jurisdiction in all areas of human life, and to make these prerogatives known to the entire Christian people. The treatise is divided into three books. Book I examines ecclesiastical authority in relation to the material sword and secular power. Book II studies the same authority in relation to temporal goods. Book III attempts to answer the objections that may be raised against the position upheld by the author. Although a disciple of Augustine (the Christian authority most often quoted in the treatise) and of Aquinas, Giles goes far beyond both of his masters in his vigorous defense of papal absolutism. His views in this matter are more akin to those of Hugh of St. Victor and Roger Bacon. The treatise *On Ecclesiastical Power* was widely used by contemporary and subsequent promoters of papalist or curialist views. It provided the foundation for Boniface VIII's famous bull, *Unam Sanctam* (1302), which marked the zenith of the papal ecclesiastical polity in the middle ages.

The following is the first English translation of Book II, chapter 6, of Giles' treatise. The translation follows the critical edition of that work by R. Scholz: Aegidius Romanus, *De Ecclesiastica Potestate* (Weimar, 1929), pp. 60-70. The italic numbers in brackets in the text refer to the pagination of the Scholz edition.

BOOK   TWO

CHAPTER   VI

That earthly power [*61*] both in itself and in what pertains to it rightly and properly serves the spiritual power because it is more particular, because it prepares its materials, and also because it attains what is best more remotely.

In various chapters of this short work we have tried to state more clearly how earthly power, because it rules over temporal matters, is rightly and properly subject to the spiritual power, so that from this we may be able to infer that the spiritual power rules not only over the temporal power but also over temporal matters, inasmuch as the ecclesiastical authority is shown to have dominion over both temporal matters and their rulers.

Now in the title of this chapter we have indicated three reasons, as it were, by which our thesis may be manifested, all of which are derived from what we see in other powers. Indeed, lest some people find it possible to oppose us in this matter, we wish to show by means of what we see in other powers that earthly power ought to be subject to the spiritual power, so that from this we may further conclude that earthly and temporal things themselves come under the jurisdiction and domination of the church. And from this it will be possible to show further that, by divine disposition, these two powers are so related to each other that one does not hinder but rather helps the other, and that one does not take away the other's right, but each one, observing the proper measure, enjoys and uses its own right. Thus, if the earthly power serves the spiritual power, it is not thereby deprived of its own right, since it is rightly and properly required to serve the spiritual power. And if, for a just and urgent cause, the church were to inject itself into the affairs of the empire or into the empire itself, even if, for a just and urgent cause, it were to transfer the empire itself, in so doing it would not be committing an injustice toward anyone, since this belongs to it by right and since no one who uses his right is said to commit an injustice. For, as we were saying in the preceding chapter, the strictness of ecclesiastical power requires that it possess all things by ruling over them, but, in order to be freer to attend to spiritual things, that it have no earthly possessions in the sense that it would concern itself with them. Rather it commits the concern of these temporal things to laymen. Nevertheless, for a just and urgent cause, as we have proved by the authority of Bede, this strictness can at times intervene; and thus the church rightly injects itself into temporal matters and into the things that pertain to the right of the empire.

Let us therefore get down to our thesis by explaining what is contained in the title of the chapter. In order to do this, we shall distinguish four kinds of powers, and in each case we shall show that some powers are higher and some lower and likewise that in each case the lower powers serve the higher. By way of describing power, then, let us say that power is nothing other than that by which something is said to have the capacity to act. Just as whiteness is that by which something is said to be white and blackness that by which something is said to be black, so power is that by which someone is said to have the capacity to act.[1] [*62*]

Now we see that natural causes have the capacity to act by means of natural powers; fire, for example, can heat by means of heat and of the heating power that it possesses, and water can cool by means of its cooling power, and the heaven by means of its power can affect the things here below. Each natural thing, then, has the capacity to act by virtue of its power and its potency. And just as natural causes are capable of acting by virtue of natural powers, so artists are capable of acting by means of the arts. Thus the lute player can play the lute properly by virtue of the art of lute-playing, whereas the man who lacks this art cannot do so. Thirdly, wise men are capable of exercising their activity by means of the sciences. Thus one becomes capable of knowing the parts and properties of mobile bodies by means of natural philosophy, and one becomes capable of contemplating and knowing what is explained in the other sciences by means of these sciences. Finally, rulers are capable of acting by means of the ruling powers, whether these ruling powers be material or spiritual; and so each one enjoys his own right and rules in virtue of his own ruling power.

Thus we have distinguished four kinds of powers: one kind is the natural powers, another is the arts, a third the sciences, and a fourth the powers by which men are ruled and governed. And each one of these powers consists in a certain order or proportion: the natural power consists in the rightly ordered production of natural effects; the artistic power consists in right reason with regard to, or the ordered making of, artifacts; the scientific power consists in right reason with regard to the consideration of knowable things; and the ruling powers consist in ordered or right reason as regards the government of men. And because we have undertaken the present treatise for the purpose of dealing with certain points concerning these very ruling powers, which are indeed powers of a certain kind, we have to examine the other powers. In the degree to which we shall gain an insight into these other powers, we shall be able to clarify certain points pertaining to rulers and to the governments of men.

Thus we see that among the natural powers some are higher and others lower. The heavenly powers, for example, are higher than those of the elements, inasmuch as the powers of the elements do not act except by the power of the heaven; for, as natural philosophy teaches, fire does not or could not generate fire save by the power of the heaven; and so the heaven and fire generate fire. And what we have said of the elements also applies to the compounds of elements, so that, according to the order that we see, a horse [63] would not be able to generate a horse save by the power of the sun. The same holds for the other animals: sun and horse generate a horse, and sun and lion generate a lion, as is explained in the study of natural things. Therefore, the heavenly power, being more common and universal, dominates all the other powers, whether they be those of the elements or those of the compounds of elements.

Just as in natural things we see that some powers are higher and others lower, so too in the arts some are higher and others lower; for instance, there is an art of bridle-making and there is likewise an art that consists in knowing how to make use of an army; and these two arts are not to be regarded as equals. Rather one is subordinated to the other: the art of bridle-making is subordinated to the art of warfare and thus makes such bridles as are useful to the soldier. It is not in this way, however, that the powers here below serve the heavenly powers; for, whereas the art of bridle-making serves the art of warfare in that it prepares its materials, the lower powers serve the heavenly powers in that they exercise a more limited causality. For it is proper to the heaven that its causality extends to all things and that it assists all things. Indeed, it assists the elements and the compounds of elements; it helps water to cool, fire to heat, horses to generate horses, lions to generate lions. For neither the horse, nor the lion, nor the other compounds could produce anything naturally save by the power of the heaven; and neither water, nor fire, nor the other elements could produce anything save by the power of the heaven.

The power of the heaven is therefore general and hence it rules; the powers of the agents here below, which are either elements or compounds, are particular and hence they serve. In the arts, on the other hand, the reason and cause for which bridle-making, for example, serves warfare is to be found, not in the fact that it is a particular agent, but rather in the fact that it prepares its materials, inasmuch as bridles could be made for many other animals besides horses, which are not used in battle or in warfare. Thus, although these lower agents are particular powers in relation to the heaven and so cannot do anything save by the power of the heaven, nevertheless it is not necessary that bridle-making be particular in relation to warfare to the extent of not producing anything except what is useful to soldiers. However, bridle-making does serve warfare by preparing its materials and, in so doing, it orders itself and the things that pertain to it to warfare. We shall say then that a horse is a certain material with which the soldier works, but it is not a material prepared and disposed to serve the soldier unless it has a bridle, just as a ship would not be disposed to serve a sailor unless it had a mast. Bridle-making thus serves warfare by preparing its materials; so also stonecutting serves housebuilding by disposing its materials, for, in preparing his materials, the stonecutter follows the requirements of the builder.

Thus we have indicated the reasons and causes for which in nature and in the arts one agent serves another. As to the sciences, we can indicate a third reason and cause for which one serves the other: [64] each one of the sciences discovered by the human mind serves metaphysics not only because metaphysics is more general and more universal than the other sciences but also because it attains what is best more perfectly. Indeed, among the sciences discovered by the human mind, metaphysics is able to study God, who is the most perfect of beings, better than any other science. And hence, since theology attains what is best more perfectly than metaphysics and any particular science, it is the queen of the sciences and engages all the sciences in its service, so that metaphysics itself is its handmaiden and servant. For metaphysics or any science discovered by the human mind studies God only in so far as He can be known by the light of reason, whereas theology studies God as He is known with the help of divine revelation. And since more can be known—as indeed it is—about God by revelation than by unaided reason, it follows that theology attains what is best more perfectly and that it is capable of knowing more about God than any other science. For this reason it is the goddess and queen of the sciences, and they are all her servants. Hence it has them all summoned as hand-maidens to the citadel and walls of the city, so that all may defend the citadel and walls of the city—that is to say, so that all may defend theology, which we refer to as a kind of citadel and a kind of walled city—and keep it from being attacked by its enemies. That is why in the Canticle it is likened to the tower of David, *which is girt with bat-tlements on which hang all sorts of bucklers and all the shields of valiant men* [Song of Songs 4:4], designed to prevent the arguments of philos-ophers from breaking in and invading it. All this can be applied to theology and to the church.

Thus we have distinguished four kinds of powers; for, we said, natural agents, artificial things, scientific reasonings,[2] and the conduct of gov-ernments and of men are all different powers. As regards the first three kinds, we have indicated three reasons and causes of subjection and dom-ination. In the case of natural agents, we indicated generality and limitation as the reason and cause for which the heavenly powers domi-nate; thus the heavenly powers dominate because they are general, and the powers here below serve because they are limited and particular. In the case of artificial things, we indicated the preparation of materials as the reason and cause; thus stonecutting serves housebuilding and bridle-making serves warfare in that they prepare and dispose the materials for both of these arts. In the case of scientific reasonings, closeness to what is best was said to be the reason and cause; thus the science that attains what is best more perfectly commands and the others serve. [65] As to the fourth kind of power, namely, ruling and governing, we shall say that all three causes concur simultaneously. For we shall say that earthly power and rule must obey and serve the spiritual power and rule for all three reasons mentioned: because it is more particular, and because it disposes and prepares the materials, and because this earthly power does not come so close to what is best or attain it so perfectly as the other.

Now ecclesiastical power is more universal than earthly power because the church is said to be catholic, that is, universal, as Isidore states in the last chapter of Book VII of the *Etymologies;*[3] for he explains that "catholic" is taken to mean universal or general, and he adds that "cath-olic" is the Greek term for universal. If then it is an article of faith that we must believe in the Holy Catholic Church, he is not a true believer who does not believe the church to be catholic—that is, universal—and holy—that is, hallowed[4] and firm because it is established on a firm rock, or else holy in the sense that it is pure and immaculate, according to the words of the Letter to the Ephesians: *That Christ might present to himself a glorious church, not having spot or wrinkle* [Eph. 5:27]. The church therefore is holy and catholic, that is, universal. But it would not be truly universal if it were not universally set over all men.

Now all the other rules are particular because there is not a single one that is indispensable to the attainment of salvation, and this is especially true of secular rules and earthly powers, inasmuch as one draws nearer to salvation by disengaging himself from them. Indeed, clerics, who are not subject to earthly power, are in a more perfect state than laymen, who are subject to it. Thus earthly power is not so universal that unless one is subject to it he cannot attain salvation. On the contrary, as we have said, clerics, who are not subject to earthly power, are in a more perfect state than laymen.

Indeed, the Lord not only always wanted clerics to be free from earthly power, He also wanted those who take asylum with clerics to gain immunity and freedom. Thus in the next to the last chapter of the Book of Numbers,[5] God ordered that forty-eight cities or forty-eight fortified places be given to the Levites who serve at the altar and by whom are meant the clerics, according to Hugh.[6] He also ordered not only that cities or fortified places be given to them to dwell in but pasture lands outside the cities as well. He likewise wanted this land to extend toward every zone of the heaven or in every direction: east, west, south, and north. In addition, he ordered that of these forty-eight cities or forty-eight fortified places, six should be [66] set apart as asylums for fugitives, so that those who had shed blood might flee to them.

Hence the persons to whom are entrusted the material sword and the judgment of blood did not have the authority to exercise this judgment against those who fled to the six fortified places of the Levites, that is to say, of the clerics. This is sufficient evidence that, if even under the Old Law the dignity of the priesthood and of the clergy was such that not only the priests and the clerics themselves were exempt from the lay power, but even those who fled to them in certain specified places were preserved from the judgment of blood despite the fact that they had shed blood and deserved to suffer this judgment, *a fortiori* now, when the priesthood is more noble and the clerical state more perfect, the clergy is not subject to earthly power. The priesthood is indeed much more noble under the law of grace than it was under the written law, for where there was the prefiguration now there is the truth, now Christ is really contained on the altar, the body that Christ received from the Virgin is really there, His own blood is there, and although the body and the blood are not there under their proper appearance but under the appearance of bread and wine, still Christ, who was only prefigured in the sacraments of the Old Law, is there according to His power and according to His substance. Indeed, the earthly power will not be able to exercise its authority even over those who seek asylum with clerics and especially over those who flee to the places dedicated to God, where clerics minister, even though they may have incurred the death penalty. All this proves and establishes the particularity of earthly power and the freedom and immunity of clerics.

Earthly power is therefore particular because it does not have authority over all men, whereas ecclesiastical power is universal. This was expressed figuratively in the Book of Numbers when the Levites, that is to say, the clerics, were given land outside the cities in every direction of the sky; herein was prefigured the fact that the church, which was to succeed to the Levites who served at the altar, was destined to rule over the whole world and over every part of it. For one is rightfully subject to another if he cannot attain salvation without being thus subject to him. Therefore the church should rule throughout the entire world and all men should be subject to it, since if they are not, they will find the gates of heaven shut and so will not be able to enter the kingdom of heaven.

Moreover, this universal dominion of the church was not only prefigured in the Old Law, it was stated among the articles of the faith. These articles are not to be interpreted narrowly but broadly, inasmuch as everything that we must believe and the whole Christian faith is based on them. Now any real Christian has to profess the article that the church is holy and catholic. But it would not be catholic, that is, universal, unless [67] it ruled over all the faithful and over all their affairs. For the church is catholic by its universal rule and the faithful themselves are catholic by subjecting themselves universally to the church. Let no one claim that he is catholic, then, unless he is subject to the universal church, and let no one profess that the church is catholic unless he profess that it rules universally. Now one is not universally subject to the church unless he subjects himself and what belongs to him to the church; first himself and then what belongs to him; for, as it is stated in Genesis, *The Lord had respect to Abel and to his offerings* [Gen. 4:4]; first to Abel, therefore, and then to his offerings. Thus the faithful should first subject themselves to the church and then what belongs to them. The faithful and their possessions both belong to the church. The Apostles too wanted to have both and to exercise their dominion over both, not to exalt themselves but to enlarge the church and make it universal and catholic. Hence the Gloss on II Corinthians, chapter 7, says that it was the glory of the Apostles to possess all things and their owners.[7]

Let us then return to our thesis and say that almost every word of this discussion proves that earthly power, both in itself and in what pertains to it, ought to be subject to ecclesiastical power. Nevertheless, to continue with our subject as outlined in the chapter heading, we shall say that ecclesiastical rule is universal and earthly rule particular, as is clear from what we already know.

Hence ecclesiastical rule imitates the heavenly powers, whose causality extends to all things, whereas earthly rule imitates the powers here below, which produce particular effects: fire, for example, heats, but of itself it does not cool; and water cools, but of itself it does not heat. The power of the heaven, however, accomplishes both, since it helps water to cool (for, according to the order that we see, water would not be able to cool without the power of the heaven), and in like manner it helps fire to heat. For all these lower powers, serving the heaven, as it were, produce whatever they produce by the power of the heaven.

So, too, earthly rulers, who serve the church in everything they do and in everything that pertains to them, must recognize that the church is catholic and universal, that is to say, that it rules universally. Earthly power will therefore be subordinated to ecclesiastical power as the particular is subordinated to the universal. This is the subjection of the lower powers to the heavenly powers. Secondly, earthly power will be subordinated to ecclesiastical power as the one who prepares the materials is subordinated to the one for whom he prepares them. For it pertains to earthly power through the church and under its authority to receive the material sword and to rule over temporal and material affairs and even over the bodies of men, as far as laymen and the affairs over which they have been granted power are concerned. [*68*]

It will be the duty of earthly power, therefore, to administer justice in these matters, so that no one may wrong anyone else in his body or in his affairs and so that every citizen and every believer may fare well. Thus the duty of earthly power is to prepare the materials in order that the ecclesiastical ruler may not be hampered in spiritual matters. For the body was made to serve the soul, and temporal goods to serve the body. Hence the body is well disposed when it serves the soul well, and temporal goods are well disposed and well ordered when they are ordered to the requirements of bodily life and to the needs of human bodies. Accordingly, the whole duty of earthly power is to administer and regulate these external and material goods so that the faithful may not encounter any obstacles in the enjoyment of peace of conscience, peace of soul, and tranquillity of mind. For in this manner not only have *justice and peace kissed* [Ps. 84:11] in the things that pertain to God (indeed, unless we live justly with God we shall not have peace with Him), but also justice in these external matters fosters tranquillity of soul and peace of mind. For, as regards suffering injustice, if all men were as perfect as Matthew urges when he says, *If someone strikes you on the right cheek, turn to him the other also; and if anyone would go* to law with you and take your tunic, let him take your cloak as well [Matt. 5:39-40], there would perhaps be no need for earthly justice. But since everyone is not that perfect and since it is good to check injustice and thus prevent victims from being harmed and offenders from inflicting harm, it was necessary to establish earthly power to preserve justice with regard to bodies and temporal matters, to safeguard tranquillity of soul and peace of mind, to safeguard tranquillity in spiritual matters.

This then is the principal function of earthly rulers: to dispose and prepare the materials for the ecclesiastical ruler. Therefore, the earthly rulers preserve justice in temporal and material matters in order to safeguard peace of mind and tranquillity in spiritual matters, so that he who rules spiritually may rule more freely. Hence, just as bridle-making equips a horse with a bridle and prepares the horse to serve the soldier more readily, so earthly power puts a bridle on laymen, lest they interfere with the church or with one another, and disposes them to submit more readily to ecclesiastical power. And just as stonecutting by its work prepares stones so as to enable the builder to make a suitable and well-ordered house out of them, in the same way, since the faithful are the members that make up the body of the church, whose cornerstone is Christ, according to Ephesians, *Jesus Christ himself is the chief cornerstone in whom all the building, being framed together, grows up into a holy temple in* [69] *the Lord, in whom you also are built together,* and so on [Eph. 2:20-22], earthly power through justice in external matters cuts and disposes these stones in order to achieve peace of mind and tranquillity of soul, so that out of them a spiritual temple may be more readily and more easily constructed.

It is clear, then, that earthly power and the art of governing the people by earthly power is an art that disposes the materials for the exercise of ecclesiastical power. That is why, just as bridle-making is subordinate to warfare and stonecutting to housebuilding, so that in their work they comply with the orders and wishes of these higher arts and dispose all their tools and all their equipment in view of these orders and wishes, so the art of ruling by earthly power and earthly power itself must be subject to ecclesiastical power and must order itself and all its tools and equipment to the service and orders of ecclesiastical power. And since the tools and equipment of earthly power are civil authority, engines of wars, the temporal goods it possesses, the laws and constitutions it establishes, earthly power should therefore order itself and all these things, which constitute, as it were, its tools and its equipment, to the accomplishment of the wishes of ecclesiastical power. Thus secular power in itself and in all the aforesaid instruments is subject to ecclesiastical power.

Thirdly, earthly power is subordinate to ecclesiastical power as that which attains what is best is subordinate to that which attains it more perfectly. We observe this mode of subordination in the sciences; for example, metaphysics, which treats of God, is the goddess of the sciences discovered by man, and all the other human sciences are subordinated to it and serve it and are directed by it. According to this mode, ecclesiastical power, which is spiritual and which deals with the things that pertain to God, is the mistress of earthly power; and it belongs to it to direct this earthly power, and earthly power must be subject to the rule of the priest.

Open your eyes, then, *and see* [cf. IV Kings 19:16], and *ask* the natural powers *and they will tell you* [cf. Deut. 32:7]; examine the mode of procedure of the arts and they will tell you; observe the scientific disciplines and they will make it clear to you. You see in the case of the natural powers that particular and earthly powers are subject in themselves and in what pertains to them to the universal and heavenly powers. You see also in the case of the arts that the arts that prepare the materials are subject in themselves and in what pertains to them to the arts for which the materials are prepared. You see furthermore in the case of the scientific disciplines that the sciences that attain what is best more perfectly command all the other sciences. And because all these things are joined in ecclesiastical power with respect to earthly power, inasmuch as earthly power is more particular and prepares the materials and attains what is best less perfectly, hence it is proved and established beyond any shadow of a doubt that earthly power both [70] in itself and in what pertains to it is subject and subservient to ecclesiastical power.

NOTES

1. Literally: "is powerful." However, because the connotations of the English word "powerful" are different from those of the Latin *potens,* the parallel established by the author between "power" and "powerful" has not been maintained in the translation.

2. The expression *raciones scienciales* has been substituted here for *raciones seminales,* "seminal reasons," which, although carried by all the MSS and kept by the editor, is wholly unintelligible in the present context. *Raciones scienciales*

occurs, with what is obviously the same meaning, a few lines below.

3. Isidore of Seville *Etymologies* vii. 14. 4.

4. The terms "holy" and "hallowed" are used here to suggest the relationship between *sanctam* and *sancitam,* from *sancio,* to ratify or confirm.

5. Cf. Num. 35:2–7.

6. Hugh of St. Victor *De Sacramentis* ii. 2. 3.

7. *Glossa ad* II Cor. 6:10, in Migne, *Patrologia Latina,* 114, col. 560.

21.

John of Paris

ON KINGLY AND

PAPAL POWER

Translated by Ernest L. Fortin

Hardly anything is known about the life of the Dominican John of Paris (or, as he was sometimes called, Jean Quidort, *ca.* 1241–1306), except for the frequent theological controversies in which he seems to have been involved. His professorial career was interrupted, at least momentarily, when as a young Bachelor of Theology he was accused of expounding erroneous doctrines in his lectures on Peter Lombard and forced to defend thirteen propositions taken from his teachings. A few years later, he rallied to the defense of Aquinas and wrote his *Correctorium Corruptorii Thomae,* a refutation of William of la Mare's indictment of that theologian, the *Correctorium Fratris Thomae.* At the height of the dispute between Boniface VIII and Philip the Fair, he entered the lists with his own controversial treatise *On Kingly and Papal Power;* and shortly afterwards,

he sided with Benedict XI when the latter reversed the policy of his predecessor and granted to the mendicant orders the power of hearing confessions. His last work was again an attempt to justify his doctrine of the Eucharist, which was being denounced as heretical. He died at Bordeaux, where he had been summoned to explain his doctrinal positions.

The treatise *On Kingly and Papal Power (De Potestate Regia et Papali,* composed *ca.* 1302) is particularly noteworthy for its forthright challenge of the theory of absolute papal monarchy championed by Giles of Rome in his book *On Ecclesiastical Power.* Its author was regarded in the middle ages as having been the first theologian to clarify and set forth systematically the doctrine of the distinction of the two powers, already intimated by Aquinas. For all John's immediate concern with the most burning political issue of the time, his tone remains serene and unimpassioned throughout. The book contains only a few barely discernible allusions to contemporary political events. Although clearly influenced by numerous other writers, John's chief authority is undoubtedly Aquinas. His book makes use of the latter's commentaries on the *Ethics* and the *Politics*, of the two *Summae*, and of the treatise *On Kingship*. While heavily criticized by the papalists, the treatise *On Kingly and Papal Power* was often read and quoted until as late as the seventeenth century. Among the author's admirers were such men as

Peter d'Ailly, Torquemada, Bellarmine, and Bossuet.

The following selections were translated from the critical edition of John's treatise by Jean Leclercq, O.S.B., *Jean de Paris et l'ecclésiologie du XIIIe siècle* (Paris, 1942), pp. 173-185 and 189-190. The italic numbers in brackets in the body of the translation refer to the pages of this edition. The sections of the treatise that have been omitted deal with the priority (in time) of kingship to the priesthood (chapter 4), the dominion of the Pope over the temporal goods of the Church (chapter 6), and the general question of papal jurisdiction in temporal matters (chapters 8-25).

PROEMIUM

IT SOMETIMES HAPPENS that, in wanting to avoid one error, one falls into the opposite error. Thus, as we read in the *Decree*, some people assert that monks, because they are dead to the world, cannot give penances or grant absolution, since these things are inconsistent with them for the very reason for which they are monks.[1] Wishing to avoid this error, or perhaps to forestall it, some people have said that monks, precisely because they have chosen the state of perfection, have the right to hear confessions, to absolve sins, and to impose salutary penances. Between these two errors, the sound doctrine occupies a middle position, asserting that this is neither inconsistent with, nor owed to, them by reason of their state, but that it may be fittingly exercised by them if their ordinaries, to whom these things belong by right, have so commissioned them. Thus in the book *On the Two Natures and One Person of Christ*, it is shown that faith occupies a middle position between two contrary errors, namely, that of Nestorius and that of Eutyches.[2] In a similar way, concerning the power of the ecclesiastical pontiffs, the truth lies between two errors. The error of the Waldenses[3] consisted in saying that dominion in temporal matters was inconsistent with the successors of the Apostles, that is, the Pope and the ecclesiastical prelates, and that they were not allowed to possess temporal riches. Hence, they say, the church of God and the successors of the apostles and the true prelates of the church of God lasted only until Sylvester,[4] at which time, in virtue of a donation made to the church by the Emperor Constantine, the Roman church began, which, according to them, is no longer the church of God. The church of God, they say, has already disappeared, except to the extent to which it is continued in them or has been restored by them. To support this claim, they cite, among other things, the words of Matthew: *Do not lay up for yourselves treasures on earth* [Matt. 6:19]; and those of Timothy: *Having food and sufficient clothing, with these let us be content; but those who seek to become rich*, and so on [I Tim. 6:8–9]; and again Matthew: *You cannot serve God and mammon* [Matt. 6:24]; and in the same chapter: *Do not be anxious for your soul, saying what shall you eat, nor for your body* [Matt. 6:31]; and these words: *Look at the birds of the air: they do not sow or reap* [Matt. 6:26]. And in Matthew, Christ said to His disciples: *Do not keep gold, or silver, or money* [Matt. 10:9]; and Luke: *If someone does not renounce all that he possesses* [Luke 14:33]; and Acts: *Silver and gold I have none*, and so on [Acts 3:6]. [*174*] From these statements they argue that the prelates of the church of God, the successors of the apostles, should not have any dominion over temporal riches.

The other error was that of Herod, who, upon hearing that Christ the king was born, thought that he was an earthly king. From this appears to derive the opinion of certain moderns who reject the first error to the point where, going to the other extreme, they assert that our master the Pope, in so far as he occupies the place of Christ on earth, has dominion over the temporal goods of princes and barons, as well as cognizance of, and jurisdiction over, them. They even say that the Pope has this power in temporal matters to a more perfect degree than the prince, because he possesses it according to a primary authority and one that is received immediately from God, whereas the prince receives it from God through the intermediary of the Pope. Moreover, [they assert] that the Pope does not possess immediate execution, save in certain cases listed in the *Decretals*,[5] whereas the prince does possess immediate execution, and that those who have stated otherwise have spoken in favor of the princes. And if the Pope sometimes says that he has no temporal jurisdiction, this is to be understood in relation to regular and immediate execution, or because he seeks to preserve peace between princes and the church, or for fear that prelates will be too inclined to inject themselves into temporal goods and secular affairs. They say further that the relation of the Pope to temporal goods differs from that of the princes and prelates because the Pope alone is the sole true master, in such a way that he may, if he so pleases, absolve the usurer from the debt due to usury, and take away from someone what otherwise belongs to him; and what he has done holds, even though he sins and should not do this save for a reasonable cause, such as the defense of the church and the like. The other prelates, on the other hand, are not masters, but guardians, procurators, and distributors. This opinion concerning do-

minion over things not only stems from the error of Herod but seems
to carry on the error of Vigilantius. For it is held and should be held
by all that anything pertaining to evangelical perfection is not inconsistent with the Pope our master by reason of his state. Now it is clear
that, if the Pope, by reason of his state as Pope and vicar of Christ, is
the master of all things, the renouncement of property and the rejection
of dominion in temporal matters are inconsistent with him by reason of
his state, since the opposite is essentially fitting for him. Hence poverty
and the lack of dominion in external things do not pertain to evangelical perfection, as Vigilantius used to say. In this connection Augustine
says in his book, *On the Christian Combat*, that there are some people
who strive for what is theirs, even though they are Catholics or seek
glory from the very name of Christ, as do heretics.[6] Among their number there once appeared in Gaul, which up to that time had been free
of monsters of error, [one] Vigilantius, who dared to place the state
of riches on the same level as poverty, just as once upon a time in Italy,
Jovinian seems to have placed marriage above chastity. This opinion has
something of the haughtiness of the Pharisees, who proclaimed that the
people offering tithes and sacrifices to God were not obliged to pay
taxes to Caesar, in order that they themselves might receive more
generous portions from them as a result of their having been made
richer, as Jerome says.[7] This opinion, too, seems fraught with danger,
because [*175*] the dominion over the things that the converts to the
faith once possessed is transferred to the supreme pontiff, and thus the
faith is rendered less attractive and suffers, since the rights pertaining
to one's condition are disrupted by it, as the Gloss on I Peter 2 says.[8]
From this opinion one must also fear lest, while transactions are going
on in the house of God, Christ should enter, angry and stern, and cleanse
his temple not otherwise than by the use of a whip, and turn the den
of thieves into a house of prayer, as Chrysostom says in his commentary
on Matthew.[9]

Between such contrary opinions as these, then—the first of which
everybody regards as erroneous—the truth, I think, holds the middle.
To possess dominion and jurisdiction over temporal things is not inconsistent with the prelates of the church, contrary to the first opinion.
Nevertheless, this is not owed to them essentially by reason of their
state and by reason of their being the vicars of Christ and the successors
of the apostles. But it may be fitting for them to possess such things
by concession or permission of the princes, if something of this sort
should have been entrusted to them out of devotion by these princes,
or if they should have received them from another source. I declare,
however, that in no way do I intend to assert anything either against
faith, good conduct, or sound doctrine, or against the reverence due to

the person or state of the supreme pontiff. If some such thing should be found, directly or incidentally, in what I have said or am about to say, I wish to withdraw it; and I want this declaration to apply and hold good, as if I were to reiterate it in connection with each one of the things that are going to be said.

*   *   *

CHAPTER I

Nature and Origin of Kingly Rule

Concerning the first point, we should know that kingship, taken in its proper sense, may be defined as follows: kingship is the rule over a perfect multitude by one man for the sake of the common good. In this description, "rule" represents the genus. "Multitude" is added to distinguish this rule from that by which someone rules himself, either by a natural instinct, as in the case of brutes, or by his reason, as in the case of those who lead a solitary life. "Perfect" serves to distinguish this multitude from the domestic multitude, which is not perfect because it is self-sufficient only for a short period of time and not for all of one's life, as is the city, according to the Philosopher in Book I of the *Politics*.[10] "For the sake of the good of the multitude" is included to distinguish this rule from an oligarchy, a tyranny, and a democracy, in which the ruler seeks his own good, as is especially true of a tyranny. "By one man" [is included] to distinguish this rule from an aristocracy, that is, the rule of the best (or *optimates*), in which a few men govern in accordance with virtue—this rule is called by some people the rule according to the decision of prudent men or the decrees of the senate— and to distinguish it from the rule of the many (*polycratia*), in which the people govern by plebiscite. Only he who governs alone is a king, in accordance with what the Lord says through Ezekiel: *My servant David shall be set over them, and they shall all have one shepherd* [Ezek. 34:23]. Such a regime is derived from natural right [*177*] and from the right of nations. For, since man is by nature a political or civil animal, as is said in Book I of the *Politics*[11]—this, according to the Philosopher, is shown from food, clothing, and protection, in which things one man alone is not self-sufficient, as well as from speech, which is ordered to others, all of which are owed to man alone—it is necessary that he live in a multitude, and in such a multitude as is self-sufficient for life. Such is not the household community or the village, but the city or state (*regnum*); for in a single household or village are not found, as they are in the city or state, all the things necessary to feed, clothe, and protect a man for his whole life. When everyone seeks his own interest, however, the multitude is dispersed and scattered on all sides, unless it is ordered to the common good by one man who has charge of this common good, just as a man's body would disintegrate if there were not in it some common force to look after the common good of all the members. Hence Solomon says in Proverbs: *Where there is no governor, the people shall fall* [Prov. 11:14]. This is indeed a necessity, for what is proper and what is common are not the same. Men differ by what is proper, whereas they are united by what is common. Diverse causes produce diverse effects; hence it is necessary that, in addition to what impels to the proper good of each individual, there be something to promote the common good of the multitude.

Now the rule of one man over the multitude in accordance with virtue is more advantageous than that exercised by many or by a few virtuous men. This is clear: 1. from the point of view of power; for power is more united when it exists in a single ruler, and hence stronger than when it is divided among several. 2. From the point of view of the unity and peace that should be sought in the rule of the multitude, which do not exist unless the people are united and unless there is concord among them. If indeed the cause of a thing's being such is itself such to a higher degree, one man ruling according to virtue will be more capable of preserving peace, and the peace of the citizens will not be so easily disrupted. 3. From the fact that a single ruler seeking the common good has an eye to what is more common than if several should govern even in accordance with virtue; for the greater the number of those who are withdrawn from the community, the less common the remainder, and vice versa. Hence the Philosopher says that, among the rules seeking their own interest, that of the tyrant is the worst, because what he seeks is more proper and what he scorns is more common.[12] 4. From the fact that, in the rule of nature, we see that the entire rule is reduced to unity, as is the case in a mixed body, where one element dominates: in a heterogeneous human body, there is in the whole man one principal member, and the soul keeps all the elements together. Gregarious animals also, for which it is natural to live in a society, are subject to one king.

From what we have said, we see clearly that it is necessary and advantageous for man to live in a multitude, and above all in a multitude that can suffice for his entire life, such as a city or a province (*regio*), and especially under one man ruling for the sake of the common good, inasmuch as man is by nature a political or civil and social animal— so much so [*178*] that before Belus and Ninus, who were the first to reign, men did not live according to nature or as men, but after the manner of beasts without rule, as did certain men of whom Orosius speaks in Book I of his work *Against the Pagans.*[13] Tully also says something similar in the beginning of the *Vetus Rhetorica;*[14] and in the *Politics,* the Philosopher says of such men that they do not live as men but as gods or beasts.[15] And since these men could not be brought by the use of common words to the common life that is by nature fitting for them, as we have seen, men who made greater use of reason and who were moved by compassion for their plight attempted by persuasive arguments to bring them to a common life properly ordered under one man, as Tully says; and once they had been brought together, they bound them by definite laws—laws to which we may refer here as the right of nations. So it is clear that this rule is derived from natural right and from the right of nations.

CHAPTER   II

Nature and Origin of the Priesthood

In addition, we have to bear in mind that man is not only ordered to such a good as may be acquired by nature, which is to live according to virtue, but that he is further ordered to a supernatural end, which is eternal life, to which the entire multitude of men living according to virtue is ordered. Hence it is necessary that there be some one man to direct the multitude to this end. If, indeed, it were possible to attain this end by the power of human nature, it would necessarily pertain to the duty of the human king to direct men to it, for we call a human king that man to whom has been entrusted the highest care of the government in human affairs. However, because man does not attain eternal life by human power but rather by divine power, according to the words of the Apostle to the Romans: *Life everlasting is a gift of God* [Rom. 6:23], it belongs not to the human king but to a divine one to lead men to this end.

This rule, then, pertains to that king who is not only a man but also God, namely, Jesus Christ, who introduces men into eternal life by making them sons of God. For this reason He is called king, according to the words of Jeremiah: *A king shall reign and shall be wise* [Jer. 23:5]. This was entrusted to Him by God, and it shall not pass away. And because it pertains to the charge of the king to remove the obstacles that stand in the way of that end, and to provide remedies and resources by which it may be attained, Christ, offering Himself to God the Father on the cross at once as priest and as sacrificial victim, removed by His death for the common sin of the human race the universal impediment, that is, the offense against God the Father. For this reason He was called a *true priest appointed for men* [Heb. 5:1]. However, since a universal cause must be joined to its particular effects, it was necessary that certain remedies be provided by which this general benefit could somehow be applied to us. [*179*] And these are the sacraments of the church, in which the spiritual power of the passion of Christ is contained, like the power of an agent in an instrument. Hence it was fitting that there be these sensible things, in order that man might be provided for in accordance with his condition, which is to be led to the possession of spiritual and intelligible things by means of sensible things, according to the words of the Epistle to the Romans: *The invisible things of God . . . through the things that are made,* and so on [Rom. 1:20], and in order that these instruments might be proportionate to the incarnate Word, the principal agent whose power they contain, inasmuch as they contain a spiritual power under sensible signs.

Besides, since Christ was to deprive His church of His corporal presence, it was necessary that He institute some ministers, who would administer these sacraments to men, and who are thus called priests, either because they dispense sacred things, or because they are sacred leaders, or because they teach sacred things—in all of which they serve as intermediaries between God and men.

These ministers had to be, not angels, but men, possessing a spiritual power that has been conferred upon them, as the Apostle says: *Every priest is taken from men and for men* [Heb. 5:1], so that the minister might be appropriate both to the instrument, in which a spiritual power is found under a sensible element, and to the principal cause of human salvation, namely, the Word incarnate, who, as God and man, produces our salvation by his proper power and authority.

From what we have just said, we may define the priesthood as follows: the priesthood is a spiritual power conferred by Christ upon the ministers of the church in view of the dispensation of the sacraments to the faithful.

CHAPTER III

On the Relation of the Ministers to One Supreme Minister,
and That It Is Not so Necessary That all Rulers
Be Ordered to One Ruler As Are the Ministers
of the Church to One Supreme Minister

Moreover, because, as the Apostle says in the last chapter of the Second Epistle to the Corinthians, this power has been given to the church *for the sake of edification* [II Cor. 13:10], it must remain in the church as long as the church is in need of edification, that is, until the end of the world. Hence power was given first to the disciples of Christ, so that through them it might be passed on to others, among whom there must always be found some higher and perfect ministers, who confer this priesthood upon others by ordaining and consecrating them. These are the overseeing bishops, who, although they are not superior to simple priests with respect to the consecration of the true body of Christ, are nevertheless superior in the things that pertain to the faithful. Bishops are great and perfect priests because they can make other priests—something that simple and lower priests cannot do. And any difficult matters that have to be attended to concerning the faithful flock are reserved to the bishops, by whose authority the priests, too, are able to perform what has been entrusted to them. And in the actions that they perform, priests use things that have been consecrated by the bishop, such as [*180*] a chalice, an altar, and palls, as Dionysius says in the chapter "On Priestly Perfections," in his work *On the Ecclesiastical Hierarchy*.[16]

Now it is evident that, although peoples are divided into different dioceses and cities, in which bishops rule in spiritual matters, there is nevertheless a single church made up of all the faithful and a single Christian people. Hence, just as in any diocese there is a single bishop, who is the head of the church among that people, so in the whole church and the whole Christian people there is one supreme [head], namely, the Roman Pope, the successor of Peter; so that the militant church derives by way of resemblance from the triumphant church, in which one [ruler] presides over the whole universe. Hence Apocalypse: *And they will be his people, and God himself will be with them as their God* [Apoc. 21:3]; and Hosea: *The children of Judah and the children of Israel shall be gathered together, and they shall appoint themselves one head* [Hos. 1:11]. Hence also John: *There shall be one fold and one shepherd* [John 10:16], which certainly cannot be understood of Christ alone, but of some other single minister who rules over all the others in His stead. For, now that the corporal presence of Christ has been removed, it happens from time to time that, concerning the things that pertain to the faithful, certain questions arise, over which the church, whose unity requires the unity of faith, would be divided by a diversity of views if unity were not safeguarded by one man's view. This one man is Peter and his successor, who possesses authority, not by virtue of a synodal disposition, but from the mouth of the Lord, who did not want the church to be deprived of things that are necessary, and who, before His ascension, said to Peter individually, in the last chapter of John: *Feed my sheep* [John 21:17], and in Luke, before His passion: *And do you, when once you have turned again, strengthen your brethren* [Luke 22:32].

Now we find this relation to one supreme [head] among the ministers of the church rather than among secular rulers, because ecclesiastical ministers have been assigned in a special way to the divine cult by the Lord as a particular people. Hence the relation of the ministers to one man stems from a divine statute. The laymen among the faithful, however, are not subject by divine right to one supreme monarch in temporal matters; rather, by a natural instinct, which comes from God, they are inclined to live politically and in a society, and so, in order to live well together, they choose rulers, and choose different ones according to the difference of communities. But that all men be reduced to one supreme monarchy in temporal matters stems neither from a natural inclination nor from divine right; nor is it as fitting for them as it is for ecclesiastical ministers.

First, because, just as among men there is a diversity from the point of view of bodies but not from the point of view of souls, which are all on the same essential level on account of the unity of the human species, so the secular power exhibits a greater diversity according to climate and differences of complexion than the spiritual power, which presents less variety in such matters. Hence it is not necessary that there be as great a diversity in one as in the other. [*181*]

Secondly, because one man is not as sufficiently able to rule the whole world in temporal matters as he is in spiritual matters, for the spiritual power can easily transmit its censure to all men, near and far, since it is a verbal censure. The secular power cannot so easily transmit its sword to men who are far, since it is manual. It is indeed easier to extend a word than to extend the hand.

Thirdly, because the temporal goods of laymen do not belong to the community, as will become clear later; rather, each man is the master of his possessions, inasmuch as these have been acquired by his own industry. Hence the temporal goods of laymen do not require a common administrator, since each man administers his own possessions as he sees fit. The ecclesiastical goods, on the other hand, have been granted to the community. Hence there has to be one man who rules over the community as common administrator and disposer of all goods. Thus it is not so necessary that one man rule over the whole world in the case of the temporal goods of laymen as it is in the case of the temporal goods of clerics.

Fourthly, because all the faithful concur in one catholic faith, without which there is no salvation. It happens from time to time, however, that questions arise over matters pertaining to the faith in different regions and realms. Hence, lest the unity of the faith be disrupted as a result of different controversies, it is necessary, as we have said, that there be one man who is superior in spiritual matters and through whose decision these controversies may be brought to an end. But it is not necessary that the faithful concur in this manner in some common regime. Rather there may exist different modes of life and different regimes according to differences of climate, languages, and the conditions of men; and what is virtuous in one nation is not virtuous in another, as is also the case with individual persons, of whom the Philosopher says in Book II of the *Ethics* that one thing is too little for one man and too much for another;[17] for example, what is too much for a trainer in a gymnasium, namely, to eat ten pounds or ten ounces, would be too little for Milo of Crotona, who used to kill a bull with a single punch, as the Commentator says.[18]

Thus it is not so necessary that the world be ruled by one man in temporal matters as it is that it be ruled by one man in spiritual matters; nor is this derived from natural or divine right. Hence the Philosopher shows, in the *Politics*, that each city or realm is the product of a natural generation, but not an empire or a monarchy.[19] Augustine says likewise, in the *City of God*, that the commonwealth was better and more peacefully ruled when each realm was bounded by the limits of its own territory. The same author says that the cause of the expansion of the Roman empire was its own desire to achieve domination even by drawing foreign nations into unjust wars.[20] Thus one does not gather from natural right that in temporal matters there should be a single monarch, as is the case in spiritual matters. Nor does what is stated in the *Decree*, where it is said that one man should rule, and not several,[21] constitute an objection to this; for [the *Decree*] is speaking there of something that is one, in which case it is not expedient for several [*182*] to rule indistinctly, as it illustrates by the example of Remus and Romulus, who ruled together indistinctly, and thus one committed fratricide on the other. The same thing is also illustrated there by other examples.

CHAPTER   V

Which Is Prior According to Dignity, Kingship
or the Priesthood

From what we have just said, it is easy to see which is prior according to dignity, kingship or the priesthood. For what is posterior in time is usually prior in dignity; the perfect is prior to the imperfect, and the end is prior to the means. Hence we say that priestly power is higher than kingly power and surpasses it in dignity, since we always find that what pertains to the ultimate end is better and more perfect, and directs that to which the lower end pertains. Now the end to which kingship is ordered is that the assembled multitude may live according to virtue, [*184*] as we have said, and this end is further ordered to a higher end, which is the enjoyment of God; and the charge of directing us to that end has been entrusted to Christ, whose vicars and ministers are the priests. Hence priestly power is higher in dignity than secular power. This is commonly conceded in the *Decree*: "The priestly order surpasses kingly power to an even higher degree than gold surpasses lead in value."[22] And in the *Decretals* it is said that, just as spiritual things are more highly prized than temporal things, and the sun is more highly prized than the moon, in the same way. . . .[23] And in Book II, Part 2, Chapter 4 of his treatise *On the Sacraments*, Hugh of St. Victor says: "The spiritual power surpasses the temporal power in honor and dignity in proportion as the spiritual life is higher in dignity than the earthly life, and the spirit higher in dignity than the body."[24] And in Book I of his treatise to Pope Eugene, Bernard [says]: "Which dignity seems to you to be greater, the power of remitting sins or that of dividing estates? But there is no comparison";[25] as if to say, the spiritual power is greater; hence it surpasses the other in dignity.

If the priest is superior to the ruler in dignity and absolutely speaking, nevertheless it is not necessary that he be superior to him in all things. The lower secular power is not so related to the higher spiritual power that it has its origin in, or derives from, it in the same way that the power of the proconsul is related to the emperor, who is superior in all things, inasmuch as the power of the former derives from him. Rather the relation is similar to that of the father's power to that of the general of the army: neither of these powers derives from the other;

rather they both derive from some higher power. Hence secular power is greater than spiritual power in certain matters, namely, temporal matters; and with respect to this it is not subject to it in anything, because it does not stem from it. Rather both stem directly from one supreme power, namely, divine power. For this reason, the lower is not subject to the higher in all things, but only in the things in which the supreme [power] has subordinated it to the higher. For who would say that, because the teacher of letters or the instructor in morals orders all the members of the household to a more noble end, namely, the knowledge of the truth, the physician, too, who pursues a lower end—namely, the health of bodies—is subject to him in the preparation of his medicines? Indeed, this should not be, since in regard to this matter the father of the family, who introduced both of them into the household, did not subordinate him to the one who exercises a higher function. The priest is, therefore, superior in spiritual matters and, conversely, the ruler is superior in temporal matters, even though, absolutely speaking, the priest is higher in proportion as the spiritual is higher than the temporal.

This is also shown by the examples of the authorities already cited. For although gold is more precious than lead, lead does not come from gold as from its cause. This is likewise expressly stated in the *Decree*.[26] It should be understood, however, that we take what has been said to refer to the true priesthood of Christ. For the priesthood of the gentiles and their entire divine cult was for the sake of temporal goods, which are ordered to the common good of the multitude, whose care devolves upon the king. Hence the priests of the gentiles were subject to the kings, and [185] kingship was higher than the priesthood, just as the power of the one upon whom devolves the care of the common good is greater and higher than that of the one upon whom devolves merely the care of a particular good. Likewise, in the Old Law, the priesthood promised immediately only temporal goods, even though these were to be provided for the people, not by devils, but by the true God. Hence in the Old Law, too, the priesthood was lower in dignity than the royal power and was subject to it, because the king was not directed by the priest to anything higher than the good of the multitude, whose care devolved upon him. The converse is true in the New Law.

One should also consider that through divine providence it came about in a wonderful way that in the city of Rome, which God has chosen to become the principal seat of the Christian priesthood, the custom gradually prevailed that the rulers of the city—albeit not out of a duty of justice, since they were, absolutely speaking, superior to the priests—as a sign of the excellence of the priesthood to come, were of their own accord more subject to the priests than in all other places, according to the testimony of Valerius: "Our city has always placed religion above all things, even the ones in which the honor of the highest majesty wished to show itself; for this reason, the magistrates did not hesitate to devote themselves to religion, thinking that, if they served the divine power constantly and well, they would rule over human things."[27] Also, because it was to come about that in France the religion of the Christian priesthood was to flourish most highly, God provided that among the Gauls, too, gentile priests, who were called Druids, determined every [phase of] Gallic life, as Julius Caesar wrote in his book *On the Gallic War*.[28] The priesthood of Christ is therefore higher in dignity than the royal power.

CHAPTER VII

The Relation of the Supreme Pontiff to the Goods of Laymen

From what we have said appears clearly the relation of the Pope to the goods of laymen; for his dominion over the external goods of laymen is far smaller [than over those of clerics]. Indeed, the Pope is not an administrator in regard to them, save perhaps in the case of extreme necessity for the church; and even in this case he is not an administrator but the declarer of right. In order to explain this, we have to bear in mind that the external goods of laymen are not given to the community, as are the ecclesiastical goods; rather they are acquired by each person through art, labor, or proper industry, and individual persons as such have a right, a power, and a true dominion over them; and anyone may order, dispose, distribute, hold, or part with what belongs to him as he sees fit without injury to others, since he is the master. Hence such goods are not ordered or connected among themselves or to one common head, having the power to administer or distribute them, since everyone is the disposer of his own possessions as he sees fit. Thus neither the ruler nor the Pope has dominion over such things or the right to administer them.

However, because it occasionally happens that, on account of such external goods, the common peace is disrupted when someone usurps what belongs to another, and because at times men, out of excessive love for what is theirs, do not share it as befits the necessity or advantage of the country, a ruler is appointed by the people and governs as a judge in such matters, determining what is just and unjust, and as a punisher of injustices, and as a measure in accepting goods from each person according to a just proportion, given the common necessity or utility. The Pope, on the other hand, is the supreme head, as it were, not only of clerics but in general of all the faithful as such; and for this reason, in cases of extreme necessity—in which cases all the goods of the faithful are common and should be shared, even the chalices of the churches—he has the power, as the general instructor of faith and morals, to administer the external goods of the faithful and decide what should be turned over in conformity with the demands of the common necessity of the faith, which would otherwise be subverted by the irruption of pagans or the like. [*190*] The necessity might also be so great and so evident that he could require tithes or definite contributions from each of the faithful, but according to due proportion, lest without reason some people should be more burdened than others in coming to the rescue of the common necessity of the faith. Such a measure by the Pope is nothing other than a declaration of the right. He could also coerce rebels or dissenters by means of ecclesiastical censure; and by the same means, if in a parish the number of the faithful has multiplied to the extent that the old revenue were no longer sufficient for the priest in charge of the parish, in such a way that, in order to care for the parish, the latter would suddenly have to keep a number of chaplains as assistants, the Pope could require the faithful of that parish to contribute more of their goods, until the proper sufficiency were reached. Such a measure would, in this case, be a declaration of the right. Outside of these cases of necessity for the common spiritual good, however, the Pope cannot administer the goods of laymen. Rather each one disposes of what belongs to him as he sees fit, and in cases of necessity the ruler disposes of them in view of the common temporal good. In cases where there is no necessity but [merely] some spiritual advantage, or when it is clear that the external goods of laymen do not contribute to such an advantage or necessity, the Pope cannot coerce anyone; but he could distribute indulgences to the faithful for the help to be offered. Other than that, nothing has been granted to him in my opinion.

NOTES

1. Cf. Gratian *Decretum*, Part II, C. 16, Qu. 1, ch. 8.

2. Boethius *Liber de Persona et Duabus Naturis*, Proemium, in Migne, *Patrologia Latina*, 64, col. 1341. Nestorius (d. *ca.* 451) was a Syrian heresiarch who denied the divine maternity of Mary and eventually the substantial unity of the person of Christ. He was condemned by the Council of Ephesus in 431. Eutyches was another fifth century heresiarch, who reacted against the position held by Nestorius and denied the duality of natures in Christ. His doctrine is known as monophysitism. Eutyches was condemned by the Council of Chalcedon in 451.

3. The Waldenses were a dissenting sect who sought to restore the Church to its pristine purity. They were founded by Peter Waldus, a merchant of Lyons, *ca.* 1179.

4. Pope Sylvester I (314–335), who reigned at the time of the emperor Constantine. The would-be donation of Constantine is a medieval invention designed to provide a legal basis for the Church's claim to earthly possessions.

5. Gregory IX *Decretales*, Book IV, Tit. 17, ch. 13.

6. Cf. Augustine *De Agone Christiano* 10.

7. Cf. Jerome *Adversus Vigilantium Liber* 1.

8. Cf. *Glossa Interlinearis in 1 Pet.* 2:13 (Antwerp: Biblia Sacra, 1634), Vol. VI, col. 1319.

9. Pseudo-Chrysostom *Opus Imperfectum in Matthaeum, Homilia* 38, in Migne, *Patrologia Graeca*, 56, col. 841.

10. Cf. Aristotle *Politics* i. 2. 1252^{b}12 ff.

11. *Ibid.* i. 2. 1253^{a}2.

12. Cf. Aristotle *Nicomachean Ethics* viii. 12. 1160^{a}35 ff.

13. Cf. Orosius *Historiarum adversum Paganos Libri VII* i. 1.

14. Cf. Cicero *De Inventione* i. 2.

15. Cf. Aristotle *Politics* i. 2. 1253^{a}29.

16. Cf. pseudo-Dionysius *De Ecclesiastica Hierarchia* 5.

17. Cf. Aristotle *Nicomachean Ethics* ii. 6. 1106^{b}1 ff.

18. Cf. Aquinas *In Libros Ethicorum Aristotelis*, Book II, Lesson 6, No. 314.

19. Cf. Aristotle *Politics* i. 2. 1252^{b}27 ff.

20. Cf. Augustine *De Civitate Dei* iv. 14.

21. Cf. Gratian *Decretum*, Part II, C. 7, Qu. 1, ch. 41.

22. Gratian *Decretum*, Part I, D. 96, ch. 10.

23. Gregory IX *Decretales*, Book I, Tit. 33, ch. 6.

24. Hugh of St. Victor *De Sacramentis* ii. 2. 4, in Migne, *Patrologia Latina*, 176, col. 418.

25. Bernard *De Consideratione* i. 6, in Migne, *Patrologia Latina*, 182, col. 736.

26. Cf. Gratian *Decretum*, Part II, C. 2, Qu. 7, ch. 41.

27. Valerius Maximus *Factorum Dictorumque Memorabilium* i. 1.

28. Cf. Caesar *De Bello Gallico* vi. 13.

22.

Dante

ON MONARCHY

Translated by Philip H. Wicksteed

Dante Alighieri (1265-1321) was descended from an ancient Florentine family that for several generations had belonged to the burgher rather than the knightly class. Apart from his love for Beatrice at a tender age, nothing definite is known about his early years. He later set out to master all the sciences of his time and prided himself on being one of the first to have assimilated the teachings of Aquinas. From 1295 onward, he took an active part in Florentine politics as a member of the guild of physicians and apothecaries, and showed himself a firm opponent of papal interferences in temporal matters. Along with two other envoys, he went to Rome *ca.* 1301, in a vain attempt to dissuade Boniface VIII from calling in a French army under Charles of Valois to liquidate the anti-Church party in Florence. In 1302 he was charged with corrupt practices ("barratry") in and out of office, as well as with offenses against the Guelf party, and condemned to pay a fine of 5,000 florins. The real reason for his conviction appears to have been his outspoken criticism of the policies of the Pope and his Florentine supporters. When he refused to submit, his property was confiscated and he himself was forced into exile. The rest of his life was spent wandering from one city to another, Verona, Padua, and Bologna among them. Henry VII's visit to Italy in 1310 revived his hopes for an improvement of the political situation in that country. These hopes were dashed when the Emperor, whom Dante had induced to besiege Florence ("destroy the poisonous hydra"), died soon after. In 1315, the sentence pronounced against Dante by his city was renewed. He later settled at Ravenna and devoted the last years of his life to the completion of his greatest work, the *Divine Comedy*.

De Monarchia (*ca.* 1312), Dante's chief political work, is divided into three books, the contents of which are described by the author himself in the second chapter of Book I. Book I sets forth the necessity of a universal temporal monarchy for the well-being of the world. Book II establishes the right of the Roman people to this dignity. Book III defends the proposition that, although he owes to the Pope the reverence that a first-born son owes to his father, the monarch receives his authority immediately from God. Book I is reproduced here in its entirety, along with the last chapter of Book III. The work as a whole, at once a treatise and a tract for the times, purports to advance "truths that have not been touched upon by others." Like the other Christian Aristotelians of his day, Dante draws extensively upon Aristotle, but he departs radically from the teaching of his master by advocating the establishment of a monarchy or world government as a means of eliminating strife among cities and nations. The seriousness of his proposal should be weighed in the light of that departure—a departure motivated ultimately by Dante's views

concerning the role of the papacy in political and temporal affairs. The alleged Averroism of *On Monarchy* is founded in part on the author's use of the doctrine of the "possible intellect" in chapter three of Book I. The accusation occurs for the first time in Guido Verani's *De Reprobatione Monarchiae* (1327), a reply to Dante inspired by John XXII and dictated in large measure by the circumstances of the latter's quarrel with the Emperor Louis of Bavaria. Although burned as heretical in the market place at Bologna in 1329, *On Monarchy* continued to exert a circuitous influence for at least two centuries. It was placed on the Index in 1554, but removed therefrom in the nineteenth century. The final rehabilitation came when Benedict XV extolled Dante's works in his encyclical letter, *In Praeclara* (1921).

The following translation is that of Philip H. Wicksteed: *The Latin Works of Dante* (London, 1904), pp. 127-172 and 275-279, with extensive revisions by the editor. The italic numbers in brackets in the text are page references to the fourth edition of *Le Opere di Dante Alighieri* by E. Moore, revised by P. Toynbee (Oxford, 1924).

[handwritten: of "need a monarch – divine right of King]

BOOK ONE

I

IT SEEMS TO BE of the utmost importance to all men on whom the Higher Nature[1] has stamped the love of truth to work in advance for their descendants, so that posterity may have from them something by which to be enriched, just as they themselves have been enriched by the work of the ancients. For let there be no doubt in the mind of

[handwritten: Kingship argument – god appoints King who should be leaders natural selection cream of crop]

the man who is imbued with public teachings and yet does not care to contribute anything to the commonweal that he is falling far short of his duty. He is not indeed *a tree by the streams of waters, bearing its fruit in its season* [Ps. 1:3], but rather a devouring whirlpool, always sucking in and never pouring back what it has swallowed. Reflecting then, as I often do, upon these things, lest I should one day be convicted of the charge of the buried talent,[2] I long not only to burgeon but also to bear fruit in the public interest and to set forth truths that have not been touched upon by others. For what fruit would one bear by demonstrating anew one of Euclid's theorems, or by setting about the task of re-expounding the doctrine of happiness already expounded by Aristotle, or by undertaking once again the apology of old age, which Cicero has defended? None whatsoever. That boring superfluousness would rather provoke disgust.

And since among other hidden and useful truths the knowledge of the temporal monarchy is the most useful and least known, and since, because it stands in no direct relation to gain, it has not been touched upon by anyone, I propose to extract it from its recesses, so that I may both keep a useful vigil for the world and become the first to win for my glory the palm of so great a prize.[3] The task is indeed arduous and beyond my strength, but in undertaking it I trust not so much in my own power as in the light of that Giver *who gives all liberally and does not upbraid* [James 1:5].

II

We must first consider then what is meant by temporal monarchy ideally, so to speak, and according to its intention. The temporal monarchy, which is called empire, is thus a single rule extending over all persons in time or in and over the things that are measured by time. Now there are three main questions to be raised concerning this temporal monarchy. First, we may inquire and examine whether it is necessary for the well-being of the world; secondly, whether the Roman people rightfully claimed for itself the office of monarch; and thirdly, whether the authority of the monarch depends upon God directly or upon some minister or vicar of God.

But inasmuch as every truth that is not a principle derives its evidence from the truth of some principle, it is necessary in any inquiry that we be clear as to the principle to which we may return by analysis in order to arrive at certitude concerning all the propositions that are afterwards laid down. And since the present treatise is an inquiry of some sort, it seems that before all else we must examine closely the principle in virtue of which what follows may be established. We should know, then, that there are some things that are not in any way subject to our power and that we can only consider but cannot do, such as mathematics, physics, and things divine. But there are other things that are subject to our power [*342*] and that we can not only consider but also can do; and in this case, the action is not undertaken for the sake of speculation, but speculation for the sake of action, for in such things the end is action. Hence, since the present matter is political, and indeed the source and principle of just polities, and since everything political is subject to our power, it is obvious that the present matter is not ordered primarily to speculation but to action. Moreover, since in matters of action the ultimate end is the principle and cause of all things (for it first moves the agent), it follows that every consideration of the means to an end must be derived from the end itself. Thus there will be one way of cutting wood to build a house and another to build a ship. Hence that which is the universal end of the society of the human race, if there is such an end, will be in this case the principle by means of which all the things that we have to prove below will be made sufficiently clear. Now it would be foolish to suppose that there is an end for this or that society and no one end for all of them.

III

Now, then, we must consider what is the ultimate end of human society as a whole; once we have seen that, more than half of our work will be done, as the Philosopher says in the *Nicomachean Ethics*.[4] And in order to clarify the point in question, we must observe that, just as nature produces the thumb for a certain end, and the whole hand for a different end, and the arm for still another, and the whole man for an end that again differs from all the others; so it orders the individual man to one end, the domestic community to another, the village to a third, the city to another, the kingdom yet to another, and lastly there is an ultimate end for which God eternal, by His art, which is nature, brings into being the human race in its universality. And this last end is what we are seeking here as the guiding principle of our investigation.

Accordingly, we have to know first of all that "God and nature make nothing in vain,"[5] but whatever comes into being is ordered to some operation. For the ultimate end in the intention of the creator as creator is not some created essence, but rather the proper operation of the essence. Hence it is not the proper operation that comes into being for the sake of the essence, but the latter for the sake of the former.

There is, then, a certain operation proper to mankind as a whole to which the totality of men itself in all its multiplicity is ordered and that is indeed beyond the scope either of one man, or of one family, or of one village, or one city, or of a particular kingdom. Now what this operation is, will become clear if the ultimate potentiality of mankind as a whole can be manifested. I say, therefore, that no power that is shared by several specifically distinct beings is the ultimate potentiality of any one of them. For since that which is thus ultimate is constitutive of the species, it would follow that one essence would be specified by several species, which is impossible. The ultimate power in man, then, is not being itself, taken absolutely—for even taken as such, it is shared by the elements; nor is it compound being, for this is also found in minerals; nor is it animated being, for this is also in plants; nor is it apprehension, for apprehension is also shared by the lower animals; rather it is apprehension by means of the possible intellect, which belongs to no other save man, either above or below him. For although there are other essences that share in the perfection of the intellect, their intellect is not a possible intellect like man's, since these essences are intellectual species and nothing else and their being is nothing other than the act of understanding without interruption; otherwise they would not be everlasting. It is clear then that the ultimate potentiality of mankind as such is an intellectual potentiality or power.

And since that potentiality cannot all be reduced to actuality at the same time by one man or by any of the particular groups distinguished above, there must be a multiplicity in the human race by which precisely the whole of this potentiality may be actualized, just as there must be a multiplicity of generable things in order that the whole potentiality of prime matter may always be in act; otherwise we would have to concede the existence of a separate potentiality, which is impossible. Averroes agrees with this view in his commentary on [343] the treatise *On the Soul*.[6] Moreover, the intellectual power of which I am speaking is ordered not only to universal forms or species, but also by a kind of extension to particular forms. Hence it is commonly said that the speculative intellect becomes practical by extension and so has as its end doing and making. I say this because there are things to be done, which are regulated by political wisdom, and things to be made, which are regulated by art, all of which serve speculation as the greatest good for which the Supreme Goodness has brought the human race into being. This already enables us to understand the statement of the *Politics* that "the intellectually vigorous by nature rule over the others."[7]

IV

It has been sufficiently shown, therefore, that the proper work of the human race taken as a whole is to actualize at all times the entire potentiality of the possible intellect, primarily for speculation, and secondarily—by extension and for the sake of the other—for action. Since it is with the whole as it is with the part and since the individual man is perfected in prudence and wisdom by means of sedentary tranquillity, it is evident that the human race is most freely and favorably disposed toward its own proper work—which is almost divine (according to the words: *Thou hast made him a little lower than the angels* [Ps. 8:6; Heb. 2:7])—in the quiet or tranquillity of peace. Hence it is clear that of all the things that are ordered to our happiness, universal peace is the best. That is why there rang out to the shepherds from on high, not riches, not pleasures, not honors, not length of life, not health, not strength, not beauty, but peace. For the heavenly host proclaimed: *Glory to God in the highest, and on earth peace to men of good will* [Luke 2:14]. That is why also He who is the salvation of men used the salutation, *Peace be with you* [Luke 24:36; John 20:21,26]. For it was fitting that the Supreme Saviour should utter the supreme salutation. His disciples and Paul likewise sought to preserve this custom in their own salutations, as everyone can see.[8]

By which means, then, the human race better and indeed best achieves its proper work is clear from what we have said. And as a result, we have perceived the most proximate way of attaining that to which all our deeds are ordered as to their ultimate end, namely, universal peace, which may serve as the principle upon which the following arguments are based. This principle was needed, we said, as a standard set before us into which whatever has to be proved must be resolved as into the most obvious truth.

To sum up, then, what we have been saying since the beginning, there are three main questions to be raised and discussed concerning the temporal monarchy, more commonly called the empire; and these questions, as we stated earlier, we propose to investigate in the light of the principle laid down and according to the order that has already been indicated. The first question therefore is whether the temporal monarchy is necessary for the well-being of the world. Against its being necessary there is no force of reason or of authority, whereas there are indeed very strong and lucid arguments to show that it is. The first of these arguments may be drawn from the authority of the Philosopher in his *Politics*.[9] For there his venerable authority asserts that when several things are ordered to one thing, one of them must regulate or rule and the others be regulated or ruled. To this not only the illustrious name of the author but inductive reasoning forces us to assent. For if we consider one man, we shall see that this is true of him; indeed, since all his powers are ordered to happiness, the intellectual power itself regulates and rules all the others; otherwise he cannot attain happiness. If we consider one household, the end of which is to prepare its members to live well, there must be one to regulate and rule, who is called the *paterfamilias,* or someone who takes his place; according to the words of the Philosopher, "every household is ruled by the oldest."[10] And it pertains to him, as Homer says, to rule over all and to impose laws on others.[11] Hence the proverbial curse: "May you have an equal in your home." If we consider one village, the end of which is convenient assistance as regards both persons and things, one person has to rule over the others, whether he be appointed by someone else or rise to preeminence out of themselves with the consent of the others; otherwise [344] not only do they fail to achieve that mutual sufficiency, but sometimes, when several strive for pre-eminence, the whole village is brought to ruin. And if we consider one city, the end of which is to live well and self-sufficiently, there must be a single rule; and this applies not only to a just regime, but even to a corrupt one. For if it be otherwise, not only is the end of the civil life thwarted, but even the city ceases to be what it was. Finally, if we consider one particular kingdom, the end of which is the same as that of the city, but with greater assurance of its tranquillity, there must be one king to rule and govern; otherwise, not only do the people living in the kingdom fail to reach the end, but the kingdom itself lapses into ruin, according to the words of the infallible truth: *Every kingdom divided against itself shall be laid waste* [Matt. 12:25; Luke 11:17]. If such is the case, then, in these and in all things that are ordered to some one thing, the proposition laid down above is true.

Now it is evident that the entire human race is ordered to one thing, as we have already shown. Therefore there has to be a single regulating or ruling power, and this is what we mean by monarch or emperor. Thus it is clear that for the well-being of the world there must be a monarchy or empire.

VI

Furthermore, the relation of the partial order to the total order is the same as that of the part to the whole. The part is related to the whole as to its end and greatest good. Therefore the order in the part is also related to the order in the whole as to its end and greatest good. From this we gather that the goodness of the partial order does not exceed the goodness of the total order, but rather the contrary. Since then we may discover a twofold order in things, namely, the order of the parts among themselves and the order of the parts to some one thing that is not a part (for instance the order of the parts of an army among themselves and their order to the general), the order of the parts to that one thing is the superior order, as being the end of the other; for the other exists for its sake and not conversely. Hence, if the form of this order is found in the parts of the human collectivity, much more must it be found in the collectivity or totality itself, in virtue of the previously advanced syllogism, since it is the superior order or form of the order. But it is found in all the parts of the human collectivity, as is sufficiently clear from what has been said in the preceding chapter. Therefore it is also found or ought to be found in the totality itself. And thus all the parts mentioned earlier, which are inferior to the kingdoms, and the kingdoms themselves should be ordered to a single ruler or to a single rule, that is to say, to the monarch or the monarchy.

VII

Moreover, the human totality is a whole of some sort in relation to certain parts, and it is a part of some sort in relation to a certain whole. It is indeed a whole in relation to particular kingdoms and nations, as shown above, and it is a part in relation to the universe as a whole. This is self-evident. The human totality therefore is said to be properly related to its whole in the same way that its own lower parts are properly related to the human totality itself. Its parts are related to it by means of a single principle, as may easily be gathered from what has been said earlier. The totality itself therefore is properly related, absolutely speaking, to the universe or to its ruler, who is God and the monarch, by means of one principle only, namely, a single ruler. Hence it follows that the monarchy is necessary to the world for its well-being.

VIII

Furthermore, all things are good and perfect when they are as the first agent, who is God, intended them to be. And this is self-evident to all save those who deny that the divine goodness attains the height of perfection. It is God's intention that every created being should reflect the divine likeness in the degree to which its proper nature is capable of receiving it. For that reason it was said: *Let us make man after our image and likeness* [Gen. 1:26]. And although *after our image* cannot be said of the things lower than man, yet *after our likeness* can be said

unlike aristotle

of anything whatever, since the universe in its entirety is nothing other than a certain vestige of the divine goodness. The human race therefore is good and perfect when, in so far as it is capable, it resembles God. But the human race most resembles God when it is most one; for it is in Him alone that the true notion of the one exists. That is why it is written: *Hear, Israel, the Lord your God is one* [Deut. 6:4]. But the human race is most one when it is all united in one, and this [345] cannot be except when it is totally subject to one ruler, as is self-evident. It is when subject to one ruler, therefore, that the human race most resembles God and, as a result, best conforms to the divine intention; and this is to be good and perfect, as was proved at the beginning of this chapter.

We are most like God when we all one

religion = sense of unity when all on the same page (pre modern stuff)

IX

Likewise every son is good and perfect when he follows the example of a perfect father, in so far as his own nature allows. The human race is the son of heaven, which is most perfect in all its work; for "man is begotten by man and the sun," according to Book II of the *Physics*.[12] The human race is perfect, therefore, when it follows the example of heaven, in so far as its own nature allows. And since the whole heaven in all its parts, motions, and movers, is regulated by a single motion—namely, that of the first moved—and by a single mover—who is God, as human reason discovers very clearly through philosophy—the human race is perfect, if our reasoning is correct, when it is regulated in its movers and its motions by a single ruler as by a single mover, and by a single law as by a single motion. Hence it appears necessary for the well-being of the world that there should be a monarchy or single rule, which is called empire. This is the argument that Boethius was sighing forth when he said: "How happy you would be, oh race of men, if the love by which heaven is ruled, also ruled your minds."[13]

moves nun des aquinas eternal divine natural human

X

Furthermore, wherever disputes may arise, there must be judgment; otherwise there would be something imperfect without its proper perfecting element, which is impossible since God and nature do not fail in things necessary.[14] Between any two rulers, one of whom is in no way subject to the other, a dispute may arise either through their own fault or that of their subjects, as is self-evident. Between such rulers, therefore, there must be judgment. And since one cannot take cognizance of the affairs of the other, one not being subject to the other (for an equal has no authority over his equal), there has to be a third of wider jurisdiction who, within the compass of his right, may exercise his dominion over both. And this person will be either a monarch or not. If he is a monarch, the proposition is established. If not, he will again have a coequal outside the compass of his jurisdiction; then a third will again be necessary. And so either we shall go on to infinity, which cannot be, or we must come to a first and highest judge, by whose judgment all disputes may be settled, either mediately or immediately; and this person will be the monarch or emperor. Monarchy is therefore necessary to the world. The Philosopher perceived this argument when he said: "Beings do not want to be badly disposed; but a multiplicity of rules is an evil; therefore let there be a single ruler."[15]

XI

In addition, the world is best disposed when in it justice is strongest. Hence Virgil, wishing to praise that age which seemed to be emerging in his own day, sang in his *Bucolics*: "Already, too, the Virgin is returning, the Saturnian kingdoms come again."[16] For by "Virgin" was meant justice, which was also called Astraea.[17] By "Saturnian kingdoms" was meant the best age, which was also called the golden age. Justice is strongest only under a monarch. For the best disposition of the world, therefore, a monarchy or empire is required.

In order to establish the subsumed premise, we have to know that justice of itself and considered in its proper nature is a certain rightness or rule excluding deviations on either side; and thus it is not susceptible of more or less, any more than is whiteness considered in the abstract. For there are certain forms of this kind, which, although subject to composition, consist in a simple and invariable essence, as the Master of the Six Principles rightly says.[18] Such qualities are nevertheless susceptible of more or less with respect to the subjects to which they are united, according to the greater or lesser admixture of their contraries in these subjects. Hence where there is least of the contrary of justice admixed, both as regards habitus and as regards operation, there justice is strongest. And then it may truly be said of it, as [346] the Philosopher remarks: "Neither Hesperus nor Lucifer is so wonderfully fair."[19] For then it is like Phoebe gazing across the horizon at her brother in the purple glow of the morning calm.[20]

As regards habitus then, justice sometimes finds opposition in the will; for where the will is not free from all greed, even though justice is present, nevertheless it is not altogether there in the radiance of its purity; for it has a subject that, however slightly, resists it to some extent. That is why those who attempt to inspire the judge with passion are rightly rebuffed.[21] As regards operation, on the other hand, justice finds opposition in relation to power. For since justice is a virtue that is related to others, how can anyone act in accordance with it if he does not have the power of rendering to each his due? Hence it is obvious that the stronger the just man is, the broader his justice will be when he acts.

On the basis of this statement, then, we argue as follows: justice is strongest in the world when it exists in the most willing and most powerful subject; the monarch alone is such a subject; therefore justice is strongest in the world only when it exists in the monarch. This prosyllogism is in the second figure,[22] with intrinsic negation, and is similar to this one: All B is A; only C is A; therefore, only C is B. That is: All B is A; nothing except C is A; therefore nothing except C is B.

The first proposition is clear from the preceding explanation. The other is manifested as follows, first as regards the will, then as regards power. In order to establish the first point, we should note that what is most contrary to justice is greed, as Aristotle points out in the fifth book of the *Nicomachean Ethics*.[23] If greed is removed altogether, nothing is left to oppose justice. Hence it is the opinion of the Philosopher that those things that can be determined by law should in no way be left to the judge, and this for fear of greed, which readily twists the minds of men.[24] Thus where there is nothing that can be desired, there it is impossible for greed to be; for when their objects are destroyed, the passions cannot exist. But the monarch has nothing that he can desire, for his jurisdiction is bounded by the ocean alone, which is not the case with other rulers, whose realms are bounded by other realms, as for instance the King of Castile's by that of the King of Aragon. From this it follows that the monarch can be the purest subject of justice among mortals.

In addition, just as greed, however slight, clouds the habitus of justice, so charity or right love sharpens and brightens it. Thus the person in whom right love is most capable of inhering is also the person in whom justice can occupy the most important place. Such is the monarch. When he exists, therefore, justice is or can be strongest. Now that right love produces the effect just mentioned may be shown from the following. Greed, scorning the intrinsic dignity of men, seeks other things; but charity, scorning all other things, seeks God and man and, consequently, the good of man. And since, among the various goods of man, the most important is to live in peace (as we were saying earlier), and

everybody experus that monarchy as a single person

since this is brought about best and above all by justice, charity will chiefly lend vigor to justice, and the stronger it is, the more.

And that of all men the monarch is the one in whom right love should most inhere, is manifested as follows. The closer anything lovable is to the lover, the more it is loved. But men are closer to the monarch than to other rulers. Therefore they are or ought to be most loved by him. The first proposition is evident if we consider the nature of passive and active principles. The second becomes apparent from the fact that men come into contact with other rulers only in part, whereas they come into contact with the monarch according to their totality. And again, they come into contact with other rulers through the monarch, and not conversely. And thus the care of all men is found primarily and immediately in the monarch, and in other rulers only through the monarch, inasmuch as their care is derived from that supreme care.

In addition, the more universal a cause is, the more fully it has the nature of a cause, for the lower cause is a cause only in virtue of the higher, as is clear from the *De Causis*;[25] and the more a cause is a cause, the more it loves its effect, since [347] such love is a property of the cause as such. Hence since among mortals the monarch is the most universal cause by which men may live well, for other rulers are so through him, as we have already said, it follows that the good of men is most loved by him.

Now who, with the exception of the man who is ignorant of the meaning of the word, has any doubt that the monarch has the greatest power to effect justice? For if he is monarch, he could not possibly have enemies.

The subsumed premise having been sufficiently explained, the conclusion is certain, namely, that for the best disposition of the world it is necessary that there should be a monarchy.

XII

Furthermore, the human race is at its best above all when it is free. This will become evident if the principle of freedom is made clear. Hence we have to know that the first principle of our freedom is freedom of choice, which many have on their lips but few in their minds. For they get as far as saying that free choice is free judgment on the part of the will. And what they say is true, but they are far from understanding what is meant by these words, as is constantly the case with our logicians in regard to certain propositions introduced by way of example in logic—for instance, the three angles of a triangle are equal to two right angles.

I say, therefore, that between apprehension and appetite lies judgment.
For first a thing is apprehended; once apprehended, it is judged good
or bad; and finally the one who judges either pursues it or shuns it.
If, then, the judgment moves the appetite altogether and is in no way
anticipated by it, it is free. But if the judgment is moved by an
appetite that anticipates it in any way whatever, it cannot be free, for
it does not move of itself, but is drawn captive by another. And hence
it is that brutes cannot have free judgment, because their judgments are
always anticipated by their appetite. And hence too it can be shown
that the intellectual substances, whose wills are immutable, as well as
the separated souls who depart from this life in grace, do not lose
their freedom of choice because of the immutability of their wills, but
retain it in its most perfect and efficacious form.

Having seen this, we may further show that this freedom or this
principle of all our freedom is the greatest gift conferred by God on
human nature, for through it we are rendered happy here as men,
through it we are rendered happy elsewhere as gods. And if this is so,
who would not agree that the human race is best disposed when it
enjoys the fullest use of this principle? But it is under a monarch that
it is most free. In order to grasp this, we have to know that to be free
is to exist "for one's own sake and not for the sake of some other,"
as the Philosopher would have it in his treatise *De Simpliciter Ente*.[26]
For that which exists for the sake of something else is determined by
that for the sake of which it exists, as a road is determined by its goal.
Only when a monarch is reigning does the human race exist for its own
sake and not for the sake of something else; for it is only then that
perverted forms of government—namely, democracies, oligarchies, and
tyrannies—which force the human race into slavery, as is obvious to
anyone who runs through all of them, are rectified, and that government
is exercised by kings, aristocrats, who are called *optimates,* and zealous
lovers of the people's freedom. For since the monarch has the greatest
love of men, as already indicated, he wants all men to become good,
which is something that cannot exist under perverted rulers. That is
why the Philosopher says in his *Politics* that "under a perverted regime
a good man is a bad citizen, but under a just one the good man and the
good citizen are identical."[27] And just regimes such as these aim at
freedom, namely, that men may exist for their own sakes. For the citizens are not there for the sake of the consuls, nor the nation for the
sake of the king, but conversely, the consuls for the sake of the citizens
and the king for the sake of the nation. For just as the regime is not
established for the sake of the laws, but rather the laws for the sake
of the regime, so too those who live according to law are not ordered
to the legislator, but rather he to them, as the Philosopher again says
in what has been left by him on the present matter.[28] Hence it is also

clear that, although the consul or the king is the master of the others as regards the way, yet as regards the end he is their servant, and [348] the monarch most of all, for he must assuredly be regarded as the servant of all men. Hence, too, we can already see that in establishing laws, the monarch is determined by the end set before him. The human race, therefore, is best disposed when it exists under a monarch; from this it follows that for the well-being of the world the existence of a monarchy is necessary.

XIII

Further, he who is himself capable of being best disposed for ruling is also capable of disposing others best. For in every action the chief intent of the agent, whether acting by necessity of nature or by choice, is to unfold its own likeness. Hence every agent, in so far as it acts, experiences pleasure. For since everything that exists desires its own being, and since by acting the agent's being is in a certain way expanded, pleasure of necessity follows; for pleasure always attaches to the thing desired. Nothing acts, therefore, unless it is already itself what the thing acted upon is to become. That is why the Philosopher says in his work *De Simpliciter Ente*: "Everything that is reduced from potency to act is reduced thereto by something that is already in act what the other is to become,"[29] for if anything attempted to act under other conditions, the attempt would be vain. And thus may be refuted the error of those who think that by speaking well and acting badly they can inform others with life and morals and who fail to perceive that the hands of Jacob were more persuasive than his words, although the former urged what was false and the latter what was true. Hence the Philosopher says in the *Nicomachean Ethics*: "For in the things that concern passions and actions, words are less convincing than deeds."[30] Hence also it was said from heaven to the sinner David: *Why do you talk of my righteousness?* [Ps. 49:16], as if to say, "In vain do you speak, so long as you yourself are other than that which you speak." From this we gather that he who would dispose others best must himself be best disposed.

But the monarch alone is the one who is capable of being best disposed to rule. This is shown as follows. A thing is easily and perfectly disposed for a habitus and an operation in the degree to which there is in it nothing contrary to such a disposition. That is why those who have never been taught anything acquire the habitus of philosophical truth more easily and perfectly than those who have been taught for a long time and are imbued with false opinions. For this reason Galen says rightly: "Such persons need twice as much time to acquire science."[31]

Since, then, the monarch cannot have any occasion for greed, or since at any rate of all men he has the least occasion, as has been shown above, which is not the case with the other rulers, and since greed itself alone corrupts judgment and impedes justice, it follows that the monarch can be either altogether well disposed or at least best disposed to rule, because of all the rest he is capable of the highest degree of judgment and justice. These two qualities belong most fittingly to the legislator and to the executor of the law, as that most holy king testified when he requested of God the things that are fitting for a king and the son of a king. *God*, he said, *give Your judgment to the king and Your justice to the king's son* [Ps. 71:1].

The subsumed premise rightly states, therefore, that the monarch alone is the one who is best disposed for ruling. Thus the monarch alone is capable of disposing others best. From this it follows that for the best disposition of the world monarchy is necessary.

XIV

Also, it is better that what is capable of being done by one should be done by one rather than by more than one. This is shown as follows. Let A be the one by which a thing is done, and let A and B be the more than one by which in like manner the same thing can be done. If then that same thing that is done by A and B can be done by A alone, B is called in in vain, because nothing follows from its being called in, inasmuch as that same thing was being done by A alone. And since every such calling in is useless or superfluous, and everything superfluous is repugnant to God and nature, and everything repugnant to God and nature is bad, as is self-evident, it follows not only that it is better for it to be done by one if it can be than to be done by more than one, but further that it is good for it to be done by one and bad absolutely for it to be done by more than one.

Moreover, a thing is said to be better for being closer to the best, and the end has the character of the best; but to be done by one is closer to the end, therefore it is better. And that it is closer is clear from the following. Let C be the end, A the being done by one, A and B the being done by more than one. It is evident [349] that the way from A through B to C is longer than from A alone to C. But the human race can be ruled by one supreme ruler, who is the monarch. In this respect it should of course be noted that when we say the human race can be ruled by a single supreme ruler, we do not mean that the minutest decisions of each municipality could emanate directly from this single ruler, since municipal laws also are sometimes deficient and need direction, as is clear from the Philosopher, who commends *epieikeia* [equity] in the fifth book of the *Nicomachean Ethics*.[32] For nations, kingdoms, and cities have their own characteristics, which have to be regulated by different laws. For a law is a rule to direct life. Naturally the Scythians,[33] who live outside the seventh circle and experience great inequalities of days and nights and are oppressed by an almost intolerable chill of frost, have to be regulated in a different way from the Garamantes, who live under the equinoctial circle and always have the light of day equal in length to the darkness of night and, because of the excessive heat of the air, cannot wear clothes. Rather we mean that the human race, in the things that are common and apply to all, should be ruled by him and guided to peace by a common rule. And the particular rulers ought to receive this rule or law from him, just as, to arrive at a practical conclusion, the practical intellect receives the major proposition from the speculative intellect, subsumes a particular proposition that is properly its own, and draws its conclusion concerning a particular action. And not only is this possible to one, but it must of necessity flow from one, so that all confusion concerning universal principles may be removed. Moses writes in the Law that this is also what he himself did;[34] for, joining to himself the sons of the tribes of Israel, he left the minor decisions to them and reserved the higher and more common ones for himself, and the chieftains made use of these more common decisions throughout their tribes according to their applicability to each of them.

It is better, therefore, that the human race be ruled by one than by several, and thus by a monarch, who is a single ruler; and if better, then more acceptable to God, since God always wills what is better. And since when there are only two alternatives better and best are the same, it follows that between "one" and "several," "one" is not only more acceptable to God, but most acceptable. Hence it follows that the human race is most perfect when it is ruled by one. And thus for the well-being of the world it is necessary that there should be a monarchy.

X V

Likewise, I affirm that being and oneness and goodness are related in order of priority according to the fifth sense of "prior."[35] For being by nature is prior to oneness, and oneness is prior to goodness; for that which "is" most, is most one; and what is most one, is most good. And the further anything is removed from the supreme being, the further also is it removed from being one and consequently from being good.

That is why in every genus of things that which is most one is best, as the Philosopher would have it in his work *De Simpliciter Ente*.[36] Hence we see that "being one" is the root of that which is "being good," and "being many" the root of that which is "being bad." That is why Pythagoras, in his correlations, placed one on the side of the good and the many on the side of evil, as is clear from the first book of the *De Simpliciter Ente*.[37] From this we can see that to sin is nothing other than to reject the one and go on to seek the many. And this the Psalmist perceived when he said: *They are multiplied in the fruit of corn and wine and oil* [Ps. 4:8].

It is clear, then, that everything that is good is good in virtue of its being one. And since concord as such is a good, it is evident that it consists in some unity, as in its proper root; which root we shall discover if we consider the nature or definition of concord. Concord is indeed the uniform motion of several wills. From this definition it becomes apparent that the unity of wills, which we are given to understand by uniform motion, is the root of concord or is in fact concord itself. For just as we would call a number of clods concordant because they all descend together toward the center, and a number of flames [350] concordant because they all ascend together toward the circumference, if they did this of their own will, so we call a number of men concordant when, as regards the act of the will, they move together toward a single thing that is formally present in their wills—just as a single quality, namely, heaviness, is formally present in the clods and another, namely, lightness, in the flames. For the capacity to will is a certain power, but its form is the concept of the good that is apprehended; and this form, like other forms, although one in itself, is multiplied according to the multiplicity of the matter in which it is received, as are the soul and number and the other forms subject to composition.

With these preliminary remarks in mind, in order to manifest what will be the major premise of our thesis, we argue as follows. All concord depends on unity in the wills. The human race when best disposed is a certain concord. For just as one man when best disposed both as to soul and body is a certain concord, and likewise a family, a city, and a kingdom, so also is the whole human race. The human race, therefore, when best disposed depends upon the unity of wills. But this cannot be unless there is one will dominating all the others and guiding them to unity, inasmuch as the wills of mortals, because of the seductive pleasures of youth, are in need of direction, as the Philosopher teaches in the last book of the *Nicomachean Ethics*.[38] Nor can that one will exist unless there be one ruler of all, whose will may dominate and regulate all the others. Now if all the above conclusions are true—and they are—it is necessary for the best disposition of the human race that there should be a monarch in the world and consequently for the well-being of the world that there should be a monarchy.

X V I

All the reasons set forth above are confirmed by a memorable experience, namely, the experience of that state of mortal things which the Son of God, who was to assume man for man's salvation, either awaited or, when he so willed, produced. For if we go through all the states and periods of man from the fall of our first parents, which was the point at which we deviated and began to wander, we shall find that the world was never quiet on every side except under the monarch *divus* Augustus, when there existed a perfect monarchy. The fact that the human race was then happy in the tranquillity of universal peace is attested by all the historians and the famous poets. Even the scribe of the gentleness of Christ[39] deigned to bear witness to it. Finally, Paul too referred to that most happy state as the *fulness of time* [Gal. 4:4]. Truly the time and all temporal things were full, for no ministry to our happiness was vacant of its minister. But what the state of the world has been since that seamless garment first suffered rending by the nail of greed[40] we may read; would that we might not also see! O race of men, how many losses must you suffer, in how many storms and shipwrecks must you be tossed, so long as, transformed into a beast of many heads, you strive after diverse things? You are sick in either intellect, sick likewise in affection. You do not minister to the higher intellect by means of arguments that cannot be gainsaid, nor to the lower by the evidence of experience, nor even to your affection by the sweetness of divine persuasion, even though through the trumpet of the Holy Spirit the words are sounded to you: *Behold, how good and how pleasant it is for brothers to dwell together in unity* [Ps. 132:1].

B O O K   T H R E E

X V I

Although in the preceding chapter it has been shown by reduction to an incongruity that the authority of the Empire is not derived from the authority of the Supreme Pontiff, yet it has not been fully proved, save by consequential inference, that it depends immediately on God.

For it follows that if it does not depend on the vicar of God, it depends on God. And so, for the perfect establishment of our thesis, we must prove clearly that the emperor or monarch of the world stands in immediate relation to the ruler of the universe, who is God.

Now in order to understand this we have to know that man alone among all beings occupies a middle position between corruptible and incorruptible things. That is why he is rightly likened by philosophers to the horizon, which joins two hemispheres.[41] For man, if considered according to each essential part, that is, soul and body, is corruptible with respect to the one, namely the body, but with respect to the other, namely the soul, he is incorruptible. For that reason the Philosopher in the second book of *On the Soul* rightly says of the soul, in that it is incorruptible: "And it alone, as perpetual, is capable of being separated from the corruptible."[42]

If man, then, is a kind of mean between corruptible and incorruptible beings, since every mean savors of the nature of the extremes, it is necessary that man should savor of either nature. And since every nature is ordered to some ultimate end, it follows that there exists a twofold end of man, so that just as he alone among all beings partakes of corruptibility and incorruptibility, so he alone among all beings is ordered to two ultimate ends, one of which is his end as a corruptible being and the other his end as an incorruptible being.

That ineffable providence, then, has set before man two ends toward which he must tend, namely, the happiness of this life, which consists in the exercise of his proper power and is figured by the earthly paradise, and the happiness of eternal life, to which his proper power cannot ascend without the assistance of the divine light; and this happiness is what we are given to understand by the heavenly paradise.

Now we have to arrive at this twofold happiness, just as we arrive at diverse conclusions, by diverse means. We arrive at the first through the teachings of philosophy, provided we follow them by acting in accordance with the moral and intellectual virtues. We arrive at the second through spiritual teachings, which transcend human reason, provided we follow them by acting in accordance with the theological virtues, namely, faith, hope, and charity. Thus, although these ends and these means have been made plain to us—in one case by human reason, which [376] the philosophers have wholly brought to our knowledge, and in the other case by the Holy Spirit, who, through the prophets and the sacred writers, through Jesus Christ, the Son of God coeternal with the Spirit, and through His disciples, has revealed the truth that is beyond our nature but necessary to us—nevertheless human greed would cast them aside if men, like horses going astray in their brutishness, were not *held in the way by bit and rein* [Ps. 31:9].

That is why man needed a twofold directive power corresponding to his twofold end, namely, the Supreme Pontiff to lead the human race to eternal life in accordance with what has been revealed, and the Emperor to direct the human race to temporal happiness in accordance with the teachings of philosophy. And since none or few, and these with extreme difficulty, could reach this port, were not the waves of seductive greed assuaged and the human race free to rest in the tranquillity of peace, this is the standard on which he who has charge of the world and is called the Roman Prince should chiefly fix his mind—namely, that on this threshing floor of mortality, life should be lived in freedom and in peace. And since the disposition of this world follows the disposition that inheres in the rotation of the heavens, in order to accomplish this end, namely, that the teachings conducive to freedom and peace should be applied by the ruler in question with due reference to time and place, it is necessary that they should be dispensed by Him who personally looks upon the whole disposition of the heavens. And this being is He alone who so preordained that disposition that by it He Himself in His providence might weave all things together in their proper order.

If this is so, God alone chooses, He alone confirms, since He has no superior. From this we may further gather that neither they who are now called Electors nor others of any kind who have been in the past should be so called; but rather they should be reckoned as the heralds of divine providence. Hence it happens that those to whom has been granted the honor of exercising this function are subject from time to time to dissent, because either all or some of them are clouded by the mists of greed and fail to discern the features of the divine dispensation.

Thus it is plain that the authority of the temporal monarch descends upon him without any intermediary from the source of all authority, which source, although undivided in the citadel of its simplicity, flows into multiple channels out of the abundance of its excellence.

And now it seems to me that I have sufficiently attained the goal that I set for myself. For I have searched out the truth concerning the three questions that were raised: whether the office of monarch is necessary for the well-being of the world, whether the Roman people rightfully claimed the Empire for itself, and finally whether the authority of the monarch derives immediately from God or from someone else. The truth of this last question is not to be taken so strictly as to mean that the Roman Prince is not subject in some things to the Roman Pontiff, inasmuch as mortal happiness is in some way ordered to immortal happiness. Let Caesar, therefore, observe that reverence toward Peter which a first-born son should observe toward a father, so that, illuminated by the light of paternal grace, he may with greater power enlighten the world over which he has been set by Him alone who is the ruler of all things spiritual and temporal.

NOTES

1. Cf. Dante *Purgatory* xvi. 79, where God is referred to as "miglior natura" or superior nature.

2. Cf. Matt. 25:25.

3. Cf. I Cor. 9:24.

4. Cf. Aristotle *Nicomachean Ethics* i. 7. 1098^{b}6.

5. Cf. Aristotle *De Caelo* i. 4. 271^{a}33.

6. Cf. Averroes *Commentarium Magnum in Aristotelis De Anima Libros* iii. 1.

7. Cf. Aristotle *Politics* i. 2. 1252^{a}31; cf. also i. 5. 1254^{a}17 ff.

8. Cf. Gal. 1:3; Eph. 1:2; I Pet. 1:2; II John 1:3.

9. Cf. Aristotle *Politics* i. 5. 1254^{a}28.

10. Aristotle *Politics* i. 2. 1252^{b}21.

11. Cf. Homer *Odyssey* ix. 114, cited in Aristotle *Politics* i. 2. 1252^{b}23.

12. Aristotle *Physics* ii. 2. 194^{b}13.

13. Boethius *De Consolatione Philosophiae* ii. Poem 8.

14. Cf. Aristotle *De Anima* iii. 9. 432^{b}21.

15. Aristotle *Metaphysics* xii. 10. 1076^{a}4. The last part of the sentence is a quotation from Homer *Iliad* ii. 204.

16. Virgil *Eclogues* iv. 6.

17. According to one account, Astraea, the star-maiden, was the daughter of Zeus and Themis and as such was identified with Dike, justice. She lived among men in the golden age and, at the end of that age, was the last of the gods to withdraw into the sky, where she shines as the constellation of the Virgin. Saturn was an ancient Italian god of seedtime and harvest, later identified with the Greek Kronos. Thrust out by Zeus, he came across the sea to Italy and brought to that country, over which he ruled as king, the blessings of agriculture. His reign was regarded as the golden age of Italy.

18. Cf. Gilbert de la Porrée (*ca.* 1076–1154), *Liber de Sex Principiis*, I, 1.

19. Aristotle *Nicomachean Ethics* v. 1. 1129^{b}28. Hesperus is the evening star, and Lucifer the morning star.

20. Phoebe, the moon-goddess, was the sister of Phoebus or Apollo, the sun-god.

21. Cf. Aristotle *Rhetoric* i. 1. 1354^{a}24.

22. Cf. Aristotle *Prior Analytics* i. 5.

The second figure of the syllogism may be summed up as follows: P M
$$\begin{array}{cc} \text{P} & \text{M} \\ \text{S} & \text{M} \\ \hline \therefore \text{S} & \text{P} \end{array}$$

23. Cf. Aristotle *Nicomachean Ethics* v. 2. 1130^{a}19.

24. Cf. Aristotle *Rhetoric* i. 1. 1354^{a}31.

25. *Liber de Causis* i. 16. This work was put together in Arabic by an unknown philosopher *ca.* 850 and consists for the most part of excerpts from Proclus' *Elements of Theology*. The work exerted a considerable influence in the Christian world through Gerard of Cremona, who translated it into Latin at Toledo between 1167 and 1187 and attributed it to Aristotle. William of Moerbeke's translation of Proclus' *Elements of Theology* into Latin in 1268 revealed to Thomas Aquinas and medieval philosophers generally the true character of the *Liber de Causis*.

26. Aristotle *Metaphysics* i. 2. 982^{b}25.

27. Aristotle *Politics* iii. 4. 1276^{b}30; cf. *Nicomachean Ethics* v. 2. 1130^{b}28.

28. Cf. Aristotle *Politics* iv. 1. 1289^{a}13–15.

29. Aristotle *Metaphysics* ix. 8. 1049^{b}24.

30. Aristotle *Nicomachean Ethics* x. 1. 1172^{a}34.

31. Galen *De Cognoscendis Morbis* 10.

32. Cf. Aristotle *Nicomachean Ethics* v. 10. 1137^{b}26.

33. In antiquity, Scythian was a general designation for the nomadic tribes of the north of Europe, beyond the Black Sea. The Garamantes were a tribe of the interior of Africa, beyond the Gaetulians, in that part of Libya today called the Fezzan.

34. Cf. Exod. 18:17–26.

35. Cf. Aristotle *Categories* ch. 12.

36. Cf. Aristotle *Metaphysics* iv. 1. 1003^{b}23.

37. *Ibid.* i. 5. 986^{a}23–27.

38. Cf. Aristotle *Nicomachean Ethics* x. 9. 1179^{b}31.

39. I.e., the Apostle Luke; cf. Luke 2:14.

40. Cf. John 19:23.

41. *Liber de Causis* ii. 22.

42. Aristotle *De Anima* ii. 2. 413^{b}26.

23.

Marsilius of Padua

THE DEFENDER

OF THE PEACE

Translated by Alan Gewirth

Little is known with certainty about the life of Marsilius of Padua (Marsilio dei Mainardini, *ca.* 1275/80–1342). As a young student, he appears to have hesitated between law and medicine and finally decided in favor of the latter. He was rector of the University of Paris from December, 1312 to March, 1313. While in Paris, he became acquainted with Peter of Abano and other prominent "Averroists." Pope John XXII promised him a canonry in 1316 and reserved for him the first vacant benefice at Padua in 1318. He spent some time in the service of Can Grande of Verona and Matteo Visconti of Milan and was sent by them to Count Charles of La Marche to offer him the captaincy of the Ghibelline League. Having failed in this mission, Marsilius returned to Paris and devoted himself to the teaching and practice of medicine. The *Defensor Pacis*, his only cine. The *Defensor Pacis*, his only

major work, was completed in June, 1324. When, two years later, his authorship became known, he fled with John of Jandun to the court of Louis of Bavaria at Nuremberg. In 1327, John XXII condemned five propositions from the *Defensor* and excommunicated its author. In 1327 and 1328, Marsilius accompanied Louis to Rome on his ill-fated expedition to seize the imperial crown. The spectacular events of those years may be viewed as an attempt to put Marsilius' antipapal doctrines into practice. Louis was crowned by Sciarra Colonna as a delegate of the people, while he himself, acting "by our authority together with the entire clergy and Roman people," deposed John XXII and named a new Pope. Marsilius was appointed spiritual vicar of the city. The following year Louis incurred the displeasure of the people and was compelled to withdraw. Marsilius returned with him to Bavaria, where he spent the rest of his life. Shortly before his death, he wrote a short summary of the *Defensor Pacis* entitled *Defensor Minor*, of which the *Tractatus de Iurisdictione Imperatoris in Causis Matrimonialibus*, composed in view of the marriage of Louis' son to Margaret Maultasch, is a part.

The *Defensor Pacis* presents itself as the work of a single author. The once common view that it was written in collaboration with John of Jandun is based on external evidence only. The book is divided into three discourses (*Dictiones*) of unequal length. The First Discourse sets forth Marsilius' views on the nature and causes of civil society by means of arguments drawn from reason (cf. I. 1. 8). Chapters 14–19, which are here omitted, deal with the general question of the efficient cause of rulership and, specifically, with the qualities of the ruler, his election, the unity of government in the state, the correction of rulers, and finally, the papal plenitude of power. The Second Discourse, which constitutes the major portion of the work, is a long indictment, based on Scripture and various other Christian authorities, of the doctrine of the papal plenitude of temporal and coercive power, regarded by Marsilius as the singular cause of strife and discord in cities and states. The Third Discourse sums up briefly the results of the preceding Discourses and draws a number of conclusions from them.

As the title of his book suggests, Marsilius writes as a defender—not indeed of the faith—but of peace, the necessary condition for the actualization of the good life. His whole outlook differs profoundly, both in its Aristotelian and in its Christian aspects, from that of the foremost Christian Aristotelian of the middle ages, Thomas Aquinas. Throughout his work, Marsilius refers to Aquinas just once, and even then only to quote a text that the latter had himself cited from some other source. His stated aim is not to set forth a complete political philosophy, but to deal with one specific evil, which Aristotle, as a pagan living in pre-Christian times, could not have foreseen: the encroachments of the papacy in the spiritual and temporal spheres and the dire consequences of these abuses for the peace of society. His one flagrant deviation from Aristotle (on the subject of popular sovereignty) finds its explanation in his doctrine of the Christian priesthood, to which Marsilius denies many of the prerogatives claimed for it by the traditional ecclesiastical polity of his time, and is not to be taken as the final expression of his own views concerning political authority. The same reason may account, at least in part, for his tacit opposition to Aquinas on the issue of natural law, the existence of which he rejects in II. 12 (reproduced below, along with the first thirteen chapters of Discourse I). His doctrines exerted a profound influence on the political theology of the Reformation.

The following translation is that of Alan Gewirth, *Marsilius of Padua,* Vol. II, *The Defender of Peace* (New York: Columbia University Press, 1956), pp. 3–55 and 187–92, with minor revisions by the editor. Gewirth's translation was made from the critical edition by C. W. Previté-Orton, *The Defensor Pacis of Marsilius of Padua* (Cambridge: Cambridge University Press, 1928). In a few cases, which are indicated in the footnotes, emendations of Previté-Orton's text have been adopted from the edition of the *Defensor Pacis* by R. Scholz (Hanover, 1932), and from Dino Bigongiari, "Notes on the Text of the *Defensor Pacis*," *Speculum,* VII (1932), 36–49. The divisions into Discourses, chapters, and sections are those of Marsilius. The italic page numbers in brackets refer to Previté-Orton's edition.

DISCOURSE ONE

CHAPTER I. On the General Aim of the Discussion, the Cause of that Aim, and the Division of the Book

"Tranquillity, wherein peoples prosper and the welfare of nations is preserved, must certainly be desirable to every state. For it is the noble mother of the good arts. Permitting the steady increase of the race of mortals, it extends their means and enhances their manners. And he who is perceived not to have sought for it is recognized to be ignorant of such important concerns."[1]

1 The benefits and fruits of the tranquillity or peace of civil regimes were set forth by Cassiodorus in this passage of his first epistle. Exhibiting through these very great goods the greatest good of man, sufficiency of life, which no one can attain without peace and tranquillity, Cassiodorus aimed thereby to arouse in men the desire to have peace with one another and hence tranquillity. In this aim he was in accord with what the blessed Job said in his twenty-second chapter: *Be at peace, and thereby thou shalt have the best fruits* [Job 22:21]. Indeed, it was for this reason that Christ, son of God, decreed that peace would be the sign and messenger of his new birth, [2] when, in the same message, he wanted the heavenly choir to sing: *Glory to God in the highest: and on earth peace to men of good will* [Luke 2:14]. For this same reason, too, he often wished peace to his disciples. Whence John: *Jesus came and stood amid his disciples and said, "Peace be to you"* [John 20:19]. Counseling them concerning the maintenance of peace with one another, he said, in Mark: *Have peace among you* [Mark 9:50]. And he taught them not only to have peace among themselves, but also to wish it to others; whence in Matthew: *When you come into the house, salute it, saying: "Peace be to this house"* [Matt. 10:12; Luke 10:5]. Peace, again, was the heritage which he bequeathed to his disciples at the time of his passion and death, when he said, in the fourteenth chapter of John: *Peace I leave with you; my peace I give unto you* [John 14:27]. And like Christ, his true heirs and imitators, the apostles, wished peace to the men to whom they sent epistles containing evangelical lessons and admonitions, for they knew that the fruits of peace would be the greatest goods, as was shown from Job and more fully exhibited through Cassiodorus.

2 Since, however, "contraries are [essentially] productive of contraries,"[2] from discord, the opposite of tranquillity, the worst fruits and

troubles will befall any civil regime or state. This can readily be seen, and is obvious to almost all men, from the example of the Italian state. For while the inhabitants of Italy lived peacefully together, they experienced those sweet fruits of peace which have been mentioned above, and from and in those fruits they made such great progress that they brought the whole habitable world under their sway. But when discord and strife arose among them, their state was sorely beset by all kinds of hardships and troubles and underwent the dominion of hateful foreign nations. And in the same way Italy is once again battered on all sides because of strife and is almost destroyed, so that it can easily be invaded by anyone who wants to seize it and who has any power at all. Nor is such an outcome astonishing, for, as Sallust attests, writing about Jugurtha: "By concord small things increase, by discord great things [3] perish."[3] Misled through discord into the bypath of error, the Italian natives are deprived of the sufficient life, continuously undergoing the gravest hardships instead of the quiet they seek, and the harsh yoke of tyrants instead of liberty; and finally, they have become so much unhappier than citizens of other states that their ancestral name, which used to give glory and protection to all who appealed to it, is now, to their ignominy, cast into their teeth by the other nations.

3 Into this dire predicament, then, the miserable men are dragged because of their discord and strife, which, like the illness of an animal, is recognized to be the diseased disposition of the civil regime. Although strife has numerous original causes, many of which are not unrelated, almost all those which can emerge in the usual ways were described by the foremost of the philosophers in his *Civil Science*.[4] Besides these, however, there is one singular and very obscure cause by which the Roman empire has long been troubled and is still troubled.[5] This cause is very contagious and prone to creep up on all other cities and states; in its greediness it has already tried to invade most of them. Neither Aristotle nor any other philosopher of his time or before could have discerned the origin and species of this cause. For it was and is a certain perverted opinion (to be exposed by us below) which came to be adopted as an aftermath of the miraculous effect produced by the supreme cause long after Aristotle's time; an effect beyond the power of the lower nature and the usual action of causes in things. This sophistic opinion, wearing the guise of the honorable and beneficial, is utterly pernicious to the human race and, if unchecked, will eventually bring unbearable harm to every city and country.

4 The fruits of peace or tranquillity, then, are the greatest goods, as we have said, while those of its opposite, strife, are unbearable evils. Hence we ought to wish for peace, to seek it if we do not already have it, to conserve it once it is attained, and to repel with all our strength the strife which is opposed to it. To this end individual breth-

ren, and in even greater degree groups and communities, are obliged to help one another, both from the feeling of heavenly love and from the bond or law [4] of human society. This admonition Plato also gives us, as Tully attests in the first book of his treatise *On Duties*, when he said: "We were not born for ourselves alone; to part of us our native land lays claim, and to part, our friends." To this sentence Tully adds: "And so, as the Stoics were wont to say, the things that grow in the earth are all created for the use of men; but men are born for the sake of men. In this we ought to follow the lead of nature, and to bring forth common utilities for all."[6] But it would be no small common utility, indeed it is rather a necessity, to unmask the sophism of this singular cause of wars which threatens no small harm to all states (*regnis*) and communities. Hence, whoever is willing and able to discern the common utility is obliged to give this matter his vigilant care and diligent efforts. For while this sophism remains concealed, this pestilence can in no way be avoided, nor its pernicious effect be completely uprooted from states or cities.

5 This task should not be neglected by anyone because of fear or laziness or any other evil disposition. For, as it is written in the second epistle to Timothy: *God has not given us the spirit of fear, but of power and of love* [II Tim. 1:7]: the power and love, I say, of spreading the truth; whence the Apostle continues: *Be not thou therefore ashamed of the testimony of our Lord*. This was the testimony of the truth, for the bearing of which Christ said he had come into the world when he stated, in the eighteenth chapter of John: *For this was I born and for this came I into the world, that I should give testimony to the truth* [John 18:37]: that truth, namely, which leads the human race to eternal salvation. Following the example of Christ, therefore, we must strive to teach the truth whereby the aforesaid pestilence of civil regimes may be warded off from the human race, especially the worshipers of Christ—the truth which leads to the salvation of civil life, and which also is of no little help for eternal salvation. Such striving is all the more obligatory for that person in whom the giver of graces has inspired a greater understanding of these things; and he who has the knowledge and the ability for this, but yet, like an ingrate, neglects it, commits a grave sin, as James attested in the fourth chapter of his canonic epistle, when he said: *To him who knoweth to do good and doeth it not, to him it is sin* [Jas. 4:17]. For this evil, the common enemy of the human race, will not be completely cut down, nor will the pernicious fruits which it has thus far produced [5] be arrested, unless the iniquity of its cause or root is first revealed and denounced. For by no other path can the coercive power of rulers safely enter upon the final rout of the shameful patrons and stubborn defenders of this evil.

6 And so I, a son of Antenor,[7] heeding and obeying the aforesaid admonitions of Christ, of the saints, and of the philosophers, moved also by the spirit of an understanding of these things (if any grace has been given me), and of confidence sent to me from above (for as James attests in the first chapter of his epistle: *Every best gift and every perfect gift is from above, coming down from the Father of lights* [Jas. 1:17]); acting from reverence for the giver, from love of spreading the truth, from fervent affection for country and brethren, from pity for the oppressed, from a desire to save them, to recall the oppressors from the bypath of error, and to arouse the resistance of those who suffer such things when they can and should combat them; and beholding in you especially, most exalted Ludwig, emperor[8] of the Romans, God's servant, who shall give to this task that external fulfilment of it which you desire, and who by some special ancient birthright, as well as by your singularly heroic native disposition and outstanding virtue, have a firmly ingrained love of wiping out heresies, upholding and preserving the catholic truth and every other worthy discipline, uprooting vice, encouraging virtuous pursuits, extinguishing strife, and spreading and nourishing peace or tranquillity everywhere—I have written down the sentences which follow, after a period of diligent and intense study, thinking that these may be of some help to your vigilant majesty, who bestows careful attention upon the above-mentioned evils and others which may occur, as well as upon all matters affecting the public welfare.

7 It is my purpose, therefore, with God's help, [6] to expose only this singular cause of strife. For to reiterate the number and nature of those causes which were set forth by Aristotle would be superfluous; but this cause which Aristotle could not have known, and which no one after him who could know it has undertaken to investigate, we wish to unmask so that it may henceforth be readily excluded from all states or cities, and virtuous rulers and subjects live more securely in tranquillity. This is the desirable outcome which I propose at the beginning of this work; an outcome necessary for those who would enjoy civil happiness, which seems the best of the objects of desire possible to man in this world, and the ultimate aim of human acts.

8 I shall divide my proposed work into three discourses. In the first I shall demonstrate my views by sure methods discovered by the human intellect, based upon propositions self-evident to every mind not corrupted by nature, custom, or perverted disposition. In the second discourse, the things which I shall believe myself to have demonstrated I shall confirm by established testimonies of the eternal truth, and by the authorities of its saintly interpreters and of other approved teachers of the Christian faith, so that this book may stand by itself, needing no external proof. From the same source too I shall refute the falsities opposed to my conclusions, and expose the intricately obstructive soph-

isms of my opponents. In the third discourse, I shall infer certain conclusions or useful lessons which the citizens, both rulers and subjects, ought to observe, conclusions having an evident certainty from our previous findings. Each of these discourses I shall divide into chapters, and each chapter into more or less paragraphs depending upon the length of the chapter. One advantage of this division will be ease for the readers in finding what they look for when they are referred from later to earlier discourses and chapters. From this will follow a second advantage: a shortening of the volume. For when we assume in later pages some truth, either for itself or for the demonstration of other things, whose proof or certainty has been sufficiently set forth in preceding sections, instead of trifling with the proof all over again, we shall send the reader back to the discourse, chapter, and paragraph in which the proof was originally given, so that thus he may easily be able to find the certainty of the proposition in question. [7]

CHAPTER II. On the First Questions in this Book, and the Distinction of the Various Meanings of the Term "State"

1 Entering upon our proposed task, we wish first to show what are the tranquillity and intranquillity of the state or city; and first the tranquillity, for if this be not clear, one is necessarily ignorant also of what is intranquillity. Since, however, both of these seem to be dispositions of the city or state (let this be assumed from Cassiodorus), we shall consequently make clear what must be revealed at the very outset; namely, what is the state or city, and why. Through this, the definitions of tranquillity and of its opposite will be more readily apparent.

2 Following the aforesaid order for the definition of the tranquillity of the city or state, we must notice, in order to prevent ambiguity from entering our project, that the term "state" (*regnum*) has many meanings. In one sense it means a number of cities (*civitatum*) or provinces contained under one regime; in which sense a state does not differ from a city with respect to species of polity but rather with respect to quantity. In another sense the term "state" signifies a certain species of temperate polity or regime, which Aristotle calls "temperate monarchy";[9] in this sense a state may consist in a single city as well as in many cities, as was the case around the time of the rise of civil communities, for then there was usually one king in a single city. The third and most familiar sense of this term is a combination of the first and the second. In its fourth sense it means something common to every species of temperate regime, whether in a single city or in many; it was in this sense that Cassiodorus used it in the passage we quoted at the beginning of this book, and this, too, is the sense in which we shall use the term in our discussions of the matters under inquiry.[10]

3 Now we must define tranquillity and its opposite. [*8*] Let us assume with Aristotle in his *Politics*, Book I, Chapter 2, and Book V, Chapter 3, that the city is like an animate nature or animal.[11] For just as an animal well disposed in accordance with nature is composed of certain proportioned parts ordered to one another and communicating their functions mutually and for the whole, so too the city is constituted of certain such parts when it is well disposed and established in accordance with reason. The relation, therefore, of the city or state and its parts to tranquillity will be seen to be similar to the relation of the animal and its parts to health. The trustworthiness of this inference we can accept from what all men comprehend about each of these relations. For they think that health is the best disposition of an animal in accordance with nature, and likewise that tranquillity is the best disposition of a city established in accordance with reason. Health, moreover, as the more experienced physicists describe it, is the good disposition of the animal whereby each of its parts can perfectly perform the operations belonging to its nature; according to which analogy tranquillity will be the good disposition of the city or state whereby each of its parts will be able perfectly to perform the operations belonging to it in accordance with reason and its establishment. And since a good definition consignifies contraries, intranquillity will be the diseased disposition of the city or state, like the illness of an animal, whereby all or some of its parts are impeded from performing the operations belonging to them, either entirely or to the extent required for complete functioning.

In this general way, then, we have defined tranquillity and its opposite, intranquillity. [*9*]

CHAPTER III. On the Origin of the Civil Community

1 Having defined tranquillity as the good disposition of the city for the functioning of its parts, we must now examine what the city is in itself, and why;[12] what and how many are its primary parts;[13] what is the function appropriate to each part,[14] their causes,[15] and their order in relation to one another.[16] For these are the main points required for the perfect determination of tranquillity and its opposite.

2 However, before discussing the city and its species or modes, since the city is the perfect community we must first trace the origin of civil communities and of their regimes and modes of living. From the imperfect kinds, men have advanced to perfect communities, regimes, and modes of living in them. For from the less to the more perfect is always the path of nature and of its imitator, art.[17] And men do not think that they have scientific knowledge of each thing unless they "know its first causes and first principles down to the elements."[18]

3 Following this method, then, we must note that civil communities had small beginnings in diverse regions and times, and growing gradually came at length to completion, just as we said happens in every process of nature or of art. For the first and smallest combination of human beings, wherefrom the other combinations emerged, was that of male and female, as the foremost of the philosophers says in the *Politics*, Book I, Chapter 1,[19] and as appears more fully from his *Economics*.[20] From this combination there were generated other humans, who first occupied one household; from these, more combinations of the same kind were formed, and so great was the procreation of children that a single household did not suffice for them, [*10*] but many households had to be made. A number of these households was called a village or hamlet, and this was the first community, as is also written in the above-cited treatise.[21]

4 So long as men were in a single household, all their actions, especially those we shall henceforth call "civil," were regulated by the elder among them as being more discerning, but apart from laws or customs, because these could not yet have been discovered. Not only were the men of a single household ruled in this way, but the first community too, called the village, was ruled in almost the same manner, although in some things it was ruled differently. For although the head of a single household might have been allowed to pardon or to punish domestic injuries entirely according to his own will and pleasure, this would not have been allowed the head of the first community called the village. For in this community the elder had to regulate matters of justice and benefit by some reasonable ordinance or quasi-natural law, because thus it seemed appropriate to all by a certain equity, not as a result of prolonged inquiry, but solely by the common dictate of reason and a certain duty of human society.

The cause of this difference of regime in a single household and in a village is and was as follows. If someone in the single and first household or domestic family had killed or otherwise offended his brother, then the head of the household, if he so desired, was allowed not to give the wrongdoer the extreme penalty without any dangerous consequences resulting therefrom, because the injury seemed to have been done to the father alone, who forgave it; and because of the paucity of men; and again because it was less unfortunate and sorrowful for the father to lose one son than two. Our first ancestor, Adam, seems to have acted in this way when his first-born son, Cain, killed his brother Abel. For there is properly no civil justice of a father in relation to his son, as Aristotle wrote in Book IV of the *Ethics*, the treatise on justice.[22] On the other hand, in the first community, the village or hamlet, such procedure was not and would not be allowed, because the case here was different from that of the family; indeed, unless injuries were avenged or equalized by the elder, there would have arisen fighting and the separation of the villagers.

Villages having multiplied and the community grown larger [*11*] because of increasing procreation, they were still ruled by one man, either because of a lack of many prudent men or through some other cause, as is written in the *Politics*, Book III, Chapter 9.[23] The ruler, however, was the elder or the man who was regarded as better, although the regulations of these communities were less imperfect than those by which the single village or hamlet was ordered. Those first communities, however, did not have so great a differentiation and ordering of parts, or so large a quantity of necessary arts and rules of living, as were gradually to be found afterwards in perfect communities. For sometimes the same man was both ruler and farmer or shepherd, like Abraham and several others after him; but in perfect communities this was not expedient nor would it be allowed.

5 These communities having gradually increased, men's experience became greater, more perfect arts and rules and ways of living were discovered, and also the parts of communities were more fully differentiated. Finally, the things which are necessary for living and for living well were brought to full development by men's reason and experience, and there was established the perfect community, called the city, with the differentiation of its parts, to the discussion of which we shall now proceed.

Let this much suffice, then, concerning the rise of the civil community.

CHAPTER IV. On the Final Cause of the City and of Its Civil[24] Requirements, and the Differentiation in General of Its Parts

1 The city, according to Aristotle in the *Politics*, Book I, Chapter 1, is "the perfect community having the full limit of self-sufficiency, which came into existence for the sake of living, but exists for the sake of living well."[25] This phrase of Aristotle—"came into existence for the sake of living, but exists for the sake of living well"—signifies [*12*] the perfect final cause of the city, since those who live a civil life not only live, which beasts or slaves do too, but live well, having leisure for those liberal functions in which are exercised the virtues of both the practical and the theoretic soul.

2 Having thus determined the end of the city to be living and living well, we must treat first of living and its modes. For this, as we have said, is the purpose for the sake of which the city was established, and which necessitates all the things which exist in the city and are done by the association of men in it. Let us therefore lay this down as the principle of all the things which are to be demonstrated here, a principle naturally obtained, held, and freely granted by all: that all men

not deformed or otherwise impeded naturally desire a sufficient life, and avoid and flee what is harmful thereto.[26] This has been acknowledged not only with regard to man but also with regard to every genus of animals, according to Tully in his treatise *On Duties*, Book I, Chapter 3, where he says: "It is an original endowment which nature has bestowed upon every genus of living things, that it preserves itself, its body, and its life, that it avoids those things which seem harmful, and that it seeks and obtains all those things which are necessary for living."[27] This principle can also be clearly grasped by everyone through sense induction.

3 But the living and living well which are appropriate to men fall into two kinds, of which one is temporal or earthly, while the other is usually called eternal or heavenly. However, this latter kind of living, the eternal, the whole body of philosophers were unable to prove by demonstration, nor was it self-evident, and therefore they did not concern themselves with the means thereto. But as to the first kind of living and living well or good life, that is, the earthly, and its necessary means, this the glorious philosophers comprehended almost completely through demonstration. Hence for its attainment they concluded the necessity of the civil community, without which this sufficient life cannot be obtained. [*13*] Thus the foremost of the philosophers, Aristotle, said in his *Politics*, Book I, Chapter 1: "All men are driven toward such an association by a natural impulse."[28] Although sense experience teaches this, we wish to bring out more distinctly that cause of it which we have indicated, as follows: Man is born composed of contrary elements, because of whose contrary actions and passions some of his substance is continually being destroyed; moreover, he is born "bare and unprotected" from excess of the surrounding air and other elements, capable of suffering and of destruction, as has been said in the science of nature.[29] As a consequence, he needed arts of diverse genera and species to avoid the aforementioned harms. But since these arts can be exercised only by a large number of men, and can be had only through their association with one another, men had to assemble together in order to attain what was beneficial through these arts and to avoid what was harmful.

4 But since among men thus assembled there arise disputes and quarrels which, if not regulated by a norm of justice, would cause men to fight and separate and thus finally would bring about the destruction of the city, there had to be established in this association a standard of justice and a guardian or maker thereof. And since this guardian has to restrain excessive wrongdoers as well as other individuals both within and outside the city who disturb or attempt to oppress the community, the city had to have within it something by which to resist these. Again, since the community needs various conveniences,

repairs, and protection of certain common things, and different things in time of peace and in time of war, it was necessary that there be in the community men to take care of such matters, in order that the common necessity might be relieved when it was expedient or needful. But beside the things which we have so far mentioned, which relieve only the necessities of the present life, there is something else which men associated in a civil community need for the status of the future world promised to the human race through God's supernatural revelation, and which is useful also for the status of the present life. [*14*] This is the worship and honoring of God, and the giving of thanks both for benefits received in this world and for those to be received in the future one. For the teaching of these things and for the directing of men in them, the city had to designate certain teachers. The nature and qualities of all these and the other matters mentioned above will be treated in detail in the subsequent discussions.

5 Men, then, were assembled for the sake of the sufficient life, being able to seek out for themselves the necessaries enumerated above, and exchanging them with one another. This assemblage, thus perfect and having the limit of self-sufficiency, was called the city, whose final cause as well as that of its many parts has already been indicated by us in some measure, and will be more fully distinguished below. For since diverse things are necessary to men who desire a sufficient life, things which cannot be supplied by men of one order or office, there had to be diverse orders or offices of men in this association, exercising or supplying such diverse things which men need for sufficiency of life. But these diverse orders or offices of men are none other than the many and distinct parts of the city.

Let it suffice, then, to have covered thus in outline what the city is, why there came about such an association, and the number and division of its parts.

CHAPTER V. On the Differentiation of the Parts of the City, and the Necessity of Their Separate Existence for an End Discoverable by Man

1 We have now treated in general of the parts of the city, in whose perfect action and intercommunication, without external impediment, we have said that the tranquillity of the city consists. But we must now continue our discussion of them, since the fuller determination of these parts, with respect both to their functions or ends and to their other appropriate causes, will make more manifest the causes of tranquillity and of its [*15*] opposite. Let us say, then, that the parts or offices of the city are of six kinds, as Aristotle said in the *Politics*, Book VII, Chapter 7: the agricultural, the artisan, the military, the financial, the priestly, and

the judicial or deliberative.[30] Three of these, the priestly, the warrior, and the judicial, are in the strict sense parts of the city, and in civil communities they are usually called the honorable class (*honorabilitatem*). The others are called parts only in the broad sense of the term, because they are offices necessary to the city according to the doctrine of Aristotle in the *Politics*, Book VII, Chapter 7.[31] And the multitude belonging to these offices are usually called the vulgar. These, then, are the more familiar parts of the city or state, to which all the others can appropriately be reduced.

2   Although the necessity of these parts has been indicated to a certain extent in the preceding chapter, we wish to indicate it again more distinctly, assuming this proposition as having been previously demonstrated from what is self-evident, namely, that the city is a community established for the sake of the living and living well of the men in it. Of this "living" we have previously distinguished two kinds: one, the life or living of this world, that is, earthly; the other, the life or living of the other or future world. From these kinds of living, desired by man as ends, we shall indicate the necessity for the differentiation of the parts of the civil community. The first kind of human living, the earthly, is sometimes taken to mean the being of living things, as in Book II of the treatise *On the Soul*: "For living things, living is their being";[32] in which sense life is nothing other than soul. At other times, "living" is taken to mean the act, the action or passion, of the soul or of life.[33] Again, each of these meanings is used in two ways, with reference either to the numerically same being or to the being that is common to many individuals and that is called specific. And although each of these kinds of living, both as proper to man and as common to him and to the other animate things, depends upon natural causes, yet we are not at present considering it in so far as it comes from these causes; the natural science of plants and animals deals with this. Rather, our present concern is with these causes in so far as [*16*] they receive fulfilment "through art and reason," whereby "the human race lives."[34]

3   Hence, we must note that if man is to live and to live well, it is necessary that his actions be done and be done well; and not only his actions but also his passions. By "well" I mean in proper proportion. And since we do not receive entirely perfect from nature the means whereby these proportions are fulfilled, it was necessary for man to go beyond natural causes to form through reason some means whereby to effect and preserve his actions and passions in body and soul. And these means are the various kinds of functions and products deriving from the virtues and arts both practical and theoretic.

4   Of human actions and passions, some come from natural causes apart from knowledge. Such are those which are effected by the contrariety of the elements composing our bodies, through their intermix-

ture. In this class can properly be placed the actions of the nutritive part. Under this head also come actions effected by the elements surrounding our body through the alteration of their qualities; of this kind also are the alterations effected by things entering human bodies, such as food, drink, medicines, poisons, and other similar things. But there are other actions or passions which are performed by us or occur in us through our cognitive and appetitive powers. Of these some are called "immanent" because they do not cross over (*non transeunt*) into a subject other than the doer, nor are they exercised through any external organs or locomotive members; of this kind are the thoughts and desires or affections of men. But there are other actions and passions which are called "transitive" because they are opposed in either or in both respects to the kind which we have just described.

5　In order to proportion all these actions and passions, and to fulfil them in that to which nature could not lead, there were discovered the various kinds of arts and other virtues, as we said above, and men of various offices were established to exercise these for the purpose of supplying human needs. [*17*] These orders are none other than the parts of the city enumerated above. For in order to proportion and preserve the acts of the nutritive part of the soul, whose cessation would mean the complete destruction of the animal both individually and as a species, agriculture and animal husbandry were established. To these may properly be reduced all kinds of hunting of land, sea, and air animals, and all other arts whereby food is acquired by some exchange or is prepared for eating, so that what is lost from the substance of our body may thereby be restored, and the body be continued in its immortal being so far as nature has permitted this to man.

6　In order to moderate the actions and passions of our body caused by the impressions of the elements which externally surround us, there was discovered the general class of mechanics, which Aristotle in the *Politics*, Book VII, Chapter 6, calls the "arts."[35] To this class belong spinning, leathermaking, shoemaking, all species of housebuilding, and in general all the other mechanical arts which subserve the other offices of the city directly or indirectly, and which moderate not only men's touch or taste but also the other senses. These latter arts are more for pleasure and for living well than for the necessity of life, such as the painter's art and others similar to it, concerning which Aristotle says in the *Politics*, Book IV, Chapter 3: "Of these arts some must exist from necessity, and others are for pleasure and living well."[36] Under this class is also placed the practice of medicine, which is in some way architectonic to many of the above-mentioned arts.

7　In order to moderate the excesses of the acts deriving from the locomotive powers through knowledge and desire, which we have called transitive acts and which can be done for the benefit or for the harm or injury of someone other than the doer for the status of the present world, there was necessarily established in the city a part or office by which the excesses of such acts are corrected and reduced to equality or due proportion. For without such correction the excesses of these acts would cause fighting and hence the separation of the citizens, and finally the destruction of the city and loss of the sufficient life. This part of the city, together with its subsidiaries, is called by Aristotle the "judicial" or "ruling" and "deliberative" part, and its function is to regulate matters of justice and the common benefit. [*18*]

8 In addition, since the sufficient life cannot be led by citizens who are oppressed or cast into slavery by external oppressors, and also since the sentences of the judges against injurious and rebellious men within the city must be executed by coercive force, it was necessary to set up in the city a military or warrior part, which many of the mechanics also subserve. For the city was established for the sake of living and living well, as was said in the preceding chapter; but this is impossible for citizens cast into slavery. For this, as the excellent Aristotle said, is contrary to the nature of the city. Hence, indicating the necessity for this part, he said in the *Politics*, Book IV, Chapter 3: "There is a fifth class, that of the warriors, which is not less necessary than the others, if the citizens are not to be slaves of invaders. For nothing is more truly impossible than for that which is by nature slavish to be worthy of the name 'city'; for a city is self-sufficient, but a slave is not self-sufficient."[37] The necessity for this class because of internal rebels is treated by Aristotle in the *Politics*, Book VII, Chapter 6.[38] We have omitted the quotation of this passage here for the sake of brevity, and because we shall quote it in Chapter XIV of this discourse, paragraph 8.

9 Again, since in some years on earth the harvests are large, and in others small; and the city is sometimes at peace with its neighbors, and sometimes not; and it is in need of various common services such as the construction and repair of roads, bridges, and other edifices, and similar things whose enumeration here would be neither appropriate nor brief— to provide all these things at the proper time it was necessary to establish in the city a treasure-keeping part, which Aristotle called the "money class." This part gathers and saves monies, coins, wines, oils, and other necessaries; it procures from all places things needed for the common benefit, and it seeks to relieve future necessities; it is also subserved by some of the other parts of the city. Aristotle called this the "money" part, since the saver of monies seems to be the treasurer of all things; for all things are exchanged for money. [*19*]

10 It remains for us to discuss the necessity of the priestly part. All men have not thought so harmoniously about this as they have about the necessity of the other parts of the city. The cause of this difference was that the true and primary necessity of this part could not be com-

prehended through demonstration, nor was it self-evident. All nations, however, agreed that it was appropriate to establish the priesthood for the worship and honoring of God, and for the benefit resulting therefrom for the status of the present or the future world. For most laws or religions[39] promise that in the future world God will distribute rewards to those who do good and punishment to doers of evil.

11   However, besides these causes of the laying down of religious laws, causes which are believed without demonstration, the philosophers, including Hesiod, Pythagoras, and several others of the ancients, noted appropriately a quite different cause or purpose for the setting forth of divine laws or religions—a purpose which was in some sense necessary for the status of this world. This was to ensure the goodness of human acts both individual and civil, on which depend almost completely the quiet or tranquillity of communities and finally the sufficient life in the present world. For although some of the philosophers who founded such laws or religions did not accept or believe in human resurrection and that life which is called eternal, they nevertheless feigned and persuaded others that it exists and that in it pleasures and pains are in accordance with the qualities of human deeds in this mortal life, in order that they might thereby induce in men reverence and fear of God, and a desire to flee the vices and to cultivate the virtues. For there are certain acts which the legislator cannot regulate by human law, that is, those acts which cannot be proved to be present or absent to someone, but which nevertheless cannot be concealed from God, whom these philosophers feigned to be the maker of such laws and the commander of their observance, under the threat or promise of eternal reward for doers of good and punishment for doers of evil. Hence, they said of the variously virtuous men in this world that they were placed in the heavenly firmament; and from this were perhaps derived the names of certain [20] stars and constellations. These philosophers said that the souls of men who acted wrongly entered the bodies of various brutes; for example, the souls of men who had been intemperate eaters entered the bodies of pigs, those who were intemperate as regards [the pleasures of] the sense of touch and sexual matters entered the bodies of goats, and so on, according to the proportions of human vices to their condemnable properties. So too the philosophers assigned various kinds of torments to wrongdoers, like perpetual thirst and hunger for intemperate Tantalus: water and fruit were to be near him, but he was unable to drink or eat these, for they were always fleeing faster than he could pursue them. The philosophers also said that the infernal regions, the place of these torments, were deep and dark; and they painted all sorts of terrible and gloomy pictures of them. From fear of these, men eschewed wrongdoing, were instigated to perform virtuous works of piety and mercy, and were well disposed both in themselves and toward

others. As a consequence, many disputes and injuries ceased in communities. Hence too the peace or tranquillity of cities and the sufficient life of men for the status of the present world were preserved with less difficulty; which was the end intended by these wise men in laying down[40] such laws or religions.

12 Thus there existed a handing-down of such precepts by the gentile priests; and for the teaching of them they established in their communities temples in which their gods were worshiped. They also appointed teachers of these laws or traditions, whom they called priests (*sacerdotes*), because they handled the sacred objects of the temples, like the books, vases, and other such things subserving divine worship.

13 These affairs they arranged fittingly in accordance with their beliefs and rites. For as priests they appointed not anyone at all, but only virtuous and esteemed citizens who had held military, judicial, or deliberative office, and who had retired from secular affairs, being excused from civil burdens and offices because of age. For by such men, removed from passions, and in whose [21] words greater credence was placed because of their age and moral dignity, it was fitting that the gods should be honored and their sacred objects handled, not by artisans or hirelings who had exercised lowly and defiling offices. Hence it is said in the *Politics*, Book VII, Chapter 7: "Neither a farmer nor an artisan should be made a priest."[41]

14[42] Now correct views concerning God were not held by the gentile laws or religions and by all the other religions which are or were outside the catholic Christian faith or outside the Mosaic law which preceded it or the beliefs of the holy fathers which in turn preceded this—and, in general, by all those doctrines which are outside the tradition of what is contained in the sacred canon called the Bible. For they followed the human mind or false prophets or teachers of errors. Hence too they did not have a correct view about the future life and its happiness or misery, nor about the true priesthood established for its sake. We have, nevertheless, spoken of their rites in order to make more manifest their difference from the true priesthood, that of the Christians, and the necessity for the priestly part in communities.

CHAPTER VI. On the Final Cause of a Certain Part of the City, the Priesthood, Shown from the Immediate Teaching or Revelation of God, but Incapable of Being Proved by Human Reason

1 It remains now to discuss the final cause for which the true priesthood was established in communities of the faithful. This was in order to moderate human acts both immanent and transitive controlled by knowledge and desire, according as the human race is ordered by such

acts toward the best life of the future world. Hence it must be noted that although the first man, Adam, was created principally for the glory of God, just as were the other creatures, nevertheless, unlike the other species of corruptible things, he was created uniquely in God's image and likeness, so that he might be capable of participating [*22*] in eternal happiness after the life of the present world. Also he was created in a state of innocence or original justice and also of grace, as is plausibly said by some of the saints and certain leading teachers of the sacred Scriptures. Now if Adam had remained in this state, the establishment or differentiation of civil offices would not have been necessary for him or for his posterity, because nature would have produced for him the advantages and pleasures of the sufficiency of this life in the earthly or pleasurable paradise, without any suffering or fatigue on his part.

2   But because Adam corrupted his innocence or original justice and grace by eating of the forbidden fruit, transgressing thereby a divine commandment, he sank suddenly into guilt and misery, and was punished by being deprived of eternal happiness, the end to which he had been ordered with all his posterity by the beneficence of glorious God. His desert for transgressing this commandment was also to propagate all his posterity in lust. Every man after him was likewise conceived and born in lust, contracting therefrom the sin which in the law of the Christians is called "original." The only exception was Jesus Christ who, without any kind of sin or lust, was conceived by the Holy Spirit and born of the Virgin Mary; which came about when one of the three divine persons, the Son, true God in the unity of his person, assumed a human nature. As a result of this transgression of its first parents, the whole posterity of mankind was weakened in soul and is born weak, whereas it had previously been created in a state of perfect health, innocence, and grace. It was also because of this guilt that the human race was deprived of its best end to which it had been ordered.

3   But it is proper to God to have compassion for the human race, which He made in His own image, and which He had foreordained to a happy and eternal life. Hence God, who "never does anything in vain and never is lacking in necessaries,"[43] willed to remedy the human plight by giving certain commands which men were to obey and observe, and which would counteract the transgression and heal the disease of the guilt resulting from it. Like an expert physician, He proceeded in a very orderly manner from the easier to the more difficult steps. For He first commanded men [*23*] to observe the rite of holocausts, sacrificing the first fruit of the earth and the first-born of the animals, as if He wanted to test human penitence and obedience. This rite the ancient fathers observed with reverence for God, with faith, obedience, and thankfulness, down to the time of Abraham. To him God gave an additional command, more difficult than the first: the circumcision of

the whole male sex in the flesh of the foreskin. By this command God seemed again to be testing even more severely human penitence and obedience. These commands were observed by some men down to the time of Moses, through whom God handed down to the people of Israel a law wherein He set forth, in addition to the previous commands, further ones for the status of both the present and the future world; and He appointed priests and levites as ministers of this law. The utility of observing all the prior commands and the Mosaic law was that men would be purged of sin or guilt, both original and actual or freely committed, and would escape and be preserved from eternal and temporal sensory punishment of the other world, although by observing these commands they would not merit eternal happiness.

4 It was such happiness, however, to which merciful God had ordered the human race and which He wished to restore to it after leading it back from the fall, following the appropriate order. Hence, most recently of all, through His son Jesus Christ, true God and true man in unity of person, He handed down the evangelical law, containing commands and counsels of what must be believed, done, and avoided. By observance of these, not only are men preserved from sensory punishment, as they had been by observance of the prior commands, but also through God's gracious ordainment they merit, by a certain congruity, eternal happiness. And for this reason the evangelical law is called the law of grace, both because through the passion and death of Christ the human race was redeemed from its guilt and from the penalty of losing eternal beatitude which it had incurred as a result of the fall or sin of its first parents; and also because, by observing this law and receiving the sacraments established with it and in it, we are given divine grace, after it is given it is strengthened in us, and when we lose it, it is restored to us. Through this grace, by the ordainment of God and with the merit of [24] the passion of Christ, our works come by a certain congruity (as we have said) to merit eternal happiness.

5 Through Christ's passion the grace whereby men are able to merit a blessed life was received not only by those who came after but also by those who had observed the first commands and the Mosaic law. Before Christ's advent, passion, death, and resurrection, they had been deprived of this beatitude in the other world, in the place called limbo. But through Christ, they received the promise given to them by God, although in the prior commands of the prophets and of the Mosaic law such a promise had been handed down to them in a veiled and enigmatic manner, for *all these things happened to them in figure* [I Cor. 10:11], as the Apostle said to the Hebrews.[44]

6 This divine procedure was very appropriate, for it went from the less to the more perfect and finally to the most perfect of the things appropriate to human salvation. Nor should it be thought that God

could not have bestowed immediately at the outset, had He so wished, a perfect remedy for the fall of man. But He acted as He did because He so willed it and it was fitting, as required by men's sin, lest a too easy pardon be the occasion for further sinning.

7   As teachers of this law, and as ministers of its sacraments, certain men in the communities were chosen, called priests and deacons or levites. It is their office to teach the commands and counsels of the Christian evangelical law, as to what must be believed, done, and spurned, to the end that a blessed state be attained in the future world, and the opposite avoided.

8   The end of the priesthood, therefore, is to teach and educate men in those things which, according to the evangelical law, it is necessary to believe, do, and omit in order to attain eternal salvation and avoid [eternal] misery.

9   To this office appropriately pertain all the disciplines, theoretic and practical, discovered by the human mind, which moderate human acts both immanent and transitive arising from desire and knowledge, and which make man well disposed [25] in soul for the state of both the present and the future world. We have almost all these disciplines through the teaching of the admirable Philosopher and of other glorious men; however, we have omitted to enumerate them here, both for the sake of brevity and because it is not necessary to our present consideration.

10[45]   With respect to this chapter and the one following, we must understand that the causes of the offices of the city, in respect of each kind of cause, differ according as they are offices of the city and according as they are habits of the human body or mind. For according as they are habits of the human body or soul, their final causes are the functions which are immediately and essentially forthcoming from them. For example, the final cause of the shipbuilding part of the city is a ship; of the military part, the use of arms and fighting; of the priesthood, the preaching of the divine law and the administration of the sacraments in accordance with it; and so on with all the rest. But according as they are offices determined and established in the city, their final causes are the benefits and sufficiencies which perfect human actions and passions, and which are forthcoming from the functions of the aforesaid habits, or which cannot be had without them. For example, from fighting, which is the act or end of the military habit, freedom is forthcoming and is preserved for men in the city, and this freedom is the end of the acts and functions of the military. So too from the function or end of the housebuilding part, which is a house, there is forthcoming to men or to the city protection from the harmful impressions of the air, the hot, the cold, the wet, or the dry, which protection is the final cause for whose sake the housebuilding office was established in the city. In the same way, from observance of the divine law, which is the end of the priesthood, eternal happiness is forthcoming to men. Similar considerations apply to all the other parts or offices of the city. And the other kinds of causes of these offices—the material, formal, and efficient causes—are distinguished in the same or a similar manner, as will appear in the following chapter.

We have now finished our discussion of the number of the parts of the city, their necessity, and their differentiation through the sufficiencies which are their ends. [26]

CHAPTER VII. On the Other Kinds of Causes of the Separate Existence of the Parts of the City, and the Division of Each Kind in Two Ways Relevant to Our Purpose

1   We must now discuss the other causes of the offices or parts of the city. First we shall speak about their material and formal causes; then we shall inquire into their efficient cause. And since in things completed by the human mind the matter actually exists prior to the form,[46] let us first discuss the material cause. The proper matter of the different offices, according as the offices mean habits of the soul, is men inclined from their generation or birth to different arts or disciplines. For "nature is not lacking in necessaries,"[47] and is more solicitous for what is more noble;[48] among corruptible things, the most noble is the human species, which, perfected by different arts or disciplines, is the matter wherefrom must be established the city and its distinct parts necessary for the attainment of sufficiency of life, as was shown in Chapters IV and V of this discourse. Hence nature herself initiated this differentiation in the generation of men, producing some who in their natural dispositions were apt for and inclined toward farming, others toward military pursuits, and still others toward the other genera of arts and disciplines, but different men toward different ones. Nor did she incline only one individual toward one species of art or discipline, but rather many individuals toward the same species, to the extent necessary for sufficiency of life. Hence, she generated some men apt for prudence, since the judicial and deliberative part of the city must be composed of prudent men; some men apt for strength and courage, since the military part is appropriately composed of such men. So too she adapted the other men to the other genera of practical and theoretic habits which are necessary or appropriate for living and living well, so that out of the diversity of the natural inclinations toward habits [27] of diverse genera and species in all men, she perfected what was necessary for the diversity of the parts of the city.

The material causes of the offices of the city, according as the offices mean parts of the city, are almost apparent already. For these are men habituated by the arts and disciplines of diverse genera and species, from whom the diverse orders or parts are established in the city for the sake of the sufficiencies or ends forthcoming from their arts and disciplines. Considered in this way, as having been established in the city for this purpose, the parts of the city are properly called offices, in the sense of services, for they are ordered toward human service.

2   The formal causes of the offices of the city, according as they are habits of the human mind, are none other than these very habits. For these habits are themselves the forms of those who have them; they fulfil or perfect the human inclinations which exist by nature. Hence it is said in the *Politics*, Book VII, last chapter: "Every art and discipline aims to supply what nature lacks."[49] On the other hand, according as the offices of the city are established parts of the city, their formal causes are the commands which the efficient cause has given to or impressed upon the men who are appointed to exercise determinate functions in the city.

3   The efficient or productive causes of the offices, according as they mean habits of the soul, are the minds and wills of men through their thoughts and desires, individually or collectively. Also, in the case of certain offices, an added principle is the movement and exercise of the bodily organs. But the efficient cause of the offices, according as they are parts of the city, is frequently and in most cases the human legislator, although formerly, rarely and in very few cases, the immediate efficient cause was God, without human determination, as will be said in Chapter IX of this discourse and as will appear more fully from Chapter XII of this discourse and Chapter XV of Discourse II.[50] With regard to the priesthood, however, there is a different manner of establishment, which will be sufficiently discussed in Chapters XV and XVII of Discourse II.

In this way, then, we have discussed the parts of the city and the necessity of their establishment from the three other kinds of cause. [*28*]

CHAPTER VIII. On the Genera of Polities or Regimes, the Temperate and the Diseased, and the Division of Their Species

1   We must now show with greater certainty what was already shown to some extent above, that the establishment and differentiation of the parts of the city are brought about by an efficient cause which we have previously called the legislator. The same legislator establishes these parts, and differentiates and separates them as nature does with an animal, by first forming or establishing in the city one part which in Chapter V of this discourse we called the ruling or judicial part,[51] and through this the other parts, as will be indicated more fully in Chapter XV of this discourse. Hence we must first say something con-

cerning the nature of this ruling part. For since it is the first part of the city, as will appear below, the appropriate procedure will be to go from the indication of its efficient cause to the indication of the efficient cause which establishes and differentiates the other parts of the city.

2 There are two genera of ruling parts or governments, one well tempered, the other diseased. With Aristotle in the *Politics*, Book III, Chapter 5,[52] I call that genus "well tempered" in which the ruler governs for the common benefit, in accordance with the will of the subjects; while the "diseased" genus is that which is deficient in this respect. Each of these genera, again, is divided into three species: the temperate into kingly monarchy, aristocracy, and polity; the diseased into the three opposite species of tyrannical monarchy, oligarchy, and democracy. And each of these again has sub-species, the detailed discussion of which is not part of our present task. For Aristotle gave a sufficient account of them in Books III and IV of his *Politics*.

3 To obtain a fuller knowledge of these species of government, which is necessary for the clear understanding of what follows, let us define each species in accordance with the view of Aristotle. A *kingly monarchy*, then, is a temperate [29] government wherein the ruler is a single man who rules for the common benefit, and in accordance with the will or consent of the subjects. *Tyranny*, its opposite, is a diseased government wherein the ruler is a single man who rules for his own private benefit apart from the will of his subjects. *Aristocracy* is a temperate government in which the honorable class (*honorabilitas*) alone rules in accordance with the will or consent of the subjects and for the common benefit. *Oligarchy*, its opposite, is a diseased government in which some of the wealthier or more powerful rule for their own benefit apart from the will of the subjects. A *polity*, although in one sense it is something common to every genus or species of regime or government, means in another sense a certain species of temperate government, in which any citizen participates in some way in the government or in the deliberative function in turn according to his rank and ability or condition, for the common benefit and with the will or consent of the citizens. *Democracy*, its opposite, is a government in which the vulgar or the multitude of the needy establish the government and rule alone, apart from the will or consent of the other citizens and not entirely for the common benefit according to proper proportion.

4 As to which of the temperate governments is best or which of the diseased governments is worst, and the relative goodness or badness of the other species, the discussion of these points is not part of our present concern. Let it suffice to have said this much about the division of governments into their species and the definition of each.

CHAPTER IX. On the Methods of Establishing a Kingly Monarchy, and Which Method Is the More Perfect;[53] Also on the Methods of Establishing the Other Kinds of Regime or Polity, Both Temperate and Diseased

1   Having determined these points, we must now discuss the methods of effecting or establishing the ruling part [of the city]. For from the better or worse nature of these methods, viewed as actions[54] emerging from that nature to the civil regime, we must infer the efficient cause by which [30] these methods and the ruling part established by them will emerge more advantageously to the polity.

2   In this book we are considering the causes and actions by which the ruling part must in most cases be established. First, however, we wish to indicate the method and cause by which this part has been established in the past, although rarely, in order to distinguish this method or action, and its immediate cause, from those by which the government must regularly and in most cases be established, and which we can prove by human demonstration. For of the former method no certain comprehension can be had through demonstration. This method or action, with its immediate cause, by which the ruling part and other parts of the city, especially the priesthood, were formed in the past, was the divine will commanding this either through the determinate oracle of some individual creature or else perhaps immediately through itself alone. It was by this method that the divine will established the government of the people of Israel in the person of Moses and of certain other judges after him, and also the priesthood in the person of Aaron and his successors. With respect to this cause and its free action, as to why it did or did not operate in one way or another, we can say nothing through demonstration, but we hold it by simple belief apart from reason. There is, however, another method of establishing governments which proceeds immediately from the human mind, although perhaps from God as remote cause, who grants all earthly rulership, as is said in the nineteenth chapter of John [cf. John 19:11], and as the Apostle clearly states in the thirteenth chapter of the epistle to the Romans [cf. Rom. 13:1] and St. Augustine in the *City of God*, Book V, Chapter 21. However, God does not always act immediately; indeed in most cases, nearly everywhere, He establishes governments by means of human minds, to which He has granted the discretionary will for such establishment. And as for this latter cause, what it is, and by what kind of action it must establish such things, this can be indicated with human certainty from what is better or worse for the polity. [31]

3   Omitting, then, that method of which we cannot attain certain knowledge through demonstration, we wish first to present those methods of establishing governments which are effected immediately by the

human will;[55] next we shall show which of these is the more certain and the simpler.[56] Then, from the better nature of that method we shall infer the efficient cause from which alone it must and can emerge.[57] From these points, consequently, will appear the cause which must move to the best establishment and determination of the other parts of the city.[58] Finally we shall discuss the unity of the government,[59] through which it will also be apparent what is the unity of the city or state.[60]

4 In pursuit of this program, then, we shall first enumerate the methods of establishing kingly monarchy, by speaking of their origins. For this species of government seems rather kindred to us, and directly connected with the rule of the family, as is clear from what we said in Chapter III. After the determination of this point, the methods of establishing the other divisions of government will be made clear.

There are five methods of establishing kingly monarchies, according to Aristotle's *Politics*, Book III, Chapter 8.[61] One is when the monarch is appointed for one determinate function with respect to the ruling of the community, such as the leadership of the army, either with hereditary succession or for his own lifetime only. It was by this method that Agamemnon was made leader of the army by the Greeks. In modern communities this office is called the captaincy or constabulary.[62] This leader of the army had no judicial power in time of peace, but when the army was fighting a war he had the supreme authority to kill or otherwise punish transgressors.

Another method is that whereby certain monarchs rule in Asia; they receive their dominating authority through hereditary succession, and while they rule according to law, this law is like that of despots, being for the monarch's benefit rather than completely for the community's. The inhabitants of that region endure such rule "without protest,"[63] because of their barbaric [*32*] and slavish nature and the influence of custom. This rule is kingly in that it is native to the country and is over voluntary subjects, because, for example, the monarch's ancestors had been the first inhabitants of the region. But it is also in a sense tyrannical, in that its laws are not completely for the common benefit but for that of the monarch.

A third method of kingly government is when the ruler receives his authority through election rather than hereditary succession, but governs according to a law which is not completely for the common benefit but rather for that of the monarch, like the law of tyrants. Aristotle, therefore, called this species of government an "elective tyranny,"[64] a tyranny because the law was despotic, and elective because it was not over involuntary subjects.

A fourth method is that whereby a ruler is elected with subsequent hereditary succession, and governs according to laws which are completely for the common benefit; this method was used "in heroic days,"[65] as Aristotle says in the chapter previously mentioned. Those days were called "heroic" either because the stars then produced men who were believed to be "heroes," that is, divine, on account of their exceeding virtue; or because such men and not others were named rulers on account of their exceeding virtues and beneficial deeds, in that they brought together a scattered multitude and assembled it into a civil community, or they freed the region of oppressors by fighting and strength of arms, or perhaps they bought the region or acquired it by some other appropriate method and divided it among the subjects. At any rate these men were made rulers with subsequent hereditary succession, because of their bestowal of great benefits or their excess of virtue over the rest of the multitude, as Aristotle also said in the *Politics*, Book V, Chapter 5.[66] Under this species of monarchy, Aristotle perhaps included that in which someone is elected only for his own lifetime or a part of his lifetime; or else he designated it through the combination of this fourth species and the one called elective tyranny, because it shares features of both.

There is and was a fifth method of kingly monarchy, whereby the ruler is made [*33*] lord (*dominus*) over everything in the community, disposing of things and persons according to his own will, just as the head of a family disposes at will of everything in his own household.[67]

5   To make clearer these concepts of Aristotle, and to summarize all the methods of establishing the other kinds of government, we shall say that every government is over either voluntary or involuntary subjects. The first is the genus of well-tempered governments, the second of diseased governments. Each of these genera is divided into three species or modes, as was said in Chapter VIII. And since one of the species of well-tempered government, and perhaps the more perfect, is kingly monarchy, let us resume our previous statements about its various modes, by saying that the king or monarch either is named by the election of the inhabitants or citizens, or duly obtains the rulership without their election. If without the election of the citizens, this is either because he or his ancestors first inhabited the region, or because he bought the land and jurisdiction, or acquired it by a just war or by some other lawful method, such as by gift made to him for some great service. Each of these kinds of monarchy participates so much the more in true kingship, the more it is over voluntary subjects and according to law made for the common benefit of the subjects; and it savors so much the more of tyranny the more it departs from these features, that is, the consent of the subjects and law established for their common benefit. Hence it is written in the *Politics*, Book IV, Chapter 8: "These," that is, monarchies, "were kingly because they were according to law, and ruled voluntary subjects; but they were tyrannical because they ruled des-

potically and in accordance with their," that is, the monarchs', "own judgment."[68] These two features, then, distinguish temperate from diseased government, as is apparent from the clear statement of Aristotle, but absolutely or in greater degree it is the consent of the subjects which is the distinguishing criterion.[69] Now if the ruling monarch is elected by the inhabitants, it is [*34*] either with all his posterity succeeding him or not. If the latter, this may be in several ways, as he is named either for his own lifetime alone, or for his own lifetime and that of one or more of his successors, or not for the whole lifetime either of himself or of any of his successors but only for some determinate period, such as one or two years, more or less. Again, he is named to exercise either every judicial office, or only one office such as leading the army.

6 The elected and the non-elected kingly monarchs agree in that each rules voluntary subjects. They differ, however, in that the non-elected kings for the most part rule less voluntary subjects, and by laws which are less politic for the common benefit, as we said before in the case of the barbarians. The elected kings, on the other hand, rule more voluntary subjects, and by laws which are more politic, in that they are made for the common benefit, as we have said.

7 From these considerations it is clear, and will be even more apparent in the sequel, that the elected kind of government is superior to the non-elected. This is also the view of Aristotle in that passage of the *Politics*, Book III, Chapter 8, which we cited above with reference to those who were made rulers in the heroic days.[70] Again, this method of establishing governments is more permanent in perfect communities. For at some time or other it becomes necessary to have recourse to this from among all the other methods of establishing governments, but not conversely. For example, if hereditary succession fails, or if for some reason the multitude cannot bear the excessive malice of that family's rule, they must then turn to the method of election, which can never fail so long as the generation of men does not fail. Moreover, by the method of election alone is the best ruler obtained. For it is expedient that the ruler be the best man in the polity, since he must regulate the civil acts of all the rest. [*35*]

8 The method of establishing the other species of temperate government is usually election; in some cases the ruler is chosen by lot,[71] without subsequent hereditary succession. Diseased governments, on the other hand, are usually established by fraud or force or both.[72]

9 Which of the temperate governments is better, monarchy or one of the other two species, aristocracy or polity; and again, which of the monarchies is better, the elected or the non-elected; and moreover, which of the elected monarchies, that established with hereditary succession ensuing or that in which one man alone is named without such succes-

sion; which in turn is divided into the further alternatives of whether it is better to name the ruler for a whole lifetime, either of himself alone or of some of his successors also, or only for some determinate period, such as one or two years, more or less—in all these questions there is room for inquiry and reasonable doubt.[73] It must be held without doubt, however, in accordance with the truth and the manifest view of Aristotle, that election is the more certain standard of government, as will be more fully shown in Chapters XII, XVI, and XVII, of this discourse.

10 We must not overlook, however, that different multitudes in different times and places are inclined toward different kinds of polity and government, as Aristotle says in the *Politics*, Book III, Chapter 9.[74] Legislators and institutors of governments must hearken to this fact. For just as not every man is inclined toward the best discipline or study, whereupon it is appropriate that he be directed toward the acquisition not of that discipline but of some other good one for which he is more fitted, so too a multitude in some time or place may perhaps not be inclined to accept the best kind of government, and therefore recourse must first be had to that kind of temperate government which is more appropriate to it. For example, before the monarchy of Julius Caesar, the Roman people were for a long time unwilling to accept any definite monarch, either with hereditary succession or even one who was named only for his own lifetime. The reason for this was [36] perhaps that there was a large number of heroic men worthy of rulership among them, both families and individuals.

11 From these conclusions, then, it emerges clearly that those who ask which monarch is better for a city or state, the one who rules through election or the one who rules through hereditary succession, do not put the question in the proper way. What they must correctly ask first is, which monarch is better, the elected or the non-elected. And if the elected, again which, the one who is named with hereditary succession ensuing or the one who is named without hereditary succession. For although a non-elected monarch almost always transmits the rulership to his heir, not every elected monarch does so, but only the one who is named to rule with hereditary succession ensuing.

Let these, then, be our conclusions about the methods of establishing governments, and that the absolutely better method is election.

CHAPTER X. On the Distinction of the Meaning of the Term "Law," and on the Meaning Which Is Most Proper and Intended by Us

1 Since we have said that election is the more perfect and better method of establishing governments, we shall do well to inquire as to

its efficient cause, wherefrom it has to emerge in its full value; for from this will appear the cause not only of the elected government but also of the other parts of the polity. Now a government has to regulate [*37*] civil human acts (as we demonstrated in Chapter V of this discourse),[75] and according to a standard (*regulam*) which is and ought to be the form of the ruler, as such. We must, consequently, inquire into this standard, as to whether it exists, what it is, and why. For the efficient cause of this standard is perhaps the same as that of the ruler.

2 The existence of this standard, which is called a "statute" or "custom" and by the common term "law," we assume as almost self-evident by induction in all perfect communities. We shall show first, then, what law is;[76] next we shall indicate its final cause or necessity;[77] and finally we shall demonstrate by what person or persons and by what kind of action the law should be established;[78] which will be to inquire into its legislator or efficient cause, to whom we think it also pertains to elect the government, as we shall show subsequently by demonstration.[79] From these points there will also appear the matter or subject of the aforesaid standard which we have called law. For this matter is the ruling part, whose function it is to regulate the political or civil acts of men according to the law.

3 Following this procedure, then, we must first distinguish the meanings or intentions of this term "law," in order that its many senses may not lead to confusion. For in one sense it means a natural sensitive inclination toward some action or passion. This is the way the Apostle used it when he said in the seventh chapter of the epistle to the Romans: *I see another law in my members, fighting against the law of my mind* [Rom. 7:23]. In another sense this term "law" means any operative habit and in general every form, existing in the mind, of a producible thing, from which as from an exemplar or measure there emerge the forms of things made by art. This is the way in which the term was used in the forty-third chapter of Ezekiel: *This is the law of the house . . . And these are the measurements of the altar* [Ezek. 43:12–13]. In a third sense "law" means the standard containing admonitions for voluntary human acts according as these are ordered toward glory or punishment in the future world. In this sense the "Mosaic Law" was in part called a law, just as the "Evangelical Law" in its [*38*] entirety is called a law. Hence the Apostle said of these in his epistle to the Hebrews: *Since the priesthood has been changed, it is necessary that there be a change of the law also* [Heb. 7:12]. In this sense "law" was also used for the evangelic discipline in the first chapter of James: *He who has looked into the perfect law of liberty, and has continued therein . . . this man shall be blessed in his deeds* [Jas. 1:25]. In this sense of the term law all religions, such as that of Muhammad or of the Persians, are called laws in whole or in part, although among these only the

Mosaic and the evangelic, that is, the Christian, contain the truth. So too Aristotle called religions "laws" when he said, in the second book of his *Philosophy*: "The laws show how great is the power of custom";[80] and also in the twelfth book of the same work: "The other doctrines were added as myths to persuade men to obey the laws, and for the sake of expediency."[81] In its fourth and most familiar sense, this term "law" means the science or doctrine or universal judgment of matters of civil justice and benefit, and of their opposites.

4 Taken in this last sense, law may be considered in two ways. In one way it may be considered in itself, as it only shows what is just or unjust, beneficial or harmful; and as such it is called the science or doctrine of right (*juris*). In another way it may be considered according as with regard to its observance there is given a command coercive through punishment or reward to be distributed in the present world, or according as it is handed down by way of such a command; and considered in this way it most properly is called, and is, a law. It was in this sense that Aristotle also defined it in the last book of the *Ethics*, Chapter 8, when he said: "Law has coercive force, for it is discourse emerging from prudence and understanding."[82] Law, then, is a "discourse" or statement "emerging from prudence and" political "understanding," that is, it is an ordinance made by political prudence, concerning matters of justice and benefit and their opposites, [*39*] and having "coercive force," that is, concerning whose observance there is given a command which one is compelled to observe, or which is made by way of such a command.

5 Hence not all true cognitions of matters of civil justice and benefit are laws unless a coercive command has been given concerning their observance, or they have been made by way of a command, although such true cognition is necessarily required for a perfect law. Indeed, sometimes false cognitions of the just and the beneficial become laws, when there is given a command to observe them, or they are made by way of a command. An example of this is found in the regions of certain barbarians, who cause it to be observed as just that a murderer be absolved of civil guilt and punishment on payment of a fine. This, however, is absolutely unjust, and consequently the laws of such barbarians are not absolutely perfect. For although they have the proper form, that is, a coercive command of observance, they lack a proper condition, that is, the proper and true ordering of justice.

6 Under this sense of law are included all standards of civil justice and benefit established by human authority, such as customs, statutes, plebiscites, decretals, and all similar rules which are based upon human authority as we have said.

7 We must not overlook, however, that both the evangelical law

and the Mosaic, and perhaps the other religions as well, may be considered and compared in different ways in whole or in part, in relation to human acts for the status of the present or the future world. For they sometimes come, or have hitherto come, or will come, under the third sense of law, and sometimes under the last, as will be shown more fully in Chapters VIII and IX of Discourse II. Moreover, some of these laws are true, while others are false fancies and empty promises.

It is now clear, then, that there exists a standard or law of civil human acts, and what this is. [*40*]

CHAPTER XI. On the Necessity for Making Laws (Taken in Their Most Proper Sense); and That No Ruler, However Virtuous or Just, Should Rule Without Laws

1 Having thus distinguished these various meanings of "law," we wish to show the end or necessity of law in its last and most proper sense. The principal end is civil justice and the common benefit; the secondary end is the security of rulers, especially those with hereditary succession, and the long duration of governments. The primary necessity of the law, then, is as follows: It is necessary to establish in the polity that without which civil judgments cannot be made with complete rightness, and through which these judgments are properly made and preserved from defect so far as it is humanly possible. Such a thing is the law, when the ruler is directed to make civil judgments in accordance with it. Therefore, the establishment of law is necessary in the polity. The major premise of this demonstration is almost self-evident, and is very close to being indemonstrable. Its certainty can and should be grasped from Chapter V, paragraph 7 of this discourse. The minor premise will now be proved in this way: To make a good judgment, there are required a right disposition (*affectio*) of the judges and a true knowledge of the matters to be judged; the opposites of which corrupt civil judgments. For if the judge has a perverted disposition, such as hate, love, or avarice, this perverts his desire. But such dispositions are kept away from the judgment, and it is preserved from them, when the judge or ruler is directed to make judgments according to the laws, because the law lacks all perverted disposition; for it is not made useful for friend or harmful for foe, but universally for all those who perform civil acts well or badly. For all other things are accidental to the law and are outside it; but they are not similarly outside the judge. Persons involved in a judgment can be friendly or inimical to the judge, helpful or harmful to him, by making him a gift or a promise; and in other ways too they can arouse in the judge a disposition which perverts his judgment. Consequently, no judgment, so

far as possible, should be entrusted [*41*] to the discretion of the judge, but rather it should be determined by law and pronounced in accordance with it.

2 This was also the view of the divine Aristotle in the *Politics*, Book III, Chapter 9, where he purposely asks whether it is better for a polity to be ruled by the best man without law or by the best laws; and he replies as follows: "That is better," that is, superior for judging, "which entirely lacks the passionate factor," that is, the disposition which may pervert the judgment, "than that to which passion is natural. But law does not have this," that is, passion or disposition, "while every human soul must necessarily have it"[83]; and he said "every," not excepting anyone, however virtuous. He repeats this view in the *Rhetoric*, Book I, Chapter 1: "Most of all" is this required, that is, that nothing be left to the discretion of the judge, to be judged apart from the law, "because the judgment of the legislator," that is, the law, "is not partial," that is, it is not made on account of some one particular man, "but is concerned with future and universal matters. Now the judge and the magistrate judge about present and determinate matters, with which love and hate and private benefit are often involved, so that they cannot sufficiently see the truth, but instead have regard in their judgments to their own private pleasure and displeasure."[84] He also makes this point in Book I, Chapter 2 of the same treatise: "We do not render the same judgments when we are pleased as when we are pained, when we love as when we hate."[85]

3 A judgment is also corrupted through the ignorance of the judges, even if they be of good disposition or intention. This sin or defect is removed and remedied by the law, for in the law is determined well-nigh perfectly what is just or unjust, beneficial or harmful, with regard to each civil human act. Such determination cannot be made so adequately by any one man, however intelligent he may be. For no single man, and [*42*] perhaps not even all the men of one era, could investigate or remember all the civil acts determined in the law; indeed, what was said about them by the first investigators and also by all the men of the same era who observed such acts was meager and imperfect, and attained its completion only subsequently through the additions made by later investigators. This can be sufficiently seen from experience, in the additions, subtractions, and complete changes sometimes made in the laws in different eras, or at different times within the same era.

Aristotle also attests to this in the *Politics*, Book II, Chapter 2, when he says: "We must not ignore that attention must be paid to the long time and many years of the past, in which it would not have remained unknown if these things were good,"[86] that is, the measures which are to be established as laws. He says the same thing in the *Rhetoric*, Book I, Chapter 1: "Laws are made after long study."[87] This is also confirmed by reason, since the making of laws requires prudence, as we saw above from the definition of law, and prudence requires long experience, which, in turn, requires much time. Hence it is said in the sixth book of the *Ethics*: "A sign of what has been said is that while youths may become geometers, and be learned and wise in such sciences, they do not seem to become prudent. The cause is that prudence is of singular things which become known through experience; but a youth is not experienced, for experience requires a long time."[88] Consequently, what one man alone can discover or know by himself, both in the science of civil justice and benefit and in the other sciences, is little or nothing. Moreover, what is observed by the men of one era is quite imperfect by comparison with what is observed in many eras, so that Aristotle, discussing the discovery of truth in every art and discipline, wrote as follows in the *Philosophy*, Book II, Chapter 1: "One man," that is, one discoverer of any art or discipline, "contributes to it," [43] that is, discovers about it by himself alone, "little or nothing, but by the contributions of all a great deal is accomplished."[89] This passage is clearer in the translation from the Arabic, in which it reads as follows: "Each of them," that is, each of the discoverers of any art or discipline, "comprehends little or nothing about the truth. But when a collection is made from among all who have achieved some comprehension, what is collected will be of considerable quantity."[90] This may especially be seen in the case of astrology.

It is in this way, then, by men's mutual help and the addition of later to earlier discoveries, that all arts and disciplines have been perfected. Aristotle indicated this in a general way (*figuraliter*) with regard to the discovery of music in the same place cited above, when he said: "If there had been no Timotheus, we should be lacking much melody; but if there had been no Phrynes, there would have been no Timotheus";[91] that is, Timotheus would not have been so accomplished in melody if he had not had the melodies previously discovered by Phrynes. Averroes expounds these words as follows in the second book of his *Commentary*: "And what he," that is, Aristotle, "says in this chapter is clear. For no one can discover by himself the larger part of the practical or considerative," that is, theoretic, "arts, because these are completed only through the assistance which an earlier investigator gives to the one following him."[92] And Aristotle says the same thing in the second book of the *Refutations*,[93] last chapter, concerning the discovery of rhetoric and of all other disciplines, whatever the case may have been with regard to the discovery of logic, whose complete development he ascribed to himself alone without the discovery or assistance of any predecessor; in which he seems to have been unique among men. He also makes the same point in the *Ethics*, Book VIII, Chapter 1: "Two persons are better able to act and to understand"[94] [than one alone]. But if two, then more than two, both simultaneously and successively, can do more than one man alone. And this is what Aristotle says with regard to our present subject in the *Politics*, Book III, Chapter 9: "It will appear most unreasonable if one man should perceive better, judging with only two [*44*] eyes and two ears and acting with only two hands and feet, than many persons with many such organs."[95]

Since, then, the law is an eye composed of many eyes, that is, the considered comprehension of many comprehenders for avoiding error in civil judgments and for judging rightly, it is safer that these judgments be made according to law than according to the discretion of the judge. For this reason it is necessary to establish the law, if polities are to be ordered for the best with regard to their civil justice and benefit; for through the law, civil judgments are preserved from the ignorance and perverted disposition of the judges. This was the minor premise of the demonstration by which we have tried from the beginning of this chapter to prove the necessity of the laws. As to the method by which a dispute or civil lawsuit is to be decided or judged when it is not determined by law, this will be discussed in Chapter XIV of this discourse.[96] Laws, therefore, are necessary in order to exclude malice and error from the civil judgments or sentences of the judges.

4   For these reasons, Aristotle counseled that no judge or ruler should be granted the discretionary power to give judgments or commands without law, concerning those civil affairs which could be determined by law. Hence he said in the *Ethics*, Book IV, Chapter 5, the treatise on justice: "We must not allow man to rule, but" in accordance with "reason,"[97] that is, law; and Aristotle indicated the cause which we pointed out above, the perverted disposition which can be had by man. In the *Politics*, Book III, Chapter 6, he said: "The first question shows plainly above all that laws rightly made should govern,"[98] that is, that rulers should govern in accordance with laws. Again in the same treatise, Book III, Chapter 9, he said: "He who orders the mind to rule seems thereby to order God and the laws to rule; but he who orders man to rule," that is, without law, according to his own discretion, "instigates a beast";[99] and shortly thereafter he indicated the ground for this: "Hence the law is reason without appetite,"[100] [*45*] as if to say that the law is reason or knowledge without appetite, that is, without any affective disposition. He repeated this view also in the *Rhetoric*, Book I, Chapter 1: "It is best, therefore, for rightly-made laws to determine as many matters as possible and to entrust as little as possible to the judges";[101] giving the reasons adduced above, the exclusion from civil judgments of the judges' malice and ignorance, which cannot arise in the law as they do in the judge, as we have shown above. And even more clearly Aristotle says in the *Politics*, Book IV, Chapter 4: "Where the laws do not govern," that is, where rulers do not govern in accordance with the laws, "there is

no polity," that is, none which is temperate. "For the law should govern all things."[102]

5 It still remains to show that all rulers should govern according to law and not without it, and especially those monarchs who rule with hereditary succession, in order that their governments may be more secure and longer lasting. This was the second reason for the necessity of laws which we indicated at the beginning of this chapter. This may be seen first of all from the fact that, when rulers govern according to law, their judgments are preserved from the defect which is caused by ignorance and perverted disposition. Hence the rulers are regulated both in themselves and in relation to their citizen subjects, and they suffer less from sedition and from the consequent destruction of their governments which they would incur if they acted badly according to their own discretion, as Aristotle clearly says in the *Politics*, Book V, Chapter 5: "For a kingdom is destroyed least of all by external forces: its destruction most usually comes from within itself. It is destroyed in two ways: one is when those who share the ruling power quarrel among themselves, the other is when they try to govern tyrannically, by controlling more things, and contrary to the law. Kingdoms no longer occur these days, but if monarchies occur, they are rather tyrannies."[103]

6 Someone will raise an objection about the best man, who lacks ignorance [46] and perverted disposition.[104] As for us, however, we reply that such a man happens very rarely, and that even when he does he is not as free [from ignorance and passion] as the law itself, as we proved above from Aristotle, from reason, and from sense experience. For every soul sometimes has a vicious disposition. We can readily accept this from the thirteenth chapter of Daniel; for it is there written that *two elders came full of wicked device against Susanna, to put her to death* [Dan. 13:28]. Now these were old men and priests and judges of the people that year: nevertheless they bore false witness against her because she would not acquiesce to their vicious lust. If, then, old priests, about whom it would least be expected, were corrupted by carnal lust, what should be thought of other men, and how much more will they be corrupted by avarice and other vicious dispositions? Certainly, no one, however virtuous, can be so lacking in perverted passion and ignorance as is the law. Therefore, it is safer that civil judgments be regulated by the law than that they be entrusted to the discretion of a judge, however virtuous he may be.

7 Let us assume, however, although it is most rare or impossible, that there is some ruler so heroic that in him neither passion nor ignorance finds a place. What shall we say of his sons, who are unlike him and who, ruling in accordance with their own discretion, will commit excesses which result in their being deprived of the rulership? Someone

may say that the father, who is the best of men, will not hand over the government to such sons. This reply, however, is not to be granted, for two reasons: first, because it is not in the father's power to deprive his sons of the succession, since the rulership is a hereditary possession of his family, and second, because even if it were in the father's power to transfer the rulership to whomever he wanted, he would not deprive his sons of it no matter how vicious they were. Hence, Aristotle answers this objection as follows in the *Politics*, Book III, Chapter 9: "It is difficult to believe this," that is, that the father will deprive his sons of the rulership, "as it would require a greater virtue than human nature is capable of."[105] For this reason it is more expedient for rulers [47] that they be regulated and limited by law, than that they make civil judgments according to their own discretion. For when they act according to law, they will do nothing vicious or reprehensible, so that their rule will be made more secure and longer lasting.

8 This was the counsel which the distinguished Aristotle gave to all rulers, but to which they pay little heed. As he said in the *Politics*, Book V, Chapter 6: "The fewer things the rulers control," that is, without law, "the longer must every government endure, for they," that is, the rulers, "become less despotic, they are more moderate in their ways and are less hated by their subjects."[106] And then Aristotle adduces the testimony of a certain very prudent king called Theopompus, who gave up some of the power which had been granted to him. We have thought it appropriate to quote Aristotle's words here because of this ruler's uniqueness and his outstanding virtue, almost unheard of in anyone else throughout the ages. This is what Aristotle said: "Theopompus exercised moderation," that is, he lessened his power, which may perhaps have seemed excessive, "among other ways by establishing the office of the ephors: for by diminishing his power he increased his kingdom in time," that is, he made it more durable; "hence in a way he made it not smaller but greater. When his wife asked him whether he was not ashamed to give his children a smaller kingdom than he had received from his father, he replied, 'Not at all, for the power I give to them will be more lasting.' "[107] O heroic voice, proceeding from Theopompus' unheard-of prudence, a voice which should be heeded by all those who wish to wield plenitude of power over their subjects apart from laws! Many rulers, not heeding this voice, have been destroyed. And we ourselves have seen that from lack of attention to this voice not the least of kingdoms in modern times almost underwent a revolution, when its ruler wished to impose upon his subjects an unusual and illegal tax.[108] [48]

It is clear, then, from what we have said, that laws are necessary in polities if they are to be ordered with entire rightness and their governments are to be longer lasting.

CHAPTER XII. On the Demonstrable Efficient Cause of Human Laws, and Also on That Cause Which Cannot Be Proved by Demonstration: Which Is to Inquire into the Legislator. Whence It Appears Also That Whatever Is Established by Election Derives Its Authority from Election Alone Apart from Any Other Confirmation

1 We must next discuss the efficient cause of the laws which is capable of demonstration. For I do not intend to deal here with that institution of laws which can be effected by the immediate act or oracle of God apart from the human will, or which has been so effected in the past. Such, we said, was the establishment of the Mosaic law.[109] But I shall not deal with it here even in so far as it contains commands with regard to civil acts for the status of the present world. I shall discuss the establishment of only those laws and governments which emerge immediately from the decision of the human mind.

2 Let us say, to begin with, that it can pertain to any citizen to discover the law taken materially and in its third sense, as the science of civil justice and benefit.[110] Such inquiry, however, can be carried on more appropriately and be completed better by those men who are able to have leisure, who are older and experienced in practical affairs, and who are called "prudent men," [49] than by the mechanics who must bend all their efforts to acquiring the necessities of life. But it must be remembered that the true knowledge or discovery of the just and the beneficial, and of their opposites, is not law taken in its last and most proper sense, whereby it is the measure of civil human acts, unless there is given a coercive command as to its observance, or it is made by way of such a command, by someone through whose authority its transgressors must and can be punished.[111] Hence, we must now say to whom belongs the authority to make such a command and to punish its transgressors. This, indeed, is to inquire into the legislator or the maker of the law.

3 Let us say, then, in accordance with the truth and the counsel of Aristotle in the *Politics*, Book III, Chapter 6,[112] that the legislator, or the primary and proper efficient cause of the law, is the people or the whole body of citizens, or the weightier part thereof, through its choice or will expressed by words in the general assembly of the citizens, commanding or determining that something be done or omitted with regard to civil human acts, under a temporal pain or punishment. By the "weightier part" I mean to take into consideration the quantity and the quality of the persons in that community over which the law is made. The aforesaid whole body of citizens or the weightier part thereof is the legislator regardless of whether it makes the law directly by itself or entrusts the making of it to some person or persons, who are not and

cannot be the legislator in the absolute sense, but only in a relative sense and for a particular time and in accordance with the authority of the primary legislator. And I say further that [50] the laws and anything else established through election must receive their necessary approval by that same primary authority and no other, whatever be the case with regard to certain ceremonies or solemnities, which are required not for the being of the matters elected but for their well-being, since the election would be no less valid even if these ceremonies were not performed. Moreover, by the same authority must the laws and other things established through election undergo addition, subtraction, complete change, interpretation, or suspension, in so far as the exigencies of time or place or other circumstances make any such action opportune for the common benefit. And by the same authority, also, must the laws be promulgated or proclaimed after their enactment, so that no citizen or alien who is delinquent in observing them may be excused because of ignorance.

4   A citizen I define in accordance with Aristotle in the *Politics*, Book III, Chapters 1, 3, and 7, as one who participates in the civil community in the government or the deliberative or judicial function according to his rank.[113] By this definition, children, slaves, aliens, and women are distinguished from citizens, although in different ways. For the sons of citizens are citizens in proximate potentiality, lacking only in years. The weightier part of the citizens should be viewed in accordance with the honorable custom of polities, or else it should be determined in accordance with the doctrine of Aristotle in the *Politics*, Book VI, Chapter 2.[114]

5   Having thus defined the citizen and the weightier part of the citizens, let us return to our proposed objective, namely, to demonstrate that the human authority to make laws belongs only to the whole body of the citizens or to the weightier part thereof. First we shall try to prove that this is so. The absolutely primary human authority to make or establish human laws belongs only to those men from whom alone the best laws can emerge. But these are the whole body of the citizens, or the weightier part thereof, which represents that whole body; since it is difficult or impossible for all persons [51] to agree upon one decision, because some men have a deformed nature, disagreeing with the common decision through singular malice or ignorance. The common benefit should not, however, be impeded or neglected because of the unreasonable protest or opposition of these men. The authority to make or establish laws, therefore, belongs only to the whole body of the citizens or to the weightier part thereof.

The first proposition of this demonstration is very close to self-evident, although its force and its ultimate certainty can be grasped from Chapter V of this discourse. The second proposition, that the best law is made only through the hearing and command of the entire multitude, I prove by assuming with Aristotle in the *Politics*, Book III, Chapter 7, that the best law is that which is made for the common benefit of the citizens. As Aristotle said: "That is presumably right," that is, in the laws, "which is for the common benefit of the city and the citizens."[115] But that this is best achieved only by the whole body of the citizens or by the weightier part thereof, which is assumed to be the same thing, I show as follows: That at which the entire body of the citizens aims intellectually and affectively is more certainly judged as to its truth and more diligently noted as to its common utility. For a defect in some proposed law can be better noted by the greater number than by any part thereof, since every whole, or at least every corporeal whole, is greater in mass and in virtue than any part of it taken separately. Moreover, the common utility of a law is better noted by the entire multitude, because no one knowingly harms himself.[116] Anyone can look to see whether a proposed law leans toward the benefit of one or a few persons more than of the others or of the community, and can protest against it. Such, however, would not be the case were the law made by one or a few persons, considering their own private benefit rather than that of the community. This position is also supported by the arguments which we advanced in Chapter XI of this discourse with regard to the necessity of having laws.

6 Another argument to the principal conclusion is as follows. The authority to make the law belongs only to those men whose making of it will cause the law to be better observed or [52] observed at all. Only the whole body of the citizens are such men. To them, therefore, belongs the authority to make the law. The first proposition of this demonstration is very close to self-evident, for a law would be useless unless it were observed. Hence Aristotle said in the *Politics*, Book IV, Chapter 6: "Laws are not well ordered when they are well made but not obeyed."[117] He also said in Book VI, Chapter 5: "Nothing is accomplished by forming opinions about justice and not carrying them out."[118] The second proposition I prove as follows. That law is better observed by every citizen which each one seems to have imposed upon himself. But such is the law which is made through the hearing and command of the entire multitude of the citizens. The first proposition of this prosyllogism is almost self-evident; for since "the city is a community of free men," as is written in the *Politics*, Book III, Chapter 4,[119] every citizen must be free, and not undergo another's despotism, that is, slavish dominion. But this would not be the case if one or a few of the citizens by their own authority made the law over the whole body of citizens. For those who thus made the law would be despots over the others, and hence such a law, however good it was, would be endured only with reluctance, or not at all, by the rest of the citizens, the more ample part. Having suffered contempt, they would protest against it, and not having been called upon to make it, they would not observe it. On the other hand, a law made

by the hearing or consent of the whole multitude, even though it were less useful, would be readily observed and endured by every one of the citizens, because then each would seem to have set the law upon himself, and hence would have no protest against it, but would rather tolerate it with equanimity. The second proposition of the first syllogism I also prove in another way, as follows. The power to cause the laws to be observed belongs only to those men to whom belongs coercive force over the transgressors of the laws. But these men are the whole body of citizens or the weightier part thereof. Therefore, to them alone belongs the authority to make the laws.

7   The principal conclusion is also proved as follows. That practical matter whose proper establishment is of greatest importance for the common sufficiency of the citizens in this life, and whose poor establishment [53] threatens harm for the community, must be established only by the whole body of the citizens. But such a matter is the law. Therefore, the establishment of the law pertains only to the whole body of the citizens. The major premise of this demonstration is almost self-evident, and is grounded in the immediate truths which were set forth in Chapters IV and V of this discourse. For men came together to the civil community in order to attain what was beneficial for sufficiency of life, and to avoid the opposite. Those matters, therefore, which can affect the benefit and harm of all ought to be known and heard by all, in order that they may be able to attain the beneficial and to avoid the opposite. Such matters are the laws, as was assumed in the minor premise. For in the laws being rightly made consists a large part of the whole common sufficiency of men, while under bad laws there arise unbearable slavery, oppression, and misery of the citizens, the final result of which is that the polity is destroyed.

8   Again, and this is an abbreviation and summary of the previous demonstrations: The authority to make laws belongs only to the whole body of the citizens, as we have said, or else it belongs to one or a few men.[120] But it cannot belong to one man alone for the reasons given in Chapter XI and in the first demonstration adduced in the present chapter; for through ignorance or malice or both, this one man could make a bad law, looking more to his own private benefit than to that of the community, so that the law would be tyrannical. For the same reason, the authority to make laws cannot belong to a few; for they too could sin, as above, in making the law for the benefit of a certain few and not for the common benefit, as can be seen in oligarchies. The authority to make the laws belongs, therefore, to the whole body of citizens or to the weightier part thereof, for precisely the opposite reason. For since all the citizens must be measured by the law according to due proportion, and no one knowingly harms or wishes injustice to himself, it follows that all or most wish a law conducing to the common benefit of the citizens.

9 From these same demonstrations it can also be proved, merely by changing the minor term, that the approval, interpretation, and suspension of the laws, and the other matters set forth in paragraph 3 of this same chapter, [54] pertain to the authority of the legislator alone. And the same must be thought of everything else which is established by election. For the authority to approve or disapprove rests with those who have the primary authority to elect, or with those to whom they have granted this authority of election. For otherwise, if the part could dissolve by its own authority what had been established by the whole, the part would be greater than the whole, or at least equal to it.

The method of coming together to make the laws will be described in the following chapter.

CHAPTER XIII. On Some Objections to the Statements[121] Made in the Preceding Chapter, and Their Refutation, Together with a Fuller Exposition of the Proposition

1 Objections will be made to our above statements, to the effect that the authority to make or establish laws does not belong to the whole body of the citizens. The first objection is that those who for the most part are vicious and undiscerning should not make the law. For these two sins, malice and ignorance, must be excluded from the legislator, and it was to avoid them in civil judgments that we upheld the necessity of law in Chapter XI of this discourse. But the people or the whole body of citizens have these sins; for men for the most part seem to be vicious and stupid: *The number of the stupid is infinite* [Eccles. 1:15], as it is said in the first chapter of Ecclesiastes. Another objection is that it is very difficult or impossible to harmonize the views of many vicious and unintelligent persons; but such is not the case with the few and virtuous. It is more useful, therefore, that the law be made by the few than by the whole body of the citizens or the exceeding majority of them. Again, in every civil community the wise and learned are few in comparison with the multitude of the unlearned. Since, therefore, the law is more usefully made by the wise and learned than by the unlearned and uncultivated, it seems that the authority to make laws belongs to the few, not to the many or to all. Furthermore, that which can be done by fewer persons is needlessly done by more. Since, therefore, the law can be made by the wise, who are few, as has been said, the entire multitude or the greater part of it would needlessly be occupied therein. [55] The authority to make the laws does not belong, therefore, to the whole body of the citizens or to the weightier part thereof.

2 From what we assumed above as the principle of all the things to be demonstrated in this book, namely, that all men desire sufficiency of life and avoid the opposite,[122] we demonstrated in Chapter IV the civil

association of men, inasmuch as through such association they can attain this sufficiency, and without it they cannot. Hence too Aristotle says in the *Politics*, Book I, Chapter 1: "There is in all men a natural impulse toward such a community,"[123] that is, the civil community. From this truth there necessarily follows another, which is presented in the *Politics*, Book IV, Chapter 10, namely, that "that part of the city which wishes the polity to endure must be weightier than the part which does not wish it."[124] For the same specific nature according to the greater part of itself never desires a thing and immediately at the same time that thing's destruction, since such a desire would be futile. Indeed, those who do not wish the polity to endure are classed among the slaves, not among the citizens, as are certain aliens. Hence Aristotle says in the *Politics*, Book VII, Chapter 13: "Everyone in the country unites with the subjects in the desire to have a revolution," and then he adds: "It is impossible that there be so many persons in the government," that is, rebellious, or not caring to live a civil life, "that they are stronger than all the others,"[125] that is, than those who wish to carry on a political life (*politizare*). Why this is impossible is obvious; for it would mean that nature errs or is deficient for the most part. If, therefore, the weightier multitude of men wish the polity to endure, as seems to have been well said, they also wish that without which the polity cannot endure. But this is the standard of the just and the beneficial, handed down with a command, and called the law; for "it is impossible for the best-ruled city," that is, the city governed according to virtue, "not to be well ordered by laws," as is said in the *Politics*, Book IV, Chapter 7,[126] and as we demonstrated in Chapter XI of this discourse. Therefore, the weightier multitude of the city wishes to have law, or else there would occur deformity in nature and art in most cases; the impossibility of which is assumed from natural science.[127] [56]

With these manifest truths I again assume that common conception of the mind, that "every whole is greater than its part," which is true with respect both to magnitude or mass and to practical virtue and action. From this it clearly follows of necessity that the whole body of the citizens, or the weightier multitude thereof, which must be taken for the same thing, can better discern what must be elected and what rejected than any part of it taken separately.

3   Now that we have laid down these obvious truths, it is easy to refute the objections whereby one might try to prove that the making of the law does not pertain to the whole body of the citizens or the weightier multitude thereof but rather to a certain few. As for the first objection, that the authority to make laws does not belong to those who in most cases are vicious and undiscerning, this is granted. But when it is added that the whole body of citizens is such, this must be denied. For most of the citizens are neither vicious nor undiscerning most of the

time; all or most of them are of sound mind and reason and have a right desire for the polity and for the things necessary for it to endure, like laws and other statutes or customs, as was shown above. For although not every citizen nor the greater number of the citizens be discoverers of the laws, yet every citizen can judge of what has been discovered and proposed to him by someone else, and can discern what must be added, subtracted, or changed. Hence in the major premise's reference to the "undiscerning," if what is meant is that because most of the citizens cannot discover the law by themselves, therefore they ought not to establish the law, this must be denied as manifestly false, as is borne out by sense induction and by Aristotle in the *Politics*, Book III, Chapter 6. By induction we can see that many men judge rightly about the quality of a picture, a house, a ship, and other works of art, even though they would have been unable to discover or produce them. Aristotle also attests to this in the place just cited, answering the proposed objection with these words: "About some things the man who made them is not the only or the best judge."[128] He proves this in many species of arts, and indicates that the same is true for all the others. [57]

4. Nor is this position invalidated by those who say that the wise, who are few, can discern what should be enacted with regard to practical matters better than can the rest of the multitude. For even if this be true, it still does not follow that the wise can discern what should be enacted better than can the whole multitude, in which the wise are included together with the less learned. For every whole is greater than its part both in action and in discernment. This was undoubtedly the view of Aristotle in the *Politics*, Book III, Chapter 6, when he said: "The multitude is justly dominant in the more important matters," that is, the multitude or the whole body of citizens or the weightier part thereof, which he here signifies by the term "multitude," should justly be dominant with respect to the more important matters in the polity; and he gives this reason: "The people is composed of many persons including the council and the judiciary and the honorable class, and all of these together are more ample than any single person or group, including the few rulers who hold high governmental offices."[129] He means that the people, or the multitude composed of all the groups of the polity or city taken together, is more ample than any part of it taken separately, and consequently its judgment is more secure than that of any such part, whether that part be the common mass, which he here signified by the term "council" (*consilium*), such as the farmers, artisans, and others of that sort; or whether it be the "judiciary," that is, those officials who assist the ruler in judicial functions, as advocates or lawyers and notaries; or whether it be the "honorable class," that is, the group of the best men, who are few, and who alone are appropriately elected to the highest governmental offices; or whether it be any other part of the city taken

separately. Moreover, even if we assume what is indeed true, that some of the less learned do not judge about a proposed law or some other practical matter as well as do the same number of the learned, still the number of the less learned could be increased to such an extent that they would judge about these matters as well as, or even better than, the few who are more learned. Aristotle stated this clearly in the place cited above when he undertook to confirm this view: "If the multitude be not too vile, each member of it will indeed be a worse judge than those who have knowledge; but taken all together they will be better judges, or at least not worse."[130]

As for the passage quoted from the first chapter of Ecclesiastes that *the number of the stupid is infinite*, [58] it must be replied that by "stupid" was meant those who are less learned or who do not have leisure for liberal functions, but who nevertheless share in the understanding and judgment of practical matters, although not equally with those who have leisure. Or perhaps the wise author, as Jerome says in his commentary thereon, meant by "stupid" the unbelievers who, however much they may know the worldly sciences, are stupid in an absolute sense, in keeping with the statement of the Apostle in the first epistle to the Corinthians: *The wisdom of this world is stupidity with God* [I Cor. 3:19].

5   The second objection carries little weight, for even though it be easier to harmonize the views of fewer persons than of many, it does not follow that the views of the few, or of the part, are superior to those of the whole multitude, of which the few are a part. For the few would not discern or desire the common benefit as well as would the entire multitude of the citizens. Indeed, it would be insecure, as we have already shown, to entrust the making of the law to the discretion of the few. For they would perhaps consult therein their own private benefit, as individuals or as a group, rather than the common benefit, as is quite apparent in those who have made the decretals of the clergy, and as we shall make sufficiently clear in Chapter XXVIII of Discourse II. By this means the way would be opened to oligarchy, just as when the power to make the laws is given to one man alone the opportunity is afforded for tyranny, as we showed above in Chapter XI, paragraph 4, where we quoted from the fourth book of Aristotle's *Ethics*, the treatise on justice.

6   The third objection can be easily refuted from what we have already said: for although the laws can be better made by the wise than by the less learned, it is not therefore to be concluded that they are better made by the wise alone than by the entire multitude of citizens, in which the wise are included. For the assembled multitude of all of these can discern and desire the common justice [59] and benefit to a greater

extent than can any part of that multitude taken separately, however prudent that part may be.

7 Hence those do not speak the truth who hold that the less learned multitude impedes the choice and approval of the true or common good; rather, the multitude is of help in this function when it is joined to those who are more learned and more experienced. For although the multitude cannot by itself discover true and useful measures, it can nevertheless discern and judge the measures discovered and proposed to it by others, as to whether they should be added to, or subtracted from, or completely changed, or rejected. For many things which a man would have been unable to initiate or discover by himself, he can comprehend and bring to completion after they have been explained to him by someone else. For the beginnings of things are the most difficult to discover; as Aristotle says in the second book of the *Refutations*, last chapter: "Most difficult is it to see the beginning,"[131] that is, of the truth proper to each discipline. But when this has been discovered, it is easy to add the remainder or to extend it. Hence, while only the best and most acute minds can discover the principles of the sciences, the arts, and other disciplines, nevertheless when these principles have been discovered, additions can be made to them by men of humbler mind. Nor should the latter be called undiscerning because they cannot discover such principles by themselves; on the contrary, they should be numbered among good men, as Aristotle said in the *Ethics*, Book I, Chapter 2: "That man is best who has achieved an understanding of all things by himself. But he too is good who hearkens to the wise words of another,"[132] that is, by listening to him attentively and not contradicting him without reason.

8 It is hence appropriate and highly useful that the whole body of citizens entrust to those who are prudent and experienced the investigation, discovery, and examination of the standards, the future laws or statutes, concerning civil justice and benefit, common difficulties or burdens, and other similar matters. Either some of these prudent and experienced men may be elected by each of the primary parts of the city enumerated in Chapter V, paragraph 1, according to the proportion of each part; [60] or else all these men may be elected by all the citizens assembled together. And this will be an appropriate and useful method whereby to come together to discover the laws without detriment to the rest of the multitude, that is, the less learned, who would be of little help in the investigation of such standards, and would be disturbed in their performance of the other functions necessary both to themselves and to others, which would be burdensome both to each individual and to the community.

After such standards, the future laws, have been discovered and diligently examined, they must be laid before the assembled whole body of citizens for their approval or disapproval, so that if any citizen thinks that something should be added, subtracted, changed, or completely rejected, he can say so, since by this means the law will be more usefully ordained. For, as we have said, the less learned citizens can sometimes perceive something which must be corrected in a proposed law even though they could not have discovered the law itself. Also, the laws thus made by the hearing and consent of the entire multitude will be better observed, nor will anyone have any protest to make against them.

These standards, the future laws, will thus have been made public, and in the general assembly of the citizens those citizens will have been heard who have wanted to make some reasonable statements with regard to them. Then there must again be elected men of the qualities, and by the method, indicated above, or else the aforesaid men must be confirmed; and they, representing the position and authority of the whole body of the citizens, will approve or disapprove in whole or in part the aforementioned standards which had been investigated and proposed, or else, if it so wishes, the whole body of the citizens or the weightier part thereof will do this same thing by itself. After this approval, the aforesaid standards are laws and deserve to be so called, not before; and after their publication or proclamation, they alone among human commands make transgressors liable to civil guilt and punishment. [*61*]

We think we have adequately shown, then, that the authority to make or establish the laws, and to give a command with regard to their observance, belongs only to the whole body of the citizens or to the weightier part thereof as efficient cause, or else to the person or persons to whom the aforesaid whole body has granted this authority.

DISCOURSE   TWO

CHAPTER XII. On the Differentiation of the Meanings of Certain Terms Necessary for the Determination of Questions Concerning the Status of Supreme Poverty

*   *   *

3 We shall begin by distinguishing the meanings of "right" (*jus*), since we shall need these in the distinctions and definitions of the other terms, and not conversely. (i) "Right," then, in one of its senses means law taken [*214*] in the third and last sense of "law," which we discussed

in Chapter X of Discourse I.[133] This is twofold, one human, the other divine, and the latter at a particular time and in a particular way comes under the last meaning of law, as has been said above.[134] The nature and quality of these laws, how they agree and how they differ, have been sufficiently discussed in Chapters VIII and IX of this discourse. But reconsidering them again in relation to our present purpose, let us say that these laws agree in this respect first of all, that each is a command or prohibition or permission of acts whose nature it is to emerge through the control of the human mind. But the laws differ in that the human is coercive in this world over those who transgress it, while the second, the divine, is not coercive in this world, but in the future world only. The word "command" also is used in two senses. In one sense it is used actively, referring to the act of the commander; it is in this sense that we say that the expressed will of a man who holds power, such as a king or other ruler, is a command. In another sense, "command" refers to what is willed by the act of the commander; in this sense we say that the servant has done the command of the master—not that the servant has done the master's act, which is to command or order, but that the servant has done what was willed by the master's act or command. And therefore, whenever this word "command" refers to the commander, it means the same as the act of commanding; whenever it refers to the subject, it means the same as what is willed by the act of commanding, and is then used passively.

This word "command," then, taken actively and in the general sense, means the legislator's ordinance or statute, both affirmative and negative, obliging the transgressor to punishment. But in modern usage it is properly taken for an affirmative statute. For usage has brought it about that an affirmative statute does not have a specific name of its own, but has kept the general name of "command"; but a negative statute does have a specific name of its own, for it is called a "prohibition."

I call an "affirmative statute" one which orders something to be done; a "negative statute," one which orders something not to be done. If such an ordinance, which obliges the transgressor to punishment, be affirmative, it is called a "command"; if it be negative, and also thus obliges, it is called a "prohibition." [215] Now "prohibition" is used in two senses, actively and passively, as is "command." These two ordinances, which oblige transgressors to punishment, are usually expressed in laws, either in their own proper species or in a similar or analogous one.[135] But in another and stricter sense, "command" and "prohibition" are used in divine law to refer only to that affirmative or negative statute which obliges the transgressor to eternal punishment. It is in this sense that these words are used by theologians when they say that commands are "necessary for salvation," that is, that observance of them is necessary, if one is to be saved. Whence in Luke, Chapter 18: *If thou wilt enter into life, keep the commandments*,[136] that is, the commands.

4 But there are certain other ordinances, both affirmative and negative, which are expressed or only implied in the laws, and which, whether referring to the same act or to a different one, do not oblige the man who does or omits the act to punishment. Very many acts are the objects of such ordinances, such as the performance or omission of an act of liberality. And it is such acts which are properly said to be "permitted by law," although this word "permission" is sometimes taken in a general sense to refer to statutes which oblige to punishment. For everything which the law commands to be done, it permits to be done, although not conversely; so too, what the law prohibits to be done, it permits not to be done. And again, of these permitted acts, taking "permitted" in its proper sense as that which does not oblige to punishment, some are meritorious according to divine law and are called "counsels," while others which are not thus meritorious are given the unqualified name of "permissions." And these terms, thus taken in their proper sense, are again used in two ways, actively and passively, as are prohibitions and commands. But these for the most part are not given specific expression in the laws, particularly in human laws, because their number is so large and a general ordinance concerning them is sufficient. For everything which is not commanded or prohibited by the law is understood to be permitted by the ordinance of the legislator. A "command" in accordance with the law, then, in its proper sense is an affirmative statute obliging its transgressor to punishment; a "prohibition" in its proper sense [216] is a negative statute obliging its transgressor to punishment; a "permission" in its proper sense is an ordinance of the legislator obliging no one to punishment. We shall henceforth use these terms in these proper senses.

5 From the above, it can readily be seen what is meant by the term "lawful"; for everything which is done in accordance with the command or permission of the law, or which is omitted in accordance with the prohibition or permission of the law, is lawfully done or omitted, and can be called "lawful," while its opposite or contrary is "unlawful."

6 From the above, we can also see what is usually meant by the term "equitable" (*fas*). For in one sense the equitable is the same as the lawful, so that the two are used convertibly. In another sense, the equitable is that which the legislator is reasonably presumed to have permitted in some case, although such an act is generally or regularly prohibited; as, for example, it is equitable to pass through another's field sometimes, or to take what belongs to another without the owner's express consent, although it is not "right" taken regularly in any of the senses given above. For the taking of another's property is regularly prohibited; yet it is equitable in the case where the owner is reasonably presumed to give his consent, even though he does not expressly give it; for which

reason there is sometimes need of equity (*epieikeia*) in such cases.[137]

Thus, then, in one sense right is the same as law, divine or human, or what is commanded or prohibited or permitted according to these laws.

7 There is also another division of right, and properly of human right, into natural and civil. Natural right (*jus naturale*), according to Aristotle in the fourth book of the *Ethics*, the treatise on justice, is that statute of the legislator with respect to which almost all men agree that it is honorable and should be observed.[138] Examples are that God must be worshiped, parents must be honored, children must be reared by their parents up to a certain age, no one should be injured, injuries must be lawfully repulsed, and the like. Although these depend upon human enactment, they are analogously (*transumptive*) called "natural" rights [*217*] because in all regions they are in the same way believed to be lawful and their opposites unlawful, just as the acts of natural things which are devoid of will are everywhere uniform, like fire, which "burns here just as it does in Persia."[139]

8 However, there are some men who define natural right as the dictate of right reason in practical matters, which they place under divine right; and consequently everything done in accordance with divine law and in accordance with the counsel of right reason is lawful in an absolute sense; but not everything done in accordance with human laws, since in some things the latter fall away from right reason. But the word "natural" is used equivocally here and above. For there are many things which are in accordance with the dictate of right reason, but which are not agreed upon as honorable by all nations, namely, those things which are not self-evident to all, and consequently not acknowledged by all. So too there are some commands, prohibitions, or permissions in accordance with divine law which do not agree in this respect with human law; but since many cases of this are well known, I have omitted to cite examples for the sake of brevity.

9 And hence too, some things are lawful according to human law which are not lawful according to divine law, and conversely. However, what is lawful and what unlawful in an absolute sense must be viewed according to divine law rather than human law, when these disagree in their commands, prohibitions, or permissions.

10 (ii) "Right" is used in a second sense to refer to every controlled human act, power, or acquired habit, internal or external, both immanent and transitive or crossing over into some external thing or something pertaining thereto, like its use or usufruct, acquisition, holding, saving, or exchanging, and so on, whenever these are in conformity with right taken in its first sense. What the use or usufruct of a thing is, together with the other lawful or rightful ways of handling things, we shall assume for the present from the science of civil acts. [*218*]

It is in this sense that we usually say: "This is someone's right," when he wishes or handles some thing in a manner which is in conformity with right taken in the first sense. Hence, such wish or handling is called right because it conforms to the command, prohibition, or permission of right; just as a column is called right (*dextra*) or left because it is situated nearer to the right or the left side of an animal. Right, then, taken in this second sense, is none other than what is willed by the active command, prohibition, or permission of the legislator, and this is what we called above the passive meaning of these three words.[140] And this too is what we previously called lawful.[141]

11   (iii) In another sense this term "right" means the sentence or judgments made by judges in accordance with the law or with right taken in its first sense. It is in this sense that men usually say: "The judge or ruler has done or rendered right to someone," when he has convicted or acquitted someone by a legal sentence.

12   (iv) "Right" is also used to refer to an act or habit of particular justice; in this sense we say that he wishes right or justice who wishes what is equal or proportional in exchanges or distributions.

NOTES

1. Cassiodorus *Variae* i. 1.
2. Aristotle *Politics* v. 8. 1307^{b}29.
3. Sallust *Jugurtha* x. 6.
4. Cf. Aristotle *Politics* v, *passim*.
5. The cause of strife to which Marsilius alludes here is described at greater length in I. 19. 12–13:
"This wrong opinion of certain Roman bishops [that is, that they have total coercive temporal jurisdiction over the Roman ruler and over every human creature] and also perhaps their perverted desire for rulership, which they assert is owed to them because of the plenitude of power given to them, as they say, by Christ—this is that singular cause which we have said produces the intranquillity or discord of the city or state. For it is prone to creep up on all states, as was said in our introductory remarks, and by its hateful action it has for a long time distressed the Italian state, and has kept and still keeps it from tranquillity or peace, by preventing with all its force the appointment or institution of the ruler, the Roman emperor, and his functioning in the said empire. From lack of this function, which is the just regulation of civil acts, there readily emerge injuries and contentions, and these, if not measured by a standard of justice or law because of the absence of the measurer, cause fights, whence there have resulted the separation of citizens and finally the destruction of the Italian polities or cities, as we have said. With this opinion, therefore, and perhaps also with what we have called a desire for ruling, the Roman bishop strives to make the Roman ruler subject to him in coercive or temporal jurisdiction, whereas that ruler neither rightly ought to be,

as we shall clearly show below, nor wishes to be subject to him in such judgment. From this there has arisen so much strife and discord that it cannot be extinguished without great peril to souls and bodies and expenditure of wealth.

"For the office of coercive rulership over any individual, of whatever condition he may be, or over any community or group, does not belong to the Roman or any other bishop, priest, or spiritual minister, as such, as has been demonstrated in Chapters XV and XVII of this discourse. And this was what Aristotle held with respect to the priesthood in any law or religion, when he said in the fourth book of the *Politics* [1299ª16 ff.]: 'Hence not all those who are elected or chosen by lot are to be regarded as rulers. Consider the priests in the first place. These must be regarded as different from the political rulers,' and so on. 'And of the superintendent functions,' that is, offices, 'some are political,' and so on. And a little below he adds: 'And other offices are economic.'

"13   Since this pernicious pestilence, which is completely opposed to all the peace and happiness of man, could well infect with a disease of the same corrupt root the other states of faithful Christians throughout the world, I consider it supremely necessary to repel it, as I said in my introductory remarks. This is to be done first by tearing away the mask of the aforementioned false opinion, as the root of the past and future evils; and then by checking, through external action if necessary, its ignorant or unjust patrons or expositors and stubborn defenders. To these tasks all men are obligated who have the knowledge and ability to thwart this evil; and those who neglect or omit them on whatever grounds are unjust, as Tully attested in the treatise *On Duties*, Book I, Chapter 5, when he said: 'There are two kinds of injustice: one, of those men who inflict it; the other, of those who do not drive away the injury from those upon whom it is inflicted, if they can.' See, then, according to this notable statement of Tully, that not only those who inflict injury on others are unjust, but also those who, while having the knowledge and ability to prevent men from inflicting injury on others, do not do so. For every man is obligated to do this for another by a certain quasi-natural law,

the duty of friendship and human society. And lest I myself, by knowingly transgressing this law, be called unjust at least to myself, I propose to drive away this pestilence from my brethren, the Christian believers, first by teaching, and then by external action so far as I may be able. For, as I seem indubitably to see, there has been given to me from above the power to discern and unmask the sophism which has sustained in the past, and by which they will strive to sustain, the wrong opinion, and perhaps also the perverted desire, of certain former Roman bishops and of the present one with his accomplices. It is this opinion and desire which is the parent of the scandals mentioned above."

6. Cicero *De Officiis* i. 7. 22. Cf. Plato *Epistles* ix. 358A; *Laws* xi. 923A.

7. Antenor was the legendary founder of Padua. Cf. Virgil *Aeneid* i. 242–49.

8. This is the only place in the *Defender* where Marsilius refers to Ludwig (Louis) as emperor.

9. Cf. Aristotle *Politics* iii. 7. 1279ª34; v. 8. 1307ᵇ30.

10. The decision to use the term *regnum* to mean "something common to every species of temperate regime" is unique among the medieval Aristotelians in two respects, for the others use the term in Marsilius' third sense alone, that is, as signifying a *royal monarchy* composed of a *number of cities*.

11. Cf. Aristotle *Politics* i. 5. 1254ª31 ff.; v. 3. 1302ᵇ34 ff.; iv. 4. 1290ᵇ24 ff.

12. Cf. below, I. 4. 1–2.

13. I. 4. 3–4; I. 5. 1.

14. I. 5. 5–13; I. 6.

15. I. 7.

16. I. 8. 1; I. 15. 14.

17. Cf. Aristotle *Physics* ii. 8. 199ª9 ff.

18. *Ibid.* i. 1. 184ª13.

19. Aristotle *Politics* i. 2. 1252ª26 ff.

20. Pseudo-Aristotle *Economics* i. 3. 1343ᵇ8 ff.

21. Aristotle *Politics* i. 2. 1252ᵇ9 ff.

22. Aristotle *Nicomachean Ethics* v. 6. 1134ᵇ9 ff. Cf. *ibid.* v. 11. 1138ᵇ6. Marsilius regularly refers to Book V of the *Ethics* as Book IV.

23. Aristotle *Politics* iii. 14. 1285ª2 ff. Cf. *ibid.* iii. 15. 1286ᵇ8 ff.

24. Reading, with Scholz, *civilium* for *scibilium*.

25. Aristotle *Politics* i. 2. 1252ᵇ27.

26. Reading, with Scholz, *huic* for *hinc*.

27. Cicero *De Officiis* i. 4. 11.

28. Aristotle *Politics* i. 2. 1253ª29.
29. Aristotle *On the Parts of Animals* iv. 10. 687ª25.
30. Aristotle *Politics* vii. 8. 1328ᵇ2 ff.
31. *Ibid.* vii. 7. 1328ª2 ff.
32. Aristotle *De Anima* ii. 4. 415ᵇ14.
33. Cf. *ibid.* ii. 1. 412ª10 ff.
34. Aristotle *Metaphysics* i. 1. 980ᵇ27. Cf. *Politics* vii. 13. 1332ᵇ3–6.
35. Aristotle *Politics* vii. 8. 1328ᵇ6.
36. *Ibid.* iv. 4. 1291ª2–4.
37. *Ibid.* iv. 4. 1291ª6.
38. *Ibid.* vii. 8. 1328ᵇ7.
39. Literally, "sects" (*sectae*). Marsilius uses this term regularly to refer to any system of religious law. See below, I. 5. 13; I. 10. 5, 7.
40. Reading, with Bigongiari (p. 37), *ex positione* for *expositione.*
41. Aristotle *Politics* vii. 9. 1329ª28.
42. This paragraph division is from Scholz.
43. Aristotle *De Anima* iii. 9. 432ᵇ22. Cf. *De Caelo* i. 4. 271ª34; *Politics* i. 1. 1253ª9.
44. Marsilius refers here only to the general argument of the Epistle to the Hebrews.
45. This paragraph division is from Scholz.
46. Aristotle *Metaphysics* vii. 7. 1032ᵇ31.
47. Aristotle *De Anima* iii. 9. 432ᵇ22. See above, I. 6. 3.
48. Aristotle *On the Parts of Animals* iv. 10. 686ª25 ff.
49. Aristotle *Politics* vii. 17. 1337ª1.
50. Reading, with Scholz, "2ᵉ" after "15°." The passages referred to are I. 9. 2; I. 12. 1; II. 15. 2 ff.
51. I. 5. 7.
52. Aristotle *Politics* iii. 7-8. 1279ª17 ff.
53. Reading, with Bigongiari (p. 39) and MSS, *perfectioris* for *perfectionis.*
54. Reading, with Bigongiari (p. 40) and MSS, *actionum* for *actionibus;* hence also *provenientium* for *provenientibus.*
55. I. 9. 4–6.
56. I. 9. 7.
57. I. 15. 1–3. Cf. I. 10. 1; I. 14. 1.
58. I. 15. 4–10.
59. I. 17. 1–9.
60. I. 17. 11.
61. Aristotle *Politics* iii. 14. 1284ᵇ35 ff.
62. Marsilius' terms are *capitaneatus* and *constabiliaria.* The former meant a position of army leadership; see Du Cange, *Glossarium,* s.v. *capitaneatus, capitaneus.* Du Cange has no entry for

constabiliaria, but for the seemingly related terms *constabularia* and *contestabiliaria* (the latter found in some MSS of the *Defensor* instead of *constabiliaria*), Du Cange refers to *comes stabuli,* meaning the custodian of the royal stable, and gives a large number of citations, s.v.
63. Aristotle *Politics* iii. 14. 1285ª23.
64. *Ibid.* iii. 14. 1285ª32.
65. *Ibid.* iii. 14. 1285ᵇ4.
66. *Ibid.* v. 10. 1310ᵇ10 ff.
67. See *ibid.* iii. 16–17. 1287ª1 ff.
68. *Ibid.* iv. 10. 1295ª15.
69. See above, I. 8. 2.
70. Aristotle *Politics* iii. 14. 1285ᵇ2; above, para. 4.
71. Aristotle *Politics* ii. 6. 1266ª9; vi. 2. 1317ᵇ21, 1318ª2.
72. *Ibid.* v. 4. 1304ᵇ8.
73. See above, I. 8. 4.
74. Aristotle *Politics* iii. 14. 1284ᵇ39, 1285ª19.
75. See above, I. 5. 7.
76. I. 10.
77. I. 11.
78. I. 12–13.
79. I. 14; I. 15. 3.
80. Aristotle *Metaphysics* ii. 3. 995ª4.
81. *Ibid.* xii. 8. 1074ᵇ3.
82. Aristotle *Nicomachean Ethics* x. 9. 1180ª21.
83. Aristotle *Politics* iii. 15. 1286ª17.
84. Aristotle *Rhetoric* i. 1. 1354ᵇ4 ff.
85. *Ibid.* i. 2. 1356ª14.
86. Aristotle *Politics* ii. 5. 1264ª1.
87. Aristotle *Rhetoric* i. 1. 1354ᵇ3.
88. Aristotle *Nicomachean Ethics* vi. 9. 1142ª12.
89. Aristotle *Metaphysics* ii. 1. 993ᵇ2.
90. For the translation from the Arabic, see *Aristotelis Opera,* ed. Manardus (Venice, 1560), Vol. IV, fol. 47v.
91. Aristotle *Metaphysics* ii. 1. 993ᵇ15; inserting, with Bigongiari (p. 42), *non* before *Phrynes.*
92. Averroes *Commentarius in Aristotelis Metaphysicam* ii. 1, in *Aristotelis Opera,* ed. Manardus (Venice, 1560), Vol. IV, fol. 49r.
93. Aristotle *On Sophistical Refutations* ch. 34. 183ᵇ34 ff.
94. Aristotle *Nicomachean Ethics* viii. 1. 1155ª16.
95. Aristotle *Politics* iii. 16. 1287ᵇ26.
96. See below, I. 14. 3-6.
97. Aristotle *Nicomachean Ethics* v. 6. 1134ª35.
98. Aristotle *Politics* iii. 11. 1282ᵇ1.

99. *Ibid.* iii. 16. 1287ª28.
100. *Ibid.* iii. 16. 1287ª32.
101. Aristotle *Rhetoric* i. 1. 1354ª32.
102. Aristotle *Politics* iv. 4. 1292ª32.
103. *Ibid.* v. 10. 1312ᵇ38.
104. Cf. *ibid.* iii. 13. 1284ª3 ff.; iii. 17. 1288ª15 ff. Cf. also Dante *De Monarchia* i. 11 and 13 (above, Selection 22).
105. Aristotle *Politics* iii. 15. 1286ᵇ26.
106. *Ibid.* v. 11. 1313ª20.
107. *Ibid.* v. 11. 1313ª26.
108. This is a reference to the leagues formed in France to protest against Philip the Fair's new taxation in 1314.
109. Cf. above, I. 9. 2; also I. 6. 3.
110. Cf. above, I. 10. 3.
111. Cf. above, I. 10. 4-5.
112. Aristotle *Politics* iii. 11. 1281ª39 ff.
113. *Ibid.* iii. 1. 1275ª22, 1275ᵇ19; iii. 3. 1277ᵇ33; iii. 13. 1283ᵇ42.
114. *Ibid.* vi. 3-4. 1318ª3 ff.
115. *Ibid.* iii. 13. 1283ᵇ40.
116. Cf. 1. 12. 8.
117. Aristotle *Politics* iv. 8. 1294ª3.
118. *Ibid.* vi. 8. 1322ª5.
119. *Ibid.* iii. 6. 1279ª21.
120. Reading, with Scholz, full stop after *pauciores*.
121. Reading, with Scholz, *ad dicta* for *addicta*.
122. Cf. above, I. 4. 2.

123. Aristotle *Politics* i. 2. 1253ª29.
124. *Ibid.* iv. 12. 1296ᵇ14.
125. *Ibid.* vii. 14. 1332ᵇ29 ff.
126. *Ibid.* iv. 8. 1293ᵇ42.
127. Aristotle *Physics* ii. 8. 199ª9 ff.; *Nicomachean Ethics* i. 9. 1099ᵇ20–24.
128. Aristotle *Politics* iii. 11. 1282ª17.
129. *Ibid.* iii. 11. 1282ª38 ff.
130. *Ibid.* iii. 11. 1282ª15.
131. Aristotle *On Sophistical Refutations* ch. 34. 183ᵇ24.
132. Aristotle *Nicomachean Ethics* i. 2. 1095ᵇ10, quoting Hesiod *Works and Days* 293.
133. Cf. above, I. 10. 3-4.
134. Cf. I. 10. 7.
135. That is, an act may be commanded (or prohibited) in a law which deals either specifically with that act or with acts similar thereto.
136. While the reference is to Luke 18:18, the passage cited is really Matt. 19:17.
137. Cf. above, I. 14. 7. Also Aristotle *Nicomachean Ethics* v. 10. 1137ª32 ff.
138. See Aristotle *Nicomachean Ethics* v. 7. 1134ᵇ19.
139. *Ibid.* v. 7. 1134ᵇ25.
140. Cf. above, para. 3.
141. Cf. above, para. 5.

24.

William of Ockham

THE DIALOGUE

Translated by Francis Oakley

For many of the events of William of Ockham's life (*ca.* 1280/90–*ca.*1349) we are reduced to more or less probable conjectures. Nothing certain is known about his early life and education. It is likely that he pursued his theological studies at Oxford from about 1309 to 1315. Although he apparently fulfilled all the requirements for the degree of Master of Theology and lectured on the Bible and the *Sentences* of Peter Lombard, he never occupied an official chair of theology at the university. His reputation as a dialectician, his vigorous criticism of his contemporaries (especially Duns Scotus), and the real or apparent novelty of his opinions seem to have aroused considerable antagonism. In 1323 he was accused of expounding dangerous doctrines by Lutterell, the former chancellor of the University of Oxford and himself a controversial figure. The following year, John XXII

summoned him to the papal residence at Avignon to give an account of his teaching and appointed a commission to examine his *Commentary on the Sentences*. None of the doctrines censured by the commission was ever formally condemned. At Avignon, where he remained from 1324 to 1328, Ockham became involved in the debate over Franciscan poverty and sided with Michael of Cesena, the Superior General of the Order, in his stand against the Pope. The question ceased to be a purely religious one when the German Emperor, Louis of Bavaria, tried to make capital of it to further his own political aims. The year 1328 appears to have been the crucial turning point in Ockham's life. Together with Cesena and two other Franciscan friars, he joined Louis after the collapse of the latter's Roman expedition and withdrew with him to Munich, where he became one of the intellectual leaders in the struggle of the Emperor against the "Church of Avignon," as he called it. Between 1337 and 1343 alone, he composed seven treatises, including the last part of the *Dialogue*, in which he set forth his views regarding political matters in the light of recent events. Louis' death in 1347 left him without a defender. There is good reason to think that he later sought a reconciliation with the Pope and his Order. A formula of submission was drawn up and presented to the rebellious monks. Whether or not Ockham signed it, or even saw it, remains uncertain. It is noteworthy that the formula refers specifically to certain errors concerning the relation between the Pope and the Emperor and to Ockham's disobedience, but not to any theological or philosophic teachings belonging to his first period at Oxford. Ockham died shortly afterwards, *ca.* 1349, a probable victim of the Black Death.

The *Dialogue* (*Dialogus de Potestate Papae et Imperatoris*) was conceived as a comprehensive work in which Ockham proposed to include all his major ideas on political matters and, more particularly, on the errors of the papacy and its rights with respect to those of the empire. It is written in the form of a dialogue in which a pupil asks questions and the master (Ockham) answers them, and is divided into three parts. Part I (1333–34), the only one to have come down to us in its totality, deals mainly with the question of definitions in matters of faith. Although aimed primarily at proving the heterodoxy of John XXII, it raises a number of more general topics, such as the nature of heresy, papal, conciliar, and ecclesiastical infallibility, the procedure to be followed when a Pope falls into heresy, and the punishment of heretics and their accomplices. Part II has not survived. Part III (*ca.* 1341–43) was to be made up of nine treatises. The first treatise deals with the power of the Pope and the clergy. The second, which remains incomplete, defends the rights of the Emperor against the Pope, the cardinals, and the clergy. The remaining treatises are either lost or were never written. In them Ockham had planned to give a historical account of the deeds of John XXII, Louis of Bavaria, Benedict XII, Michael of Cesena, and other figures involved in the controversy in which he himself had taken a prominent part. The vast dimensions of the *Dialogue,* coupled with the fact that the author often sets forth contradictory opinions without openly siding with any one of them, renders an analysis of Ockham's thought particularly difficult. While opposed to the indefinite extension of powers granted to the Pope by earlier or contemporary theologians and canonists, Ockham appears never to have shared the radicalism of Marsilius, with whose work he was well acquainted. His *Dialogue* nevertheless supplied the adversaries of the papacy with a wide variety of arguments in favor of their position. His theological doctrines also prepared the way for Luther and many of the other Reformers. Among his most convinced disciples were such men as John Buridan, Peter d'Ailly, and John Gerson.

The edition of the *Dialogue* from which the following selections have been newly translated is that of Melchior Goldast, *Monarchia Sancti Romani Imperii* (Frankfurt, 1614), pp. 922–924 and 932–935. Italic numbers in brackets in the text refer to the pagination of the Goldast edition.

PART   THREE,   TREATISE   ii,   BOOK   II

CHAPTER   26

[He inquires here whether the emperor has the plenitude of power in temporal matters to as great an extent as the pope has in spiritual matters, and he cites one opinion, which he supports with five arguments. To these arguments a reply is made later on in Chapter 28.[1]]

PUPIL: We have already inquired to what degree the emperor has power over some matters in particular, but now I ask the general question whether the emperor has a plenitude of power in temporal affairs in the same way as the pope, according to many, is deemed to have a plenitude of power in spiritual matters.

MASTER: On this point there are conflicting positions, one of which claims that the emperor has such a plenitude of power in temporal matters that he can do all things that are not against divine or natural law, so that in matters of this kind all his subjects are bound to obey him.

PUPIL: Would you try to state some arguments in support of this opinion?

MASTER: Many things can be said on behalf of this opinion:

1   For he who is limited by no human law, but is bound only by the divine and natural laws, can do everything that does not run counter to one of the latter [923] laws. Now the emperor is bound by no human law, but by the divine and natural laws, since (as is said in the *Digest*, I, 3, para. 31, and is reiterated in the gloss to the *Decretals*, i, 2, 1 in v. *ab omnibus*),[2] the emperor is not subject to the laws, and, therefore, has such a plenitude of power in temporal matters that he can do all things that are not contrary to the divine and natural laws.

2   Besides, he whose will in temporal matters is endowed by law with the force of law, possesses in these things a plenitude of power. But what pleases the prince (and especially the emperor) has the force of law. Therefore, the emperor possesses in these matters a plenitude of power.

3   Again, he whose very error constitutes law in temporal matters enjoys a plenitude of power over them; hence, the emperor has such a plenitude of power.

4   Furthermore, if somebody subject to the emperor can justly resist an imperial decree in temporal matters—one that runs counter neither to the divine nor to the natural law—it is necessary that he can so resist in

accordance with some law, since we can do rightly only that which we can do legally. Either, therefore, he can resist the emperor by divine or natural, or by human law. But not by divine or natural, since, as has been said, the imperial decree is contrary to neither of these laws. Nor by human law, since—as is said in the *Decretum*, D. 8, c. 1,[3] and was mentioned earlier—human laws are not contrary to the imperial law "because these human laws themselves God promulgates to the human race through emperors and through the kings of the world." Thus, by the law of the emperor, nobody can resist the imperial decree, since the emperor can do everything in all matters of this [temporal] kind.

5 Besides, that to which human society obliges itself, it is bound to observe. But human society binds itself in general to obey kings, and, therefore, so much the more to obey the emperor. For Augustine says in the second book of the *Confessions* (quoted in the *Decretum*, D. 8, c. 2),[4] "It is, indeed, a general agreement of human society to obey its kings." The emperor, then, is always to be obeyed in temporal things, for he can do everything that is not against divine and natural law.

CHAPTER 27

[He cites a second opinion that runs counter to the first.]

PUPIL: State the opposite case.

MASTER: The opposed position is that the emperor does not possess a plenitude of power in temporal matters so that he can do everything that is not against divine or natural law. His power, instead, is limited, in that in relation to the free men subject to him and to their possessions, he can do only such things as promote the common utility.

PUPIL: Would you cite some arguments in support of this position?

MASTER: On behalf of this position it may be argued as follows:

1 That he whose laws must be made, not for a private good, but for the common utility, lacks the plenitude of power by which he could do all things. For if he had a plenitude of power he could establish laws, not only for the common utility, but even for a private good (whether his own or another's), and also for any cause whatever, provided only that it was contrary neither to the divine nor to the natural law. But imperial laws and other [human] laws have to be established not for private convenience but for the common utility—witness Isidore, who

says (see *Decretum*, D. 4, c. 2): "The law will be just, honorable, and feasible, in accordance with nature and the custom of the land, appropriate to the place and time, necessary, useful, and clear, too, lest through indistinctness it may contain something improper; and it will be drawn up, not for any private good, but for the common utility of the citizens."[5] The emperor, then, does not have such a plenitude of power that he can do all things, but only those that contribute to the common welfare.

2 Furthermore, if the emperor has in these matters a plenitude of power, all other kings, princes, and other laymen would be subject to him just as mere slaves. For a lord does not have greater power over slaves than that of being able to order them to do everything that is not against divine or natural law—indeed, it is possible that he does not have that great a power over them. If, therefore, the emperor could do in temporal matters, not only those things that contribute to the common utility, but also any other thing at all that is not against the divine or natural law, then every other person would be subject to him as his very slave.

3 Again, the pope does not possess a plenary power in spiritual matters, for he cannot prescribe to anyone those things that are works of supererogation—such as virginity, fasting on bread and water, entering a religious order, and so forth. So much the more, then, does the emperor lack such plenitude of power in temporal things.

4 Or again, the emperor does not possess in temporal matters a power greater than that which the people had, since he owes his power to the people (as was argued earlier), and the people could not transfer to him a greater jurisdiction or power than it possessed itself. But the people never possessed such a plenitude of power that it could order any of its members to do everything that does not run counter to the divine or the natural law, for it was unable to command those things that necessity did not require to be done. On this matter, note the gloss to the *Decretals*, i, 2, c. 6 in v. *cum omnes*,[6] which says that on those things that are [not] required by necessity, "nothing can be done unless all have given their consent."[7] Thus, if the people orders one of its members to do something that is not required by necessity, he is not bound to do it unless he so wishes; and if this is so, it follows that the emperor does not possess such a plenitude of power.

5 In addition, to falsify, alienate, sell, give, or bequeath [anything that pertains to his imperial prerogatives] is against neither the divine nor the natural law, and yet the emperor cannot do any of these things. He lacks, therefore, a plenitude of power.

6 Furthermore, the emperor possesses no power that is perilous to the common good. But this plenitude of power would imperil the common

good, for it could reduce all subjects to poverty, which would certainly be contrary to the common good.

7 Also, that power, which was established only with a view to the common utility, does not reach beyond those things that are ordained to the common utility, and, as a result, falls short of all those things that are contrary to the divine or natural laws. But the imperial power [*924*] was established simply to further the common utility and does not, therefore, extend to those things that do not pertain to that common utility. This may be proved by the following argument: That which is not directed to its due end seems to lack ordination, and that which lacks ordination is not to be judged lawful. But the end for which emperors are instituted is the common utility. Anything, therefore, that the emperor does by the imperial authority and does not direct to the common utility lacks ordination and, as a result, is unlawful. And from this one may infer that the emperor, by virtue of his imperial authority, cannot do all things that are not contrary to the divine or natural laws, but only those that conduce to the common utility.

CHAPTER 2 8

[He replies here to the arguments set forth in Chapter 26.]

PUPIL: Since this second opinion seems to redound to the benefit of human society and of the common good, on behalf of which we are all obliged to concern ourselves, I should like to know how reply is made to the arguments in support of the opposed opinion. Tell me, then, how one can reply to the first of the arguments set forth above in Chapter 26.

MASTER: Reply may be made to that one by posing a distinction concerning human laws. Some of these are laws of the emperor and of other particular persons and communities subject to the emperor, and these can be called civil laws. Others, however, spring in some fashion from the whole of human society, and these seem to belong to the law of nations (*jus gentium*), since they are to some extent natural and to some extent human or positive—as may be gathered from what has already been said in Chapters 10 and 11 of this part [of the book]. So long as he observes those laws that belong to the law of nations, the emperor is in no way obliged of necessity to live in accordance with his own laws, although it is proper that he should do so. For all nations, and especially those that live in accordance with the dictates of reason, accept this law. The emperor, therefore, is bound to it also, and he is not at liberty to transgress at will those laws that pertain to it, but only in a case in which he perceives them to run counter to the common utility. It would not generally be permissible for him, therefore, to forbid the seizure of thrones, wars, the taking of prisoners, the reduction of men to slavery, reprisals, the promise of immunity to ambassadors, and other matters that seem to belong to the law of nations. Now it pertains to the law of nations that the emperor should lack such a plenitude of power as would enable him to do, in temporal matters, everything that is not contrary to the divine law and the unconditional natural law (which was spoken of above in Chapters 11 and 12 of this [part of the book]), just as it is deemed to pertain to the law of nations that some people should be free and not wholly servile. And, because the one follows from the other, it follows that the emperor is bound by this law [of nations]. But this is a human law, since it derives its force as law from the agreement of all men in proscribing the contrary.

PUPIL: How then can one reply to the second argument?

MASTER: To this it is said that what pleases the prince (that is, the emperor), justly and with reason on account of the common good, has—when he clearly states it—the force of law. If, however, something pleases him, not because of the common good but on account of a private good, it does not have the force of law because of this—that is to say, it does not have the force of law justly, but wrongly and unjustly.

PUPIL: This argument, like the opinion set forth in the last chapter, seems to detract from the integrity and authority of the emperors; for, according to what is written above, the emperor can establish no law unless it is a general one that looks to the common good. It follows from this that he cannot concede a privilege to anyone, since privileges are not common or general things, but pertain to private law (*Decretum*, D. 3, *secunda pars Gratiani*, para. 1, and D. 3, c. 3).[8] The inability, however, to grant a special privilege to anyone seems to detract from the integrity as well as from the authority of the emperor.

MASTER: To this it is replied that because any private person or particular association (*collegium*) is a part of the whole community, then the good of any private person and of any particular association is the good of the whole community and is capable of being ordained to, and of redounding to, the common good. It follows from this that if the emperor, in granting special privileges to some particular persons or associations, is not misled in his reasoning to the detriment of the common good, then the privileges are just and promote the common good. If, however, he does not intend the common good in this way, but grants the privileges because of personal affection or other less just cause, then these privileges are not just, but wrong and unjust, and, by granting them, he falls into the vice of favoritism, for which he can scarcely be excused.

PUPIL: Tell me, then, what reply is made to the third argument?

MASTER: It is said that the error of the prince probably makes law, in the sense that others are obliged to obey, unless it appears to them that the error of the prince is contrary to the divine or natural laws, or to the common good. For, if this is the case, the error of the prince does not constitute law.

PUPIL: And to the fourth argument?

MASTER: Reply is made along the lines of what was said above in response to the first argument, for a person can often resist, by virtue of human law, a command of the emperor that is not contrary to the divine or natural laws. This can be done, not, indeed, on the grounds of the civil law, but of the law of nations, just as was said. Against the same argument, it is also said that it speaks of those human laws that are called *civil* and not of the law of nations. Civil laws are the laws of emperors and kings, but the law of nations is not the law of emperors or kings in the sense that they establish it—although it can be in the sense that they may approve and observe it.

PUPIL: What does this opinion maintain concerning the last of those arguments?

MASTER: It maintains this: that human society is in general agreed to submit to its kings in those things that pertain to the common good, and, as a result, that human society is in general obliged to obey the emperor in those things that conduce to the common utility, but not in those things that clearly by no means advance the common good.

PART THREE, TREATISE ii, BOOK III

CHAPTER 6

[He replies to the third objection of the preceding chapter, indicating also that natural law is threefold and the sense in which the whole body of natural law can be called divine.]

PUPIL: Tell me in what way answer is made to the proposition that

I have accepted—namely, that neither by divine nor by human law do the Romans have the right of electing the supreme pontiff.

MASTER: To this it is replied that, if we stretch divine law to include the whole of natural law, the Romans by divine law have the right of electing the supreme pontiff.

PUPIL: This reply seems vague to me, and I should like, therefore, to have it clarified along the lines of the opinion in question. But first tell me why those who follow this opinion say "if we stretch divine law to include the whole of natural law"; and, secondly, why the whole of natural law can be called divine law.

MASTER: In the first place, three distinct senses are ascribed to the term "natural law." For in one sense natural law is said to be that law which is in conformity with natural reason that in no case fails—as, for example, "Thou shalt not commit adultery," "Thou shalt not lie," and so on. In another sense, natural law is that law which is to be observed by those who go on natural equity alone, without any human custom or constitution, and which is natural because it is [not] contrary to the state of nature as it was established and would[9] have to be followed or observed if all men lived in accordance with natural reason or the divine law.

In the second sense, but not in the first, all things are common, since in the state of nature as it was established all things had been common. And if, after the Fall, all men had lived in accordance with reason, all things would still have been common and nothing private, for property was established on account of sin (*Decretum*, C. 12, qu. 1, c. 2).[10] And Isidore speaks in this sense when he says in the fifth book of the *Etymologies* (as quoted in the *Decretum*, D. 1, c. 7),[11] that according to the natural law "all possession of all things is common and all men share a single liberty." For the common possession of all things and the single liberty of all men is not grounded upon the natural law in the first of the above senses, since, if it were, nobody could lawfully make something his own property, nor, by the law of nations or the civil law, could a person be reduced to slavery, for natural law in this [*933*] first sense is immutable and invariable and admits of no dispensation (*Decretum*, D. 5, *prima pars Gratiani*, para. 2; D. 6, *Gratianus post* c. 3).[12] But it is equally clear that some men are lawfully slaves by the law of nations—witness what the blessed Gregory (as quoted in the *Decretum*, C. 12, qu. 12, c. 68)[13] says: "It is well done if men whom nature at the start brought forth as freemen, and whom the law of nations placed instead under the yoke of servitude, are returned to freedom by the favor of manumission, as to that nature in which they were born." From these words one may conclude that by the natural law all men are free, but that some by the law of nations are slaves. And from this one may infer that natural law in this [second] sense of the term is not immutable—indeed, it may lawfully be decreed that something be done that is contrary to that law.

In its third sense, natural law is said to be that which may be deduced by evident reason from the law of nations or from some human deed—unless the contrary is established by the agreement of those to whom the matter pertains—and this can be called "conditional natural law" (*jus naturale ex suppositione*). For instance, according to Isidore in the passage referred to above, the restoration of a thing entrusted[14] or of money that has been lent and the repelling of force by force are of natural law. But they do not pertain to natural law in the first and second senses of the term, because they did not exist in the state of nature as it was established, nor would they have existed among those who, living in accordance with reason, directed their actions by natural equity alone without human custom or constitution, since among such men nothing would have been entrusted or lent, nor would someone use force against another. Such laws, then, are conditional natural laws, for once it is assumed that things and money have in fact been appropriated by virtue of the law of nations or some other human law, then it is deduced by evident reason that things given in trust or money that has been lent should be returned, unless the person or persons to whom it pertained decreed otherwise. Similarly, once it is supposed that someone may in fact use violence injuriously against another—which is not a right grounded in natural law but is contrary to it—then one infers by evident reason that it is permissible to repel such violence by force.

Because, therefore, the term "natural law" possesses these three senses, they [the supporters of the opinion in question] say that the Romans have the right of electing the supreme pontiff from the divine law, divine law being extended to comprehend all kinds of natural law. And from this it follows that they would not have the right of electing the supreme pontiff from divine law if it were extended to include natural law in the first of the above senses only (which is the sense ascribed to natural law in the *Decretum*, D. 5, *prima pars Gratiani*, para. 1, and D. 6. *Gratianus post* c. 3).[15]

PUPIL: As I have not heard this distinction concerning natural law elsewhere, I should like to raise some objections to it, so that from the solution to the objections I may better understand whether or not the opinion in question contains some truth.

It may be said, then, that this distinction seems clearly to contradict the words of Isidore in the chapter cited above [D. 1, c. 7]. First, because Isidore says: "Natural law is the common possession of all nations, in that everywhere in the unregulated state of nature some laws are accepted."[16] These cannot correspond with natural law in the second sense distinguished, because those practices the contrary of which can be lawful according to the law of nations, are not common to all nations, nor are they accepted everywhere in the state of nature, for they are not accepted in those places where, in accordance with the law of nations, their contraries are observed. Again, because in the same place Isidore says: "Now this" [that is, the law of nature] "or that which resembles it, is never held to be unjust but, rather, natural and equitable." For this can be true [of natural law] neither in the second nor in the third sense distinguished, because everything that is said to be natural law in the second sense can be unjust. This is so because its opposite can be prescribed by the law of nations, and that which is contrary to the law of nations is to be regarded as unjust. That law, too, which is said to be natural in the third sense can be unjust, since its contrary can be prescribed by natural law in the second sense. For instance, it is ordained by natural law in this second sense that no money is to be lent and no object to be entrusted, since, according to natural law in this sense of the term, such things are all held in common, and thus no money can be lent and nothing deposited. These are the considerations that lead me to query the distinction in question. Tell me, then, how one replies to them.

MASTER: These difficulties are answered in two ways—in the first place, by pointing out that certain words in the above-mentioned definition of natural law are to be understood only of natural law in the first sense distinguished, and certain words of the other senses. The words you cite, therefore, are to be understood of natural law in the first of these senses, and thus do not seem to run counter to the distinction in question. In the second place, it is said that those words that you take to be in opposition to it, apply to all the senses of natural law, and must be understood soundly. When, accordingly, Isidore says, "Natural law is the common possession of all nations," because all nations are indispensably bound by it, and, therefore, that in the state of nature it is the law of reason that in no case fails, then the law of which he is speaking is natural law in the second sense. For thus it is common to all nations in that all nations, unless the contrary is ordained for reasonable cause, are bound by it; and in this sense also, it springs from the state of nature—that is, from natural reason before the contrary is established by human decree. On that account, therefore, it was said that all things were held in common before, by human agreement, they were appropriated. Natural law in the third sense, however, was said to be common to all nations in a conditional fashion, that is, on condition that all nations decreed or did that from which [natural] law in this sense is by evident reason deduced; and thus in the state of nature, that is, of natural reason, it does not exist, but[17] it does exist when that from which it is understood in this sense is given. Similarly, in connection with the words that you cite in the second place: "Now this [natural law] and that which resembles it," and so forth, it is said that "natural" and "equitable" can be understood of natural law in the second sense since it is followed unless by some human law its contrary is for reasonable cause established. Moreover, even natural law in the third of the above senses in some way is never unjust, but always natural and equitable;[18] for it exists when that from which it is deduced by evident reason is given, and it is never unjust but always natural and equitable, because in this case it is accepted by the person or persons to whom it pertains to order the contrary.

PUPIL: These arguments seem to be misleading since they interpret ambiguously that expression [that is, *jus naturale*], which occurred only once in the words of Isidore cited above.

MASTER: This is not to be regarded as misleading, for the gloss to the *Decretum*, D. 63, c. 12 *in v. clero*,[19] indicates this when it says: "Observe that the word used here no more than once is used ambiguously"—see also D. 28, c. 16.

PUPIL: You have shown why, according to the opinion under examination [*934*] the Romans are said to have from divine law the right of electing the supreme pontiff—divine law being extended to comprehend all types of natural law. Now tell me why, according to this opinion, all types of natural law can be spoken of as divine.

MASTER: They say this because every law that comes from God, who is the founder of nature, can be called divine law. But all types of natural law do come from God, who is the founder of nature—it follows, therefore, and so forth. Again, because every law that is explicitly contained in the divine scriptures can be called divine law, for, as is said in the *Decretum*, D. 8, c. 1,[20] divine law is contained in the divine scriptures. But the whole of natural law is contained, explicitly or implicitly, in the divine scriptures, as there are in the divine scriptures certain general rules from which (either by themselves or along with other rules) it can be deduced. In view of this, therefore, all natural law, in our first, second, and third senses, is divine law, even though it may not be found explicitly in the scriptures.

PUPIL: You have explained, in accordance with the opinion in question, two things that seemed obscure. Now tell me, in accordance with the same line of reasoning, how it is that the Romans have the right of electing the supreme pontiff.

MASTER: On this it is said that the Romans have the right of electing the supreme pontiff from natural law in the third of the senses distinguished above, for, given the fact that someone is to be placed over the others as prelate, prince, or ruler, then it is concluded by evident reason that if he is not appointed by the person or persons to whom it pertains, those over whom he is to rule have the right of electing the ruler and of placing him over themselves. Thus, it follows that no ruler should be placed over them if they are unwilling. This could be proved by many examples and arguments, but I shall cite only a few.

The first is this, that nobody should be placed in command of a community of mortals, except by the choice and consent of its members. Further, what touches all should be the work of all. But that someone should be given command over others does touch all. Hence, it should be the work of all. Again, those who possess the power to make their own laws can also, if they wish, choose their ruler. But any people or city can make its own law, which is known as civil law (*Decretum*, D. 1, c. 8).[21] Therefore, both the people and the city can make their own laws and choose their own rulers. And thus the choice of a ruler always belongs to those over whom he is to rule, unless the contrary is ordained by the person or persons to whom it pertains to do so.

This last point is mentioned because, in many cases at least, they [that is, the subjects] can relinquish their right and transfer it to some other person or persons; and, in this way, although by natural law in the third sense[22] the people has the right of making the laws, it has, however, transferred that power to the emperor, and, as a result, it was in the power of the emperor to pass on the right of election to some other person or persons. Similarly, if those over whom someone is to be set in command are, in matters of this type, subject to some superior, that superior can decree that they do not possess the right of election, even though they have such a right from natural law in the third sense[23]—if, that is, the contrary has been ordained neither by themselves nor by their superior. And thus it seems to its supporters that the proposition in question is to be regarded as evident.

Now the supreme pontiff is, in a certain way, especially placed over the Romans, since they have no other bishop. They, therefore, have the right of electing him from natural law in the third sense (that is, from conditional natural law—the condition in this case being that they have to have a bishop), unless the contrary is established or decreed by the Romans themselves or by some other person who is their superior and who possesses power in this matter. For the Romans could yield to his right or themselves transfer their right of electing the supreme pontiff to some other person or persons; and they could also transfer the right of constituting the electors of the supreme pontiff. Moreover, the person who was superior to the Romans and who had power in matters of this sort could concede the right of election to people other than the Romans. Now this superior was Christ, and not the pope, and, therefore, Christ and not the pope could deprive the Romans of the right of electing the supreme pontiff. But Christ did not in fact deprive the Romans of that right. For when Christ placed the blessed Peter over all Christians, giving him the power to be, in a way, the special bishop of the people dwelling in whatever place he might choose as his seat, he did not deprive these people of that right which belongs to all those over whom some authority, whether secular or ecclesiastical, is to be placed—unless, of course, the contrary is ordained by themselves or their superior. Since the blessed Peter, therefore, chose Rome as his seat, it follows that the Romans have the right of electing the successor of the blessed Peter who is to be set over them in spiritual matters. And thus the Romans have from divine law the right of electing the supreme pontiff —if, that is, divine law is extended to include all kinds of natural law.

Pupil: It seems, according to that opinion, that it might be better to say that the Romans have the right of electing their bishop from the law of nations, since it belongs to the law of nations that all men over whom some ruler is to be placed should have the right to choose him—unless they relinquish their right, or their superior decrees otherwise.

Master: Although many things that pertain to the law of nations are natural laws in the third sense of the term, nevertheless, according to the opinion in question, it is more correct to say that the Romans have the right of electing their bishop from natural law in the third sense than from the law of nations. And the reason is that to have a Catholic bishop does not pertain to the law of nations, but belongs rather to the divine law. That somebody, moreover, who is to be placed over others should be chosen by those over whom he is to rule, although it belongs to the law of nations, pertains also, nevertheless, to the divine law, in that it can be deduced (if the texts are correlated) from those things that are contained in the sacred scriptures. And of those two assumptions from which it is deduced that the Romans have the right of electing their bishop, both pertain, although in different ways, to the divine law, but only one to the law of nations. Because of this, then, it is more correctly said that the Romans have the right of electing their bishop from divine law or from natural law in the third sense, than from the law of nations. Those, however, who do not like to wrangle over words say that it is enough for them that the Romans have the right of electing their bishop because of the very fact that they have to have a bishop, and because those over whom someone is to be placed should have the right to choose him, unless they relinquish their right or the contrary is decreed by their superior. [935] But they do not make much of the question as to whether, strictly speaking, it should be said that the Romans have the right of election from divine law or from natural law in its third sense, or, better still, from both divine law and the law of nations. Nevertheless, it does appear to some that it is more correct to say that they have the right of election from divine law and the law of nations. And thus, when one asks whether they have the right of election from divine law or human, they reply that they have it neither solely from divine law nor solely from human, but from both together—that is, if human law is taken to include the law of nations and not simply the civil or canon laws.

NOTES

1. These introductory synopses that head every chapter in Goldast's text seem to have been added by Ascensius, the editor of the Lyons edition of 1494 (the text of which Goldast reprints), for they are not to be found in the first edition of the *Dialogue* (Paris, July 5, 1476).

2. Ockham gives the reference thus: "sicut habetur *ff. de legibus,* et glossa recitat *extra de constitutionibus, canonum.*"

3. Ockham's reference: "sicut habetur *distinction. octav. capitulo, quo jure.*"

4. Ockham's reference: "ut habetur *distinction. octav. quáe contra.*"

5. Ockham's reference: "ut legitur *dist. 4, erit autem.*"

There is translated here *not* Ockham's version of Isidore's text, but the version to be found in A. Friedberg (ed.), *Corpus Juris Canonici,* 2 vols. (Leipzig, 1879-81), which reads as follows: "Erit autem lex honesta, justa, possibilis, secundum naturam, secundum consuetudinem patriae, loco *temporique conveniens,* necessaria, utilis, manifesta quoque, ne *aliquid* per obscuritatem *inconveniens* contineat, nullo privato commodo, sed pro communi utilitate *civium* conscripta." The italicized words represent variants from the text as given by Ockham. The text of the *Etymologies* printed by Migne (*Patrologia Latina,* 82, col. 203) is closer to the Friedberg version translated above than it is to Ockham's confused version.

6. Ockham's reference: "Glossa *extra de constitution. cum omnis.*"

7. Goldast omits the negative inserted above, but the gloss to which Ockham has referred and that he is in part quoting reads: ". . . in aliis quae ex necessitate *non* fiunt . . . nihil potest fieri nisi omnes consentiant."

8. Ockham's reference: "*dist. 8. secundum quod quaedam, et c. privilegia.*"

9. Goldast places the negative here rather than earlier in the sentence, but the coherence of the sentence would seem to require the emendation suggested.

10. Ockham's reference: "*12. q.1. cap. dilectissimis.*"

11. Ockham's reference: "*di. 1. jus naturale.*"

12. Ockham's reference: "*dist. 5. para.*

nunc autem, et dist. 6. para. his itaque respondetur."

13. Ockham's reference: "ut inquit 12. q. et c. *cum redemptor.*"

14. Goldast's text reads: "jus naturale est *de potestate rei, ut* commodatae" etc., but the lines that follow would suggest that this is a corruption of ". . . *depositae rei aut commodatae.*" In translating, I have assumed this emendation, further support for which can be found in the version of Isidore's words contained in the *Decretum,* D. 1, c. 7 (Friedberg, ed.): "jus naturale est . . . *depositae rei vel* commodatae" etc.

15. Ockham's reference: "*dist. 5.* para. *1 et dist. 6.* para. *his itaque respondetur.*"

16. Goldast's rendering of Isidore's words has been followed because Ockham's subsequent remarks reveal that it represents what he himself had read. According to the *Decretum,* however (and this version coincides with that of Migne, *Patrologia Latina,* 82, col. 199), Isidore's words should read: "Jus naturale est commune omnium nationum eo quod ubique *instinctu naturae, non constitutione* aliqua habetur" (italics added).

17. Goldast's text, ". . . hoc est naturalis rationis, habetur illo supposito . . . ," has been emended to read: "hoc est naturalis rationis, *non habetur, sed* habetur illo supposito. . . ."

18. Goldast reads: ". . . sed semper *ut* naturale et aequum." *Est* has been substituted for *ut,* as the meaning of the sentence would seem to require it.

19. Ockham's reference: "Hoc notat Glossa *distinctio. 63, c. nosse.*"

20. Ockham's reference: "*dist. 8. c. quo jure.*"

21. Ockham's reference: "*distinct. 1. jus civile.*"

22. Goldast reads: ". . . ex jure naturali tertio modo dicto, *vel secundo modo*" etc., but Ockham's argument throughout would seem to make natural law in his second sense irrelevant to any popular law-making power. The italicized words have, therefore, been omitted.

23. Goldast in fact reads: ". . . ex jure naturali *secundo* modo dicto," but, for the reason given above in note 22, this has been emended to "*tertio* modo dicto."

25.

John Fortescue

ON THE MERITS

OF THE LAWS OF ENGLAND

Translated by S. B. Chrimes

John Fortescue (*ca.* 1385–*ca.* 1479) was the second son of Sir John Fortescue of Winstone, who fought with Henry V at Agincourt and became governor of the fortress of Meaux. His ancestry went back twelve generations to the Sir Richard who left the Cotentin to join the forces of William the Conqueror. Our first information about him concerns his admission to membership of Lincoln's Inn before 1420. He became sergeant-at-law *ca.* 1430 and by 1437 he had been eight times elected a member of Parliament. He was a Justice of the Peace thirty-five times in seventeen counties at one time or another and received no fewer than seventy judicial commissions in the course of his long career. In addition to his ordinary duties, he acted as arbitrator in several extra-judicial disputes and was for many years trier of petitions in Parliament. His Lancastrian sympathies caused him to be relieved of his judicial duties and sent into exile in 1461. He joined Queen Margaret on the eve of, or very soon after, the battle of St. Albans and was present at the battle of Towton. He accompanied Henry VI to Edinburgh after the latter's defeat and was rewarded by him with the title of "chancellor." In 1462, he was given letters of credence to Louis XI and probably paid a visit to France at that time. He returned to Scotland early enough to accompany Margaret and Prince Edward in the journey that eventually brought them to St. Mihiel in Bar, where he remained for the next seven years, except for occasional visits to Paris, Angers, and elsewhere. He took a leading part in the negotiations that resulted in the alliance between Queen Margaret and the Earl of Warwick. He arrived with the Queen and the Prince at Weymouth on the very day on which Warwick was slain and Henry VI captured at Barnet (April 14, 1471). Fortescue himself was taken prisoner a few days later at the Battle of Tewkesbury, which was to prove fatal to the House of Lancaster. He was pardoned in October of that year, became a member of Edward IV's council, and eventually recovered his estates, but not until he had written in favor of the new king's title and refuted his own arguments against it. His death occurred between 1477 and 1479.

The *De Laudibus Legum Angliae,* Fortescue's most famous work, dates from the years 1468–71, during the author's sojourn at St. Mihiel. It is written in the form of a dialogue between "the chancellor" (Fortescue himself) and "the prince" (Edward, the only son of Henry VI). The chancellor begins by exhorting his young pupil, who is wholly taken up with martial exercises, to study the English laws (chapters 1–6), and then goes on to answer the latter's question about the relative merits of the English and the civil laws. He first explains that the king of England has no right to change the laws of his realm, and is thus led to compare the English form of government, which is both "regal and political" (*dominium regale et politicum*), with the

purely regal or absolute monarchies found elsewhere (chapters 7–18). The remaining chapters, which are here omitted, compare English law and civil law with regard to the following points: procedure of proof (chapters 20–38), legitimation by subsequent marriage (chapters 39–41), succession (chapters 42–43), guardianship of minors (chapters 44–45), theft and freedmen (chapters 46–47), legal training (chapters 48–51), and delays in courts (chapters 52–53).

The present translation is that of S. B. Chrimes, to whom we owe what may be regarded as the first critical edition of this work: Sir John Fortescue, *De Laudibus Legum Angliae* (Cambridge: Cambridge University Press, 1942), pp. 2–41. A number of revisions have been made by the editor. Also incorporated are Professor Leo Strauss' remarks on Chrimes' translation, *Columbia Law Review,* Sept., 1943 (reprinted in L. Strauss, *What Is Political Philosophy?* [Glencoe, Ill.: The Free Press, 1959], pp. 275–78). The italic numbers in brackets in the translation refer to the even-numbered pages of Chrimes' edition, on which the Latin text is printed.

INTRODUCTION   TO   THE   MATTER

N O T   L O N G   A G O, a savage and most detestable civil war raged in the kingdom of England, whereby Henry VI, there king most pious, with Margaret his queen-consort, daughter of the king of Jerusalem and Sicily, and their only son Edward, prince of Wales, were driven out, and whereby eventually King Henry himself was seized by his subjects, and for a long time suffered the horror of imprisonment, while the queen herself, thus banished from the country with her child, lodged in the Duchy of Bar in the domain of the said king of Jerusalem.

The prince, as soon as he became grown up, gave himself over entirely to martial exercises; and, seated on fierce and half-tamed steeds urged on by his spurs, he often delighted in attacking and assaulting the young companions attending him, sometimes with a

lance, sometimes with a sword, sometimes with other weapons, in a
warlike manner and in accordance with the rules of military discipline.
Observing this, a certain aged knight, chancellor of the said king of
England, who was also in exile there as a result of the same disaster,
thus addressed the prince.

CHAPTER I

And Herein the Chancellor First Proposes to the Prince
the Study of the Law

"I do indeed rejoice, most fair prince, at your very noble disposition,
perceiving as I do with how much eagerness you embrace military
exercises, which are fitting for you to take such delight in, not merely
because you are a knight but all the more because you are going to
be king. *For the office of a king is to fight the battles of his people
and to judge them rightfully*, as you may very clearly learn in I Kings
8[:20]. For that reason, I wish that I observed you to be devoted to
the study of the laws with the same zeal as you are to that of arms,
since, as [4] battles are determined by arms, so judgments are by laws.
This fact the Emperor Justinian carefully bears in mind when, in the
beginning of the Proemium to his book of *Institutes*, he says, 'Imperial
Majesty ought to be not only adorned with arms but also armed with
laws, so that it can govern aright in both times of peace and of war.'
Furthermore, Moses, that greatest of legislators, leader of the synagogue in time past, invites you to strive zealously in the study of the
law, even more forcefully than Caesar, when with divine authority he
commands the kings of Israel to read their laws every day of their
lives, saying thus, *After the king has sat on the throne of his kingdom,
he shall write for himself the laws of Deuteronomy in a book, receiving
a copy from the priests of the Levites, and he shall have it with him,
and shall read it all the days of his life, so that he may learn to fear
the Lord his God, and to keep His words and His rites, which are
written in the law* [Deut. 17:18–19]. Helynandus,[1] expounding this
text, said, 'The prince, therefore, ought not to be ignorant of the
law, nor is he permitted, on pretext of military duty, to be ignorant
of it,' and, a little further on, 'he is commanded to receive a copy
of the law from the priests of the Levites, that is, from men catholic and
learned.' Thus says he. The book of Deuteronomy, indeed, is the book
of the laws by which the kings of Israel were bound to rule the people
subject to them. Moses commands the kings to read this book, so
that they may learn to fear God and to keep His commandments,

which are written in the law. Lo! to fear God is the effect of the law, to which man shall not be able to attain, unless first he knows the will of God, which is written in the law. For the beginning of all service is to know the will of the lord whom you serve. Yet Moses, giver of laws, mentions first in this command the effect of the law, namely the fear of God, and then exhorts to the observance of the cause thereof, namely the commandments of God; for the effect is prior to the cause in the mind of him who exhorts. But what sort of fear is it that the laws promise to those who keep them? Verily, it is not that fear of which it is written that *perfect love casts out fear* [I John 4:18]. Yet that fear, though it be servile, often incites kings to read the laws, but is not itself the offspring of the law. That fear, of which Moses here speaks and which the laws beget, [6] is forsooth that of which the prophet says, *The fear of the Lord remaineth for ever holy* [Ps. 18:10]. This fear is filial, and knows not the pain of that fear which is cast out by love. For this fear stems from the laws, which teach the doing of the will of God; hence it does not deserve punishment. *But the glory of the Lord is upon those that fear Him, whom also He glorifies* [Ps. 14:4]. This fear, furthermore, is that of which Job, after he had sought wisdom in manifold ways, speaks thus, *Behold! fear of the Lord is wisdom itself, and to depart from evil is understanding* [Job 28:28]. The laws teach departure from evil —and this is understanding of the fear of God, whereby they also produce that fear."

CHAPTER II

Reply of the Prince to the Chancellor's Proposal

When the prince heard this, he, straitly confronting the old man, spoke thus, "I know, chancellor, that the book of Deuteronomy that you mention is a book of Holy Scripture, and that the laws and usages set down therein are also sacred, decreed by the Lord and declared by Moses; hence to read them pertains to the sweetness of sacred contemplation. But the law, to a knowledge of which you exhort me, is human, decreed by man, and treats of this world; and, though Moses constrained the kings of Israel to the reading of Deuteronomy, nevertheless it is beyond all reason that he should have thereby persuaded other kings to do the like with regard to their laws, since the purpose in studying the two sets of laws is not the same."

CHAPTER III

Herein the Chancellor Defends His Proposal

Further, "I know," the chancellor said, "from what you have just objected, prince, with how much attention you consider the nature of my exhortation, whereby you encourage me not a little to discuss with you, up to a point, the matters that have been raised, not merely more clearly, but also more deeply. I want you, then, to know that not only the laws of Deuteronomy, but also all human laws, are sacred, inasmuch as law is defined by these words: 'Law is [8] a sacred sanction commanding what is honest and forbidding the contrary.'[2] For what is sacred by definition must be sacred. Right is likewise said to be described as that which is 'the art of the good and the just; and of this art we are deservedly called the priests.'[3] For a priest is by etymology said to be one who gives or teaches holy things, and, because laws, as expressive of rights, are said to be sacred, hence the ministers and teachers of the laws are called priests. Moreover, all laws that are promulgated by man are decreed by God. For, since the Apostle says *all power is from the Lord God* [Rom. 13:1], laws established by man, who receives power to this end from God, are also instituted by God, as is implied by the author of the *Liber de Causis* when he says that, 'whatever the second cause effects, so also does the first cause, in a higher and more perfect way.'[4] Wherefore, Jehoshaphat, king of Judah, says to his judges, *The judgments that you give are the judgments of God* [II Chron. 19:6]. By this you are taught that to learn the laws, even though human ones, is to learn laws that are sacred and decreed of God, the study of which does not lack the sweetness of divine consolation. But still, as you know, it was not because of this sweetness that Moses commanded the kings of Israel to read Deuteronomy. For, on that account, he exhorted the kings no more than the people to the reading thereof, nor did he encourage the reading of the book of Deuteronomy more than other books of the Pentateuch, since those books no less than Deuteronomy abound in revelations of the Holy Spirit, the meditation of which is a devout exercise. Hence the reason for that command was none other than that the laws are set forth in Deuteronomy rather than in other books of the Old Testament—the laws by which the king of Israel is obliged to rule his people, a fact that the circumstances of the command obviously show us. Hence, prince, the same reason impels you no less than the kings of Israel to be a careful student of the laws by which you will in the future rule the people. For what is said to the king of Israel must be understood figuratively to apply to every king of a people acknowledging God.

"Have I not, then, fitly and usefully proposed to you this command enjoined to the kings of Israel—to learn their law? For [*10*] not only its example, but also, figuratively speaking, its authority, teach you and oblige you to act in the same way with regard to the laws of the kingdom that, by the permission of God, you are to inherit."

CHAPTER IV

Herein the Chancellor Proves That the Prince Can Become Happy and Blessed through the Laws

"The laws, most honorable prince, not only invite you to fear God and thereby be wise, saying with the prophet, *Come, ye children, hearken unto me, and I will teach you the fear of the Lord* [Ps. 33:12], but invite you also to their study, that you may obtain happiness and blessedness so far as they are obtainable in this life. For all the philosophers who have disputed so differently about happiness are agreed in this respect, namely, that happiness or blessedness is the end of all human desire. For that reason certain of them called it the *summum bonum*. The Peripatetics, however, placed it solely in virtue, the Stoics in what is honest, and the Epicureans in pleasure. But since the Stoics defined honesty to be what is done well, laudably, and out of virtue, and the Epicureans asserted that nothing is pleasurable without virtue, all these schools, as Leonardo Aretino[5] says in his *Introduction to Moral Philosophy*, agreed in the view that virtue alone procures happiness. Hence the Philosopher, in defining happiness, says that 'it is the perfect exercise of virtues.'[6]

"These premises being granted, I want you to consider what follows from them. Human laws are none other than rules by which perfect justice is taught. But, to be sure, the justice that the laws reveal is not that particular justice which is called commutative or distributive, or any other particular virtue; it is rather the perfect virtue that is called by the name of legal justice, which the aforesaid Leonardo therefore says is perfect because it eliminates all vice and teaches every virtue, so that it is itself rightly called the whole virtue. [*12*] Homer spoke of it in the same way as the Philosopher, saying that 'it is the most excellent of virtues, and neither Lucifer nor Hesperus is as wonderful as this.'[7] This justice, indeed, is the object of all royal administration, because without it a king judges unjustly and is unable to fight rightfully. But this justice attained and truly observed, the whole office of king is most equitably discharged. Therefore, since happiness is the perfect exercise of virtues, and human justice, which is not perfectly taught except by the law, is not merely the effect of virtue, but the whole virtue, it follows that he who is in enjoyment of justice is made happy by the law. Thereby he becomes blessed, for blessedness and happiness are the same in this fleeting life, and through justice he attains the *summum bonum* of this world. Not, indeed, that law can do this without grace, nor will you be able to learn or to strive after law or virtue, without grace. For, as the Parisian[8] says in his book *Cur Deus Homo*, 'The internal appetitive power of man was so vitiated by original sin, that to him the works of vice savor sweet and those of virtue bitter.' Wherefore that some give themselves to love and pursuit of virtues is a gift of the divine goodness, not derived from human power. Are not, then, the laws that, preceded and accompanied by grace, accomplish all these effects worthy to be studied with all application, since the learner of them shall obtain the happiness that, according to the Philosopher, is the end and completion of human desire, whereby he shall be blessed in this life, possessing its *summum bonum*?

"Verily, if these considerations do not move you who are one day to rule the kingdom, the words of the prophet shall persuade you and oblige you to the study of the law, saying, *Be instructed, ye who judge the earth* [Ps. 2:10]. For here the prophet does not persuade to a knowledge of any practical or mechanical art, for he does not say, 'Be instructed, ye who cultivate the earth,' nor does he persuade to a knowledge of a purely theoretical science, however suitable for the inhabitants of the earth, for he did not say in general terms, 'Be instructed, ye inhabitants of the earth.' But the prophet only invites kings to the study of the law by which judgments are rendered, when he uses these specific words, *Be instructed, [14] ye who judge the earth*. It follows on, *Lest at any time the Lord be angry, and ye perish from the right way* [Ps. 2:12]. Nor does Holy Scripture command you only to be instructed, O king's son, in the laws by which you shall pursue justice, but also, in another place, it requires you to love justice itself, when it says, *Love justice, ye who judge the earth* [Wisd. of Sol. 1:1]."

CHAPTER V

Herein He Proves That Ignorance of the Law Causes Contempt for It

"But how shall you be able to love justice, if you do not first somehow grasp the science of the laws by which justice itself is known? For the Philosopher says that 'nothing is loved unless it be known.'[9] Wherefore Fabius the Orator says that 'the arts would be fortunate if artists alone were to judge them.'[10] Indeed, what is not known is usually not only unloved but also spurned; hence a certain poet observes, 'All that he is ignorant of, the rustic declares ought to be despised.'¹¹ And this view is that not only of the rustic, but also of learned experts. For, if a metaphysician tells a natural philosopher who has never studied mathematics that his science considers things disjoined from all matter and motion according to reality and reason; or a mathematician tells him that his science considers things conjoined with matter and motion according to reality but disjoined according to reason, that natural philosopher, who never knew anything disjoined from matter and motion in reality or reason, will reject their sciences, though nobler than his own, and will deride both of them, albeit they are philosophers, for no other reason than that he himself is utterly ignorant of their sciences.¹²

"Thus, you, prince, would marvel at a lawyer of England if he told you that a brother shall not succeed in a paternal heritage to a brother not born of the same mother, but that rather the heritage shall descend to a sister of the whole blood or shall fall to the lord-in-chief of the fee as his escheat, because you are ignorant of the reason for this law. But the difficulty of such a case does not in the least perturb one learned in the law of England. [*16*] Wherefore it is commonly said that 'art has no enemy except the ignorant.'¹³ But far be it from you, O king's son, to be hostile to, or to despise, the laws of the kingdom to which you are to succeed, when the book of Wisdom aforementioned instructs you to love justice, which the laws reveal. Again, therefore, and again, most noble prince, do I adjure you to learn the laws of your father's realm, to which you are to succeed, not only that you may avoid those disadvantages, but because the human mind, which naturally desires the good and can desire nothing unless under the aspect of good, rejoices as soon as it has by instruction grasped the good and loves it, and delights in it the more as it more reflects upon it. Hence you realize that if by instruction you understand those laws of which you are now ignorant, you will love them, since they are the best; and the more you reflect upon them, the more agreeably will you enjoy them. For all that is loved transfers the lover into its own nature by usage, wherefore the Philosopher said, 'Use becomes another nature.'¹⁴ Thus, a sprig of pear tree grafted onto an apple-stock, once it has taken, so draws the apple tree into the nature of a pear tree that both are deservedly called a pear tree, and produce the fruits of a pear tree. Thus, also, a virtue practiced engenders a habit, so that the practicer thereof is thenceforth called by the name of that virtue. Hence one practiced in modesty is called modest, in continency, continent, in wisdom, wise. Wherefore, prince, when you have done justice with pleasure, and have thereby put it on as a habit, you will deservedly and lawfully be called just, and on that account it shall be said to you that *thou hast loved justice and hated iniquity, therefore the Lord thy God hath anointed thee with the oil of gladness above thy fellows* [Ps. 44:8], that is to say, the kings of the earth."

CHAPTER VI

Herein the Chancellor Sums Up the Effect of
His Whole Argument

"Are not these arguments, then, most serene prince, enough to persuade you to the study of the law? For you will thereby be adorned with the habit of justice, and will therefore be called just; you will be able to avoid the disgrace of ignorance of the law, [*18*] and, enjoying happiness through the law, you will be blessed in this life; you will moreover be adorned with the filial fear that is God's wisdom, and will unperturbedly attain the charity that is love toward God, thus cleaving to God, as in the words of the Apostle, *Thou shalt become one in spirit with Him* [I Cor. 6:17]. But because this law cannot flourish in you without grace, it is necessary to pray for that above all things; also it is fitting for you to seek the science of the divine law and Holy Scripture. For Holy Writ says that *all are vain in whom subsisteth not the knowledge of God* [Wisd. of Sol. 13:1]. Therefore, prince, while you are young and your mind is as it were a clean slate, impress on it those things, lest in future it be impressed more pleasurably with images of lesser worth; for, as a certain sage observes, 'What a vessel takes when new it tastes of when it is old.'[15] What craftsman is so negligent of his child's profit that he does not instruct him in crafts when he is young, by which he may afterwards gain the comforts of life? Thus a carpenter teaches his son to cut with an axe, the smith his son to work with a hammer, and he who desires to minister in spiritual matters is trained in letters. Thus it is proper for a prince to cause his son, who after him will rule the people, to be instructed in the laws while he is young. If the rulers of the earth observed this, the world would be ruled with more justice than it now is. And if you do as I have urged you, you will offer no small example."

CHAPTER VII

Now the Prince Surrenders Himself to the Study of the Laws,
Although He Inquires Further into Certain Precise Points

The chancellor having ceased, the prince began thus: "You have overcome me, good sir, with your most persuasive discourse, by which you have caused my mind to thirst with no small heat for lessons in the law. Nevertheless, my mind is in two difficulties in the matter, just as a boat in troubled waters knows not whither to direct its prow. One difficulty is that when I recollect how many years [*20*] students in the curricula of the law devote to their study before they attain to an adequate expertness therein, I fear lest I myself spend the years of my youth in the same way. The second difficulty is whether I shall devote myself to the study of the laws of England or of the civil laws, which are renowned throughout the world. For the people should not be governed by any save the best laws; as the Philosopher says, 'Nature always covets the best.'[16] Hence I should willingly pay heed to your advice in these particulars."

CHAPTER   VIII

As Much Knowledge of the Law as Is Necessary
for a Prince Is Speedily Attainable

To whom the chancellor replied, "These matters, O king's son, are not hidden in such mystery as needs lengthy consideration, so I will not delay in telling you how I see them. The Philosopher, in the first book of the *Physics*, says that 'we think we know anything when we know the causes and principles of it as far as the elements of it.'[17] On this the Commentator[18] observes that 'Aristotle meant by principles, efficient causes, and by causes, final causes, and by elements, matter and form.' In the laws, indeed, there are no matter and form as in physical things and in things artificially devised. But, nevertheless, there are in them certain elements out of which they proceed as out of matter and form, such as customs, statutes, and the law of nature, from which all the laws of the realm proceed, just as natural things do out of matter and form, and just as all we read comes out of the letters, which are all called elements. The principles, furthermore, which the Commentator said are efficient causes, are certain universals that those learned in the laws of England and mathematicians alike call maxims, just as rhetoricians speak of paradoxes, and statesmen of rules of law. These principles, indeed, are not known by force of arguments or logical demonstrations, but they are acquired, as it is taught in the second book of the *Posterior Analytics*, by induction through the senses and the memory.[19] Wherefore, the Philosopher says in the first book of the *Physics* that 'principles do not proceed out of other things nor out of one another, but other things proceed out of them.'[20] Hence in [*22*] the first book of the *Topics* it is written that 'any principle is its own ground for holding it.'[21] For that reason the Philosopher says, 'There is no arguing with those who deny principles,'[22] because, as it is written in the sixth book of the *Ethics*, 'There is no proof for principles.'[23] Therefore, whoever are anxious to understand any branch of knowledge must learn thoroughly its principles. For out of them are discovered the final causes, to which one is brought by process of reasoning upon a knowledge of principles. Hence if these three—principles, causes, and elements—are unknown, the science to which they appertain is totally unknown; and if these are known, the science is known, not indeed distinctly, but in a confused and universal way. Thus we declare we know the divine law when we feel we know faith, charity, and hope, as well as the sacraments of the church, and the commandments of God, leaving other mysteries of theology to the prelates of the church. Wherefore the Lord said to His disciples, *Unto you it is given to know the mystery of the kingdom of God, but to others in parables, that seeing they may not see* [Mark 4:11–12]. And the Apostle said, *Know not more than you ought to know* [Rom. 12:3], and in another place, *Knowing not high things* [Rom. 12:16]. Thus you, prince, do not need to explore the mysteries of the law of England by long study; it is sufficient for you to progress in the laws as you have in grammar. Perfection, indeed, in grammar, which flows out of etymology, orthography, prosody, and syntax, as out of four streams, you have not completely acquired, yet you are sufficiently learned in grammar to be deservedly called a grammarian. Similarly, you will deserve to be called learned in the law, if you have learned, in the role of student, the principles and causes of the law as far as the elements. For it will not be expedient for you to investigate precise points (*sacramenta*) of the law by the exertion of your own reason, but these should be left to your judges and advocates who in the kingdom of England are called sergeants-at-law, and also to others skilled in the law who are commonly called apprentices. In fact, you will render judgments better through others than by yourself, for none of the kings of England is seen to give judgment by his own lips, yet all the judgments of the realm are his, though given through others, just as Jehoshaphat asserted that *all judicial sentences [24] are the judgments of God* [II Chron. 19:6]. Wherefore, most gracious prince, you will be sufficiently learned in the laws of the kingdom of England in a short time and with moderate industry, provided you devote your mind to the apprehension of them. For Seneca said, in a letter to Lucilius, 'There is nothing that great pains and diligent care do not overcome.'[24] Indeed I know the perspicacity of your mind, and I dare say that in these laws, though the experience of them necessary for judges is scarcely attainable in the labors of twenty years, you will adequately acquire a knowledge fitting for a prince in one year. But in the meantime, do not neglect the military exercises to which you are ardently devoted, but enjoy them at pleasure as a recreation even during that year."

CHAPTER   IX

A King Ruling Politically Is Not Able to Change
the Laws of His Kingdom

"The second difficulty, prince, of which you are apprehensive, shall
be removed with like ease. For you hesitate whether you should apply
yourself to the study of the laws of the English or of the civil laws,
because the civil laws are celebrated with a glorious fame throughout
the world above all other human laws. Do not, O king's son, let this
consideration trouble you. For the king of England is not able to change
the laws of his kingdom at pleasure, for he rules his people with a
government not only regal but also political. If he were to preside over
them with a power entirely regal, he would be able to change the
laws of his realm, and also impose on them tallages and other burdens
without consulting them; this is the sort of dominion that the civil
laws indicate when they state that 'what pleased the prince has the
force of law.'[25] But the case is far otherwise with the king ruling his
people politically, because he will not be able himself to change the
laws without the assent of his subjects nor to burden an unwilling
people with strange imposts, so that, ruled by laws that they themselves
desire, they freely enjoy their properties and are despoiled neither by
their own king nor any other. The people, forsooth, rejoice in the same
way under a king ruling entirely regally, provided he does not degenerate into a tyrant. Of such a king, [26] the Philosopher said (*Politics*
iii) that 'it is better for a city to be ruled by the best man than by the
best law.'[26] But, because it does not always happen that the man presiding over a people is of this sort, St. Thomas, in the book he wrote for
the king of Cyprus, *On the Governance of Princes*, is considered to
have desired that a kingdom be constituted such that the king may not
be free to govern his people tyrannically, which only comes to pass
when the regal power is restrained by political law.[27] Rejoice, therefore,
good prince, that such is the law of the kingdom to which you are to
succeed, because it will provide no small security and comfort for you
and for the people. By such a law, as the aforementioned Saint said,
'The whole human race would have been ruled, if it had not transgressed
in paradise the commands of God.'[28] By such a law the synagogue was
ruled, when under God alone as king, who adopted it as a realm pe-
culiarly His, it was struggling; but at last a human king having been
constituted for it, on its own petition, it was thereafter humbled under
an entirely regal law. Under this law, nonetheless, it rejoiced when the best
kings ruled, but when a peevish sort ruled, it lamented inconsolably, as

the Books of Kings reveal quite clearly. But as I think I have discussed this matter sufficiently in a small work *On the Nature of the Law of Nature*,[29] which I wrote for your consideration, I desist from saying more about it now."

CHAPTER X

A Question by the Prince

Then the prince said forthwith, "How comes it, chancellor, that one king is able to rule his people entirely regally, and the same power is denied to the other king? Of equal rank, since both are kings, I cannot help wondering why they are unequal in power."

CHAPTER XI

A Reference to the Other Treatise

Chancellor: "It is sufficiently shown, in the small work I have mentioned, that the king ruling politically is of no less power than he who rules his people regally, as he wishes;[30] [28] but I have by no means denied, either then or now, that their authority over their subjects is different. The cause of this diversity I will explain to you as far as I can."

CHAPTER XII

How Kingdoms Ruled Entirely Regally First Began

"Formerly, men excelling in power, greedy of dignity and glory, subjugated neighboring peoples to themselves, often by force, and compelled them to serve them, and to submit to their commands, to which in time they themselves gave sanction as laws for those people. The folk thus subject, by long endurance, and as long as they were protected, by their subjection, against the injuries of others, consented to the dominion of their rulers, thinking it better to be ruled by the government of one, whereby they were protected from others, than to be exposed to the oppressions of all those who wished to attack them. And thus began certain kingdoms; and the rulers of them, thus ruling the subject people, usurped to themselves the name of king, from the word *regendo*,[31] and their lordship is described as entirely regal. So Nimrod first secured for himself a kingdom, though he was not himself a king, but is called by Holy Writ *a mighty hunter before the Lord* [Gen. 10:9], because, as a hunter compels beasts enjoying their liberty to obey him, so did he compel men. Thus Belus reduced the Assyrians to his behest, and Ninus the greater part of Asia.[32] Thus the Romans usurped the government of the world, and likewise kingdoms began among nearly all peoples. Hence, when the children of Israel demanded a king as all people then had, the Lord was thereby displeased, and commanded the regal law to be explained to them by a prophet—the law that was none other than the pleasure of the king presiding over them, as may be learned more fully in the first book of Kings. Now you have, most excellent prince, unless I am mistaken, the form of the beginning of kingdoms possessed regally. I shall now, therefore, also try to explain how the kingdom ruled politically first began, so that, the beginnings of both kingdoms being known, the reason for the diversity about which you inquire may be more easily made plain to you." [*30*]

CHAPTER XIII

How Kingdoms Ruled Politically First Began

"Saint Augustine, in the nineteenth book of the *City of God*, chapter 23, said that 'a people is a body of men united by consent of law and by community of interest.'[33] But such a people does not deserve to be called a body while it is acephalous, that is, without a head. Because, just as in natural bodies, what is left over after decapitation is not a body, but is what we call a trunk, so in bodies politic a community without a head is not by any means a body. Hence the Philosopher in the first book of the *Politics* said that 'whenever one body is constituted out of many, one will rule, and the others be ruled.'[34] So a people wishing to erect itself into a kingdom or any other body politic must always set up one man for the government of all that body, who, by analogy with a kingdom, is, from *regendo*,[35] usually called a king. As in this way the physical body grows out of the embryo, regulated by one head, so the kingdom issues from the people, and exists as a body mystical, governed by one man as head. And just as in the body natural, as the Philosopher said, the heart is the source of life, having in itself the blood that it transmits to all the members thereof, whereby they are quickened and live, so in the body politic the will of that people is the source of life, having in it the blood, namely, political forethought for the interest of the people, that it transmits to the head and all the members of the body, by which the body is maintained and quickened.

"The law, indeed, by which a group of men is made into a people, resembles the nerves of the body physical, for, just as the body is held together by the nerves, so this body mystical is bound together and united into one by the law, which is derived from the word *ligando*,[36] and the members and bones of this body, which signify the solid basis of truth by which that community is sustained, preserve their rights through the law, as the body natural does through the nerves. And just as the head of the body physical is unable to change its nerves, or to deny its members the powers belonging to them and the nourishment of blood belonging to them, so a king who is head of the body politic is unable to change the laws of that body, [32] or to deprive that same people of their own substance if they protest or are unwilling. You have here, prince, the form of the institution of the political kingdom, whence you can estimate the power that the king can exercise in respect of the law and the subjects of such a realm; for a king of this sort is obliged to protect the law, the subjects, and their bodies and goods, and he has power to this end issuing from the people, so that it is not permissible for him to rule his people with any other power. In this way I briefly answer the question you desire to be assured of—the question of how came it that the power of kings should differ so widely. I am firmly of the opinion that this difference is due solely to diversity in the institution of those dignities that I have mentioned, as you will be able to gather by the light of reason from what has been said. For thus the kingdom of England blossomed forth into a dominion regal and political out of Brutus' band of Trojans, whom he led out of the territories of Italy and of the Greeks. And thus Scotland, which at one time was obedient thereto as a duchy, grew into a kingdom political and regal. Many other realms also have obtained by such an origin as this the right to be ruled not only regally, but also politically. Hence Diodorus Siculus, in the second book of the *Ancient Histories*, writes thus of the Egyptians: 'The kings of Egypt did not at first lead their lives with license as other rulers, to whom will is law, but, like private people, they were restrained by the laws; nor were they thereby displeased, but thought that by obeying the laws they would become happy; for they considered those who indulged their own cupidities did much that exposed them to dangers and perils.' And in the fourth book he writes thus: 'He who has become king of Ethiopia has led a life ruled by laws, and does everything according to the custom of the country, offering neither reward nor penalty to anyone except according to the law handed down to him from his predecessors.'[37] The same is said of the king of Saba in Arabia Felix and of other kings who reigned happily in ancient times."[38] [34]

CHAPTER XIV

Herein the Prince Briefly Summarizes What the Chancellor Has Already Expressed at Length

To whom the prince said, "You have, chancellor, dispersed by the light of your discourse the darkness that dimmed the sight of my mind, so that I now very clearly perceive that for no other reason has any people ever formed itself into a kingdom of its own accord, unless in order to possess safer than before both themselves and their own, which they feared to lose—an expectation that would be disappointed if their king were able to deprive them of their means, which was not permitted before to anyone among men. And such a people would suffer still more grievously if they were ruled by laws strange, and perhaps hateful, to them; especially if their substance was thereby diminished, to avoid the loss of which, as well as to protect their bodies, they submitted of their own will to the government of a king; truly such a power as this could not issue from the people, and if not from them, a king of this sort could obtain no power over them. On the other hand, I conceive it to be quite otherwise with a kingdom that is incorporated solely by the authority and power of the king, because such a people is subjected to him in no other manner than to obey and be ruled by his laws, which are the pleasure of him by the pleasure of whose will the people is made into a realm. Nor, chancellor, has it thus far slipped my memory that you have shown elsewhere, with learned argument, in your treatise, *On the Nature of the Law of Nature*, that the power of the two kings is equal, since the power by which one of them is free to do wrong is not increased by this freedom, just as to be able to be ill or to die is not power, but is rather to be deemed impotency because of the deprivation involved. For, as Boethius said, 'There is no power unless for good,'[39] so that to be able to do evil, as the king reigning regally can more freely do than the king ruling his people politically, diminishes rather than increases his power. For the holy spirits who, already confirmed in glory, are unable to sin, [36] are more powerful than we, who are given free rein to commit any misdeed. Therefore, it only remains for me to inquire of you whether the law of England, to the study of which you invite me, is as good and effectual for the government of that kingdom as the civil law, by which the Holy Empire is ruled, is thought to be sufficient for the government of the whole world. If you satisfy me in this respect, with suitable proof, I shall at once apply myself to the study of the law, and shall not weary you any more with my queries in these matters."

CHAPTER XV

All Laws Are the Law of Nature, Customs, or Statutes

Chancellor: "You have committed to memory, my good prince, what I have so far mentioned to you, so that you deserve my explanation of what you now ask. I want you, then, to know that all human laws are either law of nature, customs, or statutes, which are also called constitutions. But customs and the rules of the law of nature, after they have been reduced to writing, and promulgated by the sufficient authority of the prince, and commanded to be kept, are changed so as to take on the nature of constitutions or statutes; and thereupon oblige the prince's subjects to keep them under greater penalty than before, by reason of the strictness of that command. Such is no small part of the civil law, which is reduced to writing by the Roman princes in large volumes, and by their authority commanded to be observed. Hence that part has now obtained the name of civil law, like the other statutes of the Emperors. If, therefore, I shall prove that the law of England excels pre-eminently in respect of these three fountains, so to speak, of all law, I shall have proven also that law to be good and effectual for the government of that realm. Furthermore, if I shall have clearly shown it to be adapted to the utility of that same realm as the civil law is to the good of the Empire, I shall have made manifest that the law is not only excellent, but also, like the civil law, is as fine as you could wish. Therefore, I proceed to show you sufficiently these two things." [*38*]

CHAPTER XVI

The Law of Nature Is the Same in All Regions

"The laws of England, in those points that they sanction by reason of the law of nature, are neither better nor worse in their judgments than are all laws of other nations in like cases. For, as the Philosopher said, in the fifth book of the *Ethics*, 'Natural law is that which has the same force among all men.'[40] Hence there is no need to discuss it further. But from now on we must examine what are the customs, and also the statutes, of England, and we will first look at the characteristics of those customs."

CHAPTER XVII

The Customs of England Are Very Ancient, and Have
Been Used and Accepted by Five Nations Successively

"The kingdom of England was first inhabited by Britons; then ruled by Romans, again by Britons, then possessed by Saxons, who changed its name from Britain to England. Then for a short time the kingdom was conquered by Danes, and again by Saxons, but finally by Normans, whose posterity hold the realm at the present time. And throughout the period of these nations and their kings, the realm has been continuously ruled by the same customs as it is now, customs that, if they had not been the best, some of those kings would have changed under the impulse of justice, reason, or will, and totally abolished them, especially the Romans, who judged almost the whole of the rest of the world by their laws. Similarly, others of these aforesaid kings, who possessed the kingdom of England only by the sword, could, by that power, have destroyed its laws. Indeed, neither the civil laws of the Romans, so deeply rooted by the usage of so many ages, nor the laws of the Venetians, [40] which are renowned above others for their antiquity—though their island was uninhabited, and Rome unbuilt at the time of the origin of the Britons—nor the laws of any kingdoms worshiping the true god, are so rooted in antiquity. Hence there is no gainsaying nor legitimate doubt but that the customs of the English are not only good but the best."

CHAPTER XVIII

Herein He Shows with What Solemnity
Statutes Are Promulgated in England

"It only remains, then, to examine whether or not the statutes of the English are good. These, indeed, do not emanate from the will of the prince alone, as do the laws in kingdoms that are governed entirely regally, where so often statutes secure the advantage of their maker only, thereby redounding to the loss and undoing of the subjects. Sometimes, also, by the negligence of such princes and the inertia of their counsellors, those statutes are made so ill-advisedly that they deserve the name of corruptions rather than of laws. But the statutes of England cannot so arise, since they are made not only by the prince's will, but also by the assent of the whole realm, so they cannot be injurious to the people nor fail to secure their advantage. Furthermore, it must be supposed that they are necessarily replete with prudence and wisdom, since they are promulgated by the prudence not of one judicious person nor of a hundred only, but of more than three hundred chosen men—of such a number as once the Senate of the Romans was ruled by—as those who know the form of the summons, the order, and the procedure of parliament can more clearly describe. And if statutes ordained with such solemnity and care happen not to give full effect to the intention of the makers, they can speedily be revised, and yet not without the assent of the commons and nobles of the realm, in the manner in which they first originated. Thus, prince, all the kinds of the law of England are now plain to you. You will be able to estimate their merits by your own prudence, and by comparison with other laws; and when you find none in the world so excellent, you will be bound to confess that they are not only good, but as good as you could wish."

NOTES

1. Helynandus (d. *ca.* 1219) was celebrated as the author of sermons, but he also wrote at least two philosophic works, *De Cognitione Sui* and *De Bono Regimine Principis*. Cf. Migne, *Patrologia Latina*, 212, col. 482–1084.

2. This maxim comes from the Accursian Gloss to *Institutes* i. 2. 3, *v.* Lex. Cf. Bracton, *De Consuetudinibus et Legibus*, i. 3: *Lex . . . significat sanctionem iustam, iubentem honesta prohibentem contraria.*

3. Justinian *Digest* i. 1. 1.

4. *Liber de Causis* i. 14. On this work, see above, Selection 22, n. 25.

5. Leonardo Bruni Aretino: Greek scholar and historian of Florence (1389-1444). His *Isagogicon Moralis Disciplinae* was edited by V. F. Tocco, *Archiv für Geschichte der Philosophie*, VI (1892).

6. Aristotle *Politics* viii. 1. 1323^{b}21; cf. *Nicomachean Ethics* i. 7. 1098^{b}17.

7. Aristotle *Nicomachean Ethics* v. 1. 1129^{b}28. Cf. Dante *De Monarchia* i. 11; above, Selection 22 (p. 346).

8. William of Auvergne, bishop of Paris (d. 1249). His *Cur Deus Homo* was possessed by Fortescue (Bodl. Rawl. MSS. C 398). The gist of the quotation, if not the exact words, is to be found on fol. 137v.

9. Cf. Aristotle *Nicomachean Ethics* ix. 5. 1167^{a}4. In its present form, however, the dictum is closer to Augustine *De Trinitate* x. 2. 4; cf. *ibid.* x. 1. 1, and Ovid *Ars Amatoria* iii. 397: *Ignoti nulla cupido.*

10. The quotation has not been identified.

11. The quotation has not been identified.

12. Cf. Aristotle *Metaphysics* ii. 3. 994^{b}31-995^{a}20; vi. 1. 1025^{b}25 ff. Also *Nicomachean Ethics* i. 3. 1094^{b}24; *Physics* ii. 2. 193^{b}22 ff.

13. This proverb was used in English by Ben Jonson, *Every Man Out of His Humour* (ed. Cunningham, 21).

14. Cf. Aristotle *Nicomachean Ethics* vii. 10. 1152^{a}30.

15. This proverb is to be found in Vincent of Beauvais' *De Eruditione Filiorum Regalium*, fol. 1, whence Fortescue probably got it.

16. Cf. Aristotle *Nicomachean Ethics* i. 9. 1099^{b}22.

17. Aristotle *Physics* i. 1. 184^{a}9 ff.

18. The Commentator, i.e., Averroes. This comment by Averroes is in the *Auctoritates Aristotelis*, which also appears to be the immediate source of Fortescue's quotations from Aristotle.

19. Aristotle *Posterior Analytics* ii. 19. 99^{b}21 ff.

20. Aristotle *Physics* i. 5. 188^{a}28.

21. Aristotle *Topics* i. 1. 100^{b}20.

22. Aristotle *Physics* i. 2. 185^{a}3.

23. Aristotle *Nicomachean Ethics* vi. 6. 1141^{a}1.

24. Seneca *Letters* 50.

25. Justinian *Institutes* i. 2. 6; *Digest* i. 4. 1.

26. Cf. Aristotle *Politics* iii. 17. 1288^{a}15; iii. 13. 1284^{a}3.

27. Cf. Aquinas *De Regimine Principum* i. 7; ii. 8. (The latter chapter belongs to that part of the work written by Ptolemy of Lucca and not by Aquinas himself.)

28. Cf. *ibid*. ii. 9 (Ptolemy of Lucca).

29. Fortescue *De Natura Legis Naturae* i. 6–15 and esp. 16.

30. *Ibid*. i. 22–26.

31. The Latin words *regere* (to rule) and *rex* (king) are derived from the same root.

32. Fortescue's information was obtained from Augustine *De Civitate Dei* xvi. 17.

33. Augustine *De Civitate Dei* xix. 21. 1; xix. 24.

34. Aristotle *Politics* i. 5. 1254^{a}29.

35. Cf. above, n. 31.

36. The word *lex* (law) was commonly said to be derived from *ligare* (to bind).

37. Diodorus Siculus *Bibliotheca* ii. 35.

38. Cf. *ibid*. iv. 76.

39. Boethius *De Consolatione Philosophiae* iv. Prose 2. 2.

40. Aristotle *Nicomachean Ethics* v. 7. 1134^{b}19.

SELECTED BIBLIOGRAPHY

PART ONE

Algazel. *Deliverance from Error.* Translated by W. Montgomery Watt in *The Faith and Practice of al-Ghazālī.* ("Ethical and Religious Classics of East and West.") London: Allen and Unwin, 1953.
———. *The Incoherence of the Philosophers.* Partially reproduced in Averroes' *The Incoherence of the Incoherence* (see below).
Alfarabi. *Aphorisms of the Statesman.* Translated by D. M. Dunlop ("University of Cambridge Oriental Publications," No. 5.) Cambridge: Cambridge University Press, 1961.
———. *The Philosophy of Plato.* Translated by Muhsin Mahdi in *Alfarabi's Philosophy of Plato and Aristotle.* Part II. New York: The Free Press, 1962; rev. ed., Ithaca: Cornell Paperbacks, 1969.
———. *The Virtuous City.* An English translation has been prepared by Richard Walzer. Translated into German by Fr. Dieterici: *Der Musterstaat von Alfārābī.* Leiden: E. J. Brill, 1900. Translated into French by R. P. Jaussen, Youssef Karam, and J. Chlala: *Idées des habitants de la cité vertueuse.* ("Publication de l'Institut français d'archéologie orientale. Textes et traductions d'auteurs orientaux," t. 9.) Cairo, 1949.
Averroes. *Commentary on Plato's Republic.* Translated by E. I. J. Rosenthal. ("University of Cambridge Oriental Publications," No. 1.) Cambridge: Cambridge University Press, 1956.
———. *The Incoherence of the Incoherence.* Translated by Simon van den Bergh. ("E. J. W. Gibb Memorial," New Series, XIX.) 2 vols. London: Luzac, 1954.
Ibn Khaldūn. *The Muqaddimah: An Introduction to History.* Especially, Vol. I, pp. 1–93, Vol. II, pp. 1–231. Translated by Franz Rosenthal. ("Bollingen Series," XLIII.) 3 vols. New York: Pantheon Books, 1958.
Ibn Taymiyyah. *The Religious Regime.* Translated into French by Henri Laoust. *Le traité de droit public d'Ibn Taimiya.* Vol. I. Beirut: Institut français de Damas, 1948.

PART TWO

Judah Halevi. *Book of Kuzari.* Translated by Hartwig Hirschfeld. New York: Pardes Publishing House, 1946. This work is available in another, but abridged, translation: *Kuzari.* Translated by Isaak Heinemann. Abridged edition. ("Philosophia Judaica Series.") Oxford: East and West Library, 1947. The latter translation is reprinted in *Three Jewish Philosophers.* New York: Meridian Books, 1960.

Maimonides. *The Code of Maimonides* (*Mishneh Torah*); *Book Fourteen, The Book of Judges.* Treatise Five. Translated by Abraham M. Hershman. ("Yale Judaica Series," Vol. III.) New Haven: Yale University Press, 1949.

Saadiah ben Joseph, Gaon. *The Book of Beliefs and Opinions.* Introductory Treatise and Treatise III. Translated by Samuel Rosenblatt. ("Yale Judaica Series," Vol. I.) New Haven: Yale University Press, 1948. This work is available in another, but abridged, translation: *The Book of Doctrines and Beliefs.* Prolegomena and Chapter III. Translated by Alexander Altmann. Abridged edition. ("Philosophia Judaica Series.") Oxford: East and West Library, 1946. The latter translation is reprinted in *Three Jewish Philosophers.* New York: Meridian Books, 1960.

PART THREE

Aquinas. *Summa Theologica.* Ia IIae, Questions 90–108, in *Basic Writings of St. Thomas Aquinas.* Vol. II. Edited by Anton C. Pegis. 2 vols. New York: Random House, 1945.

————. *Summa contra Gentiles.* Book I, chapters 63–71; Book II, chapters 31–38, 59–61, 68–81; Book III, chapters 41–45, 69–75, 84–87, 92–100, in *On the Truth of the Catholic Faith.* Translated by Anton C. Pegis, James F. Anderson, Vernon J. Bourke, and Charles J. O'Neil. 5 vols. Garden City, N. Y.: Image Books, 1955–57.

————. *On Kingship, to the King of Cyprus.* Translated by Gerald B. Phelan. Revised by I. Th. Eschmann, O. P. Toronto: The Pontifical Institute of Mediaeval Studies, 1949.

Augustine. *The City of God.* Book XIX. Translated by Marcus Dods. ("The Modern Library.") New York: Random House, 1950.

Bacon, Roger. *Opus Maius.* Translated by Robert B. Burke. 2 vols. Philadelphia: University of Pennsylvania Press, 1928.

Dante. *Epistolae.* Translated by Philip H. Wicksteed in *The Latin Works of Dante.* London: J. M. Dent, 1904.

John of Salisbury. *Polycraticus.* Book IV. Translated by John Dickinson in *The Stateman's Book of John of Salisbury.* New York: Alfred A. Knopf, 1927.

Nicholas of Cusa. *De Concordantia Catholica.* Partially translated in *A Treatyse of the donation . . . by Constantyne. . .* London: Thomas Gofray [1525 ?].

Unity and Reform: Selected Writings of Nicholas de Cusa. Edited by John Patrick Dolan. Notre Dame, Indiana: University of Notre Dame Press, 1962.

INDEX

(Names cited in the body of the translations, excluding titles of books and the names of God.)

529